PRAISE FOR
Before the Court of Heaven

2016 IndieReader Discovery Award — 1st Place - Fiction

2015 Nautilus Book Award Winner — Fiction — Silver medal

2016 Finalist — Grand Prize (Eric Hoffer Award) — Fiction

2016 Honorable Mention (Eric Hoffer Award) — Commercial Fiction

2016 Finalist - First Horizon Award (Eric Hoffer Award) — Fiction

2015 Finalist - Foreword Reviews INDIEFAB Book of the Year Award — Historical Fiction

2015 Mom's Choice Award — Gold Medal — Historical Fiction

2015 Pinnacle Book Achievement Award — Best Novel Fall 2015

2015 Beverly Hills Book Awards — Finalist — "Faction" - fiction based on true stories

A Best Indie Book of 2015 — IndieReader (5-stars)

Shelf Unbound — Notable Indie — 2015 Best Indie Books

★　★　★　★　★　★　★　★　★　★

"This is a brilliantly-written tale of internal struggle and redemption in a time of great social and political upheaval. The author does a chillingly good job of illustrating just how seductive the nationalist message was in a beaten and humiliated Germany, how it used and twisted values like patriotism, loyalty and honor to win over people who otherwise might have lived out their lives as ordinary, decent, humane people. *Before the Court of Heaven* is a powerful, intensely vivid look at Europe between the World Wars, and one man's attempt to make sense of his life, his deeds, and their meaning, to himself and to others."

— IndieReader
5-star Review

★　★　★　★　★　★　★　★　★　★

"Jack Mayer has written a strong, affecting novel that offers an arresting portrait of a deeply troubled time. His evocations of Ernst Werner Techow and other historical figures are beautifully and thoughtfully rendered. He has a remarkable grasp of period details, and he used these details to create an atmosphere of dense particularity and clarity. This is a story of immense human failure and touching redemption, and it stands among the finer recent portrayals in fiction of the most troubling era of mod   y sympathetic readership. I recomm

"Haunting echoes of Boris Pasternak's *Doctor Zhivago* and Irwin Shaw's *The Young Lions* waft through this excellent novel of the turbulent times encompassing Europe and the far reaches of the globe between World Wars I and II. Similar to those groundbreaking tales, Mayer's story is most concerned with lives rent asunder by historically catastrophic events... By keeping his focus on a small set of human beings caught up in the upheaval of entire populations, he is able to weave a narrative that is as poignant as it is riveting. The author does a superb job of pulling readers into Ernst's hopes and fears as he grapples with familial obligations, divided loyalties, and trials by fire and by courts both earthly and heavenly... Mayer's sweeping saga is simultaneously a compelling chronicle of history, a gripping tale of high adventure, and an enthralling love story in the classic tradition."

– Recommended by
the US *Review of Books*

★   ★   ★   ★   ★   ★   ★   ★   ★   ★

"On June 24, 1922, the terrorist Ernst Werner Techow murdered Walter Rathenau, the Jewish Foreign Minister of the Weimar Republic. Eleven years later, Hitler was sworn in as Chancellor. *Before the Court of Heaven* is a powerful chronicle of those fateful eleven years. But it's much more, and you may choke when reading the (authentic) letter written by Rathenau's mother to Techow's mother ... Repentance, forgiveness, atonement, redemption. The Talmud said it best: 'To save one life was to save the universe.' ... A luminous book."

– Ray Ortali, Emeritus Professor of French,
University at Albany and Publisher, *We
Love Books & Company* eMagazine

★   ★   ★   ★   ★   ★   ★   ★   ★   ★

"A fully engaging read from beginning to end, Before the Court of Heaven is a deftly crafted novel that showcases author Jack Mayer's truly impressive storytelling talents as a novelist. A terrifically entertaining read that is enhanced with close attention to historical detail, *Before the Court of Heaven* is very highly recommended."

– *Midwest Book Review*
Reviewer's Bookwatch, February 2016

★   ★   ★   ★   ★   ★   ★   ★   ★   ★

"...a compelling work... This is an excellent work of historical fiction, one that nevertheless provides the reader with an important and accurate lens into the past."

– Francis Nicosia, Raul Hilberg Distinguished
Professor of Holocaust Studies,
University of Vermont

"Period details come to life... Techow is the fascinating central figure whose story is deftly embellished. Before the Court of Heaven displays a remarkable talent for imagining the unknowable parts of Techow's psyche. It's a distinctive story poised between the drama of a Damascene conversion and a quieter, steadier about-face. Violence and atonement meld with affecting results."

– 5-Star Clarion Review

★　★　★　★　★　★　★　★　★　★

"*Before the Court of Heaven* is enthralling historical fiction based on the true story and subsequent legends of Ernst Techow... The novel is gripping from the very first line. This is an immersive, exciting, and often heart-breaking story."

– BlueInk Review (Starred Review)

★　★　★　★　★　★　★　★　★　★

"Jack Mayer has hit his stride as a sophisticated and convincing writer of historical fiction. His writing is vivid in the description of people and places and the ... violent upheavals in Germany that constitute the political landscape of this novel."

– MARJORIE LAMBERTI, Charles A. Dana Professor
Emerita of History, Middlebury College

★　★　★　★　★　★　★　★　★　★

"*Before the Court of Heaven* is enthralling historical fiction based on the true story and subsequent legends of Ernst Techow, a German assassin turned French Legionnaire... the novel is gripping from the very first line. This is an immersive, exciting, and often heart-breaking story that will engross any reader interested in this period of history."

– Blue Ink Review (Starred Review)

★　★　★　★　★　★　★　★　★　★

"*Before the Court of Heaven* is an engrossing novel that compels you to keep reading... Mayer's impressive skill as a writer allows him to seamlessly weave an engrossing, fictional account of one man's journey into a well-researched and nuanced portrayal of life in Weimar Germany and Nazi occupied Europe. Far beyond a simple page-turner, however, the book is also an impressive rendering of the historical realities of a dark era and the real uncertainties of the people living through it."

– REBECCA AYAKO BENNETTE,
Director of Jewish Studies and Associate
Professor of History (German),
Middlebury College

"Before the Court of Heaven is a captivating read... Mayer's novel takes its readers through the most tumultuous and painful decades of German history as its tormented protagonist develops... At times supporting basso continuo, at times gripping counter-point, Techow's tragic love story with his childhood friend Lisa provides an additional layer of humanity that recommends the novel to the silver screen. Mayer's characters and their stories... make the early 20th century come alive, and they stay with you long after you have finished their story. "

— Bettina Matthias
Professor of German, Middlebury College

★　★　★　★　★　★　★　★　★　★

"Before the Court of Heaven is a remarkable feat of historical and moral imagination: a captivating historical novel. The book goes personal, seeking to answer the question: how does political disaffection and resentment lead to violent radicalism. Mayer has created a spellbinding novel and a moral tale of enduring profundity."

— Robert S. Schine, Curt C. and Else Silberman
Professor of Jewish Studies, Middlebury College

★　★　★　★　★　★　★　★　★　★

"Jack Mayer's powerful historical novel provides a vivid portrait of a decaying democracy and the choices individuals must make in that context and their inevitable unintended consequences. Mayer's masterful command of the historical details of Weimar Germany's collapse and his thoughtful rendering of the book's central characters make this a rewarding and compelling read. The journey of the novel's protagonist... reveals the capacity for evil and good that can exist in one human being, as well as his or her potential for redemption. While set in another place and time, Before the Court of Heaven prompts reflection on contemporary moral challenges. Not to be missed."

— Allison Stanger, Leng Professor of International
Politics and Economics, Middlebury College

BEFORE THE COURT OF HEAVEN

A NOVEL

JACK MAYER

Author of *Life in a Jar: The Irena Sendler Project*

LONG TRAIL PRESS
MIDDLEBURY, VERMONT

for my wife, Chip and my son, Alex

Before the Court of Heaven
First Edition, October 2015

Text copyright © 2015 by Jack Mayer
Author photo by Chip Mayer
Cover design by Laurie Thomas
Interior design by Winslow Colwell/Wren Song Design

Published in the United States by Long Trail Press
Middlebury, VT 05753
www.jackmayer.net
jacklmayer33@gmail.com

The text of this publication was set in Quadraat.

ISBN: 978-0-9841113-4-3

Library of Congress Control Number: 2015915710

TABLE OF CONTENTS

AUTHOR'S NOTE

The events depicted in *Before the Court of Heaven* occurred after World War I in Germany, an enlightened culture, a constitutional democracy, with the rule of law and free elections. Ordinary people made free choices.

★   ★   ★   ★   ★   ★   ★   ★   ★   ★

On October 29, 1918, the eve of defeat in W.W. I, German sailors mutiny at the naval bases at Kiel and Wilhelmshaven. Leftist unrest finds enthusiastic recruits among the lower ranks of the military, who were war weary and intoxicated with the possibility of a leftist or Bolshevik revolution. Twelve days after the mutiny, Prince Max of Baden announces the Kaiser's abdication. The German monarchy is no more. Germany signs the armistice on November 11, 1918. The 1919 Versailles Treaty's harsh terms subject Germany to humiliation and backbreaking reparations, and contribute to post-war social disarray as forces of the left (communists of all convictions) and the right (monarchists, Nationalists, and fascists) battle for influence and control. Elections to the national assembly result in the lion's share of votes for the center-left Social Democratic Party, which nonetheless struggles for legitimacy and stability. The assembly meets in Weimar, and a constitution is adopted on August 11, 1919, ushering in a semi-presidential representative democracy. The Weimar Republic is born.

As the new German Republic takes its first democratic baby steps, forces from the left and right plot to strangle Weimar in the crib. Fearing for its survival, the government calls on paramilitary forces, the Freikorps, or Free Corps, vicious, anti-communist shadow militias, to put down leftist unrest. After ruthlessly crushing the communist threat, the Free Corps turns on the government of the Republic and attempts a coup: the Kapp Putsch – March 12, 1920. In the wake of the failure of the Kapp Putsch, a secret army, Organization Consul, (Organization C, The Black Reichswehr, 1920 – 1922), begins a determined campaign of terror and assassination to bring down Weimar. One of their victims, Foreign Minister Walther Rathenau is assassinated on June 24, 1922. Twenty-one-year-old Ernst Werner Techow is the driver for the assassination. Many individuals involved in the Free Corps ultimately make their way into the ranks of the SA and the SS.

Individuals spawn this history. Ernst Werner Techow, a young fascist, is one of those catalysts. *Before the Court of Heaven* is populated with historical characters, agents of this history. Much of Part 1 of this novel is based on transcripts from the Leipzig court proceedings of the Organization Consul (OC) trial – October 1922. Frau Rathenau's poignant courtroom letter is genuine. Techow's trial was a worldwide sensation. The beginning of Part II is also based on actual events, but then the historical trail runs cold, and the ending is a fiction.

I first heard Ernst Werner Techow's story as a sermon at Middlebury College in 1992. Rabbi Fritz Rothschild presented this sermon on Yom Kippur, the most solemn day of the Jewish year, a day to atone for one's sins, a day to grant and receive forgiveness.

★   ★   ★   ★   ★   ★   ★   ★   ★   ★

In 1992, the mayor of Mainz, Germany invited my mother, who had narrowly escaped the Holocaust, to return to her hometown to speak with school children, to tell her story, to be a living witness. The idea of going home was too painful, and she declined the first invitation. A year later, the mayor invited her again, and she courageously accepted. Thus began a remarkable dialogue with the community that had expelled her fifty-five years earlier. My mother spoke as a witness and, as Elie Wiesel observed, "when you listen to a witness, you become a witness." She was keeping history alive and preventing its recuurrence. Once again she spoke of the fragrance of the nut trees that bloomed in her front yard and of swimming in the Rhine.

I hope you read this story with an open heart so that you too will smell the sweet possibility of *t'shuvah* – turning from evil – in a world that reeks of it.

Against the brutal tide of Nazism, individuals made courageous choices to turn from evil and save lives.

It is in this spirit that I have written *Before the Court of Heaven*.

CHARACTERS
(★ Historical characters)

TECHOW FAMILY & HOUSEHOLD:
  ★ **Ernst Werner Techow** born 1901
  ★ **Hans Gerd Techow** – born 1905 – Ernst's younger brother

* **Leo Techow** – born 1899 – Ernst's older brother
* **Magistrate Alfred Techow** – Ernst's father.
* **Gertrude Techow** – Ernst's mother
* **Uncle Erwin Behrens** – Ernst's Uncle, Gertrude Techow's sister
  Frau Stimmel – Housekeeper for the Techow family

RATHENAU AND ORGANIZATION C ASSASSINS:

* **Walther Rathenau** – born 1867 – German industrialist, politician, writer, and statesman who served as German Foreign Minister during the Weimar Republic's early years. He was the highest ranking Jew in the Weimar government. Assassinated June 24, 1922.
* **Mathilde Rathenau** – Walther Rathenau's mother
* **Hermann Ehrhardt** – born 1881 – a German Free Corps commander from 1918 to 1920, he commanded the famous Ehrhardt Marine Brigade and led the violent right-wing Organization Consul (OC). He was an early Hitler supporter.
* **Erwin Kern** – born 1898 – a naval officer and one of the assassins of Walther Rathenau. Kern was a member of the Ehrhardt Marine Brigade and the Organization C.
* **Hermann Fischer** – born 1896 – a member of Organization C and one of the assassins of Walther Rathenau.
* **Ernst von Salomon** – born 1902 – writer and Free Corps and Organization C operative from Munich.
* **Willi Günther** – student member of Organization C
* **Hartmut Plaas** – 'The Fat Man' – high ranking Organization C operative from Münich

FRIENDS & LOVERS:

Lisa Schmidt – *Wandervogel* (German youth scout) and Ernst's life-long love
Fritz Sommers – *Wandervogel* and childhood friend of Ernst and Lisa
Margaret – Lisa's childhood friend

STRIEGAU PRISON:

Puck – aka **Julius Isaac** – Ernst's cellmate, a forger and career criminal

ALGERIAN DESERT:

Moulay Bassim – Tuareg elder and desert trader

MARSEILLE:

* **Varian Fry** – born 1907 – An American journalist who ran the Emergency Rescue Committee in Vichy France that helped approximately 2,000 to 4,000 anti-Nazi and Jewish refugees escape Nazi Germany and the Holocaust.
* **Bill Freier** – born 1913 as Wilhelm Spira, a Viennese political cartoonist and caricaturist. Spira fled to Paris in August 1938, where he assumed the more symbolic name of Bill Freier (meaning "more free"). Following the Nazi invasion of France, Spira became a fugitive for his anti-Nazi cartoons. He fled to Marseille where he became an expert forger for Varian Fry.
* **Mary Jayne Gold** – born 1909 was a glamorous American heiress who worked with Varian Fry. She used her considerable wealth and charm to help prominent Jewish and anti-Nazi refugees, like Marc Chagall, escape Vichy France.
* **Daniel Benedite** – born 1912 – a French journalist and resistance fighter who was a key aide to Varian Fry.

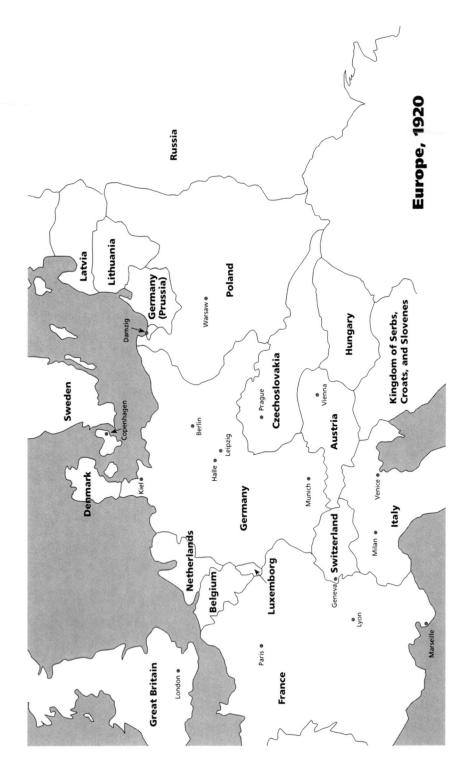

Europe, 1920

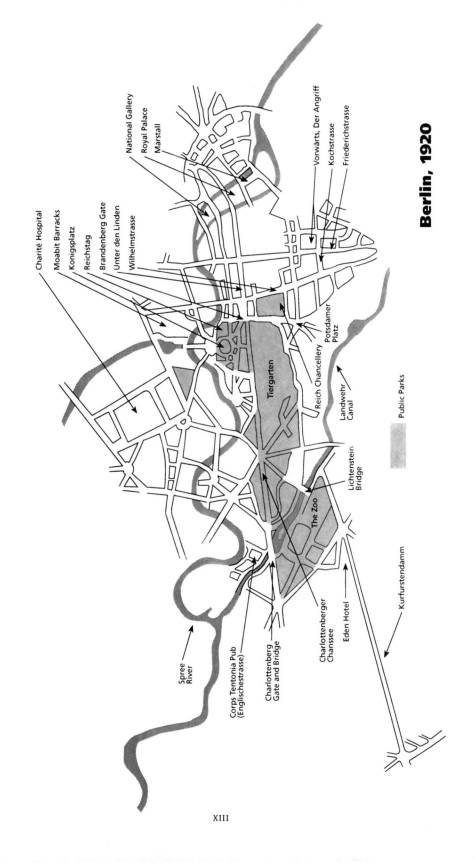

Berlin, 1920

Charité Hospital
Moabit Barracks
Konigsplatz
Reichstag
Brandenberg Gate
Unter den Linden
Wilhelmstrasse

National Gallery
Royal Palace
Marstall

Vorwärts, Der Angriff
Kochstrasse
Friederichstrasse

Tiergarten

Reich Chancellery

Potsdamer Platz

Landwehr Canal

Public Parks

The Zoo

Lichtenstein Bridge

Spree River

Corps Tentonia Pub (Englischestrasse)

Charlottenberg Gate and Bridge

Charlottenberger Chanssee

Eden Hotel

Kurfurstendamm

XIII

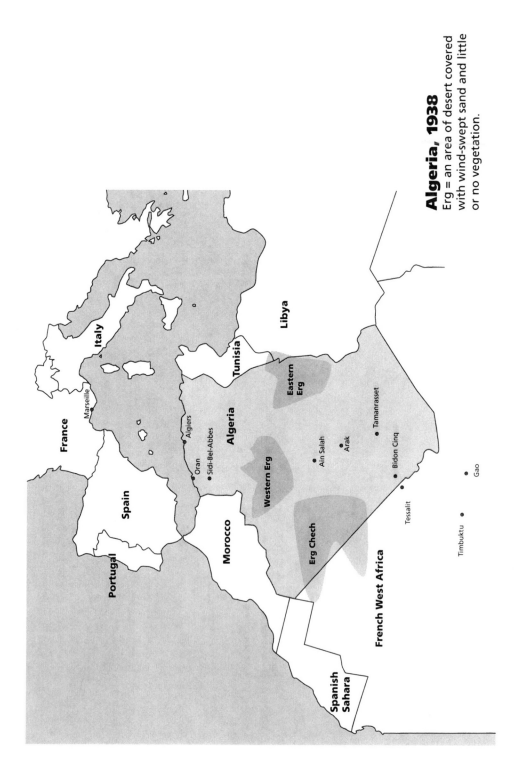

Algeria, 1938

Erg = an area of desert covered with wind-swept sand and little or no vegetation.

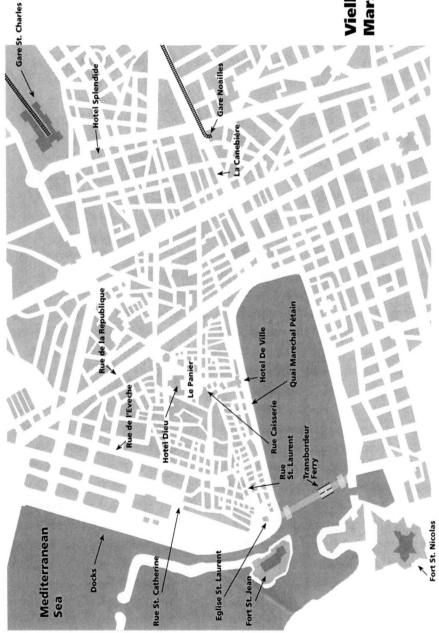

Vielle Ville,
Marseille, 1942

ACKNOWLEDGEMENTS

I want to express my deep appreciation to those who helped make *Before the Court of Heaven* possible. I owe a deep and reverential debt to my wife, Chip, and my son Alex, who lived with this novel for many years. I dedicate it to both of them. Chip was my first and last reader and my first editor, saving me from some colossal blunders. When this project was nothing more than a haunting tale, Marita Schine, my friend and research assistant, translated original German archival material, including hand-written police depositions of Techow and the other defendants, and German newspapers of the time. Every Tuesday we sat together at Middlebury College and Ilsely Library squinting at microfiche, learning about this remarkable history and filling in the puzzle of Ernst Werner Techow. Novelist and Middlebury College English Professor, Jay Parini, my generous mentor at the Bread Loaf Writers' Conference, has been bountiful with encouragement and advice. Jay introduced me to my first professional editor, Michael Lowenthal. Michael's thorough, sensitive, and thoughtful editing saved this novel from collapsing of its own weight, and helped me become a better writer. His enthusiasm and good humor made a difficult task possible and enjoyable.

Deep gratitude for my parents, Harvey and Nana Mayer, who lived through the Weimar years and the rise of Nazism. Their personal recollections and vignettes from their childhoods in Germany were invaluable for me as an author and as their son. My parents narrowly escaped the Holocaust, others in my family did not. My uncle and aunt, Eric and Lisa Mayer and Fred Stroop shared invaluable personal recollections of growing up in Weimar Germany.

David Rosenberg, Emeritus Professor of Political Science at Middlebury College, read through two drafts of the manuscript and helped shape the arc of the novel. Martin Sabrow, a noted German historian, shared archival information with me about the historical Ernst Werner Techow. Marjorie Lamberti, Middlebury College Emeritus History Professor specializing in Weimar Germany, was kind enough to read an early draft of the novel and helped me bring fiction in line with historical accuracy. Professor Rebecca Bennette, a Holocaust scholar and Director of Jewish Studies at Middlebury College, read *Before the Court of Heaven*, corrected historical inaccuracies, and blessed the book with her commendation. Middlebury College German

Professor Bettina Matthias, also reviewed the manuscript and gave the novel a lovely blurb. Otto Friedrich's compelling history, *Before the Deluge*, a vivid portrait of the political, economic, social and cultural landscape of Weimar, Berlin, provided a menu of civic and intimate vignettes of inter-war Germany. A bibliography is available on request.

Many thanks for the artistry and patience of Winslow Colwell, for book design, cover art, maps, text, and for being my computer guru. (Win was awarded the Eric Hoffer da Vinci Eye Award for designing my previous book, *Life in a Jar: The Irena Sendler Project*.) My deep appreciation to Megan Shrestha for her generous and skillful marketing assistance and computer savy. This book could not have been launched without Win and Megan's care and competence. Thanks also to Robert Schine for his contribution to the cover art – penning Frau Rathenau's letter in authentic Suetterlin script.

Anne Wallace and David Gusakov edited an early and long draft of the novel. While hiking up Mt. Marcy in New York, Adam Woods helped me discover the end of this story. Many other generous friends and family have been early readers. I thank them all for their feedback. My thanks go to: Priscilla Baker, Margie Beckoff, Mary Brevda, Win and Joanna Colwell, Carol Crawford, Victoria DeWind, Julia Eddy, Kathy Giles, Jonathan Katz, Mary Kellington, Chris Lawton, Alex Mayer, Dan Mayer, Jan and Bruce Ogilvie, Margaret Olson, Jean Rosenberg, Elizabeth Rosenberg, Peggy and Shel Sax, Robert Schine, Melita Sedic, Eva Simon, Ron Slabaugh, Homer Wells, Adam Woods, and Alex Wylie.

I am grateful for the editorial assistance of Jennifer Bates and Amy Graham who helped with the final cleanup of the manuscript. I also extend my appreciation to Ray Ortali for being a champion of *Before the Court of Heaven* and my previous book, *Life in a Jar: The Irena Sendler Project* through his on-line magazine *We Love Books & Company*.

Finally, thanks to Pete LaFramboise who educated me about the Mercedes flat-head engine.

"Art is a lie which makes us realize the truth."

–Picasso

"What are our stories if not the
mirrors we hold up to our fears?"

–Wally Lamb (This One Thing I Know is True)

PART ONE

HISTORIES

The Deed of Deeds

June, 1922

The assassins were twenty minutes late. Uncharacteristically, so too was Foreign Minister Walther Rathenau, their intended victim. Exhaust puffed from his idling limousine a block and a half away, as his chauffeur paced before the opulent entrance to Rathenau's home.

Ernst Werner Techow monitored the chauffeur from under the bonnet of the assassins' Mercedes, an open six seater. "Damn this pig," he muttered as he fine-tuned the oil feed. The idle smoothed to velvet. Rathenau's driver still paced. Ernst secured the bonnet. Kern and Fischer, immobile in the back seat, watched Rathenau's man check his pocket watch.

If Ernst's mother had known of their plan, she would have asked: whom did he think he was to do this? Did he not think of the shame this would bring on his father's memory? The past no longer mattered. Today, June 24th, was St. John's Day, a day of anti-Semitic actions, a day Jews stayed in their homes. He remembered Pastor Namann explaining to his Sunday school class that according to St. John's Gospel, all Jews in all generations are guilty of the death of Jesus. It was a day to hear frightening stories of Jews using the blood of murdered Christian children to make Matzoh for Passover. Three years earlier, Germany had surrendered to the dictates of the Versailles Treaty. Today was the day the Weimar Republic began to crumble and fall. After today, they would all know that it was not only a man he was about to kill, but the Weimar obscenity. It would only take longer to die.

He released the handbrake and adjusted his goggles. Ready.

His older brother, Leo, would damn Ernst under his breath, then try to save him like the repulsive Bolshevik missionary Leo was – the only one of the three brothers who had turned out that way. He was the same Leo who had shared his bedroom when they still lived in a mansion on Wannseestrasse behind a wrought iron gate; the same brother he almost shot two years earlier when the red flag flew over the Royal Palace.

It was best that his father was no longer alive. When Ernst offended as a child, which he did considerably more often than Leo, his father would pinch his neck, pull the hairs behind his ear, and sentence him, like the magistrate he was, to write something corrective one hundred times. *I must not kill pigeons in Mariakirche Park. I must not be disrespectful to Headmaster, Herr Strauss.* And after today: *I must not kill for the Vaterland.*

But this was the "justice of the Volk." Organization C (OC) had chosen him for this moment. Planning Rathenau's assassination and anticipating its consequences had become exhilarating, electrifying – even erotic – like waiting for Lisa at Günther's deserted apartment before an afternoon of lovemaking.

The sudden burst of flapping wings startled them all. Something scattered the pigeons at the corner of Königsallee. One by one, the birds returned, anxiously cocking their heads and pecking at crumbs. Ernst first killed pigeons when he was ten; it was after the fight with the Jew, Rothstein. Ernst had walked through the park across from St. Mary's Church to the Franco-Prussian War memorial with his new slingshot, the one he had just paid Heinrich Schliefen his last marks for. With its polished wood handle so smooth, it was the finest instrument he had ever held. The first time he used it, anticipation had caused his heart to shudder, as it did now; his arm strained to pull the elastic strap and trembled until he released the stone. It flew like a bullet into the flock, which suddenly rose into the air, clucking, flapping, dust and crumbs flying – all but one bird, lying on its side, one wing flapping feebly, turning in a slow circle. One dying bird – his clearest recollection – as provocative now as it was disturbing then.

Rathenau's auto idled, still unattended. After today, Organization C would quietly submerge again like a sated shark, and vanish until the next assassination, and the next, until Weimar was dead and the Nationalists, the true German patriots, seized power.

In the rear view mirror Ernst saw Kern, square built and fit, his fixed gaze animated only by wisps of blond hair. The murder weapon, a machine pistol, lay at his feet. Beside Kern, Hermann Fischer, tallest of the three, skeletal, smoked another cigarette. To hear Kern rant about Rathenau – the traitor, the highest ranking Jew in the Weimar Republic, the guarantor of the Versailles Treaty, the 'stab in the back' – Ernst wondered that he hadn't been murdered before now.

It was 10:25.

He tried to distract himself with Saturday's *Berliner Tageblatt*, resting on the steering wheel, but the vibrations blurred the words. Ernst eased in the choke and the print re-focused, but he could not make sense of it – could not read the words. Sweat from his palms smudged the newsprint and stained his fingers. Earlier that morning, at Schütt's Garage, the oil leak had worsened and Ernst had patched it again with heavy tape. The delay cost half an hour. For now, the convertible idled smoothly, the only life in a line of parked automobiles a half block from the main thoroughfare, Königsallee.

The chauffeur came to attention and pulled on his driving gloves. He settled behind the wheel and waited.

Assassinating Rathenau was more than killing a man, something Ernst had done before. The 'Deed of Deeds' was the murder of a traitor. Too many Germans had been seduced by his betrayal and revered him.

Ernst's chest tightened, a familiar acid tension he'd experienced before in a mutiny, in a revolution, in chaos when the bullet could strike at any moment. He calmed himself stroking the Mercedes' rich wood-grained paneling, fondling the mahogany ball of the shift lever. He recalled his father's Mercedes, purchased in 1910. A year later, when Ernst was ten, Eric, the Techow chauffeur, let Ernst 'drive' on his lap and he delighted in the other kind of fear, the carnival fright. It was the last time he'd felt the kindly embrace of a man.

"You mustn't tell your mother," Eric had said, his arms guiding Ernst's on the steering wheel.

"Can we tell Father?"

"I will mention it, but only when I am alone with him. Say nothing until then. Look out! Here come the bumps!"

Ernst had laughed out loud as the hard rubber wheels jarred and jostled over the trolley tracks crossing Königsallee at the intersection with Wallotstrasse and Erdenerstrasse – the same intersection where Rathenau would die today. He could still hear Eric singing:

> Bump, bump the horsey-rider!
> When he falls down he will cry.
> If he falls into the ditch,
> then the ravens will devour him.
> If he falls into a swamp
> then the horsey-rider goes kerplunk!

As they shouted "kerplunk!" in unison, Eric bumped him from his lap into the air. Ernst's nanny, Maria, also played Bump, bump the horsey-rider! and let him fall between her legs, into the sling of her pinafore. A playmate once told Ernst about how his father had played the game carrying him on his shoulders. He could only wonder at such affection.

If Lisa could see him now she would say he wore his 'frightful expression,' with sunken slitted eyes, flushed cheeks, lips drawn thin. She said his eyes turned from blue sky to steel, and his blond hair darkened. He had sworn to Lisa that after today he was finished with OC – begged her to believe that this was his final mission.

Gradually, the words blurred again; he toggled the choke, watched the oil gauge tremble like a dragonfly's tail and slowly fall. Ernst leapt from the car and threw open the bonnet. Oil spit from the taped junction, spraying his face and soiling the full-length leather coat Kern had presented to him that morning at Schütt's Garage, before anything had gone wrong.

Kern sprung from the back seat, over the car's doors, and in a moment was beside him. Ernst reached blindly for the oil feed and sealed the leak with more tape. The engine purred again.

"Do you know what you're doing, boy?"

"I'm twenty-one," Ernst said to the flathead engine, his fingers still working the tape. "You've only a few years on me."

"A few years perhaps," Kern said, "but one war."

Ernst straightened, tall and thin, challenging Kern's granite density. "I've killed more Communists than..."

"Relax, Techow." Kern fixed Ernst with an uncommon expression of concern. "It's your first time, isn't it?"

"No. No, I'm fine." His shoulders slumped. He took a step back. "It's just this... this car..."

"Poor choice?"

He avoided Kern's cobra eyes. "It's a piece of shit," Ernst muttered. "Küchenmeister must have run it into the ground. One would think OC could afford a fleet of Mercedes."

"Enough!" Kern bared his teeth, breathing hard. His neck muscles contracted, a red blush flushed his puffy cheeks. "If it's shit, it's high quality shit – and untraceable." He glanced at his watch then at Fischer. "Make it run!"

Ernst worked the heavy tape. He hated for Kern to be angry with him. "I'm sorry, Sir," he said. "It will run for a short time – probably long enough – no guarantees."

4

"Make it work, Techow," Kern said. "The Fat Man said it has to be today." He brushed light blond hairs from his smooth forehead and tucked them under his new leather driving cap. "It's time!" Kern backed away. Fischer threw his cigarette into the street and flashed two fingers forming a 'V'.

Ernst slammed the bonnet and wiped his hands on the rag. It was difficult to take in a breath. Clouds hung low and immobile over Berlin; overnight rain had left puddles in the deserted street. Only a few bush roses and Kern's cheeks glowed pink. Kern plucked Ernst's newspaper from the front seat and let himself into the back, once more remote.

"Arrangements have been made for the boat to Sweden," he said without looking up from the *Tageblatt*. "We leave from Warnemünde." Kern looked up into the gray overcast. "Even the rain has cooperated. Rathenau's car is open."

"Sweden?" Ernst said. "What are you talking about? I'm not going to Sweden."

"Just for awhile. OC's orders. Your trial would not be attractive."

Ernst was about to protest, but then Fischer sat forward, his eyes electric with excitement, but still bloodshot from last night's drinking. "Here he comes. Let's kill the son of a bitch."

As much as Ernst knew about Kern, that was how little he knew about Hermann Fischer. Even when drunk, he spoke little. Like Kern, his wispy hair was of the fine variety that almost disappeared in sunlight. He seemed not to have eyebrows, unless one looked from the side in just the right light. Fischer's gently curved, aquiline nose and small pointed mouth gave the mistaken impression of a man deep in thought.

Ernst gripped the shift as Rathenau strode down the walk toward his automobile.

There had never been any mention of Sweden – of exile. Weimar was to fall – he was to be a hero, not a fugitive.

Though Ernst was a block away and could not make out details, he remembered how tall and handsome Rathenau had been when the minister had visited his father six years earlier.

What if Weimar did not 'collapse' as Kern assured? Ernst might be in Sweden for years; Lisa would be left in Berlin with Fritz.

Rathenau exchanged a few words with a manservant, positioned his black fedora on his head, and folded a walking stick under his arm. Ernst thought he took a deep, refreshing breath, as if pleased with the world and himself.

The Foreign Minister glanced up and down the street, then let himself into the back seat of his automobile. He opened his newspaper and appeared to exchange pleasantries with his chauffeur. Once moving, the car passed close enough for Ernst to hear the Foreign Minister laugh aloud.

"Follow a block behind," Kern ordered.

Ernst's senses sharpened. The overcast light brightened. He thought he could hear the trill of a Zaunkönig, one of the tiny yellow 'fence kings' who sang outside his window as a child. The Mercedes growled. From behind him came the sharp metallic locking of the machine pistol's magazine. Though it was Saturday, the tree-lined Königsallee, redolent of roses and opulence, was not empty. They passed a trolley and a double line of Kindergarteners in white blouses and blue pinafores following their Mother Superior's fluttering blue habit.

He remembered the story of his favorite poet Heinrich Heine, on his deathbed. The priest told him that God would forgive him his sins. "Why, of course he will forgive me," Heine said. "That's his business." Ernst wondered if it was God's business to forgive these next few moments.

Kern leaned forward and touched his shoulder. "Now!"

Ernst floored the accelerator, hoping the oil feed would hold. The roadster surged and gained on Rathenau. They were coming up on the tram lines. Rathenau's car slowed to navigate the double bend in Königsallee. Ernst felt his heart race and misfire, the wind roaring in his ears. Hunched over the wheel, he chanted from a Free Corps marching song:

> Shoot down Walther Rathenau.
> He's a goddamn dirty Jew.

Over and over he repeated the two lines for courage.

One car length ahead and to the right, Rathenau turned to the sound of their acceleration, perhaps concerned about a collision. Ernst wished not to see his face, but could not help himself. He recognized Rathenau immediately – his expression whimsical, curious. Their eyes met for a moment, and Ernst remembered his father and Rathenau in the Techow parlor, sipping liquor from fine crystal.

They passed a street cleaner's dust heap. Rathenau smiled at Ernst and touched the handle of his cane to the brim of his black felt hat. His goatee suggested the face of Lenin. Ernst looked forward again, leaned into the steering wheel, accelerator on the floor. He could not stop from turning again and met the chauffeur's uneasy glance. Over his shoulder Ernst saw Kern stand and turn toward Rathenau.

Ernst jerked with each rapid *pop-pop-pop* of Kern's machine pistol. In his rearview mirror he glimpsed Fischer tossing the hand grenade almost into Rathenau's lap. Brakes screeched. Rathenau's car disappeared. At the intersection where Königsallee turns sharply to the right, over the trolley tracks that had bounced him as a boy, Ernst proceeded straight through onto Wallotstrasse.

"Faster!" Kern commanded.

The hand grenade detonated; the blast bruised his ears. Ernst heard one high pitched scream. A woman pointed at him, and then the intersection was behind them.

The street cleaner would later testify how Rathenau's body lifted off the seat, how his car lurched briefly forward, then stopped.

At the trial four months later, Helene Kaiser, a middle-aged nurse who had been on her way to work at the tuberculosis ward of Friedrich Wilhelm Hospital, recalled how traffic from all five streets converging on the intersection had stopped. An eerie, hushed space opened around the smoking car, "like a bubble under water," she said. Blue-gray smoke churning from the back seat dissipated so everyone could see the rounded back of a man slumped forward. She walked, then ran toward the car. Except for the smoke, the black limousine seemed strangely undamaged. She eased herself beside the toppled minister and maneuvered his head onto her lap. Rathenau's chauffeur, miraculously unhurt, pulled off his driving goggles, and Frau Kaiser remembered his face smudged black from the explosion except for twin ellipses of pink skin around his eyes. Blood flowed freely from wounds in Rathenau's jaw and neck, staining her uniform, but she stroked his forehead, murmuring reassurance as his face paled and mottled. He looked into her eyes, she testified, and held her gaze for a long moment before he died.

★   ★   ★   ★   ★   ★   ★   ★   ★   ★

Ernst drove automatically, looking at everything, seeing nothing. The steering wheel felt cold and wet. His fists ached. Two blocks beyond the intersection, the engine's hum abruptly coarsened and rattled – the exhaust thickened. The Mercedes jerked and bucked, screeched a metallic whine, and died.

Kern jumped out of the car. "Shit, Techow! There's a police station not two blocks from here!"

"You saw the oil feed!" Ernst slammed the door behind him, plucked off his driving cap and hurled it onto the seat.

He threw open the smoking bonnet, but before he could look inside, Kern

7

spun him around and grasped his shirt up short beneath his chin. "It's a fucking Mercedes, Techow. A ten-year-old could make this run."

In the years he had known Kern, Ernst had never seen his steely eyes as they were now, wild and distressed. He managed to whisper, "The Fat Man – we mustn't be apprehended."

Kern's tremulous fist slackened. There was something smooth, momentarily graceful, as Kern's body sagged for a moment, then firmed up again. He released Ernst. In that instant before he turned away, Ernst unexpectedly saw terror in his eyes.

"Take off your coat," Kern ordered. "You too, Fischer. Push the car to the curb. Techow – under the bonnet as if you're working on the engine. Hermann, disappear under the car."

Kern threw the Mauser machine pistol over a wall into a private garden. Minutes later the first police car drove by on Wallotstrasse. Three policemen ran by, uninterested in two young men working on their car.

A crowd swelled at the intersection of Königsallee and Erdenerstrasse. Police officers had already cordoned off half the thoroughfare, creating a hopelessly tangled congestion of automobiles and horse carts. Ernst, Kern, and Fischer abandoned the car and filtered through the stunned crowd at Königsallee.

Three hours later they strode through the Tiergarten, then to the Brandenburg Gate, where massed marchers, already thousands, paraded in silent witness, dolefully, under the red banners of Socialism and the black-red-gold flag of the Weimar Republic. All of Berlin knew; a church bell tolled ceaselessly. Workers who had left their factories and warehouses marched, solemn and silent, in the city center.

Ernst clasped the straps of his knapsack, bulging with clothes and food for three days – the same pack he had carried as a boy, as a *Wandervogel* scout in the Black Forest with Fritz and Lisa before the Great War, before Organization C, before Kern assured him the Republic would collapse after Rathenau's assassination. The Nationalists would seize power, the officer corps would back them, and, before the first snow, Ernst would be a hero of the Deutsches Reich, the German Empire.

But the crowd was funereal – a somber parade of working men and women, their heads bare. "This isn't what you said would happen," Ernst said to Kern.

Kern continued to lead them along the margin of the crowd. "It's only been a few hours. Patience."

"I don't like this," Ernst said.

Kern suddenly turned on Ernst and pushed him into a recessed doorway. Again his hot breath warmed Ernst's face. "Don't lose your nerve." He gripped Ernst's arms. "Just remember this. Never implicate OC – that's all you need to remember. The courts are ours." He released Ernst. "But there will be no problem. We'll all be safe in Sweden."

Ernst cleared his throat. "I'm not going to Sweden," he said. "I'll take my chances."

Kern looked at his watch and turned to Fischer. "We'll be late for the train, Hermann." He turned again to Ernst. "You're not staying for that girl, are you?"

Ernst stared back at Kern, bewildered. In that moment, he didn't care a fig for OC or Kern, or Ludendorf or the new Reich – any of it. He wanted Lisa and to hell with the rest. He backed away from his co-conspirators, into the mob.

Kern pulled him back. "The Fat Man will be most upset."

Ernst squirmed away.

Fischer pointed at his watch. "Time to go!"

"Fool!" Kern said. He and Fischer sprinted across the plaza. Ernst, clutching his knapsack, was jostled into the flow of the proletarian crowd, carried along by the current of mourners. A red banner slapped his face, and two burly men bumped him on either side. He stumbled, tripped by too many legs, lost the sky, and fell onto his knees, rolled to his side and strained to get back up again, gasping for air – for balance. He had unleashed a deluge, altered history, shamed his family. There was no undoing, no repairing the rent he had created in the world.

Undoubtedly, Lisa already knew. One had only to look out the window to know that something dreadful had occurred, something so memorable that people would recollect for the rest of their lives what they were doing at the moment when they learned Rathenau had been assassinated.

Ernst had to return to Schütt and Diestel's Garage in the Schmargendorf suburb to pay off Schütt and retrieve his tools. Likely as not the fat garage owner was still drunk from last night.

Trams stood idle on the main lines. Conductors left their vehicles in the street to join the mourners. Such an odd feeling, snaking through the interstices of the dazed crowd in the shadow of the Brandenburg Gate. He thought he must be the only person in this hypnotized city who had someplace to go. Every bump and jostle multiplied as if nerves reached out from his body like cat's whiskers.

At Lisa's dormitory, students milled on the green, clinking beer steins and exchanging gossip about the murder. Just below her window, on a table set up on the grass, a crudely lettered sign appealed for new members for the GNYO, the German National Youth Organization.

"Techow," a young Nationalist called to him. "Happy St. John's Day! Come have a beer!"

Ernst tried to smile and shook his head.

The young man caught up with Ernst. "If you're looking for Lisa, she's with Fritz. Emergency meeting of the national party. What a day, eh? The Deed of Deeds!"

Ernst wondered if they could tell by looking at him – surely a policeman could. "Yes. A great day." He hurried into Lisa's dormitory parlor where he scribbled a note and dropped it into her mailbox.

> Dear Lisa,
>   Going out of town for a few days. I'll tell you all about this when
> I return. I want you, more than anything.
>   If anyone asks, you haven't heard from me.
>   I love you. Ernst

The instant he dropped the note into Lisa's box, he saw the stern house-mother squinting suspiciously at him from across the parlor, and he felt hunted. It was the terror he felt fighting Spartakists in the streets of Berlin a few short years ago and again during the Kapp Putsch – the feeling that he was in the crosshairs of some sniper's Mauser 78. He wished for invisibility, but everyone seemed to be scrutinizing him with unusual attention.

For the next few days at least, he would be safe at his Uncle Erwin's estate in Jacobsdorf. Uncle Erwin neither knew nor cared about the world beyond his estate – and Ernst was his favorite nephew.

Schütt's Garage was deserted when he finally arrived late in the afternoon. A generator whirred in the far corner, churning and blending the penetrating scents of gasoline and oil, but the mechanics had abandoned their tools to join the mourning masses, leaving two cars with their bonnets raised.

He walked through the bays, across a small courtyard, and climbed the shadowed stairwell to Schütt's apartment. As he turned the corner atop the stairs he was suddenly face to face with Schütt, and the shock set loose a flood of adrenaline, his heart banging hard and fast. They both backed away, startled. Ernst, almost a head taller, recognized Schütt's bulging abdomen, barely contained by a grease-stained undershirt. Two days' beard stubbled his hanging jowls. Soured cognac and wine, the Schweden punch that smelled so sweet last night, fouled his breath. His yellow teeth clenched the butt of a cold cigar.

Schütt squinted at him. "It was you, wasn't it?"

"I don't know what you're talking about," Ernst said.

"I saw the machine pistol last night."

"You saw nothing last night." Ernst's nostrils flared. He dug deeply into his pocket for the roll of money. "One thousand marks, Herr Schütt. I believe we're settled."

Schütt counted the bills. "You're not going to rescue any goddamn Nationalists from a goddamn French prison, are you?"

"Herr Schütt, it would be better for you not to pursue this."

"Rathenau – an important man." Schütt's eyes jumped from window to stairwell to Ernst.

"Herr Schütt, you are dealing with dangerous people. Forget this, or risk everything."

Schütt laughed, spraying saliva. Ernst fingered the Free Corps dagger in his pocket.

"You rookie!" Schütt pulled the cigar stump from between his teeth. "You think I'd turn you in? I'd give you a fucking medal if I had one." Then he laughed and escorted Ernst into his disordered apartment. "Just one question. Why now?"

"I don't know what you're talking about."

Schütt laughed again. It was stifling in the apartment, and flies lazily buzzed about a pitcher of Schweden punch and turned-over glasses. Ernst found the box of paint and brushes he had used to alter the license plate. His temples throbbed.

Schütt sank into his sagging couch, and more flies flew up like fat dust motes. He rested his feet on a low table littered with crushed cigarettes and empty glasses. "Whoever is behind this, they surely got everyone's attention. Even my mechanics, not a Communist among them, left their jobs to join the march. They liked... no, they loved Rathenau. Stood up to the goddamn French." He broke into fits of laughter again, then belched. "How's Küchenmeister's car?"

"Where's my tool kit? It has my name on it."

"Have some punch, Techow. You've earned it. Don't worry about your tool kit. I'll find it and keep it safe for you."

Ernst circled behind Schütt and pressed the point of his dagger against his throat. Schütt's cigar fell onto his lap.

"Don't tempt me," Ernst breathed. The blade trembled. "You... you are involved in this... this endeavor, up to your asshole. You and Diestel will be part of any prosecution. There can be no mistakes. My tools!"

Schütt laughed, nervously this time, and his stubbled jowls shook like soiled gelatin. "Under the kitchen sink, behind the soap powder."

Ernst released him. "I only did this for Kern," Schütt said. "He's the only true soldier among you. It's pathetic using boys to do a man's job."

Ernst stuffed the toolbox into a canvas sack and thundered down the stairs. As the garage door closed and the generator whir was suddenly muffled, he inhaled deeply, cleansed his lungs and felt light-headed; fear of snipers gave way to a peculiar sense that he was creating something mythic – something meant to be – something beyond substance. He felt invincible. He was going to get away with it; he felt an exhilaration not unlike the night he first undressed Lisa and their naked bodies touched.

Daylight had faded, tenement shadows grown long by the time he arrived at his mother's apartment on Heydenstrasse. Through the wood panel apartment door he heard his younger brother, Hans Gerd, shouting at her and then her scolding retort. Ernst stood at the door listening, his hand unwilling to turn the knob. There was something reassuring about his mother's tirade.

Ernst held the doorknob for a long moment, summoning his courage. His pulse started its bumblebee rhythm again. He opened the door in time to see Hans Gerd storm off to his room, leaving their mother standing by the kitchen, her hands perched hard on her hips as if they pinched them thin. Ernst thought right away that she knew.

"You're late, Ernst," she said, and turned back to her stove so he could only imagine her expression. "We'll eat now. You need a haircut."

Perhaps it was the hot, flat light of sunset that made her lips and cheeks so vibrant. When she was angry, color returned to her skin, and Ernst remembered how elegant she once had been, when his father was still alive and the house had thirty rooms, and there were parties. He and Leo would sit on the first floor landing, by the man-sized Chinese vase, watching the guests and eating sweet cakes and marzipan. His mother glittered in expensive but modest gowns, tall and thin, her long face delicately poised, her hair perfectly pinned, a vision floating from one guest to another. By her mockingbird laughter, delicate and unique, he knew exactly which room she was in when he closed his eyes. Then his father died and the dream evaporated.

"Hans Gerd! Come to the table immediately!"

Hans Gerd sulked out of his bedroom, his hair wild from inattention, and sat at a small kitchen table set for three. He nodded at Ernst then turned to steady a piece of black-bread with the stump where his right hand should have been, and buttered it with his left. Ernst could feel his mother's glare, and he struggled to avoid eye contact.

"You heard what happened today." His mother's hair was badly brushed.

He studied the beans on his plate and speared three at once.

"You were in the city today, weren't you?"

"Hmm. Yes, I was." Even without looking up he could feel the chill in her eyes – the accusation in her tone.

Her serving spoon clacked a Delft Bowl, her eyes avoided his. She cleared her throat but still her voice rasped. "Were you involved in Dr. Rathenau's murder?"

Ernst noticed her hands – red and chapped. "I hear it was an assassination – not really a murder."

"Don't be stupid!" she hissed and now looked at him. "I must know if you were involved."

Ernst looked down. "Others did this!" A pigeon cooed on the windowsill. "I won't be home tonight, Mother. Hans Gerd and I are going out. I may be away a few days on a job."

"Your father..." She rummaged for exact words. "Your father would not have wanted you to break the law."

He banged the table and locked eyes with her. "Father and his law! What about Grandfather? What about 1848?"

"I'm sorry to say – your grandfather would have been a Socialist," she said, "like Leo, out there with the mob."

Almost certainly his older brother Leo was parading in the street right now with the Reds and his detestable fiancée, Katherine.

Hans Gerd began to cough until his face turned red. His mother asked, "Did you take your medicine?"

"Yes..." His lips puckered, and he coughed again.

She stared at him through the mist over her soup. "The bottle is empty. I know when you lie to me."

"Yes, Mother."

"I brought a new bottle from the Apothecary. Take some now. You are to be home by eleven."

Ernst felt the all too familiar gravity of her condemnation. She served his father and became the magistrate of their mansion. She saw into his heart, exposed his lies, and meted out justice, sometimes with a wooden spoon. With his father's death, there was a sudden vacuum she could not fill – no paid help, no galas, no receptions – and year by year she slowly collapsed. The breach of faith between them was almost too old to remember, and too large to endure. It was easier – a relief – for both of them to be angry.

★   ★   ★   ★   ★   ★   ★   ★   ★   ★

The Corps Teutonia Pub, on Englischestrasse, a watering hole for Nationalist and monarchist students, occupied a huge basement across the Landwehr Canal from the University. By the glow of the Charlottenburg Bridge, Ernst and Hans Gerd cleared a path through the brush to the canal's edge, and Ernst threw the sack from Schütt's Garage into the inky water.

Max Guderjahn, proprietor of the Pub, watched over the entrance, his huge arms folded across his chest, taking the evening air. He smiled broadly when he recognized Ernst. "Ernst and Little Brother Techow. Always a pleasant surprise! The first beer is on me, in honor of today's glorious events. You do know about Rathenau?"

"Of course," Ernst said as Max led them down the cellar steps.

"Most remarkable," Max said. "A deed among deeds. If I knew who the heroes were I would give them my Iron Cross and free beer for six months."

"I might know who did it," Hans Gerd said.

Max froze on the last step then turned to face them, his walrus mustache twitching.

Ernst dug his knuckle into Hans Gerd's back, and he winced. "I mean, Herr Max, any number of organizations... It was obviously a professional job. I heard it was a machine gun and a hand grenade. Not much chance of failure."

"No, I don't suppose so." Max's forehead wrinkled quizzically, suspicious. He turned and led them into the subterranean hall teeming with students celebrating the assassination and St. John's Day. Their gaiety, a welcome relief from his mother's silent accusation and the somber procession of workers on the streets above, allowed Ernst's anxiety to recede. His first beer quenched a deep thirst for amnesia, and each draught that followed calmed the cacophony of voices in his head – Kern, Lisa, his mother, Headmaster Strauss, Pastor Namann, and, most strident of all, his father. Three beers later, Hans Gerd sang along with the rest of the patrons, and his deformed right hand, free from its usual asylum in his jacket pocket, pounded the table in time to the music. Neither he nor Ernst had mentioned the murder.

During a lull in the singing Hans Gerd dragged Ernst to an empty table. "Well? Tell me about it?"

They leaned forward until their foreheads almost touched. Ernst felt lighter than he had in months – giddy with unexpected love for his brother. "The actual moment – the thing itself – was so simple. Worst of it was the shitting car. Fucking thing broke down two blocks away."

"What now?"

"I need to disappear for a while."

Hans Gerd leaned his head against the stump that was his right hand, a birth defect. "Will I see you again?"

"Of course you will."

"You'll need a good watch, Ernst." He unstrapped the Krug-Bauman from his wrist and pushed it across the table.

Ernst turned the gold watch over in his hands, remembering when he had slipped it from the wrist of a dead Spartakist, after the *Vorwärts* battle, just after he had killed his first man. It bore the inscription, To My Angel.

"I'm glad you wear my watch," Ernst said, "instead of the one Leo gave you. Keep it. It was your birthday present."

"I wouldn't want anything to happen to you." Hans Gerd blinked away tears. "You're the only one who really understands me."

Ernst wondered what proportion of his brother's sentimentality was love and what proportion was beer. He puzzled over how his own bond to Hans Gerd was apportioned between filial love and pity.

Regardless of how exasperating he was, Ernst felt almost paternal and Hans Gerd reciprocated with admiration, almost worship for his older brother. How many times had he saved his life? From almost being hit by a tram after running into the street as a toddler, to helping him resign from Organization C this year. It was remarkable that he was still alive. OC's leaders saw great promise in Hans Gerd – "eager, daring, great potential – just too young," was how Hoffmann and Tillessen spoke of 'the younger Techow.' At fifteen, Hans Gerd had been the youngest member of OC, and now, the only person ever allowed to resign. OC's leadership must have taken pity on him because of his age, or his deformity, or more likely, his brother Ernst. Anyone else would have been executed.

"Gimme a cigarette," Hans Gerd said.

"Bad for your asthma."

"Fuck my asthma. I'm drunk and I want a cigarette."

"I will have to tell mother." They laughed. Ernst raised his voice to falsetto. "I know when you're lying to me, Hans Gerd."

He leaned forward for Ernst to light his smoke. "Where will you go?"

"I don't suppose I should tell you, but I may stay with Uncle Erwin until the heat is off. He's always liked me. He once asked if I would consider taking over the estate from him when he retires. Imagine that."

"He's so peculiar. It's no wonder he never married."

"All the same, I like him. Sometimes I wonder what would have become of us if he were our father." Ernst emptied another glass. "You look worried, Hans Gerd. Relax. Who would betray me? With the exception of you, OC kills traitors and informers. I'm not worried worth a fig."

"And there's always Lisa," Hans Gerd said.

"Yes, there is always Lisa."

*   *   *   *   *   *   *   *   *   *

Ernst planned to leave the next afternoon for Jacobsdorf on the 2:15 train from Anhalter Bahnhof. Better to sleep at the Pub tonight than to indulge his mother's suspicions, or worse, succumb to her interrogation.

Within minutes of lying down in one of the dormitory rooms Max kept for special visitors, and in spite of a dull headache, Ernst fell into a sleep of dreams both disturbing and ephemeral. All he could recall when he sat bolt upright at dawn, chilled with sweat, was claustrophobia and contamination. After a few moments he recognized the room and remembered that Rathenau had been dead less than a day, that his deed would be the headline of every newspaper, on the lips of every person in the civilized world.

As he climbed the stairs out of the Corps Teutonia basement, the rising sun reignited his headache. White posters with red lettering had sprouted overnight on Englischestrasse lampposts and walls.

"MASSES!! HOLD YOURSELVES IN READINESS!!"

Maybe Kern's prediction, Organization C's dream, was correct, and, for a blessed moment, Ernst felt light – optimistic. Weimar would fall in a raucous revolution. He would be a hero. Lisa would marry him. Fritz, brilliant Fritz, would rise meteorically in the new Reich.

But then he crossed Charlottenburg Bridge and could see into the Tiergarten where silent demonstrators pressed together for a second day, all because of him and Kern and Fischer – three nobodies who had altered history. The city seemed to hold its breath, the streets so quiet he imagined he could hear the tumult in the Reichstag. He felt naked, villainous, and he was sure everyone in this silent mob damned him to hell.

It was necessary, he told himself over and over. Rathenau had to die.

Even the vaulted Anhalter Bahnhof train station was ghostly and silent. Children seemed to intuit the gravity of the day and clung to their parents' hands or dresses. There was a palpable air of sadness in the station, and for a moment he felt the prick of shame, but he confused it with remorse and rejected it out of hand.

Ernst left Berlin on the D-Zug train first to Jena to visit friends in the Corps Thüringen, where he stayed overnight, and then on to Jacobsdorf, near Frankfurt-on-the-Oder, where Uncle Erwin met him at the station with an enthusiastic bear hug.

Erwin Behrens was the perfect antidote to Ernst's mother – short and cherubically plump, perennially cheerful and more than a bit eccentric. The gap between his two front teeth gave him a slight lisp. Strawberry blond hair curled so tightly on his overlarge head as to resemble miniature shrimp, and his prized muttonchop sideburns bushed out too far. A long time ago Ernst's heart had opened to Uncle Erwin – the one person in the family who Ernst thought valued him as fundamentally and unconditionally good.

"Oh, how wonderful to see you, Ernst! How wonderful!" Erwin shook his hand and clapped his back. "Always welcome, any time, any time." He signaled an estate worker to carry Ernst's knapsack.

"No, no, Uncle Erwin. I can carry it myself. Really..."

"Nonsense, boy. Come to the car. We have much to discuss. Day before yesterday – quite the day, eh? And now the ragtag unemployed in the streets. Filthy Communists! Oh, sorry, Ernst. I don't usually involve myself with such things, but assassinating Rathenau – that's something quite extraordinary." He paused a moment in thought, then brightened and turned to Ernst. "Quick ride? So much more pleasant than it used to be. Ninety kilometers. Why, when I was a boy it would have taken all day. Mark my words boy, the railroad will be remembered as the single most important invention of the last thousand years."

Uncle Erwin's almost mystical trust and championing of Ernst had something to do with the ghost in the photograph.

When Ernst was much younger, before Hans Gerd was born, he was fascinated by what he called 'the magical picture' in Uncle Erwin's parlor, which came to life whenever Ernst looked askance at it, with the same peripheral vision he used to sight faint stars. In the sepia photograph, a young Uncle Erwin, a trim cavalry officer with his emblematic, gap-toothed smile, sported a pencil mustache, one hand on his horse's saddle, the other on his sword hilt. Sometimes his horse seemed to shake its mane. More regularly Ernst saw the ghostly outline of a woman hiding in the tapestry backdrop. According to Maria, Ernst's nanny, she was Erwin's fiancée, and it was either typhoid or Typhus that had taken her a week before their marriage.

"You must never ask your mother or your uncle!" Maria warned.

Of course, Ernst felt compelled to provoke his mother, so he told her about the ghost he saw. She said to stop talking stupidly. When he summoned the courage to ask Uncle Erwin, the old man looked wistfully at the photo and sighed, "Beatus." Neither Hans Gerd nor Leo could see the "ghost lady," as they called her, and Ernst could only conclude that was why Uncle Erwin favored him.

In the gloom of his uncle's living room Ernst saw the giant headline in the day old Jena newspaper. He picked it up gingerly, as if it might be electrified, and sank into a wingback chair. His heart churned as he read accounts of the assassination and the paralysis of a nation. Even the Stock Market closed for the day.

> Socialists and Independent Socialists massed in Berlin and every other city in Germany — orderly demonstrations of working people mourning the loss of their unlikely champion, this aristocrat, this intellectual, this Jew.
>
> In the Reichstag, the Independent Socialist Herr Crispien demanded that all former officers be dismissed from the Reichswehr and the police, and that the property of former ruling houses be confiscated for the purpose of reparations.
>
> If the government fails to do this, the workers would be obliged to act in self-defense and violence will be answered with violence.
>
> The Wirth government issued a Presidential decree creating a Special Law for the Protection of the Republic and a special court with broad powers to "suppress threats and organizations espousing the destruction of the Republic." Influential deputies are predicting the coming war to the death between democrats and those who follow the Kaiser. Cries of 'Revenge!' filled the Reichstag.

He laughed nervously when he read that the reward for the assassins was one million marks. Ernst fantasized himself an old man showing these yellowed pages to an adoring grandson on his lap.

His uncle bustled in, his head in a cloud of cigar smoke. "They've arrested this Tillessen fellow in Flensburg." Erwin poured Ernst a cognac. "Member of that murder organization – Organization Consul. Organization C. Heard of it?"

Ernst felt gooseflesh prickling his arms. "Just what I read in the newspaper." Tillessen? How could the police have acted so quickly? How could Uncle Erwin know? He drank half the snifter and let the burn distract him. Until now, 'Erwin was his unconditionally loving, old bumbling uncle. If he knew the truth, what would Erwin think – what he would do? Ernst wondered just how safe he was at Uncle Erwin's.

"All mixed up in this Rathenau mess, *sine dubio*. Nasty business." He raised his glass. "Prost, Ernst."

Uncle Erwin dropped onto his easy chair and it groaned. He eyed his nephew and pulled on his cigar. "I know you and Hans Gerd have been involved with that patriotic student group – and bully for you – what's that name..."

"German National Youth Organization?"

"That's it – GNYO. Good people. But this murder organization, this Organization Consul – another thing altogether. Despicable. Can't be running around murdering anyone you don't like. It's not like it's war."

Ernst emptied his glass. "This Organization C probably does think it's war." His legs trembled. "Would that make a difference, Uncle?"

"Damn right it would – but it's not... war, I mean. Bunch of silly radicals." Erwin sighed and wiped his face. "Rathenau wasn't all bad, you know. Gave those French blood-suckers a run for their money at Genoa. Even if he was a Jew. *Carpe Diem* I always say."

"But Versailles, and the Rapallo Treaty," Ernst said. "With the Bolsheviks, no less. Betrayal! It's a wonder he wasn't murdered before now."

"Calm yourself, dear boy. You're too young to understand the subtlety of politics. Can't be so pure – or so hot-blooded."

"He's a blood-sucking Jew, Uncle."

He flapped one hand at Ernst. "There, there – must be calm – civilized. Even your father, no friend of the Versailles 'stab-in-the-back,' invited Rathenau to your home. If I'm not mistaken, you've met him." Erwin re-lit his cigar. "My brother, your Uncle Peter, was chief architect for Rathenau's father, Emil – funny little man. Your father advised him about legal matters for his electric company. Everything is complicated. But, *dixi*, enough politics and murder. What about you, boy?"

"Uncle." Ernst felt lightheaded as he poured himself another cognac. He steadied his voice with effort. "In two years I graduate, and I wonder if your offer to work here on your estate is still good?"

Erwin's face brightened. "Wonderful, dear boy. Wonderful! I'd like nothing better. I could show you the books – that's really the heart of the business. Handling the workers, now that's another kettle of fish altogether – lazy bunch – Communists and peasants. Have to be tough with them. Respect a strong boss. Don't like me, but they respect me. And I pay decent wages. Nothing to complain about. Anyone who does... complain I mean, gets the boot – thrown right out."

"The Communists – they may take advantage of the turmoil to overthrow the government." Ernst searched his face for affirmation of Kern's prediction.

"Communists will riot over anything – anytime. Not a few of my workers, no doubt."

"Do you have guns?"

"Of course. Everybody has guns – and a few loyal overseers who are not afraid to use them. If things get out of hand, I know who to call in Jena."

"Free Corps?"

"Yes, of course. Can't call on those Weimar buffoons. Take them a month to send troops. By then we'd be a Bolshevik republic. You know all about the Free Corps. You were at the Royal Palace, weren't you?"

Ernst flushed with pride. "Yes, Uncle."

"Bit of unpleasantness that was, what with your brother and all. Leo's a good boy, just confused, like so many. Your mother – she's the one I feel sorry for. Ever since your father died, she's beside herself with worry – about both of you. And Hans Gerd with that deformed hand. *Dies Irae* – such tragedy – breaks my heart every time I think of it. I try to help her all I can, but she's a proud woman – too proud, if you ask me. Proud but not very strong, your mother. Does as well as she can."

"What if because of Rathenau's assassination, Weimar were to fall to the Free Corps?"

He shook his head decisively. "Never happen. Too many Socialists and Communists."

"But if some miracle were to occur – wouldn't you be glad for it?"

Erwin drank his cognac and seemed lost in thought. "I'm too old for revolutions. And it's bad for business. Sometimes, I just want to shut the gates to keep the world out."

"Aren't you a member of the National Socialist Party?"

"Yes, of course. Damned stupid name, if you ask me. Ridiculous. Who thought of that?"

"I think it was this Hitler fellow."

"Ever meet him?"

"As a matter of fact I have – about two years ago. A small man – very intense."

"Never can tell about people. Don't trust small men, I always say. Tend to be Napoleons. Can't trust them. That Organization Consul is named after Napoleon. Called himself Consul. See what I mean? Do you like it here?"

"Yes, I do, Uncle. Berlin is just too busy and noisy."

"Quality of life, my boy. Can't beat it. Halle and even Leipzig are not that far away. And Jena – a very respectable little city. Decent place to live, not like Berlin with those nasty cabarets and sexual perversions. *O tempora! O mores!* I live well here. You would like it. Can always use a good man with a university education. What are you studying?"

Uncle Erwin asked the same question every time they met. "Literature – European Literature."

"Hmm." He stroked his chin. "No matter. You'll learn what you need to."

     ★   ★   ★   ★   ★   ★   ★   ★   ★   ★

Three days later Ernst woke to a rough hand jostling his shoulders. In his dream he had been riding a swan, like Lohengrin, and had beckoned Lisa to join him. She was undecided, but now came towards him. He reached out a hand for her, but the swan began to buck and shake until he woke to the barrel of a pistol.

"There are two ways you can die today." Uncle Erwin's voice was taut, his face red-hot. "I can give you over to the workers. They will tear you limb from limb. Or I can send you into the woods with this pistol to do the honorable thing yourself."

Ernst sat up slowly, backing away from this red-eyed caricature of his Uncle who threw the morning paper into his lap.

"Ernst Werner Techow, Edwin Kern, and Hermann Fischer," he recited from memory, "have been identified as the three assassins of Foreign Minister Rathenau. Ernst Werner Techow, 21 years old, an ex-officer and active member of the secret 'Organization C' is said to have been the driver of the murder car."

Ernst shivered. "I had no choice, Uncle. You've got to believe me. They would have killed me – and Hans Gerd. How did they find out?"

"Ten conspirators arrested. One of your own comrades made a deal with the prosecutors. Fellow named Günther. Some friend."

"It had to be done."

"Be still!" The pistol barrel quivered. "I don't want to hear your rationalizations."

"They would have killed me."

Uncle Erwin's eyes grew large. "Your mother called from the police station. Do you care what's happened to her? Your mother and Hans Gerd were picked up early this morning. Like common criminals. Your mother knew nothing and she was allowed to call me for help."

Ernst felt lightheaded. A fine sweat broke above his lip, his heart a convulsing knot. Why had he not considered catastrophe? Was he so smug, so impulsive he could not conceive of disaster? There would be no failure, Kern had promised; everything had been carefully planned. And Ernst had believed him. But three days – only three days – and the conspiracy was breached. What a fool he'd been. How stupid. "What are you going to do with me?" Ernst asked.

"I've already called the police. I suggest you cooperate and your prison term may be shortened." He paced the small room, arms crossed over his chest. "Don't protect these murderers; they only do our cause harm."

Ernst's heart beat fast and regular again, but he felt like a child about to be severely disciplined – a child whose protestations only added to his shame. "Kern and Fischer are heroes. Rathenau is the traitor." He threw off the covers. "The reward is one million marks, Uncle. Do you have to share that with Günther? At least I can hold my head up knowing I served the Vaterland honorably. What about you?"

Erwin's lips trembled. His brow furrowed sadly. The barrel of the pistol tremored and slowly sank. "It isn't loaded, Ernst. I would not have wanted you to shoot yourself." His voice was husky with emotion. "I'm sorry..." His throat closed and he turned to leave. He pulled the door softly behind him and Ernst heard his fumbling key, the tumblers falling. Police sirens wailed in the distance; through the bedroom window Ernst watched a dust cloud advancing from the Jacobsdorf Road.

He could hardly think. Maybe he would be better off dead; the pain and shame would be erased in an instant.

He heard boots on the stairs, Uncle Erwin's key unlocking and, suddenly, four policemen burst into his bedroom, pistols drawn. An Inspector, black spectacled, stood at the door. His overlarge blue uniform hung from bony shoulders

Uncle Erwin mumbled explanations that Ernst barely understood. There were 'special circumstances,' Erwin explained; more than once Ernst heard his father's name. The word 'shackles' roused him as if from a stupor.

"...he's a good boy, just confused. He'll go with you on his own accord. His father was a magistrate."

Inspector Fluth, Chief of the National Police for Internal Security sighed and settled a bony finger against his gaunt jaw. He removed his police helmet and passed a handkerchief over his short-cropped black hairs. Ernst could almost hear them bristle. After a thoughtful pause, Fluth pursed his lips and nodded to the policemen.

The kitchen staff and chambermaids watched as the entourage shuffled down the broad staircase. In the courtyard, stable boys leaned on their pitchforks. When they reached the side of the police car, a six-seater Mercedes, one policeman applied the irons to Ernst's wrists.

"Back to work!" Erwin yelled at the boys, but his voice broke.

On the police sedan's back seat, flanked by two officers, Ernst sank into the leather upholstery.

After an hour of travel, Inspector Fluth half-turned to study him. Without his spectacles Fluth seemed more forgiving, even empathetic. Ernst noticed late afternoon beard stubble.

"We picked up Günther right away – within twelve hours. He confused us – bragged about doing it! Then he cut a deal. As far as OC is concerned, Günther's a dead man. Your buddies, Kern and Fischer, are still at large. We'll get them."

The Chief Inspector wiped the past few days' exhaustion from his eyes. "If you ask most of the men in my squad, they'd say get rid of all the Jews. But you can't kill just one. You have to think big; then it's a service to the Vaterland. But you," he shook his head, "you're a sucker – someone's fool. You'll get the book thrown at you. We have to – for appearances."

★ ★ ★ ★ ★ ★ ★ ★ ★ ★

2

Stillbirth

June 1922

Morning sun baked the police sedan. Turns in the road swayed Ernst between his muscular guards, as he tried not to touch either. It was arduous, and his back ached from the effort. When his father, Magistrate Techow, corrected young Ernst, he often detailed the brutality of police interrogations – beatings, electric shocks, submersion in ice water – cautionary tales that neither frightened nor corrected Ernst. None of it could possibly pertain to him. But now, as his father was fond of saying, "it all comes home to roost." He wanted to rest his forehead against the window, stare out into the pastoral landscape, and ignore Inspector Fluth's monologue. As the long miles unwound, Fluth relaxed and carried on about "the old days, when people did as they were told," turning to scrutinize Ernst every few kilometers. He could not breathe correctly; he was air hungry, his heart pounding, his stomach writhing like a bag of frogs as the car swerved and turned. By the time the road straightened and widened, he slumped back against the hot leather, exhausted, and found Fluth's reminiscences of pre-war Berlin unexpectedly calming.

Fluth had grown up in the central city, near Neukölln. Every Sunday his upward-climbing father dragged the family to Mass at Mariakirche, St. Mary's in the Spandau district, only blocks from Ernst's home. "I know just which mansion was yours – on Wannseestrasse. The windows were enormous." The Inspector recounted his family's weekly pilgrimage on the Number 5 trolley, along Schönwälder Allee to Mariakirche, and simply mouthing the names appeared to give him pleasure. Fluth described the flowers on Wannseestrasse, in particular the overabundance of Gemeiner Goldregen, 'common golden rain,' teeming yellow flowers overflowing the Techow's wrought iron fence. Fluth smiled. "Like hot lava suddenly frozen." After Mass, if the weather was fine, Fluth's family paraded about the neighborhood and he and his younger brother tried to see into the mansions.

He laughed nervously and reached into his breast pocket. "I was hoping to see a naked woman." Fluth's cigarette case sprang open and flashed golden. "Have one. You might not see too many of these in the near future." He signaled one of the agents flanking Ernst. "Undo the shackles."

Ernst caressed his wrists where the irons had squeezed for two hours, then took a cigarette. Fluth's description of the Gemeiner Goldregen brought back vivid and bittersweet memories of their mansion in early summer, and, unexpectedly, Frau Stimmel bustling from kitchen to dining room to parlor. Ernst smiled to think of her cooking and baking skills. Frau Stimmel was an ample woman with a hard and cracked face, tiny wire-rimmed spectacles, and salt and pepper hair that bulged under a white peasant scarf. A starched white pinafore overlay her blue-gray dress. Born with one leg shorter than the other, she walked with a rocking gait that amplified from her ankles to her overlarge head. Ernst called her the 'Queen of Hearts,' to which his brother Leo would say, "Off with her head!" in a good imitation of her Mecklenburg accent, which was no asset in Berlin. But Frau Stimmel reigned over the Techow mansion.

Fluth monotoned on about being the "son of a rising bureaucrat" and his personal hopes for advancement after bringing Ernst to justice. His tone was matter of fact, as if he spoke with an old friend. Ernst inhaled deeply, then studied the glowing Reemtsma cigarette, something so ordinary, so transitory. Everything else was not ordinary and it might last forever – so he stared at the ember and the lazy smoke.

"You were in the Navy, weren't you?" Fluth did not pause for Ernst to respond. "When I was a child, I wanted only to be a sailor on a battleship. I still remember my model ships. But, much to my father's disappointment, I was more suited for police work."

Ernst thought of his first toy warship, the *Brandenburg*, a wood-sculpted battleship his father gave him for his sixth birthday. That was when he discovered his uncanny ability to draw. He sketched the *Brandenburg* from every angle and filled in each scene with heavy seas or hellish combat. Ernst flipped through his memory's portfolio, another welcome distraction, examining each drawing, each painting.

His artistic abilities became apparent when his first letters were perfectly formed. First Class school master Herr Strauss called Ernst to the chalkboard frequently to demonstrate how simple it was to create perfect 𝕲𝖔𝖙𝖍𝖎𝖈 letters, if one "only paid attention and surrendered one's wildness."

Ernst had no idea what he was talking about. The perfect letters, like his drawings, just came to him, without attention, without effort, from some wild place inside. It satisfied a deep yearning he could not understand – like scratching an itch.

That was before the stillbirth in 1908, when Ernst turned seven and the discipline problems began. One day, instead of the humorous cartoons he drew all the time, Ernst sketched a particularly cruel caricature of Headmaster Herr Strauss, his trousers around his ankles, fat flies circling his prodigious behind. It bonded him with the older boys, especially Heinrich Schliefen, the implicit leader of 'the Outlaws.' It did not endear him to Herr Strauss who ordered Ernst to spend the first of many days facing the wall under a conical cap.

Ernst accumulated scale models of warships. First the Brandenburg, then Nassau, the spider-web rigged Scharnhorst and her sister-ship Gneisenau, the Koenig and Van der Tann. When he sketched and painted his fleet, he felt detached from ordinary time, alive in fertile reverie, omnipotent. He created storms and sent massive warships churning into combat, where, at his discretion, ships exploded and men died, while the lucky ones clung to life rafts.

One scene particularly obsessed him and he drew it over and over – the Brandenburg plowing through turbulent seas, her single funnel belching smoke and embers, while four paired deck guns fired a full-blooded broadside into boiling gray clouds that suggested the outline of a giant woman, her head thrown back, her mouth open. Crying? Laughing? Cloud Woman. All his other drawings he either pinned to his wall, or laid flat under his bed and across his desk, but this one he kept hidden in his closet. With charcoal, in his sketch book, he rendered Cloud Woman again and again, taking different perspectives, seeking a crucial detail that would change everything. But it never appeared, no matter how often he tried to recapture the instant that winter day when his mother started to bleed, the moment she realized she was not alone in the parlor.

On that day – it was almost Christmas – he piloted his balsa Brandenburg across the hardwood Floor Ocean, down the Hallway Canal, through the narrow Doorway Strait into Parlor Bay, where he came upon his pregnant mother staring out the tall window at snow-covered cedars. On that particular day his Lilliputian crew dropped anchor across Parlor Bay, and Admiral Ernst studied Cloud Woman through finger-circle binoculars. She gave no evidence of noticing his presence. She moaned a little and stared past the glass, swaying, stroking her overlarge womb with the same vigor that Frau Stimmel polished the silver bowl. The blue of her sunken eyes disappeared in shadow.

She was crying or laughing; he didn't know which. Ernst raised the *Brandenburg's* big guns and swiveled her turrets. He meant her no harm, wanted only to frighten her, to protect his battleship. Suddenly, thunder pummeled boiling seas, whipping up winds, like torrential weeping. Cloud Woman reeled, listed heavily; a rivulet of blood ran down and pooled by the leg of the chair that steadied her, a spreading dark stain on the burgundy carpet. Had his tiny crew fired a broadside without his order? Mutiny? He lowered the big guns and steered *Brandenburg* in a large circle, full steam ahead with great pistons whooshing.

"Ernst!" she cried through her pain. "Get out!"

From nowhere, Frau Stimmel swooped upon him, seized him by the collar, and dragged him to Eric in the garage. All she could say, in her harsh Mecklenburg accent was, "for shame, for shame!"

★   ★   ★   ★   ★   ★   ★   ★   ★   ★

Reshackled, Fluth led Ernst into Police Headquarters on Alexanderplatz, past the spear-point iron fence, through the brick façade, and into a granite fortress. When they were children, his older brother Leo scared him with stories about Grandfather Heinrich and the interrogation and torture he had endured in this very building during the 1848 revolution. Grandfather's oil portrait dominated the Techow-Behrens gallery in the Wannseestrasse parlor, a rakish young man with a white feather stuck in his Bohemian cap, a sign of the student rebels. In his father's words, "your grandfather was a fierce fighter for Germany," and regardless of where Ernst stood in the parlor, Grandfather Heinrich's eyes fixed right on him. He seemed to challenge Ernst. "What is wrong with you?"

At the rear of the Alexanderplatz station, Ernst's wrist and leg irons were removed, and he was led down a narrow staircase to a dark holding cell that he estimated to be three by four meters, an aspect he had never considered before. Rough-dried concrete walls closed in from three sides. A prison guard slouched at a desk across the basement eyeing him – with contempt?... with curiosity? He returned to his newspaper.

Ernst sat on a wooden bench, the seat worn smooth and concave by legions of the damned. Though it was mid-summer, the cell felt damp and chilly, and his hands sought the warmth of his pants pockets. In the bottom of one, his fingertips discovered the thin sketching charcoal that he always carried, that had been missed by the searchers. The black stub in his hand felt ember-warm with possibility, with relief, an unexpected friend in this pitiless place.

Above the water spigot, cold only, he found a smooth square of concrete and began to draw from memory.

He had drawn Lisa's face so often that just a few strokes of the charcoal brought her to life, feature by feature until she became fully formed. As her image appeared on the cement, she became three dimensional in memory, an ache in his heart, a throbbing tenderness.

He drew a younger Lisa – the one he had first met, so absurdly, at youth camp. Each year, in August, he had been sent away to Sturmbund youth camp. It was Uncle Erwin's idea, and his father readily endorsed it. The Headmaster, Herr Kremer, had warned that unless Ernst's behavior improved dramatically, he would be expelled. It was not an academic problem; with almost no effort he maintained average grades. But, as Kremer would later testify at his trial, Ernst provoked fights, was disrespectful, and drew vile and pornographic caricatures of people in authority.

When first informed at the age of ten that he would be sent away for the summer to become a *Wandervogel*, Ernst stamped his feet and threatened to run away. His father pinched Ernst's neck harder than ever before and, for the first time, said he would not hesitate to send Ernst to the Glockenschule, where discipline was enforced with hard labor and physical punishment. It was one step away from prison, and his father made it plain to Ernst that he would have no compunction about committing him "at the next provocation."

Becoming a *Wandervogel* was not helpful. The year before the war began, twelve-year-old Ernst had earned the dubious distinction of becoming the youngest of Heinrich Schliefen's 'Outlaws.' To earn this distinction, this recognition of his Aryan manhood, he had only to beat up the Jew Rothstein. Ernst could hardly have considered his initiation a fight – it was more sport. The Outlaws had surrounded Rothstein, and Schliefen pushed Ernst to the fore. Ernst was still a slight boy with narrow shoulders and thin arms – hardly a fighter – but he felt a giddy release as he realized that Rothstein would not fight back, so he pummeled him. He felt purified afterward – cleansed of the judgments of headmasters and parents, embraced by the Outlaws' unconditional acceptance. As for Rothstein, his face bloodied and swollen, he was as inconsequential as the pigeons in Mariakirche Park. Today's beating was his punishment for being 'other,' and it was a legitimate price to pay for Ernst's coveted social advancement.

Now Ernst was Schliefen's boy. The Outlaws taught Ernst how to roll cigarettes and steal from stores; he drank beer with them in abandoned lots and joined in their petty vandalism. His unique contribution was to forge letters and signatures, to untangle trivial infractions, which was for Ernst child's play – drawing.

Wandervogel were Scouts and Maidens – wandering birds, hiking, camping, and imbibing the pastoral culture of 19th century Germany, recapturing a past when everything was pure and good and Aryan. Ernst was only twelve that first year of camp in 1913, when he first saw Lisa. A tall, thin girl, she balanced on one foot in the middle of a field, her golden braid hanging over her shoulder. She had just arrived as a new Maiden, and had already broken the silence rule at role call. Her punishment was to stand alone on one leg for half an hour in full view of the other scouts. It was meant to be a humiliation, but Lisa smiled and lifted her hands into balletic poses. The tittering of the campers enraged the head counselor who put Lisa into the tool shed.

Something thrilled deep inside him. He followed her when he next saw her as they both left the dinner tent, not knowing what, if anything, he would say. She turned to him, and their eyes met. He could only stutter and stammer, "You are... I see that... You have... You have a strong leg." She laughed; they both blushed. As other Maidens surrounded Lisa and dragged her away she looked back at Ernst, smiled and waved.

His heart went up in flames.

He watched for her every day, knew when she entered a room or strode across the soccer pitch. Any time they met, he was sure that her smile for him was different than for anyone else. A day before the end of camp he waited for her after dinner, praying she would be alone, if only for a moment.

He was desperate to speak to her. She wandered away from the other Maidens and walked into a copse of trees near the dinner tent, looked back to see that she was alone, then sat behind a thick pine tree.

He crept behind another tree nearby and watched as she unfastened a brooch from her collar. Ernst was startled to see her prick the soft flesh of her thumb, then suck the wound.

He cleared his throat, and she jumped.

"Are you watching me?" she said, her eyes cold for a moment until she recognized him and smiled sheepishly.

"Could I... Would you... Could we talk – just for a little?"

She reattached the brooch, watching him through upturned eyes of bluest blue. "So now you know something strange about me," she said.

Her eyes made him uncomfortable and inflamed. "I guess."

"Why don't you sit down. Over here." She patted the grass next to her and looked down, embarrassed. As Ernst sat, she looked up again, into his eyes, her lips drawn into a tight line as if about to do something daring. "Now you must tell me something disturbing about you."

"Fair enough," Ernst said, perplexed. "My brother is deformed. He has only one finger on his right hand, his left side is bigger than his right, and he is abnormally active."

She turned to face him and sat up straight-spined. "My turn." Her tone became stern. "I was mute when I started the First Class. The only sound I made was to cry when Father beat me with a switch, or when Aunt Ida brushed my hair too hard. Your turn."

"I killed pigeons in Mariakirche Park." Her eyes were pools.

"I dressed up like a man." She blushed.

"My mother had a miscarriage."

She looked at him quizzically. "That's not strange."

"But I saw it." He regretted his words, then felt a curious comfort in sharing the secret. "I saw the blood."

Lisa's eyes grew wide. "What was it like? I mean, was she on the floor? Did it hurt?"

"I don't remember anything except the blood."

"How did it happen?"

Ernst felt light-headed and faint, suddenly awash in sweat. "I... I don't know. Nobody knows." He felt suspicious of his own memory, as if he might be lying, but no other remembrance came.

"Probably too horrible to remember," she said.

The memory was so close to recall that he was sure that if she pressed him... but he was grateful to leave it undisturbed. "Your turn," he said.

Her brows knitted with anxiety. "Just last month, Max – my chauffeur – when he drove me here from Halle, he tried to kiss me and touch me in a bad place. Then he gave me 10 marks not to tell."

"Where is it?"

"The bad place?"

"No, no, no... the 10 marks."

"It's in my book of Heine."

"You like Heine? He's my favorite poet."

"The rules are you must tell me something disturbing. Heine is not disturbing." She paused for a moment, and Ernst thought she had forgotten where she was. Then her brow furrowed again. "I hurt myself with needles."

"I saw. Why would you do that?"

"I don't know." Lisa kneaded a finely embroidered cloth. "I do know. Do you want me to tell you?"

Lisa slumped forward in the grass, her spine bent over her folded legs like a windswept sapling. "Mother died when I was five. It was very fast. I heard her cough on Sunday in church, and she had a fever on Monday. She died on Tuesday." Lisa looked up at Ernst – her blue eyes moist and pleading. "The next day, Aunt Ida moved into the house. That was the day I stopped speaking. I was only five, but I remember how Ida tried to brush my hair exactly the way Mother did, with the same brush Mother used, but she hurt me with the brush and I cried and cried. Every day she would brush my hair and every day I cried. But I would not speak."

Lisa seemed in a trance, unblinking.

"When did you speak again?"

"Three years later."

He shook his head and wondered if she was sane. Who ever heard of such a thing? "Three years?" he said.

"Father was angry after Mother died. He hated that I wouldn't speak. He beat me, but still I said nothing. I don't know if Ida was as afraid of Father as I was, but I think so."

"What made you start speaking again?"

"The needles. They helped me stop what I call 'my deadness.' I prick myself."

"Didn't you even talk to *yourself?*"

"I did. Every night – when I was alone in my bedroom. I would light a candle and recite, in my quietest voice, a nursery rhyme. One night Ida suddenly came into my room and I immediately fell silent. She put a pile of sheets on my dresser and left as if the candle was not lit, as if I was not awake. I took it as a sign from her that she forgave my bad behavior, that she understood. The next day she asked me if I wanted to learn how to embroider. I was seven."

"Then you spoke?"

"No. But she taught me the stitches." Lisa unfurled the handkerchief she had been kneading, an embroidered garden of fruits and vines. "That first night, in the parlor, Ida showed me how to thread floss through a needle. The next night she helped me mount a linen handkerchief, like this one, on a hoop, and I threaded several stitches of the brightest red I have ever seen. The white linen looked so sad, so empty, until each red stitch burst into being. I felt joyful for the first time in years.

"The three of us sat in the parlor each evening. Father corrected my school essays and my numbers like a stern headmaster. One night, after I had begun learning stitches with Ida, he shook the pages of my writing at me, as was his habit, expecting me to spring up for them. Just then I pricked my finger on the needle and found myself so distracted that I ignored Father and pushed another stitch through the cloth, until he hissed at me and agitated the papers again.

"At first it was an accident, but it so distracted me from my deadness. I sat beside Aunt Ida after that, and learned first simple vines – a fern stitch that snaked about the perimeter in fire red. Then a back stitch, a seed stitch, a looped seed and satin stitch. Whenever I thought of Mother, or when Father made me afraid, I pricked myself again. Sometimes I would actually bleed and stain my work, but I never thought it was strange or unusual.

"One night when Father had become angrier than I've ever seen him, something about the French and the Russians, I pricked myself again, but this time I spoke. I asked Aunt Ida to teach me the Palestrina knot. It was so beautiful, like a row of pearls. I had been watching her perfect it and finally asked her.

"I remember she only looked at me strangely. Then she smiled and taught me the Palestrina knot. That night, for the only time I can remember, Father returned an essay without criticism and said, 'This is a good piece of work.' I remember as if it was yesterday. He had a second glass of brandy that night and went to bed early. He said he didn't feel well."

"What did your mother die of?"

"Pneumonia." Lisa reached under her blouse and brought out a locket on a golden chain. She opened the clamshell mechanism and held the photograph out for Ernst to see. "Ida says I have her eyes. Do you think so?"

Ernst leaned forward to where he could smell her faint perfume, what he later knew to be Lillé, that would always recall this moment, and he squinted at the tiny photograph.

Two Maidens called to Lisa from the edge of the woods. She jumped up and waved to them. "I never told a boy what I just told you. Good-bye, Ernst."

★　★　★　★　★　★　★　★　★　★

After camp came the despondency of September, the disappointment of Berlin, of his father, of Hans Gerd, of school, of ordinary life. He longed for

32

flaxen-haired Lisa and waited each day for her next post.

When her perfumed letters arrived it was as if she touched him. She wrote about what made her mad, what made her happy, of her difficult father. She wrote that she was grateful to tell her story, in her own words, to a boy she cared about.

His own writing was obtuse. The words sounded reasonable enough in his head, but on the page they turned horrible, or worse, simpleminded, so he always included a drawing – of his cat, or the Mercedes, once a self-portrait. Over the long weeks between her letters, Ernst sketched moments from their summer together. He strove for photographic loyalty, spending weeks on a single image – a pencil drawing of Lisa reading a book, a charcoal of Lisa kicking a soccer ball into the goal, and it was as if she was with him.

*   *   *   *   *   *   *   *   *   *

During the first three days of his incarceration, Inspector Fluth stood silently as lesser detectives questioned Ernst. They asked the same questions over and over, never letting him sleep more than two or three hours before they shackled him again and led him to the interrogation room. Fluth watched as if he had never seen Ernst before, as if he didn't care or expected nothing. At times he leaned his head back against the stone wall and closed his eyes. But today Fluth strode into the interrogation room alone, his eyes framed and focused by new black spectacles, and he threw a copy of the Berliner Tageblatt onto the desk. Willi Günther's picture filled the front page under the headline "Common Murderer?" The stenographer readied her pen and ink. Fluth's probing stare worried Ernst; he wanted the other Fluth back.

"Günther is a lying shit-head, isn't he?" Fluth leaned close.

Ernst smelled sour garlic and tried to remember his previous testimony, to separate what he should have said from what he actually said. "I don't know. I was only the driver."

"We broke him. Yesterday. We know everything – Tillessen, Hoffman, your brother, Hans Gerd – all singing like nightingales. You're to be charged with capital murder."

Ernst shivered and felt the pit of his stomach shrink hard and fast. The cells were damp; it would be bad for Hans Gerd's asthma.

"I picked up Ilsemann myself." Fluth backed away. "When we finally extracted the truth from Günther, he bragged about it, told us everything." Fluth cleaned his teeth with a wooden pick and studied Ernst. "Want to talk about Organization C?"

Ernst shook his head and stared at the dull metal of his shackles.

"Günther – he's somewhat... you know, not right in the head. You were stupid to include him. Same goes for your deformed little brother."

Ernst leapt to his feet and thrust his manacled hands over the table towards Fluth's throat. He tripped over his shackled feet, and two guards restrained him. The inspector flinched back and shed his glasses, but only to clean them on a gray cloth.

"You should learn to control your temper, Herr Techow. It will be the death of you."

"Leave Hans Gerd out of this. He's sickly and a child."

Fluth nodded. "Do you know what we found in that sickly child's room at your mother's flat?" He leafed through pages in his folder. "Ah – here it is – a loaded Bajard pistol, a box with 9 mm parabellum cartridges and 2 magazines." He laid the inventory before Ernst. "Well armed for a sickly child."

"That's my service revolver and ammunition. Perfectly legal."

"Perhaps. I am only deposing you and gathering the weight of evidence. Given Hans Gerd's... how shall I say – peculiarities, this is substantial. He was the youngest Organization C inductee, wasn't he?"

"If you say so."

"No, Techow, Hans Gerd says so." He adjusted his glasses again and resumed his unblinking stare. "I'm going to take a piss, Techow. Think about what you just learned."

If Hans Gerd were with him now, arrogant brat that he was, Ernst would cuff his ears. Fluth didn't know the half of it, but it was just like his younger brother to brag about Organization C.

Hans Gerd had been born too early, with a lung condition and only one rudimentary finger on his right hand. After his birth, Frau Stimmel's eyes bulged with anxiety as she waddled up the thickly carpeted staircase with kettles of boiled water, stopping to pant halfway where the Chinese porcelain vase, as big as a cannon, guarded the first landing. Ernst was frightened as well when he first saw his baby brother, who resembled a hairless puppy with a deformed paw. Hans Gerd's breathing was so labored that he was taken right away to hospital where he spent the first two months of his life.

From the moment of his birth, Hans Gerd's high-pitched wailing set Ernst's nerves on edge. Try as Maria, the nanny, and Frau Stimmel might, the sickly baby kept to no schedule, sleeping briefly, restlessly, then waking furious. Everyone's sleep was disturbed. As a fragile toddler Hans Gerd picked at meals, then demanded food an hour later. He tantrumed daily. So delicate was his sleep that when he took his short, blessed naps, sound was forbidden.

Uncle Vaclav in Prague said of Hans Gerd: "He comes from wild eggs!"

When Fluth returned, he read aloud Hans Gerd's deposition, more diatribe than confession, naming names in OC and bragging of his own membership. Ernst couldn't think who angered him more, Fluth or Hans Gerd.

After the morning interrogation Ernst was left alone and granted permission to write a letter to his mother. As he sat in his cell, his pen poised over blank paper, he tried to imagine her receiving this letter, and no words came. Should he seek forgiveness, or reaffirm his resolve to tear down his father's world? Should he express defeat or persistence with only the faintest hope of victory? He remembered how Maria had read aloud to them from Heinrich Hoffmann's children's poems *Struwwelpeter*, Slovenly Peter. His mother insisted that she had grown up with these gruesome rhymes and ghastly drawings and that, in fact, *Struwwelpeter* was a "salutary tonic to encourage good behavior."

Ernst particularly remembered *The Story of Little Suck-A-Thumb.*

> *The door flew open, in he ran,*
> *The great, long, red-legg'd scissor-man.*
> *Oh! Children, see! The tailor's come*
> *And caught our little Suck-a-Thumb.*
> *Snip! Snap! Snip! the scissors go,*
> *And Conrad cries out – Oh! Oh! Oh!*
> *Snip! Snap! Snip! they go so fast,*
> *That both his thumbs are off at last.*

The drawing of little Conrad, blood spurting from where 'scissor-man' had cut off his thumbs, delighted the children and horrified Maria. Ernst had concluded that scissor-man had lopped off all but one of Hans Gerd's fingers and that this accounted for his deformity.

He could not write the letter. He sketched Lisa diving into a lake instead.

★ ★ ★ ★ ★ ★ ★ ★ ★ ★

The next day, Fluth swaggered into the deposition room with a leather satchel under his arm and greeted Ernst with a queer smile. "A confession will help you, Techow," he said, and laid his glasses on top of the satchel.

Fluth began the day's session with simple questions about the murder car, the machine pistol, and Ilsemann. He was merely the chauffeur, Ernst said again, merely a driver following the orders of his former officer, Lieutenant Kern. Ernst felt how Fluth played him, but he clung to his testimony. No, he said, he was not involved with the planning of the murder. All he knew of Organization C was what he read in the newspaper. Ernst felt a rising anticipation that maybe he would be pitied, even absolved. Perhaps no cause was worth this distress, he thought, and he felt the shame of his defeat.

Fluth suddenly froze. There was only the sound of a torpid fly trying to reach the caged incandescent bulb and falling back onto the table. Quick as a pouncing spider, Fluth slapped his hand over the fly, which buzzed madly.

"Lisa Schmidt?" He squashed the fly then smiled and plucked a letter from his satchel. He made much of smelling the perfume while looking at Ernst. "I'm only trying to help you, Techow," Fluth said. "It's best to come clean."

"You son of a bitch!" Ernst said. He narrowed his eyes, pursed his lips, and felt how easily he could have killed Fluth, with his bare hands. No, he would not be defeated. Overpowered perhaps, but not defeated.

"I don't want to embarrass you. But you leave me no choice." Fluth backed away from the table and paced as he read aloud.

> "My Dearest Ernst,
>
> I was remembering that night at the Megalomania Cabaret and Margo Lion – how uncomfortable Fritz was and how drunk we all were. It was the night I told you I couldn't marry you. And since then something has seemed to go stale between us. Oh, we still have wonderful sex. I crave your touch, your kisses, the feel of you inside me..."

Fluth looked over the top of his glasses. Two guards tittered by the door. The stenographer's steady scratching stopped.

> "It's that murder organization – I know it. Ever since you began driving for them something has changed. You seem distant, devoted more to Kern than to me. That night when I turned you down, before we got drunk at the Megalomania, I wanted you to fight for me. I wanted you to cry for me, to plead with me, to give up Kern and whatever silly plots he hatched. I wanted you to love me more than Germany. If you loved me enough this would not be

a difficult choice. But something in you rebels against everything except chaos itself. You seek the chaos and I don't understand — I don't feel safe.

I miss our lovemaking in Günther's apartment, when we had nothing on our minds except Heine and Goethe. You say you are a Nationalist — we are all Nationalists — but we don't stick out our necks, we don't sacrifice everything and everyone we love. You say you'll quit Kern and his fellows, but only after one more job. When will it end? There will always be one more job. I can't stand the thought of losing you, but you must fight for me, or you will be throwing me away — throwing us away — and that is unforgivable. Please come back to me before it's too late."

"Good advice." Fluth folded the letter and dropped it back into his bulging satchel, then cleaned his glasses again with the gray cotton square.

Ernst felt the flush of shame and let his head fall into his shackled hands. His life was over; even the fear of a beating or electric shock receded as if a numbing fog suddenly filled the room. He did not have to listen to Fluth.

In his mind he drew a sketch of Lake Schoenplatz. He conjured the smell of that warm dawn five years ago in the summer of 1917, their last together as *Wandervogel*. A few bright stars still flickered. Leaves crunched as he raced through the woods toward Lisa's silhouette etched against the dawn blue lake, her proud posture accentuating the curve of her breasts.

She giggled when he arrived and shook her finger at him. He was late — they'd be discovered. He presented her with a bouquet of daisies. A chorus of birds already sang in the dawn as they walked hand in hand along the edge of the water.

She asked him the strangest question that morning. "What would you do if you knew you could not fail?" He remembered how she took his cigarette and brought it to her lips like a novice, squinting when the smoke stung her eyes. She puffed out the smoke, which had never entered her lungs

Without a moment's thought he said, "I would be an artist. I would paint the light — like that Frenchman, Monet. That's what my father told me about Monet and others like him. He paints the light." Ernst took back the cigarette. "My father loves Monet. More than he loves me, more than he loves anything, except maybe the law." An all too familiar sadness pressed down like a heavy blanket in summer.

They walked in strained silence. He heard only the crunch of dead leaves, until Lisa began, in a dreamy voice. "I would want to have an affair — a perfect affair — with a married man, so I would be in love but free." She must have sensed Ernst's unease. "I mean, I wouldn't really do it. I mean, I'm still only 15. But just for one day, I'd like to be as outrageous as Margaret."

A warm breeze blew, and he slipped into Lake Schoenplatz in his underwear. She dove in wearing only her bra and panties, swam over and kissed him for the first time. A brief kiss on the lips and then she swam away, laughing, but he was transformed.

Returning from the lake, their light steps crunched leaves and pine needles on the forest trail leading to the dirt road. He remembered how her fingers responded to his touch. They would not see each other for eleven months, an eternity, Ernst said, and her fingers caressed his.

At the edge of the pine forest, Lisa bent to pluck a wild Heckenrose, and she held it out to Ernst. He kissed it and held it out to her lips; she smiled and kissed it as well. Oh, if Fritz could only see them now, he thought. But Fritz was the lucky one; he lived less than a kilometer from Lisa in Halle. During all the eleven months when Ernst would ache for her, his only relief her infrequent letters, Fritz could see her every day if he so desired. If she so desired.

Behind them on the dirt road, the purr of a lorry grew insistent. They crouched low in the grass, holding hands until the ice truck passed. As the dust settled, a small vortex of turmoil persisted – a tiny, mad flapping.

Lisa pulled him onto the road to look at the wounded bird. He wished they had continued on. When Ernst had killed pigeons with a slingshot, he felt curiously alive, potent, watching each pigeon die. But he was no longer a boy, and, though he could not understand why, he felt powerful tenderness for this bird.

"Let's put it in the grass," Lisa said. She looked to Ernst, her blue eyes lightening with the sky.

"I think we should put it out of its misery," he said and rummaged along the roadside until he found a splintered branch. He prodded the thrush in such a way that he could feel its waning life. How many pigeons had it been? Too many. The thrush still fluttered, its black eyes shining, beak open a sliver. He couldn't stop now – otherwise it was all a mistake, from killing pigeons to killing Rathenau.

Lisa bent to scoop up the bird. "At least it can die in the cool grass."

Too fast, Ernst skewered the bird through the breast and staked it to the ground. Its wings jerked upward and a trickle of blood stained its beak. "Sometimes killing is the kindest thing you can do," he said. "Besides, it's only a bird."

Back in Berlin, missing her viscerally, he produced sheet after sheet of charcoal sketches of Lisa diving as she had that magical morning. He drew quickly, desire propelling his charcoal, longing that could not be contained to the page. Each drawing exposed another mood, the angle of her head, the fullness of her lips, the arc of her body, a new dimension to her breasts. The faintest suggestion of her nipples became progressively and unmistakably erect.

The best of these drawings, those that excited him the most, he kept on the high shelf in his closet where his fingers easily found them at private moments. In the bathroom, late at night, Ernst drew rapidly on toilet tissue, sketching anonymous women with Lisa's hair, in various states of undress. In time he became facile at birthing her modular figure and created a modular man to join her, courting, seducing, at first seen only from behind. Gradually, Ernst turned the couple to the side like a sculptor turning clay, and a penis appeared, exaggerated. The woman's head progressively arched back, with her mouth open, eyes closed, the youth holding her tightly, the sway of his back impelling the thrust of his pelvis.

After each orgasm, Ernst felt the predictable shroud of shame fall over him, and he flushed his toilet pornography into the sewer.

It always troubled him, how ashamed and confused he felt, how he had crossed that sharp divide between Lisa as perfection, as love itself, and the possibility of touching her, feeling her real breasts, not those of the imaginary woman he drew on toilet paper. He remembered the surge of excitement and courage that swelled in him, as if any liberty were feasible.

*　*　*　*　*　*　*　*　*　*

Fluth shook Ernst's shoulder. "Pay attention, Techow! I said your mother was confident that you would confess."

3

Casualties

1914 – 1918

The silence of his isolation cell disallowed distractions that might have saved Ernst from being taken hostage by his deepest anxieties, regrets, and impotent rage. In the awful quiet, his mind droned self-indictment, stigma, and failure. How could he have been so confident of success, so deluded, so in need of Kern's approval? How could he have been taken in by OC's promise of 'The Great Turning,' the fall of Weimar? Everything was to change, suddenly, convulsively, and the past was to be swallowed whole – gone. Now it seemed that he was the only one swallowed whole.

After completing a charcoal portrait of young Lisa, her cheeks still plump with early adolescence, he found another area of smooth cement and began to sketch again. He started with a crucifix over a hospital bed in which lay his best friend, Fritz, his bandaged head like the white dot of an exclamation point. Another past swallowed whole, Ernst thought as his head rested against the cool concrete, his eyes closed. It was their second summer together, in 1914, a month after the war had begun, and he and Lisa leaned over Fritz Sommers's unconscious body. Then, too, everything changed.

War fever infected every child of wealth who came to the Sturmbund that euphoric August, a frenzy that especially bonded the twelve- and thirteen-year-old Scouts and Maidens. For eleven long months Ernst anticipated seeing Lisa again, and, as August drew closer, she hijacked his waking thoughts and stole his sleep at night.

A month before the start of camp, on June 28th, a nineteen-year-old Serbian Nationalist, Gavrilo Princip, assassinated Archduke Franz Ferdinand in Sarajevo. A nineteen-year-old had changed history. Three days before the start of camp the Austro-Hungarian artillery began to fire, and the war was on. When the Scouts and Maidens gathered, their meeting was charged with enthusiastic banter about mobilized brothers and fathers. Jubilant anxiety made for unconditional camaraderie amongst otherwise awkward adolescents. War and infatuation.

On their second day, the Scouts and Maidens marched to the local Farm Market. Fritz Sommers, a new boy in Ernst's group, was stout in a strong way, with bristly blond hair. He was either very serious or nervous; Ernst couldn't decide which. Fritz's wide eyes gave him the look of perpetual surprise, and his piercing blue eyes compelled attention. Ernst stood at the fruit stand close to Lisa's Maiden's Group, waiting to buy her an orange, when Fritz appeared out of nowhere and quickly engaged her in animated conversation. Ernst clearly heard Fritz tell Lisa about his high grades, explaining about the special testing he'd undergone and his special classes in Halle.

She, too, lived in Halle, not far from Fritz, and they laughed about shared recollections of their home town. Fritz asked if she had read Bernhard Kellermann's newest novel.

Lisa touched his shoulder and said, "*Der Tunnel? A great book."

They chattered about Jack London's latest American novel *John Barleycorn* that they had both read in English class. In a very few moments they looked like old friends.

Ernst balled his fists. How could her sweet smile for Fritz be so painful, like something precious stolen from him? Lisa was his girl, though he was not exactly sure what that meant. He walked by them and jostled Fritz with his shoulder, just hard enough, he thought, to interrupt their conversation. But he caught Fritz off balance, or maybe bumped him too hard, and Fritz staggered backwards into the fruit stand, which collapsed. The heavy wooden awning fell, hit Fritz across his forehead and knocked him senseless. Apples, oranges and a pineapple spilled around him, a trickle of blood oozed from his nose, fruit rolled down the cobblestone street. The vendor, his eyes were wide with rage, produced a club he kept hidden for thieves and vandals and took off after Ernst, yelling for the police in a Slavic accent.

Ernst sprinted around a corner into the arms of the head counselor, Group Leader Hoff. The vendor and a policeman came upon them moments later. Restrained by the constable, but still waving his stick and his fist, the vendor screamed at Ernst in rudimentary German. "My stand! My stand! Ruined! Ruined!"

Lisa ran up, breathing hard. "It was an accident. I saw the whole thing."

Hoff reassured the vendor that his loss would be redeemed by the Sturmbund, then he scowled at Ernst, clearly doubting Lisa's alibi.

At the Catholic hospital Ernst and Lisa sat in hard wooden chairs at Fritz's bedside watching him sleep. The nurse, an elderly Sister, swirled into the room, a cyclone of black and white. Her heavy crucifix sparkled like lightning and pendulumed over Fritz as she slipped a thermometer under his tongue then held his wrist for a pulse. Sister's heavy lidded eyes, framed tightly by her wimple, scorned the two adolescents, and Ernst felt certain that she willed the fury of Judgement Day at him. He could hardly breathe, and after she left, he felt compelled to walk about. He stopped at the room's only opening, a small square window in the door – a glass canvas. Ernst watched heads pass expressionlessly on urgent missions. Others drifted by more slowly, their faces masks of anxiety or sadness. When he turned back, Lisa was watching him; she turned away, awkward or coy.

A shaft of sunlight, speckled with dust motes, lit a square on the floor. "Do you like the painter, Monet?" Ernst asked.

"I know his name, but I don't think I've seen his paintings."

"He paints light, and wind, and air. It's really quite remarkable."

"Can you do that?"

He shook his head and felt a familiar, deep longing for that skill. "I'm just a doodler, not a real artist."

"No, Ernst," she insisted. "You're really, really good. You have natural talent. You should take lessons, or something. Really! I'm not just saying that."

"My father met Monet in France. A business meeting. He used to take me to the National Gallery to see his paintings. It was as good a time as I've ever had with Father. He would lecture me about" – he caricatured a deep, erudite voice – "the painting of the light." Ernst paused to recapture the memory – precious but pierced with an icicle of sadness, of longing. "But he never looked at me, only at the paintings. He spoke as if to another grownup. He never asked if I liked the paintings, but of course, I did. More than anything, I wanted to paint like Monet."

Lisa took his hand, like a friend, and looked into his eyes. "Aunt Ida always told me to follow the demands of my heart. I think that's good advice, don't you?"

Ernst felt her blue-green eyes caress him in a curious and sublime fashion that offset the sterility of the pale green room.

Fritz began to snore like an old man. Lisa laughed first and covered her mouth. Ernst could hardly contain his own laughter and they both burst out loudly until Fritz stirred and they hushed. He moved his head back and forth, and partway opened his eyes. Lisa and Ernst leaned forward, but Fritz's eyes closed again and he resumed his ponderous sleep.

Lisa cleared her throat and suppressed a new wave of giggles. "It's not right," she said. "We should be serious."

★　★　★　★　★　★　★　★　★　★

Three hours later, Fritz woke up, dazed and confused. The doctor pronounced him 'damn lucky,' and the Sturmbund driver came to pick them all up. Ernst was so relieved that he hadn't killed Fritz that he apologized to him several times on the dirt road back to camp, something he did not do often, or easily, at least not at his own initiative. Fritz was gracious in his pardon and Ernst felt the warmth of his forgiveness. It was neither what he expected, nor what he was accustomed to.

Ernst, Lisa, and Fritz became fast friends, and every Wednesday, when the Maidens and Scouts had common activities, the three of them were inseparable. Too old for the enchanted world of wood nymphs and heroes, evil dwarves, and Valhalla, they passed notes during Wednesday Culture Club. Wandervogel sang patriotic songs, celebrated the physical supremacy of the pure German, and endured lectures about "The Evil Trinity" – Jews (bankers in particular), genetic degradation caused by inbreeding with defectives and finally materialism and modern culture. Fritz paraphrased it as "Dirty Jews, dirty genes, and dirty pictures."

On the last Wednesday before the end of summer, as they climbed the hill to Siegfried's Lodge, Lisa casually announced, "I have given you each new names. Ernst, you will be Ruby and Fritz you are now Ivory."

"You're changing my name?" Fritz snorted.

"I've thought about this for a good long time," she said. "Ernst, you have Ruby red intensity – like a red comet. And Fritz, your intelligence and... and your strength are Ivory white."

★　★　★　★　★　★　★　★　★

That same summer, Ernst's older brother Leo enlisted as a Naval Cadet and Fritz's older brother Cedric entered the army. In October, Lisa wrote Ernst with bad news.

Dear Ruby,

Cedric is dead. Fritz is devastated. I was going to meet him last Sunday,

43

secretly, to fly my newest kite, but he never came. Fritz is never late. He is as predictable and regular as my grandfather clock. I knew something terrible had happened. His house is a short trolley ride away. Fritz and I fly kites some Sundays after church, when my father thinks I'm at the park with Margaret (who would tell him the same if he asked. Margaret and I love conspiracies).

Outside Fritz's house, a mansion really, the flag was only half way up the pole and a black cloth hung over the door. I knew right away. His mother let me in. She looked awful. Pale as a ghost with red eyes. She told me right away at the door. Fritz was in his room and I went up there. We just sat together on the floor and he whittled a stick with his Scout knife. It's the first time I saw Fritz so different – confused, short of words, in pieces. He wasn't Ivory – more like a dark blue. Next Sunday we will fly my new kite, which we have named Cedric's Kite, and the wind will be Cedric because we cannot see him, but know he's there. It's so sad. I wish you were here to paint the wind, like that Monet artist you love so much.

It seems that everybody is losing people to this war. But I still believe – no, I'm sure – we will win. And Cedric will be a German hero. It's just so sad. Please dear Ruby, write to Fritz.

I am thinking of you. I hope Leo is well. This summer you said you didn't miss him, but I think you must. The Navy is so heroic, how can you not be proud?

The world is a mess. I'm afraid our carefree Wandervogel days are over.

With Love,

Lisa

Ernst read her letter several times trying to feel Fritz's loss, imagining how he might feel if Leo were killed. Though he felt badly about Cedric, reading of Lisa and Fritz flying kites together in Halle disturbed him the most. When Fritz wrote to Ernst, he said Lisa's father cloistered her and they hardly ever met anymore. She was, he said, under virtual house arrest.

But now he knew different. That night, and for many more that followed, he could not escape the image of Fritz and Lisa running together through the park, flying a kite, holding hands, kissing. It was acid in his heart.

★   ★   ★   ★   ★   ★   ★   ★   ★   ★

Magistrate Alfred Techow, thin and angular like his wife, was a handsome man whose face gave up no emotion. His blond mustache, now going gray, disguised and gave substance to a narrow upper lip. He wore the same mask in the courtroom and at home, a stern façade of discipline and joylessness. Ernst's mother at least had a second disguise, the charming, ebullient hostess at parties, but for Ernst she was no less severe than his father. Magistrate Techow wore a starched white shirt and cravat every day, even on those special Sundays when he took Ernst to the National Gallery and sported a walking cane whose carved handle resembled the head of a duck. Sundays at the National Gallery were some of Ernst's happiest moments.

Each time they entered the Impressionist gallery, Ernst marveled at his father's magical transformation. Standing before a Cezanne or a Pissarro he smiled, and his head shook ever so slightly in amazement. Sometimes he would sigh. In that moment, Ernst recognized the young man's face from the wedding portrait in the parlor –Lieutenant Alfred Techow posing with his young bride, Gertrude.

"See how the light is painted?" He talked more to the paintings than to Ernst, almost in a whisper, as if in a trance. "See how he paints the wind filling the sails, ruffling the water. Can you imagine that? Painting the wind – painting the light." Ernst stood very close, but his father did not touch him.

Everything changed when they came upon the Fauves, and Magistrate Techow railed against these 'Wild Beasts,' aghast at their primitive, child-like paintings and strong colors. Their work was decadent, he said, a threat to the very soul of the nation. Ernst wondered if these artists, Matisse, Derain and Braque, were also once misbehaving boys like himself. He liked their compositions, though he knew not why, and he wondered if one day, he too would become a 'Wild Beast.' Or maybe he already was one.

After two hours at the museum, his father would take him to a small café, where they ordered fantastic cakes – a light genoise layered with raspberry cream encased in a shell of white chocolate, or his favorite, chocolate hazelnut cream cake covered with schlag. His hot chocolate came in a tall, fragile glass with handles, topped with clouds of whipped cream with two mint leaves like angels' wings.

*   *   *   *   *   *   *   *   *   *

A week before Christmas, 1916, Ernst saw his first bread line from his father's car window. It was during his school vacation, and his father ordered him to spend the week with him at the Board of Trade, "to expose you to useful occupation." Though he had heard rumors of hunger in Berlin, and the newspapers carried grim statistics, Ernst had seen no evidence of it until now. The Mercedes paused at the intersection of Hebbelstrasse and Fritschestrasse, and Ernst studied the line of cloaked human forms bundled in gray and brown, faces turned away from stinging sleet. The queue inched toward a door under a huge crucifix. A child turned toward him, its face a coin of light with large eyes. The very next day, his father's chauffeur, Eric, appeared with a bulky bandage on his arm and drove with some discomfort. He explained how a crazed man with a dagger had tried to steal a sausage from the rack at Gruenspecht's butcher shop and how, in the melee that followed, Eric had been stabbed. For the first time in Ernst's life, the streets of Berlin felt threatening.

That night at the dinner table his father was disturbed. "Damnedest thing, about Eric."

"Alfred, please! Language." Frau Techow, eyes wide, threw admonishing looks at Hans Gerd and Ernst.

"For goodness sake, Gertrude. The word 'damn' is used all over these days, with the possible exception of your Ladies of St. George." His spoon clattered against the bottom of his soup bowl. "Each day there are more beggars before the court house."

"There are always beggars downtown," his mother said. She dabbed at her thin lips with a linen napkin.

"My point is that there are more beggars," he said, "and more thieves. One of the older judges, Hartmann, was robbed at knife-point two days ago. Some of the judges carry pistols."

"There is ample food in the army," she said. "Why are those men not fighting for Germany?"

"Unfit for military service. Dregs of society."

"Then let them starve."

Frau Stimmel, smiling, her cheeks apple red, bustled excitedly into the dining room, rocking back and forth, balancing a steaming plate. She put the roast down beside Ernst's mother. "When Master Leo comes home next week, we shall have the schnitzel he so loves." She stood back, pleased with herself. "Herr Gruenspecht assured me of fresh veal, though it is so hard to find these days."

"Thank you, Frau Stimmel," Herr Techow said. "That will be all. There's no need for you to slice tonight."

"Yes, of course, sir." She swallowed her smile and backed into the kitchen

46

again.

His mother cut into the crisped brown end of the roast, shiny with grease. The first slice peeled away, brown in the center, his father's favorite cut, and she laid it on his plate.

"There will be more trouble after the war," she said. "Mark my words. There are blood suckers about. Immigrants, corrupt politicians, war profiteers. The Bolsheviks supply such easy answers for the riffraff. When the army returns they will have to fight this cancer. A cancer – that's what it is – a cancer slowly eating away from within."

"Hans Gerd, sit up!" his father said, then returned attention to his wife. "These are critical times. We must trust in Hindenburg and Ludendorf."

"It's the Social Democrats who will be the death of us." His mother carved slices for Ernst and Hans Gerd.

"I don't like roast!" Hans Gerd whined. "And the butcher is a Jew."

She shook the knife at him. "Herr Gruenspecht has the best meat." She considered her youngest for a moment, then continued. "Your brother Leo will be home for Christmas. You will not embarrass me at the table when he visits."

"There are some reasonable Social Democrats." Ernst's father ignored the domestic drama. "Father, God rest his soul, would have been a Social Democrat. I wonder what he would have made of this."

"He never would have tolerated treason," Frau Techow said. "Take that Karl Liebknecht, for instance. Now there's a dangerous man. He still publicly speaks against the war. He's a traitor and a Jew. Why do we tolerate traitors?"

"Liebknecht's father is an honorable man." Magistrate Techow ate the first piece of glistening roast end. "There are a few Jews who are human – like Herr Gruenspecht. Father also bought his meat there. Liebknecht's son is another matter. He's in prison where he belongs. We've no use for the likes of him."

"Traitors should be hanged."

"We are a civilized people, my dear. We must deal with our adversaries in a civilized manner."

"We should cleanse ourselves of the Jews," his mother said. "I suppose there are other butchers."

Hans Gerd clenched his eyes and stomped his feet. "I. Don't. Like. Roast!"

"Then eat potatoes!" His mother removed the slice of meat and replaced it with a steaming potato. "Perhaps, if you listened to our conversation you would learn something. Someday you may fight and even die because of what is happening now. Listen! And learn!"

"I don't care," he muttered. Hans Gerd prodded the potato with his fork.

His mother's words chilled Ernst. She turned her attention to him. "What did you do today?" she demanded.

"I was at father's office, reading and typing on the new typewriter. I wrote a letter back to Fritz."

Her stern countenance dissolved. "How is the poor boy?"

"He said Christmas would be difficult without Cedric. But he's strong – disciplined. He says things are getting back to normal."

"Such a dear young man." She filled Ernst's milk glass. "I wish you were more like him."

A week before Christmas Ernst's older brother Leo arrived at the Potsdamer Platz Bahnhof, handsome in his naval uniform. He stood at rigid attention, altered, subdued, not the same Leo who enlisted six months ago. Ernst searched for that Leo, but his eyes were not the same. He clicked his heels, bowed to their father and shook his hand. "It's good to be home, Sir."

Ernst had seen the beginning of Leo's transformation already a year before he enlisted, when his 'new friend' from the University, Katherine Smoltz, began to take up his time and interest. The one and only night she had come to dinner, she explained her Socialist philosophy to the family, using oversimplified language, as if anyone who did not agree with her required only more rudimentary explanations. His father muttered and said "hmmm," but was otherwise silent. It was plain that Katherine led the 'new Leo' by the nose, confusing and transforming him with her peculiar ideas. Now it was naval discipline that exacted yet another disturbing maturation, leaving almost no trace of his brother. Leo bathed every day. He hung his clothes carefully on hangers, and he was formal and short with Ernst. But when the Judicial Trade Board came to the Techow mansion that Sunday, Leo came alive in his new incarnation. He was the center of their fawning attention, indulging the old men's animated questions about his ship, the *Bayern*, poised at the Kiel Naval Base for orders to attack the British Blockade.

★   ★   ★   ★   ★   ★   ★   ★   ★   ★

Their father's final illness began with a cough the first week in January. Leo had just returned to Kiel and a brutal wind raked Berlin. Newspapers reported homeless Berliners frozen to death in the parks and alleys where

48

they slept. Influenza was epidemic.

Hans Gerd was almost thirteen, and each pubertal growth spurt accentuated his asymmetry, as if his left side waged a civil war against his slower growing, impoverished right half. His tendency to frequent bronchitis kept him in bed for weeks at a time, where he followed the War's progress on huge maps pinned to his wall. He kept a war diary of battles, and his maps of Europe and Russia were studded with straight pins flying colored thread to identify battalions, divisions, armies. Bent pins were naval battle groups; Leo's *Bayern*, a large safety pin, stuck resolutely in Kiel's harbor and never moved. Cobbler's tacks with flattened heads marked U-boat attacks on allied shipping.

During one of Dr. Katzenstein's regular visits to attend Hans Gerd, the portly doctor examined Ernst's ailing father and diagnosed a mild case of 'British flu.' As was his custom, the good doctor administered an injection to Magistrate Techow and left two vials of tablets to be taken two and three times a day.

His father recovered rapidly and was well enough one week later to attend a trade conference in Munich. While strolling through the greenhouse at the Four Seasons Hotel he stepped on a board and a nail pierced his shoe. Just a bother, he later said, nothing more. A week after the conference, the featured speaker, the controversial industrialist and chairman of AEG, Walther Rathenau, came to the Techow mansion for a private conversation with Magistrate Techow.

Ernst was struck by Rathenau's imposing stature, a tall, handsome man with broad shoulders, a bald pate and a goatee. His brow was furrowed, his expression severe. Through the closed parlor door Ernst heard a vigorous debate, but when the two men emerged they smiled and exchanged small talk.

Rathenau noticed Ernst and went to shake his hand. "Your father tells me you are a talented artist. May I see some of your work?" Ernst swelled with pride. His father never asked to see his 'work.' Rathenau admired a few of Ernst's charcoals and drawings with care, nodding thoughtfully, saying "hmm" frequently enough that Ernst felt he was not just being polite. He shook Ernst's hand again and said to his father. "He's quite good. He'll make you proud one day."

A few days later, Ernst was surprised to find his father at home when he returned from school. Frau Stimmel was flustered, but said it was merely a relapse of the 'British Flu,' not to concern himself, and to begin his assignments immediately. She stirred a hot toddy with tincture of Valerian for Herr Techow and ordered Maria to keep Ernst and Hans Gerd quiet.

The next day Dr. Katzenstein came to the house. Ernst listened by his father's bedroom door as he confirmed that this was, indeed, a relapse of the flu and ordered a mild purge followcan'ted by Quinine, 1 grain with 2 drams of solution of Acetate of Ammonia every hour for three hours, and then every four hours. Sodium Salicylate was to be given every two to four hours as needed. He would return the next day; he was confident that his important patient would be much improved. Frau Techow expressed her relief, and Ernst felt soothed as well.

But he worsened. After midnight Ernst awakened to the distressed voice of his mother. He listened from outside his door in the hallway. "Alfred, Dr. Katzenstein must come tonight. I've never seen you quite so ill."

"Don't be ridiculous," his father said. His voice trembled.

"Maybe you have pneumonia. That's what happened to Frau Schlössel. She was in hospital for weeks. Almost died."

"Chamber pot! Right away! It's urgent!" Ernst heard metallic clinking, then his father straining and groaning. "Damn it to hell. I have to piss, but nothing comes!"

"Alfred! Language!"

"Help me change my night shirt. I'm soaked with sweat."

"Here, let me..."

"Ow! Will you be careful!"

"Your foot! It's quite swollen."

"It's the least of my problems. In the morning, you can call Katzenstein. I'm not that ill. It's time for more Salicylate."

Ernst's mouth went dry as he heard a glass filling with water. A moment later his father gagged and sputtered trying to swallow.

The next day, Dr. Katzenstein came to the house, and the postman delivered a letter from Lisa.

Dear Ernst,

I'm sorry not to have written in such a long time. I've been feeling sad and I'm not sure why. Margaret has been a wonderful friend. She understands me. I almost feel as if she's my sister. It's hard for me to sleep and then I have bad dreams. Even awake, I feel under an evil spell. I worry about getting sick and dying, like Mother, so I don't step on cracks in the sidewalk, or kill spiders, or walk under ladders.

I was glad to hear about Leo's visit, though it was hard for you. You sounded disappointed and I wanted to respond as soon as I could. But I have to be secretive. I don't know if I ever told you, but Father found one of your letters and he asked me who E. Techow was. I assured him that your name was Elizabeth, a friend from camp. I'm writing this letter at night by electric torch. I'm sure if Father knew you were 'Ernst' he'd be furious. Isn't he ridiculous? It would be funny if it weren't my life, which has become more and more intolerable.

Father watches me the way he watches his ticker tape, ready to take severe action at the slightest provocation. We are studying the stock market in school and I find it fascinating that gamblers run the country. Fritz says these blood-suckers profit from the war. It is VERY disturbing to me that Father, who makes my life so miserable, could be one of the very parasites that we learned to hate as Wandervogel. Remember the Unholy Trinity? Dirty Jews, dirty genes, and dirty pictures? Well, add a fourth – dirty war profiteers – Father! I hate him! People are starving in the streets and Father becomes richer and richer. I can't wait to go to university.

I'm sorry that Leo was a disappointment. Everybody changes when they grow up – some become better, but, I think, they are always different. I try to imagine you in a uniform and I think you will be quite handsome. I know that you will always be different than anyone else, and you don't like to be told what to do. I admire that in you. But Ruby, please, try to find the meaning in your life. Don't become wild and lost the way some artists do. (There seem to be more and more wild people wandering the streets these days, especially those returning from the War. I wonder what will become of them?)

Find some meaning with people who love you, like me and Fritz. It can be a lonely life without that. For some people I suppose it's God. The Sisters try to plant that in me, but I would rather smoke cigarettes and laugh with Margaret.

Write me again and tell me about your innermost, inside, deep feelings. Don't get lost, Ruby. Wandervogel forever!

With Love

Lisa

P.S I think maybe we'll win the War. The revolution in Russia. What a gift for us! (Who could have predicted it?). How quirky history is. All of a sudden the Czar's army is gone. I hear we now have more troops on the Western Front than the British and the French and all their allies combined. The momentum is with us! We're going to win!

Ernst smelled her perfumed letter, felt her substance, as if she were in the room. He searched for his 'innermost, inside, deep feelings.' And he caught glimpses – the 'painting of the light,' his father's smile at the National Gallery, Lisa's kiss at Lake Schoenplatz. That night, lying awake, he tried to recapture the taste and feel of her lips. In his mind's eye they made love and then lay together in the dark, whispering their affection, their fidelity, and he forgot about his sick father.

He awoke early enough to hear the milkman's horse shake its halter. Empty bottles tinkled their bright carillon as they were exchanged for the dull resonance of full ones. Lisa's letter lay next to his pillow and he read it again. Outside his room he heard heavy, uneven footsteps that could only be Frau Stimmel's, but that was odd. What was she doing upstairs so early? Reluctantly, he left his warm bed and cracked his door enough to hear his mother's whispered command.

"Dr. Katzenstein must come immediately! Do you understand? Immediately!"

"Yes, yes, I understand." Frau Stimmel was panting. Ernst saw the alarm in her face, her eyes wide as pfennigs, her upper teeth overbiting her lower lip. He shivered in the morning chill.

From the wedge of light under his parent's door, his father's voice came unnaturally slow, his words fat. "The Salicylate... it does nothing."

"Dr. Katzenstein is coming, Alfred." His mother's voice high pitched like a bird call, flying from one side of the room to the other.

"Call the court."

"Yes, dear, of course, but no one is there yet. I will be sure to call. A few days of rest will do you good. Do you want to see the boys before they go to school?"

"Gertrude, I'm not dying! Tell them I'm sick and I am not to be disturbed."

His mother left the bedroom and floated across the hall in her pale night-gown to the top of the stairs. "Frau Stimmel, a pot of chamomile!" She stared across the banister into empty space, the light from below etching shadows on her face.

Dr. Katzenstein rang the doorbell, his generous shadow filling the frosted glass door, while Ernst and Hans Gerd ate breakfast, though it could hardly be called that: oatmeal and slices of wheat toast set down by a distracted Frau Stimmel. Wiping her hands on her apron, she wobbled to the anteroom to admit the doctor, and a gust of cold air swept in with him. She fussed with his cane, mantle and hat, mumbled a few words, then sent him immediately

52

up the stairs.

Frau Stimmel limped through the dining room muttering to herself and bustled into the kitchen. A moment later she reappeared and set down the pitcher of milk, some of which splashed onto the table.

Hans Gerd steadied his toast with his deformed right hand and spread butter with his other. Frau Stimmel left again, and he eyed his older brother and asked, "What's really wrong with Father?"

"The Flu. It's just the flu," Ernst said. The house was colder than usual.

"Then why is everyone so crazy?"

"No one is crazy. He's just sick. You should know better than anyone. Dr. Katzenstein is always coming to see you. Why not Father when he's sick? It's no big deal."

"But Father is never sick,"

"Everyone gets sick."

"Emil's father died last week." Hans Gerd poked at his oatmeal. "He came back from the war with the fever and was in the hospital for a long time. Last week he just died."

"So? What does that have to do with anything?"

"A lot of people are dying," Hans Gerd said.

"Shut up!" Ernst tried to butter his toast; his knife tore the bread.

"You wouldn't even care if Father died," Hans Gerd said.

"You're talking stupid shit."

"But you hate him. I know you do."

"I don't hate him. Sometimes he makes me mad, but he's my father."

"You hate me. What if I died?"

"I don't hate you, little brother. You just piss me off. You piss off everybody. You're weird."

"I can't help it." He paused. "It was my birthday yesterday. You forgot."

Ernst felt ashamed. Usually Maria reminded the boys of birthdays, and four or five days were sufficient for a handmade card and a little present from the gift shop nearby. But this week was distorted. There was no reminder and, of course, everyone forgot.

"I'm sorry, little brother. It's been a bad week."

"You know what I want for my birthday? I want you to stop calling me 'little brother.' Can you do that?"

"It's an old habit – but I'll try."

"As long as you feel guilty. That's what really counts." Hans Gerd continued to stare at Ernst. "Do you know how old I am?"

"Uh... You're twelve, no – thirteen."

"Good guess. Thirteen." He coughed again. "You don't give a shit about anyone except yourself, do you, Ernst?"

"That's not true. I care a lot about..."

"You don't have to answer; it wasn't that kind of question. Just a fact."

They both suddenly heard Dr. Katzenstein bellowing upstairs. "The clinic! It is urgent! There is no time to lose!"

"I'm going to school." Hans Gerd slipped from the table, grabbed his heavy coat and books and fled the front door without brushing his teeth. Maria would be angry.

The doctor was on the upstairs telephone in the hallway. "Hello? This is Dr. Katzenstein. Dr. Blau, please. It's urgent!"

Ernst left the breakfast table and stood at the base of the stairs looking up through the spindle wood of the banister at the corpulent doctor, the earpiece trembling.

"Dr. Blau? Katzenstein here. I'm at the home of Magistrate Techow on Wannseestrasse. I fear he has tetanus. He needs antiserum immediately. I want him treated at your clinic."

Tetanus! The scourge of the front lines. There was no cure. Even with the best of care, soldiers died from tetanus, not from their wounds, as if the European armies were really at war with this bacterium. He felt unsteady and leaned against the lintel of the door, felt the room darken as his field of vision shrank to a binocular tunnel, and he sank to his knees sweating.

"...a puncture wound of his foot... insignificant... a healthy man." Katzenstein's words filtered through Ernst's fogged brain. "Damnedest thing I've ever seen. I would hate to be wrong on this, Dr. Blau. His only chance is the antiserum. I will need an ambulance. I'm just now administering a purge. He is in extremis. Please hurry."

Dr. Katzenstein called down the staircase. "Frau Stimmel, I need you immediately!"

She tottered out of the kitchen and gamely climbed the stairs, her face flushed and anxious.

"Frau Stimmel! More permanganate." The doctor's disembodied, goateed face hung over the banister.

"Oh, yes, of course." She stopped and turned around by the Chinese vase and limped down. At the bottom she saw Ernst and grabbed his arm. "Come with me, this instant!" She dragged him into the kitchen.

A kettle of boiling water whistled on the stove. She carefully poured the scalding water into another pot with granules of potassium permanganate; the water turned deep purple.

"Take this upstairs immediately! Tell the doctor I'm coming right away with the muslin." She eased him out the door with the sloshing purple liquid. He ascended the stairs carefully balancing the heavy pot.

"Do not spill any!" she shouted after him. "It stains horribly."

He passed the Chinese vase and gave it a ritual kick. Today was not a day to tempt fate. A spot of permanganate stained the tan rug. What the hell, he thought.

He knocked lightly at his parents' bedroom. After a moment, Maria opened the door and tried to take the pot from him at the threshold.

"Thank you, Ernst," she said. A salted tear had crusted under her red eyes.

Ernst looked past Maria, across the white sheet covering his father, at the bright purple stain where his left leg lay uncovered from the knee down, resting on two pillows. His foot was clearly swollen, the detail of toes and tendons lost in purple edema. At the other end of the bed, his father's head was propped on pillows, one eye opened more than the other. He must have heard, for when Maria said his name, it triggered a spasm of muscular contraction that rippled from the purple spot, beneath the sheets and emerged as a spastic contortion of his face that pulled his mouth down sharply on the left and shut that eye. Katzenstein tried to usher Ernst out of the room.

"Be a good lad and wait downstairs. Your father will be all right. You should probably go to school, don't you think?" The doctor glared at Maria and signaled by tipping his goatee toward the door.

"Yes, of course, Herr Doctor." Maria turned Ernst with her gentle arm around his shoulders. "Take Hans Gerd to school, Ernst. Please!"

"He already left." Ernst resisted and looked past Maria to see another spasm. "Father?"

"Your father is quite ill, young man." Dr. Katzenstein interposed himself between Ernst and his father and shepherded him from the room. "Your father needs expert care in a clinic. You can visit him soon and..."

"I want to see him now!" Ernst pushed against him, forcing his way back into the room.

"You'll make him sicker!" the doctor said.

"Where's my mother? Father?"

A moan arose from the sheets. The old bed creaked as he writhed.

Katzenstein's eyes grew wild. "I must insist that you leave! You will kill your father if you don't!"

Ernst looked from his father to the doctor and back again, confused. He saw his father raise his right hand. It hung half suspended over the sheet for what seemed like a long moment, then fell against his chest. A gurgled moan caught in his throat, as if he were trying to speak while being strangled.

Ernst shuddered and allowed Maria to lead him from the bedroom. The purple spot on the sheet burned in his mind like the after-image from a photographer's flash tray.

Maria led him to his room and sat next to him on his bed, her arm around his shoulder. She rocked him gently, crying. He knew he would never see his father alive again.

Frau Stimmel's face appeared at his door. She was breathing hard from another rapid ascent. "Maria," she whispered. "The doctor requires your assistance." She ducked back out into the hall.

Maria was careful to close the door gently, almost reverentially. Far away a siren began to wail. Was he already dead? Was Ernst complicit? Countless times he had wished for his father's death, had wished himself born into another family.

He felt light headed again and lay back on his bed; he felt his life capsizing. His whole misspent childhood loomed before him as a sacrilege, a desecration of his own making. The morning sun lit up the shelf over his desk, lit up Ernst's warships: a defining light, brief and clarion. Already the shadow from the next shelf began to darken his lovely, troubled, fleet. The *Brandenburg*, his flagship, lay on her side – her back broken, gathering dust, never to be repaired. Sunlight reflected the dust-dimmed colors of his painted navy, blurred now with tears. It was the painting of the light.

The siren droned closer. Ernst lunged off his bed and crossed the room in two furious strides. His right arm swung in a roundhouse arc, palm open, catching *Brandenburg* full astern. She crashed into *Nassau*, *Koenig* and *Van der Tann*, sweeping away *Scharnhorst* with her spider web of rigging, dragging her sister ship *Gneisenau* across the shelf. In a tangled mass they flew out into space and smashed against Leo's empty desk. The siren blared at full intensity then stopped as the ambulance skidded to a halt on gravel.

He collapsed onto his bed weeping for everything he had lost.

4

The Red Kite
1918

He had no tears during the grand funeral in Mariakirche or at the graveside, or the memorial at the Board of Trade, or the reception that followed at the house. Ernst floated in a bubble of willful amnesia, voices around him hollow and muffled. He drew caricatures of Leo, Hans Gerd and his mother, Uncle Erwin, Uncle Peter and Pastor Namann. It was only when he wrote to Lisa that his father had died on February 3, 1918, that his tears suddenly dropped onto the paper unbidden, inextinguishable, and strangely comforting, as if for one moment, his overfull heart had finally overflowed.

Though he told no one else, bad news travelled apace. His classmates somehow all knew and avoided him. Heinrich Schliefen and the Outlaws treated him as if he were contaminated.

During the reading of his father's will, it was revealed that he had secured Ernst a position in the Officer Training Corps of the Naval Cadet School. He was informed that his acceptance was contingent on excellent grades. Ernst worried that the war might end too soon. This was his chance for glory, for pride.

To the astonishment of all who knew him, he plunged into his studies, though he was still trapped in a boundless sea of anesthesia, focusing all his attention on his studies and drowning his feelings. Nietzsche spoke to him of emotional pain and strength – of the hideousness of pity. He carried Faust in his rucksack, to read when remembrance threatened to overwhelm him. Instead of menacing the streets with Schliefen's Outlaws, he squirreled away in the library and excelled in mathematics and history. When images of his dying father and the purple stain bludgeoned into his consciousness, he banished them by sheer force of will and took solace in imagining how proud his father would have been of Ernst the obedient student. (Herr Kremer, though pleased, could neither fathom, nor trust, this sudden conversion from delinquent to academic.) It was not out of love for his father, but from the pain of his premature death, a snuffing out of any possibility of his redemption as a man and as his father and the inescapable thought that one day he, too, would die unfinished.

At home, Ernst felt anchorless. Without his father, there was no one to restrain or correct him, no one to rail against. The rare times she was downstairs, his mother hovered ghost-like, her speech slurred from sedatives Frau Stimmel administered every six hours by the clock. She had become a chemist, dispensing a mixture of Veronal and Medinal in water to bedridden Frau Techow, along with codeine and bromides to Hans Gerd, whose asthma worsened. As the acute pall of grief gave way to time, relatives and friends stopped visiting. The silence of the house deepened as if the estate on Wannseestrasse had sunk to oceanic depths where light faded and life became scarce, the crushing pressure unbearable.

Contrary to Ernst, Hans Gerd's behavior problems escalated. He failed his grade and had to repeat the year. Without his father to establish order and enforce hygiene, his flaming red hair grew wild and hung over his face in curls. Ernst retreated to his room to draw or read; he desired more than anything to abandon this house forever. He wrote Fritz to arrange a visit to Halle. He needed to see Lisa.

Fritz responded that Lisa had told him of his father's passing. He was sorry for his loss. Then, in the next paragraph he confirmed that Easter vacation would be a fine time to visit. He and Lisa and Margaret had devised a plan for how to evade Lisa's father's surveillance.

Ernst asked Frau Stimmel, who stomped her short foot and refused. In the household vacuum, she had seized the mantle of authority. "It's too upsetting to your mother." She stretched for a plate high on a shelf. "She needs you." Her fingers groped in vain. "Ernst Werner! Get me that yellow plate. Careful – it was your grandmother's."

The kitchen was hotter than usual. "What about me? Does anyone care about me? Just two days?"

"Impossible." Frau Stimmel moved erratically, as if distracted or confused.

"One day?"

"You must be here on Easter Sunday."

"One day – Saturday. I'll return in the evening. Mother won't even know I'm gone."

"Pastor Namann will know if you are not at Easter Service." She stirred the pot then tasted the chicken stock. "I shouldn't allow this. Nothing makes sense."

"Please, Frau Stimmel." He hated begging.

She looked from him to the bubbling stock and back. "You must promise to be back by Saturday evening." She put more kindling in the kitchen stove. "I just don't understand anything anymore."

★　★　★　★　★　★　★　★　★　★

Fritz met him at the Halle train station and they embraced. Ernst's eyes unexpectedly filled with tears and he wiped them roughly away. They held each other at arms length. Fritz wore a well-tailored jacket and cravat. Over the eight months since the end of summer Ernst had grown almost a head taller than Fritz, who had become more stout and broad-shouldered. Ernst rubbed his friend's freshly shorn, stubbly head.

"Getting ready for the army?"

"I like it. It's easy, very vogue."

"You look like a teddy bear."

Fritz growled.

"What's in the rucksack?" Ernst asked.

"Lunch for the *Wandervogel* – Rhine wine, Rye bread, Bavarian soft cheese, and a red kite." Fritz linked arms with Ernst and led him toward the depot. "Ernst, I'm so sorry about your father. It must have been horrible."

The train began to leave the station, accelerating, and Ernst felt the sky and the platform begin to tilt and whirl. He stopped. "I need to sit for a moment, Fritz."

On a platform bench he put his head between his knees as the train clackety-clacked out of Halle. When it was quiet again, the spinning stopped and his stomach settled.

"It was so unexpected, Fritz. I didn't get to say goodbye." Travelers hurried past. Sparrows flitted and pigeons cooed among the steel girders.

"Same with Cedric," Fritz said. "One day he was alive and the next day... gone. It's hard to make sense of it."

Ernst looked for sadness through Fritz's thick glasses, but his hazel eyes only blinked and shifted, as if alert for an ambush. "When will we see Lisa?"

"We have to kidnap her," Fritz said. "It's very dangerous work, but we are *Wandervogel!*" His left hand saluted backwards, comically.

"Her father?" Ernst asked.

"Worse than ever."

"Do you two still fly kites?"

"Not for a long time. She's chaperoned everywhere."

"How do you get in touch with her?"

"Margaret. The families know each other from church and she's in Lisa's class at her new private school. I give a letter to Margaret and she passes it to Lisa. Lisa responds the same way."

"What does Margaret get out of this?"

"Cigarettes – a pack with every letter – and the thrill of conspiracy. Margaret has completely deceived Lisa's father. She looks quite innocent. But she has, shall we say, complex tastes. Margaret is involved with a married man, and I allow them to use my bedroom when my parents are away on father's business trips." He winked at Ernst. "They bring their own sheets."

"You have a way about you, Fritz. You make connections."

"The statesman's tools – motivation, persuasion, consummation."

Bahnhof Halle bustled with Easter travelers, families wearing ordinary weekend overcoats, carrying suitcases no doubt stuffed with Easter finery. Fritz and Ernst exited into the bright sun on Bahnhofstrasse. An unshaven beggar appealed to them and Fritz pushed him aside. Shiny black taxis lined up at the curb. A poster, half torn, announced a sold-out concert of Maestro Busoni and The Berlin Philharmonic. Someone had painted graffiti to read **Kaiser Wilhelm Sold Out!** Beside that, a faded poster showed a stern-faced army officer in a piked steel helmet pointing his finger at everyone, **"What have you done for the Vaterland?"**

Beneath the pointing soldier, on the sun-warmed curb, two skeletal women sat on the pavement holding out wooden bowls. Between them, a girl – it was hard to know how old – leaned against one of the women, her sunken, dark eyes more compelling than the begging bowls. Ernst felt her accusing gaze. Her legs were like sticks and oily strands of hair stuck to her smudged cheeks. He had read that starvation made children look half their age. He had to look away.

"Do you wear that silly cravat every day?" he said to Fritz.

"As a matter of fact, I do. I rather like being in style."

"How vain you've become."

"Think on this, Ernst. You know that in the land of the blind, the one-eyed man is king. Well, in the land of the hopeless, the vain man is king."

Ernst laughed. "I really don't take you seriously."

Fritz twirled an imaginary mustache. "I know." He rolled his eyes. "I am so – what's the word? Impeccable."

"An impeccable asshole," Ernst said.

60

"Come on, there's our tram." He pulled Ernst toward the streetcar. "Your train doesn't leave till 7:10 tonight; we have all day."

They rode the #12 tram to within a block of Lisa's mansion. At a specified Linden tree, Margaret waited, a tall girl with heavy glasses and mouse-brown hair draped over her delicate shoulders. Her cheeks still betrayed early adolescence and until she smiled, Margaret seemed quite ordinary and young. She took off the glasses and straightened from the tree, squaring her shoulders. She smiled, dimples dotting each cheek. Ernst saw a sensual beauty transform her face. Just to the left of her nose, she had a small dark mole. More than anything, Ernst found her curious, but also compelling. Interesting. She wore a tightly fitted green dress and, about her shoulders, a burgundy shawl that concealed her breasts. It was arousing to imagine Margaret with a man in Fritz's bedroom.

Fritz stroked his shorn head twice, a nervous gesture. "Margaret, this is Ernst, my best friend."

Her smile coquettish, she locked eyes with Ernst and shook his hand a little too firmly, a little too long. Fritz dropped a pack of cigarettes and something wrapped in brown paper into Margaret's handbag, and she was distracted. "Lisa has told me all about you." She looked back at Ernst and tilted her head. "The third bird?" Her laugh was throaty and rough. "Berlin?" One eyebrow lifted.

"Yes... Yes," Ernst stammered. "Ber – Berlin. This morning – by train."

She studied him and her dimples deepened. She shifted from one hip to the other.

"Margaret will pick up Lisa," Fritz interrupted. "Lisa has explained to her father that they will go shopping downtown. Everything has already been purchased so that dear old dad will see the fruits of a prodigious day at the shops. One hour, Margaret? Good luck."

"Thank you, Fritzy." She stroked his cheek, then kissed the air between them. She turned and walked off, her hips swinging, both boys staring after her. As she rounded the corner to Lisa's front door, her hips stopped mid-swing, her body slumped, and she became as plain as paper.

* * * * * * * * * *

They waited more than an hour for the girls. Fritz fiddled with the kite, red canvas emblazoned with a fierce imperial eagle. He looked up frequently, watching for them to come through the wrought iron arch that opened into

Halle Municipal Park and Boathouse. Ernst skipped stones onto the Lake's wind-whipped, white-capped surface, and most stones crashed against the wavelets. Geese scattered skyward, screeching from the inlet, circling the lake.

Ernst pretended not to see Lisa walk through the arch arm in arm with Margaret. They both wore red kerchiefs like peasant women, two red heads bobbing together talking and smiling. Margaret's hips swayed again. Lisa's pale yellow dress was speckled with thousands of red dots, like Monet's *Field of Poppies*, Ernst thought. The fitted bodice wrapped skin-tight about her waist upward to her breasts. Her skirt fluttered like a flag in the south wind. Lisa waved and he waved back, then skipped another stone. He had to contain his eagerness.

They met lakeside and Lisa hugged Margaret goodbye.

"You are an angel, Margaret!" Fritz called to her.

"My pleasure." She blew them a kiss and walked off. She stopped and lit a cigarette in the lee of a linden tree. Margaret smoking in the middle of a public park on the day before Easter. Outrageous even for Berlin, but in Halle?

Lisa wrapped her arms about Ernst's shoulders and kissed his cheek. His arms circled her thin waist and held tight.

"Ruby! Ivory! My sweet boys. Oh, how are you? Tell me everything! I want to know everything."

She backed away and Ernst let his arms fall awkwardly to his side. "I've missed you terribly." He blushed.

"And oh, how I've missed you."

For a moment there was only her voice and his pulse hammering in his ears, the curious tilt of her head, her secret smile. She grabbed their hands and pulled them up a grassy knoll overlooking the boathouse.

"This is the *Wandervogel* spot, Ruby. Ivory and I discovered it last fall and claimed it for the three of us. It's our private country."

"Colonial expansion," Fritz pronounced. "The first territorial seizure in our conspiracy to take over the world and fill it with *Wandervogel*."

"Cut the crap, Fritz." Ernst felt suspicions. "That was six months ago? You never told me."

"Relax, Ernst. It was nothing; just a silly game." Fritz opened his rucksack and pulled out a red and white checkered tablecloth containing cheese, a small crock of butter and rye bread. They spread the cloth and had to sit on it to keep it from blowing away.

"And now, the libation." Fritz dramatically drew out the Rhine wine.

Lisa pulled off her kerchief and her blond hair fluttered behind her. "Hush," Lisa whispered and gathered them to her side. "Close your eyes. Listen to the wind." As they did so often during their summers, they sat holding hands in a circle, Ernst's and Lisa's hair dancing in the south wind.

She bent forward and touched her cheek to Ernst's hand. "I'm so sorry about your father."

"Just bad luck."

Lisa stared out over the lake. "It's more than that. I still cry about Mother, and she died more than ten years ago. It makes me sad to think of her, but I also love the idea of loving her and the way she loved me."

"Do you pray for her?" Fritz asked.

"When I was young I did, until I got so angry with God. Then I stopped." She turned to Ernst. "Do you pray about your father?"

"It doesn't even occur to me to pray," he said. "At some places, Grünewald, The Havel, The National Gallery, I get a strange, religious kind of feeling. But I really don't don't think about it now." He paused and prepared his announcement. "I've been accepted for officer corps training at the Naval Cadets in the fall. But my grades have to be excellent."

"Do mine ears deceive me?" Lisa's brow furrowed. "Ruby, the serious student? I guess I don't really know you anymore."

He felt stung. "Of course you do," he said.

"Ivory's always the same," Lisa said. "Aren't you, Fritzy?"

An uncomfortable silence hung until Fritz said, "Lisa and Margaret are going to University in Berlin next year."

Lisa in Berlin! In the Fall! Ernst's face flushed.

Fritz poured wine into their three tin *Wandervogel* cups. "A toast to our Naval cadet and our university student! And to Lisa's liberation from the dungeon of her father's castle."

Ernst reached into his rucksack for his book of Heine poems. He tapped his tin cup again. "Another fortifying beverage, my good man." Fritz's eyes looked enormous behind his glasses and Ernst stifled an impulse to laugh. They drank another cupful of wine. "I'll read the first poem! It's called *Which Way Now?*" Ernst closed his eyes, took a deep breath and began. The words soothed him in a manner not unlike his drawings.

They took turns reading poems and toasting the Army, the Reich, Margaret, the Impressionists, and more than once, *Wandervogel* . Ernst closed the book of Heine and returned it to his pack. Numbed by wine and wind, words and sun, the celebration depleted, they sat unmoving.

"How many days, Lisa?" Ernst asked.

"One hundred and forty-eight days until winter term starts. I shall live in a charming third floor garret and hang my underwear on a clothes line at night out the window."

"Wake up, Lisa," Fritz said. "You shall live in a crummy little dormitory room like every other first-year and dream about a crummy little apartment in Charlottenburg. Besides, your crummy old dad will never let you live in a crummy old garret all by yourself."

"And will you visit dear old dad when he comes to the stock exchange?" Ernst asked. "It's not that far to Behrenstrasse."

"I'll be busy that day." She brightened. "Margaret and I will be roommates. I can't believe we're talking about living in Berlin. It's just too amazing."

Down the hill by the boathouse, Ernst noticed a dark man in a battered khaki coat rooting through a garbage barrel. He nudged Fritz's arm and nodded in his direction. "Returnee?"

"Looks like it from the trenchcoat."

"Millions of them will be coming home from the war," Ernst said. "No food, no jobs, no place to live. You politicians better come up with something fast. Remember that kid at the railroad station this morning?"

"I try not to see the beggars," Fritz said.

"Better wear dark, dark glasses – at least in Berlin."

"A defeated army is still an army," Lisa said. "There's no telling what they could do – public works, get rid of the Bolsheviks. It's just a matter of creativity and will."

"Speaking of creativity," Fritz said, "I read in the newspaper about a new show by that maniac Picasso and his insane friend, Bricque or Bracque... something like that. Have you ever seen such trash? Kindergarteners can draw better pictures."

"Do you think Picasso and What's-his-name are laughing at us?" Lisa said. "I always wonder if these new artists are really the ultimate anarchists. Our class from school went to see an exhibition here in Halle and I just laughed. Head Mistress got really angry at me, but it was ridiculous. One painter just splashed paint on the canvas and gave it a name. Is that art? Am I stupid? I just don't get it. Ernst, you're an artist. What do you think?"

Ernst could only think of his father in the National Gallery railing at The Fauves – the Wild Beasts. "I don't understand it. But it's interesting – in a weird way. I don't know. It's complicated. I understand the urge." There was an uncomfortable silence. Ernst jumped up. "Hey, we have this great wind.

Let's fly this kite." He began unraveling the ball of string and lifted the canvas kite into the wind where it flapped and strained like a royal topsail.

"Excuse me, *Wandervogel*," Fritz said, "but this vintage beverage has distended my bladder." He wobbled down the hill to the boathouse.

"You boys are disgusting," Lisa said. She took up the ball of string and slowly unwound enough length for the crimson kite to launch.

"When did you start flying kites?" Ernst asked.

"I was about five or six. Aunt Ida told me that kites fly on the spirit winds of people."

"Your mother?" Ernst asked.

"Yes, Mother's. Aunt Ida said the spirit and the soul are the same, and cannot die."

Another gust fluttered the tablecloth. Bread crumbs blew away.

She stood before him, looking up at the kite. Before timidity could restrain him, Ernst laid his hands on Lisa's shoulders, ready to pull them away at any suggestion of discomfort, but she only watched the red kite. He started to knead her shoulders, the way Maria did for him when he was upset as a child.

"How well do you remember her?" he asked.

"I remember her like a five year old remembers the world. She's always young and I feel that I know this beautiful woman in a mysterious way."

He too would remember his father as vital and young. "And when you fly your kite?"

"She's the wind and we talk."

She looked at him. He felt the pull of the kite string and the magnetic tug of her eyes. "Then I name the wind... Lisa," he said and blushed again.

She leaned forward and kissed his cheek, and then their lips brushed like butterflies. He could taste the wine on her breath. Her lips whispered against his. "In Berlin, Ruby."

"In Berlin."

Fritz stumbled out of the boathouse and when Ernst saw him, he backed away from Lisa.

The sun glowed through a layer of nimbus clouds advancing from the south. The approaching storm suffused the wind with a fruited scent. Ash leaves trembled, their silver undersides glittering like coins. Lisa ran down the knoll pulling the red kite, which jumped and jerked and surged higher and higher. Ernst hastened after her, keeping a respectful distance until the kite was a red dot under the clouds and she stopped, the string taut against her chest.

"Take it, Ernst!" She pressed the ball of twine into his hands and right away the vigor of the wind surged through him.

"It pulls hard," he said.

She laughed. "You've never flown a kite before, have you? Close your eyes, Ruby. Think of your father. Do you see his face?"

5

Kiel Naval Base
September – November, 1918

His commission was approved and on September 3rd,1918 Ernst was assigned to the Naval Cadet Officer's Corps in Kiel, Leo's naval base – a choice posting. No doubt it had something to do with his father's influence. He could not help but suffer the irony that on the very day Lisa arrived in Berlin for university, he left for Kiel, and they were just as far away from each other as they had been. Ernst thought fate had played a cruel joke, that they should have missed each other by so small a margin.

It was a week before the brothers first met for dinner, and Ernst was dazzled by Leo's uniform and his still shiny second lieutenant's bars. They sat on the veranda of a popular dockside tavern favored by officers.

Leo was going bald and kept his light brown hair short like Fritz, like most military men. They hardly resembled each other. Where Ernst was reedy and tall like his father, Leo stood half a head shorter, and he had inherited his Uncle Erwin's broad shoulders and stout constitution. "Kiel's big fish have overtaken its little sprats," Leo expounded. Long before they built battleships here, everyone knew Kiel for its sprats, its canneries. The waterfront reeked of fish. No longer. Now the sprats counted for nothing compared to the big iron fish, and the harbor smelled of coal-fired engines and dry-dock welding fumes. Leo's brow crinkled as he looked across the fjord at the fleet. "There's something you should know right away, Ernst. Something big is about to happen. Something dangerous. You and I are sprats. It's best to stay sprats. Be very careful."

He felt his brother watching him, studying him. Leo told Ernst about the growing unrest among the seamen, about injustice, and abuse. But he never said what he really thought about it. He only explained the problem, as if reading from a newspaper. Then he said something that unnerved Ernst. "I think Father would have understood."

"Don't speak for Father."

"His name still carries weight. How do you think you got this posting?"

The knowledge that his father directed his life from the grave rankled Ernst, but it had become an unexpected opportunity. And he wished for Lisa to see him in his naval uniform. He wanted not to think of the stern father he could never please.

"Oh," Leo said before they parted for the evening. "And use protection when you visit Fraulein Sylvia's girls."

* * * * * * * * * *

"Techow! You miscreant!" First Lieutenant Manfred rounded the barracks corner and loomed over Ernst and three sailors playing cards. Ernst grabbed his white officer's cap and sprang to attention, scattering his playing cards across the table and floor. His three partners, stokers from the engine room crew of which Ernst was the Cadet Officer, sprang to attention and saluted their company commander. Manfred returned their salutes with an angry chop. "In my office, Techow. Now!" The lieutenant wheeled and marched off.

Seaman Solwitz gathered the cards, swearing under his breath. "Cunt! Can't even play cards. What the hell else is there to do?"

Seaman First Class Marcus Varren, a chemist's assistant from Dresden, put two cigarettes in his mouth and lit them both. He passed one to Ernst. A dark port wine birthmark stained Varren's left scalp, forehead, eye and cheek, like a purple continent on a fleshy globe. "Cadet Officers are not to play cards with working class scum like us."

"Where's it say that?" Solwitz muttered.

Varren spit. "In their black hearts." His lips chewed nervously, like an insect, while his dark eyes kept scanning, blinking.

"Fuck him," Solwitz said. He stared hard after the departing Lieutenant.

Ernst buttoned his tunic then polished his shoes by rubbing each briefly on the back of a pant leg. He straightened his spine and centered his peaked cap.

"Some day," Varren eyed Ernst, "you'll have to make a choice. Swine like him will be shot from behind. When it all boils over, the officer corps can never be sure who to trust, and then," he pointed his finger like a revolver, "Bang! The revolution begins and scum like Manfred are the first to go."

With Varren still jabbering at his side, Ernst walked toward Lieutenant Manfred's office. Though still an officer in training, Ernst found easy rapport with common seamen – and Varren, a leader among them, seemed to cultivate his camaraderie.

"Varren, lighten up. Everything is not class warfare."

"If you would come to a meeting of the People's Naval Division you'd understand. Quantitative change suddenly becomes qualitative change."

"Varren, sometimes you sound like a ventriloquist's dummy."

"Fuck you, Techow." Varren grabbed the cigarette out of Ernst's mouth and flicked it away. "I'm trying to save your ass. You think Lieutenant Manfred gives a shit about you? You're the lowest noncom in the fleet, just one tiny step above us sailors. You're nothing but a Cadet Officer, and only because your father's a rich judge."

"My father is dead," Ernst said.

"He rules from the grave." Varren's restless lips chewed up and down. "How many rooms in your house?"

"I really don't know."

"Exactly. The rest of us don't have that problem. It's a number less than five."

Varren turned abruptly and walked the other way.

★ ★ ★ ★ ★ ★ ★ ★ ★ ★

Lieutenant Manfred's office door stood ajar and his aide was absent from his desk. Manfred returned his salute and closed the door behind him. "At ease, Techow. Please, sit down. Smoke?" A gold plated cigarette box sprang open in his hand.

"No thank you, sir." Ernst sat at attention expecting the worst. He looked straight ahead, past Manfred's eyes through the window behind the Lieutenant's head, where the forecastle of a battleship loomed – its 380 mm guns, some of the largest in the world, pointed straight at him.

"Relax, Techow." Manfred lit his own cigarette.

Shorter than Ernst, with a beefy face and broad muscular shoulders, the company commander's clean shaven face was pitted with acne scars. His light brown hair, already thinning, lay in wisps across his forehead, and dark, oval eyes, too small for his face, squinted at Ernst through the smoke.

"I have something urgent to discuss with you. You may disavow this conversation if it in any way disturbs you. I will, of course, also have complete deniability. Do we understand each other?"

"Yes, sir."

"Good." Manfred tapped his cigarette's ash into the glass ashtray. His manicured fingernails reflected the window's light. "You're a first class Cadet, Techow. You show great promise and you come from a good family. You are a class above the ordinary sailor. You have much to learn, but you've shown yourself to be intelligent, and, I hope, savvy. You do understand the difference, don't you?"

"I'm not sure I know what you mean, Sir."

"Intelligent people sometimes make impractical choices." He paused. "Let me be blunt. What is your position on the political issues the seamen raise?"

"I'm not sure what you mean, Sir."

"I know what goes on in the barracks, Techow. I have eyes and ears everywhere. Have you been to the Monday night meetings at The Warehouse? The People's Naval Division, I believe it's called?"

"No, Sir."

"Though I, of course, have never been, my eyes and ears have attended every meeting and I'm deeply troubled. Talk of Bolshevism, a Soviet Revolution, the oppressed masses rising up and overthrowing the monarchy – murder, conspiracy, violent overthrow of the state. It's really rather remarkable." He sat back and studied Ernst. "And it's treason." He offered the cigarette box again. It glittered, reflecting the bare bulb that hung over the Lieutenant's desk. "Gauloises. It's one of the few things the French make that is superior to our own. Please, take one." Ernst plucked a cigarette from the box and tapped one end on his thumbnail. The Lieutenant leaned over with his silver lighter. "This war won't last much longer, and we've lost. The Allied blockade is strangling us. The economy is in ruins. For now, we in the military still eat well, but civilians don't. And hunger breeds revolution."

Ernst knew his mother, for now, was insulated from privation by virtue of meat, milk and eggs from Uncle Erwin and a survivor's pension worth less and less as the economy faltered. Across the fjord, in the city center of Kiel, the suffering was more plain. Children begged openly in the streets. Ernst avoided the city. He stayed near the naval base where alcohol flowed freely at the Hofbrauhaus, and Fraulein Sylvia's whores were eager for the extra marks necessary to feed their families.

"We were so close to victory." Manfred leaned back and launched a smoke ring to the ceiling. "Ludendorf's spring offensive – a mere 50 kilometers from Paris. Fifty kilometers. I find it astounding that the margin between victory and defeat can be that small." Manfred inhaled deeply, then launched a series of smoke rings. "After Jutland, the High Command never let us out of port to engage the British. They were fools – what a wasted opportunity. Instead we sit on our asses and let Bolshevism seep in. It's over. I understand that Ludendorf and Hindenburg have told the Kaiser that the war is lost."

His voice wavered; his eyes were glassy and red. For a moment Ernst was horrified that Manfred might weep. "There is talk of an armistice," Manfred said. "The lame-brained who cannot see reality think it is a trick that will allow us to regroup and renew the fight." He shook his head and pursed his lips. "A fool's dream and the officers know it. Germany will sue for peace on the Allies' terms. Nobody will admit that publicly, but everyone knows the end is nearing. And then, what will become of our soldiers and sailors? Will they go back to their homes, scrounge for food, look for non-existent work and continue their lives as if the Bolshevik Revolution never occurred? Of course not. There may be civil war and I need to know which of my officers I can trust." He leaned forward and ground out his Gauloise. "Are you with us?"

Ernst nodded, first tentatively, then vigorously as he felt Manfred's affection. "Yes, Sir." Ernst picked tobacco from the end of his tongue and rolled it between his fingers. "I'm an officer in the Navy, Sir, not a politician. I will do my duty."

"That is the answer you are expected to give." He leaned forward again and articulated each word slowly. "I need to know what is in your heart."

Lisa had asked him the same question in her letter – about his 'innermost, inside, deep feelings'. It was about truth and loyalty, which were not at all the same. Was there room enough in his heart for both Lisa and Manfred?

"It is my duty, Sir, to defend our Vaterland from those who would destroy it from within or without." He thought of the unholy trinity. "Jews, Bolsheviks, racial mixing, pornographers – whomever."

Manfred smiled and sat back again. "I think I read you correctly, Techow. You have not disappointed me. Do you know Captain Ehrhardt?"

"He's somewhat of a legend, Sir. The officers seem in awe of him."

"Captain Ehrhardt is forming a Brigade of officers and men with shared convictions. This is very unofficial and not sanctioned by the military – at least not yet. As you have undoubtedly surmised from the morale in your unit, we cannot count on enlisted men. It seems quite likely that in the near future the military may have to serve a Socialist government. We must seize the initiative at the turning. Do you understand?"

"The turning, Sir?"

"The nation is ripe for convulsive change. We must anticipate the worst. The Supreme Command itself recognizes the problem. They've chosen Major von Schleicher to organize volunteers – Freebooters – into what is being called the Free Corps 'Storm Battalions.' The Ehrhardt Brigade will be one of those battalions. Freebooters will not be government troops. There will be no traitors or pacifists to betray us."

"Why are you telling this to me, Sir?"

"I need a driver – someone I can trust – someone clever who can fix an engine, who has ears and intellect, someone who knows Berlin. I need you, Techow."

Ernst blushed. "I'm honored."

Manfred smiled. "Nothing will change for now, Techow. When you are needed, you will be called. Oh, and don't be playing cards with the enlisted men. Stay clear of Marcus Varren. He's a very dangerous man. That's all for now, Techow. Dismissed."

★　★　★　★　★　★　★　★　★　★

Captain Volker of Ernst's Battleship *Helgoland* assembled his officers and non-coms for an urgent briefing. Ernst stood in the back of the crowded stateroom, which was clamorous with urgent conversation, breathing in a heady amalgam of tobacco smoke and ardor.

It had been two weeks since Ernst's private talk with Lieutenant Manfred. He wondered how many men in this room knew of the Free Corps. How many, like Manfred, anticipated the next war?

The room hushed as Captain Volker strode through the bulkhead in a crisp new uniform. He removed his dress cap and signaled his officers to be seated. His gray hair, thinned to a rim around his balding head, was slicked down in perfect order.

"Gentlemen." His Executive Officer and First Mate began distributing sealed packets to senior officers. "At 0200 we steam out of port and engage the blockade at first light."

A cheer erupted from the officers who had anticipated this moment since their victory at Jutland, more than two years earlier.

"All units are to be on board by 1600 hours today. Senior staff will meet in my wardroom at 1330 hours. Exec?" He replaced his cap and barely concealed a cocksure smile as he surrendered the lectern to his Executive Officer, saluted and left.

The naval base at Kiel suddenly bustled with activity. Trucks filled the mud rutted roads carrying food, ammunition, and coal to feed the men, guns, and boilers of the great ships waiting in the cold October rain.

Shivering in the dampness, Ernst walked briskly back to the Seamen's barracks reviewing the details of the briefing, planning his words to Varren and the boiler crew. There would be no meeting of the People's Naval Division that night.

But Ernst was troubled. Manfred himself had said that the war was over. Was this a suicidal mission? It was not for him to reason why, but he knew this was a desperate gamble, for even if they broke the blockade and defeated the British fleet, nothing could reverse the disasters on the Eastern and Western Fronts.

"Varren!" he shouted into the barracks. "Varren, where are you?"

"Takin' a dump," Varren called from the lavatory.

"Every man is to report to his station on board, immediately." He looked around at the lounging seamen, some just rousing from a nap after lunch.

"Achtung!" Ernst yelled with the deepest voice he could muster and stood at rigid attention. The motley boiler men slowly lumbered to their feet. "It is now 1330 hours! You have until 1430 to be on board at engine room stations. Boilers to full steam by 1630."

The men grumbled and reached for their uniforms. The toilet flushed and Varren came out of the lavatory fastening his seaman's pants. "Another fucking drill? Do something worthwhile, Techow. Tonight, come to the meeting at the warehouse, 2100 hours – don't be late." He winked at Ernst.

Ernst remained at attention. "Seaman First Class Varren, you will come to attention and salute an officer."

"You're the one who's always telling me to relax, Techow." He offered a spiritless salute. "What stick is up your ass?"

"1430 on board! Make sure everyone's there, Varren, or I'll bust you." He turned and left for the ship.

An hour later in the engine room, Ernst's crew lined up before Helgoland's three great boilers. A stoker threw the last shovelful of coal into the red-hot glow and the third heavy door clanged shut. The cathedral-sized engine room darkened and cooled. Except for the scant illumination of incandescent bulbs, the battleship's bowels churned in near darkness. Steam hissed from valves and disappeared into blackness above. The men had obviously dressed quickly; some had not shaved for days. Stokers' yellow leather aprons phosphoresced in the perpetual twilight of the ship's hold. From far overhead came the drumming of feet on steel, with shouted orders barely audible. The air reeked of hot coal and steam. Condensation dripped from great pipes that thrummed with the engine's lifeblood. Sudden avalanches of coal cascaded into vast bins on each side of the boilers.

Twenty men stood at their stations and it was immediately clear to Ernst that Varren's fire safety position was empty.

"Goddammit!" he screamed over the turbine's cacophony. "Where is Varren?"

A steel door slammed shut high above; all heads turned toward the staccato clank of boots descending metal steps. Through the iron mesh of catwalks, ladders and stairs, Ernst recognized Varren. "There will be sanctions," he yelled up at him. The adrenaline in his brain infused him with power he was unaccustomed to wielding. He felt animated with courage and potency, disgusted by these dirty men in this hell-hole.

Ordinarily they would run through their exercise by rote: fire up the boiler, test the governor valves, lubricate every moving part. Fire safety pumps would hum into action, limp hoses grow turgid. Three hours later they would be back in their barracks.

But not today. Word must have gotten out; the chain of gossip preempted the chain of command, and Ernst could feel a peculiar zeal among the crew. The men moved as if galvanized by the pulse of Helgoland's massive pistons. Ernst suppressed a smile as Varren finally took his station.

"As you seem to know already, this is not a drill. We are finally going into action. 0200 hours."

There was no cheering, not even ardor. Their eyes looked troubled as they came to attention. They exchanged confused glances. Varren broke ranks and moved among the various stations, sharing words with the stokers, the coal boys, the engineers, the fire safety gang. As he passed each group, they slumped impotently and avoided Ernst's gaze.

"As you were, Varren!"

High above the steel shell of the boiler room, a choral chant began and barely penetrated the hiss and pump of the pistons.

"Our orders are to break the British blockade. We steam into the North Sea at 0200 hours along with the rest of the fleet from Wilhelmshaven and Hamburg, and engage the enemy at first light. This is what we have been waiting for."

Varren picked up the nozzle of his turgid fire hose. "There will be no engagement," he said calmly.

Ernst could hardly believe what he was hearing. "As you were, Seaman Varren!"

High above, on deck, Ernst heard faint singing – as of a chorus. Solwitz, Ernst's card partner and a baritone in his church choir, dropped his shovel onto the steel floor and began to sing.

> Arise ye prisoners of starvation
> Arise ye wretched of the Earth
> For justice thunders condemnation
> A better world's in birth.

One by one, the other nine yellow-suited stokers let their shovels clatter onto the deck and stepped away from their stations to gather in front of the boilers. One by one took up the chorus of The Internationale, tentatively at first, then with gusto. The harmonic resonance of the steel hull echoed and amplified their small chorale until it melded with the engine's rumble.

"Back to your stations!" Ernst's wide eyes swept the semi-circle of mutineers, his breath coming hard. He had lost control. He was disrespected. His authority – his potency – was gone. "Varren, this is your doing, isn't it?"

They sang louder, gaining courage and voice. Each man moved to a new position, as if they had practiced this choreography for weeks. Varren and two yellow stokers uncoiled three fire hoses. Varren's lips chewed nervously. He did not sing. Without taking his eyes off Ernst, he signaled with his head and one by one, the great boiler doors swung open.

"This is high treason, it's mutiny, you bastards!" Ernst drew his service revolver and leveled it at Varren. "A state of war exists. This vessel is technically speaking already in combat. I am completely within my right to execute you immediately. Marcus! Cease and desist! All of you, return to your stations!" The boiler fires baked Ernst's face from each side; rivulets of perspiration soaked his chest and ran cold down his abdomen. The pistol stock felt slick in his hand and trembled. "I will shoot, Varren. Put down the hose! Return to your stations, all of you! Immediately!"

"This is our moment." Varren glared into his eyes. "Which side are you on, Techow?"

"Join us, Techow," Goldmacher pleaded. "Join us. You're one of us."

"Put away the gun," Solwitz said. "You're aiming at the wrong people."

Ernst looked down the barrel of his pistol, alone and terrified, the gun weighty in his hand. "This cannot be permitted!" He leveled the pistol at Varren. His arm ached. "This is the Imperial Navy. I must shoot, Marcus." Boiler fires roared; steam hissed and rumbled. Ernst squeezed the trigger.

At that instant, from all over the ship, fire emergency gongs rang and jets of water erupted from the three hoses. Varren swung the surge of water into Ernst and it caught him in the middle of his chest, throwing him back onto the steel deck with the force of ten men. The bullet ricocheted off the bulkhead; his revolver spun away from his hand and clanged across the steel. Varren struggled to direct the gush of water into the glowing mouth of the first boiler; his companions turned on the other two. In rapid succession, ear shattering explosions of steam spewed out and each boiler cracked with a sharp metallic rupture, then hissed, filling the engine room with super-heated steam and burning coal fumes, a toxic fog that spilled into the hold and burned Ernst's nostrils. Over the mad hiss of the boilers came shouting, and the climbing footfalls of the crew mounting ladders, crossing catwalks. Water pressure in the hoses dropped and they came to rest. Only the ebbing steam sizzled as the great boilers cooled. Far above, Ernst heard the muti-neers regrouping in song until the engine room bulkhead doors slammed shut and their chorale was overwhelmed by the hissing yellow mist, per-cussed by emergency bells.

Ernst lay in the warm water, his skin burning, each bell-stroke a sharp pick in his temples. Something ached above his eyes and he had to wipe away blood to see. The force of the hose had thrown him along the bolt-studded deck into the bulkhead; his back and legs throbbed, his knuckles bled freely. Was this just his ship? He wondered about Leo, on the *Bayern*, across the har-bor. How could they have turned on him? His "officer authority" meant noth-ing. But in the end he had pulled the trigger, and that troubled him more than anything. Yet, the law would forgive him; the law encouraged him. How could he be so troubled by two things so opposite? He knew full well he should just do his duty, free himself from the conflict in his mind, in his heart.

As the mist condensed, he could make out the three hoses, tangled on the deck like dead serpents bleeding trickles of black water. A sudden chill passed through him, though the water was warm, and he drew his knees up. The last piston ground to a halt and the emergency bells ceased; his teeth chattered. Once again it was quiet enough to hear The Internationale reverber-ating from several decks above.

He struggled to his feet. Each step up the ladders was excruciating. His bruised ribs ached with every breath and he could feel burns starting to blister on his face.

He staggered through the hatchway into the late afternoon light, gasping at the fresh air. The deck was deserted. *The Internationale* resounded from the piers and warehouses. Volleys of rifle fire and automatic weapons filled the twilight, some of it quite close to *Helgoland*. He was too rattled to be afraid. A red flag flapped rebelliously from *Helgoland's* stern flagpole, and Ernst looked up at the bridge from which another red flag, this one torn, draped over the side. The signal-flag lines had been cut and lay like crepe paper decorations bow to stern. A distant cheer suddenly rose from across the fjord and a massive red flag ascended the courthouse flagpole.

A sudden burst of automatic rifle fire erupted from the pier and Ernst, ducked behind the forecastle. He peered around the edge and saw three sailors run from the cover of packing crates and scatter across the wharf. One limped, then fell, a dark stain spreading from the back of his leg. He tried to crawl, but two Naval policemen were on him in a moment. One kneeled to handcuff the fellow, the other swung his rifle butt into the man's head.

"Techow! Over here, Techow!"

Ernst recognized Lieutenant Manfred striding toward him, accompanied by two officers; only then did he become conscious of shivering.

"You're hurt." Manfred led him into the gray superstructure to the ship's darkened wardroom, where a dozen officers moved with waxen slowness. The room had lost its heat. Manfred threw a blanket around Ernst and eased him onto a bench. "Get him tea." Manfred looked around but no one moved. "I said get him tea! And a change of clothing."

If he'd shot Varren an instant sooner, maybe the rest of the engine room crew would have surrendered to him. But he could not have prevented what happened on the rest of the ship. And there was gunfire from their sister ship, *Thuringen*, and gunfire from the port wharves. As a corpsman attended his burns the tea started to warm him, relax him. Captain Volker came in looking drawn, gray hair escaping like smoke from under his cap, which tilted at a nervous angle. The radioman pushed through the crowd and handed him a transmission. Captain Volker began reading the cable without waiting for order, before the room had quieted and Ernst missed the beginning.

"...a mutiny of sailors throughout Kiel, Wilhelmshaven and Hamburg. Every ship has experienced desertion. A force of three thousand mutineers has seized City Hall in Kiel. You will all remain at your posts. Firearms are to be issued to all remaining loyal personnel." He looked up at his officers, his mouth turned down, and he said, "Await orders. That's all." He left quickly, and Ernst thought he must be feeling ashamed.

Except for white steam billowing from *Helgoland* and *Thuringen*, the dying hemorrhage of their ruptured boilers, the Kaiser's navy showed few signs of life, or, for that matter, destruction. Soon enough the last clanging alarm bells stilled. Here and there a gas lantern glowed in a stateroom, but, as night fell, the Imperial Navy was dark. Ernst thought of Fraulein Sylvia's girls and, with the world seemingly collapsing, had the peculiar thought that revolution might not be as good for Sylvia as war had been.

★ ★ ★ ★ ★ ★ ★ ★ ★ ★

Two days later his burns were healing but Ernst had still not heard from Leo. His fellow officers on the *Bayern* could not account for him, but one said, with some disgust, he would not have been surprised if Leo was with the mutineers. What worse shame could there be, than his brother, another officer, in league with the enlisted men.

Ernst had to know about Leo. Was he hurt, a hostage? He asked Lieutenant Manfred for any information he might have about Leo. In return, Manfred hoped Ernst might glean some information from his brother about the mutineers and their plans.

The next day he went into Kiel with forged documents, wearing a sailor's tunic and cap, his unshaven face and crusted burns an adequate disguise.

Kiel was a witch's brew of revolutionary democracy and radical Bolshevism. There were so many sailors drunk with schnapps and beer as to give new meaning to being drunk with power. At City Hall, at least a thousand sailors packed the square, staggering, cheering, wailing revolutionary slogans and songs. Ernst searched the crowd for Leo.

Plastered on the walls of most public buildings were multiple copies of a bright two-paneled poster in red, green and black. In the first panel a worker oiled the wheels of a green locomotive belching steam. In the second, the same worker gave a speech before an audience of workers, his green jacket the same dazzling green of the locomotive, and his boots as black as the engine's driving wheels, his arm raised for emphasis in front of the Red banner hanging behind the heads of the workers. The caption read:

> "Earlier I was an oiler. I oiled the wheels.
> And Now I'm in the Soviet. I decide the Issues."

"Ernst!" A familiar voice from the dark corner of a building. "Over here." Ernst searched anxiously in the darkness.

"Ernst, it's Leo."

"Leo... My God." His brother's face was unshaven, streaked with dirt. He wore a plain seaman's coat and cap.

They embraced. "I'm glad you're here," Leo said.

Ernst remembered how angry he was with Leo and pulled away. "How could you do this?"

Leo looked confused. "You mean you're not..."

Ernst looked hard at Leo. "You're a traitor, Leo."

"You're wrong, Ernst." A rabble of intoxicated sailors staggered by on their way to the rally. "Grandfather would have been here with his white rose. Do you really believe in the officers?" Leo asked. "All they care about is their privilege."

In the square a block away, a bonfire blazed, casting animated silhouettes, a battleship's complement of seamen.

"I believe in the Vaterland, Leo." Ernst closed his wool coat up to his neck. "I'm for Germany, not Bolshevism."

"Where did your sudden patriotism come from? I thought you were only for yourself."

"It's not patriotism. Patriotism is simple-minded. When Father died I questioned a lot of things in my life. Everything I ridiculed at camp suddenly made sense."

"Not that *Wandervogel* shit."

"It's not shit, Leo."

"Frolicking in the woods with your girlfriend – what's her name – Lotte? Is that who you're doing this for? Your girlfriend?"

Before he knew what or why, Ernst swung his fist and caught Leo's jaw. His brother sprawled on the ground, propped himself on an elbow and rubbed his bloody chin.

"I came here to find you," Ernst said. "Because I care about you." He could have punched him again.

They stared at each other. Leo reached up his arm. "Give me a hand."

Ernst pulled him to his feet.

Leo held onto his hand. "I'm sorry, Ernst. I provoked you. But I'm more sorry that you're with them." He felt his jaw again. "Thank God I'm more durable than Hans Gerd. No need to call Dr. Katzenstein." He laughed.

Ernst took back his hand and opened his cigarette case. He offered one to

Leo. "You can't help being an asshole."

Leo shook his head. "Father wouldn't have liked you to smoke."

They stared at the bonfire. Ernst could only see the shadows as demonic, as the mob gyrated. "Leo, do you remember at camp how they talked about the coming of that special person who would..."

"Ernst, that was a fairy tale. This is real life. When I was a boy, the Führer sounded fine, in principle – stern, but just – a national hero, a father figure, a saint. But now – wake up, Ernst. There is no such man, the world is different, and we have just lost the war."

"We almost won. We came that close."

"But we lost. And now – look around. We're on the verge of civil war."

"It's that Katherine. She turned your head with this communist nonsense."

"Katherine has taught me to see the world differently, but I don't do it for her." Leo leaned against the brick wall that flickered with light from the bonfire. "Do they like you, Ernst – the officers?"

"Yes, they do. They're good to me. They believe in me."

"You always needed more of that than I did – and got less of it. I never could figure out what it was you did to make Mother so angry. It was so clear with Hans Gerd, but you... I just don't know. It didn't seem fair. And you and I – we're always on the wrong side of each other. It's like the line in our bedroom." Leo stroked the bruise on his chin and winced. "I'll take that cigarette."

Ernst felt in his heart how melancholy overcame outrage and he saw in Leo's eyes a sadness that transcended pity, that longed to heal a deep wound inexplicable to either of them. "What will you do?"

"Me? I'll do what I can for the cause. For what is right and just. And when this mess is over? I'll find a job – anything, and live quietly with Katherine." A trench rocket arced over the bay and lit the night phosphorescent green, a stunning and ominous sight.

"Leo, don't follow the sailors. Please. For me – for Mother. It's very dangerous."

"Don't worry. I'm a sprat, remember? How about you?"

Out of the shadows a husky sailor lurched up to Leo and muttered into his ear. His sea coat showed scars where he had ripped off military insignias.

Leo ground his cigarette under his heel. "It's time to go, Ernst. Council meeting. I'll see you in Berlin?" He hugged Ernst for a brief moment and whispered in his ear, "Don't be on the wrong side."

6

Revolution!

October – December 1918

C ables and newspapers coming into the naval base carried disturbing reports. Bolshevik revolutionaries controlled many cities, the Ruhr Valley, the North Coast, and most ammunition dumps and railroad junctions. The officers felt betrayed when they learned that Friedrich Ebert, the impoverished saddle maker who rose to leadership of the Social Democratic Party, had been named Chancellor.

On November 9, 1918 the day of the General Strike, the day the Kaiser abdicated, two days before Germany surrendered and the Great War ended, the three thousand sailors who made up Leo's People's Naval Division stormed the Royal Palace, and Berlin's civil war began.

They were led by Dorrenbach, one of the ringleaders of the Kiel mutiny. The most disturbing image for Ernst was a newspaper photograph of the Bolshevik flag flying where Kaiser Wilhelm's colors had hung the day before. The Berlin garrison at the Royal Palace was ordered to hold their fire, and there were no casualties. Ernst read the story over and over and wondered how long this new government's restraint would last and what his role would be.

Karl Liebknecht and Rosa Luxemburg directed the Spartakist seizure of the palace. Perhaps Leo was there when they declared a Soviet Republic that same day.

Ernst felt his dread multiply. There was betrayal in the Vaterland, and it could not be permitted. But he was the point of the spear that would thrust into the heart of the revolt. Events were spinning out of control and Ernst could only hold fast to the purpose he was entrusted with, its burden and responsibility. He would be tested, and he could not bear the shame of being found wanting.

He worried about Lisa and about the well-being of his family on

Wannseestrasse, but there was no way of communicating with them. Ernst worried that mansions were particularly at risk from the Spartakists. The city had broken down.

It seemed as if nothing could stop the nation's descent into chaos. The best information about the fighting in Berlin was not good at all, cobbled together as it was from the partisan news-sheets, rumors and military cables that came across Lieutenant Manfred's desk. There was no mail; telephones went silent. Scuttlebutt persisted of drunken gangs of Spartakists rampaging through the streets, looting and raping. Even if the Ebert government was successful in restoring order, which Ernst doubted, he wondered what this new Republic would mean for his mother's suddenly precarious finances. Manfred had great hopes for the Free Corps as Germany's salvation, and he never stopped reminding Ernst that if the Bolsheviks won the peace, then Germany would forever be lost.

On December 16th, yet another contingent of Dorrenbach's sailors stormed the Chancellory, seized the switchboard and sealed the building. Otto Wels, Chancellor Ebert's military officer, was seized along with two of his subordinates and held hostage in the Royal Palace.

According to Manfred, the General Staff had finally reached the limit of its patience and requested Free Corps assistance. Ernst drove Manfred to an urgent meeting with the mysterious Captain Ehrhardt, commander of the Ehrhardt Naval Brigade Free Corps. He was not invited into this meeting, and he only saw the reclusive Captain's shadow through the door.

Two days later Berlin ordered the mobilization of the Ehrhardt Brigade to join forces with General von Lequis' Imperial Horse Guards, the Hussarenregiment. As a boy Ernst had seen this legendary unit in a parade. They carried erect lances on splendid horses in perfect order and wore tall fur hats and twilight blue uniforms, with a kinetic yellow stripe running down their trousers. The day they left for Berlin, Manfred addressed Ernst's unit. The Spartakist occupation must end, he said, and he used the word 'liquidation'.

Their first night in Berlin they bivouacked at the Moabit barracks and then deployed on a cold night to set up an encampment in Berlin's Tiergarten. The venerable park in the middle of the city was transformed by the Free Corps into row upon row of kerosene-glowing tents, like fireflies. They looked like an army, and Ernst felt their potency, but a part of him was saddened to see their desecration of his lovely Tiergarten. He was caught up in the deluge of events, unable to contact Lisa or his mother. Leo was God knows where. Ernst smoked too many cigarettes, drank too much coffee. Every day he alternated between nervous attention and fraught vulnerability. But, he told himself again and again, there was no backing away from his duty to Germany, and to himself.

Sleep was impossible that night as Ernst could not keep Lisa's and Leo's faces out of his thoughts. More than likely Leo was in the Royal Palace, and Ernst's Free Corps unit would be chosen to take it back. Ernst didn't want to appear afraid before his first possible combat, but he could not stop wondering: what if Leo was actually there? And if Ernst failed his duty? What would the officers think of him? a coward? a crybaby?

Sergeant Baer, an oversize man whose neck was almost as wide as his head, jarred Ernst awake from a dream in which he, Lisa and Margaret swam naked in the ocean.

"Wake up kid. Happy Christmas Eve. It's two AM. Today we see how tough you are."

Ernst sat up trembling from cold and anticipation. Seeing Baer's shaggy outline, backlit by a kerosene lamp, summoned a terrifying childhood vision: St. Nickolaus's dark companion, Knecht Ruprescht, looming over him, stinking of tobacco and cheap wine, with a sack to take away bad children.

It would be unmanly to admit the fears that preyed on his sleep, in concert with the cold December air and the hard ground. Ernst checked his rifle's magazine again and whispered a prayer for Leo.

Moonlight smudged the western sky through thin overcast. The cold lights of Berlin twinkled between naked beech trees, and his winter tunic could not soften the pre-dawn chill.

His unit's call-up came and he checked the magazine one more time before running to the lorry he would drive, his helmet awry on his head, the straps undone. The Tiergarten teemed with the dark shadows of Freebooters taking up guns in kerosene-lit tents – shadows and ghosts moving slowly toward dark lorries parked like freight cars along Charlottenburger Chaussee. So new was this army that its soldiers had to wear their old service uniforms, mostly naval, some Reichswehr. Ernst's fellow Freebooters jumped into the back of his lorry, smoking and laughing.

"Come on, Norbert, one more."

"OK. What's the difference between a whore and a Frenchy's mother?"

"Give up."

"Two Francs."

"Old and stupid." Baer spit out the back. "You need new jokes. What happened? You used to be funny."

Norbert raised his middle finger. "So get yourself a new belt man."

Manfred closed the partition between the cab and the soldiers in back. "Baer and Norbert are like an old married couple," he said to Ernst. "Bickering the whole shitting war while they fight their way through France and survive. It's a fucking miracle. They're charmed and they don't know it. Ignorant bastards. "

In the shower room at Moabit two days before, Ernst had seen these battle-hardened veterans naked in the steam. Heimler's abdominal skin, just above his navel, was twisted to one side by chiseled scar tissue. Baer pointed at two perfect pink ovals, one on his left hip, the other in his right side. "Fucking machine gun," he said. "Can you believe it? One bullet here took a piece of my hip bone; the other didn't hit a goddamn thing going through. I was right in between. That was a lucky day."

Most were at least ten years older than Ernst. Despite their rough lives, they lavished their 'baby Ernst' with a rough and tumble kindness that he welcomed, but to which he was unaccustomed. They called him their 'mascot' but then spoke to him as a brother officer. They taught him, they coddled him, and yet they respected him. It was like drinking cool water in the desert.

The Freebooters seemed completely imperturbable; not even the anticipation of combat disturbed their rambunctious equanimity. At first Ernst thought that, like most mercenaries, they didn't care for anything except their wages, food and drink, but he began to recognize their intense national pride and their passion for destruction. After the Great War, they were the professionals. Ernst wondered if, deep inside, they didn't share at least a modicum of the terror that made his throat itch and parched his tongue, or if the War had sterilized their fear.

He drove behind an identical lorry filled with another unit of Freebooters, eager to kill Communists and 'restore order' in Berlin and perhaps, in themselves. They smoked cigarettes and cigars and spat out the back of the truck.

The truck column moved slightly faster than a funeral cortege down Unter den Linden, over the Spree Canal, to the iron gate surrounding the Royal Palace. Across the broad avenue, in the predawn darkness, Berlin Cathedral glowed white, a beacon of reassurance that God was with them, Ernst hoped. Immediately after stopping, each lorry's metal gate fell open at the back, and a thousand combat boots ran across the cobblestones, their leather boots punctuating the cold night. Shouts of command and the clatter of metal echoed off the cathedral walls.

Ernst lined up with his fellow Freebooters. Lieutenant Manfred faced them at the head of the column. Baer stood in front of Ernst, completely blocking his view, a machine gun barrel strapped to his back as if it was a mere carbine. Norbert, equally tall but thinner, carried the gun's swivel base and stock. Ribbons of machine gun bullets hung around their necks like coarsely knit scarves. As they marched forward Baer teased Ernst about green recruits who soil themselves in their first battle, and Ernst swore to himself that would not happen.

A new clattering began. The castanet staccato of horse hooves from far down the broad avenue leading to the Palace grew louder until it dwarfed their marching boots. Ghostly even in their colorful uniforms, the first Hussaren Horse Guards clattered past, their ceremonial lances replaced by the latest issue semi-automatic carbines. Generators hummed and massive lamps cast eerie shafts of light.

As Ernst turned the corner onto the broad square before the Royal Palace, six field artillery pieces were already in place on the lawn, their barrels horizontal for point blank range. Soldiers with machine guns and howitzers maneuvered into position. Ernst's company occupied the right flank between the Palace and the iron gate, behind the cover of formal sculpted bushes.

Baer and Norbert hacked a hole out of the bushes with knives to position their machine gun, taking obvious delight in vandalizing royal shrubbery. The grass was damp, and Ernst's knees were already wet and cold. Corporal Meisner tapped his shoulder and thrust a tarpaulin at him. "Sit on this, Techow, so we'll know if you piss your pants."

At 0400 a white flag emerged from the Palace door followed by a party of three sailors who carried it to the Horse Guard's lines. Ernst watched a brief interchange, then heard swearing. The Horse Guard's regimental commander cuffed one of the sailors on the side of his head as if he were a misbehaving boy and sent them all back. Several other attempts at negotiation ended in failure.

At 0730 a captain of the Hussaren goose-stepped up to the Palace gate and stood at attention until a sailor opened a French door on the second floor balcony.

"You are hereby notified that if you do not unconditionally surrender in the next ten minutes we will commence hostilities. This is your final opportunity."

Without waiting for a reply he turned ceremonially on his heels and goose-stepped back to his regiment. The sailor closed the door behind him and a legion of faces retreated from all the windows.

A white stallion, speckled with gray under his belly, reared up and neighed. Other Hussaren horses, sensing battle, began to snort and stamp their feet. Ernst tried to sight his rifle, but his chest shivered and the metal tab tremored, as it had when he almost shot Varren. *Please, Leo, don't be inside.*

At precisely 0740 the first howitzer fired. The shell splintered the oak doors through which the nobility of Europe had strode for decades. An overhanging balcony, supported by two columns in the form of toga-clad female figures, sagged to one side after one young goddess broke at the waist and the other lost her left arm.

Cracks of rifle fire echoed from the second floor. Ernst crouched behind the trunk of the sculpted bush and sighted toward his chosen window, waiting for the command.

"Steady, Techow," Baer whispered from his left side, where he lay prone behind his machine gun, Norbert at his side cradling a ribbon of cartridges. "Steady."

Child's play, he thought, suddenly remembering how he and Leo played with wooden guns in the park across from Mariakirche. How easy and glorious it had all been, shooting each other, dying and sacrificing. But his wooden gun was now heavy with iron, a live cartridge poised in the chamber, and, likely as not, Leo was in the Royal Palace.

A face appeared at the glass beyond his rifle sight. He thought he recognized the port-wine birthmark on Varren's face, just before the figure disappeared.

"Fire!"

The order came from the Hussaren commander and quickly passed down the line. A thundering volley of rifle and machine gun fire erupted around the Palace, and every window burst in turn, in a wave, as if the shouted order itself had destroyed the glass.

Ernst fired and felt the gun's recoil. The window was gone, and he fired into a square black hole in the Palace – volley after volley. There was no return fire.

"Hold Fire!" Lieutenant Manfred yelled above the cacophony. A line of fifty Hussars charged the gate on foot and quickly disappeared into the smoking building. Moments later a guardsman emerged and waved the rest inside. With a chilling yell, 700 Hussars streamed into the Palace.

It was suddenly quiet. Guardsmen ran past shattered windows, their rifles at the ready. Smoke fogged the air. Baer gave Ernst a thumbs up sign, and he couldn't help but smile.

"The cowards!" Baer spat. "Give up without a fight. Bolshevik traitors. Shoot 'em, I say. Every one of 'em. You OK, Techow?" He barked as if still berating the Bolsheviks. Then, in a mocking sing-song, "Is our little baby gonna to be sick?"

Ernst's throat tightened. He could not speak, so he raised his middle finger to Baer, who smiled avuncularly.

"Ehrhardt Brigade!" Manfred shouted. "Move out – to the stables. On the double. Follow!"

Behind them another unit of Freebooters double-timed toward the Royal stables; Manfred held his service revolver high, and the Ehrhardt Brigade followed. As they must have done in countless battles during the Great War, Baer and Norbert ran in tandem with the heavy machine gun between them, cartridge belts flapping on their shoulders.

They established new positions outside the Marstall, the Kaiser's elaborate stables on Schlossplatz, where, the Hussaren reported, the sailors had fled through an underground passage from the Royal Palace. Ernst remembered how Leo had ranted about the Kaiser's horses living better than most Germans.

Minutes after Ernst took his position next to Baer and Norbert's machine gun, a howitzer fired, gouging a hole in the side of the stables. Round after round of howitzer fire exploded at point blank range. The Marstall shuddered, and ornately carved wood fragments flew into the air.

Minutes after the shelling started, another white flag emerged from the heavily damaged Marstall, and Ernst hoped the battle was won. Along with his fellows he loosened his helmet strap and allowed the tension in his body to relax.

"Twenty minute truce," Manfred announced. "Hold fire!"

Only now did Ernst see that a large crowd of civilians had assembled behind the soldiers and artillery pieces, as if they were spectators at a sporting match. Women and children stood in the mob's front line.

"Long Live the Revolution!" "No Monarchist counter-revolution!"
"Death to Monarchists!"

The crowd surged forward and began to infiltrate the rear units. Commoners mingled among the Hussaren and Freebooters, whose weapons were still hot. One by one, women and children in threadbare coats – chanting, insulting, pleading, cajoling – seeped into the ranks.

"Let me shoot the bitches," Baer yelled.

"Hold your fire!" Manfred said.

Ernst froze at his position even as the mob surged around him.

A gray haired woman crouched beside Ernst and looked into his eyes. "Go home young boy. You don't have to fight. We want only to be treated well – just like you."

She reminded Ernst of his mother. But his mother would want him to be resolute, as his father would have. Be true to the Vaterland. This was one thing he could remain true to. There really was nothing else. Leo was so very, very wrong. Pity had to be put aside, like an annoying Hans Gerd, baiting him. He remained in his kneeling position, his rifle trained on the Marstall, trying to block out the woman's voice.

"The war is over," she said. "Please go home. You are our returning sons and husbands. For heaven's sake, no more fighting. What's your name, young man?"

"Steady, Techow," Baer said. "Don't let that old cow turn your head."

A pair of women, perhaps a mother and daughter, their long skirts frayed and their feet muddy, thin shawls tied over their heads against the cold, stood over Baer.

"Monarchist pig! Don't you know when you're beaten? Go home!"

"Miserable lout! Killer! The people will prevail."

Baer stood slowly. His towering shadow fell over the women, who stepped back, looking up. The daughter pulled her mother away by the elbow.

"I am a Freebooter!" Baer yelled to the point of hoarseness, his face strained red, eyes wide. "We are the Free Corps!" A cheer arose from the company.

"For shame!" The old woman shrieked up at Baer.

"I am the destroyer!" Baer bellowed. One thousand eyes turned to him. "After me, Germany is reborn!"

Manfred yelled for Baer to stand down.

Then the unthinkable happened. Not in his company, but among the regular army regiment beside them, several young soldiers unfastened their helmets and dropped their rifles. First one, then another, they retreated into the mob, who cheered each desertion.

Emboldened, the crowd streamed further into the armed ranks, between the horses of the Hussaren and the machine guns, chanting slogans. Like a surging tide, the first of the mob reached the stables and went inside.

Suddenly, the mutineer's white flag was torn down and armed sailors ran from the dark stables into the civilian mob. They grabbed women and children as shields and, as they backed into the stables, several rifle shots were fired at the soldiers.

Ernst worked his rifle's bolt, but no order came to return fire. Down the line a commotion swirled among soldiers in the adjacent company. Ernst strained to see into the crowd.

A cheer rose up from the demonstrators, and they hoisted a young soldier into the air; more broke ranks, and more cheers followed. One by one they abandoned their weapons and joined the rabble of mothers, wives and daughters chanting as raggedly as they were dressed.

"Join us! Join us!"

Inconceivable as it seemed, even some Hussars fled into the crowd that became more vitalized by each conversion. The women kissed them and young girls danced for them, gyrating like stage dancers in a Berlin cabaret.

"Join us! Join us!"

His resolve frayed, and Ernst prayed there would be no order to fire. The crowd cheered, louder and louder, chanting in unison as each success inspired them.

Up the line, Hussar horses, spooked by the mob, reared up on hind legs, their terrified neighing punctuating the rhythmic chants. One stallion broke loose from its handler and charged away from the Guards, bucking and prancing.

"Idiots!" Baer said. "They're burning their asses with cigarettes."

"Join us! Join us!"

The crowd surged forward, closing in more boldly on the Hussars. More dropped their weapons, while some just ran away; another horse bolted. A young boy, no more than eleven, his face smudged and his hair wild, stumbled and fell across Baer's machine gun and began to cry. Baer growled and pushed him away. A teenage girl lifted him up, and they continued toward the stables.

Messengers ran from one unit commander to another. Manfred stood before the company surrounded by demonstrators, their hands clenched in fists over their heads.

A red flag slapped across the Lieutenant's face. "Stand down! That's an order! Safety all weapons. Back to the lorry. Techow! Take us back to barracks."

"Just one burst, Lieutenant," Baer said. He cradled the machine gun in his arms and faced the surging crowd. "Just one. They'll scatter like the cowards they are."

"I said stand down! There is no discussion. Do not fire."

The unit gathered around Baer who stood half a head taller than Manfred. Cheers from the victorious mob threatened to drown out the Lieutenant's words. Ernst felt the humiliation, not just of the defeat itself, but even more, that it should have come at the hand of this treasonous rabble. But, he had to admit, he was relieved that he did not have to shoot anyone – it was so confusing, it was right and it was not right, both correct and terrible. He thought of the bird he had killed, with Lisa, not so many summers ago. "Sometimes, killing is the kindest thing you can do," he had said. He was sure then. Not so much now.

Manfred draped his pistol hand over Baer's shoulder in a fatherly manner. "This was the army's last fight. It was our first. Next time your orders will come from me and there will be no mercy."

7

Free Corps
January 1919

Two days after their humiliation at the Marstall, Ernst stood under the triumphal arch of the Charlottenburger Gate in the middle of Charlottenburg Chaussee, waiting for Lisa. Manfred had granted him an evening leave. A couple kissed in the shadowy refuge beneath the snow-dusted bronze statues of King Friedrich I and his wife Sophie-Charlotte, after whom the district was named. Electric lights, strung like pearls on the Charlottenburg Bridge over the Landwehr Canal, faded into the snowy mist that engulfed the Tiergarten. It was already dark at five o'clock, and fat snowflakes drifted under streetlights, powdering and cleansing the busy square. Where he stood, Ernst felt the singular stillness of the hub of a wheel, yet inside his heart he had to calm a raging impatience, desire, and longing. The fog of his breath danced ghostly. The snowfall muffled a trolley's rumbling, softened the bleating horns of automobiles that circled the square like a merry-go-round. In sharp contrast, the jingle of student bicycle bells sounded sharp and crisp.

"Ruby!" Lisa hailed him from across the square. Most women stepped cautiously, trying to keep their shoes dry, but Lisa leapt off the curb into the slush, weaving between carriages and automobiles, her yellow hair tucked under a blue beret.

"Ruby, Ruby!" She rushed to him and threw her arms around his neck and kissed his cheek. Her scent tingled his skin.

"Ruby..." She pulled back and Ernst brushed the snow from her shoulders. "You were there, weren't you?" She was suddenly serious. Traffic spun around them. "I mean at the Palace... at the Marstall?"

"Yes, I was there."

"I'm sorry, Ruby." She let her head lean on his shoulder.

Relief washed over Ernst as they held each other. Tears (from where?) welled up as he rocked with her gently in the snow; he opened his eyes wide so the air would dry his tears.

All too soon she pulled away, cocked her head and studied him from cap to boot. "I knew you'd look handsome in a uniform." She kissed his cheek again. "Come, let's eat, I'm starving." She took his hand, led him into the giant snowflakes, and they darted among the cars and horses in a mad dash.

"Where are we going?" Ernst said.

"How much time do you have?"

"Until eleven o'clock. You?"

"Curfew is ten. Let's go to the Corps Teutonia. Just a few blocks." She took his arm and they crossed Charlottenberg Bridge.

"You wore your *Wandervogel* boots," he said.

"It's snowing. And they make me feel good."

They turned on Englischestrasse, and immediately the narrow street along the Landwehr Canal swarmed with students. Posters plastered over brick walls carried the news of a demonstration at noon two weeks ago to support the People's Naval Division, a German Worker's Party meeting for students, a recruiting poster, and last month's schedule of performers at the Black Cat Cabaret.

"It's fabulous living here, Ruby. There's a girl in my dormitory from Turkey. And so much political agitation. My concentration is now Political Science, just like Fritzy. We have lots of classes together and, of course, there's the GNYO. Fritz is already a big shot. I'm only a little fish. But I'm second in the class ranking – second only to Fritz. Friendly competition, though."

Fritz had said nothing to Ernst of going to university in Berlin. Ernst couldn't help worry that they were lovers.

The door to the Corps Teutonia Pub opened just as they reached it, and two students stumbled up the stairs and out into the snow, their laughter as warm as the yellow light inside. He followed Lisa down the steep and narrow stairway into a cavernous basement, aroused by her motion, even in her heavy storm coat and hiking boots. She pulled off her beret and shook out her hair, then loosened her coat. Several young men in the pub turned away from their conversations to watch Lisa slip off her jacket and reach up to hang it on an immense pegboard shrouded with an array of worn coats and scarves.

At one of the long tables, the University Soccer Team celebrated their mid-winter 'Salute to Sloth'. Steins of beer lined up on the table, and the singing had just begun.

Ernst followed Lisa a bit warily, along a wood-paneled wall covered with posters. They paused in front of two posters, tacked side by side for the Free Corps.

VOLUNTEERS

From the west – March to the East!

FLAME THROWER PERSONNEL

Enlist in the Flame-Thrower section of

THE LUETTWITZ CORPS

Immediate pay plus 5 marks daily bonus.
Free food and uniform.

COMRADES

The Spartakist danger has not yet been removed.
The Poles press ever farther onto German soil.
Can you look on these things with calm?

NO!

Think what your dead comrades would think!
Soldiers, Arise! Prevent Germany from becoming
the laughing stock of the earth. Enroll NOW in

THE HUELSEN FREE CORPS

Recruiting offices: Bauer Cafe, Unter den Linden,
Potsdam Beer Garden

"That's you, Ruby. Everybody here talks, but they don't do anything. You really are doing something. I'm so proud of you. Come, let's find a table."

The football players had found their voices. Ernst felt uneasy surrounded by students, some of whom might have been in the Spartakist mob at the Marstall. Lisa led him to an empty booth, and they sat opposite each other.

"What was it like?" she said and leaned forward.

"We were betrayed. It's that simple," he said. "That mob should never have been allowed to infiltrate our lines. And General von Lequis was a coward. He was dismissed you know, afterwards. We were backup for the Hussars, and they fell apart. It was just hateful."

"When I heard about it, I couldn't believe it. Most of us at the university support the army, although some joined the demonstrators. I'm glad you're all right."

He wanted to collapse into her arms, tell her how frightened he was, how he worried that Leo was with the mutineers, how he might have been ordered to shoot women and children. Relief at reunion with Lisa was short-lived, as he felt the softness of their reunion congeal into a hard new truth –Fritz – here in Berlin, at the university with Lisa.

A student waitress dropped two menus on the table. "Beer?" She stared off at the soccer team.

"How about wine?" Lisa said. "We'll have the Rhine wine."

He felt his elation return, as if Fritz were a cloud that only briefly blocked the sun. Something chemical happened in him when he looked at Lisa, and he worried that his smile must look idiotic. He cleared his throat. Students in another booth turned and stared at him. It was probably the uniform – his so obvious, theirs flannel and cotton shirts and easy pants. Did they think him a country bumpkin, not clever enough to be in University?

After an uneasy silence, Lisa said, "Magister Bruno, my Latin teacher, is completely daft. He wears baggy pants and his buttons are often undone." She averted her eyes again, as if looking at Ernst was forbidden. "I went to a reading by my literature professor, Gustav Wein. Perhaps you've heard of him – he won the Golden Eagle last year. He's quite good, really."

As Lisa fished for words, Ernst forced himself to attend, all the while absorbed by the delicate curve of her neck, the glow of her hair, the blue of her eyes. Her heavy red sweater, close-fitting, emphasized her breasts. Yes, he agreed with Lisa, Keats had the devil in him.

The footballers sang and pounded their steins on the table. Little by little, Lisa tore a paper napkin into thin strips.

"What do people say, now that it's over?" Ernst said.

"You mean us – us students?"

"No. I mean people – regular people – out there."

"Mostly disgusted. If Ebert and the army can't even take on a ragged mob of mutineers..."

"I have to leave Berlin again, tomorrow," he interjected. "We're being sent north. I can't tell you where." Everything was possible in Berlin, he recalled Lisa saying, and he burned to ask about Fritz. Maybe it was better not to know – to keep hope alive. He searched her face, tried to connect with her restless eyes (her guilty eyes?) and knew more certainly than anything that he had to be with her, to fit into her world. He did not want her pity; he needed all of her.

"Noske, the 'Bloodhound', has called up all the Free Corps," Ernst said. "I'm not sure you're supposed to know that either, but what the hell."

Their words ran dry again. The waitress brought the wine. He reached deep for the courage to ask the only question that clawed and clamored for voice. "You and Fritz – are you – you know, special friends?"

Again she averted her eyes. "You mean, is he my boyfriend? No, no, no. We're both much too busy."

"But you do see a lot of Fritz."

"Oh, yes. Every day. He's amazing – already Secretary Treasurer of the National Student Party on campus. I go to all the meetings."

He hardly tasted the cheap wine. Their meals came and they ate silently, awkwardly.

Anticipation was such a cruel deceiver. He had imagined this reunion with choreographic perfection, every clever bit of dialogue perfectly delivered, easy, beautiful words about the mystery of their relationship, the meaning of the wind and kites, hopes for the future of Germany and how many children they would have. Now the moment had come and it was all wrong. How could he have run out of words?

"What are you thinking?" She caught his eye.

"Nothing," he sighed. "Nothing, just thinking." He twirled his wine glass. "What's new with your father?" He could think of nothing else to say.

She shrugged and prodded a small red potato. "He sends me money every month and thanks God the dormitory is strict. I have to stay in the dorm for two years then Margaret and I will get a flat together."

Silence again. Lisa pushed her plate back and twirled a strand of hair. She looked at Ernst and tried to smile, then looked down again. "Have you ever been with a woman?" she asked, then drained her glass.

"What do you mean?" He looked up, hopeful.

"You know – had sex?"

It was quite warm in the pub. "Prostitutes," he said softly.

"So you've never really made love, just, you know... fucking."

Lisa leaned forward, her breasts pressed up against the table again, and he could feel them in his groin. "How about you?"

"I've always said no."

He wanted to ask who, and wished she had never been asked. "I'm glad." He looked down again.

Their silverware ticked time on the crockery. All around them the babel of the rathskeller multitude grew louder as more and more voices joined the

'Salute to Sloth'.

Ernst leaned closer to Lisa, shrinking their intimate bubble. "If I were here, I would court you."

"Ruby." She reached her hands across the table and took his. "You're a dear boy. Someday the time will be right." She stroked his cheek with her hand.

"Promise me one thing," he said. "When you fly a kite, think of me in the wind."

"I will." She pulled her hands back, into her lap. "Ruby – please be careful. I would hate it if anything happened."

A wraith shadow fell over the table. An intense dark student, thin, with pince-nez glasses and a black goatee, leaned over. "Well, well, if it isn't the illustrious Lisa Schmidt. Comment ça va?"

"Hello, Walter. This is my friend Ernst." She did not seem pleased to see him.

Walter seemed surprised to recognize Ernst's Free Corps uniform and belatedly extended his limp hand. He turned to Lisa again. "Can I get your notes from Latin? I missed class because of the demonstration." He said it with provocation.

"Yes, of course," Lisa said, "in class on Monday."

"I thought, perhaps I could get them sooner – maybe at your dormitory? I hate to be unprepared. Maybe tomorrow we could meet?"

Walter's piercing eyes glanced at Ernst, then back to Lisa.

Ernst stood, rattling the plates, and balled his fists. "She said Monday!" The men were face to face.

"Yes, yes, of course, Monday. No problem." Walter backed into the flow of students, then was gone.

"Thanks. He's a real wolf. Tries to get a date with every pretty freshman. Maybe I should be flattered, but he's got a reputation and besides, he's a Socialist."

"You do favors for Socialists?"

"It's OK for school stuff. We find Walter to be an amusing diversion. Most of us are loyal."

"What about the professors?"

"Mostly Nationalist or monarchist. Except Professor Heiding, but he teaches Marxist Philosophy."

Their conversation loosened and flitted from Heine to *Wandervogel* to Impressionism, to funny stories of their summers together.

"What about your art work?" Lisa asked.

"It's not really art – just drawing. After being in the National Gallery, I know that I am no more than a childish doodler. I could never achieve anything with my drawing."

"But, you never know. I mean, you should keep doing it – you never know what will come of it."

"You never know what will become of anything. But you must know when to give up."

They talked for two hours, a philosophical intercourse with Lisa the optimist in her rose-colored glasses holding out for the grace of humanity, while Ernst remained the troubled realist, the pragmatist who still felt something unreal as they spoke, even with their renewed connection blowing over embers of affection they shared. Maybe there was something to be hopeful about.

It was almost Lisa's curfew, and the young women in the Corps Teutonia were leaving. Ernst reached across the table and took her hands. They were warm and responsive.

"Lisa, I have such strong feelings, sometimes I don't know what to do with them." As soon as he spoke the words he wished he could reel them back.

She pulled her hands back onto her lap. "I'm sorry, Ernst." She sheepishly averted her eyes. "There's something I should tell you. Fritz and I have been – you know – sort of seeing each other. Don't ask me to choose between you. I can't and I won't." She smiled wistfully for a moment. "Margaret says she would choose you." Lisa looked guilty, as if she had disclosed too much, violated a confidence. "I love you both as my dearest friends. It would all be spoiled by... you know, sex or something. These are confusing times, and I'm not bold like Margaret. Please, Ruby, I want you both. While you're away, keep writing letters to me."

"Yes, of course the letters." Her revelation stung him to the quick, but he resolved to be indomitable, to be opaque. He would give up nothing to Fritz.

"I keep them all. I love your sketches and doodles and drawings. They are the essence of you in two dimensions." She touched his cheek. "It's wonderful what you do, Ernst."

He was glad for her to use his name. "You mean the drawings?"

"No, that you're a Freebooter. That's wonderful. I mean, so are your drawings and letters, but... you know..."

"Yes, of course."

At her dormitory, Lisa said good night with a hesitant kiss against Ernst's cheek, so much less than he had prayed for. He walked back to the barracks breathing the cold night air as deeply as he could, chilling the deep hurt in his chest.

Snow covered the Revolution like an eiderdown, softening the cacophony of Berlin's concrete and steel. He still had an hour, so he walked through the Tiergarten. No trace of their occupation remained. His new service boots crunched the snow. Couples arm in arm seemed to be everywhere, mocking him. He was glad to return to the Moabit barracks, to the brotherhood of Freebooters, to Manfred, where the world was simpler, where neither defeat nor humiliation could crush their spirit. It reminded Ernst of the time he spent as a boy with their chauffeur Eric under the Mercedes' bonnet. The flat-head engine was sensible, predictable, reliable, and riding in the car was always thrilling.

★　★　★　★　★　★　★　★　★　★

Spartakist demonstrations began again on January 4, 1919, and two days later another general strike paralyzed Berlin. Once again, stores and factories closed. Transport and electricity were idled. Karl Liebknecht and the other left-wing leaders decided the time for a Soviet revolution had come. Hundreds of thousands of Berliners surged through the streets occupying railroad stations and newspapers, and a unit of riflemen, wearing baggy pants and half-buttoned coats, seized the biggest prize of all, the Brandenburg Gate. They were a ragtag army, with berets and old fedoras in place of steel helmets, galoshes and exhausted trench boots marching out of step, and rifles held at every angle. Artisans and factory girls marched side by side, waving red flags, chanting slogans and trading insults with the Social Democrats who marched the other way on Wilhelmstrasse.

"Spartakus Week" had begun, and The Free Corps would be tested.

Ernst's unit was recalled from Upper Silesia and the Polish frontier for service again in Berlin. This time they were billeted in Dahlem, a suburb of Berlin, at the St. Cecilia Preparatory School for Girls.

The first night at the school he slept poorly and was awake an hour before reveille. On the wall in front of his cot, hanging slightly askew, an ornately framed photograph of two schoolgirls in white pinafore uniforms, flanking a matronly teacher. A feminine scent still haunted the bathroom, but soon enough the musky barrack odor of unit 3, Marine Brigade Ehrhardt, would prevail.

He stared at the white plaster ceiling, following a diagonal crack that split the room, listening to the heavy breathing of his comrades.

Dahlem, even more than Berlin, was favored by the birds, and though it was snowing, some already sang in anticipation of the dawn. Ernst knelt by the window and looked onto the snow-covered walks crisscrossing the quadrangle in the courtyard of the girls' school. No matter how cold, one could always count on the finches, a charm of which quarreled in the bare tree outside the window. As spring neared, their yellow coats would brighten, but these showed only the palest jaundice of mid-winter. In the middle of the courtyard stood a larger than life alabaster St. Cecilia, a lyre clutched to her bosom. Angels sat at her feet looking up adoringly.

If only thoughts could be projected through the air – if only Lisa could feel him in her morning sleep. He closed his eyes and saw her, imagined her soft breasts pressed against his chest, her eyes closed, mouth waiting for his kiss.

Heavy clouds darkened the dawn and shook loose a freezing rain, too fine to see, except directly under an incandescent lamp near the building. Ernst heard a door open and saw a smudge of yellow at the base of a dark wall; a shadowy figure strode purposefully across the courtyard, his boot heels clicking on the wet pavement. The officer – it was Lieutenant Manfred – met another officer, a Captain, perhaps the mysterious Captain Ehrhardt, commander of the Brigade. After a few words the Captain handed Manfred an envelope, the two men saluted, and Manfred returned to the glowing door.

Each step creaked as Manfred ascended the carpeted stairway to his private room at the landing – the housemother's room. Frilly lace still framed the door on which a talented amateur had painted a deer leaping over a red heart, with 'Vogel' on a nameplate underneath.

"Lieutenant," Ernst whispered. "What's up?"

"Techow, what are you doing prowling about?"

"Couldn't sleep. Just had a funny feeling."

"It's going to start getting rough – today or tomorrow. We're joining Stephani's Potsdamer Free Corps and Maercker's Rifles in a definitive action. Are you ready?"

"I was ready at the Palace and the Marstall. You needn't worry about me."

"I just wanted to be sure. I have to know that every man in my company will do what is necessary." He looked carefully at Ernst's face in the dim light. "Have you ever killed a man?"

"No, Sir."

"You will today. Stay close to me."

"Yes, Sir. I will, Sir."

"Try to rest another hour."

There was no going back to sleep. Heimler stumbled out of his bunk mumbling to himself and shuffled to the toilet. After a moment, Ernst heard his urine stream, and Heimler humming. Hans Gerd did that every morning – walking by Ernst's bedroom early, humming on his way to the toilet. During a brief visit home after seeing Lisa, Hans Gerd told Ernst that he was his hero. He couldn't believe it. He was so proud of his brother the Freebooter. One never knew with Hans Gerd – he could change his mind a hundred times a day – but Ernst was heartened and appreciated how much he actually loved his troubled brother.

He wondered if he should pray and laughed at this sudden burst of religiosity. Baer wouldn't pray. He always said, "When it's time to die, I'll die". Norbert wouldn't either. What if God took the wrong side? He'd never gotten solace from the church before. His prayers were not likely to be genuine now. Any God worth his salt could see through the façade of Ernst's faith.

The crack in the ceiling ran straight like a kite string, disappearing behind the wall, and instead of praying, he tried to feel the wind.

8

Vorwärts
January 1919

I t calmed Ernst to drive the Free Corps lorry. Though sequestered in the cab from the rough and tumble Freebooters in the back, he felt attached to these men with their raw courage, their intemperate male energy, which he found simultaneously appealing and disturbing. He felt joined to something of wild substance, something fundamentally necessary for the survival of the nation, as well as for his own survival, both physical and spiritual. In the wake of Germany's defeat, the unacceptable alternative was chaos, Bolshevik revolution, disorder. Forces pulled so powerfully, especially on the young, that one had to choose between irreconcilable alternatives. Most distressing of all for Ernst was Leo and that his own family should be riven by the turmoil. Had Leo been at the Royal Palace, at the stables? He was not among those listed as dead, and no doubt he was still with the revolutionaries.

This day his lorry followed a unit of the elite Freikorps Maercker's Rifles, highly disciplined Freebooters who sat at attention in four orderly rows, their Gewehr '98 Mauser rifles between their knees at exactly the same angle. Lieutenant Manfred rode beside Ernst in the cab, loading 9 mm Parabellum rounds into a Mauser C/96 "broom handle" pistol. Each member of Ehrhardt's Brigade was issued one for close quarter fighting. Once the ten round magazine was full, Manfred loaded the metal clip from above. Between them on the seat lay a long barreled version of the Model 08 Machinenpistol with a flat shoulder stock and 32 round snail magazine. The Free Corps drew financial support from the tottering Reich government as well as from wealthy patrons. The power brokers saw them as their mercenary army, available without questions of loyalty, to restore order – politics by harsher means. Consequently, Freebooters carried the world's finest munitions into battle.

"How scared are you, Techow?" Manfred continued loading bullets.

He felt an unexpected tenderness in Manfred's question, but resisted temptation. "I'm not afraid, Sir."

"Of course you're afraid. Only Baer is not afraid and that's because he has gasoline for blood."

"Baer is one of the most courageous men in the unit. Isn't he?"

"Baer is so full of hate and anger that he feels no fear. If he is truly unafraid, he's not courageous. If you're not scared it isn't courage."

Ernst felt relieved, as if he no longer had to hold a mask up to his comrades. He could tell Lisa he was afraid, maybe not Fritz. But Manfred saw through him in the way a father might know his son. He wanted to ask if Manfred felt afraid, but could only say,

"Yes, Sir. Thank you, Sir."

"Don't get me wrong, Techow. To save the Vaterland, we need a whole army of Baers, and one day we'll have it. But I suppose we need people like you as well, who still have some heart."

It was late in the afternoon when they drove down the nearly deserted Linden tree-bordered boulevards. Ernst imagined their line of military trucks incising Berlin's quiet streets like a scalpel slicing a painted canvas. Their parade was only acknowledged by the stares of a few commuters who doubted the general strike, men on bicycles who defied it, and an orderly queue of gentlemen, under black umbrellas, clearly not Socialists, waiting for a trolley that would not come to take them home. As they drew closer to the city center the ambience grew more charged, with only rare civilians, units of soldiers, and armored cars.

They drove across Potsdamer Platz, occupied and barricaded by government Reichswehr troops. The Grand Hotel Esplanade on Bellevuestrasse and The State Library were ringed with helmeted Reichswehr, their bayonets fixed, draped in green rain slickers behind sandbagged barricades. Barbed wire coils that stood taller than a man connected one bare tree to another along what Ernst remembered so recently as a plush boulevard. To the north he heard the occasional crackle of rifle fire and rattle of automatic weapons. They passed the remains of Wertheim's Department Store on Leipzigerstrasse, its huge windows smashed and a black stain, perhaps dried blood, on one door. Without the splash of Wertheim's color and the animation of afternoon shoppers and government bureaucrats, the deserted streets insinuated menace.

"The rioters are insane," Manfred said. He offered Ernst a Gauloise from his gold cigarette case. "Liebknecht calls them his 'troops'." He laughed and lit both their cigarettes.

A burned out automobile, its hood open, still smoldering, blocked one lane of traffic and several cars parked along the curb had smashed windscreens. Ernst noticed a civilian running down the street clutching his fedora onto his head with one hand, his briefcase and closed umbrella in the other. He ducked into the Interior Ministry as they passed.

Manfred leaned his head back and closed his eyes. "You know what I would have done when the Spartakists called for the general strike? I would have invited their leaders to a 'negotiation', and then informed them that the strike was canceled. If Liebknecht says no, I shoot him. If Red Rosa says no, I shoot her. The third then says yes. Two people dead instead of civil war and thousands dead. Preventive murder – the decent thing to do. But do you know what is the ultimate irony – the true inhumanity? If we shoot Liebknecht and Red Rosa the world will condemn us. If we kill thousands of unknowns, little people of no consequence, the world will hardly notice."

Hearing Manfred go on about Liebknecht and Red Rosa inflamed Ernst's own anger and resolve. None would doubt his loyalty and in any case, he had no real choice in the matter. He was a Naval Cadet. It was his father's gift, his inheritance. He felt the weight of that control from the grave and that made him angry as well. This was what his father wanted, and he had never asked Ernst. Perhaps Lisa was right, and he should have taken art lessons – a better gift from his father? And now, here he was in Berlin, and he would kill a Spartakist today.

The motor's drone lulled Ernst into a trance-like state as he followed the truck ahead through strike-paralyzed Berlin. It was not at all the city he had known as a boy, sitting on Eric's lap, 'driving' inside the security of his arms, a boy in a nesting box, with an overlarge car hat drooping across his forehead and goggles sagging onto his nose, as he felt the power of the engine vibrate through the steering wheel and the power of tender arms around him.

With the streets empty, free of distractions, Ernst noted the profusion of electric wires running along the street like musical staff lines, with sparrows and finches as the occasional notes. Three men in dark overcoats, one ringed by a blue scarf, waved small German flags at the corner of Leipzigerstrasse and Markgrafenstrasse. Ernst wondered whose side they were on.

They passed another unit of Reichswehr. Manfred shook his head more in sadness than in anger. "Look at them! Useless! They lost the Brandenburg

Gate four days ago. How could a Jew Communist control Brandenburg Square?"

Manfred resumed his idle drumming on the dashboard. The repetition reminded Ernst of Hans Gerd tapping his teeth with his fingernail in maddening cadence.

The 'crack – crack' of small arms fire reverberated through the streets, impossible to localize in urban canyons, ominous and louder as they drove into the heart of Berlin.

Suddenly, a black shape, which became a dark bearded man, sprinted from an alley just ahead on the left. His shabby black coat, hanging just above his trench boots, flapped behind him as if he were a running crow seeking flight. He sprinted into the boulevard and heaved something overhand, then pivoted and turned to escape. Even before the grenade exploded, gunfire came from a lorry ahead and the fleeing Spartakist suddenly arched and froze as if he had run into a glass wall. Other bullets found their mark, and he twisted to each wound.

The truck ahead swerved out of line; its tires screeched and suddenly a flash of light, followed by a concussion, shook the street. Flames and black smoke billowed over the lorry. Ernst's ears stung, and he braked hard. Though one ear was deafened by the blast, he heard the clattering of weapons and swearing from inside the lorry as the column halted.

Maercker's Rifles abandoned the crippled truck. One of the soldiers ran to the Spartakist martyr and fired his semi-automatic rifle several times into the man's body. Another Freebooter dragged him back. Orders echoed up and down the line, and within seconds a perimeter unit of Maercker's Rifles took up positions as the medics evaluated the casualties. No one tended the driver; he was clearly dead. The officer riding beside him – covered with blood, his face singed black – was eased out of the smoking cab and laid out on a stretcher. A Reichswehr ambulance backed up, and he disappeared into the bay.

Ernst's trembling foot slipped off the clutch, and his lorry lurched and stalled. If the dead Spartakist had stayed in his bathroom one minute longer this morning, or thrown his grenade ten seconds later, it might now be Ernst's body that the column swerved around.

How could this be happening only a few kilometers from his home? His Mother and Hans Gerd might be eating supper now. Or Hans Gerd might be studying in his room, maybe slamming his math book from frustration. It would be just like Mother to insist that, regardless of the chaos that swirled about them, Hans Gerd must carry on with his routine.

Further into the city, near Belle-Alliance-Platz, government troops thinned and crude Spartakist barricades closed off empty side streets. The column of trucks slowed and turned onto Friedrichstrasse and then east onto Kochstrasse – Newspaper Row – where it came to a halt. Random gunshots crackled like sticks breaking underfoot in a dense wood. He could be in the gunsight of a Spartakist right now. Ernst set the brake and tightened the strap on his helmet.

"Relax, Techow," Manfred said. "It won't be until tomorrow morning."

Freebooters spilled from the trucks, the stamp of boots and rattle of gear drawing heads to windows across Kochstrasse. Units of Major von Stephani's Potsdamer Shock Troops were already in marching formation.

Between the canvas-covered lorries Ernst saw the façade of the Social Democratic *Vorwärts* Newspaper offices and presses. A defiant red flag hung limply from the flagpole. Barbed wire and scrap wood barricades surrounded the red brick four story building, number '5', with the masthead and a quote by Schiller – **"Thoughts are free!"**

"Only about 350 Spartakists inside," Manfred said. "There's 1200 of us." He slid the 'broom handle' into its holster.

"How do you know their numbers?" Ernst asked.

"Major von Stephani. He's got steel balls. A few days ago he dressed as a Spartakist and just walked in like he belonged there, saw their defenses, counted defenders, then said goodbye and left."

The order to regroup in combat units cascaded down the line behind the lorries. The Spartakist defenders could not see how many soldiers were arrayed against them, but could imagine the worst from the number of trucks that lined up across Kochstrasse. They heard only crisp shouts of command and the fugue of metal on metal that followed. Howitzers, positioned between trucks with their barrels leveled point blank, trained on three sides of the building. Flame throwers and riflemen guarded the fourth side, the alley in back. The only sign of life from the building was the occasional and brief appearance of a face in a window. The *Vorwärts* electricity had been shut off, and as twilight darkened the street, only flickering candles came on. The order to bivouac passed down the Free Corps line. Most of them laid out bedrolls under the lorries. Sentries walked the perimeter.

With the end of the rain, a sinister silence descended, disturbed only by finches and bluebirds returning to birdbaths and feeders on the courtyard lawn. Didn't the birds realize something was amiss? Usually there was constant activity in the *Vorwärts* courtyard, even on Sunday. The stately oak doors had not opened in over twelve hours.

"First thing in the morning, Techow," Manfred said. "Get some sleep."

"I have third watch."

"Too bad. See you in the morning. And remember, tomorrow, stay close."

★　★　★　★　★　★　★　★　★　★

When he was awakened at 0300 for his watch, the city was hushed. Powerful searchlights still illuminated the *Vorwärts* building, bathing it in a silver glow. Pre-dawn chill condensed into a thin fog reflecting light that seemed to drape the building with gauze. Ernst wondered how he might paint that effect, how the hard silver hue of electric arcs became a luminescent shawl. In a reverie he lounged against the front fender of his lorry, watching windows, wondering who was the Spartakist on third watch inside and whether he watched Ernst. At that moment a candle appeared in one window – it went out and reappeared in another. He thought he could make out a face pressed against the glass, then the candle went out again, and it was dark.

A black and white cat crept across Kochstrasse, rubbed its head against Ernst's leg and meowed. It purred loudly enough to wake a sleeper. Ernst petted the cat and she arced her spine to each stroke, eyes closed, pushing her head against his open palm. What would it be like to stroke Lisa, her skin as silken as this fur. She was alone in her bed, not very far away, and yet a million miles. He could only imagine – joyful for the possibility, and heartsick that maybe nothing would ever happen – that they were two shooting stars, doomed to pass each other in space and time.

The cat insisted on Ernst's full attention. It was well fed, well cared for. "Are you a Spartakist cat? If you are, kitty, you'd better not go home today." The cat rolled on the ground between his boots, playfully batting at his hands with closed paws.

A sentry approached on his rounds. "All quiet?"

The cat hastened away. "All quiet."

★　★　★　★　★　★　★　★　★　★

By 0730 when the rising sun shone briefly between two buildings, the fog was already dissipating. Baer shook Ernst awake after only an hour of sleep. He sat up in his sleeping roll, dreading the day. Freebooters huddled together about gas stoves, whispering, eating bread and cheese with cold wurst. Norbert prepared a teakettle.

"Today's your day, Techow," Baer guffawed, and his elbow hit Norbert's side.

"Ow! You big oaf." Norbert carried the kettle with a pot-holder. He had a white kitchen towel tucked in his belt that made him look like a maid with pants and a man's head. "We let you sleep 'cause you're still growin'," Norbert whispered. "More tea?"

Heimler cleared the breech mechanism of his rifle yet again and polished the metal barrel. He always said his was the cleanest Gewehr '98 in the Free Corps.

The sun felt warm on Ernst's face, and the hot tea warmed him inside, but he didn't have much appetite for the bread or cheese, and finally he ate a piece of wurst only because Norbert told him it would stop him from wetting himself.

"Techow," Manfred approached him. "Lorries ready to go in five minutes."

Up and down the street, truck engines coughed to life, and soon a dirty fog of exhaust hung over the column. Like a theatrical curtain parting, the empty lorries drove off, and the Spartakist defenders of the *Vorwärts* finally saw the troops and firepower arrayed against them. Twelve hundred helmets dotted sandbagged barricades. Howitzers separated units. Rifles and machine guns bristled. Finches bickered and sang as the sun knifed through the clouds. The black and white cat scurried across Kochstrasse, its belly low to the ground, dragging a dead mouse back home.

Ernst parked his truck with the others several blocks away and returned clutching his rifle in the back of one lorry with the other drivers. Most were young like him. Some were students.

Manfred stood by his unit's sandbagged position, signaling for Ernst to come.

He jumped the sand bags and wedged himself between Manfred and Baer.

"We're the second wave – after Stephani's Potsdamers."

Ernst tightened his helmet strap again, threw the bolt, checked his magazine and licked his dry lips. Baer leaned into him and thumped his back, "Good luck, kid," he whispered. "Stay with the Lieutenant – and stay dry."

At precisely 0800 the first two howitzers fired. The finches scattered skyward like shrapnel. The front entrance blew apart, now only a smoking hole in the splintered oak, with **"Thoughts are free!"** swinging back and forth on a nail.

Two more howitzers fired, puncturing the wall twice more, and disintegrating the makeshift barricades and barbed wire. At the same moment, small arms fire began: a withering barrage of rifle, machine gun and mortar fire shattered every window simultaneously, as it did at the Royal Palace.

After the first barrage, a white flag emerged from the smoldering entrance. A Spartakist fighter carrying the flag carefully negotiated the rubble-strewn portal.

"Terms of surrender! Terms of surrender!"

"Ha, that's a laugh," Baer said. "Can I take him out, Lieutenant?"

"Shut up!" Manfred said.

The field radio crackled. "Potsdamer 2, 5 and 9. Ehrhardt 1 – move out."

Manfred drew his pistol and stood. "We move, gentlemen. Behind the Potsdamers."

"Next time we'll be first," Baer said. "It's like a beautiful young woman – you want to be the first to take her."

Major von Stephani's First Potsdamers cleared the sandbags and broke into a run across Kochstrasse into the courtyard. Like a well-choreographed soccer team taking the field, they dispersed with intention to each blasted opening. Rifle muzzles flashed from shattered windows, answered by another blistering Free Corps volley that poured into the building. When Ernst looked back on this morning, the defining smell of cordite would be the trigger for memory.

The charging Potsdamers reached the building without casualties, at least none that Ernst saw between rounds. When the last Potsdamer was inside, Ernst followed Manfred over the sandbag barrier. Rifle fire was deafening, mostly from the Free Corps units, with some returned from upper floors of the building. He ran behind Manfred, bent forward, driven by the piston of his heart. Only 50 meters to the smoking entrance. Bullets zipped – a ricochet off the lamppost – the ground spit gravel.

Ernst's vision constricted, darkening at the periphery, magnified in the center where all he saw was Manfred's back and one smoking gap in the wall. He ran for the smoke – ran past cedar trees, the same trees that grew outside his home along the wrought iron fence on Wannseestrasse. A bird bath in the middle of the sidewalk appeared and was gone – everything was the *Vorwärts* smoking puncture wound. Manfred disappeared. Ernst followed into blind darkness.

His eyes slowly accommodated. Semi-automatic rifle and pistol fire echoed and amplified from hallways and stairways, impossible to localize.

"Move 'em along!" A Potsdamer officer yelled at a line of Spartakist prisoners, hands over their heads, being led into the library. Ernst still squatted on the floor, one hand gripping his still hot rifle, the other palm down on cool stone.

"Manfred! Where's Manfred?" A signal man across the lobby held a field radio.

Sunbeams streamed through doorways into the corridors and through the glass cupola four levels above the central stairway, highlighting particles of dust, reminding him of the light in church when he was a boy. Then, as now, the dust motes were angels, and he could almost hear Pastor Namann droning prayers over the din of battle. And it still seemed to Ernst that the density of angels defined his good luck and the holiness of the day. In the lobby of the Vorwärts, angels filled the light.

"Right here." Manfred appeared from behind a column and took the radio. "Yes Sir, we're in. No casualties." Rifle fire still echoed from the upper floors.

"Yes Sir, third floor." He returned the radio and signaled the Ehrhardt Brigade.

The unit regrouped around Manfred, crouched together on the patterned marble. Baer, carrying only a machine pistol, looked all wrong with such a small weapon in his massive hands.

"We're to take the third floor," Manfred said. "Techow, stay close! Use your pistol! Let's go!"

One by one they ran up the burgundy carpeted stairs to the third floor. Sporadic gunshots reverberated down through the stairwell's spiral opening and echoed off the marble. Someone screamed above Ernst's head, not unlike the pretend screams of boys playing at war. A man wept from the hallway to his left. Pistols in hand, one by one they took the stairs, amidst the clamor of gunshots and orders and palpable cries of pain, shifting from floor to floor.

At the third landing Manfred waved his arm to both sides signaling the unit to spread out. Ernst followed Manfred down a silent and eerily deserted corridor. At the first office, Manfred signaled a halt and fired his pistol into the door lock. Several Freebooters kicked in the door and stormed the inner office. A brief burst of pistol fire, a scream, a groan, and the Freebooters returned. At the next door, Ernst followed Baer. Manfred exploded the lock again with his pistol, and Baer crashed through the door.

Inside was a large suite of offices, richly carpeted. Painted in bold black letters on frosted glass were the words 'MANAGING EDITOR'.

Suddenly a door flew open at the end of the waiting area. Time slowed by half. A rifle barrel came through the door, followed by a dark head with a beard, twisting into position to fire. Ernst's pistol was already raised and sighted on the Spartakist's chest.

"Look out!" someone shouted.

Ernst squeezed his trigger three times, and the man froze and dropped his weapon, a look of utter astonishment on his face as he slowly sank. A gasp wheezed from his mouth, blood leaked from one corner of his lips, and he collapsed. Baer fired into the room the Spartakist had leapt out of, shattering the frosted glass. Two young men – boys really, no older than Hans Gerd – cowered in a corner, their guns thrown down across the room, their hands raised.

"Surrender! We surrender! Please don't shoot."

Baer was first in the room. He backed the terrified youths against the wall.

"Baer! Don't do it," Ernst said.

"Please don't shoot," one boy said. He was too young to have a beard.

"You shouldn't be here, boys. You should be in school." Baer fired once and the smooth-faced boy clutched his stomach and looked at Ernst, pleading as he fell. He writhed on the floor, mouth open, unable to draw his last breath.

Baer wheeled, his face crazed. "We're here to clean house!" He spat near Ernst's boot. "Not babysit." He turned back and fired into the second boy's chest. The boy gasped and fell into a spreading pool of his friend's blood. Baer fired again into the first boy's head, and he was still.

Ernst started to retch and felt Baer's massive hand grab his collar and drag him out. He stumbled, another wave of nausea sweeping over him. In the corridor he came to his senses hearing another firefight erupt on the stairwell: Spartakists from the fourth floor shooting down on the Freebooters.

"Techow, cover from there!" Manfred pointed to a protected doorway.

Ernst could neither banish the pleading boy's face, nor did he want to die here. He cursed himself. Why was he here? Was this his fight? Now, he had no choice, if he wanted to stay alive. His mouth was dry; he felt a sharp pain in his chest as he drew a deep breath. Sunlight poured through the shattered cupola onto the balustrade across the circular stairwell. He crouched and aimed his pistol up at the fourth floor, blinking frequently to keep his eyes moist. Shadows moved. Ernst saw the top of a Spartakist's head, took a deep breath and squeezed the trigger. The man's head exploded. Manfred ran into the open with two other men, all firing their automatic weapons up the

staircase. Baer, Norbert and Heimler dashed up behind. Baer tossed a hand grenade over the railing. Ernst felt the concussion an instant before the blast sent scraps of wood and plaster raining down the stairwell. His ears ached.

Shouts and epithets flew from the upper floor, along with the sounds of running boots and the rat-a-tat-tat of machine pistols in closed spaces.

"Hold fire! Prisoners!"

Spartakists started to appear with their hands on their heads, followed by Heimler with a pistol.

"Floor secured, Sir," Baer called over the banister.

"Well done! Fall in!" Manfred ordered.

Baer smiled. "Just for you, Techow – we took prisoners." Baer slapped his back. "You did good in there." He grabbed Ernst's crotch. "Not even wet."

"Fire fight in the press room! Fall in!" Manfred ran down the stairs, the burgundy carpet littered with debris. A dead Spartakist lay head down, a trickle of blood still flowing. Ernst thought it fortunate the carpet was red and seemed only damp. The pleading boy's face returned as Ernst ran down the stairs.

A unit of Stephani's Potsdamers re-grouped on the marble lobby floor. Manfred conferred with another officer, their hand motions detailing strategy. A continuous line of Freebooters passed sandbags to erect a barrier in the wide corridor outside the press room, a huge warehouse space connected to the main building.

A small caliber field cannon was in place in the center of the corridor and Baer and Norbert planted their machine gun beside it. An instant later the first cannon round shattered the barricaded door. Cordite acidified the air. Without thinking, Ernst looked over the sandbags to see the damage and was abruptly dragged down by Manfred. After the third round the doorway blew into the cavernous press room. Withering rifle fire suddenly poured out of the Spartakist's last stronghold. Baer's machine gun rattled. Tiny explosions pocked the walls, floor, and ceiling. He felt the thump of bullets into the sandbags he crouched behind. The Free Corps cannon and Baer's machine gun continued firing. Ernst sat back against the sandbags, his rifle across his chest, tart sweat on his upper lip.

"How's it goin', Techow?" Manfred said.

The boy was pleading with him, he was dying, and he knew it, but he was still imploring Ernst – to do what? There was nothing he could do. Maybe the boy was pleading with Ernst never to forget that moment. That would at least give significance, purpose, to his final anguish. But he had to push thoughts

of the boy aside, and maybe the only way to blot this memory was to accept that it would always be with him, but to package it, store it somewhere deep, reconsider it only if absolutely essential or unavoidable. His eyes burned. It was more vital to remember to blink.

"I said, how's it goin', Techow." Manfred sounded angry.

"Good, Sir. Good."

Baer and Norbert moved their gun up a few meters, then resumed firing. The din was tremendous, each cannon explosion followed by its echo, overlaid with the next detonation. So relentless was the hail of Free Corps fire that return fire from the press room ceased.

"Potsdamers!" the officer called out. "Now!"

A ferocious roar burst out as they leapt the sandbags and sprinted for the blasted open doors past the cooling machine guns and field cannon.

Manfred led the Ehrhardt Brigade over the sandbags. As each Freebooter cleared the ruined press room threshold he fired his rifle and turned to one side or the other. Ernst ran past Baer who gave him the thumbs up and smiled.

Inside, he felt dwarfed by the huge presses and rolls of newsprint, two meters high, rolled in place as barricades, pocked with cannon holes and bullet specks as if splattered with ink. His vision constricted again as he ran through the chaos of small arms fire. His boots crunched glass.

Groans of pain, screams, weeping, and confused yelling assaulted Ernst from everywhere in this cavernous space. Suddenly, his tunnel vision fixed a Spartakist, rifle in one hand, raising both arms. Ernst squeezed his trigger and the man fell. Only then did he understand the man's words jumbled up with the cries of the dying. "We give up!" The Spartakist had been trying to surrender.

The battle was over except for occasional pistol fire. Smoke hung like fog. Spartakist prisoners shuffled slowly in a line, their hands on their heads. One after the other, they looked more pathetic than any one alone, a dejected, defeated rabble, their uniforms hardly more than tattered clothes. It had been days since any had shaved; every face was bearded, distinguished only by blond or brown, except those too young for facial hair and one woman. Her hair had already been shorn off close to her scalp by a Potsdamer, so she looked like a young boy.

The prisoners dragged out the dead. Any wounded or dying were dispatched with a coup de grace to the head. On the lobby's marble floor, sticky with blood, he immediately recognized the two boys Baer had executed in

the Managing Editor's office. Ernst looked up. So much dust had been raised that it looked as if all the heavenly host floated in the light.

On the street corpses were laid out in a line, like Kiel sprats in a can, their heads all pointing toward the street so those passing would take warning. Ernst walked down the line and assured himself that Leo was not among the dead. Nor was he with the prisoners – deep relief on both counts.

A golden glint caught Ernst's eye from the line of bodies – a gold watch-band on a wrist among the anonymous dead. More were being dragged out and lined up, and no matter how hard he tried not to, his eyes locked onto that wrist, a speck of brightness among the dead. Better him than someone else, he rationalized, and easily slipped it from the limp wrist and pocketed his booty.

Across the courtyard five men stood against the brick wall of the building, blindfolded, their hands tied behind their backs. One man tried to flee, stumbling blindly, twisting his bound arms from side to side. There was laughter, and then the Potsdamer officer raised his pistol and shot him three times. The other four stood still, trembling, awaiting their fate. On his order, a volley of rifle fire erupted and the remaining four collapsed. Ernst felt his own stomach knot.

The finches returned, first one at a time, then more, as if nothing unusual had happened. The crows knew better and gathered for the blood.

*   *   *   *   *   *   *   *   *   *

Two days later the Ehrhardt Brigade marched into central Berlin behind General Noske himself. Cheering crowds of Berliners, those courageous enough to venture out, lined the streets and celebrated the Free Corps and the end of "The Red Terror".

The Free Corps re-established its headquarters in the familiar Moabit barracks just across the Spree River from the Tiergarten, and to Ernst it felt like coming home.

9

Home

January, 1919 – March 1920

From the frosted barracks window, Ernst looked across the Spree onto the Tiergarten. Columns of black smoke flattened over the Eastern districts, where mobs had tried to destroy his lovely Berlin, block by block, square by square. And though their leadership was defeated, they continued to thrash about like decapitated serpents destroying their own nests. He felt no pity for these terrorists. He felt no pity for the immigrants – Slavs, especially Poles and Silesians - Jew and Pole – displaced by the War or the Soviet Revolution in Russia, crowded into once respectable housing, breeding as if the Republic owed them a living. And how do they repay Weimar hospitality? They take up the Red flag of Bolshevism, pollute German culture, and try to replace it with a Soviet Republic. Something had calcified in his heart. He knew he could kill again, and it would be easier.

Baer and Norbert strutted about the barracks as if they had defeated the Bolshevik infection once and for all, but Ernst knew better. The day before he had overheard Lieutenant Manfred rebuke a junior officer who had congratulated him on their victory. Manfred said it was only the beginning. He likened the revolution to an abscess that once drained "must be made to bleed a good long time to cleanse the body of lingering poisons."

It was almost 10 AM when Manfred called Ernst into his office.

"Techow." Manfred motioned for Ernst to sit. "I need a driver who knows Berlin, to assist the Horse Guards at the Hotel Eden tonight."

"I know where that is, Sir. What am I to do?" He relished Manfred's approval, felt a filial pleasure in his trust.

"Drive, that's all. But keep your eyes and ears open. I want to know what's going on. Captain Pabst is the commander. No need to snoop, just tell me what you see."

The Corps Teutonia Pub was the favored watering hole for Freebooters and Nationalist university students in Berlin. The owner, Max Gudergahn, a generous Free Corps supporter, served one complimentary beer to every Freebooter in uniform, provided they buy at least one more. Baer, Norbert and Heimler finished their first round while Ernst surveyed the rathskeller with apprehension. What if Lisa were here? What would she make of Baer? And, though the possibility weighed on him daily, he didn't want Lisa to dash his hopes and tell him that she and Fritz were a committed couple. There were very few students, no sign of Lisa, and Ernst was relieved. As heroic as the Freebooters were in principle, at a distance, on wall posters, Ernst felt something unsettling and shameful about being in their brotherhood.

"Drink up, Techow." Baer roared for the barmaid.

"Just one. Manfred ordered me to drive tonight for the Horse Guards at the Eden."

"The Eden?" Norbert said. "Horse Guards get to stay at the fucking Eden and we have to sleep on wood and straw at Moabit?"

"War is hell," Baer said and emptied his glass. "I heard from Gerhard in unit 5 that the Horse Guards caught Red Rosa and Liebknecht."

"I don't know a thing about it," Ernst said.

Baer shrugged his shoulders and turned back to Norbert. "Take heart, Norbert. I hear we move to Döberitz – new barracks – very fancy." He leaned into his face. "Another girl's school."

"Promises," Norbert said. "Which November criminal told you that?"

"Look at that bevy of beauties." Heimler slicked down his hair and raised his stein toward a booth of four young women students across the hall who giggled at his attention. "I'm going to introduce myself. Excuse me, gentlemen."

After Heimler left, Ernst asked, "Have you ever met Captain Ehrhardt?"

Baer stiffened. "I've seen him from a distance, but never up close."

"Best not to ask too much about Ehrhardt," Norbert said. "There's all kinds of stories about him. He's a spook. Tell him about Kern."

Baer grunted and shook his head. "Ehrhardt's boy. Used to be in our unit, maybe he still is, I don't know. A lieutenant. One night I'm smokin' a cigar outside the barracks, and I see him talkin' to a Captain. I'm pretty sure it's Ehrhardt. He gives Kern something and the next day Kern packs his bags and leaves. That's the last we see of him. Must have been – what, three months ago? Just before the mutiny."

Norbert leaned forward. "You also want to be careful how you talk about Kern."

"Kern is a slippery bastard," Baer said. "Even me... I kept my mouth shut around him and I ain't scared of nobody. Remember Kreitz?"

Norbert shook his head. "Kreitz. Shit."

"Who's Kreitz?" Ernst said.

"Guy about our age – not your age, Techow – our age. Fought in France, lots of scars – a real tough guy. Kept to himself. Used to go out alone most evenings – not very friendly. One night Kern leaves with his buddy, Fischer. Now there's a spook. Didn't hardly say nothin' – never smiled. Tall, skinny guy, hooked nose like an eagle, blue eyes – cold. Anyway, they leave just after Kreitz and follow him. Kern and Fischer come back late. Next morning Kreitz is missing. Kreitz's name isn't even read at roll call. Just disappeared. I asked Manfred about Kreitz and he says there never was nobody named Kreitz and I should forget about him."

"What happened to him?"

"Baer checked with the police a few days later and sure enough an unclaimed body, cut up real bad, turns in the Tiergarten that matches Kreitz's description, near as they could tell."

"What did the police do?"

"Nothin'! They tell Baer to mind his own business." Norbert looked both ways then said in a whisper, "The Feme. Court, Judge, executioner – it's only rumor, but I think Kern is a Feme executioner. And Ehrhardt is mixed up with them, too."

"Feme?" Ernst said.

Baer leaned closer and said, "Vigilante courts from the Dark Ages. And the only sentence handed down by the Femegericht? Death."

"I don't know about this Feme shit," Norbert whispered. "But I don't ask no questions. Baer was stupid to go to the police."

"I was just curious, you asshole. First and last time I help the police." Baer's voice dropped to just above a whisper as he continued. "Anyway, next day, Kern pulls me aside and says if I don't want to end up like Kreitz to mind my own business. He told me Captain Ehrhardt would be unhappy to learn I was pryin' into his affairs."

"How did he know?" Ernst asked.

"Kern knows everything."

★　★　★　★　★　★　★　★　★　★

The company car, a two year old dark blue Mercedes Benz – Mark II, whose origins were as mysterious as Captain Ehrhardt, reflected a street lamp outside the Corps Teutonia Pub. Its interior was richly padded leather, and the stick shift sported a polished walnut knob. Ernst admired the car as he leaned against the brick wall of the Technicon Mechanical Engineering building and smoked a Gauloise. It was only 2100 hours. He had an hour to kill and needed to clear his head of Baer and Norbert, and the beer.

Behind Ernst on the wall hung at least twenty identical white posters with bright red lettering laid over a sultry pair of black-stockinged legs. No one tore down these posters.

Who Has the Prettiest Legs in Berlin?

Visit the Caviare-Flapper Dance at the

Wandervogel Club and Cabaret

8:30 PM – Every night!!

Ernst smiled and crushed the Gauloise under his boot heel. It was suddenly fashionable to be a *Wandervogel*. A dandy in spats, top hat and evening clothes, teetered down Gessenstrasse from the Charlottenburg Theater steadied on his arm by a fancy lady friend, coiled by a white boa.

Ernst settled into the fine leather of his driver's seat and idled the luxury automobile. He marveled at the soothing hum of its perfectly timed engine. Only a few days before he would see Lisa again. Anticipation coursed through his veins with the excitement of coffee and the intoxication of wine. Lisa was his last thought before sleep and the first on awakening. Anytime he felt distressed he would think of her and be calmed.

It was above freezing, so he drove slowly with the window open to take the pulse of his city. He knew where he was by smell alone; Middle Eastern cooking filled one street, oriental cuisine another. In spite of the fighting, Berlin still churned with business and throbbed with nightlife. Every language could be heard, especially in the student district.

Mounted policemen patrolled the streets. On the larger squares two or three government soldiers kept watch with rifles, but except for them there was no sign of the 'Revolution' seven blocks away. The 'Revolution' had been so orderly, so German, that here, in the university, as in most of Berlin – indeed most of Germany – normality had never seriously been breached.

At night, the five-story Hotel Eden, lit up by yellow search lights, dominated the nearby Zoo district. Before the Great War, carriages and limousines loaded and unloaded wealthy and influential visitors of every stripe from dignitaries to scoundrels. Sometimes Ernst and Leo would watch the parade of opulence through Leo's binoculars from the gates of the Zoo. Inconvenienced by Spartakus Week, the privileged had fled the 'Grand Dame' and were replaced by the elite Horse Guards, well armed by the very same plutocrats they had dislodged. In the place of carriages and limousines, armored cars and troop carriers lined the circular driveway.

Ernst pulled up to the side entrance and waited, trying to re-imagine the glamorous parade that once was a nightly fascination. A Horse Guard sentry approached the car, and Ernst showed his identity papers.

"Techow, Ehrhardt Brigade."

The sentry scanned his clipboard. "Yeah, I got you. Prisoner transfer." He looked at his watch. "Shouldn't be long. Stay in the car."

Ernst left the car idling so the heat would stay on. He leaned back fondling the polished wooden shift knob, then stroked the soft leather seat. Suddenly, soldiers burst out of the side entryway and formed a cordon. He looked at his watch, the gold Klug-Baumen he'd slipped off the wrist of the Spartakist corpse less than a week ago. It was a heavy watch engraved on the back "to my angel".

Once the guards were in place, the side door opened again, and a small, dark man stumbled out supported by a Horse Guard. Almost immediately, a hulking private stepped out of the line, and, muttering an obscenity, jabbed his rifle butt into the prisoner's head. He collapsed into a black heap. No officer intervened. The body was dragged and then bundled into the car in front of Ernst's, which drove off in the direction of the Tiergarten. The sentry motioned Ernst forward.

Again the door opened, and this time Ernst could see quite clearly the sepia interior of the hotel. A slight woman limped through the door, her head bent to one side as if dazed, one eye swollen shut, her opposite cheek bruised. She too, was supported by a soldier, and again the same avenging private swung his rifle butt with the same result. This time Ernst was close enough to hear the soft thump of the wooden rifle stock against her temple. She, too, crumpled like a marionette whose strings were cut. The back door of his Mercedes was opened and she was pushed inside. Ernst felt ashamed of his first thought, that her blood would ruin the leather upholstery.

"Techow?" the officer in charge settled beside him in the passenger seat, a Luger pistol in his lap. "I'm Lieutenant Räathe. Drive on."

Two Horse Guards sat in the back propping the battered woman between them.

"Private Runge is too enthusiastic," he said to Ernst. "After the beating she took, it was hardly necessary to club her at all."

Ernst wondered who she was, what she had done to deserve this brutish assault. He felt only curiosity, not pity, knowing her crimes must be significant. As he drove through the Potsdamer Platz he glanced in the rear-view mirror at the semi-conscious woman who began to look familiar behind her mask of bruises. She groaned each time the motion of the car jostled her or a turn caused her head to fall to one side.

"Techow, take us to the nearest quiet bridge where we will not be seen."

He drove to the Liechtenstein Bridge that crossed the Landwehr Canal. It was almost midnight. Heavy mist lay like steamed milk over the water and seeped onto adjoining streets. He stopped at the midpoint of the span, in the darkness between two streetlamps' gauzy circles of light.

"Do you know who she is, Techow?" Lieutenant Räathe said. He looked both ways on the bridge, satisfied himself that they were alone, then half turned and leaned over the front seat. He put his pistol to the woman's forehead and pulled the trigger. Ernst jumped at the explosion and felt a faint spray of wetness on the back of his neck. The Luger's report muffled in the mist.

In the rear view mirror he saw a splash of blood flicked with bone on the leather seat where her head had been.

"Did that frighten you?" Räathe tilted his head. "That was Rosa Luxemburg. You're quite the celebrity, Techow. You gave Red Rosa her last ride – and in a Mercedes to boot. She would have appreciated the irony." Räathe laughed and opened the door. "Get her out – over the side."

Ernst turned around as her head whisked by, a blur of hair and blood. When the car was empty Ernst had to contain an impulse to flee. No matter how he tried not to look, his attention returned to the bloodstain. Dense night air filled the car, washed out the smell of urine and sweat. He heard the soldiers grunt as they lifted her onto the cement bridge railing, then the splash of her body into the canal.

"Thank you, Techow," Räathe said. "This was just the right place. Now back to The Eden."

Räathe lit a cigarette, and the sudden flare of his lighter illuminated the bloodstain for a moment. The two Horse Guards in the back stayed far to each side of it.

★   ★   ★   ★   ★   ★   ★   ★   ★   ★

Newspapers carried reports that Karl Liebknecht was shot dead while "trying to escape" and Rosa Luxemburg had disappeared into a crowd of angry citizens demanding "vengeance on Red Rosa". According to the *Berliner Tageblatt* and the *Vorwärts*, Lieutenant Räathe, his two sentries and driver, Ernst Werner Techow, "had to surrender their prisoner to the crowd." Räathe gave a detailed account of the armed vigilantes who stopped their auto and demanded the prisoner be given over to their justice. "Better one dead," Räathe said, "than scores had we refused and it became a fight." Ernst corroborated the story.

Events moved quickly, and Ernst's leave was cancelled. He would not see Lisa. Though he was bitterly disappointed, their enforced separation kept his anticipation, and perhaps his fantasy, alive. The following day he was driving his unit north to join the rest of the Ehrhardt Marine Brigade in Upper Silesia fighting Polish insurgents in the former German territory.

Ernst's unit was on the move constantly, never staying more than a few weeks in any area of fighting. Letters were the only possible means of communication, and they were none too reliable. In any event, he never had a postal address for long. Each mail call he waited in vain for a letter from Lisa, but none came. His mother wrote regularly, and Hans Gerd sent a letter to say he was so proud of Ernst. All his friends at school were green with jealousy. Uncle Erwin invited Ernst to help him on his estate after he was demobilized. He wrote glowingly of the benefits of country life:

> In Jacobsdorf one hardly knows there is a revolution, except for a few mentally ill peasants and immigrants. I'm sorry to send so many letters and to keep repeating myself, but the Communists are interfering with the mail!! O tempora! O mores!
>
> Someday I will retire, and though I will always live on my estate, I was hoping you might take over the property management – keep it in the family. Think it over.

Fritz managed to get a few letters through, and in September he wrote that Lisa had a new steady boyfriend, someone named Horst. Ernst was disappointed, but also glad it was not Fritz. Horst was a chemical engineering student who already had a job with I.G. Farben waiting for him after graduation. Safety, thought Ernst, with scorn – that's what Lisa really wants – and needs. Fritz's letter ended with a troubling observation.

> ...Aside from his aggressive temperament, muscular arms and broad chest, Horst is likable enough. He was elected treasurer of the GNYO, which makes me very uncomfortable, but I hide it well – like a diplomat should. Horst is the old fashioned jealous type. He has his own apartment in a Nikolassee tenement. Lisa stays with him frequently. He's quite possessive. She seems to love him very much. Goo-goo eyes – the works. It's quite disgusting....I'm glad you're not here to see it.

Ernst felt vexed but drew solace knowing that Fritz had lost her as well; shared misfortune renewed their bond of brotherhood.

★ ★ ★ ★ ★ ★ ★ ★ ★ ★

It had been a long year of fierce campaigns against Polish insurgents in Upper Silesia and the territories and Communists from Bremen to Wilhelmshaven. Periods of danger and intensity alternated with long intervals of monotony and introspection. Trying to put Lisa out of his mind was arduous, but as the months went by in the rural desolation of Silesia without a letter from her, he found himself dismissing thoughts of her with an angry epithet. Drawing became his sanctuary again, and he sketched everything and everyone. He visited Wanda, a prostitute and camp follower from Danzig who kept a room in the nearby village of Wyzgoda. After having sex she listened to his heartbreak, caressed his cheek and stroked his chest. He often stayed on to sketch her and talk; she never charged him extra. Some of his drawings of Wanda were sensual and provocative, others studied her smiling, frowning, sleeping.

He received regular letters from Fritz, whose loyalty to Ernst had never wavered, letters filled with news of the university and Berlin and Fritz's political philosophy. He mentioned Lisa less and less and finally only to say that he hadn't seen her except in class. He too, missed her and worried about her, but there was nothing to be done. Margaret was not happy about Horst at all. Horst himself resigned from the GNYO and Lisa no longer came to meetings. She was still a very strong student, and Fritz and she were number one and two in the class. Fritz urged Ernst to return to school: he was far too bright to be a Freebooter. The Nationalist movement needed his intellect more than his rifle. In his last letter Fritz wrote that Hans Gerd was taking a strong interest in the GNYO and had formed his own group in the Gymnasium. He called Hans Gerd "a late bloomer with potential for the movement".

Lisa's letter finally came in February, a month before Ernst returned to Berlin. After a paragraph of banal details about the new semester, Lisa had obviously stopped and returned some time later to write again. Her next paragraph's script was constricted, irregular, more difficult to decipher. She was no longer seeing Horst; as a matter of fact, they had had a fight and he had struck her in the face. It was probably for the best, she wrote. It would be awful to be married to such a monster. Each time Ernst read her account he imagined her bruised face; his mind produced awful images of Horst slapping Lisa then forcing himself on her. And there were other images, disturbing in their own way, of Lisa and Horst, naked in a passionate embrace. But he also allowed himself the exhilaration of possibility reborn.

> ...What frightens me the most is how Horst and my father are misshapen reflections of each other. At the end, Horst started pushing me around – he was often angry, and kept me from my friends. He insisted I spend every night with him. I was so confused and afraid – not in my right mind. He hated Margaret, and Margaret tried to convince me to leave him. She finally took me out of his Neukölln apartment a week ago. I think she rescued me. Thank goodness for Margaret. What an extraordinary friend.
>
> I'm so sorry to have lost touch with you and Fritz. Will you forgive me? I would love to see you when you're next in Berlin – the National Gallery? I want you to show me those 'paintings of the light' you are always talking about.
>
> With Love, Lisa.

★ ★ ★ ★ ★ ★ ★ ★ ★ ★

Brimming with optimism like the spring buds, Ernst returned to Berlin from Upper Silesia in a March snowstorm. It was a confused time. Evergreen trees planted at regular intervals on Schönwälder Allee leaned over from wet snow. Finches glinted bright yellow. Umbrellas sprouted like mushrooms, and by noon the snow had melted into slush. Ernst was eager to go home, if only for dinner and a hot bath, to soak away the soil of Silesia. Now that he'd been away for so long, home meant something warm and comforting, relief instead of constraint, irritation and repulsion. He left a note for Lisa at her dormitory saying he was back, bivouacked at Camp Döberitz, 25 kilometers west of Berlin, and wondered how she would respond.

A wave of nostalgia swept over Ernst as he took a seat on the number 5 trolley, crowded with commuters returning home. As it rumbled along Schönwälder Allee through the northern Spandau District, the screech of its steel wheels welcomed him home. It seemed the number of automobiles had doubled since he had left. Students, bundled against the March weather, leaned into the wind. A lone mother pushed a covered perambulator against the snow, and beggars and amputees sought the shelter of recessed doorways. Every few blocks he saw one of the new breed of beggars – the 'Cornerstander' for hire holding a carefully lettered sign announcing his particular métier: Carpenter, Violin Lessons, Russian Language Tutoring, 'Philosopher for Hire.'

As the trolley rattled out of downtown, fewer and fewer bullet holes scarred the buildings. It stopped for passengers at Hohenzollern Ring at a kiosk that glowed golden in the snowy twilight. Through the wet distortion of the window Ernst saw newspapers lined up on the rack, their headlines blurred. He purposely covered his Freebooter uniform with his heavy winter coat so none of the passengers would know. He felt vulnerable – alone and unarmed. Perhaps the scruffy man asleep across the car was a Spartakist survivor going home to have supper with his mother. This was how life went on with appalling normality in the shadow of war.

Ernst patted the small rectangular box in his pocket containing Hans Gerd's birthday present, the Krug-Bauman watch. He had kept it in his knapsack through all the fighting in Bavaria and the territories. When he remembered Hans Gerd he decided it would be a perfect gift, even with the inscription "to my angel" on the back. His little brother needn't know the details.

At Mariakirche he stepped off the tram and stood for a moment, noting every lamppost, the benches, pigeons. As he left the tram, the flood lights arced on and the church's stone façade shone white. Heavy snowflakes floated like angels in the beam. Automobiles left tire tracks in the snow. He turned up his collar and walked through the darkening park accompanied by homeward bound clerks and executives from the central city, all homogenized under umbrellas. It amazed him that people still went to work as if fighting Communists was just another remote complication, a brushfire that someone else was bound to extinguish. How could these be happening simultaneously – bobbing umbrellas and the rattle of machine guns?

He turned at the wrought iron gate on Wannseestrasse, the song of the street left behind, and followed the driveway, leaving bootprints in the unblemished snow. When his father was alive, Eric would have cleared even a trace of snow from the driveway. The snow-covered cedars needed pruning and shaping; the grass had been left too long and poked through the snow like whiskers.

Ernst stood at the door and before he could ring the bell, the curtain behind the glass drew back and Hans Gerd stared through. His mouth opened when he recognized his brother, and he yanked open the door.

"Ernst, you're here!" Hans Gerd began to hug him, but at the last moment dropped his arms and Ernst shook his good left hand instead.

"Hans Gerd. Goodness, how tall you are! You need a haircut." His face had filled out. Wild red hair masked the disparate size of his eyes.

"Should I tell Mother you're here?" Hans Gerd asked, barely able to stop moving as if he contained something that squirmed.

"No. Not just yet. How is she?"

Hans Gerd hung Ernst's coat on a hook. "A little better, I guess. She's back with her St. George ladies, so at least she's going out, thank goodness. She still drives me mad."

"How's school?" Ernst took off his wet boots.

"Everybody asks me the same question, 'how's school', like that's all that matters. They're not interested in the real me, the..."

"Stop it, Hans Gerd! I just asked you about school."

"It's OK."

"What's OK?"

"I'm handling things just fine." Hans Gerd turned away crestfallen and started for the parlor.

"Hey, listen, I'm sorry. No need to be so sensitive."

Hans Gerd turned back and, even in the dim light of the entrance, Ernst could see his eyes narrow and burn. "Fuck you, Ernst! Do I ask you what grades you got in the Free Corps? How's your Lieutenant? No."

"Relax. OK? Last time I saw you, you were a wild child. I was worried."

"What's in the package?" Hans Gerd pointed at Ernst's hanging coat.

"You don't miss a thing, do you? It's your late birthday present."

Slowly, Hans Gerd's face softened and he even smiled as he rummaged through Ernst's coat. In a moment he found the rectangular box wrapped in plain brown paper, tied with baling twine.

"Go ahead, open it."

Hans Gerd's eyes danced with anticipation. The twine easily fell away and he tore open the paper. The golden watch sparkled in his hand and his eyes shimmered. "Wow, it's amazing!" He dangled it by the leather clasp then wrapped it around his wrist. "It fits just right." He inspected the watch face. "Krug-Baumen. How could you afford it?"

"Let's just say I got a good deal on it. It's not new. Enjoy it. It'll last a long time." He finger combed his wet hair. "How are Maria and Frau Stimmel?"

Hans Gerd looked over his shoulder to ensure privacy and said, "Mother let Maria go last month – just after my birthday. You know we sold the car?"

"I figured. No chauffeur and Mother can't drive. Too bad about Maria. I was hoping to see her again."

"I think she was glad to go back home. Before she left she wouldn't stop crossing herself."

Ernst was about to walk into the parlor when he stopped and put his hand on Hans Gerd's shoulder. "I don't think Mother would like to see me in my uniform. I'll take a hot bath, change clothes, and sit for a moment."

"Do you want to be alone?"

"No, come on up." He wrapped his arm around Hans Gerd's shoulders, and the two quietly climbed the stairs. At the Chinese vase they stopped and glanced at each other, laughed and kicked it, then sprinted up to the next landing.

His room was unchanged. On the second shelf, where his model ships had once anchored, a pile of his drawings curled and gathered dust. His bed and Leo's were perfectly made.

"Is Mother going to sell the house?" Ernst asked.

"Probably, but you know how Mother is – she never comes right out and says anything."

"What do you think?"

"I think I would love to live in Berlin Center, near Ku'damm, even if it meant a small flat. It is so dead here. A cemetery would be more exciting."

"Do you still get into fights with her?"

"All the time. About stupid things."

"Who wins?"

"Who do you think? She just says something like, 'if your father was alive' or 'haven't I suffered enough?' That one really gets me." Hans Gerd pulled the window curtains apart and looked into the dark. Snowflakes melted on the glass.

"Do you miss Father?" Hans Gerd pressed his face to the window.

"Yeah, I do. You?"

"Yeah, I guess. I mean, we never did much stuff together, except at Christmas." He stared into the dark. "I just miss him." His lips twitched, and he let the curtain fall. "I'll tell Mother you're here, OK? Oh, and Uncle Erwin is here also. He visits quite often."

"Tell her I'll be right down, after I take a bath. Light the boiler?"

"Yeah, sure." He was about to leave when he turned back to Ernst. "Leo and Katherine are coming later – just for dessert. Thought you should know."

The bathroom walls were thin enough to hear Hans Gerd telling his mother of Ernst's arrival. He slid under the hot water, warmth and comfort seeping into his body as steam rose from the surface. He closed his eyes and listened for ghosts, but the house was silent. On a shelf behind the tub sat an old bath toy, a balsa battlecruiser. He floated it on the warm soapsud surf of his ocean, and for a moment time rewound.

Ernst dressed for dinner as he expected his mother would wish, but he found the starched clothes hanging in his closet irritating after the softness of well-worn military cotton. It took several attempts before his fingers remembered how to properly tie his cravat. His church shoes, polished and waiting beneath his bed like the forepaws of a loyal dog, were still too tight. He walked down the staircase astonished that he had once belonged to this world.

At the bottom of the stairs he saw his mother staring into shadows, perfectly still in her black and gray silk dress, her mouth set. She had lost enough weight that she looked taller, her face pinched.

"Hello, Mother," he said.

She startled and looked at him. "Ernst! Welcome home!" She smiled for a moment.

Ernst covered the few steps between them and carefully embraced her, kissing each cheek once. Her hands felt cold on his neck.

"I was worried about you." She studied him as if she didn't quite recognize him. "What with all the fighting. You are fine, aren't you?" Her eyes glistened.

"Yes, Mother, I'm fine."

"You must tell us about everything. Oh, Ernst, here's Uncle Erwin."

Erwin beamed as he walked through the parlor door. An exuberant smile wrinkled his eyes and rounded his rosy cheeks.

"Ernst," he said. "It has been such a long, long time. *Tempus fugit.*" As was his habit, he pumped his nephew's hand just twice. "You look excellent. Excellent. The service has been good to you! You are being careful, aren't you?

Your mother worries so."

"I'm fine, Uncle Erwin. I'm not a new recruit anymore."

"Come, we must eat," his mother said. "Frau Stimmel has prepared your favorite – roast beef."

"That was Father's favorite, not mine." He wished he could call back the words.

Frau Techow's head jerked back momentarily on her long neck. "No matter. Perhaps you could carve tonight. That would be nice."

Frau Stimmel bustled through the door with a pitcher of water. Her face twinkled at the sight of Ernst. "Herr Ernst, how good to see you. I've made your favorite tonight, Schnitzel."

"I thought – wasn't it roast beef? But schnitzel is even better. Thank you, Frau Stimmel." He and Hans Gerd exchanged puzzled glances. "At least I don't have to carve. I'm glad to be home."

"Why has it taken you so long to come visit?" Frau Stimmel scolded as she fussed with the silverware and glasses.

"You know how it is in the military. It's hard to get away. But now, I will visit more regularly." Why did he even have to explain? He wasn't at University, or traveling on vacation. Frau Stimmel was hopelessly lost in the last century.

Hans Gerd extended his wrist and burst out, "Mother, look at the watch Ernst got me for my birthday."

She studied the gleaming watch. "My, my, a Krug-Baumen." She looked nervously at Uncle Erwin. "Where did you get it?"

Ernst sat at his usual seat. Uncle Erwin took his father's place at the head of the table. It bothered Ernst that anyone would sit there, even Uncle Erwin. "I got a special deal, in Silesia. One doesn't ask too many questions. Let's eat – I'm famished. This is a special treat." He winked at Frau Stimmel. She smiled and clapped her hands like an excited child, then wobbled back to the kitchen.

"You look like you've actually gained some weight," his mother said.

"We eat a lot of potatoes and drink beer."

"Not too much, I hope."

Ernst could feel her eyes scrutinizing him across the table.

Uncle Erwin cleared his throat. "I remember learning to drink beer in the army," he said and tucked a linen napkin under his chin. Hans Gerd fidgeted in his chair. "Relax, Gertrude. Just part of growing up, *Sine dubio*. Shall I say grace?"

"Bless us our Father," Uncle Erwin began. "Give us strength for each new day, each new battle, to be better Christians. Thank you for the bravery of men like our Ernst, who fight for our noble Vaterland; watch over him always. Bless this food, that we may be worthy of thy grace. Amen."

Hans Gerd scooped a mound of whipped potatoes onto his plate.

His mother unfolded her napkin carefully in her lap and sat tall and straight. "Have you seen Fritz and that girl, what's her name?"

"Her name's Lisa."

"I don't think I ever knew her name, did I?"

"Yes, Mother, you did."

"How is Fritz? I always liked him so much. Such a good family."

"Fritz is fine. He's at the University. Very active in politics. So is Lisa."

"What kind of politics?"

"Our kind, Mother."

"Is this Lisa his girlfriend?"

"No, she's definitely not his girlfriend," he said as Frau Stimmel returned with a silver tray of steaming schnitzel. She speared the top cutlet with a cooking fork and laid it onto Ernst's plate.

"I asked Herr Gruenspecht for his best cuts," she said. "Cooked just the way you like it."

Each mustard brown cutlet, coated with herbed bread crumbs, shimmered with grease. As Ernst cut through the thin breaded crust into a ribbon of fat, a flood of memories suffused in him, growing more perceptible and heavenly as he chewed that first forkful.

"Delicious, Frau Stimmel," he said. She smiled contentedly and returned to the kitchen.

Hans Gerd leaned over and speared a chop. "Schnitzel isn't your favorite," he whispered. "It's Leo's. I think you should tell her."

He responded so his mother would not hear. "It's not important. I, too, like Schnitzel."

"Were you in many battles?" Hans Gerd asked.

"Quite a few," he said.

"Tell me about Munich. I think that must have been the worst... I mean with the hostages and all."

Ernst began to tell Hans Gerd of drinking beer in Munich when his mother interjected. "Ernst! Please." Frau Techow's frosty blue eyes froze him. "I don't think we need to hear this at the table. Think of what kind of example you wish to set."

Ernst fell silent. His comrades didn't treat him harshly like this. The tinkling of fine silver on porcelain and the clock's loud meter ordered the troubled silence. Ernst concentrated on his schnitzel bone.

"Leo will be here later with his fiancée, Katherine," Frau Techow tried to sound upbeat. "She's a lovely girl – just has some mixed up ideas. Please, Ernst, no fights."

"It seems you Freebooters are either heroes or villains," his uncle said, "depending on which newspaper you read. I don't believe any of it."

"But don't you agree, Uncle, the Free Corps is necessary to maintain order."

"Yes, I suppose so," Uncle Erwin said. "What is it really like, mano a mano?"

Ernst felt sorry for his uncle trying so hard to please, to smooth over the ruffled atmosphere, that he demeaned himself. "I can only speak for my unit, but we have a brotherhood – a comradeship, that I have never known."

"When I'm old enough, I'll be a Freebooter too," Hans Gerd said. "Tell me about Captain Ehrhardt. All my friends are in awe of him. We call him the 'Führer of Youth' and 'The Consul' – the ideal man." Hans Gerd dropped his fork onto the plate, slid from his chair and faced Ernst. "Watch me, Ernst. 'The Consul' has this thing he does with his hand." Hans Gerd stroked his good hand down his nose and over his mouth. "We all do it in school. Everyone wants to be like 'The Consul'."

"Hans Gerd!" His mother pointed for emphasis. "Sit down!"

"Captain Ehrhardt says we young people will be the saviors of Germany." Hans Gerd speared another Schnitzel. "We can't wait to join up."

"You cannot be a soldier with asthma," his mother said.

"I don't need your permission, you know, once I'm seventeen."

"Ernst, talk sense into your brother. Don't fill him with foolish stories."

Ernst shifted uneasily in his chair. "Lots can happen in two years. Maybe there won't be any need for Freebooters anymore."

"I don't want to miss my chance," Hans Gerd said.

Ernst remembered feeling the same way about the Great War and how he had just missed it for his age. He understood how frustrating this was for Hans Gerd.

Frau Techow cleared her throat. "Everybody cannot be a soldier. I'm not sure I like Ernst being a Freebooter, but I do understand." She cut a small piece of schnitzel onto her plate and served herself a half spoonful of potatoes. Ernst could see that his mother hardly filled her dinner dress. Between small bites she twirled her wedding ring, which wobbled on her finger between prominent joints. Brown age spots dotted the top of her hands. "When will you return to university?" She dabbed her mouth with a linen napkin. "You know how important it was to your father that you finish university. Leo is back in school, you know."

Ernst swirled his mashed potatoes with a fork. "Good for Leo. Maybe he's come to his senses. Tell me about him."

She smiled. "You know how Leo is – he doesn't explain much. He's studying Sociology. He and Katherine intend to marry. I told him we couldn't afford a very big wedding." Her smile vanished, and she looked down at her plate.

Harsh ticking from the mantle clock divided the silence.

"They want nothing to do with the Church. That's unfortunate – Pastor Namann could have helped with special arrangements. Everything is so expensive these days."

"What does Katherine do?" Ernst asked.

"A student. I believe she wants to be a social worker. She wants to work at soup kitchens." The words came out with bitterness.

"Too many soup kitchens, if you ask me," Uncle Erwin said, as he spread whipped potatoes onto a forkful of Schnitzel. "Too much government interference. Too many hand-outs. *Labor omnia vincit* – work conquers all things. If you feed these beggars, why should they work? There's plenty to be done. Put them to work, I say. More hungry people now than under the Kaiser."

After an uncomfortable silence Ernst asked, "Mother, what are your plans for the house?"

Frau Techow's fork stopped in midair and she looked at Uncle Erwin. He nodded to her and kept eating.

"Why do you ask?"

"It's an awfully big house for just you and Hans Gerd. Frau Stimmel can't possibly manage the house alone."

"I manage this house, not Frau Stimmel."

"Yes, Mother."

"Your mother and I have been discussing options," Uncle Erwin emphasized 'options'. "Given that your mother doesn't drive, the chauffeur and the car had to go. Maria left of her own accord and, frankly, good riddance. Help is frightfully expensive and not very dependable."

"I was going to tell you later tonight," his mother said.

"Maria was my favorite," Ernst felt angry with Uncle Erwin for not understanding about Maria, though he agreed with the rest of his rant. "I knew it was only a matter of time," Ernst said. "Your pension is worth, what? Maybe one tenth what it was last year? And who knows where this inflation will end. Goddamned Versailles. A stab in the back."

"Ernst! There will be no swearing at my table." She occupied herself with cutting smaller and smaller pieces of meat.

Breaching the two swinging doors, Frau Stimmel, still radiant, returned with a pot of tea and a plate piled high with dessert cakes. It occurred to him that Frau Stimmel probably had no idea that she would soon lose her position.

Everyone was silent as she set down the tea kettle and cakes. "Will that be all?"

"Yes, Frau Stimmel. Thank you."

After she retreated to the kitchen, Ernst leaned across the table, whispering. "Mother, when will you tell Frau Stimmel?"

His mother laid her fork down with deliberate firmness. She looked up at Ernst. "In good time. Your Uncle and I have made plans. Next month Hans Gerd and I are moving to Heydenstrasse, number 7." She said it loudly to be authoritative, then realized her mistake and let her voice fall to a whisper. "The apartment is large and sunny. There are 3 bedrooms, so you will each have a room."

"Heydenstrasse..." Ernst said, "that's only a few blocks from where the fighting was."

"It's perfectly safe. The fighting is over."

As soon as Frau Stimmel came in to clear the dinner dishes and set out dessert plates, the silence resumed, as if she were the condemned clearing dishes from her own last supper. Eyes that had danced at the beginning of the meal were now puffed and red, although the thought of Frau Stimmel crying seemed as ridiculous as the Rock of Gibraltar crumbling. It occurred to Ernst that he didn't even know her first name. She shuffled back into the kitchen.

The room was silent except for the mantle clock and a slight wheeze at the end of Hans Gerd's expirations.

"You will go to the University soon, won't you Ernst?" his mother said. "It's what your father wanted."

"When the time is right. He also wanted me in the Navy."

"Don't wait too long. Sometimes the right moment passes and you will regret it for the rest of your life."

"*Carpe diem*." Erwin shook his knife.

"Mother, I will know when the time is right. If necessary I can work to pay my own fees and living expenses. I'm quite independent."

"It's not what your father would have wanted."

"Stop it, Mother!" He glared through slitted eyes. "First you say 'it's what your father wanted', then you say 'it's not what your father wanted.' Stop using him to make me feel guilty. You don't know what he would have wanted."

"Certainly not for you to be with those riff-raff. He wanted you to get a degree. If you feel guilty, perhaps it's because I'm correct."

"Now, Gertrude," Erwin began.

"Then be right for your own reasons," Ernst retorted. "It bothers me to remember father that way."

Leo, his face freshly shaved, hair slicked down, suddenly appeared at the doorway. "Mother? Ernst!" He rushed in, his hand extended. "How wonderful – everyone here. Hans Gerd." He tousled his younger brother's hair and dropped a gift-wrapped box on his plate.

"For me?"

"Late birthday present. Uncle Erwin." He circled the table and shook his hand. Leo's smile and charm instantly warmed the dining room. He was so much more relaxed than anyone else, and not at all the ominous mutineer Ernst had met at Kiel Naval Base. It felt to Ernst like the old Leo, with his hair cut short and rosy cheeks, the carefree juvenile who slept in the bed across the room. Leo was irresistible.

"Cigar?" Uncle Erwin offered.

"Katherine would have my head," he whispered and laughed. "But brandy would be lovely."

Katherine had been standing in the doorway, her luxuriant dark hair falling in waves onto the shoulders of a blue print dress – plain but attractive, sensibly long. She smiled demurely, the faintest blush of lipstick and rouge hardly necessary to accent her beauty.

"Katherine," his mother said. "Don't be shy. Please sit here, next to me. We ladies must stick together."

Katherine's eyes twinkled. Ernst noticed she winked at Hans Gerd, and he blushed and smiled.

"Katherine," Leo said, "you remember Ernst?"

Ernst stood briefly and bowed. She was more beautiful than he remembered.

Leo sat in his usual seat, next to Ernst, completing the lineup of the three boys across from their mother.

She passed the cakes to Katherine who took one and gave the plate to Hans Gerd. Blushing again, he took two cakes and, by force of will, sat on his hands and waited until everyone had been served. Frau Stimmel, impassive, poured tea and for a moment the world was old again.

Hans Gerd fumbled with Leo's present. The only finger on his right hand grasped the string while his left hand sawed at the red ribbon with his table knife. Ernst laid his Free Corps dagger in front of Hans Gerd, whose eyes lit up. It shone lustrous, silver, flawless. With it, he cut the lace ribbon like warm butter.

Uncle Erwin reached out his pudgy hand. "Might I see your dagger?" He lifted his eyeglasses to his forehead and studied the blade. "Fine piece of work. What's this insignia?"

"Swastika, Uncle. Sign of the Ehrhardt Brigade. It's painted on our helmets."

Uncle Erwin passed the knife back to Ernst. "I hear that the Free Corps will be disbanded. Versailles and all that disagreeable business." He lit a fat cigar and blew a smoke ring.

Hans Gerd opened Leo's present and his expectant expression collapsed. He held up a new gold pocket watch. "Thanks, Leo. It's great." His shirt sleeve hitched up, revealing Ernst's Klug-Baumen. Uncle Erwin cleared his throat; Katherine sat up and fussed with her napkin. "It's from Ernst," Hans Gerd said. "I'll carry them both. Ernst's is a Krug-Baumen, used, and this watch looks brand new."

Leo looked embarrassed and forlorn. He emptied his brandy snifter and turned to face Ernst. "I'm glad to see you in normal clothes and not that uniform. Tell me you're not still a Freebooter."

"I am. Nothing has changed."

The distance between them suddenly became uncomfortably small.

"I was hoping you'd cooled down," Leo said. "I did, and life is much better. Isn't that right, Katherine?"

"Yes, Leo's quite sensible now." She smiled and drank her tea

Leo's new watch flanked Hans Gerd's plate like a utensil. Nobody seemed to have anything to say as they busied themselves with Frau Stimmel's dessert cakes.

Leo broke the silence. "Might I try one of your cigarettes?" Leo said to Ernst. "French, I see." Uncle Erwin leaned over with his lighter again. The dining room filled with smoke, and Hans Gerd's cough worsened.

"There won't be much fighting with the Versailles limits on the army,"

Leo said. "I'm surprised the French allow your little Free Corps to exist at all."

In other circumstances Ernst would have punched his brother, but he saw his mother's electric stare and answered. "We're hardly little. There are more than 50,000 of us – the best of the officer corps and loyal men."

"The French could squash you like mosquitoes. They're happy to have you do their dirty work."

"I say bring back the Kaiser," Uncle Erwin said. He puffed vigorously on his cigar. "You two don't remember the glory days, before the war. If we had won – and we very nearly did, never forget that – what a different conversation this would be."

"They were good days," his mother said. Her eyes lost focus. She smiled and thawed ever so slightly.

Leo cleared his throat. Katherine's eyes grew wide, and she warned him with a surreptitious shake of her head.

"But we lost." Leo said it gently, as if the reluctant messenger of bad news. "No amount of yearning for the old days will bring the Kaiser back. And Ernst, the Treaty of Versailles will not be undone."

"You accept things as they are," Ernst said. "I see a new Germany rising out of the ashes. A phoenix. Something mystical, Leo – a chance for greatness."

"Sounds like Pastor Namann and Bismarck all rolled into one sickly sweet glop of Nationalist nonsense."

"Let's not have an argument," his mother said. "More tea?"

"It's not an argument, Mother," Ernst said. "We just have very deep differences of opinion."

"I must say," Uncle Erwin said, "there are excesses on both sides, but I rather think Ernst is clear-headed and courageous."

Hans Gerd coughed again and said, "I'm going to be a Freebooter, Leo. I don't care what you say."

"What about the children?" Katherine said. "Will the Free Corps feed the children? They are the most helpless."

"If we feed all the beggars," Hans Gerd said, "then we'll pity them, keep them helpless. They'll just be beggars all their lives. And their kids will be beggars."

"But Hans Gerd," Katherine said, "first we must give them food and love and education, if you see what I mean. We must help them to be like us."

Hans Gerd pulled his deformed hand out of his pocket and laid it across the table in front of Katherine. She blinked quickly. "When people look at me, this is all they see. I can tell by their eyes, they see me as deformed, crippled, less than they are. I won't ever be like you, and the beggars you help with handouts and pity, will never be like us."

"I hope you're wrong, Hans Gerd," she said.

"What about Jews, Slavs, immigrants, Communists?" Hans Gerd said. "Will they be like us also? Where do we stop?"

"Well spoken, Hans Gerd," Ernst said. He felt proud of his little brother.

Leo carefully crushed his cigarette and finished his brandy. Ernst thought Katherine must be stinging from Hans Gerd's verbal slap in the face, and by a young boy at that. His mother offered more cakes and invited everyone into the parlor, hoping, no doubt, that a change in venue would dissipate, or at least disguise this discomfort.

Leo and Katherine gave their regrets. Ernst saw their prearranged signal to leave. The snow had deepened, and travel would be difficult, and anyway, they only wanted to say hello to Ernst and give Hans Gerd his birthday present. Ernst lit another Gauloise, glad that Leo had suffered a defeat and was retreating.

Kapp Putsch
March 1920

At the Camp Döberitz garrison, Ernst and five thousand fellow Freebooters of the Ehrhardt Brigade and other Free Corps waited for their regimental commander's return. Disturbing rumors of disbanding or demobilizing the Free Corps had circulated for more than a week.

Baer leaned his chair back outside the barracks, his cap shading the sun. A black Mercedes pulled up to the CO's office. "That'll be Erhhardt," he announced. A rabble of men rushed from their barracks and surrounded the car.

Sitting at a card table, his sketch pad in full sun, Ernst's eyes flitted from the paper to Heimler and back again, his charcoal floating with consideration. He made quick marks on the paper and rubbed shades with his finger. "Damn it, Heimler! Hold still!"

"I don't have time for this shit," Heimler said and disengaged from his posing beside Baer to join the others.

"Pathetic!" Baer spit. "No fuckin' dignity!"

Ernst caught a glimpse of the reclusive captain stepping from his staff car. Ehrhardt stroked his face several times in the manner that Hans Gerd had imitated and spoke briefly to the Freebooters around him, who raised fisted arms and cheered. Norbert was there, eyes wide, smiling, shouting as he loped back to Baer. Simple Norbert, so like a child – illiterate, blessed with uncomplicated courage, honesty and loyalty.

"We're not dissolved! We're not dissolved!" His smile bared yellow and black teeth, more like weathered wood than enamel.

"Fuck you, Norbert." Baer leaned back in the sun again and closed his eyes. "Are we still on for tomorrow?"

"0900," Norbert said.

Baer sucked on his cold cigar and spit again. "I'm sick of this shit – sittin' on our asses for two weeks. I'm bored!!" He yelled at the sky, eyes still closed. "When do we fight?"

"Soon enough." Every man turned to a new voice coming from the barrack doorway – Edwin Kern's penetrating baritone.

"Kern!" Baer rocked forward and sat up. "Where you been?"

"Munich." Kern worked his perfect teeth with a wooden pick. His voice reverberated off the corrugated tin walls. In spite of being shorter than most Freebooters, he had something commanding about him that gripped Ernst's attention. His muscular frame filled a crisp uniform. Light blond hair crowned his round face, wispy and tussled like a juvenile bird's fluff. Though it was late in the day, he was clean-shaven. Small eyes, recessed under a shelf-like forehead with platinum eyebrows, singled out Ernst; he approached the card table.

"New man?" He continued to scrutinize Ernst, who had to look down at his sketch pad.

Heimler stood and extended his hand. "Good to see you, Kern."

Kern ignored Heimler but extended his own hand to Ernst. "Kern, Erwin Kern."

Kern's grip was painful. "Ernst Techow."

"Ah, yes. The driver. Lieutenant Manfred recommends you highly." He picked up Ernst's sketch pad and considered Heimler's portrait. "You have many talents."

"Thank you." Ernst found himself sweating, even in the coolness of this faux spring day.

Kern turned to Baer. "Captain Ehrhardt expects tomorrow's parade to be a spectacular display. Spit and polish. No fuck-ups."

"What are you talking to me for?" Baer asked. "And what happens after our little pansy parade. Are we ever going to do anything?"

"Patience."

"I'm not a patient man."

"Neither was Kreitz." Kern looked at Baer until he turned away, his head lowered. "You don't think I returned for a parade, do you?"

Kern replaced his officer's cap. "Good day, gentlemen." He walked toward Captain Ehrhardt's office.

Norbert slapped Ernst hard on the back; it was good-natured, but too hard. "I think you made a friend."

"Is that good or bad?" Ernst said, as he chilled from drying sweat.

Ernst lay on his bunk reading Faust again, as he had over and over this past year, a pursuit that – at least for his own sense of identity – distinguished him from these earthy, often crude, sometimes vulgar men. He still craved their favor, and his charcoal portraits bound them to him. They wanted to be captured on the sketchpad, as if his renderings made them heroes and lifted them out of their gritty existence.

Heimler walked through their sleeping quarters and playfully snatched Faust from Ernst's hand. "Come on, Techow," Heimler said. "Blau is fighting Melman. You can read that shit anytime. This is real sport."

Ernst leaned forward to grab for the book, but Heimler parried his grasp and sent Ernst tumbling off his bunk. "You son of a bitch!" He scrambled across the floor toward Heimler who waved Faust provocatively.

Seemingly out of nowhere, Kern appeared behind Heimler and gripped his shoulder. Heimler's face twisted in pain as Kern squeezed.

"Leave us alone, Heimler," Kern said.

Heimler shrank backwards towards the door, massaging his shoulder.

"The book, Heimler." Kern held out his hand.

Faust shook with a fine tremor until Kern received it, and Heimler scurried to the door.

Ernst sat on the edge of his bunk, breathing hard, feeling the fever of fury and shame flushing his face. His heartbeat hammered in his ears, yet another reminder that he was no physical match for these men. He felt weak.

"Techow." Kern stood over him. "I bring you greetings from Fritz Sommers – an old friend of yours, I believe?"

"Yes, Fritz... an old friend. But... how did you know... I mean..." Ernst looked up, but in the darkness of the barracks he saw only Kern's shadow.

"Herr Sommers – Fritz – recommended you as a man of intelligence who could be trusted."

"Thank you, Herr Lieutenant."

"Please. There is no need for such formality among brother officers. Call me Kern. The others do. You may smoke if you like."

Ernst took a Gauloise and offered his cigarette case to Kern who waved it away. "I don't smoke – and, in any case, I would not smoke French cigarettes."

Ernst slipped the case into his tunic pocket.

"You wish to enroll at the University – German Literature, I believe."

"That's correct, Sir." How did Kern know so much?

"It's quite expensive to live in Berlin," Kern said. "Your mother lives on a fixed income. Inflation is most unkind to old veterans and widows."

Ernst felt Kern's caustic gaze. His neck muscles tightened, and he moved away from him to lean against the wall of his bunk.

Kern stood absolutely still, his high black boots planted shoulder-width apart, his right hand resting on the pistol butt in his belt. "Captain Ehrhardt and Major Stephani are organizing an association of Free Corps fighters that cannot be disbanded by the cursed Versailles dictates. Are you familiar with The National Unity Society – the Nationale Vereinigung?"

Ernst nodded. "Fritz has written about their activity."

"Good. One could consider our new association, the Association of Nationally Minded Soldiers, to be similar to the Nationale Vereinigung, somewhat of an underground Free Corps. Of course, for public purposes we are nothing more than a social club of veterans. Captain Ehrhardt and Lieutenant Manfred represent Berlin. I am in Bavaria much of the time. I would like to offer you a job."

"What exactly would I be doing?"

"First I must know your intentions, if the Brigade is disbanded."

"I will pursue my studies."

"And your political goals, if you have any?"

"I am a German patriot, Lieutenant... Herr Kern. I will do whatever is necessary for the good of the Vaterland."

"The Association has need of a driver. You would be able to continue your studies; we would pay your expenses – a modest stipend. In return you would be expected to drive specified cargo when called upon. It would not be often. Does this interest you?"

"Yes, of course. I am honored to be considered."

"Are you a member of the League for Defense and Attack?"

"I'm not familiar, Sir. We've been away so long, one loses touch."

"Yes, of course. Things happen so quickly. Alfred Roth is the mastermind behind this Bund. His philosophy is compelling." He reached into the pocket of his officer's jacket and unfolded a single sheet of paper. "The constitution of the Schutz und Trutz Bund. Please keep it."

The document, by the Bund, the German Nationalist Protection and Defense Federation, had been printed on a crude press, the type set imprecisely, the ink smudged.

"Herr Roth has been a vocal proponent of a racially pure Germany since before the War. These days, especially since the disaster of Versailles, the 'stab in the back', his theories draw more favorable attention. Read this and perhaps we can discuss it. I think you will find it provocative."

Ernst folded the paper and wondered if this was an order or merely a suggestion. Kern's demeanor suggested the former.

★   ★   ★   ★   ★   ★   ★   ★   ★   ★

The next day's parade was cancelled. In its stead, Manfred ordered his men to bathe, shave, and assemble in dress uniform for an armed night march on Berlin. When the assembled Brigade heard their orders, they raised a deep and vigorous cheer. At midnight the Ehrhardt Brigade set out in orderly columns punctuated only by the tread of boots on pavement. After a few kilometers in the ephemeral silence, their ranks relaxed and to help the kilometers go by, Ernst told Norbert the story of Faust. Norbert was especially interested in Faust's pact with the devil.

"I would do that," he said.

"It doesn't end well," Ernst said.

"Nothin' ends well. Everybody dies. Might as well get what you can while you're alive. Whoever gives me what I want – God, the Devil – I don't give a shit."

Ernst didn't have the heart to argue with Norbert. He was just too ignorant, too consumed with his own small life. It would be like explaining Kierkegaard or Nietzsche to a toddler.

As they neared Berlin, the crescent moon disappeared over the Western horizon, and uncountable stars sparkled like finely ground salt on black velvet. Families living along the route of march would long remember the menacing percussion of boots and the ghost-like army that passed in the night.

An early spring breeze stirred the Brigade's red, white and black flags. Streetlights turned night-shadowed faces blue-gray and reflected off their helmets, large red swastikas painted on each side. They marched through the night, and before dawn they tightened their formation and began to sing:

> Comrade, give me your hand
> Steadfast we'll stand together.
> Let those fight us who will
> Our spirit marches forever.

Swastika on helmet,
Colors of Red, White, Black
The Ehrhardt Brigade
Is marching to attack!

At 0600 just west of Berlin, at the Pichelsdorfer Bridge, Captain Ehrhardt called a halt for breakfast. It was here that company commanders opened their specific orders of how they were to seize Berlin and replace the government.

The Freebooters cheered again, as if they had already toppled Weimar, already sent the Socialist Ebert and his vermin packing. According to Lieutenant Manfred they were under the supreme command of General von Lüttwitz and Captain Ehrhardt, and they answered only to Wolfgang Kapp, a Prussian administrator and mastermind of the coup. In one hour they would be at the Tiergarten where they would await Chancellor Ebert's resignation.

In fact, Ebert's government had anticipated this desperate gambit and had already fled Berlin, but not before setting in motion a vigorous appeal for a General Strike. White posters with red lettering exhorting Germans to defy the rebellion had sprouted overnight.

WORKERS! PARTY COMRADES!

The military putsch is here. The Baltic Freebooters who were afraid that they would be dissolved have made an attempt to overthrow the Republic and establish a dictatorial government with Lüttwitz and Kapp at its head.

WORKERS, COMRADES!

We did not make a revolution only to have it overthrown by a bloody Freebooter regiment. We will not negotiate with the Baltic criminals.

WORKERS, COMRADES!

The work of an entire year will fall into ruins. Your freedom, bought at such a heavy price, will be destroyed. This goes for everybody. Therefore the most drastic counter measures are required. No factory dare operate as long as the military dictatorship of Ludendorff prevails.

THEREFORE QUIT WORK! STRIKE!

Throttle the reactionary clique! Fight with every means for the maintenance of the Republic. Lay aside all petty discord.
There is only one way to prevent the return of Kaiser Wilhelm II:

Paralyze all economic activity!
No hand dare move!
No proletarian dare help the military dictatorship!
General strike all down the line!

PROLETARIANS UNITE!
DOWN WITH THE COUNTER-REVOLUTION!

(The Social Democratic Members of the Government: Ebert, Bauer, Noske, Schlicke, Schmidt, David, Müller. The party leadership of the Social Democratic Party, Otto Wels.)

Ehrhardt was true to his word. After 0700, with no response from the government to the ultimatum he delivered on behalf of Wolfgang Kapp, Marine Brigade Ehrhardt marched through the Brandenburg Gate and seized the awakening capital. They were 5,000 men strong. Weimar's military, their allegiance in doubt, stood down. Reichswehr troops were nowhere to be seen. Marine Brigade Ehrhardt's entry into the city was unopposed.

Spirits were high but restrained, and Ernst felt the powerful tide of history about to turn. The Brigade maintained discipline in the ranks as they marched through an ominously silent city. All felt the eyes of war-weary Berliners who lined the route of march and gawked at another army.

The Brigade's optimism faded quickly. By mid-morning it was clear to Ehrhardt's invading army that the popular support they had anticipated would not materialize. Instead, they felt the anesthesia of a burgeoning general strike becoming deep and widespread. Chancellor Ebert had rolled the dice in a colossal, fraught gamble, and Berlin ground to a halt. As the sun came up, streets and boulevards that normally hummed with commerce remained as deserted as dawn on a Sunday. Automobiles were scarce; trolleys remained in their garages. A lone horse-drawn wagon clomped along the empty boulevard undisturbed. As the Brigade turned right onto Wilhelmstrasse, a mere five blocks from the Reich chancellery, they confronted a troop of twenty Civil Guards marching up the street towards them. Ernst's leading squad of Freebooters unslung their rifles, and tension spread down the line of march. Bewildered by the ominous formation bearing down upon them, jackboots still echoing on the cobblestones, the Civil Guard froze. Ernst saw that they were old men in uniforms, decades past soldiering. A motley assemblage, they broke ranks, hands high in the air. Their ancient Gewehr '98 rifles remained strapped to their backs. The menacing machinery of the Ehrhardt Brigade halted in a wave from front to back, and Kern approached the confused old men. Some words were exchanged, and the Civil Guard lowered their hands and smiled, then laughed out loud to each other. Even at a distance, Ernst could hear both reprieve and apprehension in their levity.

"Good Luck!" the old leader said. They backed away to one side, and he waved the Ehrhardt Brigade on.

They marched down Wilhelmstrasse in tight formation, proud and unopposed. Ernst felt a surge of strength, of energy. Now that Horst was gone from Lisa's life, he couldn't suppress a smile, anticipating once again, his reunion with Lisa. Anything was achievable, and he relished – no, it was more than that – he thrived on the intoxication of possibility. Just as a tide was turning for Germany, so it turned inside him. His time with the Free Corps had been a suspension – an alternate reality – exciting, fulfilling, even necessary as a regimentation and a purposefulness that had soothed first the bewildering grief of his father's death and then the hurt of Lisa being with Horst. Now he would return to University; he would fulfill his potential. Maybe even his mother would be pleased. To feel her pride in him would be novel. And he would continue to serve the Vaterland. He wondered at the mysterious request by Captain Ehrhardt and Lieutenenant Manfred to participate in something secretive, something vital to the rebirth of Germany. So much was possible, and he prayed, "Dear God let Lisa be mine". He felt in the hands of a higher power, something mythic, Olympian, and he marched with his head held high.

Exactly in accord with von Lüttwitz's plan, the main line of march divided into five detachments, each assigned to a different sector of the city. Ernst's unit followed Kern and Manfred toward the Chancellery. At the North end of the Chancellery building Baer and Norbert set up their machine gun; perimeter patrols were assigned. A detachment of Freebooters had already circled the Chancellery with barbed wire. There was still no sign of the Reichswehr, and Ernst, his appetite for blood dulled, was relieved.

Wolfgang Kapp's first executive order was to fire all government employees who participated in the strike. The next day government functionaries, now of the new Kapp regime, returned to their posts, escorted through a barbed wire tunnel by Freebooters. Weimar fell without resistance.

*   *   *   *   *   *   *   *   *   *

Though Kapp could coerce some bureaucrats to return to work, he was less successful with ordinary Berliners. The general strike was stunningly effective. A quarter of a million gathered in a mass demonstration where effigies of Kapp and Lüttwitz were hung from streetlamps. Berliners sat in darkness in their apartments without water, gas, transportation, mail, telephone service or garbage removal. All communication was by courier. Over the following days Ernst drove through the paralyzed city for Lieutenants Manfred and Kern, carrying messages, orders, and sacks of Reichmarks.

On the fourth day of the putsch, Ernst filled out government payroll forms in Manfred's office as Kern paced.

"Will you please sit down!" Manfred said sharply. "You're making me nervous."

"You should be nervous," Kern said scornfully. "It was too easy. Governments don't fall without bleeding. General von der Goltz gave clear orders to shoot all strike leaders immediately. Why did Lüttwitz rescind the order? 'We're to be civilized,' he said?" He pounded his fist on the desk, and Ernst jumped. "What is wrong with him? You know what Ehrhardt says. Blood is the cement of the Revolution. Who shrinks from letting it flow is no revolutionary, only a Burger gone mad."

Manfred looked from Kern to Ernst. "Techow, you said you knew someone in Lüttwitz's office?"

"Yes, Sir," Ernst said. "Willi Günther, an orderly working for Lieutenant-Colonel Bauer – ordnance – he works in General von Lüttwitz's anteroom."

"Is he trustworthy?"

"I don't know him well. He's an acquaintance of my friend, Fritz Sommers."

"His name again?" Kern had his pen ready.

"Günther. Willi Günther."

"Techow," Manfred said, "I'm assigning you to von Lüttwitz's office – as my personal aide. Talk to Günther. We need a source in the General's office. I don't trust that Prussian son of a bitch."

★　★　★　★　★　★　★　★　★　★

After one spring-like day, the dreariness of winter returned to Berlin, as if the weather too was disgusted with the Kapp Putsch and had collaborated with the general strike. The wind that blew up deserted Kurfürstendamm carried with it the cold smell of the North Sea, and to Ernst it tasted like despair.

It was Ernst's first day in General von Lüttwitz's office. He was eager for this to be over so he could see Lisa, but he also wanted Kapp to succeed. Willi Günther leaned back in his chair and crossed his high black boots on a cluttered desk as if he was someone important in the Ministry of Commerce. Ernst sat beside him, eating his lunch. The walls were thin and the shouting from the office forceful. The passion of debate carried easily through the frosted glass door. Günther showed Ernst a list of participants – two labor leaders and three influential Reichstag deputies.

"Now that I've shown you the list, I have to kill you," Günther laughed. "Just kidding. Any friend of Fritz Sommers is OK with me," Although six years older than Ernst, Günther appeared much younger because of his round baby face and short blond hair. He had a small scooped out nose that seemed made for someone else. They had been together all morning, and Günther could not stop talking. His conversation was largely inconsequential, his humor ironic and clichéd, all of which Ernst found annoying. Günther could make a joke of anything, and Ernst thought his façade so manifest that it had to camouflage fear or sadness or anger. Possibly all three.

Günther's highly polished boots reflected the dim lamps of the Chancellery. His pants, not regulation Reichswehr, still had the sheen of wool before its first washing. Günther's standard issue Reichswehr tunic, starched white, was buttoned up to his neck.

"I had pneumonia and a recurrence of malaria in January," Günther said as he wiped a scuff from his boot. "I would have been with you Free Corps madmen had I not been so ill. Pneumonia is nothing compared to malaria. Contracted it in Turkey, during the war. Dreadful disease. Racking chills – swollen liver. I fought with the Ulan regiment – the Lancers – since 1914. Wounded at the front." He pulled up one sleeve and pointed to a small scar on his forearm. "They reassigned me to the Third Mechanized Infantry in Turkey. Turkey – what an awful place – littered with dirty little Arabs who would slit your throat as soon as look at you." He stopped, both to pour a dark liquid from a Reichswehr canteen and to allow his military record to linger like fine cognac. "Fritz Sommers is an old friend of yours?" He unwrapped a small glass jar of caviar and cut a slice from a Schwarzbrot with his swastika-emblazoned Freebooter dagger. He spread the caviar on the crusted heel and offered it to Ernst. "Authentic Russian. Would you like some?"

Ernst had long since wearied of listening to Günther, but he was intrigued. "Where did you get caviar?"

"Connections. Whatever you would like, contact me first and see if I can't get it for you at a better price. Sugar, butter, caviar, 9mm parabellum cartridges – whatever you like. Or need. No reason to live poorly just because times are hard." He bit into the caviar-coated bread, staining his perfect teeth black. "Tell me about you and Fritz."

"We were *Wandervogel* – spent our summers together. He's my best friend."

"Do you know that girl who's always with him, Lisa something? She's a looker. I wouldn't mind getting into her pants."

Now he hated Günther, but he needed his cooperation and that rankled him. "She was with us each summer. We three were best friends."

Günther squinted his piggy eyes at Ernst. "Were?"

How easy it would be to kill Günther. Ernst's threshold for mayhem had virtually disappeared, a realization that troubled him. "I mean we are good friends. I just haven't kept up as much with Lisa as with Fritz. What do you mean she's always with him?"

"Ever since that unpleasantness with that Horst fellow. You know about that little episode? Well now that she's done with Mr. Big Shot, she has returned to the GNYO and is always with your friend Fritz. I see them together frequently."

Ernst felt as if Günther was fishing. His heart in his throat, he asked, "Are they, you know, a pair – I mean a couple?"

"It's so hard to tell these days. I mean in Berlin anything goes. Boys and girls, girls and girls, boys and boys."

"But what have you heard?"

"It's none of my business. Probably none of your business either." Günther raised one eyebrow and looked askance at Ernst. "But I can find out for you, if you like."

"No... no, it really doesn't matter."

"You're sure?" Günther's eyes bore down on him again.

"Yes – really – it's nothing."

"It's never nothing, but forget I said anything. You're back at the University, aren't you?"

"Yes, as soon as this is over."

"You don't sound very optimistic. What's your connection with Kern?"

He seemed to know much more than he should. Ernst could see how Günther could be a valuable source of information as well as sugar, butter, caviar and 9mm parabellum cartridges.

"Kern is an officer in the Brigade. He offered me..." He stopped and reconsidered how much to share of Kern's discussion of the underground network.

"Yes? He offered you?"

"Uh... he offered me a more permanent position in the Brigade, but I really want to get on with my studies."

"So you refused?"

"I'm thinking it over."

"I see. You will join the GNYO, won't you? Dues are very reasonable."

"Yes, I suppose I will. Fritz will keep pestering me about it."

"Good. You and that girl Lisa will be reunited. How touching." He looked at Ernst with a disturbing leer and smiled.

In General von Lüttwitz's office, chairs scraped against the floor and what had been muffled angry debate suddenly metamorphosed into polite cocktail chatter. Behind the frosted glass, distorted shadows appeared and disappeared, grew larger and smaller in the glass. Günther quickly shifted his boots onto the floor and swept his caviar and bread crumbs into the side drawer. When the door opened Günther leaned over an open folder showing Ernst a table of figures.

★ ★ ★ ★ ★ ★ ★ ★ ★ ★

After four days of a general strike, the Kapp-Lüttwitz putsch teetered on the verge of collapse. A series of conflicting and confused orders flowed from Lüttwitz and Kapp's offices. The Prussian State Legislature was dissolved. Two days later all imprisoned Prussian cabinet officers were released as a gesture to the strike leaders. That same day Kapp issued an order seizing all matzoh flour for the approaching Passover services. Jews and Bolsheviks were to blame for the general strike.

By the fourth day, Günther's hair was disheveled, but he refused to acknowledge defeat. "It is the process, Ernst, a natural and destined unfolding. Kapp is a creator – he is setting the 'great awakening' in motion. But the time isn't right. And he's not the chosen leader. Someone else will come to finish his work. Do you need anything, silk stockings? Opium? Parabellum shells will be coming after the strike ends. Prices will never be lower."

One of the security guards came to Günther's desk and pointed at Ernst. "You. Come with me. Chancellor Kapp requires your assistance, immediately."

Günther mumbled about inflation and the rate of exchange. The young guard, more anxious than urgent, escorted Ernst across the Chancellory to the Chancellor's office, where they intruded on the stout dictator and his daughter hastily throwing possessions onto a sheet stretched out on the floor. At Kapp's command, Ernst helped them knot the four corners, and then he was ordered to carry it down the broad staircase. He and another guard hoisted the bundle on top of an idling taxi and tied it down with rope. Kapp stood atop the Chancellory steps and, to an audience of his daughter, Ernst and his security detail, he summed up his government's five day history. He had accomplished all his aims, he said, and therefore he was relinquishing power to General von Lüttwitz. His last order was to allow Captain Ehrhardt's Marine Brigade to march out of Berlin in military formation. Ernst thought him pathetic and found it difficult to watch and listen to his masquerade.

More to the point, Ernst was sorely disappointed. He had held high hopes for this coup, and now it was a failure. Another loss, another support kicked out from beneath – his father to death, Germany to the Bolsheviks, and most onerous of all, Lisa to Fritz. All was lost, and he felt numbed. It was only the physical requirements of the moment that mattered, and for now, that was the only available anodyne for his pain.

Late on Wednesday the Ehrhardt Brigade formed up again, their boots still polished from their unopposed march five days earlier. Against a twilit sky, their red, white and black flags fluttered again as stern-faced Freebooters once more marched through the Brandenburg Gate. A sullen crowd lined Unter Den Linden and Charlottenburger Chaussee, gathering to witness their departure. Ernst felt deep humiliation and anger as he heard Baer's grit-toothed obscenities. This detestable rabble – Bolshevicks, Jews, immigrants, trade unionists, social democrats – the whole treasonous lot of them was watching, and no doubt gloating, as Marine Brigade Ehrhardt retreated. This riff-raff's general strike had defeated the most elite army available to restore order. He thought they must feel smug for having defeated the Free Corps with nothing more than silence and idleness.

Ernst's unit was toward the rear of the column. Though this moment was a humiliating ending, it was also a beginning. Despite what Günther had said of Fritz and Lisa, Ernst cleaved to a glimmer of hope over his dark horizon. Without it there was nothing. Before the spring leaves unfurled, he would meet Lisa again – at the National Gallery as she had written – and then he would know if life was worth living.

As they neared the triumphal arch, a young boy stepped out of the largely silent crowd and began to boo and laugh and point at the retreating Freebooters. He danced a funny jig. Two troopers immediately ahead of Ernst broke ranks and swung their rifle butts at the young boy, hitting him in the head and stomach. As he went down, they kicked at his body with their jack boots. He was rescued, dragged by his heels back into the crowd where his single 'boo' spread quickly down the line. Hissing and booing were picked up by others.

Baer could no longer contain himself and turned to the onlookers, snarling. "You fucking scum!" He leveled his semi-automatic rifle and fired a long burst into the crowd. There were screams and shouts of confusion. Ernst could see casualties. A deafening chorus of boos and catcalls.

Norbert pulled Baer back into line.

Manfred bellowed, "Order! Form up, Brigade! No firing!"

The march continued. Somewhere at the head of the column Ernst heard the first singing and quickly, the whole column intoned with an almost dirge-like quality. The crowd screamed their disapproval, and it only energized the Freebooters, as they left Berlin behind. Their chorale continued, no longer funereal, but rousing and deep from the chest, though the road out of Berlin was soon deserted, as if the rabble didn't really care anymore, another insult. They marched to the same rousing chorus that had conducted them into Berlin five days and a revolution earlier.

> Comrade, give me your hand
> Steadfast we'll stand together.
> Let those fight us who will
> Our spirit marches forever.
>
> Swastika on helmet,
> Colors of Red, White, Black
> The Ehrhardt Brigade
> Is marching to attack!

II

Bleigiessen

April – June 1920

After the Kapp Putsch, the Ehrhardt Brigade was briefly demobilized. The prevailing consensus from newspaper editorials, weeklies, and posters was that the fledgling Weimar Republic had survived the first test of its legitimacy. Rumor had it that Captain Ehrhardt was in hiding in Bavaria where he continued to conspire for the fall of Weimar. Wolfgang Kapp had escaped to Sweden and General Luttwitz to Hungary. In Thuringia and Saxony, local commanders ruthlessly put down the strikers. But it was a different story in the Ruhr Valley where the Red Ruhr Army rampaged over a huge area encompassing Hamm, Bochum, Essen, and then routed the Reichswehr in Munster. Newspapers began calling events an armed insurrection. By the end of March, the entire Ruhr valley was controlled by the Red Ruhr Army. Once again, the Free Corps, including the resurrected Marine Brigade Ehrhardt, battled the leftists insurgents, but not Ernst. At the end of March, when the Free Corps was licking its wounds, Ernst was granted an honorable discharge. Lieutenant Manfred had made the recommendation after Ernst consented to be "available" as a driver or accomplice in some unspecified future at the university. In their conversation, he had suggested the Free Corps would probably soon be dissolved. The government, he explained, would grant effortless transfer to the Reichswehr for Free Corps members in good standing. "You're worth more to me at the university," he said.

Ernst was not disappointed; he was eager to serve the cause in another way. His self-assessment oscillated, sometimes several times each day, dizzying his sense of balance, of rationality. Some days, some hours, even minutes, he felt like a coward, shamed that he was not a good Freebooter. With almost as much frequency, he felt unshackled, liberated to be true to himself, free of the sustained anxiety, free of Baer and Norbert. But the tension between those see-sawing feelings rankled him, with each nagging suspicion, each internal verdict a scolding imperative that undermined the other.

Ernst returned to Berlin, to his mother's new apartment on Heydenstrasse. The university was closed for Easter vacation, and Lisa and Margaret were at home in Halle. In her last note to Ernst, she wrote that they would meet when she returned. He tried to register at the University, but the registrar was closed, as were dormitories and classrooms.

Another difficulty engaged his more immediate attention. Coming home was not a return to a fabled cocoon of safety and warmth. Rather it was getting accustomed to his mother's new and much restricted life. She welcomed him warmly enough, but he wondered if that was because he was a buffer, a correction for Hans Gerd. She had always made excuses and exceptions for Hans Gerd, because of his deformity. But his oppositional and hyperactive nature tested her beyond containment and they fought often. In the expansive space of Wanseestrasse Hans Gerd's excesses dissipated more easily, but in a three room flat he was often intolerable. After Ernst's first argument with Hans Gerd, the day after he returned, she made it clear to her boys that her life was complex enough without mediating their disputes. Hyperinflation made her work as an aide at the Charité Hospital a crucial supplement to her rapidly devaluing pension.

Less than a week after moving in (he stopped referring to it as his 'coming home') Ernst passed "Gruenspecht's Fine Kosher Meats" on Rheinbaben Allee, and, between plucked chickens and shiny veal flanks on hooks in the window, he saw his mother waiting behind another Hausfrau. She was calculating with a pencil on the butcher paper on the counter.

Ernst walked in to greet her, and his sense of smell was suddenly drenched by the sweet pungency of hanging meat, so familiar and evocative of childhood trips to this same butcher with Eric. Sawdust covered the damp hardwood floors. He heard Herr Gruenspecht greet his mother by name, and he saw her lips clench and her face pale, as if she was a shy woman.

She ordered a chicken and wurst, watching the scale carefully. As the butcher wrapped the meat, Ernst called to her. She turned with the resigned disdain of a cornered thief.

He must have looked perplexed for without his even asking she said, "Kosher meat is the best. Herr Gruenspecht's prices are very fair. And he's always been our butcher."

They walked home together, and she talked about her patients at the

Charité Hospital. Tuesday through Saturday she worked as an aide on the pulmonary ward, mostly tuberculosis, feeding and bathing patients, helping with dressing changes and enforcing strict adherence to visiting hours and infection control.

"At first I was afraid I would be recognized," she said. "But everyone on the ward – nurses, patients, visitors – wears cotton masks to prevent infection."

When she talked about the Charité, he felt her tenderness, her heart for the strangers she cared for. He wondered why he never felt this compassion either from her or for her. It still felt like a judgment.

★   ★   ★   ★   ★   ★   ★   ★   ★   ★

A few days later, when he knew Lisa and Margaret would be returning from Halle, Ernst had prowled into their dormitory lobby and waited in an overstuffed chair. He hid from the House Mother behind a newspaper. He wasn't sure if he wanted to do this, but impulse trumped caution. He needed to know where he stood. Even if she said nothing, he would know by her eyes, by the curve of her lips, the warmth of her fingers.

At the moment of recognition Lisa froze and her mouth opened slightly. She dropped her bag and ran to Ernst, her arms open, and they embraced. Though it was only a brief moment, it seemed to Ernst that they stood in each other's arms, swaying slightly back and forth without speaking, for a long time. It was the House Mother, clapping her hands furiously, who finally broke them apart. She shot a disturbing look, her finger directing Ernst to leave immediately.

He pulled back and held Lisa's shoulders for a moment, and she smiled as wickedly as he. The House Mother advanced. He folded a paper into her palm. "Saturday, at the National Gallery – it's all on this note. I'm at my mother's apartment." He raced out the side door.

Ernst wove in and out of the National Gallery's Greek columns like an embroidery needle. It was an auspicious day, the first time in over a year and a half that he would be alone with her. Billowing cumulus clouds could easily be mistaken for wind gods blowing branches newly covered with spring leaves, bowing whole trees to the east. Lisa would say it was a good day to fly a kite.

As a boy, he and Leo had played tag amongst these columns, darting in and out as their father slowly ascended the thirty-seven broad steps. The day

152

was cool and a fresh west wind blew his hair, which was already growing out from the close cut of the Free Corps. He ambled in and out, from shade to sun, sun to shade, his hands in his pockets, inhaling deeply. For a moment the wind carried a scent of lilac and he thought an invisible perfumed woman had blown by. Possibility was afoot.

In that narrow passageway between the colonnade and the museum wall, a gaunt and bearded one-legged man leaned on a crutch holding out his field cap to Ernst. Around his neck was a sign – **"Veteran of The Great War"**. One of 'The Shakers', though this one looked genuine enough. The police would remove him soon.

It had been almost a month since his discharge from the Brigade, yet Ernst still felt somewhat uneasy in civilian clothes. He turned his head from side to side trying to relieve the abrasion of a starched collar. He looked out over the procession of automobiles that moved up Dorotheenstrasse, weaving in and out among trolleys and horse-drawn Landaus. And then he saw her. Distinct in the crowd, Lisa's red beret shone like a lone poppy in a meadow.

Her face lit up when she saw him, a willing sparkle in her eyes. She was about to speak, but Ernst held his finger to his lips. He bounded down five separating steps, linked his arm in hers. "Say nothing," he whispered.

She laughed, and they ran up the remaining steps. The guard took their tickets, and they laughed some more, only to be stopped by two more uniformed guards, a man and a woman, with pistols and truncheons strapped to their belts.

"Please," the man said. "It is necessary to search you. A requirement of the exhibit."

Lisa's smile vanished as the woman with the pistol approached her and patted her down for weapons. The male guard did the same to Ernst.

"I'm sorry for any inconvenience," the guard said, "but the French government is quite sensitive. You may go in."

It was no secret that the German People's Party and the German National Youth Organization had made threats against this exhibit. Lisa related how Fritz himself had given a speech warning generally about moral decay among modern artists and poets, and specifically about this exhibit of degenerate art. Some of the less restrained GNYO students threatened violence if painters like Picasso, Chagall, Leger, and Miro were displayed. Even Monet might not be safe, they said. Ernst had read these views in various broadsheets, on wall posters, and in the right wing press. All he could think of was simple Norbert and violent, irrational Baer, and he was reminded again of why he was no longer a Freebooter.

The coat check man wore a mask over his left eye and cheek. He looked otherwise handsome, but Ernst knew he was a veteran whose face had been so deformed by his wound that only this artfully sculpted mask allowed him to walk among the public. He carried his disability with dignity, and except for a peculiar nasal quality to his voice, there was no other hint of deformation. Ernst thought of the misshapen hand that Hans Gerd kept hidden in his trouser pocket, and the pink and brown scars on the naked Freebooters. They all wore masks to hide their deformities, whether from a birth defect, the lost war or the cruel peace.

Lisa's turquoise dress fluttered as Ernst led her down a long corridor.

IMPRESSIONISM AND BEYOND

The placard over the door was painted in a modern font, cardinal red and chartreuse. In the first gallery room, on a wall of vibrant paintings, hung one dark square and he immediately led her to it. "Here it is," he said. "Don't you think it's extraordinary?"

Lisa turned to the painting, a scene in the Luxembourg Gardens by John Singer Sargent. In the dark canvas world it was evening, and the full moon that had just risen over the hedges lit up a white concrete walkway. In the foreground a man in black escorted a gentlewoman, her gossamer white gown shimmering in the pale moonlight, the smoldering tip of his cigarillo a tiny orange glow. All else was dark except the moon's liquid reflection in a fountain behind them.

"That's what I thought when I saw you coming up the street," Ernst said. "A splash of light and color. You were floating amongst all those drab people, in all that darkness."

Lisa smiled as she studied the painting. "It's sort of spooky – like she's a ghost." She turned to look at Ernst. "I take back what I said the last time. You look better without a uniform." She stood up close to him and her long fingers took each side of his open collar and straightened his shirt gently. "I'm so glad you're back."

Her hands felt warm against his chest and Ernst thought how much had changed since the last time. He had lost her, found her and then lost her again, this time, he had thought, forever.

He took her hand and led her into the next room. The parquet floors and white walls conspired to hush conversation. People stood alone or in pairs, like scattered soft sculptures.

She stood before a painting Ernst knew well. "Boudin." He leaned close and read, "*Deauville: Flag-Decked Ships in the Inner Harbor.* Whenever I come here I can still hear my father. He would say, 'see how he paints the light and the wind – the flags – the water.'" Ernst looked longingly at the picture. "I miss him. This was all it took."

Lisa shuffled uncomfortably and said, "I'm sorry."

"But these paintings were his greatest gift." Ernst looked from Lisa to the painting. "Aren't they incredible?"

"Ruby, all these artists. They're French. Don't you feel funny admiring our enemies?"

"I can't help it. They do something to me."

"Fritz says it's decadent, bourgeois."

"I don't care what Fritz says."

"You're not becoming a Social Democrat, are you?"

"On the contrary. I feel more Nationalistic than ever." He debated whether to tell her about his undercover assignment with the Association of Nationally Minded Soldiers, the nascent underground Free Corps.

She looked around to make sure no one was near and whispered, "Are you still in the Free Corps?"

"Demobilized. Dishonorable Ebert gave me an honorable discharge. Kern, one of the officers, wants me to be available for this Association. They pay me a stipend for not much work."

"How's your brother?"

"Leo? He's graduating next month – he'll be a teacher."

"Is he still a Communist?"

"Socialist, maybe. I think it was because of Katherine, his fiancée. They're both at Heidelberg." He told her about his move into the tiny three bedroom, third floor walk-up on Heydenstrasse and about Hans Gerd and his mother, and how strange he felt there.

In the next room a class of young children in white blouses and blue shorts followed a tall woman like ducklings. Ernst led Lisa past them into a large gallery dominated by a Japanese footbridge in the middle that arched across a lily pond and into an area resembling a fragment of Monet's garden at Giverny. On a curved wall was the mural sized painting of the *Nympheas* – *Water Lillies*. Lisa sucked in her breath when she saw the six meter long, parabolic painting.

"It's huge." Her eyes swept the curve. "I see why you love this."

Beside the pool a few people sat on benches facing the mural, listening to the faint bubbling of an electric water pump.

They sat together, their eyes riveted to the luminous painting. "If I ever see that Horst guy," Ernst said, almost in a whisper, "I'm going to punch him."

"You'd better have Fritz with you. Horst is a monster – and he has a bad temper."

He turned to her. "Was it awful?"

She kept looking forward, blinking back tears. She nodded and her chin quivered. "Fritz asked me a strange question yesterday. 'If you could kill someone and not suffer any punishment, who would it be?'"

"And?"

"I said nobody – I couldn't do it. But I've been thinking about it. And now I think I could kill Horst, and that's frightening."

For Ernst killing was not frightening, or extraordinary, or even morally complicated. Fritz's question made no sense to a soldier. It was not hypothetical. But, more to the point, it was not something he wished to dwell upon. He stood up and held out his hand. "Come, my lovely Brunhilda." He bowed. "Let us shed this mortal coil and cross the bridge into Valhalla."

Ernst led her across the gentle arch of the footbridge to the opposite side of the gallery room.

"Sometimes I wish I knew the future," she said. "Like with Bleigiessen. When you were little, did you do lead pouring?"

"Bleigiessen? I've heard of it, but I never did it."

"Goodness, I haven't thought of that in a long time." She looked wistfully at the Japanese bridge as if it spanned the years to a better time. "When I was a child, every New Year's Eve we melted a lead soldier on a spoon – it had to be a German soldier – and dropped it into a glass of water. It exploded and hissed as it froze and whatever shape it took foretold the future – what the New Year would bring. We did it by candlelight and it was scary and exciting."

"Will you have dinner with me next Friday?" The question came out awkwardly, and he blushed.

She held out her hand royally. "That would be lovely, kind knight." Ernst dropped to one knee and kissed her invisible ring.

"Good," Ernst said. "That will be good. You know Willi Günther, from the GNYO. He said I could use his apartment while he's away on business. Can I make you dinner?"

"Just the two of us?"

He nodded hopefully. "Bleigiessen after dinner? You can show me how.

I'll get everything we need. I still have toy soldiers – somewhere."

She blushed. "That will be fun."

He took Lisa's hand and they walked down the long hall to **The Hermann Stein Sculpture Garden**, a suddenly exploded inner space as large as six gallery rooms, two floors high, with natural lighting by skylight.

As they entered, the soundscape suddenly swelled, and he could feel the immensity of the space.

Ernst pointed diagonally and pulled Lisa along. "Something else you must see."

"Ernst, please," she whispered. "Slow down. It's a museum, not a race track."

He slowed. "I'm sorry. I get carried away."

They circled the courtyard, passing sculpted stones as curious as exotic bushes and trees, until they stood before two naked lovers, entwined in each other's arms, their lips about to touch.

"*The Kiss*," Ernst said. "Look at the hands. Rodin sculpted hands like God."

"Who are they?" Lisa asked.

"Paolo and Francesca – but I don't know any more than that."

Lisa slowly circled the stone lovers. "Dante."

"Dante?"

"The Inferno. These are two tragic lovers – Paolo and Francesca."

"Two lovers in Hell?"

She cocked her head sadly. "They will never complete that kiss. Moments before their lips touched they were murdered by Francesca's husband and Paolo's brother. Their particular Hell is to be doomed forever to be so close yet never kiss."

Ernst's brow furrowed. "I never thought of them as tragic. I always envied them."

As they left the sculpture garden Ernst was aware of a man walking briskly, overtaking them. He felt targeted and immediately experienced himself on a battlefield with his rifle. He was about to turn and face the man when he was called from behind.

"Techow?"

It was Hermann Fischer, a Freebooter he hardly knew in their brigade. His odd central hair whorl caught Ernst's attention immediately, a little spiral of blond hair, now slicked down. He wore a dark suit and cravat and carried a raincoat over his arm.

"Marstall," Fischer said.

"Betrayal," Ernst responded.

Fischer gave Ernst a sealed envelope from his breast pocket. "For Günther", he said. "Something for you as well." He tipped his head at Lisa, with a leering smile and walked on.

"Who was that?"

"From the Brigade."

"What was that about the 'Marstall' and 'Betrayal'?"

"Code words. We're only being careful. It's nothing, really."

Her eyebrows knotted. "What did he give you?"

"He owes Günther money. Günther always has some scam going." This was the first time he was called to act for the Association. It was nothing – he was a mere courier. He was not tempted by the envelope, but wondered what in it was for him.

For their lunch Ernst bought a bag of hot chestnuts from a vendor at the base of the museum's steps. The wind blew briskly enough to fill the air with dandelion fluff. Across Dorotheenstrasse they sat in the park on a bench and peeled the mealy nuts, while disappointed pigeons pecked at the shells, hoping for bread.

"It's a good wind," Lisa said. "Oh, if we only had a kite."

Ernst pulled a handkerchief out of his pocket. "Let's make one." With his Free Corps dagger he cut two green twigs from an overhanging tree and laid them across each other on the handkerchief. Then he tied each corner onto the sticks with pieces of yarn from Lisa's bag. Lisa fastened the miniature kite onto the skein of her burgundy knitting yarn and held it up beside Ernst's face.

"Burgundy – it's a good color for you. What do you think?"

He laughed and blushed again.

"When you blush," she said, "it's almost the same color. They say blushing is your heart wanting to see the world, instead of relying on your senses."

Ernst was euphoric. "Or, maybe it's just your heart showing off." He blew into the tiny kite and it billowed like a spinnaker. "Let's try it."

"What the hell." She laughed and ran across the field.

The tiny kite spun on its burgundy tether, corkscrewing behind Lisa as she ran. It rose, then spiraled down, then rose again, each time gaining more altitude until it disappeared. The burgundy string seemed to end in a billowing cloud.

She called to him. "We're flying a whole cloud, Ernst."

He stood behind her, and she leaned into his chest. He reached one hand up along hers to the yarn; his other arm circled her waist.

A young boy, perhaps five or six, stood by them looking up into the sky to see what it was on the end of their string.

"What are you doing, mister?"

"We're flying that cloud. Want to try?"

The boy backed up, eyes wide, and started to walk away. "No, mister. No thanks." He ran off, back to his mother.

The cloud pulled ever so slightly against them and Ernst felt anything was possible.

$$\star \quad \star \quad \star \quad \star \quad \star \quad \star \quad \star \quad \star \quad \star \quad \star$$

Though living at home was awkward, uneasy, it was less fraught than he had anticipated. His mother was so consumed with her own affairs that she left him alone, a relief at first. But periodically he felt ignored, sometimes actively shunned and often confused. Was she indifferent? Had he done something terribly wrong? Or was this just the person Gertrude Techow was, and he could only see it now, as an adult?

Contrary to Hans Gerd's expectations, living close to Kurfürstendamm was not exciting, and, in any case, he had little of his own money to spend. His mother's cooking was not Frau Stummel's. They argued regularly. At times she seemed afraid of Hans Gerd, and that distressed Ernst the most. She gave Hans Gerd the largest bedroom of the three so he could not complain of yet another inequity in his miserable life.

Whenever Kern asked, Ernst would drive a large flatbed truck lettered **'BAVARIAN WOOD PRODUCTS'**. He was called upon at least once a week. Guns and drugs were easily hidden in a nest under logs and planks that discouraged border guards. Ernst contributed a portion of his monthly stipend from the Association to his mother's rent and food budget, and a portion he kept for books and other fees.

Studying literature again opened a window into a long neglected chamber in his mind and heart. Mostly it was liberating, but it also caused him to wonder about fighting and killing and how that reality in his own life could coexist, however uneasily, in the same soul as poetry and art.

After he'd been home for a month he met Kern again. He was dressed in mufti when he approached Ernst at the University and asked him to undertake an important task for the Association – to take careful notes of the trial of a young man, Simon Wolff, who was accused of stealing morphine from the Charité Hospital's pharmacy. The Association needed a discrete presence and a daily summary of the young man's testimony.

Ernst sat in the back of the small courtroom hunched over a notebook trying to keep up with the head judge's reading of the indictment. He could only see the back of the defendant's head, but Simon Wolff looked like a boy, a tuft of dark hair standing up from the back of his head. A woman sat behind him, almost certainly his mother, her gray hair tied in a bun. She leaned forward as close as possible to her son. The first witness was called, and Ernst was confused when he heard his own mother's name and looked up from his notes to see her enter the witness box. He shifted himself on the bench so the large man in the row ahead blocked him from view. She answered the judge's questions with reserve and had to be reminded to speak up.

"I work on the TB ward – the same floor as the Pharmacy. It was a Tuesday, I first noticed the young man..."

"Is that young man the defendant?" The judge leaned forward.

"Yes, your Honor. Simon Wolff. He was reading a magazine near the pharmacy window." She picked at the skin of her neck. "I asked if I could help him and he answered no, but I could tell he was quite uneasy. The next week he was there again, this time engaged in conversation with one of the assistant pharmacists."

"And why should you remember such a banal detail?" Simon Wolff's counsel, Dr. Lütgebrune, interrupted.

"When I approached, they both looked at me with suspicious glances and moved farther down the hall. Later that afternoon I picked up a crumpled paper behind the trash basket outside the pharmacy. I was about to discard it when I recognized the letterhead of the University of Berlin. My son attends the University so I looked at the letter. It was addressed to Simon Wolff, informing him that his dormitory room and student fees were overdue and he would not be able to register for the fall semester. I threw the letter into the trash without thinking of it again.

"A week later I was questioned by a police inspector. All I could tell him was about a suspicious young man and the letter. I remembered the name – Simon Wolff."

"And did you identify Simon Wolff two days later at the police station at Belle-Alliance Platz?" the judge asked.

"Yes. I did."

Ernst could not get his pen to write down that it was his mother's testimony that led to Wolff's apprehension. Was this why Kern gave him the job? Had Ernst just incurred a debt? After her testimony his mother sat directly behind Frau Wolff as the State's Prosecutor began a withering examination of her increasingly terrified son. Was Simon Wolff a member of the Association of Nationally Minded soldiers, also known as the Association of Former Ehrhardt Officers?

"Objection!" Dr. Lütgebrune, the flamboyant defense attorney for Nationalist causes, sprang to his feet. Despite his advanced age, his presence loomed large. He was a tall man with broad shoulders and a precisely trimmed goatee. A shock of white hair fell across his rugged forehead and he pushed it back, then stroked each side of his mustache.

"Objection overruled."

"Just what kind of organization is this, Herr Wolff?" The prosecutor stared out at the spectators as he asked the question.

The boy mumbled something about not really knowing much at all.

"Speak up, Herr Wolff!"

"I really don't know..."

"We can't hear you, Herr Wolff. Just what kind of organization is this Association?"

"I have already explained the fraternal nature..."

"Have you ever been a member of the Marine Brigade Ehrhardt?"

"No, no, never."

"You are already in serious jeopardy due to the stolen morphine found in your room. Your cooperation will only lessen your sentence. Did you steal the morphine for Captain Ehrhardt?"

"Yes, sir," he mumbled.

"The court cannot hear you."

"Yes, sir, I was ordered by the Association to steal the morphine."

"Why, Herr Wolff?"

"For the Upper Silesian campaign. For the defense of German soil..."

"Did you know that stealing narcotics is a serious offense?"

"Yes, sir, I did."

"But you stole the morphine anyway."

"I had no choice. I was forced to do it."

"You could have come to the police. Why didn't you?"

Young Wolff, his eyes darting back and forth from the prosecutor to Lütgebrune, and then around the courtroom, licked his lips. His breath came short, and he blinked frequently. "It would be a betrayal. They would kill me."

"Come, come, Herr Wolff. You described this as a fraternal brotherhood of former soldiers. Social organizations do not kill their members."

"This is different," he whispered.

"Speak up, young man!" The court president thundered from the bench.

"This is different. They have killed others – they mean what they say."

"Who are these people, Herr Wolff?" the prosecutor said.

"I... I cannot . . I cannot say, sir."

"But you already did. In your pre-trial depositions you named," he looked at his notes, "let me see, Ehrhardt, Tillessen, Hoffmann, von Killinger, Plaas, von Salomon, Manfred and Kern. Would you like to add to this list? It might lighten your sentence."

Ernst looked up, startled. The boy blinked urgently.

"No!" He had a wild look in his eyes. "They said it would never be used! They lied! I hadn't yet talked to my lawyer."

"I object, your honor," Lütgebrune rose again. "The prosecution is badgering the witness with irrelevant details about a social club."

"Sustained!"

"The prosecution rests, Herr President. The defendant has already admitted guilt to the charge of theft and transfer of a controlled narcotic. His signed confession has been entered as evidence. We merely wish to suggest a more nefarious conspiracy behind this theft."

On cross examination, Dr. Lütgebrune, his chest thrust forward, thumbs hooked in the pockets of a checkered vest, asked Simon Wolff what the morphine was to be used for, and the prosecutor leapt from his seat to object. The presiding judge overruled him and, in a more kindly tone, encouraged the wilted young man to answer his lawyer's question honestly.

"The morphine was for the men of the Free Corps." His mouth twitched as he tried to be brave. He sat taller in the severe wooden chair of the witness stand. On the judge's order the bailiff brought him a glass of water, and he could continue.

"The Free Corps were fighting in Upper Silesia – fighting the Poles and the Russians – protecting the Vaterland. They needed medical supplies. Were it not for Versailles, the government would be providing such necessities to these front-line soldiers, but Weimar is..."

The presiding judge leaned over the bench and said, "Young man, please slow down. The stenographer is unable to keep up. Just relax, breathe deeply and tell the truth. Now proceed." He smiled and waved his fingers at the boy.

"Yes, sir. Thank you, sir. Weimar is reluctant to violate the Versailles treaty, so patriots must take matters into their own hands."

"Was it the right thing to do, Herr Wolff?" Attorney Lütgebrune emphasized the word 'right', then let his voice drop at the end of the question, in an avuncular manner.

"No sir, it was not right, but it was necessary."

"Necessary?"

"Yes, sir, for the survival of the Vaterland – for national defense."

"You believed you were acting for the national defense, and not for personal gain?"

"Yes, sir."

"How much did you earn from the transfer of the morphine from the hospital to the soldiers in Upper Silesia?"

"Nothing, sir. I did it for the Vaterland."

"We should give you a medal, not prosecute you." He looked at the Chief Judge. "I have no further questions."

The Chief Judge and the lawyers debated the 'necessity defense' for the deliberating judges. Dr. Lütgebrune argued vigorously that in times of national emergency, violating the law for the greater good of the nation, in deference to a higher law based on universal principles, was not only permissible, but honorable.

The prosecutor vigorously rejected this notion, suggesting that chaos would result. If every political party in Germany exercised its will in response to a 'higher law' the national system of justice would collapse.

While the judges deliberated the verdict, Ernst moved up to the row behind his mother. He was about to touch her shoulder when she leaned forward. "My name is Frau Techow – Gertrude Techow," he heard her say. "You are Simon Wolff's mother?"

The woman turned to Frau Techow, nodded and dabbed at her eyes. Ernst sat back.

She continued. "I wanted to tell you, as one mother to another... I am so sorry for having testified against your son. I thought it was a simple case of theft. I didn't know the rest. My own son, Ernst, is not much older than your Simon. He was in the Ehrhardt Brigade. He works for the same Association as your son. It could be my Ernst in that docket instead of your Simon."

"I don't understand." Frau Wolff opened a crocheted handkerchief that she had worked into a ball.

"Your Simon is a true son of Germany – a good young man – like my son, Ernst."

"Thank you Frau Techow." Her eyes were rimmed red.

"If you like, I will sit by you when the judges come in. I think it will be soon." Frau Techow laid her hand on the woman's arm.

The Judge's door opened, and the three presiding judges processed into the courtroom followed by the court President, all dressed in black robes and white wigs. The President rapped his gavel.

"The Court is in session." He struck his gavel again, replaced his pince nez glasses, and read from a document. "Have the justices come to a conclusion in the matter of The Weimar Republic vs. Simon Wolff?"

The three judges stood, and the one closest to the President said, "We have, Herr President."

"The accused will stand and face the panel."

Simon Wolff stood, unsteadily, holding onto the back of his chair. Ernst could clearly see the tremor in his legs.

"How do you find?"

"We find the defendant, Simon Wolff, guilty of one count of transferring a regulated narcotic without proper authorization."

A murmur spread through the courtroom. He had been charged with twelve counts of drug smuggling, three counts of theft and twelve counts of violating the narcotics code.

Ernst looked back and forth between Frau Wolff and Dr. Lütgebrune, who smiled coyly. The lawyer locked his thumbs in his vest and puffed out his chest.

The judge pounded for silence. As the crowd hushed, the President of the court, his pinched face pale and small in his black robes, read from a prepared text. "The judgment of this court is accepted. Simon Wolff, you are sentenced to time already served and a fine of 1,000 Reichmarks payable over twelve months."

Again the gavel fell, and the dark judges fluttered out of the agitated courtroom.

Simon Wolff hugged his mother and sobbed openly, spasmodically, like a frightened child who very nearly fell off the precipice and knows it.

Ernst leaned forward. "Mother!"

She turned, twin streaks of tears glistening, a bewildered furrow in her brow. She hugged him and would not let go, her own tears coming freely. Ernst could not remember feeling his mother's arms so fiercely about him, and all he could feel was heartache for what had never been.

As they walked out of the courtroom Ernst explained that he was reporting on the trial for the Association. "They will be pleased," he said.

"Were you here for the whole trial?" Her demeanor chilled again.

"Yes. I heard your testimony. It's not important, Mother. Justice was served. Are you going home?"

"No, I have to return to the hospital. I work until seven." As they left the building the sudden glare of the day blinded them until they could accommodate the light.

At the bottom of the courthouse steps she stopped and turned to Ernst. "When you drive that truck – is it for the same Association that boy talked about?"

"I drive for the Bavarian Wood Products Company. That's all."

She stopped abruptly and dug her fingers into his arm. "Ernst Werner Techow, tell me the truth!"

He looked away. "Try not to worry, Mother. By the way, I won't be home for dinner tonight."

She looked warily at Ernst. "That boy, Wolff. Is he a hero or a traitor?"

"I suppose he's both. But he's only a boy. I'm sure he'll be fine." Her trolley screeched to a halt, and before she mounted the steps, he added, "He shouldn't have named names."

★　★　★　★　★　★　★　★　★　★

Günther's apartment on Lindenstrasse, a frequent gathering place for students to drink beer and argue the politics of the day, was uncharacteristically empty and not well kept. As instructed, Ernst laid the thick envelop on Günther's dresser. In the envelope he counted 40,000 Reichmarks wrapped in a paper tape on which was written 'ERZBERGER!!!' In the same envelope was Ernst's itinerary for delivery of 'pine logs and boards' to Upper Silesia.

Ernst paced the living room, picking up Günther's clothing where he had strewn it on the sofa, the overstuffed chair, and the floor. He checked his watch. Lisa would arrive any minute now. He'd been here frequently, but without the distraction of other students and their spirited discourse, he noted details in the apartment as if for the first time. It was larger than he remembered, dark with the drapes pulled closed across a wall of windows. Ernst pulled them open, squinting in the late afternoon sun, grateful for the warmth. A photograph of Kaiser Wilhelm II hung on the wall opposite the window and the setting sun reflected off the glass in such a way as to animate the dark picture. Beside the portrait hung a large red flag with a white disk in the center, upon which was imprinted a black swastika. Student posters from the recent revolution hung on the walls.

WANTED: DEAD

RED ROSA AND THE
SPARTAKISTS.

VERSAILLES !

The Stab In The Back
DO NOT SIGN THE TREATY!!!
Rally: St. John's Day, June 24, 1919
The Reichstag

As six o'clock approached he could feel his pulse quicken and the apartment felt too warm and still smelled of cigarette smoke. He opened a window and the screech of a trolley's wheels swept in on a warm breeze. In the small kitchen just off the entrance hallway Ernst stirred and tasted the pasta sauce – a recipe from his mother's new cookbook – and uncorked a bottle of burgundy. His father had always warned that "a bottle of good red wine must be allowed to breathe for half an hour before pouring." He wasn't sure if that injunction pertained to 'not so good red wine'. It was too late to do anything about the stack of soiled dishes in Günther's sink.

Ernst combed his hair once more in the mirror in the bedroom. From downstairs he heard the slam and latch of the heavy front door to the building, followed by light steps running up the stairs, then slowing to a walk the last few steps, followed by a pause and a faint knock. He waited a decent interval behind the door, took a deep breath and opened it. It was hard to tell in the shadow of the hallway, but Lisa seemed to be blushing, a coy smile on her colored lips. She tilted her head to one side, and the apartment light cast shadows under her cheekbones, the leisurely curve of her neck accentuated by a low cut white blouse.

"Bon soir, Mademoiselle!" Ernst bowed formally and offered his arm like a gentleman at a club. "Voila, Mädchen. Behold, zee flat of Günther. Merveilleux, n'est-ce pas? May I take zee lady's wrap?"

When she took off her red beret, Ernst thought her hair a golden waterfall. "Günther lives here all alone?" she said, looking around, her eyes wide. "Fritz told me about this, but I've never been here. It's huge. It must cost a fortune. How does he do it?" She walked into the center of the living room and turned all around. Privacy was a rare commodity; students lived seven, even ten to a small flat.

"Günther is well connected," Ernst said. "Maybe too well connected. Hasn't he offered to get you perfume or caviar?"

"He has asked me for a date." She walked to the row of windows, where a hint of early twilight glowed over the silhouetted apartment building across the street. The last rays of sun still poured through the window, momentarily revealing her breasts through her silk blouse.

He felt aroused. "And you said...?"

"I said no thanks. I'm Fritz's girl. I just let him go on thinking that."

"But you're not, right?"

She turned back to him, silhouetted by the sun. "I'm here, aren't I?"

He imagined for a moment what her blouse would feel like, silken, smooth, like his mother's favorite scarf. A whiff of her perfume set his skin tingling with goose flesh, the hairs on his forearms erect.

They drank their first glass of wine and ate small helpings of 'Ernst's Pasta Surprise.' Neither was too hungry, but they eagerly exchanged news and stories. She was back in the GNYO and glad for it. Fritz was becoming a campus hero because of his activism. Margaret's married man had cut off their affair and she was very sad. "I'd love to see the drawings you made, while you were away."

He thought of all his drawings of Wanda and the sweet solace of her paid-for love. No one would ever see those. Thinking of her, he recalled the same arousal, the same physical agitation begging for relief. Best to think of something else. "How is it with your father these days?"

She laughed, more contemptuous than amused. "He's angry with me for breaking up with Horst. He doesn't know what happened. Maybe I should tell him, but I'm afraid he would make me come home. So we play a little game. He doesn't want to know. He pretends I'm his innocent little girl. He wants to believe a fiction – and no fool is as easy to fool as a willing fool."

"Who said that?"

"I did, silly – just now. Do you think I'm brilliant?" She posed like a movie queen.

"You're sensational." Their eyes met, and her dramatic persona melted. He poured another glass.

Lisa leaned back against the sofa cushion. "What's your mother like?"

He didn't know why, but Ernst began with the stillbirth and how everything went wrong after that. He meant to tell a version of his history in which she was to blame, but curiously he found himself feeling proud of his mother and what she had had to overcome. He explained about Hans Gerd and how his father's death had capsized her life. He described her work at Charité Hospital and her commitment to the patients.

"I'd like to meet her."

It was Lisa's presence, her question that summoned Ernst's tender assessment. But it was incomplete, and he felt he had to warn her. "She can be a bit stern."

"Was she a good mother – I mean when you were small?"

"My father was sterner. Is that a word – sterner? It ought to be. He used to pinch me, right here." He reached behind Lisa's neck and gently pinched where his father hurt him so often. He felt the silk of her collar and her hair. His breath stopped.

Her neck muscles stiffened ever so slightly, just enough for him to feel. She sat up to finish her second glass of wine. Ernst watched her cross the room to the heavy drapes and pull one side around her. He could see only her bare feet and slender calves. He wanted to go to her but felt the weight of those drapes. He plucked a cigarette from his metal case, leaned into the candle and sucked in the flame. The smoke would calm his heart.

"What do you see out there?" Ernst asked.

"The glow of Berlin – and one, two, no three stars."

"I remember the summer stars. Millions of them."

A police siren warbled, peaked and faded. "It's a selfish thing, a city," she said. "There's too much light in the city. Except for three stars, it blots out the rest of the universe."

"Some people are like that – shining too brightly – but we say they are geniuses."

She turned around and pulled back the curtain. "Fritz is brilliant like that."

Ernst winced and could think of no reply.

"So is Margaret. Margaret developed much earlier than I did – breasts at twelve. We played dress-up." She held onto the drapes to steady herself. "You wouldn't understand. Girls do that." She navigated the room, a little unsteady, and sat next to Ernst on the couch. "I was skinny and flat-chested for the longest time, but Margaret wriggled into my dresses and we would pretend to be a Bohemian couple." She picked a cigarette from Ernst's open case and held it at her lips until Ernst fumbled with a match; his hand trembled and she gently puffed on the flame. "Cinnamon sticks were our Turkish cigarillos and we talked about handsome revolutionaries and the new artists and Jazz." She pronounced it 'Yats'. "I didn't know a thing about Jazz, but Margaret had a 'friend' – we were only fourteen. On overnights at my house her man friend would come for her after ten, when everyone was asleep, and she would climb out my window. He took her to the clubs and cabarets. At two or three in the morning she would throw a pebble at my window and I'd let her in again. Then we would talk until morning."

Ernst craved the feel of her blouse again. There was no doubt she was a woman now.

"I can tell Margaret anything – my most closely guarded secrets. And she is so honest. One of those times, when we played at being Bohemian, I blurted out that I didn't believe in God. I'm not sure if I was trying to play the part of an intellectual snob, or if it really came from me, but I remember Margaret's face suddenly turned very serious." She furrowed her brow. "I remember being afraid of her for the first time."

"What did she say?"

"She was surprised that I hadn't heard that God had been killed in the Great War." Lisa leaned back beside Ernst and curled her feet up, like a cat. "Margaret says things like that. Things that make you think for a long, long time."

The light was fading. They both stared at half drawn drapes until Lisa said, "How long have we known each other, Ernst?"

"Six years, since 1914."

"Remember how we first met?"

He laughed. "Pretty stupid, wasn't it." He pointed to her glass. "More?"

"What the hell. But I have to be back in the dormitory at ten o'clock. Not sober, just back."

A slight tremor in his hand tinkled the bottle against her wine glass.

"I just remember you pushing Fritz into the fruit stand to get my attention. I knew that's what you were doing. You were very sweet and a little crazy."

"I just bumped him! He fell."

She giggled. "I think you were jealous even then. All that fruit – oranges, apples rolling all over the street – and that angry little vendor."

"I was really scared," Ernst remembered with a chill. "I thought Fritz would die. But I didn't want you to like him. I thought you were the prettiest girl in all the camp."

Lisa sat forward, serious, studying Ernst. "You were so angry," she said.

"You're very complicated, Ernst. It's as if there are two of you at war with each other. The strange thing is that I first met the angry Ernst and still, I liked you right away. My father is an angry man. Horst is an angry man. I mean, all I knew was that you almost killed your friend, and I felt drawn to you. Isn't that strange?"

"You also stick yourself with pins," Ernst sat forward and their faces were but inches apart. He could smell the wine on her breath.

Lisa whispered. "And now I know the other Ernst, the artist who loves Monet, the gentle Ernst. And I'm drawn to that Ernst as well. Just as you think things are one way, suddenly they're another. It's so confusing. I much prefer the gentle you, but I understand the angry you."

The spell dissipated and Lisa backed away ever so slightly. Ernst cleared his throat and said he'd be right back with something special. He returned with a tray and set it down. On it he had set out a flickering candle, a silver spoon, a glass of water and four lead toy soldiers from his boyhood collection.

"Meine lieben Damen und Herren. Mes dames et messieurs –" He held the tray aloft on one palm. "Bleigiessen."

Lisa clapped. Her eyes twinkled. "I have a memory of my mother doing this with me before she died. I remember it was dark, only the candle. Mother hummed or sang very quietly – chanted or something mysterious."

Lisa selected a soldier – a lancer – and laid it in the spoon. "Turn off the light, Ernst. This one candle only." As she held the spoon over the candle, the soldier began to glisten and soften, slowly melt into a silver pool. Shadows flickered on the wall. "I'm thinking about this year – 1920." She tipped the spoon; the molten lead popped and hissed as it hit the water. She carefully retrieved the sudden sculpture from the waterglass, her fingers glistening as if ignited by the silver creation, turning it over and over until she saw it for what it was. "Ah. There it is. A horse jumping through a cloud. See, these are its front hooves and here is its face and mane, and this is the cloud."

Ernst turned it over in his hand and marveled at the likeness. "What does it mean?"

"Mi Caballo blanco," she said. "My White Horse. It's a Spanish song I learned from my aunt Clara when I was young. She lived in Chile and visited us every winter. She brought marvelous foods and magical stories. The words mean 'My white horse is as white as the dawn. We always travel together. He is my best friend. On the wings of happiness my horse races on. And in the arms of sorrow he bears me as well.'" She looked at Ernst and smiled. "It's a good omen. Now you do it."

As the lead melted, Ernst felt as if he, too had begun to transform into something undefined, liquid, from the hard Freebooooter, the angry Ernst, into – what? He had no idea, but it felt like a tide pulling him along. Anything was possible. He wondered how he might paint the sphere of lead, unsteady in the spoon, how to capture the silver candle reflection, like a water world lit by the sun. He thought of Lisa – what would be their story? How would his own life change because of Lisa? He tipped the spoon and the molten lead exploded in the water and hissed. Ernst examined his Bleiguss in the candle's light, their faces nearly touching, sharing the same heady wafts of wine breath.

"I see a woman, her hair and long dress blowing in the wind. She's running; here's one hand on her head, maybe holding a hat."

Lisa carefully turned it over in her hands. "Yes, I see her." She laid it gently in his palm and folded his fingers, as if they were the lid of a jewelry box. "What does it mean?"

"She looks like you." He blushed. "I think maybe she's you." He wanted her more than anything. Thoughts of her eclipsed every other, and he wondered how much was the wine, and how much what was to come. Ernst lifted his wine glass. "To your white horse."

"... and the girl in the wind – whoever she is."

They toasted their good fortune.

"Now," Lisa said, her words becoming thick. "This is very serious." She giggled. "This time you have to close your eyes. Empty your mind of everything except your breathing. This Bleiguss will tell you what is to become of your whole life. This part is the scariest because the year Mother died, I wondered if she saw that in her Bleiguss. It always scared me when I was younger. It's been many years since I did this."

"I think we should drop the lead into wine instead of water. Is that legal?"

"You see," she sat up, excited. "You think like an artist, Ruby. In wine it will surely be true."

Lisa heated another soldier and closed her eyes. The molten bead burst in the wine, spraying fine red mist on the glass.

"It's a tree being blown by a strong wind," she said. "Maybe the same wind that blows your girl. Look, here is the trunk, this smooth part, and here, where it feathers out, the leaves and the thinner branches. These are the roots. It's very definitely a tree."

"A sturdy image – resilient."

"Now you."

Whatever twilight had penetrated the drapes was now gone. They moved closer together over the candle, side by side.

Ernst melted a Hussaran Horse Guard and closed his eyes. His Bleiguss was a complex configuration, spherical but without smooth facets. Tiny lead filaments extended like wild hair. As he turned it over, the candle's light seemed to refashion the metal. Suddenly a face appeared, ageless, certainly not the face of youth or beauty. More features emerged: a bearded man, with a full round face, a pug nose, deep eyes, his hair in a storm about his face and over his head. "An odd looking man with a beard," he said. It was unavoidable, and once he saw the wild man, it could be nothing else.

"Yes, I see him – clearly. A formidable face."

"Should I be nervous?" he whispered.

Lisa continued to study the leaded bust. "Of course not. It's only a silly New Year's Eve game."

It unnerved him. He got up from the sofa and felt a powerful urge to throw it in the garbage. "I'll take these back to the kitchen," he said and cleared the dishes. They hadn't eaten much.

When he returned the head was gone and Lisa stood at the window again, the drapes drawn wide. It seemed so natural to walk up to her. "Do you remember when I first kissed you?" he asked.

She turned to him. His arms encircled her waist and she folded hers on his chest. He stroked the smooth silk of her blouse, inhaled the suggestion of perfume.

She closed her eyes. "At the lake. I remember hiding under the rock overhang, treading water. It was so cold."

"... and I kissed you – like this." He leaned forward and gently kissed her.

Their lips remained together, barely touching, and she whispered, "I thought I kissed you."

He pressed his body to hers and she did not pull away. They swayed as if to some mysterious music. Ever so slowly their lips parted, and they searched each other's eyes.

Their shadow flickered on the wall. He closed his eyes and recited Heine's verse.

> She thinks she's a lotus blossom,
> Whose petals will open soon,
> While he, her pale companion,
> Fancies himself the moon.

The lotus shyly bares her
cup to the moonlight above,
But instead of the seed of life, she
Receives a poem of love.

They lingered at the window, holding each other close. He told her how he had longed for her all these years, afraid of her rebuff – how he thought of her every day. She twisted from one side of his head to the other, kissing, sighing that she had always wanted him. He eased her onto the sofa and held one wine glass between them. She drank, then he, his other hand stroking her hair, fallen in a golden swirl onto her chest where he cupped her breast in his palm. Lisa leaned back on the cushion, her eyes closed. He slowly undid the buttons of her blouse. Her arms rested at her side. She moaned softly with each caress of her breasts.

"Come with me," he whispered.

They drifted into the bedroom in each other's arms. Slowly, deliberately, he eased her blouse from her shoulders; it floated to the floor. She lay back, and he loosened his belt, then lay down beside her, finding her lips again, turning into her caress, her thighs parting to enclose him.

Abruptly, Lisa rolled from under Ernst's weight. She kissed him and sat up. He looked at her quizzically. She held up her hand, as if to say, stop.

"Don't you want to...?" he asked.

"Yes... oh yes, I do." She kissed him again. "But I do not want a child – or an abortion." She retrieved a condom from the pocket of her skirt.

They removed brassiere, pants and underwear until they were both completely naked. In the candlelight their bodies shone like animal fur, faint color in the darkness. They stood together, he aroused, she willing, their hands exploring, fondling, groping. Lips wet, hot breath, her groans and his a duet. They lay down together rolling over once, twice, their lips locked in unquenchable desire.

The telephone rang. Ernst started to sit up, but Lisa held him back. She lay on top of him. They kissed again. She whispered, "Oh, Ernst," kneeling over him, her thighs straddling his hips. "You are so beautiful."

"I don't want this to end," he whispered. "Ever."

Her hair hung like a yellow curtain over his chest. Her breasts felt firm, nipples hard and sensitive. Her breath became short and excited. Ever so slowly, she eased him deeper and deeper inside her then lay onto him, into his lips, caressing his head. Ernst rolled to be over her.

"Slowly, my darling. I want this to last a long time."

And it did. They climaxed together in the most exquisite pas de deux.

Afterwards, Ernst still inside her, they lay facing each other, looking into the pools that were their candlelit eyes, tender kissing and stroking. And that was how they fell asleep.

★　★　★　★　★　★　★　★　★　★

Two days later the body of Simon Wolff was found hanging in the courtyard of the Charité Hospital. A note was tied to the dagger that protruded from his chest:

> He betrayed the cause
> was found guilty
> and judgment was executed
>
> — The Feme

12

Organization C

June 1920 – August 1921

When Ernst left the Free Corps, a beer at the Corps Teutonia Pub could be had for less than one mark; three months later it cost five marks. Still the students came: some to forget, if only for an evening, some to grieve or grumble about defeat, to mourn the one year anniversary of the "stab in the back" Versailles Treaty – disarmament, territorial concessions in Europe and Africa, crushing reparations, Allied occupation of the Rhineland, guilt and humiliation. Indignity metastasized deep and wide with escalating bitterness as the consequences of Versailles were felt and the economy reeled. Pub conversations revolved around strategies to bring down Weimar.

In the aftermath of the Kapp putsch, the new Socialist chancellor, Hermann Müller, hoped that public disgust with extremism from the right and the left would translate into a victory at the polls for moderate Socialism and the 'Weimar Coalition'. He called for the election on June 6, 1920, a week before university examinations. In those frenzied weeks before the voting, Fritz was a cyclone of activity. He organized student rallies, gave speeches at sports clubs, pubs, student clubs, book clubs and garden clubs, and he met daily with GNYO committees and worked past midnight with planning committees. It was by now well known that he had been chosen to be the student aide to the leading Nationalist in the Reichstag, Karl Helfferich. As head of the German National People's Party (DNVP) Helfferich railed against the fulfillment of Versailles and filed a very public and provocative lawsuit against the democratic Catholic leader, Matthias Erzberger, a signatory to the Versailles Treaty.

After the election Fritz collapsed and slept for two days, then plunged into preparing for his examinations. Two weeks later, when Ernst met him for lunch at the Corps Teutonia, he saw the toll these past weeks had taken on his old friend. Fritz had grown stout from too many wurst und bier meetings, dark circles hung below his sallow eyes, but his enthusiasm was undiminished.

He could hardly contain himself. "Twenty-six percent!" His bloodshot eyes sparkled. "We more than doubled our vote from four to nine million. We have one quarter of the seats. There is no Weimar majority. It's astounding – a political revolution."

"What's astounding is your incorrigible optimism," Ernst said.

"If you came to more GNYO meetings you'd share my optimism. We can broker a coalition and win a majority in a year."

"And it will last six months."

"Under Versailles what's the alternative?"

Fritz thought like a politician. Ernst harbored more romantic ideas, still resonant from his *Wandervogel* days. "Something that will last a thousand years."

"Free Corps days are over, old friend. It's time for political solutions."

Fritz launched into his well-practiced exhortation about the 'stab in the back', the Nationalist agenda, Polish and Russian immigrants, Slavs, Jews, racial purity and mental defectives.

Though agreeing in principal with Fritz's vindication of the Nationalist cause, Ernst found he had nothing else to speak about with his old friend. Their relationship had become one-dimensional, banal, neither fulfilling nor jovial as it had once been. He supposed that was a consequence of growing older and growing apart. Compounding his discomfort, when Fritz held forth, Ernst felt inadequate, as if it was his failure. Such a vital time in German history, yet Ernst felt uninspired by current events. The only passion that was aroused was that for Lisa. Conversing with Fritz had become more a sparring match than a friendship, and now that Ernst felt confident about Lisa's feelings for him, he felt a devilish desire to tell Fritz about their evening together. But something held him back – a superstition that relishing his victory would only condemn it to failure. He itched to tell Fritz about Kern and Manfred and Ehrhardt, as if they were still *Wandervogel*, intent on impressing each other. But on pain of death he was not at liberty to talk about the Association, especially not since von Killinger had taken command in München. So Ernst had to content himself with an uncommon, if private, sense of superiority – or even simple pity – that Fritz was ignorant of his tryst with Lisa. And for all his connections, Fritz was certainly ignorant of the secret army with cached weapons, waiting, submerged like crocodiles in the swamp of Weimar.

Ernst interrupted him. "Your skin is pale. Ivory is your nickname, not your skin color. You should enjoy life a little – get more fresh air."

"I'll leave that to you. After examinations you, me, and Lisa should get together again. Like the old days. It's been too long."

"Does Lisa still come to your meetings?"

"Less than she used to," Fritz said. "She's very serious about her classes. I admire that, even in a woman." Fritz spoke matter-of-factly and wiped beer foam from his lips, then detached from Ernst again in a diatribe about Nationalist strategy and his role as president of the GNYO, a jumble of names, vote counts. Finally, something seemed to snap in Fritz, and he stopped his train of words to ask, "What about you and Lisa? Are you seeing each other?"

"Some," Ernst said, and knew in that moment, he would never tell Fritz.

Fritz looked sad or confused, maybe conflicted about whether to continue the conversation, Ernst could not tell. Then he smiled and said, "You look well tanned. What's your secret?"

Ernst showed Fritz his dark left arm and much lighter right arm. "I drive a truck for occasional jobs. Very asymmetric exposure, and very boring. I don't recommend it."

"But good money, eh? Who did you say you drove for?"

"Bavarian Wood Products. It's good part-time work."

★   ★   ★   ★   ★   ★   ★   ★   ★   ★

More than a year later, in May 1921, the beer was no better, but cost twenty-five marks, five times as much. Lisa was studying at Heidelberg for a term, and Ernst missed her terribly. When they were together at the University they went out several times a week but Lisa asked that they not sleep together for now – it was too distracting, too complicated. Their night of Bleigiessen and love making was extraordinary – a perfect jewel, she said, and that was how it should remain for now. Until her studies were complete, she was not prepared for anything more committed.

Ernst elbowed through the Corps Teutonia dinner crowd, acknowledging greetings and relishing the familiar fetor of stale tobacco and beer. Attached to Ernst's monthly check from the Bavarian Wood Products Company in May was a letter from Kern. Ernst had been recommended for membership in Organization Consul – OC – a secret Nationalist organization formed by

Captain Ehrhardt and his lieutenants after the Kapp Putsch. Tonight, at a secret Stammtisch, 'trunk table' meeting, where OC operatives in Berlin regularly gathered, he was to be inducted in a clandestine initiation ceremony. Kern's note went on to say that because of inflation, Ernst would henceforth be paid in Swiss francs, and he urged Ernst to change any savings, along with those of his mother, into Swiss francs, Dutch stocks or durable goods.

Captain von Killinger had assumed control of the military division of Organization C, and he would be present tonight, representing the new leadership of Captain Alfred Hoffmann and Lieutenant Karl Tillessen. Each German city had its own OC with its Stammtisch, and representatives of each frequented the others. Ernst sometimes attended the Berlin Stammtisch on the second Thursday of each month. It satisfied a hunger to honor that recent chapter of his life, to be the veteran with his mates, who had faced death together. There was no easy separation from the ties that bound him to those who would always be comrades, if not friends. Kern often came from Münich and talked about a national web linking a powerful cadre of underground Nationalists, of an instant army ready to mobilize, and, most critical of all, of brilliant leadership. It was a necessary counterweight to Fritz's misplaced optimism that politics would carry the Nationalist cause to victory. Ernst met the Kerns and von Killingers from every region of the country. Last month, Hartmut Plaas, 'The Fat Man' from Münich, had visited the Berlin Stammtisch for the first time. The recording secretary of OC-Hannover visited the same night. Another Ernst, Ernst von Salomon, also from Münich, came to the last four meetings, and he and Ernst took an immediate liking to each other, if for no other reason than their shared literary taste. At their first meeting they argued about Goethe and Rilke, and though von Salomon talked and smoked too much, Ernst felt a fondness grow between them.

With the notable exception of Captain von Killinger, the OC plotters were often physically small men – bureaucrats and politicians – not at all the brutes of the Free Corps. Von Salomon proved the stereotype, weighing no more than 130 lbs and standing half a head shorter than Ernst. Von Salomon's forehead slanted back to his short-cropped sandy hair, making his face protrude from his skull. Ernst thought his an almost simian profile.

Each month twenty or more eager students and hardened junior officers ate sausage and drank beer at the Berlin OC Stammtisch, where Heinz Ehrentraut, the pompous head of Berlin's OC, was called 'The Rector' because he had been a notoriously harsh headmaster at a school for delinquent boys in Mainz. He, too, was a slight man with a small head, bespectacled, his bony face pointed, bird-like.

On the night of his induction into OC at the Corps Teutonia, Ernst finished a cigarette in the dark hall leading to one of 'Max's rooms'. He took a deep breath as he ground the butt under his heel. This was going to be embarrassing, he thought, and he wondered why he merited the honor.

Through the door to The Kaiser Room he heard lusty singing. He held the doorknob and listened for the next chant to begin before he let himself into the room and turned his back on those assembled to close the door quietly, as if he was intruding. It felt hotter in the room, and he was already sweating. There was one empty chair at each end of the long elliptical table, and students sat behind the elite. Ernst had to look twice before he recognized his former Ehrhardt Brigade Comrade, Gustav Steinbeck from Dresden. In the intervening years he had grown an extra chin, his face was wider, his large head almost bald. As head of the GNYO, and a rising star in Adolf Hitler's National Socialist German Workers Party, the NSDAP, his presence added weight to Ernst's induction. Steinbeck recognized Ernst and signaled a greeting as he sang a rousing funny new song.

> Why should we cry when a putsch goes wrong?
> There's another one coming before very long.
> So say good-bye – but remember, men,
> In a couple of weeks we will try it again!

Steinbeck pulled out one of the empty high-backed chairs and motioned to Ernst. "Ernst, come sit here beside me, in the seat of honor. Beer? It's ghastly hot." Steinbeck tapped his watch and whispered in Ernst's ear, "Almost late to your own induction. Tsk, tsk. You haven't changed, Techow." He slapped his back. "A toast, gentlemen! To our esteemed driver – our courier par excellence, veteran of the 'naked firefight in Silesia'." There was a round of laughter, the stomping of heavy booted feet and the thumping of beer steins on the table. "And tonight – our newest 'rook', Ernst Werner Techow."

Applause thundered, and they emptied their beer glasses.

At Ernst's left elbow, von Salomon held forth as usual with a few students sitting behind him. When Ernst sat down he turned his attention to him. "Welcome, Techow. I was just explaining to these young pups how Kapp shrank from putting even a single parliamentarian up against the wall. A lost opportunity, don't you think?" Von Salomon seemed to be probing Ernst.

"Here! Here!" Günther exclaimed. "I overheard every meeting with that damn fool. My desk was right outside von Lüttwitz's office all during the Putsch."

Thinking back to the times he had eaten lunch with Günther during the Putsch, Ernst recalled hearing almost nothing through the door. But tonight he could forgive even Günther, who was, after all, no more or less an opportunist than anyone else at the table, just more dramatic. And the use of his apartment was gift enough to keep Ernst silent while knowing the truth.

Opposite Ernst, at the other end of the ellipse, another high-backed throne chair waited, empty. At each end of the table was a candelabra fashioned to represent a three dimensional swastika. The candelabra's arms made a horizontal cross, and four black candles, unlit, turned up from each crooked arm.

Steinbeck touched his shoulder. "Ernst, do you know Herr Plaas?"

Ernst reached across the table to shake the fleshy, cold hand of Hartmut Plaas, also known as The Fat Man. Plaas occupied two places beside von Salomon and, even with his jacket off and sleeves rolled up, he sweated heavily. His stubbly blond hair glistened with the sheen of the over-nourished. Plaas did not smile.

"We have met before, Herr Plaas." Ernst said. The Fat Man's handshake was soft, like a woman's.

"I am eminently memorable," he said with a thick north German accent, "and you are not, yet I remember you clearly." His grip slowly tightened. "Why is that?"

Ernst could almost hear heads turn toward them, and he felt an unsettling silence. "When I first met you," The Fat Man continued, "I told Tillessen you would go far – that we needed men such as yourself." Ernst's hand slid from his fleshy grip. "And now, here you are."

The door opened, letting in the pub's giddy disorder. The shadow of Captain von Killinger filled the bright doorway, completely soldierly in bearing, his black tie and dinner jacket a uniform. Everyone in the room rose in silence until he motioned and said, "At ease." Von Killinger's aide, wiry and small, took his cape and gloves. Ernst thought of Zamboni, the strong man at the circus, and suppressed a smile.

The 'Rector', Heinz Ehrentraut, head of Berlin's OC, his bird-like head bent forward and tilted to one side as if his neck was too weak, cleared his throat and stood in place, studying his notes. "We are deeply honored to welcome Captain von Killinger, our distinguished chief of the military division from

Münich. He has been kind enough to witness tonight's ceremony. Let us proceed with the induction, and then Captain von Killinger has a few remarks."

"Many thanks, Herr Ehrentraut." Von Killinger clicked his heels and bowed a few degrees and turned to Ernst. He stared hard at him from the far end of the ellipse. The table was cleared of everything save the two candelabras, three bottles of Scotch whiskey, and a shot glass before each man. The bar maid and students were asked to leave. The electric lights were extinguished, and the black candles were lit. The room went silent. Each man sat straight-spined, hands in his lap, head bowed. From his vantage point Ernst could see every man's profile; he noticed Günther's eyes flitting like a weasel's as if he was taking mental notes. Ernst felt a hypnotic sense of sanctification as the full significance of the ceremony soaked in.

The room flickered with candlelight. At a signal from 'The Rector' each man produced his Free Corps dagger and laid it down before him like a crucifix. The light of eight black candles glinted off sixteen polished blades. The whiskey bottles passed around the table, and each man filled his glass. After several moments of silence, The 'Rector' produced a small handbook and opened to a dog-eared page.

"We are men of the Volkish race of Germans. Proud and brave – tempered in battle – hardened in peace."

They chanted in unison. *"We are the front line soldiers of the thousand year Reich."*

"Our spiritual aims include the cultivation and dissemination of Nationalist thinking; warfare against all anti-Nationalists and internationalists; warfare against Jewry, social democracy and leftist-radicalism; fomentation of internal unrest in order to attain the overthrow of the anti-Nationalist Weimar constitution."

"We are the front line soldiers of the thousand year Reich."

"Our material aims are the organization of determined, Nationalist-minded men into shock troops for disrupting meetings of an anti-Nationalist nature; maintenance of arms and the preservation of military ability; the education of youth in the use of arms."

"We are the front line soldiers of the thousand year Reich."

"Only those men who have determination, who obey unconditionally and who are without scruples will be accepted into this secret organization. All members will swear the Oath."

Each man held his dagger's blade before his eyes and pressed the swastika to his forehead. Ernst's hand shook with a disconcerting mixture of pride and trepidation. He felt in the grip of something so powerful, brimming with such potential energy – poised to change the world. Their eyes closed; they recited from memory:

"I swear unconditional obedience to the Supreme Leader. I swear to remain absolutely silent in regard to all activities of the organization, or death shall be my lot. All traitors will fall to the Feme."

"Ernst Werner Techow – rise."

He stood, his dagger still before his eyes, the swastika warm against his skin.

"Ernst Werner Techow, on this ninth day of June, 1921, I confer upon you the sacred trust of membership in the Organization Consul."

At 'the Rector's' signal each raised his shot glass to Ernst and, starting with von Killinger, one by one each drank quickly, then turned his glass upside down, the percussive ripple circling the table.

After another moment of silence, Von Killinger reached his hand over the candelabra and, looking directly at Ernst, extinguished each candle with the palm of his hand, darkening half the table.

"Herr Techow. You will do the same with the candles at your end. Do it quickly, without consideration, without fear. It is the way to execute necessary, though painful deeds and minimize pain or second thoughts."

In a trance Ernst lowered his palm onto the candles, each in succession. He felt the compulsion to obey, winced from the flame and hot wax, smelled the smoke of each dying light. The last candle spluttered out, and the room was dark except for the line of light under the door.

After a decent interval, Ehrentraut turned on the electric lights. "Captain von Killinger," he said. "We eagerly await your remarks."

Von Killinger rose and cleared his throat. "Captain Ehrhardt sends his regrets. He hoped to be here as well, but some unpleasantness in Münich demands his attention. I congratulate our newest member, Ernst Werner Techow. Of note, OC inducted his younger brother, Hans Gerd Techow, in a similar ceremony only a few months ago. Your little brother precedes you. We expect great achievements from you both. Your reputation is good. Your former commander, Lieutenant Manfred, speaks fondly of you, almost as a father. Lieutenant Kern likewise holds you in high regard. He sends his good wishes and asked me to inquire if you still carry Faust with you?"

Ernst felt light headed. Hans Gerd inducted into OC? How had the little shit kept that secret? His tongue was always far ahead of his brain. He blurted out everything impulsively, could not be trusted with any confidence. And his self-esteem was so fragile, so stunted, like the missing fingers on his hand, that such recognition would be the headline of his day, broadcast to all who would listen, especially his older brother, the naval cadet, the Freebooter. In his absence had Hans Gerd matured so quickly, evolved so strikingly that he would be courted by the likes of OC? How little he knew his younger brother. But instead of feeling pride or brotherly love, what registered in that moment was irritation, dismay that Hans Gerd could no longer be dismissed or pitied. Hans Gerd was a force to be reckoned.

Von Killinger cleared his throat. "Herr Techow, are you ill?"

Ernst came to his senses with a start. "No. No Herr von Killinger. I'm honored to be thought of so kindly." He reached into his rucksack on the floor for the well-worn copy of Faust and held it aloft like a trophy. Cheers and applause sprouted around the table.

"Whom else do you admire, Herr Techow? Literarily."

"Heine is another favorite," he said.

Von Salomon cleared his throat and coughed.

"Herr von Salomon is troubled," von Killinger raised one eyebrow. His smile was cold. "Perhaps our literary friend will share with the Stammtisch his discomfort."

Von Salomon blushed, a most unusual occurrence. "Heine was a Jew."

Ernst felt the blood drain from his face, embarrassed, exposed, humiliated. "I didn't realize..."

"It is of little consequence. After all, we are hardly a literary society." Nervous laughter. "Have any of you read Stefan George?" Von Killinger looked around the room. Von Salomon, Voss and Günther nodded.

> Blond or black sprung from the same womb
> Unrecognized brothers seeking yourselves and hating.
> You ever wandering and hence never fulfilled!

His eyes fixed again on Ernst. "You really should read him, Herr Techow. He speaks to the heart of our future. Now that you know Heine is a Jew, perhaps you will jettison him and pick up George." Von Killinger reached into his leather case and passed a slim volume hand to hand to Ernst. "Herr Techow – please. Read from the marked page."

Ernst's hands trembled as he opened the worn book to a leather thong marking a page with heavy underlining.

"Out loud, please, Herr Techow. I would wager that even our erudite, pseudo-intellectual von Salomon has not read George carefully."

> *The racially pure German yearns for The Man! – The Deed! Perhaps someone who sat for years among your murderers and slept in your prisons, will stand up and do The Deed.*

"Thank you, Herr Techow. I hope you will read his poetry. Please keep the book for now. Take your time. The Fat Man will see that I get it back." His unblinking stare circled the table. "Gentlemen, the wheel must be turned to bring about the thousand year Reich. I am here tonight to discuss with you the deeds that will turn that wheel." He stood behind his chair, almost at attention, his powerful hands gripping the high back. For a moment, Ernst wished he were on the other side of the door, drunk with beer instead of revolution.

"Kapp and the old officer corps were too political, the Free Corps not political enough. We have learned much. The moment is ripe, gentlemen, for our particular blend of shrewd politics and ruthless action. No longer will we be Weimar's mercenaries. It is time *we* set the agenda.

"Impulsive action and patience." Von Killinger raised both hands, palms up, weighing each on the scales of history. "At times we must disappear, and at other times deliver swift, fatal blows. Captain Ehrhardt's sense of timing is beyond questioning. Impatience is our greatest enemy. Our path may be twenty years long or it may be six months long. Every act must be *The Act*. We are at war, though only we know it, and for now, that is how it must remain."

Cigarette smoke curled into a cloud just below the ceiling and shrouded the light fixture.

"Eventually, the accumulation of deeds will tip the scale." His left hand sank as his right one rose. "And then the call will go out to our fighters to dig up their guns. But not until the time is ripe. Until then they remain in readiness. When the chaos arrives, we must be prepared to seize the initiative."

The 'Rector' struck a match to light a cigar and broke von Killinger's spell. "And what is this unique action?" Ehrentraut asked. To Ernst his bird face looked all the more ridiculous for his cigar.

"Murder," von Killinger said as matter of factly as if he'd said 'Mother'. He retrieved a folded paper from his jacket pocket. "Here is the list." He held the paper up for all to see. "You can probably guess the names: Erzberger, Scheidemann, Rathenau, Zeigner, Lipinski, Cohn, Ebert, and all the rest of the 'men of November', those who signed and accepted Versailles, those who betrayed the nation. These are the individuals whose murder will destabilize Weimar. One by one they will be removed, until the critical assassination – the deed among deeds. At that moment, Weimar will be thrown into such turmoil, such instability, that it will collapse."

"And the Communists?" Ehrentraut asked.

"Ah, but that is the beauty of this strategy – the reason it cannot fail. The murder of distinguished republican leaders will create chaos. If we don't seize the government outright, our actions will cause the left to react so recklessly that they will bring down Weimar themselves; they will do our dirty work. And then we shall strike, with overwhelming force. "

"Our people will be pursued by the police," Ehrentraut persisted. "There will be investigations – trials."

"The judicial system is already in our pockets – or at least sympathetic. For those who find our politics disturbing, there are other means of..." he searched the smoky ceiling, "shall we say, encouragement. OC is well funded, as each of you know from your bi-monthly stipends. Two hundred thousand men at arms, at our beck and call."

"Who is to be the first?" Günther asked.

"Erzberger. Matthias Erzberger." Ernst shuddered at the name of the most notorious Versailles traitor.

"And who will carry out the deed?"

"It has already been decided. Erzberger is as good as dead."

*　*　*　*　*　*　*　*　*　*

The Techow apartment at Heydenstrasse 7 needed cleaning. The sofa, which had faded from vibrant burgundy to dusk-red, was littered with Hans Gerd's history paper. A few pages had fallen onto the Oriental rug, the Wannseestrasse rug from the parlor. It was far too large for the apartment and remained partially rolled against one wall. Someday, Ernst's mother said, she would live to open it fully again.

Lisa completed her semester at Heidelberg and had returned home to Halle for the summer. She promised in a letter that this was the last time she would return home. She was completely fed up with her father's controlling and condescending attitude, his tacit support for Versailles, and his profiteering on the stock exchange, but she needed for him to pay one more year's University fees. "Next Christmas vacation, Ernst, we will spend together. I promise."

Ernst hunched over the small desk in his room trying to concentrate on Stefan George. His initial impression was that Von Killinger's praise was justified – George's poetry was evocative, pleasing – but it did not move him like Heine. It was the same with the paintings – so-called "degenerate art," according to Fritz. But it was these debauched artists who inspired him in a visceral way that more acceptable painters did not.

"Hans Gerd!" Ernst heard the slap of his mother's wooden spoon on the kitchen counter. "Clean up the living room, this instant!"

No response. Ernst closed the book and rubbed his eyes.

"Hans Gerd! Feet off the sofa! When is this paper due?"

"Calm down, Mother. Ernst! Help me with my algebra!"

"Can't," Ernst called from his room. He reluctantly put down George.

"I need your help now!" Hans Gerd whined. "You never help me. I've got a final exam in two days."

"I always help you, you moron! Why are you starting so late? You should have been preparing two weeks ago."

Hans Gerd appeared at Ernst's doorway and whispered, "Ernst. What did they say about me at the Stammtisch?"

Ernst had just returned from the monthly meeting of the Berlin OC, where Hans Gerd had been an unpleasant topic of discussion. He studied his brother and concluded, with uncanny relief, that his tempestuous brother had not changed that much after all. It was crystal clear to Ernst that Hans Gerd's induction into OC several months earlier had been a mistake. Although as president of his Gymnasium GNYO chapter Hans Gerd was superb, he was only sixteen, and still far too impulsive and hot-blooded. With luck and OC's forgiveness, he would make a good lawyer someday, when he could put his love of argument to use, if he ever calmed down enough.

Hans Gerd closed Ernst's door for privacy. "Are they angry with me?"

Ernst tipped back in his chair, crossed his feet on the desk. "What do you think?"

"It was an accident. I got carried away arguing with the moderates."

"That's it, Hans Gerd. Right there, two of your biggest problems. You 'got carried away' and you 'got into an argument'. Your mouth works faster than your brain."

"I said I was sorry."

"You put people at risk. You exposed one of Hoffmann's pet projects. If you were older and not my brother, the Feme would have dealt with you already."

"Should I be scared?" It was an odd question. Hans Gerd seemed congenitally incapable of fear, and even as he asked he struck a defiant pose.

"Resign from OC, Hans Gerd. They'll make an exception. I've already spoken with Tillessen. He's not happy; he says I will have to make it up to him."

Hans Gerd puckered his lips and nodded. "Next year, in the University, things will be different."

"You'd better do well on your Abitur exams or there will be no university for you."

⋆　⋆　⋆　⋆　⋆　⋆　⋆　⋆　⋆　⋆

Lisa returned from Halle in the fall, and they resumed what she liked to call their 'developing relationship,' only kissing and fondling. She said she needed time before resuming a sexual relationship, but she could not say why. Ernst did not press her – he was glad for the intimacy they did share. He did sometimes worry that there was someone else, not Fritz, but maybe someone from Heidelberg. She wouldn't say any more, only that they had to delay their intimacy. She said it was all confusing and overwhelming. She was still warm and loving when they were together. There was something enigmatic about her, but not disturbing.

Though Ernst desperately wanted to propose marriage, he was reconciled to waiting. This night they were to meet at his apartment, where she would meet his mother for the first time. Ernst was late. He let himself in silently and stood in the entryway listening. He was relieved to hear Lisa and his mother engaged in casual conversation.

She commented on an embroidered tea cozy, and his mother explained the stitched sequence. "I remember watching my mother stitch this when I was a girl. There's the house I grew up in. These are my two brothers, Erwin and Peter, and me holding the fishing rod. Everyone says I look like a boy. My brothers are very successful. Erwin owns a large estate in Jacobsdorf and Peter is chief architect for Walter Rathenau's AEG electric. As you know, Rathenau is a very important man. Perhaps you've heard of Peter's assistant, Walter Gropius – a most inventive architect whom Peter is helping." Ernst heard the tinkle of their fine china tea service.

"The detail," Lisa said. "It's wonderful. I see here that she separated the floss into individual strands."

"You've embroidered?"

"Yes." Lisa laughed nervously. "My Aunt Ida taught me."

187

"And your mother?"

There was an awkward silence. "Mother died when I was quite young."

Ernst heard his mother open the bottom drawer of the bureau and he could imagine her lifting out the neatly folded wedding tablecloth embroidered with sailing ships along the border. Ernst visualized the two women running the edge of the cloth between their fingers, clipper ships and schooners, wind-full sails, banners flying. Unfurled, the tablecloth was at least three meters long, a decorative spread for an aristocratic table. "This is my mother's finest piece. She started it on the day Ernst was born – see here in the corner – October 12, 1901. Ernst would sit on her lap and watch her stitch. My mother wanted him to have this on his wedding day."

Ernst cleared his throat with resolve and called into the flat,,"Hello! Anyone home?" Before they could respond he turned the corner and saw the stark whiteness of the tablecloth bridging the two women. There was something different about Lisa, something uneasy, or guilty – and then it came to him. "Lisa? Your hair! When did you... ?"

"Today. I had it bobbed. Isn't it fabulous?"

Ernst stared at her shorn head. "It's... it's very modern."

His mother gathered the cloth. "Ernst, help me fold this. We've had a lovely talk. Lisa, would you like some more tea."

"Yes, Frau Techow. That would be lovely."

He looked from Lisa to his mother and wondered about the facile intimacy of women. They seemed completely at ease, and only his entrance disturbed their equanimity.

Ernst felt for the ring in his vest pocket. He had bought it months ago, waiting for the perfect moment, and now he was wondering if tonight was that moment. He was fervent in his desire to marry her. If only she would, everything would be right, but once again he felt her strange hesitancy or some other discouragement.

He looked at his watch when he was sure his mother would notice and said, "We're to meet Fritz in half an hour. We really should be going."

Once in the street, Lisa broke the silence. "I'm sorry you don't like my haircut, but I wasn't about to ask your permission."

"It's not bad," he said perfunctorily. After another block Ernst said, "How was it up there – I mean my mother?"

"She's very nice. I was nervous at first, but..."

"Lisa. That tablecloth – it could be ours."

"Yes, she told me about it. Your grandmother."

For another long block Ernst said nothing, and he could feel the chill between them. Finally, as they crossed Potsdamer Platz he could no longer hold himself back. "Lisa, would you ever consent to marry me?"

They stopped on the traffic island in the middle of the busy square, and she turned to him. She looked deeply into his eyes, and the two of them were a mystifying tranquility in the clamor and dissonance of traffic and pedestrians. She took both his hands. "Maybe some day. I think it would be nice. I really do. But not now." Berliners crossed Leipzigerstrasse in both directions; then the automobiles took their turn. A car horn blared. "I love you, Ernst. But I'm not ready." She held his face and kissed him full on the mouth. "Don't ask me to marry you. I'm not ready to make that commitment." She looked at him quizzically. "And neither are you."

He began to protest, but she placed a finger across his lips. "After Fritz, I'm the top political science student in our year. I won't become a Hausfrau – not yet."

"Nothing would change," Ernst said. "We would just be promised to each other." He searched her face.

"There's another reason." She looked down. "It's the Association. They frighten me. There's a whole part of you I worry about."

"I only drive a truck for them."

"Only drive a truck?" She studied him again. "You know what the damnedest thing is? I think you're lying, and I don't care. Your secrets are weirdly exciting. You're so unlike Fritz. I want you, and it scares me."

"I will wait." His face softened. "We're fated to be together. I feel it."

"I hope so. But I just don't know."

Ernst took her hand and held it to his lips. The moment passed, and they re-joined the flow across Leipzigerstrasse. His heart ached as if he had been disciplined by a loving parent. Yet, he also felt curious relief: relief that he didn't have to mutate into someone he was not, and that was almost as disturbing and incomprehensible.

The marquis of the Megalomania Club suddenly appeared, its garish lights just flickering on as daylight waned. Ernst's reverie ended. At the triangular intersection, a newspaper man in a worn out uniform of the Great War hawked the evening paper.

"Chancellor Wirth survives no confidence vote! Stinnes and Stresemann vote with majority! Chancellor Wirth survives no confidence vote! Stinnes and Stressemann vote with majority!"

Fritz waited for them under the marquis, looking every bit the dandy with spats, a dinner jacket and cravat, a buttoned vest and a bowler hat. He raved about Lisa's bobbed hair and ran his hand playfully over her head. Ernst felt his chest tighten.

"Everybody will want to touch you now that it's cut so short," Fritz said. "How sensual!"

Fritz's charisma chilled Ernst, and he realized that he still dreaded their rivalry. Fritz could be so damn charming. By contrast, Ernst felt wrinkled, disheveled in a plain white cotton shirt, sleeves rolled up past his elbows, an open corduroy vest – a country bumpkin next to Fritz's urbanity.

The 'supper crowd' at the cabaret scene was tame compared to the late night crowd, often referred to as 'Noah's Zoo' because every variety of human relationships came by two's and sometimes three's and four's. Berliners passing the Megalomania's entrance gawked, hoping to glimpse the inside of the notorious cabaret. Those fortunate enough to have tickets for the supper show represented the spectrum of moneyed Berliners, from politicians and former royalty resplendent in jewels and fine furs to bureaucrats and clerks draped in department store bargains and rhinestones.

Cabaret star Margo Lion, French born, thin, dark and sensuous, was the featured act. The life-sized billboard photograph depicted the fabulous Miss Lion scantily clad in lingerie. Pursed lips and one curled finger invited them into the rebuilt theater. Fritz contemplated her lusty image, and Ernst discerned what he thought must be a steamy combination of longing and lust.

The Club host, clearly disenchanted to see how young they were, confirmed their reservation and signaled a waiter. A thin young man with slicked back brown hair and a skin-tight tuxedo led them to their table past eddying currents of eager patrons. Glasses tinkled and a champagne cork popped, followed by a sudden cheer. A quartet of musicians, one violinist and three recorder players, each sporting a bulbous red clown nose, had just finished their performance. Some patrons booed, others clapped politely, but most continued their table talk as if "Les Beaux Eaux" had not performed at all.

When they were left alone at their table in partial darkness, Lisa grabbed Ernst and Fritz's hands. "Isn't this just wicked?"

The ceiling disappeared in blackness, and Ernst felt suddenly puny. He was amazed how many small round tables fit into the hall, like lily pads floating in a dark pond, each sprouting a candle lantern. Off to the left a luminous bar lined one wall.

Lisa leaned forward. "Fritz, don't stare! Those two men behind us? They're lovers."

"Lisa!" Fritz said.

"How can you tell?" Ernst asked.

"They're holding hands under the table. See? Don't be so obvious! Oh, you boys."

"That's disgusting," Fritz said.

Lisa tilted the lamp shade to illuminate Fritz's face. "You're blushing, Ivory."

"Lisa, stop it. Now you're embarrassing me."

"Blushing," Ernst said, "it's your heart aching to see the world."

"Blushing," Lisa said, "it's your heart showing off to the world."

"Aching to see!"

"Showing off!"

A rancid smile curled Fritz's lips. "That's cute. How long have you rehearsed?"

Lisa's hand found Ernst's under the table and squeezed. "I don't know what you're talking about, Ivory," she said.

"You're so adorable, Lisa. Why do you waste your time with a deadbeat like Ernst?"

She flipped her head up to imitate Margo Lion. "Ivory, dahling, don't be jealous. It's soooo boring."

After Lisa's second whiskey sour they relived their calamitous first meeting at camp almost ten years earlier and laughed so loud that patrons nearby disciplined them with stern looks. Ernst let two beers shroud his sadness and numb his discomfort over Lisa's ambivalence about marriage. He found it curious that he was not more hurt or angry, or anything except drunk. Only later that night, in the vulnerable moments before sleep, would that initial feeling of devastation and rejection return.

Ernst asked Fritz and Lisa if they knew Stefan George. Fritz, who had no time for reading anything outside of his courses except newspapers and Reichstag transcripts, only vaguely knew about the poet. Lisa, however, had read George's polemics and his translation of Dante, but she was more taken by Nietzsche, who, she pointed out, inspired George.

"Do you read poetry to each other?" Fritz asked bitterly. He took a Gauloise from Ernst's pack.

For a moment Ernst felt a malignant shadow block Fritz's sunny disposition.

"You know we've been seeing each other," Lisa said. "We're not getting married, or anything. It's just a close – you know – just a relationship. That's all."

Ernst's appetite was gone. He signaled the waiter for another round of drinks and lit another cigarette.

Fritz laughed and coughed from the cigarette smoke. "All right, all right. It's just that people talk, and you know how it goes."

Ernst studied his friend as the waiter cleared their plates and put down another round. Enough of the boy remained in Fritz's face for Ernst to remember their innocence and their adventures. Now that he was a man, there was a second, unfamiliar Fritz, not unlike the two Ernst's. He wondered if Fritz noticed, or cared. "Loosen up, Fritz." He put his arm around his shoulder. "You're too serious. Remember, I knew you before you had hair under your arms."

Lisa tried to hold back a laugh with her hand, but it burst out.

After another beer Fritz returned to politics, boasting about his new position in Deputy Helfferich's office.

Ernst's head felt fuzzy. He leaned across the table, face to face with Fritz and said, "What card games do Helfferich's assistants play?"

"What?"

Ernst leaned back and puffed out his chest, mocking self-importance. He rolled up his napkin and held it to his mouth like a giant cigar. "All those fat cats you want to be with. What card game do they play?"

"Well, I suppose Skat."

"Exactly. Freebooters play '66'." Ernst lit another cigarette. "Most people play '66'. Helfferich, for all his blather about the Volk, is still a Skat player." He shook a wobbly finger and squinted at Fritz. "Be careful, old buddy, old pal."

"I don't play cards. And, in any case, I have integrity."

"Everybody has their price," Ernst said.

"What's yours?"

Ernst's merriment collapsed, and he felt something sinister between them. "I keep my business to myself."

Fritz leaned forward, his forehead almost touching Ernst's. "Word has it you're a member of Organization C. Is that true?"

Ernst sobered quickly and ground out his cigarette. "The less said the better, for all of us."

But Fritz persisted. "I'll bet they pay you well."

Ernst's brow wrinkled with suspicion. "Modestly."

"Look," he put his hand on Ernst's shoulder. "I'm all for this OC business, as a precaution, as a back-up police force, or even a small army. I'm the politician. You're the soldier." He held both hands up as a scale of justice or reason perfectly balanced. He winked at Ernst and resumed his beer. "Who is behind OC, Ernst? I hear Hugo Stinnes mentioned, and other industrialists."

"Yes." Ernst considered his words carefully. "Herr Stinnes has been a generous patron of many Nationalist causes."

"Günther is a member, isn't he?"

"You know I can't say."

"It's you who should be careful, Ernst. Günther is involved with some very dangerous, possibly criminal elements." Fritz fumbled in his breast pocket. "This came several days ago from the Reich prosecutor."

Ernst read the letter, folded it and returned it to Fritz. "I've heard these allegations before."

"They're not just allegations. I've made inquiries through Helfferich's office."

Lisa tapped her empty glass with a spoon. "I'm still here, boys! What's going on?"

"It's nothing, really," Fritz said.

Lisa sat up sharply, her eyebrows angled with pique. "In your thousand year Reich will we women be just the mothers, cooks and cleaners? Don't you think we're every bit as capable as you? Maybe even more so?"

"I'm still first in the class."

"And I'm second," Lisa said, "so fuck you, Fritz."

"Ten thousand marks," Fritz said. "Günther stole ten thousand marks from the National Party. Nothing has been proven, yet. But Günther's the one. There's evidence. And, he's not who he says he is. I checked his military record. He was jailed for a month and demoted by the court of the Guard-Infantry during The War for desertion in the field and forgery. And it's well known that he's up to his neck in the black market."

"Who isn't these days?" Ernst said. "Look, Fritz, I don't know what Günther did or didn't do, and the money, I've heard, was well used. Don't pursue this. You put yourself at great risk. Please. Take my word."

Ernst felt that peculiar elation, the power that came with special membership in a secret, shadowy organization that inspired dread. For a rare moment he thought Fritz looked wounded, insecure, and Ernst felt washed in tenderness for his childhood friends, felt an imperative to protect them.

He grabbed Lisa and Fritz's hands and pulled them into a circle at their small table. Their three heads almost touched. "I don't mean to be so – so zealous. But I believe in this – very strongly. Something momentous is about to happen." Their beer and whiskey breath intoxicated him in a different manner. "You are my best friends. I would never lie to you. What I tell you now is in strictest confidence. People's lives are at stake." He looked at each, and they nodded.

"Yes, Fritz, I am a member of OC, as well as their driver. I was inducted last year. At each Stammtisch I hear a lot. There's a lot of money. I hear names. Powerful people – respected people – in government, especially Helfferich, Stinnes, and the estate owners. They need us. They need our secret army." A troubled shadow fell over Lisa's face.

"The Reichswehr has allowed us to steal weapons," Ernst continued.

"Not so loud!" Lisa hissed.

Fritz leaned forward. "The Reichswehr?"

Ernst looked behind him then turned back. "Pöhner, the Bavarian police chief, is one of our leading patrons. Police funds are diverted to Captain Ehrhardt. Bavaria is a haven for OC and the underground Free Corps. We also sell stolen weapons to the highest bidder, a very lucrative trade. I know, because I drive those guns from place to place. The overthrow of Weimar – a worthy goal. And they pay me well."

Lisa squeezed his hand. "It may be necessary, but I wish you weren't one of them."

Was this why Lisa rejected marriage, put their intimate relations on hold? Would she even admit it to be true? It felt odd for Ernst to think of himself as "one of them" but he supposed he was, though his role as driver was slight. And he was glad for that.

Fritz hiccupped, sat upright and saluted backwards, his eyes losing focus. "We're all on the same side, aren't we? I would never betray your trust, Ernst."

Margo Lion was scheduled to open at 8 PM. At 8:15 the stage manager, a mousy little man with a pencil-thin black mustache and sharp nose peeked out from the curtain, his beady eyes searching. Ernst could almost see his whiskers.

At last, the three piece band played a brief fanfare, after which the snare drum continued until, with a crash of cymbals, the curtain opened revealing the sensual Margo Lion. A cheer went up from the audience and another when she began her most popular song.

Can't imagine why I chose to leave him
how could I have been so cruel
After all he loved me without question
Still I left him like a fool
If I woke him late at night complaining
I'm on my last cigarette
He'd say I'll be over in a minute
darling please, don't get upset

Peter, Peter, I must have been blind
Peter, Peter, I was so unkind
Peter, Peter, tell me what to do
Peter, Peter, I'll make it up to you

If I told him that I'd been unfaithful
He would shake his head and say
darling, just as long as you feel happy
that's the man I threw away
Now whenever I'm in bed with others
on some lark or idle whim
I pretend the man I'm with is Peter
Oh, how my heart aches for him

Peter, Peter, may I have this dance
Peter, Peter, give me one more chance
Peter, Peter, tell me what to do
Peter, Peter, I'm still in love with you

The maudlin lyrics weighed heavily on Ernst's heart. He tried to catch Lisa's gaze, but hers wandered. He hoped against hope that she thought of him as her 'Peter'.

Cheers and catcalls followed each number. Just in front of the stage, three burly men dwarfed a table, each drinking from a pitcher of beer. By the end of Lion's third number, the loudest of the men, a husky lout with short-cropped hair, started singing along, badly.

Bouncers stood nearby, but it would have been a battle royale to eject them. After her next number Miss Lion hushed the audience and asked the big man his name.

"Peter!" He toasted her. The audience whistled and applauded.

"Ah!" Margo put her hands on her hips and, in her sexiest velvet voice, whispered, "Struwwelpeter?" The crowd hooted and howled. "Come, Slovenly Peter, come up here with me, and let's sing this next song together." She turned again to the audience. "Let's have a big hand for Struwwelpeter."

As he joined in the applause, Ernst leaned into Lisa, "Maria, our nanny, used to read Struwwelpeter to us. She didn't much like it – said it was too frightening for children."

"Then why did she read it?" She spoke loudly over the applause.

"Mother insisted. She said it was 'a corrective for bad behavior.'"

"It obviously didn't work in your case." Lisa giggled. "Remember the Story of the Little Suck-a-Thumb? Oh, what was his name? Caspar? No – it was Conrad. That's it – Conrad, who gets his thumbs cut off by the scissor-man because he refused to stop sucking them. I can still see the blood spurting from the stump of Conrad's thumbs and those giant scissors." She shuddered. "Oooh!"

Drunken Peter stumbled up the stage steps to encouraging applause. He tottered beside one of the sexiest women in Europe, shielding his eyes from the stage lights. After she reviewed the chorus of I Am A Vamp with him and the audience, she instructed Peter how to stand with his hands primped on his hips, swaying back and forth like a seductive woman. He started singing:

> I am a vamp, I am a vamp
> half woman, half beast
> I bite my men and suck them dry
> and then I bake them in a pie
> I am a vamp, I am a vamp
> that's all I can do
> I'm not mild-mannered like you
> and oh no and oh no
> my passion takes over and off I go
> I should really be kept in a zoo.

She sent him staggering back to his seat, no less drunk, but thoroughly pie-eyed and tranquilized by the lights and her perfume.

Margo Lion's first set finished to thunderous applause, foot-stamping and cheering, but Fritz abstained. When the applause finally stopped he said, "You know, it isn't right to be enjoying this. It's obscene – degenerate."

"Oh, Ivory," Lisa's words came slowly. "I'm buying tonight, so you have to keep your prudish opinions to yourself." She sipped at her third Whiskey sour. "Unless they exactly coincide with mine."

Margo Lion closed her performance with a song "for the Nationalists and those waiting for a Führer" – "Little Attila"

> Nowadays there are no mighty conquerors
> don't bother looking for a lover like that
> You can find a banker or a general
> one will be bald and one tremendously fat
> The younger men come and go
> and you know they all come too soon
> Older men treat and are sweet
> and they're soft like a macaroon
> Oh yes I've looked high and low throughout
>   each part of Germany
> but oh, no cock ever crowed loud enough for me.

> There are no more Attilas here amongst these dreary men
> the warrior from days of yore will not appear again
> I don't need a flotilla or a villa by the sea
> but oh for a scintilla of some hot virility
> But look around what's to be found is pitiful, 'oi vey'
> Oh I'd kill to be marryin' a barbarian today
> So I retreat to fantasy
> for there I have a man for me
> A cute little brute, who knows how to shoot
> my Attila, my Hun.

At the end of the song Fritz stood and booed loudly, as did a few individuals at other tables. Margo Lion bowed low and smiled, apparently relishing the rancor she had created.

As they left, Fritz muttered again about "cheap culture and indecent lyrics," then couldn't help but laugh. Lisa swayed between them, arm in arm. She laughed until they were outside, on Potsdamer Platz, where the cool night air sobered her. Horns blared, the news man hawked the last of his papers, and the stench of automobile exhaust hovered in the air.

Fritz hailed a cab, but at the last moment Lisa said that she and Ernst would walk back to the University. Fritz looked hurt, but Ernst slammed the door and the cab left.

Ernst kissed Lisa good night in the shadows outside her dormitory, a passionate embrace, disinhibited by alcohol and Margo Lion. He fondled her breasts, and she pressed herself into him. He felt himself harden and knew that she felt him grow against her pelvis. They leaned against a quaking aspen, and she was eager for him.

"When?" he said.

"I want to." She kissed him again.

"There is the woods."

"No. Günther's apartment. In his magical bed. But not tonight."

"I'm going to ask you again," Ernst whispered into her ear as her hands caressed his buttocks.

"To go to bed?"

"To marry me."

$$\star \quad \star \quad \star \quad \star \quad \star \quad \star \quad \star \quad \star \quad \star \quad \star$$

On August 26, 1921, Ernst waited in Münich at the Bavarian Wood Products Company for two fugitives requiring rapid transport to the Hungarian border. When they appeared, only hours after Erzberger's assassination, Ernst recognized one of them as Karl Tillessen's younger brother, Heinrich, who was no older than Ernst. He drove them to the Münich police station where they were met by Chief of Police Pöhner. The Chief shook their hands and gave them forged passports. They were not five minutes in custody; they left the police station in the cab of Ernst's truck with new identities, new clothes, money and a suitcase. It all transpired so quickly that as Ernst drove away Heinrich was still counting Reichmarks.

Ernst wondered if it was different killing an important man. Was it different than killing in battle, killing unimportant people, killing anonymously? He wondered when he would consider his own responsibility in killing inconsequential people. Seen in another light he had committed random murder. And was not that the heart of the problem – the assumption that they were inconsequential, the assumption that killing is not murder. They had had hopes and dreams no different than his own. It was the important people who sent them, or seduced them into dying for their causes. By that logic, that moral sense, it probably *was* more just to kill the torchbearer, to discourage those who followed behind.

After driving several silent hours Ernst finally asked, "How did it feel to kill him?"

"Like nothing," Tillessen said matter of factly He stared straight through the windscreen, his expression blank.

"Would it have been so easy if it were not Erzberger?"

"Makes no difference. I do what I'm told."

The other youth, more sullen than Tillessen, with even less to say, smoked cigarette after cigarette, his arm hanging out the window.

Ernst knew not to search his soul too carefully. There were too many insoluble questions, moral cul-de-sacs and labyrinths. He didn't know enough to make a judgment, he told himself. He would have to contain the contradiction, otherwise he would have to seek a purpose for it all and that, he knew, was impossible. As a balm, he let his thoughts drift to Lisa and what it would be like with her again in Günther's bed.

Ernst drove them out of Bavaria, through Austria and across the Hungarian border. During the two days of their journey Ernst watched their faces to try to understand what it was like to be a murderer on the run, your identity severed. They would never walk truly free again. They would always be looking over their shoulders for the police, or the thug sent to render more primitive justice or vengeance. At the Hungarian border the two youths were briefly taken into custody then released, as they had expected.

Ernst turned his truck north again, with relief. He still had to deliver 'machine tools' to Upper Silesia, which in this case, he knew to be one hundred '98 rifles, three machine guns and 10,000 rounds of ammunition.

The Hungarian border guards seemed to know not to search his truck too carefully.

13

Assassins

June – July 1922

Over the next year Ernst threw himself into his studies and was glad for the relative sense of normality and invisibility he enjoyed as a student. Every few weeks Kern contacted him, either by letter or courier, with orders to drive the Bavarian Wood Products truck for OC. After two years of rule under the Weimar constitution, everything in Germany was a hopeless muddle. Hyperinflation escalated at a dizzying rate, with the value of the Reichmark in 1921 declining on some days 50% from morning to afternoon. A few industrialists like Hugo Stinnes paid themselves in U.S. dollars and became so wealthy that Stinnes's personal worth exceeded that of the German Reich. The extreme left and right continued to agitate and encourage dysfunction as a means toward their disparate ends – revolution vs. restoration of the monarchy. In this fragmented society, Ernst found relief in his mindless occupation – driving a truck – a contribution to the cause that answered the nagging question that he heard in his father's voice, "What are you doing for the Vaterland?"

Hans Gerd passed his Abitur and was a first-year at the university, where he became friendly with Fritz through his involvement with the GNYO. Lisa and Fritz vied for top honors in the Political Science Faculty, a friendly competition that made Ernst nervous.

Ernst went to some GNYO meetings but found them tedious. What he did pay heed to was Lisa and Fritz, gauging their interaction, guessing their feelings. There was something thrilling about watching Lisa from a distance, hearing the voice he loved speaking with determination and authority. He also felt aroused by her body, watching her move, reveling in their secret. As an officer of the GNYO, she sat with Fritz and Hans Gerd at the head table where the debates occurred. On generous days he carried his jealousy as a mysterious weight, burdensome but bearable. On covetous days, memory and longing, anxiety and uncertainty could crush him from inside, and neither Fritz nor Lisa would know what had killed him.

There was no further mention of marriage, but their passion needed to be satisfied. Every few months, when Günther's apartment was available, Ernst and Lisa visited his prodigious bed. The last evening, as they lay together after making love, Lisa said, "I know it shouldn't make a difference, but you're not like the other men in my life – Father or Horst. They wanted to fight for me – possess me like a prize."

"And sometimes they hit you."

"I hate it," she said. "I'm drawn to it, and I hate it. But it's different with you. I know you more like a brother." She said it a little sadly. "And I should be glad – I want to be glad."

"But?"

"But I'm just not sure. There are places in you I don't know – dark places – as if we're in two different worlds."

He felt her shiver and embraced her more resolutely. "What about Fritz?" he asked.

"Oh, he's a dear boy. I think he's quite jealous of us, but he's too old-fashioned to say anything."

"And if he weren't?"

"What?"

"Old-fashioned."

She kissed him. "It's a silly question."

Ernst wasn't quite sure what she meant, but he dared not probe deeper. "Does your father know about us?"

Rain tapped gently, persistently, on the window. "I told him a few months ago," she said. "He wanted to know what you were studying. I should have lied. We had a horrible fight." She turned over, and they curled like nesting spoons. "He said I was a romantic, like Mother, and romantics don't live long. I said you were a patriot, and he slapped my face. He said patriots are chumps, and they're not fit for his daughter. The weird thing is that Margaret said she understands my father. She doesn't like him, but she understands. She says he's afraid for me, and it's the only way he can protect me, the only way he can love me. She called it 'desperate acts of love'."

"It's you and your father who are in different worlds. You want to be in politics, and all he knows is Hausfrau and grandchildren. He wants to fix you but doesn't know how."

"When I was a little girl I had a fish for a pet." Her voice was dreamy, far away. "I loved my fish. His name was Oscar – a beautiful goldfish. I changed his water and fed him every day. Oscar and I talked about everything. His bowl looked so empty and sad, and my doll furniture was just sitting there, so I gave him a sofa, a chair, a bureau, even a floor lamp. I loved Oscar so much that one day I couldn't bear to be separated from him – me in the air, Oscar in the water. I reached into the bowl and touched him. I scooped him up, and he flopped in the bowl of my hands. I kissed him and stroked him, then put him back into his world. A few days later he was swimming slowly, tilting over just the slightest bit, and he had already knocked over the chair and lamp. I took him out again to kiss him, and he didn't wiggle quite so much. The next morning Oscar was dead. Aunt Ida was all agitated and said we should flush him down the toilet, but I grabbed the bowl and ran into the woods behind our house. I dug a little hole and buried Oscar, wondering that he was now in yet another different world, and no matter how hard I tried, no matter how much I wanted him, Oscar would always be separated from me."

"But you loved him – that's what matters."

"I killed him. That matters also."

"It wasn't your intention."

"I think it's that way with Father. Margaret is right. I know he loves me, and I know he's afraid for me, wants to protect me. It wasn't Father's intention to hurt me, but he did. Sometimes I wonder if my memory of Mother is warped. Maybe I remember her as gentle and kind so she can protect me, even from the grave, with gentleness, with something that remedies the violence of men."

"Your father can't hurt you anymore."

"But I came from him – I have him inside me – I'm made of the same stuff that he's made of. And that's what is so disturbing. Maybe that's why I chose Horst and let him beat me as well."

They said nothing for a long time, but he could tell by her breathing that she was awake. How much did he want to possess Lisa? How much to rescue her? How much for her to rescue him? It was baffling and disconcerting. So often he had no words, no clear images or concrete thoughts, only deep currents of desire, primal like a magnetic field. He felt incomplete without Lisa, wondering if she could fill the emptiness inside. To clear his mind for other thoughts, he scolded himself. Wishing, dreaming, praying – this was the way children and the God-fearing looked at the world, a prayer for each one's personal interest and comfort, prayers for success as God's endorsement of each sinner's goodness. He knew that surety was fallacious, yet also seductive, and now here she was in his arms, and everything seemed all right. Best not to think beyond the moment, he told himself. His eyes stopped probing the darkness and he fell asleep.

★　★　★　★　★　★　★　★　★　★

Ernst sought out Willi Günther at the Corps Teutonia Pub in early June. He found Günther engaged in spirited conversation with an attractive young woman who had blue eyes and a sparkling complexion .

"... in the Turkish campaign. I was wounded, twice, but insisted on staying with my unit. I was decorated..."

"Willi." Ernst pulled on his shoulder. "May I speak with you – alone?"

"Certainly. If Fräulein will excuse me." He kissed her hand and bowed. She blushed and smiled shyly.

Ernst pulled him into the hallway. "Turkey? Wounded? Medals? Why don't you tell her you deserted in Turkey, were 'wounded' by a camel's bite, and were this close to a court-martial?"

Günther smoothed his rumpled uniform. "What's the harm? I think she'll sleep with me tonight."

"Günther, you are disgusting."

"Disgusting? The next time you fuck your girlfriend in my bed, change the sheets. That's disgusting. Now, what's so urgent?"

"Do you know a student, Stubenrauh?"

Günther rolled his eyes. "Indeed, I do."

Ernst leaned close to Günther and whispered. "Do you know that he's talking about a plan to murder Rathenau?"

"First of all, dear Ernst, it's not murder. It's assassination. There's a world of difference. And yes, he spoke to me a few days ago. How did you know?"

"Hans Gerd. He said you knew all about it. You've got to dissuade Stubenrauh."

"I told him I'd check with OC and not to do anything until then. But he's a loose cannon." Günther cocked his head and squinted at Ernst. "Do you have a problem with Rathenau's elimination?"

"Don't be obtuse. My only concern is Hans Gerd. Whom did you tell?"

Günther shook his head. "It's all taken care of, Ernst. Don't worry yourself. Now, if you don't mind, I will rejoin my new friend."

The next evening, after a Stammtisch meeting, Ernst and Hans Gerd ambled home across the Charlottenberg Bridge, intoxicated with beer and the warm June breeze. At the other end of the bridge, two men leaned over the railing, smoking cigarettes, staring into the Landwehr Canal. As the brothers approached, the shorter man turned, and his face caught the street light.

"Ernst Werner Techow! What a surprise!"

The moment Ernst recognized Kern and Fischer, a surge of surprise, then fear, swept over him. But when Kern grasped his hand and draped his arm over Ernst's shoulder, the discomfort dissipated.

Ernst allowed himself to be led down Charlottenberger Chaussee. He hadn't seen Kern in two years. What was so important as to bring him to Berlin? It certainly wasn't just to chat with Ernst. And why was Fischer with him?

Fischer introduced himself to Hans Gerd, and they followed several paces behind. "We have some business to discuss," Kern said to Ernst. "Are you sober enough to talk and walk at the same time?"

Ernst felt military prerogative straighten his spine. "I'm fine."

"When this job was proposed, I thought of you right away, Techow. I need a dependable driver for a 'Nationalist purpose'. Tillessen suggested you, also – something about a debt of gratitude to OC?"

It was Hans Gerd. They were playing their OC and Feme card in exchange for something big. "I'm flattered. What do you require?"

"We are to assassinate Walther Rathenau."

Ernst stopped and turned to face Kern. "Rathenau?"

Kern pulled him along. "You shouldn't be surprised. We need a dependable driver."

"Well... I... I..."

"I understand your debt of gratitude to Tillessen involves your brother."

Ernst sobered quickly and felt the chill return. Hans Gerd spoke with Fischer not three paces behind.

"Herr Tillessen assured me you were the right man for the job," Kern said. "You can think about it overnight. June 24th, Johannestag, the Feast of St. John the Baptist. It was the day the Feme dispensed punishment in medieval times. Tillessen likes the poetic justice in selecting that day. He thinks it may be the Deed of Deeds. Did you know Rathenau predicted this would happen? He did – to that Frenchman, Loucheur, during the Wiesbaden negotiations. Said it very matter of factly – he expected the same fate as Erzberger, Kurt Eisner and Liebknecht." He turned around. Something about Kern made it crystal clear to Ernst that there was nothing more to discuss. "Come, Fischer, these boys have to get home." Kern and Fischer crossed the busy Charlottenburg Chaussee and disappeared in the traffic.

"Is that the guy from the Brigade?" Hans Gerd asked.

Ernst nodded. "That's Kern." He looked wistfully across the square. "A most remarkable man." Hans Gerd would never appreciate the range of possibilities in that word – remarkable. And he could never imagine the depth of trepidation Kern could inspire. Ernst worried for his younger brother. But there was no end of things to worry about, from inflation to national disgrace. And to add insult to injury, every German was subjected to the irritating Weimar wrangling and maneuvering, analyzed in microscopic detail as if clarity could make sense of a mortally divided nation and Reichstag. Were it not for Hans Gerd, Ernst would have declined this mission. Powerful forces were at work, and it was best to stay out of their path. As his big brother Leo had remarked so long ago in Kiel, better to be sprats than big fish.

"What did he want?"

"Nothing. Just renewing an old friendship." And calling in an old debt.

★   ★   ★   ★   ★   ★   ★   ★   ★   ★

Two nights later, Ernst met Lisa for dinner at the Corps Teutonia. He was torn between wanting to tell her – to tell the world – and trembling when he contemplated her response. Though she was certainly sympathetic with the Nationalists, Lisa was always more ambivalent about what it actually took to achieve their goals. He understood her squeamishness about violence, but politicians like Rathenau chose their profession. They had begged citizens to vote for them; they wanted to be public. They all knew the risks.

Lisa greeted him with a perplexed expression. "Are you sick? Ernst, you don't look well."

"There's something I have to do for OC." Lisa's complexion darkened like the moon eclipsed by a cloud. "I may be gone for eight or nine days. Don't look for me. If necessary, I'll leave a message in your mailbox."

"What... What is...?"

He covered her hand with his own. "When it's over, you'll know. Until then... "

She pulled her hand away. "When?" The word was ice.

"This is a matter of utmost importance. A Deed of Deeds."

"And nobody else can do it?"

"Somebody has to do it, and Lieutenant Kern and OC have chosen me."

"Why you?"

"I don't know."

"You're lying."

He gripped her hand again. "Keep your voice down," he hissed. "I have no choice." He felt shamed that he was angry with Lisa, and that he had to keep silent. He was a good soldier – doing his duty without question. Once upon a time that was enough reason.

She searched his face. "What does Kern give you that I can't?"

He could not tell her about Hans Gerd. "It's hard – it's complicated to say no to Kern. It feels like saying no to myself." The words were out of his mouth before he could consider them. Before he could scrub them clean for Lisa's benefit. Certainly not for his own.

"Nonsense! I'm beginning to think that OC is really a secret organization of wounded men. You pretend to be saving the nation, but really you are trying to save yourselves."

"Lisa, Please. Listen to me. After this, I'm through with them. Give me the benefit of your doubts." He brought her fingers to his lips. "I swear it, Lisa. I swear it."

"I believe you." She drew her hand away from his, gently, but resolutely.

"Will you still go with me to the Summer Festival tonight?" Ernst asked.

"No." She gathered her books and put on her blue beret. "I have a bad feeling, Ernst. Be careful. Much is at stake."

"Try not to worry. You will be proud of me."

*   *   *   *   *   *   *   *   *   *

Three days before St. John's Day – three days before Rathenau would die – Günther had located Schütt and Diestel's Automotive Garage in the Schmargendorf district of Berlin. Ernst and Günther negotiated with Schütt in the tiny office he and Diestel shared. Two ancient desks were invisible under papers weighted down by spark plugs and a piston head. The carpet was so worn and dirty as to be indistinguishable from the wooden floor boards. Though the scent of gasoline and oil was normally pleasing and evocative to Ernst, in here it was so strong that his head ached.

Günther explained the importance of Schütt's cooperation. He was sorry he could not give Schütt more specific information, but it was a matter of national urgency. Schütt was reluctant; he wanted more money, but Günther lowered his voice and closed the door to their office. "Herr Schütt, you are providing assistance to Lieutenant Kern of the Organization C – of the Ehrhardt Brigade. Need I remind you of the Feme?"

Schütt leaned forward, his beer belly resting on a pile of invoices. "Are you threatening me, you little shit? Get out of here." He pointed to the door where Kern stood pulling on tight black gloves.

"I assure you, Herr Schütt," Kern said, "this is necessary – for national purposes." Schütt stepped back from his desk. "You will be paid generously for your trouble."

"And if I refuse?"

"There is no refusing, Herr Schütt. Time is short. If you cooperate your life may be long."

"Diestel and I have to discuss..."

"There is no discussion, Herr Schütt. There is no choice. Ernst will return in a few days to work on the car. Save a space in the garage. And we three will need to sleep in your extra room. Ernst will give you the details. Good day, Herr Schütt."

Two days later Ernst, Kern and Fischer picked up the Mercedes in Schwerin, but it needed oil, which troubled Ernst. Under the bonnet, he felt all along the idling engine until he found an amber drop just under the oil feed. He wiped it away, and another drop started to form. Eric had taught him that the simple answer to an engine's complaint was often correct, but also short-lived. Life, he said, was the same, but that meant nothing to young Ernst. A simple tightening of the oil feed would suffice for now, but he would check it at intervals on their way back to Berlin. He could almost hear chauffeur Eric's instruction. "Listen for at least five minutes. It's like listening to a forest at night. At first you hear very little. But if you're still and patient, you hear more and more."

Ernst's hand tremored as he closed the bonnet and wiped a smudge off the chrome handle. He ran his palm over the wood paneling inside the Mercedes, and it felt warm, purring like a panther.

Keeping a worried eye on the oil gauge, Ernst drove Kern and Fischer back to Berlin through a stormy evening. Did Kern share any of Ernst's dread? Their silence in the back seat reminded Ernst of what Kern referred to as "a strong-willed conviction to the deed." Sometimes Ernst understood this and aspired to such courage, but more often he was mystified.

It was still raining when Ernst left Kern and Fischer at Zirkus 10 and continued on to Schütt's Garage in Schmargendorf. He had to knock repeatedly on the metal garage door until the housekeeper's torch blinded him through the little window. She said he was late, but Schütt was expecting him and she trudged up the stairs to the apartment over the garage to inform him of Ernst's arrival. By the time Schütt came into the bay, pulling his suspenders over a dirty undershirt, Ernst had parked the Mercedes over a mechanic's pit. Schütt drank from a bottle of Schweden punch, hot wine and cognac.

"Want some?"

Ernst shook his head. "I have work to do on the license. I could use better light, though." He arrayed his paints on an artist's cloth and began to work a brush in turpentine.

"You should have chosen a better appointed garage."

He had no patience for this repulsive excuse for a man. "We chose you, Herr Schütt. Get used to it. Bring that lamp over here."

"Are you ordering me around in my own garage?"

After spending the last week with Kern, Ernst felt ferocity surging through his veins once again, upending any apprehension or doubt. "You will do exactly as I say, Herr Schütt."

"First tell me what you're up to. Günther said something about freeing prisoners from French jails in the Ruhr Valley. I would drink to that." He did.

"If you would like to believe that, then so be it – we are freeing prisoners. Now, get me the lamp."

"I'm not your shitting servant, Techow! Get it yourself."

Ernst walked across the garage and dragged the heavy lamp to the Mercedes, murky and ominous in the dark bay, flanked by two cars in various stages of disrepair. "Incidentally, Herr Schütt, Kern and Fischer will be here soon, and we will sleep in your extra room. Our mission starts tomorrow morning, and we cannot afford to be late."

"You'll sleep on the goddam floor, you pimp." He drank again, then picked up a half-smoked cigar from a tool box.

"I don't think you'd say that to Lieutenant Kern."

Ernst lifted the bonnet of the Mercedes and examined the oil-stained engine block by electric torch. There had been more exhaust today as they returned from Schwerin, but the engine ran smoothly enough. The oil level was down about 300 cc. "Give me a can of your best motor oil," he said, as he wiped his hands on the stained cloth.

Schütt grunted at a shelf, spit at the floor and left.

With the engine running, Ernst watched the oil feed where the bleeding continued, though ever so slowly at an idle. He tried to tighten the junction again, but it felt wrong; almost certainly the screw thread was stripped. He wound heavy tape around the junction, swearing under his breath, glad Kern wasn't there to see this sophomoric repair.

There was still artistic work to be done. A strange use of his skill on paper and canvas. Strange and demeaning. It occurred to him as he altered the number plate that this was forgery, not creativity, and that made it tedious, swept his brushwork of meaning. After two hours, the new plates were so perfectly rendered that only careful inspection could have detected the counterfeit. By the time Kern and Fischer returned to the garage at one in the morning, the plates were reattached, and Kern praised Ernst's handiwork. With Kern's arrival Schütt's disposition improved, if only for Kern's benefit, and Fischer happily accepted his offer of Schweden punch. The two climbed the stairs to Schütt's apartment, one squat and fat, the other tall and lean.

The one lamp Ernst used to paint his forgeries cast dramatic shadows in the garage. The scent of oil paint blended with gasoline and solvents. Kern removed a machine pistol bundled inside a soft oil cloth from the boot of the car. He admired the weapon, running his fingers over the gun metal, then folded it back into the cloth and tucked it under his arm.

"You know, Ernst," he said, just louder than a whisper. "Whatever happens tomorrow, I've grown quite fond of you. You've always been a good soldier."

Ernst felt his face redden, and he busied himself with cleaning up his painting material. He felt lighter than air, but so different than the way Lisa made him feel. Somehow it was not just desirable, but necessary, that Kern like him – a disquieting thought. "Thank you, sir. It means a lot."

Kern held out his hand. "We should shake hands on tomorrow. It is your bond, your word of honor. It means you understand just what you are doing, and you do it for the Vaterland."

Though feeling at Kern's mercy, Ernst never-the-less clasped his hand without hesitation. "What if I had refused?" Ernst asked. He felt Kern's grip tighten.

"I knew you wouldn't." Their eyes met again. "Word of honor," Kern said. "Word of honor."

*　*　*　*　*　*　*　*　*　*

Twenty-four hours later Rathenau was dead, and they were fugitives:

Ernst on his way to Uncle Erwin's estate, Kern and Fischer fleeing north to Rostock to meet a fishing boat that would take them to Sweden.

Ernst left Berlin on the D-Zug train the morning after the assassination, heading to Jena first to spend the night at the Corps Thuringen Pub, owned by a good friend of Max Gudergahn. Ernst felt numb. He smoked constantly, like the Erzberger assassins he had driven to Hungary the previous summer. Every sensory cell stood alert. Darkness was less black, light intolerable. Policemen made him nervous. At least in Jena no one knew him; he didn't have to talk. Anyone who knew him would see immediately that something was amiss. The dormitory room upstairs from the pub felt like a cell, and Ernst cringed at the thought of being incarcerated in a cement cell even smaller than this room. Was it worth it? Did he do this for Kern, for himself, for Lisa, for the Vaterland? The proximate reason, the reason easiest to comprehend, was that he did it for Hans Gerd. One does what one must for family. But that rationalization did not long satisfy the insistent pecking of guilt at his heart. Not for Rathenau, but for the dozens – could that be? Had he killed dozens? What was the point? He could have been a nobody – but now that was impossible. He was moved by forces beyond even basic understanding, and maybe it was time to just let go – to float with the rapids, wherever they carried him. He was tired of trying to understand, to figure out the truth, to discern a good enough reason. This was easier, if no more reassuring. He would have settled for a long night of sleep. The beer finally put him out, until he awoke at 4 AM with a pounding headache. He needed a dose of Pyramidon.

He walked the darkened streets of Jena searching for an open Chemist, every pulse in his head a jolt of pain. Also against his will, he relived the final few seconds of the assassination, played it over and over in his mind: Rathenau touching his hat and smiling at him as their cars passed. The unexpected weight of shame that settled on him left the same acid taste in his throat as when Baer executed the two boys in the *Vorwärts* fight – another endlessly looping memory. He walked for two hours, aimlessly, no longer thinking of the Chemist. Hans Gerd was safe; Ernst was done with OC. Ernst's fevered mind settled all claims on his free will. He had had to do this, and now he was finished – ready to disappear – ready to forget everything and start anew. The arguments clashed in his head, and he cursed OC and Kern and Fischer – and Rathenau – but, most often and most mercilessly, he cursed himself. He was on fire, every pulse of pain an alarm bell.

Finally, dawn glowed behind the city, and the morning paper was delivered to a kiosk. That was when he saw the front page photograph of Günther.

Only twenty-four hours after Rathenau's assassination, the police proudly showed off the 'confessed assassin'. In fact, Günther's apprehension required no brilliant police work. The very night of the murder, Günther addressed the teenagers of the German National Youth Organization at the home of Studienrat Rentsch, Assistant Master of Secondary Schools and chairman of the GNYO Hansa. Günther proclaimed himself one of the assassins, and the pubertal boys cheered him wildly. One of the students, Simon Brent, told his parents of Günther's 'Deed of Deeds', and they went to the police. Ernst worried that perhaps he should have gone to Sweden after all.

Two days later, at Uncle Erwin's estate in Jacobsdorf, Ernst came to breakfast and found Erwin's newspaper on the table beside a warming cover over his toast. The kitchen maid brought hot coffee. On the front page were police artist portraits of Kern and Fischer. For three days, Günther had persisted in a fiction about his role in the assassination and managed to throw the police off their trail. But from the moment of Günther's arrest, Detective Otto Gribbetz doubted his story and pressed him about details he did not know. Finally, by the third day, the inspector broke Günther with threats to reveal his sordid past. According to the newspaper, Günther mumbled to himself for over an hour, and his sanity was questioned, but then he named Kern and Fischer.

The chase was on.

⋆　⋆　⋆　⋆　⋆　⋆　⋆　⋆　⋆　⋆

After Ernst's arrest the next day at his uncle's estate, Inspector Fluth questioned him for hours at the Alexanderplatz police station in Berlin about Kern and Fischer. Ernst kept to his story; he was only the driver and knew nothing of either the plot or Kern and Fischer's whereabouts. He worried what Kern and Fischer would say about him if they were apprehended. There was no distraction in his cell, nothing to read, and between drawing charcoal wall sketches of Lisa, Ernst wondered if he might not go mad.

On his fourth day at Alexanderplatz, a sympathetic guard gave him a day-old newspaper about Rathenau's burial and the chase for Kern and Fischer. The pictures of Rathenau's Reichstag funeral, the first such state funeral since Bismarck, compelled Ernst's attention. It kept his terror at bay to read each article several times until he knew every detail of the ceremony. Rathenau's 80 year old mother sat in the ex-Kaiser's red brocade chair in the

Reichstag gallery, her grief evident even under a black veil. Communist and Nationalist ministers wore silk hats. The coffin, draped with the black-red-gold Republican flag, sat in state behind the speaker's rostrum under a large black canopy. A sea of flowers and plants decorated the chamber. The speaker's rostrum and Government Bench were shrouded in black and hung with wreaths and ribbons in the Republican colors. Musicians from the Berlin Philharmonic Orchestra played the Egmont overture, after which President Ebert spoke. Ernst read Ebert's funeral oration several times, lingering at the paragraph addressed to him.

> ...The accursed murderers' bullets struck not only the man Rathenau but all Germany. The bloody murder was directed against the German Republic and against the idea of democracy, whose convinced champion Rathenau was. It was an assassination attempt against the nation, which robbed the nation of one of its best patriots, one of the finest brains and protagonists of Germany's reconstruction....

There was a twenty-four hour work stoppage to honor Rathenau, and the stock market closed.

A day after Günther fingered them, Kern's and Fischer's pictures were on every public building in Germany, the bounty on their heads already 500,000 marks each. Ernst fervently hoped they were either in Sweden or dead.

But their escape had not gone well. It was only in prison that Ernst read the newspaper accounts of the apprehension of the assassins. Kern and Fischer were twelve hours late getting to Rostock on the day of the murder, and the captain of the fishing boat that was to meet them had gotten nervous and left. The next day near Lenzen, at the ferry landing on the Elbe, they were recognized by a detective on holiday. Fischer produced a hand grenade, and Kern seized a young girl of seven. They forced the ferry captain to take them across immediately, and they were halfway across the river when the police arrived at the ferry slip. Once across the Elbe, they released the girl and fled.

To everyone's surprise, Kern and Fischer eluded the police for almost three more weeks. The Berliner Tageblatt featured stories about the other arrested co-conspirators, editorials about OC, feature articles celebrating Rathenau. Ernst himself was identified as "a disturbed young man," the son of the late Magistrate Alfred Techow.

Kern and Fischer were finally surrounded in the Rüdelsberg Castle in Saaleck in the Hartz Mountains. They had traveled almost 1,000 kilometers on stolen bicycles. Neither had shaved nor bathed. They had stolen what food they could. Each had lost almost twenty pounds.

A massive police posse surrounded the castle. Kern and Fischer fled to the tower and threw defiant papers from the ramparts. They must have known they had nothing to lose – they were already dead men.

DOWN WITH WEIMAR
DEATH TO THE NOVEMBER TRAITORS.

An occasional gunshot came from below.

In the late afternoon, as the setting sun illuminated the tower, Geren Hauser, a police sharpshooter, shot Kern through the heart as he released another blizzard of notes. The police battered down the door and stormed the castle tower, where they found Fischer lying on the bed as if asleep beside his companion, Kern, with a bullet hole in his temple.

14

Trials

October 1922

St. Luke's Little Summer began on Tuesday, October 3rd, the same day the Rathenau murder trial convened. The odor of manure wafted on a warm southwest wind from Schmargendorf, where Catholic farmers ceremonially fertilized their fields in obeisance to the Bishop's injunction to "prepare today for the bounties of spring, trusting the dormancy of winter and the process that goes on unseen except in the eye of God".

The largest courtroom in Germany, Leipzig's Kaiser Hall in the Supreme Court building, was chosen for the Rathenau assassination trial. Reichswehr security police in crisp uniforms with polished leather guarded the building. The coat of arms of the dukedoms of Saxony, freshly painted and mounted on polished oak panels, circled the inner walls of the courtroom. Even the sensational war crimes trials had not attracted as many journalists. The world press compared it to a theater, the dais a stage for the Judges and prosecutors, and a huge hall for over seven hundred spectators with a single overhanging gallery. Citizens of Leipzig expressed concern about the 'circus atmosphere.'

The Kaiser Hall was overfull. People stood in the aisles and along the walls. The tall doors slowly closed, the shaft of daylight they admitted narrowed, then vanished. A cordon of security police stood at regular intervals around the inner perimeter. To provide enough space for the unusual number of journalists, the Reichspresident had ordered extra tables placed directly in front of the dais between the judges, who could not see them, and the defendants. Because there were so many defendants, a long table had been brought in with extra chairs and, in front of that, smaller tables for the seven defense attorneys. On the right, beside the dais, hung a large map of the assassination site, showing the Königsallee with a great red mark, like a bullet hole, at the intersection of Erdnerstrasse.

Shortly after 8:30 on the first day, the defendants, led by an armed bailiff, filed into the courtroom. The galleries suddenly hushed into excited whispers as Ernst, followed by Hans Gerd, led a parade of the accused. Von Salomon came next, primping his hair with a comb. Ernst heard him joking with Hans Gerd about "this gala affair" and how they would be introduced – the most eligible bachelors in Germany.

"Except, of course," Hans Gerd said, "for the Fat Man." Ernst recognized his brother's nervous laughter.

The Bailiff hushed the two defendants, then cleared his throat three times for silence. He announced the accused:

"Ernst Werner Techow – Student – Berlin. Hans Gerd Techow – Student – Berlin. Ernst von Salomon – Bank clerk – Frankfurt am Main."

Von Salomon clasped his hands over his head like a sports hero. There was laughter, a smattering of applause, and the staccato rapping of Dr. Hagens's gavel.

"Waldemar Niedrig – Private Detective – Hamburg. Christian Ilsemann – Salesman – Schwerin. Gustav Steinbeck – Student – Dresden. Karl Tillessen – Student – Frankfurt. Hartmut Plaas – Journalist – Frankfurt. Friedrich Warnecke – Salesman – Hamburg."

After a pause two policeman entered, a protective cordon around the next defendant, Günther, whose glasses rode too low on his nose.

"Willi Günther – Student – Berlin."

Immediately, two young men leapt from their seats in the rear of the chamber shouting, "Traitor! Jew swine! Feme death to Günther!" Six police-men hustled the two away, and order was restored. The bailiff continued:

"Richard Schütt – Garage owner – Schmargendorf – Berlin. Franz Diestel – Garage owner – Schmargendorf – Berlin. Werner Voss – Salesman – Berlin. Günther Brandt – student – Dresden – still a fugitive."

As Ernst found his seat, the last chair at the defendants' table, a surf of whispers diffused through the vast courtroom. Heads nodded in his direction, and he thought almost a thousand spectators watched him as if the courtroom was a creature with compound eyes, swarming and hostile. Perspiration coated his forehead and upper lip, and he blotted at them with the handkerchief his mother had given him the day before, one of his father's, with the monogrammed 'AT' in one corner. She seemed numbed to what was actually happening and concerned herself with mundane details, bringing food to her two boys when she could visit, but it was a long journey, more than 150 km, and expensive. She worked extra hours at the hospital. At the Leipzig prison she could only visit one of her sons at a time. At least with

Ernst, she never shed a tear. He understood her stoicism to be a transparent barrier, an entreaty not to touch her heart.

Before him on the table sat a copy of the indictment, a black notebook with his name handwritten on the first page, a document he knew only too well from the preparatory sessions with defense lawyers. He focused on it as substance, as paper and ink, to quell all other thoughts or feelings.

Next to Ernst, Hans Gerd snickered into his good hand at von Salomon's jokes; he kept his right hand hidden in his pocket. Plaas, The Fat Man, crisp and suave in a new suit, smiled at the press photographers, who took so many pictures that the smoke of flash powder hung under the courtroom lights like a lifting fog. Warnecke adjusted his tie and flattened his hair. Hans Gerd leaned over and elbowed Ernst in the side.

"Relax," he whispered. "Lütgebrune said this will be a walk in the park."

"For you, maybe. I could get the death penalty."

"OC owns the courts. Ebermayer is nothing. He's a relic."

"I'll try to remember that."

"You're superstitious. Is that it? You think if you're too cocky things will go badly?"

"You don't need to make me feel better," Ernst said.

Hans Gerd smiled, and his head resumed its bobbing, his knees knocking back and forth.

Perhaps it was for the best that Hans Gerd did not understand, or chose to ignore the full gravity of their situation. His baby brother did not take fear or anxiety or even confusion well, and Ernst took comfort in knowing his brother felt neither afraid nor hopeless.

Spectators were well dressed and expectant, like a theater audience before curtain time. Those further back focused opera glasses on the diminutive bailiff as he read from the dais. A simple wooden barrier with a swinging gate separated the spectators from the players. Hans Gerd joked that it was the zoo fence between the dangerous animals and the aroused crowd of onlookers. Von Salomon bared his claws and growled like a lion.

Ernst thought he caught a brief glimpse of Fritz in the courtroom, but it was difficult to be sure. His mother had told him that she would not be humiliated in court. Ernst was glad she would not be there; lying would be that much more difficult in her presence.

During pre-trial hearings, Chief Prosecutor Ebermayer had offered into evidence a copy of the letter Ernst had written in prison to his mother detailing his reasons for carrying out the murder and condemning Uncle Erwin for his betrayal. Ernst's lawyer, Dr. Hahn, had seemed completely at ease and told Ernst not to worry.

"My dear boy, what you said is immaterial, either in the letter or in your depositions. Just do as you've been told. This trial will be a farce, we will see to it. Appeals will take years, and Weimar does not have years to survive."

★ ★ ★ ★ ★ ★ ★ ★ ★ ★

On this first day of proceedings, Chief Justice Dr. Hagens sat alone on the dais. His wizened face and small head, bedecked with a black pillbox cap, sat nobly, almost disembodied, over the velvet collar of his maroon robe. A tall, thin man with wisps of white hair leaking like steam from under his cap, he read the Bill of Indictment against the thirteen defendants.

Uncle Erwin arrived early, his rosy cheeks and red hair glowing in the artificial light. From his aisle seat in the first row, reserved for him as a witness, he waved to his nephews, who spurned his greeting. Leo sat beside Erwin, and the two engaged in a spirited conversation. This nettled Ernst, particularly because each, in his own way, had betrayed him.

A wave of silence spread from the back, and the courtroom stilled. Frau Rathenau had arrived, pale and hunched over. In the hushed courtroom Ernst could hear the metallic tap of her cane on the marble steps leading up to the gallery. Her manservant assisted her to a reserved seat in the center balcony. After she sat down, heads bobbed and conversation resumed. Ernst was certain she stared directly at him.

A few rows behind Uncle Erwin he suddenly saw Lisa in a powder blue coat, her blond hair tucked up under a navy beret, finding her seat. She seemed to be alone. He couldn't help but worry that Fritz must be thinking their competition was over and Lisa would fall like a ripe cherry into his hand. When Fritz visited him in prison he appeared too cheerful, too optimistic about Ernst's prospects. But it was hard to read Fritz's heart.

Over the weeks in prison, when he tried to find sleep, Ernst cried more than a few bitter tears about his lost opportunity with Lisa. It was over, as if a limb had been amputated. Loss clung to him, and it ached like a bout of influenza that never improved. Often at night he had chills and sweats. His only choices now, with what remained of his free will, were to believe the fiction of OC and the collapse of Weimar, or to kill himself. He wondered what it would be like to die by hanging.

The last time he saw Fritz, a week before the trial, he and Lisa came to visit him together. Fritz sat up close to the bars of the visitor's cell, and with pressured speech and clipped words he inundated Ernst with a steady stream of Nationalist rhetoric.

"...German soil that would have been lost without the Free Corps... Ruhr fighters and soldiers of the Black Army... Schulz and Tillessen shot this parasite Erzberger..."

Behind Fritz, bent over and small, Lisa stared at Ernst as if he were already condemned. She caught his eye, and her counterfeit attempt at a smile only amplified her anguish.

Fritz stopped mid sentence. "Ernst! You've not heard a word I've said. The future is bright – the Free Corps, The Viking Bund, Storm Troops – more than ever, we are ready to take up our buried arms. It won't be long."

"I'm listening, Fritz."

"Above all, stay loyal. Say anything – anything except OC. Lütgebrune and Hahn are the very best lawyers. Be strong, we are all behind you. Isn't that true, Lisa?"

Ernst couldn't help but think of Simon Wolff and the boy's acquittal by the Weimar court, only to die at the hand of the Feme.

"Fritz, might Lisa and I have a few moments alone?"

"Yes, of course. How selfish of me. Be brave, Ernst." He reached through the iron barrier, and his handshake felt as cold as the bars. The guard rapped his stick against the wall.

"No touching!"

Lisa took Fritz's chair. They were alone except for the guard in the far corner.

She leaned in close, and Ernst could see how pale she had become. "Fritz is so proud of you. He tells everyone that you and he are best friends."

"And you? Are you proud of me?"

She looked into her lap again. "As you said – it needed to be done." She twisted a handkerchief then looked at him, pleading. "It didn't have to be you," she whispered urgently, as if she could reverse time. "You killed us." She dabbed her eyes.

"Lisa. Darling. There is still hope. I have to believe this will be the end of Weimar. My hope, my prayer is for chaos. The courts belong to us."

"And if Weimar doesn't fall?" An awkward silence swelled. "If you had the chance, would you do it again?"

Ernst could not answer truthfully. To his Free Corps comrades it would have been an enthusiastic, though disingenuous, Yes! But to Lisa there was no unquestionable answer. He did believe in the 'Deed of Deeds' as an abstract concept, as a hope, a dream. But he also knew, from the deepest well of his being, that he could never do this again – not out of fear, but out of shame about himself, about Lisa, about his family. Without an unequivocal answer to Lisa's question he knew any rationalization was a lie. That he had participated in the murder of Rathenau meant nothing to him, but because it was Rathenau the consequences would be crushing. Nothing good could ever come of this. He had sacrificed his future, maybe his life, for the cause. For OC.

Lisa shifted in her chair, and a long silence stretched out until the guard gave them the five minute warning. "Margaret and I are living together on Prinzmetalstrasse, near the university. Here's our address. Write, if you can. She asks about you and sends her best." Two tears coursed down her cheeks, and she suddenly got up to leave.

He was drowning, and his only hope, his lifeboat, would be the miracle of chaos.

⋆　⋆　⋆　⋆　⋆　⋆　⋆　⋆　⋆　⋆

Just before she took her seat in the courtroom that first day, Lisa removed her beret, and her golden hair cascaded onto her shoulders. She caught Ernst's eye and signaled with a shy gesture in front of her chest. With neither consent nor intent, his mind ran over and over how to undo the past, so he could touch her again, and he suffered the heartache of impossibility. As the proceedings began, Fritz suddenly appeared, moving down Lisa's row to sit beside her. She had saved him a seat. Ernst forced himself to look away.

Frau Rathenau sat motionless, barely breathing. So pale was her face that it appeared as white wax embedded in black. No matter where Ernst looked he felt her raptor scowl and the hatred and sadness that he thought must be focused on him.

Schütt and Diestel sat on the far left of the table, apart from the other defendants. They clearly wished to dissociate themselves from the jokes and laughter of their youthful co-conspirators. With the exception of Niedrig and Tillessen, the other defendants were all young men who gave an impression of confidence, or at least swagger. Tillessen, accused of not reporting an assassination threat, seemed unduly concerned and sat straight-spined, like a soldier, staring fixedly at the bunting behind the judge's dais. He looked impassive, so much like his younger brother, Heinrich, Erzberger's assassin, whom Ernst had driven to safety in Hungary a year earlier.

As previously announced, at precisely 8:45 the double oak paneled doors at the head of the great chamber opened and the crowded courtroom hushed once more. Everyone rose to their feet. Von Salomon remained seated to finish a joke for Hans Gerd, then languidly and defiantly pushed back his chair so it grated against the floor, and stood to face the dais. The senior prosecutor, Dr. Ludwig Ebermayer, a handsome man with rugged features and a thick salt and pepper mustache, strode into the courtroom draped in a maroon robe with velvet collar, followed by his assistant, Dr. Goldsticker. Seven counselors for the defense followed, led by the tall and dignified Dr. Lütgebrune, his pure white hair in sharp contrast to his black robe. He stroked his mustache and fondled his goatee as he walked. The audience buzzed, then hushed again, as the nine judges, led by President Hagens, entered the chamber. Hagens and the two Judicial Commissars, Doehn and Zeiler, also wore maroon robes with velvet collars, and they sat on the specially constructed dais overlooking the lay judge bench.

At the lower dais, the six lay judges in black robes took their seats behind name plates. President Hagens stood at his seat; except for the defendants, everyone was still as he read the Chief Prosecutor's indictments.

"Ernst Werner Techow – Accomplice to the murder of Dr. Rathenau together with the deceased Fischer and Kern.

"Hans Gerd Techow, Willi Günther, Christian Ilsemann, Gustav Steinbeck, Waldemar Niedrig, Friedrich Warnecke and Ernst von Salomon – Aide to murder.

"Hans Gerd Techow, Willi Günther, Christian Ilsemann – Complicity in murder.

"Hartmut Plaas, Werner Voss – Neglecting to inform about intentions to plan a deed dangerous to the public such as high treason, murder or robbery.

"Karl Tillessen – failure to report an assassination threat and under investigation for aiding in the murder of the Mayor of Kassel.

"Werner Voss – neglecting to inform in a timely manner and numerous transgressions involving weapons trade in Beuthen, Upper Silesia, Düsseldorf, Neisse.

"Günther Brandt – Complicity in murder – the son of Prof. Brandt in Kiel. A former naval officer, now a student. He remains a fugitive from justice."

Dr. Hagens went on to report the sequence of events of the murder and the alleged participation by the thirteen defendants. He pointed to the street map of the Grünewald suburb on the wall. Thereupon, he officially opened the trial by stating that the proceedings against Ernst Werner Techow and his co-conspirators could begin. One of the two substitute judges, Dr. Zeiler, gave the oath with a religious formula, and von Salomon turned his back. Lay Judge Müller gave a civil oath. Von Salomon poked Hans Gerd in the ribs, and the two laughed together.

* * * * * * * * * *

Ernst was the first defendant called for questioning by the court. As he stood, he felt the blood drain from his face and felt unsteady for a moment. He hadn't anticipated the duress he would experience in the courtroom; the crowd felt like a predatory organism. The spectators grew clamorous as he stood, and President Hagens gaveled the chamber to silence. Ernst took a deep breath and prepared to recite the testimony he had rehearsed with Dr. Hahn and repeated to himself much of the previous long night. It kept his mind occupied, and he embraced the challenge much as he would the ear stoppers that save one from excruciating noise. Uncle Erwin sat forward cupping his hand to his ear.

Chief Judge Hagens looked down from the highest dais, over half spectacles, and began the questioning. "You belong to the German National Youth Organization and the German Folkish Defense Organization? To which other parties do you belong?"

Ernst fastened on Lütgebrune's eyes. "No party."

"How did you become a member of the OC?"

"I refuse any statement." Ernst clenched his fists. Dr. Hahn had counseled that he nurture a feeling of rage at the court, as a way of conquering fear or insecurity.

"What was your role in the Kapp Putsch?" Ebermayer asked.

"I was a truck driver." Ernst glared at the prosecutor.

"Yes, of course." Ebermayer looked over some papers on his table. "The Bavarian Wood Products Company, I believe."

"That's correct."

"And the Ehrhardt Brigade? Weren't you an officer in the Sturmkompagnie – a unit known for its aggressiveness?"

"I was a driver in Berlin with the Brigade."

"And your leader was Manfred von Killinger, the man who was taken into custody under suspicion of collusion with the Erzberger murderers?"

Ernst was ready. "Von Killinger was released – there was no evidence..."

"He is the director of the Organization Consul – OC – isn't he?"

"You seem to know these things, Herr Ebermayer. I'm sure I know nothing of Organization Consul except what I read in the newspaper." Ernst stoked the boiler of his anger and smiled.

There was snickering from the defendants' bench.

Ebermayer turned on Ernst. "This is your deposition, Ernst Werner Techow." He waved papers at him. "Your freely given statement to the police after you were apprehended. At that time you seemed to know all about Organization Consul. Have you forgotten?"

Ernst looked at the high, slow turning ceiling fans and let them distract him. During preparation, Lütgebrune reminded the defendants not to be concerned about inconsistencies in testimony. Depositions, he explained, are obtained under duress. Memories are imperfect. Stories change.

As Ebermayer castigated Ernst, Von Salomon produced a box of chocolates, which he passed up and down the defendants' table. Tittering and clucking spread through the galleries. Schütt and Diestel sat impassively and refused the candies.

Ebermayer pressed on. "Members of Organization C are sworn to absolute obedience, to remain taciturn about any events in this organization. Is that not correct?"

"If you say so." There was a ripple of laughter from the gallery, and von Salomon pushed a chocolate cream in front of Ernst.

"You have made several long trips for Organization C?"

"I refuse any statement."

"Did you receive any payments from the OC?"

"I received my expenditures and salary from the Wood Products Company."

"Who issued these moneys to you?"

"I refuse any statement."

"Could you tell us how you learned of the plan to murder Minister Rathenau?"

On this point he could relate the truth. It was a relief. "One day my brother came to me and told me that Günther, whom I knew briefly, but who was not a real acquaintance of mine, wanted to talk to me. Günther had heard about a plan from a student, Stubenrauh, to assassinate Dr. Rathenau."

"Exactly what was this plan?"

"To assassinate Minister Rathenau."

More laughter in the court, and Ernst felt emboldened. Hagens's gavel cracked like the Mauser Machinenpistol.

"During your preliminary hearings you stated that you absolutely objected to Stubenrauh's plans."

"Of course. Stubenrauh is a young hothead – an impulsive, immature young man who wanted to make a name for himself."

"Isn't that true of all of you?"

"If you refer to our passionate belief that our Vaterland has been betrayed by Versailles and the Weimar...

"Young man!" Hagens gaveled sharply. "The Weimar Republic is not on trial. You will confine your remarks to the acts with which you are charged – no more and no less."

Ernst's lawyer, Dr. Hahn stood quickly. "Your honor, if it please the court."

President Hagens nodded in his direction.

"Your honor, counsel intends to introduce the defense of necessity whereby the current political situation plays a critical role. My client felt himself morally bound to act for the preservation of the Vaterland, thus justifying any act, no matter how brutal."

Chief Prosecutor Ebermayer rose to his feet. "If it please the court. The necessity defense requires imminent, clear and present danger to the perpetrator and that there are no other means of preventing such harm. Clearly, Herr Techow, the wealthy scion of a magistrate, is hardly threatened by Weimar."

Hans Gerd cleared his throat excessively, and the other defendants – except for Schütt, Diestel and Tillessen – all laughed. Every pair of opera glasses was raised. Hagens pounded his gavel, and decorum returned. "Herr Techow. Kindly confine your remarks to the assassination. What was Stubenrauh's plan?"

"He was going to kill him in the Reichstag." Ernst bit into the chocolate cream and felt further emboldened.

"That was his plan?" Hagens said with gentle skepticism. "Surely there was more."

"He only wanted a gun," Ernst said. "I implored Günther to dissuade Stubenrauh from his plan. Stubenrauh was only eighteen years old. He had just been dismissed from the Cadet Institute. He was an agitated young man."

"What about Lieutenant Kern? Didn't he order you to facilitate a meeting with Stubenrauh?"

"I explained to Kern that I hardly knew anything about Stubenrauh, but I could easily introduce him to Günther."

"Was that when Kern sought your services as a driver?"

"Kern mentioned that he was expecting a car from Dresden that was going to be used for national purposes."

"Specifically, what did that mean?"

Ernst found he was a facile liar. "It had been decided to free some prisoners from the occupied area – patriots whom the French had falsely accused and sentenced. I believe Herr Ditmar was one of them – one of our war heroes imprisoned in Naumberg prison."

"But when Kern inquired so intensely about Stubenrauh, did you not think that he was planning something in that direction?"

"I was under the impression that Kern wanted only to stop Stubenrauh."

"Did you volunteer to drive for Kern?"

"He ordered me to go by train to Dresden to buy the car. He gave me 1,000 marks and a letter to Günther Brandt."

"The same Herr Brandt who is still a fugitive from justice?"

"I suppose so. I knew Brandt from the Ehrhardt Brigade."

There was a modest burst of applause from the spectators, and President Hagens gaveled it to silence.

Ernst continued. "We went to a restaurant in Freiburg and met Herr Küchenmeister in order to negotiate a deal for his car. Brandt came back about six hours later and told me we had to go back to Dresden because Küchenmeister's brother was part owner of the car, and he wanted us to clear its use with him. There we met Steinbeck by chance on a streetcar."

"You met Steinbeck by chance? Dresden is a large city."

"It is rather remarkable," Ernst said, and von Salomon laughed. "But that is what happened."

"And this Küchenmeister? Is he just an ordinary guy?"

"He had a car – we needed a car – that's all I know."

Ebermayer interrupted Ernst's testimony and called Detective Schleinitz from Dresden to the stand. He read a police dossier detailing the contents of a weapons cache found by the police at Johannes Küchenmeister's property in Freiburg. The walled-in stockpile contained 107 caribiner model '98 rifles, 6 light and 6 heavy machine guns.

Ebermayer returned to Ernst. "Do you still think of Küchenmeister as just another guy?"

"He buried guns. So what? The Free Corps has buried guns all over Germany and Upper Silesia. Burying guns is a patriotic act." His disdain for Ebermayer had become palpable, genuine, and it impelled his voice.

"We may need them again – perhaps to save the hide of Weimar, as we have before. What's the big deal?"

Hagens pounded his gavel once. "Herr Ebermayer. Stay with the testimony. You are dangerously close to political matters."

Ebermayer bowed to Hagens. "My apologies, your honor. If it please the court." He turned back to Ernst. "Did you consider Kern your immediate superior?"

"Yes, I did."

"Because of your membership in OC?"

"No. As I have said before, I did not belong to OC. But he was the commander, the leader of this undertaking, and that was why I followed his orders."

"Who supplied the money?"

Ernst shrugged his shoulders. "I never asked about the money. I know nothing about the money."

"You were on the payroll of the Bavarian Wood Products Division, were you not?"

"Yes, I was a driver for them."

"And did you know that the Bavarian Wood Products Division is involved in Nationalist, rightist..."

Lütgebrune jumped to his feet, his face flushed. "Objection, your honor! The Prosecution is introducing irrelevant hearsay evidence about political organizations that have no bearing upon the matter at hand. You yourself admonished counsel about introducing political considerations into a criminal proceeding."

Hagens leaned over to confer with Fehrenbach, all the time glaring at Lütgebrune, who returned the judge's stare with equal intensity. "Continue with your testimony, Herr Techow."

Von Salomon opened another box of chocolates and sampled one, then passed it to Niedrig. Plaas, The Fat Man took two, and even Tillessen took one. He almost smiled.

Later in his testimony Ebermayer asked Ernst about Erich Baade and a silver suitcase full of money. Tillessen eased to the front of his chair, alert like a fishing heron; Plaas licked his lips and blinked quickly. Ernst could feel their eyes on him. Lütgebrune sat straight and still, his head cocked forward. It was most unwise to incriminate Erich Baade, district leader of the Group of the German Folkish Defense Organization. If only they knew how close to the brain of the hydra Erich Baade stood.

Ernst said, "I don't know anything about a silver suitcase."

Ebermayer turned on his heels, and his eyes bored into Ernst. "When the truth comes out it will go hard on you, boy!"

Lütgebrune jumped to his feet. "Your Honor! Harassing the witness!"

"Herr Ebermayer, stay with the crime. Drop the politics."

"Your Honor," Ebermayer said, "the prosecution has gathered substantial proof of involvement, even promotion, of this assassination by various right wing national groups."

Hagens was visibly upset. He conferred for a moment with Judicial Commissars Doehn and Zeiler on either side.

"Our court is charged only with a criminal proceeding, and that is what we shall pursue." He turned to Ernst. "Proceed with your testimony."

Ernst smiled. Lütgebrune and Tillessen sat back, content. Plaas selected another chocolate.

Ebermayer continued. "Did Kern tell you the night before that Rathenau was going to leave his house at ten?"

"No. I knew nothing of Rathenau or his schedule."

"Yet, in the morning at the garage you said 'it will take half an hour to fix the oil feed. We may already be too late.' That is what you said, is it not?"

"I just said that we might be coming too late for our appointed starting time – to go to the territories."

"Yet other testimony and your own initial deposition indicate that you knew it was Rathenau's car and that he was to be assassinated."

"I retract that testimony," Ernst lashed back at the prosecutor. "It was obtained under duress."

"Have you not also been asked whether you would have the necessary presence of mind, and answered you could guarantee for your nervous stability?"

"I did not say that."

"Your honor," Dr. Hahn stood at his seat, calm and academic in his reserve. "Intimidating the witness."

Hagens glowered down from the dais. "I would remind you, Dr. Hahn, that your client, the witness, is a defendant charged with a capital crime. Proceed, Dr. Ebermayer."

"Thank you, your honor. On Wednesday, before the assassination, you said to Miss Lisa Schmidt, 'In the next few days you will hear from me. I will then leave Berlin.' What did you mean by this?"

Lisa, interrogated by the police? He was heartsick, felt his composure erode. "Well, I meant.... I was referring to the territories – freeing the prisoners."

"After the assassination, you returned to the garage at Schmargendorf, did you not?"

"Yes."

"And didn't you say to Herr Schütt, 'It worked. Rathenau is stretched out'?"

"I don't remember."

"Why did you return to Herr Schütt's?"

"I left some of my personal belongings there."

"The paint and brushes you used to paint over the license plate?"

"Yes."

"And the machine pistol and the car coats?"

"I was only the driver. I don't know what happened to them. Kern gave all the orders. Schütt noticed my excitement, and I told him that Kern and Fischer had just assassinated Rathenau. Schütt reproached me heavily, and I answered him, 'I did not know this was going to happen.' I did not want this either." Ernst was doing Schütt a favor, and he expected Schütt to reciprocate in his own testimony. They had all been prepared.

Ebermayer strode purposefully to the table devoted to Reich evidence. The paper he sought was on top in a file. He studied it for a moment and then handed it to Ernst. "You have written a letter on July 5, 1922 to your mother – state's evidence #14. This letter leads one to conclude that you were fully aware of your participation in this assassination."

"No. The purpose for my letter was only to inform my mother about my reasons."

"But that means that you resigned yourself to Kern's wishes and that you decided to participate in the murder as the driver of the car."

"I only followed Kern's orders. I had no choice."

Counsel Bloch, representing Tillessen, Steinbeck and Plaas, stood at his seat waiting to be recognized. The left-wing press referred to him as 'Organization C's barrister'. Dignified, with a shock of white hair and pince nez spectacles, older even than Lütgebrune, Bloch cleared his throat, and Hagens recognized him. He spoke in a surprisingly robust and gravelly voice. "How binding was any oath that you might have sworn to the OC, if you had to give another oath to Kern?"

Ernst remembered the necessary response and shrugged his shoulders, like a boy. "As far as I know Kern did not even belong to the OC."

There was a murmuring through the courtroom. Hagens gaveled for silence.

Bloch continued. "Had you belonged to OC, the oath that you swore would not have committed you to participate in the Rathenau murder."

"That's correct. But I don't belong to OC."

Bloch turned slowly on stiff hips and waved his hand. "No further questions."

Ebermayer resumed his questioning, pacing before the defendant's table. "Didn't you tell Schütt 'something had to happen. Our money was running out'?"

"Yes. Kern told me that".

"What does that mean? Whose money was running out? The OC's?"

"No, no. Just in general, all the rightist circles."

Hagens interrupted Ebermayer's cross examination. "Herr Techow, you told the court that you were not convinced of the necessity of the assassination. Why then did you go along?"

Dr. Hahn's legs quivered with the urge to leap up and object, but Lütgebrune laid a restraining hand on his forearm.

"I was under the impression that Kern would have carried out the murder all by himself if I had not gone along. In any event, I could not disregard his orders."

"Then what was your motivation to comply with Kern?"

"I was under his influence, and I could not go back."

"So was it some kind of psychological pressure?"

"Well, yes, I believe it was. When I was in his vicinity I felt protected by him." Although he was coached to say this, Ernst winced at the inherent truth of this testimony.

"Didn't you concern yourself with the fact that Kern would pursue his goal to his death?"

"I gave Kern my word of honor."

"And this word of honor, given in relation to a murder, was sacred to you?"

"I didn't know it was to be a murder. And, yes, my word of honor is always sacred to me."

"And you preferred to keep this word even though you then complied with the worst crime possible?"

Ernst looked to his lawyer, Dr. Hahn, who nodded. "Yes. There was no talking back to Kern. He gave an order, I followed it."

"When exactly did you know about the murder plot?"

"I knew nothing of the plot until I met with Kern and Fischer at the Corps

228

Teutonia Pub a few days before. Kern talked about someone's plan, young Stubenrauh's, to shoot Rathenau. The murder was to trigger an uprising from the left. The Free Corps and other armies of the right would be called upon by Weimar to crush the leftists, and then we would have a National government. Kern mocked his plan."

"By National government you mean a National Rightist government?"

Ernst felt emboldened again. "Your words, not mine."

Hagens nodded for the prosecutor to continue. Ebermayer folded his hands behind his back, his head down, and strode the length of the defendant's table. "Herr Techow, what do you know of Dr. Rathenau?"

Hahn was already on his feet when President Hagens interrupted the Chief Prosecutor. "Dr. Ebermayer, Dr. Hahn is going to object and suggest you be more specific. Is that not correct, Dr. Hahn?"

"If it please the court." He sat down, one leg tapping.

"Specifically." Ebermayer acknowledged the defense counsel with a wave of his hand. "Have you ever read anything by Minister Rathenau?"

Ernst's mind drew a blank. He felt exposed. "I can think of nothing specific. But I read the newspapers, and I listen to lectures and presentations..."

"Right wing newspapers and lectures by Nationalists like Kern and your co-defendant, Herr Tillessen?"

Lütgebrune jumped to his feet. "I object, your honor!"

Ebermayer appealed to the dais. "Your honor, the defendant has already testified in his deposition that he knew of Minister Rathenau from articles in Zukunft, a right wing newspaper."

Hagens nodded to Ebermayer. "You may continue."

Ebermayer returned to Ernst. "What did you learn about Rathenau from Kern?"

"The Rapallo Treaty, that Rathenau negotiated and signed for Germany, and his policy of fulfillment of the Versailles Treaty. He has done great harm to Germany. Rathenau himself is an agent of Lenin. The Rapallo Treaty is proof of his support for Bolshevism. Rathenau's sister is in fact married to Radeck, Lenin's envoy to Berlin."

There was a rustle of laughter from the galleries, and Hagens gaveled.

Ebermayer made a steeple of the fingers of both hands and brought them to his lips. "I see," he said mockingly. "Go on."

"Rathenau is well known to be one of the three hundred Elders of Zion. He and other powerful Jews worldwide are plotting to overthrow governments and establish a world Jewish order. Rathenau himself acquired his position as Foreign Minister by means of a twenty-four hour ultimatum to President Ebert."

"Hmm," Ebermayer nodded his head. "This is something I had not heard."

"There are many things you and your Weimar apologists have not heard." This was his moment. The whole world was listening. "Rathenau was part of a world-wide Jewish conspiracy, a Bolshevist, an agent of Lenin. His goal was to engraft Bolshevism onto Germany forever." Ernst's face flushed; his voice escalated. He pointed at Hagens for emphasis and blame. His heart raced and pounded. "And now this self-same government that is under the influence of the Bolsheviks – whom Rathenau brought into the government in the first place – and the betrayers of Versailles... this self-same treasonous government puts us on trial? Patriots each and every one..."

Hagens' gavel fell repeatedly. A fracas broke out in the galleries. A young man with a close-shaved head unfurled a Free Corps banner and began chanting.

"Down with Weimar! Long live Techow!"

The doors flew open and a cordon of policemen streamed into the court-room. Four officers confiscated the banner and hustled the chanting youth out of the room. Some minutes later order was restored.

Hagens leaned forward and spoke to Ernst like a kindly schoolteacher. "Young man. The Treaty of Rapallo was beneficial for Germany because it clarified that Russia could not demand any payment of reparation. I believe even Zukunft acknowledged that."

Ernst felt confused, unable to focus his memory; he continued in a weakened voice. "Yes, but the Entente thought that the treaty also contained a military component and that was harmful in the eyes of the Entente."

Ebermayer was on his feet again. "And why should a devoted rightist like yourself care a fig for what the Entente thinks?"

Ernst could neither think nor hold Ebermayer's penetrating gaze. "It's very complicated," Ernst finally said in a quieter voice. His temples throbbed with headache.

President Hagens interrupted again. "Rathenau was a leader of German industry. Did you really think that this man favored Bolshevism? I would also remind you that Rathenau and your father were on the same Board of Directors. No doubt he was a guest at your house on more than one occasion. Maybe you even met him. Your uncle, Peter Behrens, served Rathenau as chief architect for AEG. Your family is, in fact, quite connected to the Rathenau family. You do know, of course, of Rathenau's invaluable service to Germany during the Great War? He organized the provision of war material. He was an indispensable patriot."

"Yes, I know these things," Ernst said.

"If you knew these things, why did you take part in the murder?" Hagens was exasperated.

"I had given my word of honor. I could not betray..."

"But this word of honor was forced from you the night before when you were under intoxication. Five or six bottles of Schweden punch, I believe. Is your word of honor given in such circumstances more important than the life of a human being?"

Ernst wanted to say he had not been not intoxicated; he knew exactly what he was doing, and it had to be done. But it was necessary for OC's disguise that these overzealous student perpetrators be characterized as drunk the night before.

Von Salomon pushed over the box of Sarotti chocolates and whispered loud enough for the press to hear. "Have another chocolate cream, Ernst. They are heavenly."

$$\star \quad \star \quad \star \quad \star \quad \star \quad \star \quad \star \quad \star \quad \star \quad \star$$

After Ernst's first examination, expert witness Prof. Dr. Strassman from Berlin was questioned about the cause of Rathenau's death, and he explained that altogether five shots had been fired. They all went through the whole body. The first bullet was already the mortal one; the fifth penetrated below the chin and destroyed the jaw. Some further injuries had been caused by the hand grenade, and they were on Rathenau's left hand and right foot. The fusillade must have begun when the pursuing car was just ahead of Rathenau's vehicle. Ernst recalled Rathenau's smile and how he had touched his hat.

Mrs. Helene Kaiser, the nurse who came to Dr. Rathenau's aid at the moment of the attack, testified next. She wore her nurse's uniform, the same blue and white striped full-cut dress with long sleeves and starched white apron she had worn the day of the murder. The galleries found her costume amusing. She described waiting for her streetcar at the corner of Erdenerstrasse, when she became witness to the murder. Sister Kaiser described the already familiar course of events: She ran into the street, almost instinctively, she said, climbed into Rathenau's car and extinguished the burning upholstery. Rathenau sat rigidly upright, ominously stiff. She laid him across her lap and supported his bleeding head. "He looked at me with his eyes," she said, looking down into her lap as if Rathenau's head was still there. "He seemed to smile, and then I thought he died."

Rathenau's driver, Herr Prozeller, identified himself as a chauffeur, an employee of Rathenau's AEG which owned the car. The murder took place behind his back. He heard three shots, and then several more, and then the detonation of the hand grenade. The memory of this bloody event still haunted him, unnerved him, and he spoke in a halting voice.

★ ★ ★ ★ ★ ★ ★ ★ ★ ★

On Thursday, the second day of the trial, Hans Gerd was questioned. Unlike Ernst, he seemed as eager as a gladiator for the Christians. He joked with von Salomon, who brought yet another box of chocolates. Later in the morning von Salomon distributed lollipops among the defendants.

So far Ernst's mother had not attended the trial, and he was glad for it. He wondered if she was sorry that he and Hans Gerd were her children.

President Hagens asked Hans Gerd, "Did your brother tell you details of the plan."

"Ernst?" Hans Gerd said. "He treats me like a baby. Told me it was none of my business. Ernst is like that – arrogant, except with his girlfriend."

Ernst jabbed his elbow into Hans Gerd's thigh.

"Wasn't the murder discussed at Schütt's apartment the night before? You were present on Friday, June 23rd."

"It was early Saturday morning – about 1 AM Kern and Fischer had just arrived from Schwerin. We all met in Schütt's apartment for drinks, but I only overheard Kern talk about cars and a gun. Nothing specific. When I wanted to find out more Kern told me I should have another Schweden punch and not concern myself with it. Günther told me that Kern and Fischer were planning a 'wild thing.' I suspected then that it was the Rathenau assassination."

"What was your job?" Hagens asked.

"I was told to procure paints, brushes, ink and a special pen for Ernst to work on a fake license plate. Ernst is very good. You should see his drawings – quite lifelike."

"Herr Techow." Hagens leaned forward. "Try to stay focused on your testimony."

"Focus, Hans Gerd," von Salomon whispered. "Focus!" The defendants laughed.

"Defendant von Salomon!" President Hagens rapped his gavel. "This court has been patient with your antics, but I will find you in contempt if your behavior persists. Herr Techow, please continue."

Hans Gerd tried to keep from smiling, but it was impossible, and he covered his mouth like the embarrassed teenager he was. His testimony corroborated Ernst's in most details. Prosecutor Ebermayer made much of several inconsistencies, and Lütgebrune objected whenever OC was mentioned.

★　★　★　★　★　★　★　★　★　★

Uncle Erwin was to testify the next day. Just before his appointed time, Ernst saw him enter the Kaiser Hall accompanied by his mother, arm in arm, brother and sister, heads erect and proud. She wore a black dress with a gray collar as if she were in mourning. Ernst was disappointed to see her in the courtroom. Perhaps she only came for Erwin's testimony. He'd known for a long time that, in spite of Uncle Erwin's patronizing attitude toward his younger sister, he was the weak sibling; it was he who needed her the most.

Erwin's suit was new, and he seemed to have lost weight. He fumbled with the latch on the witness box and tripped on the step up. He mumbled to himself and sighed before taking the oath. Ernst turned his chair away from him altogether. The facts of Erwin's discovery of Ernst's participation in the murder were reviewed sympathetically by Ebermayer and Hagens. Several times counsel had to implore the witness to speak up.

"Well, of course, I completely understand the emotional turmoil of youth today." Erwin grasped both his jacket lapels. "*O tempora! O mores!* I was once young myself, you know. But I don't condone murder. No, no, never murder."

"Herr Behrens, did you receive threatening letters after it became known that you caused your nephew to be apprehended?"

"I did. Anonymous letters signed by 'A German woman' and 'A Brave German national.' Letters that threatened my life, my estate, my family, though, of course I have none except my dear sister and brother, who incidentally works for Rathenau's AEG company. Irony only compounds sadness."

Ebermayer continued pacing slowly, his benevolent patience inviting Erwin's story, like a maestro conducting an adagio. "I understand, Herr Behrens, how difficult this is for you."

Ernst could not contain his curiosity and saw Erwin shake his head and press his lips together so tightly they almost disappeared; the corners of his mouth twitched downward. Ebermayer allowed the silence to linger.

"He's a good boy," Erwin finally said. "I want you to understand, I love my nephew. He was entrusted to me after his father's death." He stopped again.

Ernst did not want to hear this. That Uncle Erwin's words could bring him to the point of tears only made him loathe his uncle more intensely.

"I had grown so fond of the boy, I wanted to make him my heir. I still find it hard to believe that he could commit himself to such a heinous crime. He acted irrationally, out of fear – in an altered state. He never would have done this if he was not under the spell of that... that madman Kern." He leaned forward with fervent innocence to appeal to Dr. Ebermayer. "Ernst's father was an intimate friend of Doctor Rathenau's father. Minister Rathenau visited the Techow mansion as well. I knew Minister Rathenau myself, and I am ashamed that my nephew should be implicated in his murder." Erwin pulled a white handkerchief from his pocket and wiped perspiration from his face.

"Perhaps I should not have turned him in. I don't know. Once the newspapers named him I felt there was nothing I could do. I feared for his life. Look what happened to Kern and Fischer, on the run, hunted down like animals."

"But Kern is now regarded as a hero by some," Ebermayer said.

"*Extinctus amabitur idem.* Safely under the ground a bad man can be loved, or blamed, for all things. I reject the whole business of murder. Don't get me wrong. I am a patriot – a Nationalist – but this Organization C – it has no place..."

"Objection, your honor!" Lütgebrune was on his feet.

Hagens leaned forward and spoke sympathetically to Erwin. "Herr Behrens, I must ask you to confine your remarks to the question and the situation at hand. I know how you feel about Organization C – we all have questions -"

"Your honor!"

"Be seated, Herr Lütgebrune! I am sustaining your challenge!" He turned to Erwin again, and his voice softened. "We are not able to try Organization C at this hearing. They will have their day in court, Herr Behrens. I guarantee you that. Please continue."

"Ernst is an angry young man, as are so many others. He was under quite a lot of strain. His father's death. His military service was quite dangerous and stressful. A brave boy – he did his duty as he saw fit. All that Free Corps business. The Ernst Techow who acted under Kern's spell is not my nephew. They say that anger is brief madness. But strip away the anger, and I think you will find a frightened, fatherless boy. I heard he said it himself – he was afraid that if he did not participate in the plot Kern would have killed him and his brother, Hans Gerd."

"Objection!"

"Sustained. Herr Behrens, only tell us what you know, not what you heard."

"Yes, of course, of course." Erwin became more animated, his eyes widened, and he leaned forward gripping the witness box molding. "I remember...and...and I remember now that Ernst told me he thought he was driving for a prison rescue. Yes, that's it – a rescue of Germans in French prisons, in the Ruhr Valley, I believe." He shook his head as if scattering the cobwebs of memory.

"Herr Behrens." Ebermayer said it softly, as if the two were sharing a beer at Kempinski's. "You never mentioned the rescue alibi in your deposition. I realize you are fond of your nephews, but it is best not to fabricate excuses. Do you have anything further to tell the court?"

Uncle Erwin flushed and picked at his shirt as if it might have lint. "I have nothing further to add, only plead with the court for leniency. Ernst is a good boy – angry, confused, easily manipulated, but a good boy." He hesitated. "I had hoped that some day he would work on my estate – perhaps manage it after I'm gone."

Erwin was excused from the stand and had difficulty finding the step down. His handkerchief was out again, and this time he wiped his eyes. Ernst's mother came forward from the spectator's seating, through the wooden gate separating the judges and lawyers. A policeman moved to stop her, but Dr. Ebermayer raised his hand, and the constable allowed her entry.

She steadied her brother and held him under the arm, escorting him past the lawyers, through the gate held open by Dr. Ebermayer, into the hushed auditorium. Erwin walked bent over, weeping freely now, letting her lead him through the lofty exit doors.

As he watched Uncle Erwin retreat, Ernst's anger was momentarily replaced by bittersweet sadness, wondering how twenty-one years of love could be blinded in a stroke by betrayal. Kern had once explained it to Ernst in simple terms. In the history of a nation, the personal gave obeisance to the political, and when Ernst remembered Kern's injunction, he could resume his resentment.

★   ★   ★   ★   ★   ★   ★   ★   ★   ★

Günther sat between two policemen like a solitary planet, spinning on his skewed axis, largely ignored by his co-conspirators. His attorney, Gollnick, called the medical examiner, Dr. Schutz, a psychiatrist who explained that, after several interviews with the defendant, he found Günther to be "not quite right."

Dr. Schutz explained Günther's romantic disposition and his transfer to Turkey during the Great War where he "strutted about" with self-bestowed badges of honor until he was finally taken into custody for embezzlement and desertion and sentenced to prison.

Schutz continued, "Defendant Günther's former comrades are of the opinion that Günther is not a fully responsible person, and that he had suffered mental distress because of a train accident and several bouts with malaria. I have no doubt he suffers delusions."

Schutz concluded that "this examiner thinks of Günther as a sociopath who is not intellectually but ethically incapacitated. I am an absolute opponent of the notion of limited responsibility, because it can be too easily misused. But if I am asked about it now – I have to state that Günther only bears limited responsibility. According to the new penal code, he would be considered to be of limited responsibility."

As the court argued his sanity, Günther took more of an interest in the proceedings, and he even tried to engage Warnecke in whispered discussion. He too came with a box of Sarotti chocolates, a gift from a supporter.

After much wrangling, Dr. Hagens addressed the issue of Günther's fitness to be tried. "According to present day thinking," he said, "Willi Günther is under all circumstances of sound mind and may be called as a witness in his own defense. Herr Gollnick, please proceed."

There was animated discussion at the defense table, with Dr. Lütgebrune rising to state that the defense objected vigorously to Günther's inclusion in the trial, considering him to be a seriously deranged and unreliable witness.

It was late in the day, and several defendants, including Günther, looked pale and soon developed colicky abdominal pain. Günther and Warnecke seemed to have difficulty finding a position of comfort, and more than once each had to leave the court to use the toilet. Later that night, Ernst woke suddenly to a deep aching in his bowels and just reached the toilet. Half an hour later his stomach muscles suddenly cramped again; he felt cold, soaked with sweat, and he vomited. Swallowing became difficult and his face grimaced from even a sip of water. The prison doctor imposed a state of quarantine, mumbling about cholera and poisoning and wouldn't it be easier and cheaper if they all just died.

Dr. Castelli, Professor of Medicine at the Charité, came to consult on the outbreak. In front of a cortege of eager medical students he poked and prodded at Ernst's abdomen, more mindful of a differential diagnosis than of the discomfort he caused.

"Bacillary dysentery, amoebic dysentery, catarrhal or diphtheritic, mechanical or chemical irritants, ptomaine poisoning, phlegmonous gastritis and toxic gastritis. One must consider the context of the illness, the epidemic yet selective nature of the outbreak, and one must consider opportunity. If you had been reading the newspapers you know that these defendants, but not Schütt or Diestel, who remain well, ate chocolates. Arsenic is a sweet toxin, easily camouflaged in chocolate."

Ernst doubled over in pain again and felt the blood drain from his face. Castelli pronounced it arsenic poisoning and scribbled a prescription for Castelli's purge, which was almost as unpleasant as the condition it was meant to cure. The dispiriting weekend in the infirmary profoundly exhausted him.

His mother visited him in the prison infirmary and sat at his bedside, kneading her perfumed handkerchief. She was mostly silent. Ernst feigned sleep. When she did speak it was to exhort Ernst to understand how deeply Uncle Erwin cared about him, but he turned his back. There would be no forgiveness; no atonement would be acceptable. To contemplate Erwin's betrayal only worsened his condition, as did his craving of Lisa's solace.

As angry as he was, that was also how sorry he felt, though he didn't exactly know why. It was impossible to speak with her and keep those dueling emotions at bay. Of course, he understood that she had been victimized by a life once privileged, suddenly upended. Perhaps that was why she angered him so – she was a relentless reminder of the vagaries of life, the unpredictability, the injustice. He felt small and inadequate, a testament to his mother's admonition that he would never amount to anything. And now, when he had reached for something great, something grand, the 'Deed of Deeds', he was being ground into nothingness. A failure again, no doubt, in his mother's eyes.

She left him a paper bag filled with a fragrant mixture of chamomile, peppermint and fennel, for a soothing tea, and she was visibly relieved to extract a promise that he would drink it every few hours. Then she did something unexpected, something rare. She kissed his forehead. Ernst could not recall the last time he had felt his mother's lips, but her awkward sweetness wakened a primordial memory, precious and innocent, but elusive as smoke.

The next day Lisa visited briefly, this time alone. She sat beside Ernst and stroked his head as they talked. For the first time since his incarceration almost four months earlier, Ernst felt the cruel consolation of her touch, smelled her forbidden fragrance and the sweetness of her breath. Under the leering eye of the guard, who cautioned her about any displays of affection, the kiss he yearned for would not be forthcoming. She seemed to have gotten older, and there were creases near her eyes. She wore no makeup.

"How many children do you want to have?" Ernst asked dreamily as she soothed his hair into place.

"Two, maybe three. How about you?"

"Two, maybe three. We'd have lovely children."

The silence stretched out too long. The clatter of metal instruments on a tray echoed from the hallway.

Ernst rolled to his side and propped his head on one elbow. "Do you think we'll have children?"

"Margaret asked me the same question. I mean, about you and me. She likes you. She's sick to death about this mess."

"I don't care what Margaret thinks. What do you think?"

"Ask me again when all this is behind us. I can't think of the future. The present is too complex."

Ernst lay back again and closed his eyes. Lisa's fingers lingered on his cheek, and he memorized their touch.

"You've changed the future, Ernst." Her eyes brimmed full. "Most of us just live day to day. Something big happens – like Rathenau – our lives change. History changes us, we don't change history. But you, you yourself have changed the future – you've changed the world. It's extraordinary. I don't know what's right anymore. Maybe there is no right anymore. What a sad thought."

He took both her hands and her eyes cast downward.

"It's not cheap to change history," she said. "You pay a high price. In books one reads about revolutionary heroism. It's almost romantic, but really it's not. Revolutions are disorders. People die."

Her five minute visit was over. Ernst felt another wave of cramping and nausea, and the tears that threatened when Lisa left spilled down his cheeks. He was glad no one was there to see them. He had changed history, and there was no turning back the clock. Now he faced the biggest challenge of his life, and there was no place for tears – or regrets.

After the poisoned chocolate incident, Lütgebrune, representing all the attorneys for the defendants, cited the Weimar penal code and filed a motion for a retrial. President Hagens denied the motion, saying "the defendants are not dead, which may be of considerable disappointment to certain factions." There were rumors of the "Black Hand" of OC, along with newspaper and magazine stories about the medieval Feme.

Ernst felt the inevitability of a guilty verdict and prison – the rest of the trial seemed a mere formality. When he was sick it was a relief to abandon thinking about this formalized courtroom drama, even though he was the protagonist. He was at the mercy of Weimar. But Weimar was also at the mercy of OC, and one day in the near future that reality would come to fruition and correct this inequity. It was as if the arsenic-laced chocolates had poisoned his spirit as well as his body, and though he sat at the defendant's table day after day, listening to one testimony after another, he felt as if he never completely returned to the courtroom. His ears heard the words, but concentration became laborious, almost superfluous.

Sensing Ernst's detachment, the other defendants spoke less and less to him. Hans Gerd gave up trying to reassure him or to engage him with von Salomon's foolishness.

Karl Tillessen, covert chairman of OC, testified next, and his was a bravura performance as a veteran officer and a patriot who distanced himself from the assassination. "For religious reasons alone I detest murder as a person and as a Christian." A faint smile never left his lips.

Hellmut Plaas, The Fat Man, followed Tillessen on the stand, and his testimony was similar. He requested and was granted permission to remain seated – for health reasons. In a satiny voice, saccharine and cold, he denied participation in the Rathenau conspiracy. "Murder is murder," he said softly. "I detest all assassinations."

When Ernst woke before dawn the next day, he remembered that it was his twenty-first birthday, and he felt sure no one except himself would acknowledge it.

The tenth and final court session on Friday brought considerable excitement. Defense attorneys deluged the court with a flood of legal briefs to prove their clients' innocence or attempt to lessen the sentences. In response to a question by Günther's lawyer as to why the charge of manslaughter had not been considered, Ebermayer retorted that this was a "classical case" of premeditated murder.

Lütgebrune stressed again the extenuating circumstances of blind obedience to a senior officer, a quasi-military obligation to follow orders without question. The court refused this contention and noted that at least in the case of Tillessen, he was senior even to Kern and did not sufficiently bring his 'military rank' to bear.

Finally Lütgebrune introduced the defense of necessity. Citing the example of passengers crowding the lifeboats of the *Titanic*, he noted that acts of criminal violence, such as shooting men attempting to board lifeboats intended for women and children, are condoned in circumstances of imminent danger to 'prevent greater harm.' In this case, Lütgebrune went on to assert, the defendants had acted out of necessity to prevent the harm they deemed probable from the drift of Weimar towards Bolshevism. He noted that a large proportion of the German population shared this fear and, as the collapse of the mark only emphasized, the republic stood on the verge of overthrow, with the forces of Bolshevik revolution poised to create a German Soviet.

★　★　★　★　★　★　★　★　★

On Friday afternoon, Dr. Ebermayer made his closing speech and demanded the "death penalty for Ernst Werner Techow as accomplice to murder." Ebermayer explained that this had not been a political assault, but murder, even if some political motivations played a role. Because of that he also demanded loss of civic honor as well as prison terms for the other conspirators. The sentences he asked for the others were, by contrast, milder but still substantial.

When Ebermayer mentioned the death penalty for the first time, Ernst leaned forward on the table, face flushed. He hid his face, pretending to write, but his pen only scribbled and finally drew the profile of a dog's head that became a caricature of Ebermayer, extending his nose, enlarging his ears. Hans Gerd and von Salomon looked on and laughed, but Ernst roiled inside, and the lines of his drawing became taut and tremulous.

Ebermayer's speech lasted three hours. He began by quoting Rathenau himself – Rathenau as analytical defender of these young people who murdered him. Ernst's pen tore the paper.

"Ironically, it is Rathenau's own words that hold the key to understand the motives of the defendants:

> "The dying and dead middle class is the most dangerous part in the organism of our state. By itself, the decrease of the "mark" value should not be a catastrophe. But in such periods when stocks are going up and everything gains in value, the middle class however, the civil servant, the officer, the retiree, the scholar and people on fixed incomes cannot live, cannot achieve what they long for. You see reactionaries, rightist radicals and Nationalists ready to act. The civil servants raised their children in decent conservative faith. Now the circle of University students turn into hotbeds of the tempted who used to be raised with high self-esteem. Yes – you can understand the mood of these young people, how they suffer from these conditions they find themselves in – a system that contradicts what they have considered to be good and beneficial and under which members of their family suffer. So it is easy to understand from a psychological point of view that they see a direct connection between the system and the suffering, and that they are spurred to deeds which the war has taught."

There was absolute silence in the courtroom. Try as he did not to, Ernst could not help but pay rapt attention to Rathenau's own words, which he recognized as truth.

Ebermayer looked up from the text. "From this circle of people come Rathenau's murderers. And we have to ask: is it possible that the plan for that assault came about without outside influences, without instigation? Or has it been proven that there is a strong group of organizations that have written the "death sentence" of leading politicians onto their banner? In either case, it is a fact that anti-Semitic hatred has created such a poisoned atmosphere that these plans of murder could have been contemplated."

In moving language Ebermayer maintained that his sole objectives were prosecutorial fairness and full disclosure of the facts of the case. Justice demanded complete knowledge, and he laid out the course of events, organizing successful and failed evidence.

The other sentences sought by the prosecution seemed mild, Ebermayer admitted. He ended his speech with an exhortation aimed at Hagens and the panel of judges.

"We believe we have established the guilt of one man in murder and some of his circle of co-conspirators. But we have not identified the source of this evil. There is every reason to believe that the organizations behind this murder reach into every level of government and industry. It is an old sore that festers and threatens a fatal infection of the Republic itself. I must urge, no, demand of the courts to continue this investigation until this abscess had been completely drained, lest it poison us all!"

★ ★ ★ ★ ★ ★ ★ ★ ★ ★

After Chief Prosecutor Ebermayer's closing speech, President Hagens called on Ernst to respond to a final set of clarifying questions.

Ernst strove to pay attention, to rise above the numbing of enduring helplessness and fresh despair. At best he would go to prison, if he escaped the capital justice of Weimar or the simple vengeance of the Feme, and he understood now why prisoners hung themselves. For two weeks Ernst had listened to such an elaborate parade of lies and half-truths, his own and those of his fellow defendants, that he no longer knew, nor cared to distinguish, truth from fiction. His brain grew weary from play-acting Lütgebrune's script, and arsenic poisoning left him exhausted and apprehensive. The Feme haunted his daydreams and nightmares with intrusive thoughts that displaced any fragment of memory or shred of hope for Lisa.

On this last day of the trial, Ernst felt Frau Rathenau's stare especially piercing and persistent. Von Salomon called her the "old crone" and noted that she had not moved for three hours. "Someone should see if she isn't already dead," he joked, and Hans Gerd laughed. Ernst wondered what went through her mind, wondered how the two mothers, his own and Rathenau's, suffered at his hand. It was necessary, but it was hurtful in a most uncompromising way.

"Herr Techow?" Hagens' commanding voice wrenched Ernst back into the courtroom. "Herr Techow? Are you ill again?"

"No. No. I'm all right. Would you repeat the question?"

"Why had you given Kern your word of honor when you were not convinced of Kern's motivation? Did you really believe it was a practice run?"

"It went very fast. Kern held out his hand and said, 'Let's shake on it.' It was a matter of honor. I had to do it, whether I wanted to or not."

"And by 'do it' you mean participate in the murder of Foreign Minister Rathenau?"

Ernst breathed deeply. Something broke inside, and he knew the struggle was over; the best he could hope for was mercy from Weimar – and OC. Had

Kern been correct Ernst would have been an honored man, a hero of the Reich. Instead he felt the dim-witted shame of a schoolboy caught stealing cigarettes, and he barely whispered, "That is correct."

"So, it was not because you had given him your word of honor previously to help him under any circumstances?"

"No – I only gave Kern my word of honor once, and that was on that evening."

"Let me sum up," Hagens said. "When Kern confronted you with his murder plan you were not convinced? But then when Kern held out his hand the night before and said, 'Let's shake on it,' you did? Is that correct?"

The memory of Kern's handshake, so unexceptional at the time, so automatic, returned with ferocity. Did OC, or the Feme condemn for betrayal of the dead? And Weimar? Would his confession provoke the death penalty or spare him from it? He was confused, frightened by the fear that Kern had inspired, unsure if he could even trust his attorneys, who seemed more devoted to safeguarding OC. "I don't want to say why I hesitated. It would shed a bad light on Kern."

President Hagens gaveled once. "Defendant! Kern is dead! You would sacrifice yourself in order not to shed a bad light onto a dead person? That is nonsense! Explain yourself. In what way did Kern exert influence on you?"

Ernst had to puzzle out the question.

"How then did you give your word of honor?"

"I already gave a statement about that." He tried to remember the automatic answer he had memorized, then paused and breathed deeply. "But it was not the truth."

"Then deliver a truthful statement now."

"Kern would have killed me," he finally said in a near whisper. "It was a matter of life and death."

"Speak up Herr Techow."

"Kern would have killed me." This time he said it with conviction, but sought only mercy, or pity. Maybe it was even true.

"Does your assumption that Kern might have killed you depend on knowing special circumstances, or is it only based on his character?"

"I prefer not to talk about it."

Hagens' voice crescendoed. "You prefer not to? Think of your family, your mother. They are closer to you than this deceased criminal Kern."

"Kern said, 'If you refuse I will shoot you.' I believe he would have."

"And your previous testimony? Are you saying now that this confession supplants all previous alibis?"

Ernst nodded and managed to say, "Yes, this is what happened." Curiously, a single tear rolled down his cheek and fell onto the pine table top. "I'm sorry. I'm sorry."

There was a sudden commotion at the defense table. A letter passed back to Dr. Hahn from Bloch. Lütgebrune nodded agreement. "If it please the court." Dr. Hahn held aloft a page of elegant stationery. "I have a letter that I believe has a direct bearing on the sentencing considerations of this tribunal. I have been asked by Frau Rathenau to read this. Frau Techow has given her consent."

Dr. Hahn detailed the relationship between the Rathenau and Techow families. "How unspeakable the tragedy," he noted, "that despite thirty years of family ties, the son of Alfred Techow, a confidant of the slain minister's father, had become a party to assassination. The fathers share ideas, port and cigars – one son kills the other."

Ernst hushed Hans Gerd and von Salomon; the other defendants turned silent. Tillessen sat bolt upright as always, a faint smile still fixed on his face.

For the first time in two weeks of proceedings, Frau Rathenau's chair in the gallery was conspicuously empty. Dr. Hahn adjusted his reading glasses. "Frau Rathenau addressed this letter to Frau Techow on July 3, only nine days after the assassination."

> My Dear Frau Techow,
>
> In grief unspeakable I give you my hand, you, of all women the most pitiable. Say to your son that in the name and spirit of him he has murdered, I forgive, even as God may forgive, if before an earthly judge he make a full and frank confession of his guilt and before a heavenly one repent. Had he known my son, the noblest man earth bore, he would rather have turned the weapon on himself than on him. May these words give peace to your soul.
> Mathilde Rathenau.

The silence, as dense as fog on the Havel, was metered by the subtle beat of ceiling fans. A woman coughed in the shadow under the balcony. It seemed a signal for everyone to exhale at once, their breath becoming the rustle of clothes, the clearing of throats, sniffles, white handkerchiefs fluttering.

Dr. Hahn folded the letter carefully, then wiped his pince-nez. "Ernst Werner Techow has confessed the whole truth to his earthly judges, and he will answer before his Heavenly Judge. I ask the Court to pass judgment in the spirit of Frau Rathenau's letter."

Ernst looked to the empty chair from which Frau Rathenau had presided over the court as surely as the judges. He resisted her words, but they pried into him like a thief picking the lock of his heart.

★　★　★　★　★　★　★　★　★　★

On Saturday, October 14, just before the judges returned to convene the court's last session, unexpected silence spread from the back of the chamber, punctuated by the tap of metal on wood. Frau Rathenau, garbed as usual completely in black, on the arm of her manservant, walked down the aisle with her silver-headed cane. A path opened up for her through the spectators taking their seats, and by the time she reached the front row, the courtroom was silent. For the first time since her brother's testimony, Ernst's mother attended the trial, seated besides Uncle Erwin in the seats reserved for them. Frau Rathenau turned toward his mother. Two rows behind, without Fritz, Lisa sat forward on the edge of her chair, transfixed as was everyone close enough to hear. Uncle Erwin turned to Frau Rathenau, wobbled to his feet and bowed. His mother continued to stare straight ahead as if unaware of her presence, but Ernst could feel her disquietude. She reached into her sleeve for a perfumed handkerchief and dabbed her nose. But the silence must have been so compelling that she had no recourse but to turn and face the woman in black.

"Frau Techow." Ernst was surprised to hear so delicate a voice come from Frau Rathenau's severe face. "I'm glad you came today. I wanted to wish you peace. Be assured, I take no delight in your son's punishment."

Ernst did not want to witness this, but he could not look away. His mother dabbed at her nose again; her face flushed. She stood awkwardly, her eyes grounded on the silver tip of Frau Rathenau's cane.

"Thank you, Frau Rathenau. You are too kind."

"The young are impatient and reckless." She sighed deeply. "You and I are both mothers, and we bear the pain. I wish it were not so." She reached out a trembling hand, and Ernst's mother slowly brought hers to meet it.

Frau Rathenau turned and, on the arm of her manservant, tapped her way slowly up the stairs to her balcony seat. The tumult of the crowd resumed, except for a respectful corona of silence surrounding the two grieving mothers.

Von Salomon leaned over and whispered loudly to Ernst. "Pay no mind Ernst. The old crone is an Elder of Zion."

None of it made sense, and Ernst could only find the display disgusting. Clearly Frau Rathenau meant to shame him more profoundly and publicly. And no doubt she was part of the Elders of Zion conspiracy. It was so much less painful to hate than feel the responsibility of profound failure. Any regret on his part now would only lend legitimacy to the state that bore down on him relentlessly.

Ernst made use of his right to speak before sentencing. He stood before the hushed courtroom and cleared his throat several times. He had hardly slept, his cell was drafty, the blanket too thin, and in what seemed like never ending twilight sleep he had seen Frau Rathenau's mournful stare as if she watched him from the shadows of his cell. The great hall was still. He straightened his spine and returned Frau Rathenau's gaze, then sought Lisa on the floor below. He had decided upon his confession in the sleepless hours before dawn, though as he tossed and turned he could not find the words; now they came automatically, the version he had learned to assert.

"I would like to say that I have not told the full truth. You cannot imagine the terrible self-reproach that I have inflicted upon myself because I have helped Kern and Fischer in their deed. It was my choice to participate. I gave Kern my hand, my word of honor, by choice." Photographers flashed their powder. Murmurs swept through the galleries. "I have tried to lighten my conscience by telling the truth," Ernst continued over the clamor, "and that is why I am turning myself over to you seeking for fair justice."

Over and over the judge's gavel fell to bring order. Journalists bolted the courtroom to telephone their scoop. In the commotion Ernst watched Frau Rathenau rise from her chair with obvious pain and leave the gallery.

When order was restored Dr. Hagens read the verdict of the Supreme Court.

"One of the most condemnable crimes known in history has been the subject of this trial. Through a cowardly assassination, the voice of one of Germany's most noble statesmen has been stilled.

"So the deed is atoned for by the other murderers, the sad, pitiful 'second harvest,' the sentencing of the young helpers and tools – accomplices – whom the older officers taught in cold blood and then left indifferent to their fate. Behind the 13 defendants lurk the invisible defendants, the real murderers, who come from the secret organizations, the rich proponents of German Folkish murder propaganda, German Nationalists in agriculture and heavy industry – people who do not hesitate to spend huge sums on political propaganda to disseminate their racist thinking."

Chief Judge Hagens opened a sealed envelope and read the verdict and sentences. "Hans Gerd Techow, aged seventeen, guilty of helping to plan the murder, is hereby sentenced to four years imprisonment."

Ernst stared into the silent audience and saw Lisa bring a handkerchief to her eyes.

"Willi Günther – eight years penal servitude and ten years loss of civil rights. Ernst von Salomon and Waldemar Niedrig – five years penal servitude and five years loss of civil rights. Christian Ilsemann, guilty of illicit possession of weapons – two months imprisonment. Richard Schütt and Franz Diestel, owners of the motor-car garage – two months imprisonment. Karl Tillessen, guilty of not informing the police – three years imprisonment. Hartmut Plaas, guilty of not informing the police – two years imprisonment."

Friedrich Warnecke, Gustav Steinbeck and Werner Voss were acquitted.

Finally Hagens turned to Ernst. "The Court considers it apparent that the defendant, Ernst Werner Techow, had full knowledge of the murder plan; he agreed to drive the vehicle and helped to ready it. The court finds Ernst Werner Techow guilty as an aide to murder. Ernst Werner Techow, you are hereby sentenced to fifteen years penal servitude in the maximum security prison at Striegau and ten years loss of civil rights."

For the last time the convicted defendants, each considerably more sober, each absorbed in his own thoughts, were led from the Kaiser Hall. Two photographers who had maneuvered past the police cordon suddenly flashed their powder, almost simultaneously, as Ernst followed Hans Gerd to the courtroom door. As his vision slowly returned, he felt the curious relief of knowing; the reality, the oblivion of prison, loomed large. Who would think of him in six months? A year? After fifteen years, who would remember Ernst Werner Techow, the phosphorous flare that flamed briefly in the Weimar night then fell unnoticed?

Ernst's last glimpse of Lisa burned in his memory as brightly as the photographer's flash. At the wooden barrier, where she stood as they were led out, her red dress throbbed like a beating heart in the chaos of spectators leaving the courtroom. When he caught her eye, her forehead creased and one hand covered her mouth, her other hand before her as if to say, *No, stop, please come back, there's been an error.* Then her hand recovered its sanity and, ever so slightly, she waved, until he reached the very edge of the courtroom where he turned a last time and tried to stop, but the Bailiff prodded him through the door.

PART TWO

CRUCIBLES

15

Striegau Prison
October 1922 – April 1924

Three days after his twenty-first birthday, with his ankles and wrists shackled, Ernst watched Leipzig grow small and disappear through the barred rear window of the prison lorry carrying him to Striegau Prison, near the Polish frontier. At the start of their journey from Leipzig, the older of the two warders in the lorry told Ernst about the Sisters of the Convent of St. Hedwig, nuns of the Benedictine order.

"Used to be their cloister and winery – about 800 years ago. St. Hedwig, she was the patron saint of Striegau. I wonder what she would think if she returned from the dead?" They laughed as if at a bawdy joke. "Last century the Burgers of Striegau had to choose between the Sisters' fine wine and a prison." He lit his pipe. "Sent the nuns packing. Turned the convent into the fine establishment you're about to inhabit. Better for the economy. Which it certainly is, but it's a dump. We made a deal with the devil – a good deal, but it was with the devil. A prison and a stinkin' gas works. Who cares. It keeps Striegau on the map and food in my belly."

During the long ride the two warders alternated recitations of Striegau's brutality. Ernst tried to ignore them. He stared fixedly out the window at the rural countryside in the ripeness of autumn, trying to subdue a circus of disturbing thoughts – of Lisa, Fritz, his mother, Hans Gerd, Uncle Erwin, confinement.

As the olive green prison lorry approached Striegau, the stench of sulfur slowly banished the sweet and sour scent of harvested fields preparing for winter. "Gas works." The younger warder laughed, obviously enjoying Ernst's discomfort.

"It takes some getting used to," the older one said. "Some never do. Most days just smell like purgatory. Then there are the 'special' days – not more than 30 or 40 each year." His eyes bugged out. "You can smell Hell itself."

They both burst into laughter.

Ernst wanted to ask which sort of day this was, but what did it matter. He would learn soon enough.

The lorry bounced and shook as it passed through Striegau's iron gate. Ernst saw out the back window the receding inscription *O Maria*. Inside the prison his leg irons were removed and a stack of prison clothes laid across his shackled wrists. Two warders led him through the dark basement corridor past a line of gargoyle heads carved out of the native rock that stared down. In addition to sulfur, Ernst identified a gruesome brew of mold, sweat, and the septic stench from ceramic pots in each cell, which served as plumbing.

Though he had considered it before, Ernst felt the true weight of fifteen years bearing down on his outstretched arms like sacks of ground limestone. He wondered about the thirty-six-year-old who would walk free of these gates in his skin. How long before Lisa could no longer visit a caged animal? How long before she simply, and horribly, forgot? Against his will Lisa's face, her voice, her Lillé perfume demanded his attention and locked horns with the terror of Striegau, each painful in its own particular substantiation. He had known this could be his fate. Perhaps if he had been sure this would be the outcome he never would have travelled this road. After all, he was an artist, not a criminal. But he was also a patriot, and he had convinced himself that the son of a magistrate would never rot in a prison cell all his young life. Could he wait fifteen years to walk in the street, to drink beer, to eat with friends or family? Fifteen years without a woman's caress?

At the end of the hall an office door stood ajar under a sign:

PRISON DIRECTOR DRONSCH

The warder knocked at the open door and bowed slightly. "Herr Dronsch," he said. "If you please, the new prisoner – Techow." The other warder smacked the back of Ernst's legs with his truncheon, bringing him to his knees, and pressed his face against the stone wall. "Don't move!"

By the time Dronsch called him into his office, Ernst's knees ached.

More prisoners inhabited Striegau than hairs on Prison Director Dronsch's head. Shorter than Ernst and many times more stout, Dronsch had a prodigious head, perched like a boiled cabbage, that crushed his neck into his broad shoulders. His glasses, frail wire-rimmed affairs with thick lenses, made his eyes look small and porcine. Behind him on an oval mirror hung a black coat with a silk collar under a hard black bowler like an inverted exclamation point.

There was nothing else on the wall, and his desk was empty except for Ernst's file and the photograph of a schnauzer. Dronsch's black bowler over the mirror juxtaposed silver and black, one reflecting light, the other bulging like an abscess. Without looking up, Dronsch waved Ernst to a hardwood chair and finished reading his file.

"It seems you will be our guest for the next fifteen years." His baritone voice was mellifluous, forgiving, completely unexpected. "A long time – for a Nationalist, that is. If you were a Bolshevik you would be on your way to the gallows." His head still tipped down over his file, the Director's little eyes swiveled up to peer over the rim of his glasses.

"Cigarette?" He offered a dull tin case to Ernst. "Smoking is strictly forbidden here." He bobbed the case up and down, as if fishing with a shiny lure. "Go ahead. It may be your last. Your health will improve."

Though he hungered for Dronsch's cigarette, Ernst waved him away and slouched in the hard chair, the prerogative of humiliated children and the condemned. It was the only way he could insult the man.

"If you cooperate while you are here, you will be rewarded." Dronsch drew deeply from the stub of a cigarette, then crushed it into a copper ashtray. "If not, I will squash you." He smiled, his voice still silken. Ernst looked to the mirror and the bowler. "We have more than the average number of suicides here at Striegau. It's only fair to tell you that I'm a Social Democrat, but I don't care a fig for politics. My only concern is my business – this institution. Your business will be the prison laundry – every day. But you are already a lucky man." He stopped to consider his words. "No, I retract that – you are less unfortunate. Your cell mate is Puck." He laughed as if enjoying a private witticism, and Ernst thought he heard Mephistopheles. "Puck requested you." Ernst steeled himself.

"You've had the tour; now it's time to introduce you to your fellows. Your arrival has caused quite a stir. We're not accustomed to such celebrity."

Dronsch stood and, without so much as a glance behind, plucked the bowler off the mirror and dropped it onto his head with a thump. With difficulty he slid his arms inside his black coat. It must have been at least fifty pounds ago that the buttons met. He shivered. "I don't think anyone ever gets used to the cold and damp."

Dronsch snapped his fingers, and two warders responded immediately, as if they too were prisoners. He led the way, followed by Ernst and the warders. A double set of locked gates removed any lingering doubt that Ernst was about to leave one world and enter another. As the second gate slammed behind, Striegau unfolded before him, huge echoes of metal and stone, cold space and rows of cell doors stacked in tiers three stories high, as if a narrow cathedral. He tried to imagine the Sisters of the Convent of St. Hedwig praying.

As they continued down a steel lattice corridor lined with cells, the air became unbreathable. The guards complained more than once.

"Techow!" A disembodied voice shouted through bars somewhere behind.

Another voice picked up his name and passed it along the cell block like a football chant. "Techow! Techow!" It jumped across the metal passageway to the facing cells and up two levels through the filigreed iron catwalks that floated like geometric spiderwebs above the cement floor.

"Techow! Techow!"

Tin cups rattled, and a line of noses and mouths pressed through the bars, sucking air and bleating.

"Traitor!" one voice called from a cell. Another picked up that chant and then another. "Traitor! Traitor!" The unnerving cacophony re-echoed off the metal and stone.

"Techow! Techow!"

"Traitor! Traitor!"

He preceded the guards up a metal stairway to Cell 594. As they passed cell 502 a bony chin and bearded mouth suddenly jammed out as far as the bars would allow and spat in his face. Ernst's first sensation was of contamination, then dread and fragility – vulnerability, like his Free Corps days, in the company of the hardest of men. Here life was fragile – a fly in a spider's web – caught for fifteen years, if he survived. There was little to hope for and everything to doubt.

At the rear of cell 594, in the glow of a flickering candle lantern, the back of a large man hunched over a writing table hooked to the wall by chains. He did not stir as the medieval tumblers fell in the lock, and the barred door creaked open.

"Puck!" The guard removed Ernst's shackles and pushed him into the cell. "Here's your assassin."

Almost by reflex, Ernst sneered at the guard. "Son of a whore!"

In a flash, as if eager, the guard brought his truncheon around and struck Ernst across the stomach. He doubled over gasping for breath, and the guard pushed him onto the cement floor behind Puck.

From the darkness of his pain Ernst heard Puck humming a low, lilting melody, his head swaying back and forth in time as if Ernst was not there. Ernst groaned and slowly raised himself onto his cot. The cell door clanged and the tumblers rattled again. The warder's boot steps echoed down the corridor.

"Man was created on the last day of creation," Puck finally said in a soft baritone just above a whisper. "Even the flea was created before you."

"Fuck you," Ernst wheezed, clutching his stomach.

Puck remained turned away, hunched over a piece of paper in the shadow. "Humility," he said, "will serve you better than hostility."

"Who asked you?"

Puck put down his ink pen, struck a match and lit another candle. He reached into his well-worn jacket, a double-breasted gabardine, a size too large, stylish before the Great War.

"Cigarette?" He held out a dulled silver case.

Ernst looked up to see if he was mocking him again.

"Dronsch said smoking was forbidden."

"Dronsch says many things, but in the end, what counts – the only reality – is what actually happens. Words are butterflies, actions are steel bridges."

Puck's eyes reflected the flickering candle, in a dark Sargasso Sea of hair and beard. His forehead glowed golden, like a yellow continent. His hands, disembodied points of light, danced with the candle flame

"Ernst, we all know who you are and why you're here."

The way he articulated Ernst's Christian name was disturbingly paternal. "Apparently." Ernst retrieved his bundle of clothes from the floor. Black and gray striped blouses and trousers, two pair each of gray stockings that had been washed so often that the fibers frayed. No frequency of washing would ever whiten them. On a crude metal shelf that also hung by two chains over Puck's cot, gold glowing letters speckled the spines of books. Ernst studied the titles. Involuntarily, he reached for the volume of Heine's poetry, but caught himself barely in time, and his ashamed hand flattened his hair instead. Ernst considered his striped prison garb, laid out on his cot like a zebra skin. His own trousers and shirt that he had worn during the trial felt like holy vestments, his last earthly possessions. In his trouser pocket he found his talisman, the scrap of paper Lisa had given him when she visited in the infirmary, on which she had written, **'COURAGE'**. He could almost read the word with his fingers.

Ernst studied the cell and noted the small rectangle of twilight lying on its side, high on the wall. So thick were these ancient convent walls that half the light through that one brave window soaked into the stone and was lost to the cell.

"As you have already learned," Puck said, "the warders will eagerly maim you at the least provocation. The Bolsheviks will kill you today, if they have half a chance. The Nationalists and fascists – they will take you in like a bitch in heat."

Ernst accepted one of Puck's cigarettes and drew the smoke deeply.

Puck turned back to his paper and continued. "Your associates here from Organization C and the Ehrhardt Brigade – they know everything and understand nothing. Choose your friends carefully, Ernst. You have fewer than you think, and you cannot choose your enemies."

Ernst paced the cell trying to block out Puck's words and worried that maybe he was a madman. The cubicle measured five meters on a side: five strides from one red brick wall to the other, five strides from the cold steel bars denying privacy to the black stone wall with the slitted window above his head. A step stool under the window gave enough height to see out, and he wondered what speck of the world he would see for fifteen years.

"Stick with us common criminals, Ernst. Our real crime is being unlucky enough to be caught. Just business. Nothing worth killing for."

"I'm a Nationalist, a patriot. Not a criminal."

Puck nodded and stroked his barbarous beard. "Whatever you believe. You alone confessed."

Ernst studied Puck, seeking expression under his jungle beard. He could almost discern thin straight lips. He looked old, in the ageless fashion of St. Nicholas, his hunched habitus adding years, but Puck's age was incalculable.

"You're trying to figure how old? Thirty-five, give or take. Surprised? One does not age well in gaol."

Puck resumed writing in a cloth-bound ledger, the scratch of his pen like a squirrel gnawing at an acorn. Ernst felt the burning contusion on his abdomen.

Suddenly, a warder's stick clanged on the bars, jolting him. "Techow!" He shone an electric torch in his eyes. "Your clothes."

Ernst kept Lisa's note and changed into his striped prison uniform. The blouse was too large; it hung like a shroud, and the trousers were too long. He looked down and thought he had shrunken into a child again. The warder grabbed Ernst's clothes through the slats of the cell and stuffed them into a sack.

When the dinner gong sounded that evening, Ernst stood at the door to his cell as he had been instructed. "Aren't you coming?" he asked Puck, who continued reading on his bunk.

"I don't take my meals in the dining room." The warder's key rattled, and their cell door opened. "But Striegau is notable for its cuisine. For a prison, I mean. You'll be surprised. Bon appetit."

Ernst joined the lineup of prisoners. On the command of the head warder they marched in two single files, clattering across the steel catwalk, down metal stairs, to a huge hall, St. Hedwig's nave and transept, where, seated by cell number, all three hundred prisoners took their meals together. Puck had explained to him that more than a year before, after a series of disturbances, Dronsch had imposed a silent rule in the dining room. Each man sat hunched over, curved like a question mark, scooping soup from bowl to lips with rhythmic regularity, the only sound the sipping of 300 mouths. Above them, on a suspended balcony, guards with machine pistols, Model o8 Lugers fitted with flat shoulder stocks and snail magazines taking thirty-two rounds, watched from wooden pews. Any utterance was punished by a sharp truncheon blow from the warders who ringed the dining area.

The next day, after the noon meal all three hundred men marched again to the exercise yard, the Sister's ghostly garden. This time Puck marched along, in front of Ernst, humming his funny tune, ledger tucked under his arm, his gabardine jacket anomalous in twin lines of gray striped men. Ernst waited alone at the entrance to the yard as the inmates broke ranks and swarmed like striped bees into a new social order. Three distinct swarms formed, and Ernst felt confused and forsaken.

Under the courtyard arch, a crude iron rendering of St. Cecilia, patron saint of music, presided over 'the yard' in one of the few places on earth where there was no music. Her blacksmith creator had managed only a crude sneer instead of the intended blissful smile, and St. Cecilia's lyre hung from her hand, ponderous, pulling her shoulder down. Her stare bore down into Ernst from every angle, a countenance of languor, defeat and condemnation.

As he searched for Puck, Ernst was approached by a pair of men who might have been piano movers or loggers before Striegau. They backed him into the fence before he could resist.

"I spat in your face today," the taller man said. "It was a waste of good phlegm!" In a moment, fists flew out of a mélange of striped cloth, beards and pale flesh, and a sharp blow struck Ernst below his eye. For a moment there was only impact, no pain, then another blow to his abdomen, swollen and sore from the warder's truncheon, and he crumpled. His vision tunneled, then blackened.

Awareness slowly returned. Ernst saw Puck as a floating head, heard his voice, diffuse and far away, then suddenly sharp and clear.

"Techow is off limits." Puck said it with soft authority. "Stanley will bear me out. Hadn't you better be across the yard with the others?"

It seemed to Ernst as if a puppeteer pulled their strings and backed them away awkwardly, their brows furrowed, perplexed, opening up the narrow sky again. The warders arrived moments later, truncheons already raised until they saw Puck, and their intent withered, their arms fell. The lead warder simply nodded his head as Puck eased Ernst to his feet. Still dazed, he let Puck lead him to the Nationalists who were already faced off with the Bolsheviks. Puck raised his hand and patted the air between them as if to say, 'there, there, it's all right'.

Each evening at seven, Puck's special dinner tray was eased through the food slot, and he set it reverentially on his cleared table. He sat before it, eyes closed, head bowed, and mumbled a queer chant, then drank a small tumbler of brown liquid. He winced, smiled, and sighed.

"Hospital diet," he said when he caught Ernst's curious glance that first night. "Compliments of the house. Passable brandy or whiskey; Dronsch surprises me. The doctor writes orders each month – *spiritus frumenti* – for medicinal purposes."

The pleasing odor of gravy and wurst wafted from Puck's tray. "Did you make friends with the Nationalists?" Puck asked. "It was the safest place to leave you today."

"Tell me about Buchmann and Georg."

"Natural leaders. I'm sure you are their newest darling. I have a – how shall I say it – a mutual understanding with those two. You see, Ernst, my only ideology is greed. Buchmann says I have neither a sense of history nor destiny; my only value lies in the services I provide. I'm contemptible, but necessary. Buchmann is in for three years. Extortion, racketeering, gun running."

"And Georg?"

"He looks so innocent, so boyish. He can hardly grow a beard. He murdered a left wing labor leader. Walked up to him in the Tiergarten and shot him in the head with a pistol as his wife and child looked on. Then he calmly walked away. Ten years."

"I didn't thank you for helping me today," Ernst said.

"I wasn't helping you. I was helping myself."

Puck cleaned the gravy from his plate with Schwarzbrot and left his tray at the bars. He consulted his pocket watch. "I always am asleep by nine. I have a routine." He stripped down to long underwear and folded his desk against the wall, stood on the step stool, ghost-like, and stared out the high window, then disappeared under a dark quilt. After a few minutes Puck's heavy breathing filled the cell.

For Ernst sleep was elusive. Consumed by his aloneness, his head aching from the afternoon's blows, he curled into a fetal ball for warmth beneath the thin prison blanket, trapped in a lightless void, where even anticipation was a withered memory.

★ ★ ★ ★ ★ ★ ★ ★ ★ ★

Officially, prison visits at Striegau were limited to 60 minutes for parents and spouses, 45 minutes for siblings and close relatives, and not more than 30 minutes for non-blood related persons. The actual length of visit was determined by the prisoner's record and a generous gratuity. In any case, the 'Visitor Chamber' was none too congenial, relegated as it was to a large windowless room where hardback chairs faced each other across a steel fence that forbade privacy, though fingers could touch through the mesh. Ernst wondered at the added cruelty – and perhaps he would have preferred not to feel Lisa's warm hands, not to be tormented by the curve of her neck, the smell of her breath, her perfume, now that she was so utterly gone. Better to bury a memory, than care-take its agony.

A month after beginning his sentence Ernst was allowed his first visitor, his mother, who brought a "late birthday present," a large package of Lebkuchen. While Ernst waited for her at the fence, the Visitor Chamber warder explained to Frau Techow that the cakes were too large, that he was obligated to cut each one open to search for contraband. The other visitors stopped their conversations to watch, and Ernst felt her humiliation, and his own. Her fingers stumbled as she unwrapped the tin and removed cake after cake as if they were newly hatched chicks and placed them on a newspaper for the guard to impale and dissect. The warder nodded, and she gathered the fragments in a white cloth bundle tied with an orange ribbon.

Ernst knew how mortifying this was for his mother, and he admired her fortitude. She gave away nothing of the seething he knew to be churning inside her. "Now may I give this to him?" she asked.

"I will see he gets it." Ernst knew the guards would eat half of them.

257

When they finally sat facing each other, her red eyes darted back and forth to the other visitors in hushed conversations nearby. She held her perfumed handkerchief under her nose, something she did when he was a boy and they lived on Wannseestrasse, and that was reassuring. Then it was her way of keeping working class odors at bay. He was not sure what it meant today. But the same perfume he smelled then was as evocative and provocative as Proust's madeleine.

"Are they treating you well?"

"As well as can be expected, Mother. I see the mark has dropped again. It must make your finances difficult. Are you making out all right?"

"I'll be fine." She was pale, her voice strained, hoarse with tension. With one hand she drew the collar of her coat together and licked her lips repeatedly. It was just as cold and damp in the Visitor Chamber as elsewhere in Striegau. She coughed once and then again, in a paroxysm that seemed to hurt her chest.

"Are you sick, Mother?"

"No, just a touch of the grippe. I'm fine, really."

Women on either side of her hunched forward in heavy dark coats, carrying on animated conversations with husbands and sons, all in identical striped prison garb. It seemed to Ernst that among the line of shrouded women none looked more shrunken or more defeated than his mother.

"Your Great Aunt Gertrude, for whom I was named, died last week." Ernst had to strain to hear her. "I don't think you would remember her. Just another old lady." She summoned her courage and cleared her throat. "I've taken another job at the hospital – at the laundry. The pay is almost as much as your stipend was before. The Association sends a small sum each month. It's quite thoughtful."

"Are you still working on the tuberculosis ward?"

"Oh, yes. There seems no end to new cases. It's steady work. They are overwhelmed and understaffed."

"It's dangerous work, Mother. No one else will work there, that's why they want you. Can't you ask to be transferred to another ward?"

"I don't think there is work on any other ward. And I like my job – the doctors have come to rely on me. I feel I make a difference, and the money helps."

"Have you called Uncle Peter?"

"I did, and he has made some calls – perhaps some special privileges, a boost to Lütgebrune's appeal."

"No, I mean for you. He's loaded, so is Uncle Erwin. Borrow some money. Damn it, what are you waiting for?" He let his voice grow too loud and suddenly felt the nakedness of their conversation. He leaned into the fence. "Take care you don't get run down."

"It's nothing. We do what we have to do." She set her jaw. "Uncle Peter sends his regards. He will try to visit, but he is enormously busy. Peter invited me to the wedding of his assistant at AEG, Walter Gropius. He married Gustav Mahler's widow, Alma. It was quite an event. Such glitter and excitement. So many interesting people – intellectuals."

"I'm sure you looked wonderful, Mother."

Her eyes looked up dreamily. "Yes, of course." She turned her wedding ring round and round.

"Try not to worry, Mother." He said it for himself as much as her. "In the end, we shall win." Buchmann was to Ernst's left, and he paused in his conversation and nodded agreement. He leaned over and smiled at Ernst and his mother. He was missing his two front teeth, and his breath was foul.

"Take heart, Frau Techow. We shall all be out of here before long. You can count on it. Your son is a hero. We'll take good care of him."

There was no need to reply. He returned to his conversation with a woman who, curiously, took notes.

"This never would have happened if your father was still alive." One hand still gripped the other; two fingers turned her ring. "He never would have let them make an example of you. The other magistrates from the Trade Court are making a special appeal – for a lesser sentence. They're quite optimistic."

Ernst could hear the hollowness of her reassurance. "How is Hans Gerd?"

"He's adapting to life in Landsberg. His asthma is not so bad. I worried so, because of the dampness, but Uncle Peter was able to secure him a comfortable cell and some special considerations because of his health. I visited last week. Hans Gerd sends you his best. He so admires you and misses you. He said you shouldn't be sad." She looked at him with questions in her eyes. "Are you very sad?"

Her question felt like tenderness. Ernst was perplexed and left it unanswered. "What do you hear from Leo?"

"Oh yes, of course, Leo." She smiled for the first time. "Leo and Katherine will be married – in the summer. Leo has a job at the Reichsbank. Imagine that. Your brother, the Socialist, working for the bank. But they're very happy."

Ernst shook his head. "Poor Leo – I just don't know." But he did know.

What he wouldn't give to be sensible, moderate Leo, with a good job, a new wife, and the world at his command. The contented Kiel sprat.

"Now, Ernst. Don't be that way." A few moments of troubled silence passed between them. "I have something else for you." She looked over her shoulder to see that the warder was not watching, and she opened her handbag, her church purse from Wannseestrasse that held Lindt chocolate to sweeten church attendance. Now the leather, like his mother's skin, was dull and scuffed. Instead of milk chocolate, she produced a folded sheet of stationery that she pressed quickly through the lattice work of the fence. Ernst took it reflexively. "Frau Rathenau's letter."

The parchment paper felt warm and heavy.

"I wanted you to have it," she said. She fumbled with the catch of her purse and stuffed her perfumed handkerchief back inside, then thought the better of it and retrieved it again. "Is there anything you need? Are you warm enough? These stone buildings can be so drafty."

★　★　★　★　★　★　★　★　★　★

After Puck's intervention in the yard that first day, the warders and other prisoners seemed to respect a protective zone around Ernst, and no more blows fell on him. Ernst hardly spoke to Puck those last two months of 1922, and then only to answer in monosyllables. Nothing distinguished one day from another, and Ernst lay on his cot face down, sketching Lisa on the slate floor with the same stick of charcoal he was arrested with. The slate was dark gray, and details were obscured. After each drawing was complete he washed it off with a wet cloth and began again. At first he couldn't think of Lisa without longing, an ironic ache that was not altogether unpleasant. But as the weeks passed, and the charcoal stub steadily shrank until it was no larger than a cigarette butt, her image frayed. There were no letters, and visits from non-related persons were forbidden during the first 6 months of incarceration. More than once he wondered if there was any point in remaining alive.

"You'll need another charcoal," Puck said one day.

"I suppose," Ernst said.

"She's a lovely woman. Who is she?"

"A friend."

"You have lost more than your freedom."

Ernst only grunted and continued to fill in the chiaroscuro of her neck. His will counted for nothing in Striegau; these impermanent drawings were the ghostly vestiges of love and passion, the withering remains of his creative impulse. And, when his charcoal finally crumbled into dust, the agonal expiration of his spirit. The only sexual thought he had was that it would be fifteen years before he would sleep with a woman. Each moment of his life was prescribed, reduced to bare necessity – folding gray striped laundry, eating tiresome food, shivering each night under a thin blanket, defecating into a foul ceramic pot and waiting in vain for Weimar to collapse.

As a New Year's present, Puck gave Ernst two new charcoal sticks. He wrapped them in a sheet of white paper and asked for a portrait in return. "On the paper, Ernst. Don't destroy this one."

Drawing Puck was a welcome respite from the repeated portraits of Lisa on the dark stone beside his cot. As he drew him, Ernst puzzled over his cellmate, trying to understand his unique connections in Striegau. Each day in the yard Puck sat at a folding table while one customer after another, inmates and warders, brought him some kind of business, and Puck scribbled in his ledger. Messages and packages passed in and out of cell 594 as if it was a general post box. One of the packages contained two books, which Puck added to the overfull shelf above his bunk. Among his fellow prisoners, Puck, in his dark gabardine jacket and navy blue trousers, was as distinct and seemingly necessary as a hive's queen bee, the inmates his workers, the warders his soldier bees, facilitating and protecting Puck's marketplace.

Ernst asked him about his business and he shrugged as if it were a mere trifle. "It's only because I know a lot of people on the outside. Specialists." He had an impish twinkle in his eyes.

Puck's routine at Striegau was precise and unchanging. At five o'clock each morning he wrote in his journal. At precisely nine o'clock, Puck was let out of their cell to walk unattended to the print shop, where he operated a hugely profitable "business" for Dronsch, and then he "took lunch" until recreation in the afternoon.

For most prisoners, life was compressed into the two hours allotted each day to be outdoors in the yard. When the weather allowed, chess and checkers were popular, while a few inmates ran along the periphery fence for exercise, and newspapers and gossip were exchanged. On the simplest level, Puck linked the men with access to money to their basic needs such as tobacco and newspapers. Buchmann and Georg were most interested in Adolf Hitler's new weekly, the *Völkischer Beobachter* – The People's Observer – which Puck obtained at a dear price, along with copies of *Die Rote Fahne* – the Communist Party paper, for Stanley and the Communists. Puck accessed the world beyond Striegau's walls in multiple and unique ways, and he provided the illusion of potency in their lives, which for Buchmann and several wealthier clients included occasional procurements of cocaine.

One evening during his third month at Striegau, Puck's supper tray appeared at the slot as usual at precisely 7 PM, with a steaming bowl of potato leek soup, carrots and turnips and a slice of beef in gravy that filled the cell with succulence.

"How do you do it?" Ernst asked.

"How do I do what?" Puck licked his mustache hairs.

"Special food, schnapps, tobacco, books…"

His eyes glistened. "That's why they call me Puck."

"Shakespeare's fairy. But Striegau is no comedy."

"Ah, but it is," his voiced lilted. "Just because you carry suffering in your heart does not compel the play itself to be a tragedy. You are not that powerful. But you are well read. I knew it from the first day when you looked longingly at my books." He lit a cigarette, offered the case to Ernst and he accepted. "I haven't had a cell-mate for many months. Solitude suits me. But I am able to exercise some choice in the matter. As you know, I am well-connected here." Puck leaned his head against the stone wall and without opening his eyes he asked, "I know you are self-absorbed with your own particular misery, but don't you ever wonder why I'm here?"

"Not really."

"Perhaps curiosity has not served you well in the past." Puck leaned forward and stared at Ernst. "No matter – you have the choice to exercise your curiosity now. You do find this a curious place, I trust. A far cry from Wannseestrasse, n'est-ce pas?"

"How much do you know about me?"

"I have access." He leaned back against the brick wall, his hands folded over his ample abdomen. "I can teach you not only the ways of this place, but how to make sense of it and much more."

"Speak plainly, Puck."

"I've been in Striegau for eight years this time. Just long enough to avoid that stinking rich man's war." He giggled. "The first time I was here for 5 years. My crime – do you want to know?"

Ernst did, but he said nothing.

"I'll tell you anyway. I am a forger, an embezzler, a smuggler. I'm making Dronsch quite a lot of money. In my line of work one becomes well connected and, sometimes, wealthy. It's one of only two kinds of writing that pay well – forgery and ransom notes. Perhaps in the future I'll try my hand at ransom notes." He laughed at his joke. "The chaos of war is dangerous, but it can be fruitful for my kind. However, the moral code amongst us tends to fray in wartime. We become like sharks with blood in the water. But Striegau is just the opposite – everything is predictable and calm." He ran his finger around the rim of his plate and licked off the gravy. "And my food is quite satisfactory."

"Dronsch said you requested me. Why?"

He smiled again. "Why has it taken you three months to ask?"

Ernst stood at the bars and looked through the steel mesh floors two stories below.

"No matter," Puck continued. "Time is elastic and not particularly relevant here. I'm glad that newspapers come one or two weeks late. I find it a luxury to digest and ruminate over events without having to react – or participate. It allows for perspective." Puck fogged his glasses with his breath, then polished the lenses with a strikingly white handkerchief. "I was drawn to your trial. Followed it carefully, in all the newspapers. Dronsch said you would probably be sent to Striegau." At that moment, the harsh prison lights dimmed. "Your trial was quite the cause célèbre. I know you have that letter. I have seen you read it."

Ernst felt his face flush and ground out his cigarette.

"No matter. It was a front page story. Everybody has read Frau Rathenau's letter to your mother. It was after reading that letter that I asked Dronsch for you."

"You needn't have made it your business. The press had their circus with it."

"Oh, but I am a student of human nature, and you are not an ordinary man. You've read Shakespeare. You are partial to Heine's poetry, and you assassinated a beloved political leader. A Jew no less."

Ernst strode across the cell to Puck, his fists balled up. "I didn't kill Rathenau. I drove the fucking car. That's all." He towered over Puck who continued polishing his wire-rimmed spectacles.

"Of course. Of course. You only drove the car." Puck laughed from his ample belly. "But now you are not so sure of yourself. Perhaps you do need to – how did Frau Rathenau put it? – repent before the court of heaven?"

Ernst's fists unknotted, and his arms fell to his side. Puck's voice was almost hypnotic, and it disarmed his anger, soothed his anxiety.

Puck replaced his spectacles and smiled, his yellow teeth askew like ancient headstones in a neglected cemetery. "You'll be here for a long time.

Do you want to suffer? Or would you like some meaning? You're an artist. I can teach you something practical, like the finer points of forgery. Or, perhaps you'd be interested in something more complex, like redemption? Or anything in between. Another cigarette?"

Ernst leaned over Puck's table into the candle to light the cigarette then climbed onto the footstool and stared out into the silver and blue Striegau night. He could see no sky. He would see neither sunrise nor sunset for fifteen years. Cobblestones reflected the incandescent street lamp like an insect's compound eye.

"In this world there is justice and compassion," Puck continued. "They mix together uneasily. If God had created the world only on Frau Rathenau's principle of compassion, of forgiveness, sinners like you would overrun it. There would be no punishment, no restraint. Conversely, if the world were created only on the principle of strict justice, no human could stand the test. We would all be judged harshly."

Ernst had to concede that Frau Rathenau's letter intruded into his thoughts with some frequency, something he would tell no one, certainly not Puck. It was baffling. "Which weighs more, justice or compassion?"

"Ah," said Puck. "You pose a scholar's query. And for you the question is more than academic. Your very soul depends on the conclusion you reach. That is why you need me."

An old ragman pushed his cart slowly across the cobblestoned street, the wheels ticking.

Puck selected a book from his shelf. "*To The Youth of Germany*. I suggest you read this. It's by Walther Rathenau."

"Why should I want to read this propoganda?"

"It would benefit you to know the man you helped murder. Think of it as the foundation for... for whatever follows."

"I still think you're full of shit, Puck."

He laughed again. "But you're not completely sure, are you?"

★   ★   ★   ★   ★   ★   ★   ★   ★   ★

Dronsch's rules allowed only immediate family, parents and siblings to visit once a month during the first half year of a prisoner's incarceration at Striegau. He had explained this rule as "compassionate reality" that allowed more distant family, friends and lovers to think realistically of the prisoner's situation, so there would be no fantasied expectations. Ernst's mother came every month and she looked increasingly tired and strained. In April she admitted that for the last few weeks she had walked more than three kilometers to the hospital each day because the cost of a trolley ticket was now over three million marks. How was she financing her trips to Striegau? It was Uncle Erwin, she confessed.

"I didn't beg," she said. "He feels terrible about your plight. You must believe that."

Though he could not forgive Erwin's betrayal, Ernst was relieved that his mother had enough food and heat, thanks to his uncle's generosity. She also brought news of a young woman, a co-worker on the tuberculosis ward named Elizabeth, who shared their flat and helped with rent.

"There has been an outbreak of measles in Berlin," she said and became animated again. "Elizabeth and I have been helping out on the Children's Ward. It's quite sad. The children are terribly ill. Some of them have died, others need to be held, fed and changed. I find that I have a way with babies."

Ironic, Ernst thought, considering she had never held or fed her own children. He was glad for her and sorry for himself. And now, to add insult to injury, he and Hans Gerd were "cared for" by the penal system and its minions, Weimar's frigid Kinderfräulein.

Ernst scratched each day into the stone wall behind his bunk, a last measure of anticipation that mattered enough to mark the passage of time. At her visit in March his mother brought regards from Lisa and Fritz. She made arrangements to bring Lisa with her in April, when she would be allowed a thirty minute visit. His mother brought news of a poster that had been all over Berlin announcing a meeting of the GNYO and listing the 'Martyrs of the Reich'. Ernst and Hans Gerd were near the top of the list, she said with pride, but Ernst could see it was only a brave effort for his benefit.

As Lisa's first visit approached, Ernst's mood lifted. Though he told himself he could reasonably expect only disappointment, he felt irrepressible expectancy, a feeling that had atrophied from disuse.

Every chair but one in the Visitor Chamber was occupied, and the hum of seven conversations ran together like an orchestra warming up. The same energy that kept Ernst from sleeping that night stole his appetite and made him lightheaded. As a first time visitor Lisa had forms to complete, identification to be confirmed, before she could be escorted to the door of the chamber. Right away Ernst could see in her eyes that she was frightened. She looked back and forth for him. She blinked frequently, kept her arms folded across her chest. Ernst recognized the same powder blue dress she had worn to the National Gallery, the one he had slipped off her silky shoulders at Günther's apartment. At the instant of recognition they smiled, and Ernst felt the first stab of sadness. She sat down stiff backed at the edge of the chair, her brow furrowed as if she might cry. Her hands went up to the mesh fence almost automatically, her fingers curled around the wire. His hands met hers, and in an impulsive moment she leaned forward and kissed his fingers. Neither noticed that surrounding conversations had hushed, and visitors and prisoners alike watched their forlorn pas de deux.

"All my letters were returned," she said.

"The first six months – no contact." Their eyes met, and she was everything again, as if no time had gone by, as if no court had sentenced him. Gone was the steel fence, the inmates, gone the visitors, the jumble of voices. But then, as if just waking from sleep, he remembered where he was, and every cell in his body registered the agony.

Lisa seemed to feel the same end of reverie and pulled her hands from the mesh. "You're... you're a hero... a hero at the university." She looked into her lap. "At each GNYO meeting Fritz reads a list of those in prison, and always your name is first. The Reichmark is in free fall – unemployment – we have meetings all the time. Fritz says it won't be long..."

"Before what?"

"Before Weimar falls – before you're out of prison." She looked hopeful.

But her words rang hollow, parroting the automatic language of Fritz, of Manfred, Kern or Tillessen – radicals utterly convinced of their irrefutable correctness and entitlement. "I have a lot of time on my hands here. I read the newspapers – all of them, and history books. I don't share your optimism."

She leaned up close to the mesh and searched Ernst's eyes. "If you could take back your part in this, would you?"

"I would make a pact with the devil if I could live that day over, if you and I could have an ordinary life."

"I don't think anyone will be having an ordinary life," she said.

Something had changed, had hardened in Lisa. "Puck – my cell mate – a very odd fellow – says that Weimar is concrete and steel, and our aspirations are butterflies."

"You must not lose hope, Ernst." Her fingers grasped the wire again, desperate.

"What is there to hope for?" He kissed each finger.

"I don't know. But... but don't lose hope." She smiled a little. "Look here," she dug into her coat pocket and produced a small, dense spherical object wrapped in tissue paper, hefty for something so small. "A good luck charm. I found this yesterday in an old handbag. Do you remember?" She unwrapped the Bleiguss head from their first time making love, so many possibilities ago.

Ernst looked to see if the two warders were watching, and Lisa passed the lead ball through the wire mesh. Surreptitiously, he let it fall into his pocket.

"Do you want to hear news of school? or Berlin?" She squirmed uncomfortably. "Or is it better not to know? I'm sorry Ernst, but I don't know how to do this."

"I want your letters, your visits. I'm greedy for you."

"I'll try... I'll try my best," she said. She talked about Fritz and her classes, which only made Ernst feel more and more insubstantial. She left before the end of her allotted half hour, and Ernst saw her break down in tears as she quit the Visitor Chamber.

* * * * * * * * * *

By the end of his first year, Puck had provided Ernst with sketch pads and all the charcoal he required. Water colors materialized at the end of summer, and inmates and warders bartered cigarettes and expedited mail delivery for portraits. The view from their cell window became a favorite subject of his water colors, a series in the spirit of Monet's Haystacks, each in a different reflection, each cobblestone a unique permutation of light. In rain, or after snow melt, the wet stones glowed with red and orange hues of dawn and twilight. A few of the iron spikes surrounding the prison pierced his view, and twenty meters behind them the red brick wall of the Gas Works changed hue with the shifting glow. Though not a speck of sky was visible, Ernst learned to differentiate the near ground of the courtyard from the middle space behind the iron fence. The miniature wedge of space held light like a fishbowl, as if it were a medium different than air. In the exercise yard, Ernst found that sketching and painting was a way of maintaining seclusion.

In the fall of 1923, Adolf Hitler's National Socialist German Workers Party, the NSDAP, alternately called "the Browns" for the brown shirt uniforms they wore, or "the Nazis," were the talk of Striegau. Bavaria seemed to be fulfilling the heady dreams of the Nationalists, and, according to Buchmann and Georg, Hitler had tens of thousands of Storm Troopers at his beck and call. Lisa's letters were animated again, but mostly with star struck acclaim for the new party and its leader. Ernst dared to feel cautiously optimistic, but he also worried that her attraction to National Socialism was perhaps more a preoccupation with Fritz, though he would never ask at her visits. She came every month, Fritz less often, every two or three months.

On November 8, Hitler and more than six hundred Brown Shirts detained Bavaria's separatist Governor Kahr at the Bürgerbräukeller. The *Vorwärts* printed Hitler's speech, which ended with a prediction that "there shall have arisen once more a Germany of power and greatness." An editorial noted that while Hitler was cheered, Governor Kahr slipped out a side door. The next morning, led by Hitler and Gen. Ludendorff, more than two thousand Brown Shirts marched out of the Bürgerbräukeller and set out to conquer Munich.

But Hitler's bid for power, what the Weimar newspapers scorned as a "Beer Hall Putsch," turned into a fiasco. Shots were fired. Hermann Goering was wounded in the hip and groin, Max von Scheubner-Richter was killed instantly, and Hitler fell and dislocated his shoulder, then disappeared in a private car.

The Nationalist mood at Striegau turned bleak again, and Ernst's mood darkened. Each day working in the laundry became like every other, and he lost track of time. His drawings were refuge, but scant relief. Lisa's next letter was more than a month in coming. Her handwriting was different – smaller, more unsteady. She wrote very matter-of-factly, like a newspaper account of Lisa and Fritz at GNYO meetings and rallies. In the recent student elections she had been chosen Vice-President, and Fritz, President. At the end of her letter, in her more familiar hand, she told him of sudden attacks of melancholy that would last for days then ease, but never completely lift. "It is still hard when I think of you," she wrote, then ended her letter, "With Love."

After that, there were neither letters nor visits for two months, and then, on a late summer day, Lisa unexpectedly came to Striegau alone. Since her last letter Ernst had tried to bury her memory, and there were even a few days when he didn't think of her at all. But when he entered the Visitor Chamber, expecting his mother, there she was, more enchanting than ever. The pain of resurrected passion, grievous for having been buried, twisted searingly.

She bit her lip and twisted an embroidered handkerchief. "I would have visited more often," Lisa said. "But what with all the excitement about the Nazis... so much happening... "

"Why didn't you write?"

"I couldn't." She looked left, then right, and finally into her lap where her fingers writhed, and Ernst knew.

"I've been dreading this moment," he said.

She kept her eyes averted. "I came alone – by train." Then, almost as an afterthought, she said, "Fritz and I are getting married."

He had steeled his heart against the actual words. There weren't that many ways to say it. Still his eyes filled, and he could only shake his head and look down to conceal his heartache. He inhaled deeply, seeking the stench of the Gas Works to shrink his swollen throat and dry his eyes. It would not do for his mates to see him weep.

"I'm not surprised," he whispered. He pursed his lips together. "I'm only sorry about us."

Her finger tips curled through the fence. "Oh, Ernst, it's not right. I'm so, so sorry."

She leaned forward, and he felt deluged with her scent. Their foreheads touched, their eyes caressed. His fingers wrapped around hers, and their lips met through the metal, her breath warm in his mouth.

The warder's truncheon rapped hard on the fence, and a jolt of steel vibrated into Ernst's face. They pulled back from each other.

"None of that, Techow! What do you think this is, a brothel?"

★　★　★　★　★　★　★　★　★　★

By February 1924, well into his second year in Striegau, Ernst began to feel the inevitability of forgetting. It cut both ways. Friends and relatives stopped writing, few visited, and those who remained faithful – his mother and Uncle Erwin – brought fewer regards from those who did not. Ernst felt himself becoming transparent.

Puck asked nothing of him, seemingly immersed in his business dealings, his days in the print shop and his punctual routine. Ernst thought he, too, had lost interest. But for the anchor of their banal conversations, Ernst thought he would disappear altogether in the gas-laden air.

Uncle Erwin escorted his mother on her monthly visits, but Ernst had refused to see him until now. At this visit his mother gave Ernst a suede pouch, rich with the scent of the tanner, on a leather drawstring. His Uncle had fashioned the pouch himself, she said, of chamois leather from his own sheep on his Jacobsdorf estate. She pleaded for Ernst to accept his gift as a token of reconciliation and to speak with his uncle. Reluctantly, Ernst agreed, and Erwin came into the chamber with his perennial smile and began his foolish chatter as if they had last spoken only a week before.

"Casein and blood," Erwin said as he settled on the hard chair. "Milk and blood of the lambs. Softens it right up. Brings out the velvet texture."

Erwin stayed his allotted forty-five minutes, babbling news of his estate, Ernst's brother Leo, Berlin, the economy and, "*Deus misereatur*", the National Socialists. Then he was gone, leaving an afterglow redolent and soft as his handmade chamois. Ernst was unable to marshal his anticipated anger; in fact he savored their reunion. That night before falling asleep, he rubbed the chamois between his fingers and passed it across his lips, delighting in the déjà vu of scent and memory.

Lütgebrune's first appeal failed, but he assured Ernst in a letter that the next would surely succeed. Ernst was not so sanguine, and he began to anticipate the cruel expansion of time that torments prisoners after the illusion of rescue vanishes. Thirteen more years seemed impossible, and again he had to quell thoughts of suicide.

A deepening depression set in as Ernst's second winter locked up in Striegau began. Imperceptibly, the stone walls chilled until one day in March, when Ernst touched the wall to engrave another mark on his calendar, he might as well have touched ice. Constant cold settled deeply into his bones, and his thin blanket was inadequate. One cold evening, Puck returned from the print shop with a down jacket, used but warm.

"Here. Take it. You need it. If you catch pneumonia and die I might get an idiot or an ax murderer for a cellmate."

"So you're really doing this for yourself?"

"Don't be an asshole. It's cold. Dronsch is a prison warden, not a philanthropist. He saves Weimar millions on heat in Striegau. You have inadequate clothing."

"Yes, it's always cold, and I hate it."

"Then why didn't you ask me for something like this. You know I can procure things that others cannot."

"I don't want your charity – or pity."

"You may not want it, but you need it. My charity, that is. I certainly don't pity you. Pity is for those who are pathetic or who are victims. I wouldn't insult you with either epithet."

Ernst was truly perplexed. "Then why do you do it?"

"Charity is a thing unto itself. An inclination of the soul. Additionally, I am studying you. I see another Ernst under your façade. I have great hopes for that Ernst."

He took the jacket, mumbled his thanks, and tried to get to sleep, warm for the first time in months. But it was more than cold that kept him awake.

Sleep was more and more elusive, and when it came he woke an hour or two later staring into the blackness. He derived less and less pleasure from his drawings, and only continued because his artwork secured his solitude – kept his Nationalist "friends" at bay in the exercise yard, or at least gave him a reason to shun their company.

Spring brought only relief from the cold, not from his melancholy. The sweet thawing scent of manure and loam reawakened a spirit in Ernst that felt expansive, that needed to be free, and only compounded the vile stench of the gas and the inhumanity of incarceration. On those days when the sweet winds brought the odor of reawakening to every prisoner, Ernst felt the weight of Striegau, as different from simple confinement as despair was from melancholy.

To add to his misery after lights out, he suffered visions of Lisa and Fritz gaily drinking at the Corps Teutonia, together in bed fondling each other, naked, and sometimes he became aroused, which was most disturbing of all. What little sleep he was granted was plagued by recurring nightmares of Baer's murder of the two boys in the *Vorwärts* assault. Over and over he was tormented by the pleading eyes of the younger boy trying to draw his last breath, felt it as his own and woke gasping.

One night Puck shook Ernst awake, and he was so relieved that he told Puck of his nightmare, told him of the *Vorwärts* action. In the glow of a candle, Puck's head bobbed knowingly as if he considered a family secret or transcendent truth, as if hearing confession. Ernst felt a curious comfort, a parental intimacy.

"Memory," Puck finally said, "is the guarantor of conscience. It's a measure of your integrity that you have this nightmare." He pulled Ernst's thin cover up over his shoulder and patted his back gently, humming his curious tune. Ernst's relief was so profound that he welcomed Puck's touch and readily fell into a deep sleep.

As much from boredom as curiosity, Ernst now recognized Puck as his only source of solace, and watched him more closely, observed him like a scientist. His own fragmented sleep cycle had meshed with Puck's. Ernst was up each day at five as Puck slid from his goose down comforter and lit two candles mounted on scrap wood. He hummed his funny little song while washing his face in the basin and arranging the sheepskin on his stool. As best Ernst could identify, the words were an obscure Germanic dialect, but the melody seduced him with its tragic sweetness. He couldn't be sure, but he thought Puck smiled under his wild beard, and Ernst wondered if he woke each morning, as Ernst did, forgetting, for one blissful moment, that he was in Striegau.

16

Awakenings
April 1924 – January 1930

E rnst's name and reputation still had gravitas in Striegau, but his star was already dimming. At first the Nationalists courted Ernst, gave him every benefit of their growing doubt. He stayed close to them in the yard, but their prattle sounded increasingly clichéd and common. Their naive repetition of slogans felt more like propaganda than principled crusade. His ambivalence did not stem from what they espoused, a cause he still clung to as noble and necessary. Without a doubt Fritz articulated the same thoughts, only with more refined language, with more political strategy and less brute simplicity. And now, since Fritz and Lisa had wed, Buchmann's rhetoric only reminded Ernst of the greatest betrayal of all. He was still deeply depressed, he told Buchmann, and they left him more or less alone.

Bolsheviks and Nationalists could agree on one thing – the problem of Günther – and his murder became a collaborative effort of left and right. In a rare display of common cause, Stanley, Buchmann and Georg shared a brief conference in the yard, surrounded by their lieutenants. According to Stanley and the Bolsheviks, Günther was guilty – in decreasing order of detestability – of being a Judas, a Nationalist and, finally, a mental defective. Bolsheviks and Nationalists had a score to settle with Günther. More to the point for Buchmann and Georg, OC had ordered his murder, and that was reason enough.

For any one person to be identified as Günther's killer would have earned him the death sentence, but a collaborative plan would shield the knife wielder, and at worst there would be a two week lockdown.

As OC's point man in Striegau, Buchmann ordered Ernst to walk the fence with him on a day in April when spring was in the air. "I'm hoping you will wield the knife, Techow. An honor, my young friend. It may jolt you out of your funk."

As they walked, Buchmann continued in zealous, pressured speech. "OC has ordered this to be done in the next two weeks. An easy way to prove yourself."

"I've proved myself more than enough. And what do I have to show for my efforts? Thirteen more years in this shit hole with criminals and deluded patriots. Puck is the only sane one here, and I'm not so sure of him."

"You cannot possibly understand what is going on outside of these walls. The end of Weimar is rapidly approaching, and you'll want to be poised on the right side of history. You are the man for this job, Techow. Günther is more than flesh and blood, and so are you."

"Yes, of course. We're all fucking metaphors. Everything is a fucking metaphor to you and Georg. I'll grant you, Günther is an opportunist of the worst kind, and a rat and a snitch. But he's also mentally unbalanced. Killing Günther would be gratuitous."

"Hardly," Buchmann said. "If Günther's betrayal goes unpunished, the reputation of OC falters. There can be no pity, or our entire effort is undermined. You're not going soft on us, are you? Someone from OC will deliver the weapon, soon. You are certainly in a favored position to receive it and hold it until the time is right. We need to know that we can count on you."

Ernst glared at St. Cecilia. Proving himself seemed to be the theme of his life.

Buchmann suddenly turned in front of him, close enough for Ernst to smell his fetid breath. His powerful hands gripped Ernst's arms. "You little prick!" He spit his words at Ernst. "We've coddled you – let you be a baby and cry about your bad fortune and your girlfriend. Time's up! You need to establish 'weight' in here, and soon. Your reputation will not carry you much longer. Do I make myself clear?"

He stared dumbly at Buchmann, feeling like a wandering asteroid among the galaxies of the right, the left and the criminal. Maybe Buchmann would kill him, and it would be a blessing. What immobilized him, confused him and kept him from suicide, was that somewhere in his reckoning a faint star of hope still burned, hope that Buchmann was correct. That he would one day walk free of Striegau a hero of the Reich. Unlikely, but not impossible. "Yes. I understand."

"You will receive and hold the blade until the appointed day. Because of Puck, your cell is never searched. The warders leave you in peace. It won't be long, but you must not fail this small test of character."

Two days later the warders fetched Ernst for an unexpected visitor. The Fat Man, Hartmut Plaas, sat on a chair that disappeared under him with his eyeglasses tilted up high on his forehead, writing in a little notebook with the stub of a pencil. He perspired, even in the cold dampness. As Ernst sat down, Plaas's porcine eyes swiveled towards him from his jowly head.

"Techow, so good to see you." Plaas half stood with effort and affected a slight bow of diffidence. Ernst was glad not to shake his cold doughy hand. "You are in our thoughts and hearts."

"Thank you." Ernst noted that the prisoners who flanked him were Gruber and Leicht, both OC members.

Plaas leaned forward, his eyes darting. "I believe you are expecting something from me today for our friend Günther. Please move your foot up to the mesh."

Ernst did as he was told and met the tip of Plaas's large black shoe at the wire. He felt Plass moving his shoe up against his and then back and up again. Suddenly, Ernst felt something hard and blunt strike his toes, and he allowed the wrapped knife to slide under his shoe. The transfer was over in less than a minute. Plaas withdrew his foot and sat back smiling. "I know." He primped his hair. "It's like getting fucked, isn't it?"

At that moment Gruber, to his left, leapt to his feet, his chair scraping harshly against the concrete floor.

"How dare you! You insult my wife, my family – you bastard!" He clawed at the fence, which gave little ground, and his visitor backed away, calling to the guards for assistance, his palms upwards, completely bewildered by this outburst. But it was enough time and distraction for Ernst to slip the knife into his shoe.

Günther's assassination was set for two days later. Ernst wedged the knife under a thick volume of Goethe. Puck kept his expected silence. He resolutely refused to even discuss any plot against Günther.

The next day Buchmann walked the perimeter with Ernst again. "The dagger is yours to wield. You have first refusal. Everybody will be glad you did it, even the warders." He sensed Ernst's ambivalence and pressed on. "You do hate the weasel, don't you? He betrayed you. Were it not for him you might not be here now. Maybe you'd be married to that lovely girl who used to visit – what was her name? Elsa? Elisa?"

"Lisa." He felt a murderous impulse.

That night, in their cell, Ernst asked Puck again about the impending murder. "Don't you think it reasonable retribution? Justice?"

Puck continued practicing a forged signature and ignored him.

"What would you do in my position?" Ernst pleaded.

"I am not in your position. I hardly know your mind, much less your heart. Perhaps, if you opened that book to me I could respond."

"You're fucked up, Puck. You just care about yourself."

"I'm sorry you think that. I aspire to something Hillel, a wise teacher said about 2,000 years ago. He said, 'If I am not for myself who will be for me? But if I am only for myself, who am I?' The art of living a good life is to find someplace in the middle, where you gain more than you lose. But you have to lose something."

Puck continued writing the signature over and over, occasionally holding a 20X magnification lens over his work. "If you have done wrong, counteract it by doing right."

"I have done no wrong!"

"Then you have nothing to correct."

When Ernst returned to the yard the next day Buchmann greeted him. "Everything is ready," he said, as he walked with Ernst. "It is only for you to plunge the knife. We will create the necessary disturbance. Nothing can go wrong. The knife stays in Günther."

"I've decided to decline," Ernst said.

Buchmann looked down gravely and sighed. "You're making a colossal mistake." Buchmann spat at his feet.

Ernst returned to his charcoal of St. Cecilia.

★ ★ ★ ★ ★ ★ ★ ★ ★ ★

Each day just before being let out into the yard, Ernst stood at the cell's skyless window and tried to foretell the day's complexion from the quality of reflected light. On the day of Günther's murder, he correctly guessed bright sunlight alternating with wispy cumulus shadows and a light southern breeze. The thermometer at the entrance to the yard hovered just above freezing.

Günther entered the yard in animated conversation with himself, his hands simultaneously conducting and articulating. Georg intercepted him and draped his arm over Günther's shoulder. He slowly moved him from the fence to the empty space between the Bolsheviks and Nationalists. At a nod from Buchmann, the first act of 'Rugby' began.

Ernst listened from behind as Günther explained to Georg the deception

276

of pyramid schemes, which he had used to great success in the East, in Egypt in fact, where the Nile contained bits of gold and he had seen the Foreign Legionnaires panning for it far upstream of Cairo. Slowly, the Bolshevik and Nationalist clusters circled closer. Ernst watched from the fence. On Buchman's signal, a huddle of Nationalists collapsed around Günther, followed by the Socialists completing the rugby scrum. There was no screaming, no unusual sound except spirited conversation all around, then Ernst heard the thud of impact, like the sound of a melon dropped on concrete, then a gasp, covered by laughter and loud discourse. In the center a dark mass writhed and convulsed, then was still.

As fluidly as they had blended, the two factions separated, swirling about their natural nuclei, leaving a crumpled form between them, a stain of steaming blood melting the frozen ground. Moments later the guards realized something was amiss. The natural geography of the yard was altered. A whistle blew, then another. A short burst of machine pistol fire erupted from a guard tower; batons flashed. Within minutes the exercise yard was cleared of everyone except Günther.

★   ★   ★   ★   ★   ★   ★   ★   ★   ★

Dronsch's response was half-hearted, as if he was just as happy to be done with Günther. The necessary lockdown proceeded in a perfunctory fashion. He apologized to Buchmann, Georg and Stanley; as the leadership of their respected factions, they would have to be in solitary for a decent interval. There were some ancillary benefits. It was a good time for some warders to take a vacation, and the more recent prisoners needed a healthy dose of dread.

Two weeks later, as they emerged from solitary, each inmate, left and right, cheered his man, and Dronsch docked all inmates one meal for their display. There were no exceptions and, just this once, Puck's evening meal was not delivered.

Puck was unperturbed. "Dronsch had to do it," he said. "To re-balance the world. It's just business."

By the next day it was as if nothing unusual had occurred, as if Günther had never been at Striegau. The lockdown was already memory. Georg, who had grown only the scantest of facial hair during his time in solitary, shaved it clean.

The grinding routine resumed, and there was only sameness, boredom and the caustic harshness of laundry bleach. Every day, for six hours a day, Ernst washed and folded black and white striped shirts and pants in the prison laundry. Conversation was forbidden, and nothing changed except the sulfur content of the air and the temperature. As the heat increased, the warders, that unpredictable human interface between Weimar and her prisoners, became more brutal and arbitrary. At each meal there was at least one beating, often indiscriminate. Even Ernst's protection failed him, and he was truncheoned one day at breakfast for dropping his tin cup during the prayer. Buchmann and Georg's rhetoric grew ever more tiresome and predictable. More and more Ernst contemplated how many different ways there were to kill oneself in Striegau. He wondered if Günther's death, abrupt and brutal, was not preferable to the agony of slowly dying from the inside out: soul first, then the heart and finally the body.

The next morning when Puck rose at 5 AM, Ernst sat up in his bunk and watched him light his two candles. "Every day you wake at five, write letters or something, read books by candlelight. It's as if you have a clock inside your head. Why do you do it?"

"I'm escaping Striegau." Puck laughed, and his shoulders shook.

Ernst reached under the change of clothes on his shelf and retrieved the chamois pouch Uncle Erwin had made him. In it was the Bleiguss from his last New Year's Eve with Lisa. It rolled over in his palm, and he studied the face, which bore a surreal resemblance to Puck.

Puck checked his pocket watch, the chain strung ostentatiously across his timeworn gabardine. "First, correspondence." He unlatched and lowered the hinged wooden panel on a chain and set out a blank piece of writing paper.

Ernst heard the scratching of his pen.

Hunched over close to the paper, Puck paused and asked, "What are you waiting for, Ernst?"

"What?"

"Everybody is waiting for something – for love, for release from prison, for money, success, revolution, heaven – always the promised land just over the next horizon, just barely in sight, around the next corner. Everyone is busy waiting – for eternity. But this world is not a waiting room for eternity." Puck resumed writing then paused again. "Eternity is here – now. That's why I live an ordered life. Given my circumstances, I choose to live this way. I am, in a sense, not in prison at all."

Ernst laughed. "You're true to your name, Puck. Mischievous, a trickster and clever. I think you are as amused by life as the rest of us in Striegau are crushed by it. I suppose that is a choice. I find it amusing." Ernst carved another calendar day with a butter knife in the carbonate wall. "But save your philosophizing. Wouldn't you rather be home?"

Puck laid down his pen and held his hands over his eyes. "Just now I don't have a home."

"But, what about Dahlem? What about your little cottage on a garden lane?"

"The cottage in Dahlem belongs to a Herr Isaac – same last name as mine. He's a good Protestant. He also happens to live in Tunisia. So I became him. Simple document alterations. It was a convenient fiction, and it works."

"Where are you really from?" Ernst asked.

Snoring drifted from the next cell.

Puck blew out one candle and peeled off his spectacles. He turned and sighed in a way that Ernst thought was either resignation or relief, perhaps both. "No one else knows this," he whispered. "It's been two years – you and I. I suppose I trust you."

Puck's eyes were dark caves in the bearded forest of his face; his wild hair cast weird shadows. "I was born in Lithuania. We lived in Prienai, near Vilnius on the Nemugas River. My brother Jacob took me to the river almost every day. I still remember very clearly sailing a block of wood with a sail cut from an old sheet. I was only five years old, but I remember the Nemugas. That year, 1893, my parents moved us to Eishyshok, a big shtetl, almost 4,000 Jews. But still a shtetl. We lived and died by the grace of Russians, Poles, Lithuanians, Austrians, Germans. In the Jewish cemetery there was a head-stone from the year 1097. I remember Eishyshok was a devout town, but our piety did not save us from one pogrom after another. I grew up afraid. Most of my relatives considered fear a fact of life. 'Every day God rolls the dice', my mother would say and shrug her shoulders as if that was just the way of the world. 'There is no point in leaving', my father would add. 'We have no money. And anyway, who would take us?' I thought they were crazy and the day we arrived at Eishyshok, I began to plot my escape."

"You are a –" Ernst paused then whispered, "a Jew? I've shared a cell with a Jew for more than two years?" He felt in equal parts disgusted and astonished.

"You have," Puck whispered. "And I'll thank you to keep it to yourself."

Ernst was stupefied. "You're a Jew?" he whispered hard. "This is a Protestant Gaol. What am I doing..."

"Papers mean nothing. My 'papers' say I am a Protestant from Dahlem. I made them myself, because Dronsch and I have an understanding, and the food is better at Striegau than at the Catholic prison in Lichtberg."

"Why do you tell me this? You know what I think of Jews."

"Yes, I know – and now you are imprisoned with one. I would, of course, appreciate your discretion. It would be detrimental to business, not to mention my life. Do you still want to hear my story?"

"Not particularly." Ernst felt the fool, manipulated. Their cell suddenly seemed too small. He felt soiled.

"I'll tell you anyway," Puck said.

Something searing and impulsive gripped Ernst. He swung off his bunk and grabbed one of Puck's candelabras. He raised it over his head, but Puck hardly reacted.

He sat back against the wall by his desk and drew his blanket up over his chest. "Are you going to kill me for being a Jew?" He closed his eyes. "Yiddish was my first language," he continued as if Ernst did not stand over him with murderous intent.

His white-hot fury spent, Ernst let the candelabra slowly sink to his side. The part of him that was intrigued by Puck, a deep and visceral force, betrayed the reflex that hated Jews.

"My father was a book binder and, consequently, there were always other people's books in my house in various stages of repair. These books and my oldest brother, Jacob, were my sustenance.

"My parents were Orthodox Jews, and in the shtetl we were shielded from the broader culture. The synagogue was the center of life. Father prayed every day, rising before sunrise, about this time, to wrap ritual leather straps about one arm and around his head. Each had a little box on it containing the holiest Jewish prayer – the Shema." He closed his eyes; a thin chant issued from deep in his chest in Hebrew, then in German. "Hear O Israel, the Lord is Our God, The Lord is One.

"When my father prayed, he rocked back and forth. Davening he called it, swaying, dancing, mumbling prayers. Jacob explained it to me in modern terms. He said you have to find the 'frequency of God' when you pray, like tuning that new invention, the radio, and it was slightly different in everybody, that's why everybody in Shul – in the synagogue – sways to his own rhythm. It's like forging a signature; everyone has his unique hand. It is only for the forger to discover his subject's 'frequency'. The rest is details. But that is for another day."

"Puck," Ernst whispered intensely. "Does anyone here know you're a Jew?"

"I hope not." He laughed again, and his eyes twinkled. "You're the first and only person here who knows this. Not even Dronsch. That would be quite a scene."

"What makes you think I won't blackmail you?"

"I put myself at your mercy. I calculate the risk is small. I already know you fairly well, Ernst. Though you have been asleep these two years, you have read Faust at least five times. Why not read *Werther*, Goethe's novel for love-lorn men? How many corpses have been fished out of the Landwehr Canal with that book stuffed in their pockets? No, it is not your style. I think you are inspired by Faust. A hopeless romantic. A poetic scholar with an unscrupulous bent. A tragic hero who, in spite of his noble sentiments, becomes involved in brutal deeds. Is not Striegau for you like Faust's *Walpurgis Night*? Seeking forgetfulness?"

"I have an identity. I'm a Nationalist."

"Yes, yes, of course. That's your disguise. Wear it as long as you must – as long as it fits."

Morning light oozed azure from the horizontal window. Puck stood on the stool and breathed in the faint scent of dawn. "No gas today, Ernst. It's a good sign." Puck stepped down and leaned against the wall, the window over his head like a blue crown. "It's odd to think it, but there is some good to be extracted from the misery of Striegau. Action tends to cloud thought. If you let it be so, Striegau is a place of stillness, of inaction."

"We Nationalists are still active." Ernst forced back the mesmerization, the enchantment of Puck's words. "Georg and Buchmann are in frequent contact with The Party. We are part of the revolution. It continues from Striegau."

Puck stroked the bush of his beard and nodded. "Hmm. Words, Ernst, only words." Puck returned to his desk, and the scratching of his pen resumed.

Ernst grasped the cold bars, as he had countless times, and stared across the dim hallway into the dark cell opposite. He looked as far as he could up and down a line of cell doors, like identical freight cars on a long train.

Only their cell flickered in the dawn with Puck's candlelight. Dust motes floated in the window's blue radiance, like sailboats on The Havel, like angels in Pastor Namann's church.

"You said you were very religious when you were little," Ernst said, almost in a trance, staring through the bars. "Do you still believe in God?"

Puck stopped scratching with his pen. "Do I believe in God? When I was a boy I believed in God, as a child does – probably the way you did – the wizened old grandfather endlessly wise, compassionate, but stern, sitting on a throne in the clouds dispensing justice with wisdom. And then my oldest brother, Jacob, died.

"I was thirteen when it happened. Our family visited relatives who shared a small house in Preila, on the Baltic." Ernst turned from the bars and saw Puck staring into the candle flame as he remembered. "There was a beach nearby where the current was swift, and huge rocks with fascinating tidal pools dotted the breakers. The tide was low, the pools exposed, and Jacob took me out to explore. There were crabs and brine shrimp in the pools and other tiny creatures swimming for their lives.

"In my sleep I still see the rogue wave that took him, a freak occurrence. It crashed over the rocks we were on and dragged Jacob out to sea. One moment he was not six meters away at the tip of the breakers, and I saw the wave coming. The next moment I was sprawled over the rock, bruised and cut, and Jacob was gone. God cheated me. God took Jacob from me.

"I concluded that to God our world is nothing but a tidal pool, and what seems a long lifetime is a brief few hours between tidal sweeps. The best and the brightest in our world account for nothing to God – only a more clever brine shrimp, a quicker crab. It was the beginning of my feud with God.

"I left home two years later. I stopped praying and refused to go to the synagogue. I was fifteen and expelled from school for forging bank checks – my first attempts – very crude. I'm embarrassed just to think of it."

"You didn't answer my question. Right now, do you believe in God?"

Puck rubbed his eyes. "I'm angry at God. So, yes, I believe in God. I'm not angry at nothing. I'm angry at God."

Ernst considered the cruel twist of fate that had led his father to step on a nail and die of tetanus, and Lisa's mother to die of influenza when she was only four. Every death was unfair – a pretext to fight with God.

"When did you first go to prison?" Ernst asked

"1908 – a brief interlude for illegally transporting whiskey. Obviously, not my trade. But I did find prison to be an excellent academy to refine my true calling as a forger."

"I used to transport guns." Ernst relished this bittersweet memory of himself before the assassination.

"A convenient point of entry into the underworld," Puck continued. "The years leading up to the war were lucrative, but that's not anything I comment on in this environment. There, I've shared another confidence with you."

"Why do you?" Ernst felt his interest heighten.

"It's my way of showing you I mean no harm. Like when a dog rolls over to expose its belly to another."

Ernst sat on his bunk but leaned forward as if to exchange a secret with Puck. "If you could escape, would you?"

"No." He answered quickly as though he'd considered this before. "Not unless the doors miraculously open, and an angel takes me from here – like Michelangelo's St. Peter, rescued from prison by the archangel." He chuckled to himself again. "I don't give it much thought. Do you?"

"Do I think of escape? Certainly. Who wouldn't?"

"It would be a mistake. Striegau has much to teach you." He lifted one eyebrow.

Ernst felt as if a slightly opened door had shut hard. He leaned back and closed his eyes. "There is nothing I wish to learn here."

"Do you remember the bible story of Jonah and the Whale? Such a lovely child's story – until you have to live it." Puck lit a cigarette. "Jonah – the reluctant prophet. He refused God – would not go to forewarn the people of Nineveh. He tried to hide, to escape from God, to evade responsibility, and ended up in the belly of the whale – Striegau. Why do you think that fantastic story is so compelling? Because each of us is Jonah, turning existence into a system of hideouts, trying to flee the truth – to flee God. When Jonah emerged from the whale he had turned from evil, what we Hebrews call T'shuvah. God gave Jonah a second chance, and this time he went to Nineveh – he saved the city. Jonah was no hero, no pure man. He was deeply flawed. But when he turned from evil – T'shuvah – he repaired the world – Tikkun Olam."

"Jonah was a Jew and a traitor," Ernst said. "He saved the city of his enemy. Where's the redemption in that?"

"Most people don't know the story well enough to entertain that complication. Tell me, did your pastor teach that Jews had horns?"

"I've heard that. And that they control the finances and destiny of the world."

"Ah. Finances and destiny – more subtle than horns."

"More consequential."

"Not all Jews, though. Certainly you don't think I..."

"I don't know what to think anymore. I don't understand you, Puck."

"You keep saying that. I'm not here to be understood – certainly not by you. We – you and I – are here to learn, not understand." Puck put down his pen and leaned against the wall. "Or, if you like, to be washed out by the next wave that sweeps our tidal pool. I choose to believe the former. My father used to tell me, over and over, that in studying Torah – you do know what the Torah is, don't you?"

"That odd Hebrew scroll?"

"Yes, that odd scroll. The wisdom of a 5,000 year-old people. Quite remarkable, but of course, I didn't appreciate it as a child. My father told me that when you learn Torah and carry out the word of Torah, you cross over into a world of spiritual meaning."

"And what is the word of Torah? The Protocols of the Elders of Zion?"

Puck flapped his hand at Ernst. "Rubbish! A fiction."

"Then tell me the word of your Torah."

"Saving one person's life is the same as saving an entire world."

"That's it?"

"Some commentary also. But what follows from that is profound."

A metal gate clanged far below. The change of shift began. Striegau would rouse in a few minutes.

"Frau Rathenau's letter to your mother. I see you reading it quite often. I think it must challenge you. It must defy something fundamental."

"I just don't understand it."

"Ah. Trying to understand again? At the time of your trial, the Jewish observance of Yom Kippur had just ended. It is the holiest day in the Jewish year – a time to ask God's pardon for our sins – a time to forgive our fellow humans their transgressions, asking them to forgive ours. Just as with Noah, it is a time for T'shuvah – turning – turning from sin to righteousness. It's our choice – a way of repairing the world, one life at a time. Frau Rathenau is an observant Jew. Her letter is the ultimate act of forgiveness – of repair. Do you remember first hearing it?"

Ernst knew the letter by heart, kept it folded under his prison-striped clothes. He recalled hearing it for the first time as it was read in court, a memory he rarely allowed himself. "While the letter was read," Ernst said, "Von Salomon leaned over to me and said she did it for publicity. He distracted me – saved me from weeping in court."

Puck smiled and sat back again. "Your tears, Ernst – pearls of grace. I was right about you. You are Jonah in the belly of the whale, suspended between life and death, between action and passivity, waiting, transforming. I believe God sets out a particular task for each of us. Like Jonah, your path, your task, may not be what you want, or what you understand, but God keeps pushing you toward it. Like a finger in your back. It may seem that the task chooses you, but ultimately, like Jonah, you must choose to follow it or flee from it. The choice is yours."

"There is no choice in prison. One does what one is told."

"There is always choice. Of course, each choice carries consequences. One does not have to do as one is told here. The consequence? Solitary, or a week on the shit squad – disagreeable, to be sure. Similarly, one does not have to feel imprisoned. The consequence?" He cackled. "None. I keep two scraps of paper, one in each pocket." He reached into one pocket of his baggy trousers and unfolded a crumpled fragment. **"For my sake was the world created."** He reached into the other. **"I am dust and ashes."** Puck flashed his yellow smile, and his eyes sparkled again. "Both are true. When you can live with that contradiction, you will realize it is not a contradiction at all. Then you will be free everywhere, even in Striegau."

In the yard that day Ernst wandered the perimeter fence in a daze, thinking about Puck's revelations and their conversation. Later that night he read again from Lisa's last letter, posted after she announced her engagement to Fritz.

...I know this is a painful time for you, but this world is capricious and cruel. What's happened to you is unjust and I am deeply sad for you. But what's happened to us brings me even more grief. It's like getting a fatal disease – an unearned death sentence. Maybe someday it will be clear why all this is happening. It makes no sense. Please do not be angry with me for choosing Fritz, but these days it is easy to feel afraid.

I remember when I was sick with the influenza in the 12th Class. Father was furious with Aunt Ida for letting me visit a sick friend, for attending the 12th Class Revue, for missing school. From my bedroom I could hear him storming at Ida, cursing and finally the crash of a crystal decanter. I was sure I was going to die, and I was afraid and sad. For two days I had chills and coughed and cried. Father paced the floor in the parlor and yelled for the doctors, then yelled at the doctors and at Ida as if he could bully the influenza germ. Then suddenly, I was better, and father went back to work that same day as if I had never been ill. A few days after I recovered, Aunt Ida got sick and died in five days. Sweet Ida, my second mother. Father blamed me for infecting Aunt Ida. I don't think he knows how to be sad, or maybe it was too painful, so he got angry.

I thought God unjust, and a world governed by an unjust god is not a safe place.

Keep this letter and read it to me again in ten years....
I love you, Ernst. I have always loved you. I will always love you.
   Lisa

   ★   ★   ★   ★   ★   ★   ★   ★   ★   ★

After Puck's confession, their relationship thawed, and the few months of spring felt like new growth after a long winter. He and Puck discussed everything from the 'painting of the light' to the relative merits of Heine and Stefan George. Puck was fluent in all matter of Bohemian avante garde sensibilities, yet grounded with a somewhat mystical detachment. Ernst felt memory return, felt his spirit quicken. He began to take pleasure in his drawings again.

One warm day after his mail delivery, Puck dropped a copy of Rathenau's book *In Times To Come* onto Ernst's lap. "It is your good fortune to discover Rathenau." He chuckled. "After only two years of wandering – not even searching."

In his readings Ernst began to construct a very different picture of the man he had helped assassinate. Rathenau was complex. He had lived his life pulled between conflicting desires. On the one hand he had played a leading role during the Great War in the world of men and action, and he had done so with energy and creative intelligence. Yet, his intellect was starved. He was not content and longed for the reclusive world of philosophical inquiry.

One particular passage made a deep impression on Ernst.

> *It is possible that modern man will be forced by his despair to seek refuge in chaos. He may perhaps be driven to question all ideals, even to ask whether those values, (which Christ, remember, did not recognize as values: fatherland, nation, wealth, power and culture) are really lofty and fundamental enough to justify in the world the hatred and envy, the injustice and oppression, the intrigue and violence and murder carried on in their name.*

One night several weeks into their nightly conversations, Puck announced, "No more laundry. I've secured you a job in the print shop. I will teach you the art of forgery. You need a vocation, Ernst, and that is the only useful one I can teach you. You'll also have the time and good light to read, which I know you will appreciate." Puck unwrapped a book from beneath his bed. "I believe you are ready for this, the mystical side of Rathenau – most peculiar and somewhat disturbing." He laughed – his eyes flickered like cat's eye marbles in the candlelight. "You'll be surprised to discover that the man you murdered did not even believe in death. Rathenau's strangest book – *The Mechanism Of The Mind*."

Ernst interrupted. "Puck. Do I amuse you?"

He considered for a moment. "I don't seek entertainment from my fellow man. No, Ernst, you don't amuse me. You challenge me."

"Have there been others?"

"A few, with mixed results. We humans have to take risks. How it turns out is in the hands of – oh, I don't know – let's call him God. It is my nature to study and argue. It's the Hebrew in me. My father did that at Shul – the synagogue – in Poland. Each week on Sunday morning, the men would gather to argue Torah. We Jews are great debaters. When a Jewish child comes home from school the mother says, 'Did you ask any good questions today?' It's our mission to argue as passionately about Jacob's behavior with Rachel as we do with the particulars of the Red Heifer needed for ritual slaughter. It matters not how great or little the question. What matters is that your mind and heart are engaged in the debate.

"These Sunday mornings were most remarkable for me as a boy. I was allowed to play under the table at my father's feet, half absorbed in my toy soldiers and farm animals and trying to hear if my father prevailed with his arguments. It was exhilarating when he carried his position – my armies advanced, my cows marched in a straight line."

"What happened? Why aren't you still there arguing?"

Puck seemed to stare through the wall, into another time. "God had other plans for me." He lit his second candle. "When we moved to Eishyshok I was too big to play under the table. There were more Jews, and my father studied in a large basement room with fifteen or twenty other men. It was an embarrassment to hear them still arguing in Polish. I was a German. Everything German was marvelous and modern – telephones, radios, incandescent lights, phonographs, automobiles. I wanted more than anything to leave behind the old-fashioned, embarrassing world of my father. It was as if I'd fallen into a rabbit hole, like Alice, and woken up in Wonderland. I've been trying to get back ever since, but of course, one can never go back up the hole."

Puck inhaled the damp night air and sighed, as if he unexpectedly smelled the first lilac. "I suggest we leave moral ambiguity behind for now and concentrate on simpler skills – forgery, counterfeiting, money laundering, and other 'tricks.' Everyone needs a profession they can fall back on when times are hard."

"You seem to have great confidence in me."

"You are a skillful artist. You have the proficiency necessary for a forger and a lifetime of burden on your soul."

Ernst yearned for the relief Puck offered. It would be a godsend never to return to the accursed laundry. He lay back on his bunk, drained. "How does one begin?"

"The way I learned the Hebrew alphabet from my mother," Puck said. "She sang 'Oyfn Pripetshok' to me each night as I went to sleep." He hummed the familiar tune.

"That song. You were singing it the day I first came to Striegau. I hear you humming it often. It sounds German, but the words don't make sense."

"Yiddish. Let me sing it to you in German. The words are beautiful – and sad." Puck's thin voice began:

> On the hearth a little fire burns,
> And it is hot in the house,
> And the 'rebbe' is teaching the little children
> The a-b-c.

> See now little children, remember dear ones,
> What you are learning here;
> Say it over and over again:
> 'A' with a 'komets' spells 'O!'

> Study children, do not fear,
> Every beginning is difficult;
> Happy is the one who studies Torah,
> Need a man more?

> When you will grow older, children
> You will understand,
> How many tears lie in these letters
> And how much weeping.

> When your children will be exiled,
> And be tortured,

May you gain strength from these letters,
Study, look into them now.

"As a child," Puck almost whispered, "I never understood how tears could lie in letters of the alphabet, but now I do." His voice grew husky with emotion. "But that is for another day. For tonight be content with the simple lessons of a forger. Close your eyes. I will tell you the a-b-c's of forgery. Tomorrow, in the print shop, we will begin with basic exercises. In Striegau, time is long."

Puck blew out the candles and allowed the darkness to settle before beginning. "Forgery requires the same skills as art reproduction. To imitate good art you must see good art and appreciate its subtle characteristics. Likewise, you must avoid bad art. Unlike a painting, an expert forgery should not call attention to itself. An obvious statement, but if you forget the basics you end in Striegau. True fidelity in a signature is the sum of common qualities and individual variations. And, of course, the document itself must be photographically correct, down to the watermark and any scars the paper may bear. There are certain questions a skillful reproduction artist asks himself."

Ernst stared like a blind man into the blackness of their cell, lulled by Puck's voice.

"Is the signature genuine? Is it in the natural position? Are the witnesses' signatures genuine, and were they written in the order they appear? Does the signature touch the other writing, and was the signature written last? Is the writing of the body of the document genuine? Is any of the writing disguised or unnatural in any way? Are there remains of pencil or carbon marks, which may have been an outline for the signature or other writing? Was the document written before the paper was folded?

"Examining a signature in preparation for forgery, you are like a land surveyor with level and theodolite, measuring slopes, calculating cosines and tangents..."

★   ★   ★   ★   ★   ★   ★   ★   ★   ★

"Let's start with an experiment." Puck stood behind Ernst in the print shop, hidden from the door by the press. "Draw a series of ovals, first in a counterclockwise direction, and then another set of ovals in a clockwise direction. Vary the speed and avoid pressure. That's it, nice and smooth. Which is easier?"

"The clockwise ovals," Ernst said.

"Slow the revolutions. Notice how much less firm and clean the line quality becomes, how much less symmetrical the ovals themselves are – either too narrow or too round. Uniformity of size is jeopardized. Notice the axis of your favorite ovals. It seems to be about 20 degrees sloping to the right of vertical. Now try to change that axis without moving the paper or lifting the pen or altering your writing position. What happens?"

"They lose their symmetry."

"Exactly. Flat over here," Puck pointed with a sharp pencil, "abrupt curvature here."

"What's the point of this?"

"Each of us has a distinctive slope to our handwriting. It can only be varied within narrow limits and still maintain its integrity. Speed of writing also affects the outcome. Every writer has a normal tempo. If it is artificially slowed, it betrays itself by a less firm and harmonious execution, a loss of uniformity in letter sizes. Now let's see if your hand is 'garlanded' or 'arcaded'."

A warder entered the print shop, and Puck slipped a prison work order over the sheet they had been working on. His voice rose in timber.

"Are you stupid? I said fourteen point type for the heading, then change for the text..." He looked up at the warder. "Can I help you?"

The guard poked through the papers with his stick. He was young and nervous; he had not yet acquired the mask of brutality. He reached into his tunic and drew out a large envelope, which he laid down before Puck.

"Ten days?"

Puck examined the papers and shook his head, his lips moving silently. "Three weeks, at best. Everybody has to have it 'right now.' This is a busy time."

The warder wrote a number on the envelope and raised his eyebrows expectantly.

Puck pursed his lips, reconsidering. "Special order? Ten days is certainly possible."

The warder left without another word, and Puck turned to Ernst. "Business is brisk, my overhead is low. Dronsch takes most of it. I could be making millions outside."

"Millions aren't worth much these days."

"Swiss francs, Ernst. Always deal in Swiss francs – or dollars, if you must, but the Swiss are impeccably private. To Swiss bankers, money is anonymous – money has no history." He put the envelope into the bottom drawer of his desk and returned to the table.

"Let's continue. Now, instead of superimposed ovals, let your ovals become spirals to the right with a gradually increasing creeping movement. There! Stop. Two things have happened. The height of the ovals continually declines, until here." He pulled out a calipers and measured. "You finally reach 4 mm, close to the standard of 3 mm quoted in most texts. And, look, you are an 'arcade' style writer. Notice how these coiled ovals begin to resemble the letter 'n'. The opposite, usually with left-handed writers, is for the ovals to resemble the letter 'u'. They are called 'garland' writers. Every signature is either garland or arcade."

★   ★   ★   ★   ★   ★   ★   ★   ★   ★

"Graphologically, we are not concerned with the absolute size of the writing as a whole, but with the sizes of the basic letters i, m, n, and u. These four letters fix the standard of size. If you recall, the tendency is for the writer to decrease his letter heights to that average height of 3 mm. In German Gothic there are three sizes of letters, the proportion of which run 3:9:15. The proportions of the Latin script are almost identical, though the medium and large letters are a shade more exaggerated – to about $2^{1}/_{2}$:6:10.

"So you see it is not the absolute size of the basic letters which is of importance, but the proportion between the various groups of letters. And, of course always remember that capital M is a 'privileged letter'."

★   ★   ★   ★   ★   ★   ★   ★   ★   ★

Time accordioned. Long hours compressed and became animated by the excitement of learning 'graphology'. ("So much more dignified than 'forgery'," Puck liked to say). And drawing with fine instruments further highlighted Ernst's fascination with the craft. He felt synchrony with the pens, familiarity with line, pressure, shadow and contrast.

One day, between press runs, Puck turned over an old page, brown with years, on which flowed the writing of three distinct hands. "One can produce a psychological profile of the writer simply by examining his writing style. This is the signature of an old client of mine, Herr Trautwein. He was a warder until he retired after unexpectedly receiving a windfall profit from a 'stock certificate.' A nervous fellow, with little formal education, but he has a distinctive signature. Use the lens. See here how his rapid, nervous hand leaves its mark with an irregular broken line? It is almost like being introduced to Herr Trautwein himself.

"It is the contrast between thin and thick lines that matters the most. Pen pressure is all-important, and varying it comes with practice. The 'weight of hand' is something you will learn from repetition and experience with different types of writers. Some writer's pens dance over the paper with a springy rhythmic motion, still others with a stately manner suggesting strength, but not speed. Those who cannot maintain a constant pen pressure produce a ragged line.

"Nothing is hidden or deceitful to the skillful forger. Isn't that ironic? Character is revealed, disguise stripped away. Authenticity is at once betrayed and illuminated."

Ernst thought of his own identities, wondered how many were forgeries – his public persona that had endeared him to Lieutenant Manfred, Kern, OC, Buchmann, the Nationalists at Striegau. Lisa's lover a long time ago. His father's son – waiting, patiently waiting for his regard, his touch. His mother's son – waiting, patiently waiting for even more. How had Puck said it? 'Wear your disguise as long as it fits.' Puck deciphered and exposed Ernst's 'weight of hand' through his camouflage.

"One of my favorites is Lord Byron." Puck held his pen in an awkward grip and flourished the poet's signature. "Byron had a characteristic hand called 'pasty writing' as a result of adopting a long pen-hold, grasping the pen at considerable distance from the nib. His hand left a broader trace than normal, since it lies more nearly parallel to the paper." Puck repeated the near perfect imitation, leaning the pen even more, thickening the stroke. "Notice the tendency to 'blind' all the loops." He held the 20X lens up for Ernst to examine. "Look at the lower edges of all the horizontal lines. They appear exceedingly ill-defined and irregular."

"But this is completely dependent on the width of his nib, isn't it?"

"Ah, so one would think, but remember Ernst, we seek proportion. And the nib width leaves a different impression on the paper, which we can calculate exactly with the 40X lens. If I had access to all my tools, I would use a binocular microscope, but this is sufficient for our purposes."

★ ★ ★ ★ ★ ★ ★ ★ ★ ★

In May 1924, Ernst received a letter from Hans Gerd, written six months earlier from Landsberg Prison. Ernst paid close attention to his brother's erratic handwriting, child-like but small, crowded onto six pages, most of it copied from his journal:

> ... so you would have a real sense of what my life is like here. You know
> how I have always been overly active – a whirling dervish. You used to call
> me Struwwelpeter and fidgety Philip. I feared I would go crazy in gaol, but I
> find that writing calms me, keeps me focused on the real world.
>
> This old fortress, high above the River Lech, is an unusual prison. A
> new prisoner, Adolf Hitler, has just arrived. You must know of the Hitler-
> Ludendorf-Putsch in November. The beginning of the end for Weimar. He is
> treated as an honored guest, with his own room, a special diet and time and
> space for writing. They say he is writing an important book – one that will
> change the world. He is a rather remarkable man. His conviction and sen-
> tence was for violating Article 81 of the Penal Code – 'for attempting by force
> to alter the Constitution of the German Reich.'. He could have been sentenced
> to lifelong imprisonment, yet this little man from Bavaria gets only five years
> with possibility of parole after six months.

On the last page, Hans Gerd added a personal note:

> I tell you, Ernst, the tide is turning. Prison has been the most incredible
> experience for me. Never have I been so focused and motivated as I am here at
> Landsberg. It's as if I have been transformed by what I can only call a heroic
> experience, something out of Siegfried or Parsifal. Adolf Hitler is a remark-
> able man.
>
> I think about you often and look forward to our reunion, when the
> Weimar betrayers will be ground into dust. Please write to me as often as
> you can. It does get lonely, especially late at night. You know how the dark
> affects me.
>
> With love, Hans Gerd.

Puck's newspapers told him of Hitler's November putsch, deridingly
called a "Beer Hall Putsch" by the leftist press. The Nationalists were jubilant.
Two thousand Nazis confronted the Munich police – shots were fired – sixteen Nazis and 4 policemen were killed. Hitler himself was injured and arrested and sentenced to five years in Landsberg Prison. And Hans Gerd was there.

In reply, Ernst told Hans Gerd of the Nationalists at Striegau in the most
general terms that would pass the censor, and save him from having to reveal
his doubts. He wondered what Hans Gerd would make of Puck. Most likely

he would find him loathsome, or at best incomprehensible, as Ernst sometimes did. Certainly it was challenging to reconcile Puck's world view with that of Buchmann and Georg. Ernst found Puck's 'truth' obscure and philosophical, especially when compared to the familiar and well-worn rhetoric of Buchmann and Georg. What the Nationalists said made sense. An effect had a cause – Versailles, immigrants, Jews – like that paragon of logic and power, the Mercedes flathead engine.

But something irresistible attracted him to Puck's abstract philosophy. He was intrigued by Puck's struggles with faith. And yet Puck seemed, paradoxically, to possess spiritual wholeness. He much preferred Puck's troubling duality and nuance to Buchmann's and Georg's oratory and surety.

★　★　★　★　★　★　★　★　★　★

Several months later, during a press run, Ernst opened the desk drawer and pulled out two sheets of paper from between cardboards. "What do you think of this?" He pushed them across the table to Puck, who lowered his glasses from his forehead.

"I'll have to examine them with the lens, but it looks very good." He held them up to the light. "The watermark is not very well done. Which method did you use?"

"Whitney-Woodman."

"And if I were not a drunken policeman, how could I easily finger you, right there in the middle of the night at a border crossing?"

Ernst had thought the forgery perfect, but Puck exposed the duplicity in less than a minute. He dipped a glass rod into the diluted caustic soda solution that Ernst had used to remove adhesive from bindings, and he applied a drop over each watermark and then held them up to the light. In a very few seconds it was obvious that the forged watermark had begun to fade and almost disappear as the grease dissolved into the paper fibers.

"But you needed caustic soda," Ernst said. "No policeman carries caustic soda."

"Water works as well, only slower. I thought you would appreciate the drama."

"What about the signature and the document itself?"

"Passable, Ernst, passable, though I'm sure I can find at least ten problems." His 40X lens scanned from one document to the other. "No forgery is perfect. Truth is eventually revealed." Puck ascertained that the warder was bored, distracted by his magazine, and he slid a thin file folder from under the desk blotter. Inside was a German National Railroad Bond drawn on the Reichsbank in Jena. "I think you are ready for the real world," he whispered. "This one has to be perfect. Here is the new signature and change the date."

"How long?"

"A week, ten days."

★ ★ ★ ★ ★ ★ ★ ★ ★ ★

On the morning of the first day of spring in 1927 Dronsch himself came to the print shop with the news. Puck's sentence had been reduced by two years in consideration of his excellent behavior and some vague connections with the Commissioner of Prisons. He was free to leave in two weeks.

Puck did not move as Dronsch set the release papers in front of him. "Signed by Commissioner Einhaldt." There was finality and sadness in Dronsch's voice.

Puck peeled off his glasses and closed his eyes. "This is good," he said in a barely perceptible whisper. He reached across the desk with both arms to embrace the surface that had been his friend and companion these past twelve years. His breath came in short sobs, stifled whimpers. Ernst looked away so as not to trespass. He stood on the footstool to look out the window. Laced with the ever-present sulfur fumes, the spice of manure stirred his blood, as it had for the past five springs.

"I will need to make preparations, Herr Dronsch."

"Of course. Tomorrow, come have a drink with me in my office. There are some final transactions. I fear for the commerce of Striegau."

"Not to be concerned, Herr Dronsch. I have groomed Ernst to be my agent, and yours, in Striegau. Business will not suffer."

Ernst was bewildered. He had so much more to learn.

That night, long after the prison went dark and the only sounds were the distant boiler hum and heavy breathing from the next cell, Ernst tossed fitfully.

Puck whispered. "Are you awake?"

"It's hard to find sleep tonight."

"I will miss you, Ernst."

"And I, you."

"I left my pen nibs and lenses in the Print Shop." Ernst heard Puck's throat thicken. "They're for you."

"I couldn't."

"It's business. I trust you to handle the commerce of Striegau to your, and my, advantage. That, if nothing else, will keep us connected."

"Will you be all right?"

"Better than all right, Ernst. There are millions to be made out there. Millions."

A deep-seated sadness closed in on Ernst. "Perhaps you would visit once in awhile?"

"Perhaps."

★   ★   ★   ★   ★   ★   ★   ★   ★   ★

Two weeks later Puck left Striegau. Shortly thereafter, Uncle Erwin came to visit with bad news. Ernst's mother had been diagnosed with tuberculosis the week before. Yes, the diagnosis was secure. The head of the hospital's pulmonary service, Herr Doktor Schlössel himself, had been consulted. She was quite ill and being vigorously treated with mercury, orally as well as by injection. The prognosis was guarded, but she was rallying when he had left her bedside that morning.

Dronsch allowed Ernst to use the prison telephone for daily conversations with the medical staff about his mother's condition. Cell 594 had never been so lonely.

A week later Frau Techow began to improve, and Doctor Schlössel himself talked to Ernst on the telephone. Her x-rays confirmed that her dangerous acute course was now turning into a more manageable chronic form of the disease.

"The chief aim in treatment," Dr. Schlössel explained in clipped High German, "is to increase the natural defensive powers of your mother's constitution. We must bring her general health to the highest possible standard by attention to her hygiene and diet."

Ernst tried to ask a question, but Docktor Schlössel's lecture continued.

"Fresh air by day and night is the most important factor in recovery. Your mother is receiving the most efficacious medicinals: creosote carbonate, iodine by inunction and camphor. Your Uncles, Peter and Erwin Behrens, are arranging for sanatorium care at Davos – the very best. You will be gratified to know that your mother will participate in a study I am conducting utilizing Maragliano's serum. Of course we have administered active immunization with Koch's old tuberculin.

"I understand you are in gaol, and I am, of course, aware of your crime. It is only right you should know that I am a Jew." There was a long pause. "This does not seem to be an issue for your uncles or your mother. Is it for you?"

The static silence was unbearable. "No, no, of course not. Thank you... thank you, Herr Doktor."

"I expect that your mother will be feeling well enough to travel to Davos in the next few weeks. Until then she will stay in hospital." Again the sizzling silence. "Your mother has been an angel of mercy to my patients, Herr Techow. It is the least I can do to repay her kindness all these years. Good day."

★ ★ ★ ★ ★ ★ ★ ★ ★ ★

In the press room, which Ernst took over from Puck, officially contracted printing ran off the archaic press, and between press runs Ernst forged identity papers, land deeds, mortgage claims and birth certificates. Dronsch was pleased and expressed his gratitude by extending all of Puck's privileges to Ernst. A week after his departure, Puck mailed his old gabardine jacket to Ernst to wear. "So they know you are taking over for me."

One warder paid monthly for Ernst's masterpiece, an official document of probate redirecting his father's wealth to him. A lump sum payment was only days away, and the warder's brothers and sister filed an official complaint, so surprised were they by their father's generosity to his least favorite child. Forensic experts examined the documents and found them to be in order, down to the watermark. It had been five years since his first lesson in ovals.

After Puck's release, Striegau was wired for electric lights. The low wattage filaments provided barely enough illumination for reading and burned out quickly from overuse. But complete darkness was a thing of the past. Another gift from Dronsch was a reading lamp with double wattage so Ernst could keep his books updated with the volume of trade. At night, looking down the long corridor, each cell was dark, except for Ernst's where a stab of light cut the murkiness. In the yard Ernst sat behind Puck's wobbly table with his old ledger, and his customers came one at a time. Though he continued Puck's enterprise in Striegau, and business was very good, he and Dronsch never warmed to each other.

Dronsch respected Ernst's request that no one share his cell. Ernst spread out his work and, though he missed Puck, he savored the solitude. In the yard he was now preoccupied with Striegau's commerce, legal and dubious alike, and he no longer congregated with the Nationalists. One day he found himself thinking genially of the Jew Rothstein, whom he had beaten as a boy to

297

gain the favor of the "outlaws.' Rothstein had kept to himself. He was other. In the schoolyard he had made himself small, squatting in a corner near the protection of the teacher's table where he read books, his lips dancing, his head swaying the way Puck described his father and brothers swaying in their Jewish church. There was no understanding Rothstein or those like him, but after five years with Puck, Ernst felt a curious kinship with both Jews.

As the Reichmark recovered and the economy retreated from the brink of collapse, the level of violence declined, and fewer political prisoners came to Striegau. In the yard the two political solar systems shrank and lost their exclusivity. Buchmann and Georg had been released, and no one of equal stature replaced them. Common criminals once again made up the majority of the inmates. It was good for business. Their needs were perhaps more complex and material, but their visitors paid cash.

Hans Gerd was released from Landsberg Prison in 1926 and renewed his university studies at the Faculty of Law. He visited Ernst every few months, more often after examinations. Still on the go, as if motor-driven, he spoke in torrents, inundating Ernst with his enthusiasm for the National Socialists and Herr Hitler. No longer did he conceal his deformed hand in his trouser pocket; he waved it in the air with impunity.

Hans Gerd devoted his weekends, his vacations and summers to Hitler's party, and in the summer of 1928 he announced to Ernst that he had taken a job in the office of Ernst's old friend, Fritz Sommers. And, of course, Fritz's lovely wife Lisa had inquired about Ernst. Did Ernst know that they had a son named Adolf, a beautiful child who looked exactly like Lisa?

Hans Gerd didn't stop for Ernst's wounded countenance, nor did he notice his brother's furrowed brow. Lisa's visits had ceased after she and Fritz married. There were no more letters. Try as he might, he could not imagine Lisa pregnant or holding a baby, not even his baby. The only reason he tried at all was to indulge an insubordinate hope that lingered, that would always endure.

"It won't be long before you get out," Hans Gerd continued. "The end of Weimar is near. Herr Hitler is the new Führer – I'm certain of it. And so many others agree. My best subject is Constitutional and Governmental law. The Party is eager for my services. Fritz – I mean Herr Sommers – has offered me a clerkship after I pass my Referendar this summer. And Fritz assured me that he is looking into your sentence. Don't lose hope – be strong. You're a hero."

Hans Gerd rattled off incomprehensible details of his last course, the progress of the German National Youth Organization, Hitler's latest statement about the Sudetenland, and, almost as an afterthought, their mother's illness and her progress at Davos. One day Davos would be part of Greater Germany, he said, and did Ernst know that Dr. Schlössel was a dirty Jew.

"He should be run out of the country and good riddance. It's appalling that Uncle Peter and Uncle Erwin continue to pay the doctor good money."

If Ernst paid attention to everything Hans Gerd said, his visits would have been exhausting. But he let Hans Gerd's words and tangential thoughts go. It was enough to see his flesh and blood, even across a fence, as a simple reminder of his connection to something outside of Striegau.

★ ★ ★ ★ ★ ★ ★ ★ ★ ★

At his next visit, Hans Gerd was giddy with expectation. "Fritz said to expect a development in your case."

Not long thereafter, one week after Christmas, Dronsch came into the Print Shop and asked the warder to leave the two of them alone. Dronsch looked more pale than usual.

"The Commissioner of Prisons has commuted one quarter of your sentence and has reassigned me to another prison. It is in my power to commute one quarter of your sentence for good behavior. You needn't thank me. The only pity is that I can't have you transferred with me. I shall have to start over." Dronsch laid Ernst's release papers on the desk. "It seems you have powerful friends outside. I have a few final jobs for you before I sign the last document. It's the least you owe me."

"Who... Who was it? Puck? Fritz?"

"I don't know – and you are not meant to know."

He dropped his bowler onto his head and was gone.

It had been seven years since Ernst had shaved, and the razor pulled and scratched, leaving stubble and tiny specks of blood like puddles in a cut cornfield. He dabbed at the blood and was surprised how his face had aged. Crow's feet radiated from his eyes, and the fold from his nose to his mouth had deepened.

On the day of his release in January of 1930, Ernst was hardly concerned with the outside world of men into which he was freed, into which he would disappear. After seven years, the one longing that sat with him as faithfully as a good mother, was to see the sun rise and set over a land that held no expectations, no grudges, a land where memory was ephemeral, or at least forgiving. And identity itself could be authentic.

17

Betrayal

January 1930 – April 1931

As the last of Striegau's gate bolts fell into place behind him, Ernst was puzzled that he could summon neither anticipation, nor elation, not even simple relief, only intense loneliness as bone-chilling as the day's January mist. He looked back, momentarily afraid of leaving the sanctuary that lay behind the medieval gate with *O Maria* engraved over the lintel. He set down his valise, turned up his collar, and searched for a cigarette. It was cold enough for a storm coat. He was glad for Puck's gabardine and the old down coat he slept in, and that was how he left.

He had anticipated returning to Berlin by train, anonymous, allowing the miles to re-inflate the world he had been kept from. He imagined each click of the wheels chiseling away the crust of his time underground. Looking down Driestrasse he squinted into the sun cresting the prison's south wall. He had not seen the sun at such a low angle for more than seven years. From the same direction, a shiny black Mercedes sedan materialized from the shadow of Striegau's brick wall, a dark mass, slowly rolling to meet him. He could not see through the tinted glass if there was a passenger. The automobile stopped, and the chauffeur, in a military style cap and black overcoat, opened the passenger door for him.

"Herr Techow, may I take your bag?" He bent to pick up the nearly empty valise, and Ernst stepped back. "My name is Heinrich. Herr Sommers has sent me to bring you to Berlin. I think you will find the Mercedes more comfortable than the train."

"Fritz?"

"Yes. Herr Sommers has made arrangements for you to stay at the Hotel Metropole until you find suitable lodging. Frau Sommers expects you for dinner tonight."

His heartbeat quickened to think he would see Lisa, and he thought of her pushing a perambulator or holding Fritz's child.

Heinrich slid back the partition and indicated a small bar with seltzer, a bucket of ice, cognac and scotch.

Snow-covered fields, shrouded in fog, passed in dumb succession, the soothing hum of the engine an invitation to forget. He was glad to travel behind the dark glass, unseen.

Ernst looked down at his trousers, confounded not to see prison stripes. He blinked, half expecting them to return, expecting the whiskey bottle to turn into Puck's wax draped candelabra. Unconsciously his hand ran along the smooth wooden trim of the bar. He dropped three ice cubes in the glass and felt Heinrich watching him in the mirror. Though they had been driving for some time, Ernst realized he still sat forward, and it required an act of will to allow the soft leather to cushion him. He found Uncle Erwin's suede pouch in his breast pocket and inhaled its sweet reassurance. His eyes teared. He was going home, unsure of exactly what that meant.

As the mist burned off, the sun, almost overhead after three hours of driving, cast terse shadows. Rough roads smoothed and broadened as traffic increased towards Berlin. He needed another drink when they passed the first road signs for the central city. He had not expected his passion for Lisa to return so quickly, so forcefully. He felt it first and most powerfully in Striegau when he was packing his valise to leave and he came upon her old letters, the ones he kept bundled with Frau Rathenau's letter in rough baling twine. He had only to see Lisa's distinctive handwriting, small script with a peculiar back slant, to conjure her whole in his heart's imaginings.

As they neared Berlin he tapped on the glass panel. "I was hoping to go to my brother's flat." He fumbled in his pocket for a scrap of paper. "Haasestrasse, number 35."

"Your brother will be at the Sommers's residence. I was instructed to bring you."

"And if I refused?"

"Frau Sommers was confident that you would not refuse."

Ernst leaned his head against the tinted glass and watched the rural fields morph into suburbs that turned into city streets and bridges. This morning, when he woke up in his cell, he told himself to shun Lisa; seeing her would only cause pain. But now he felt powerless to stop himself, and anxiety slowly became anticipation. Heinrich stopped at the curb of a newly restored townhouse on Reichskanzlerplatz, in the West End of Berlin. Leafless linden trees, planted symmetrically at the turn of the century, dreamed a tree's reverie of heart shaped leaves and fragrant yellow flowers.

"They are expecting you, Sir." Heinrich bowed low as he opened the door. Such deference was a new and not unwelcome feeling, but his instinct was to be suspicious.

He followed Heinrich and his valise up the five steps into a small ante-room. Ernst felt demeaned by his lamentable attire: a pair of trousers, one size too large, from Uncle Erwin, and a cotton shirt in want of ironing. He tucked in his blouse and slicked back his hair. Heinrich rang the buzzer on the wall and remained at attention.

The door opened immediately as if she had been waiting. Her hair glittered soft gold – the way it always had. Heinrich bowed and backed out of the house. For several moments they looked at each other, and he noticed the details of her aging – the corners of her eyes wrinkled, her forehead creased. He didn't know what to do, or think.

"Ernst! Welcome!"

He felt the déjà-vu of his dreams – her white silk blouse, the shadow of a black brassier, her hands coming forward to him, but now, instead of fading away, he felt her hand on his arm, and she took his coat. Without looking she reached behind her to hang his coat on one of several delicately carved wrought iron hooks, but it fell. They both stooped to retrieve it, and their foreheads touched. He smelled her Lillé perfume, and the soft sweep of her hair twisted his heart.

She stood slowly, staring at Ernst, hugging his jacket to her breasts.

"I was so surprised about your release – so unexpected." Her hand seemed to float towards him, and he resisted the impulse to take her in his arms. He felt the warmth and softness of her fingers as her breath came harder, her blue eyes opalescent, electric.

She dropped his hand, awkwardly, and turned to hang the coat. "Fritz will return soon – with Hans Gerd. Leave your suitcase there, and come sit down. You must be tired. Can I get you something to drink? A cigarette?"

"Yes," Ernst said, still staring at her. "That would be lovely."

She smiled. "What would be lovely?" and led him into the parlor.

"A drink, a cigarette, sit and talk, whatever. It would all be lovely."

He stood again when she returned from the dining room with a finely cut decanter and a gold cigarette case. She paused, eclipsing the setting sun, her breasts momentarily silhouetted through her white blouse, like the first time they made love. Childbirth had not changed her athletic figure; her calves were still finely sculpted above thin ankles and black velvet shoes.

Her hand trembled as she lit then passed a lipstick-stained cigarette to him. "Fritz would rather I didn't smoke. He says it's unseemly, not very Party-like."

"You always looked good with a cigarette."

He could scarcely take his eyes from her as she sat beside him at the edge of the sofa, poised to stand. For a moment he felt the pain of reunion and cursed himself for coming, for daring to enter this mausoleum in his heart. She seemed just as uneasy, her eyes seeking his, then fleeing to the seltzer water or the ash tray. She tapped her ashless cigarette.

"Where is Adolf?"

"There is a Nursery School. We have a Kinderfräulein, Marlis – Frau Staats. She's been with Adi four years – since he was born."

"What kind of child is he?"

"Just like Fritz. Very intelligent." Her momentary smile drew taut into pursed lips, and she sighed. Lisa straightened her spine and cleared her throat. "Fritz says you will stay at the Metropole."

"I really don't know. I only left Striegau this morning. Things are a little muddled... I mean I'm still somewhat muddled." He looked away. "It's not easy..."

She laid her hand on his arm. "I'm sorry, Ernst. I wanted to tell you – before Fritz came home."

"Do you love him?"

Lisa's hand slid off his arm and curled into a fist. "Fritz is very successful, a rising star in the Party." She finished her cognac. "We have a good life. Adi will have a good life."

"But do you love him?"

"We've been together a long time. And everything changes when there is a child." Her eyes found his, and Ernst had to turn away.

"In Striegau I read newspapers. Times are hard. I've seen the pictures in the newspaper – the lines outside unemployment offices. Many suicides."

"It's true. Even people we knew. Remember Lotte, in my Mädchen group? She's a prostitute. And Bernhard carries a pistol and is rumored to be in the underworld. There are tent colonies in Grünewald. A few weeks ago Fritz took me to see one. Very orderly and neat, but desperately poor. They have their own mayors and town councils, communal kitchens and garbage collection teams. The women cook turnips, children play in sandlots and the men sit – just sit with the saddest expressions. Some play chess or checkers or '66', most just sit and stare. Fritz says they're ripe for National Socialism."

"And you? What do you think?"

"They just make me very sad."

It was difficult for Ernst to reconcile economic collapse with the opulence of the Sommers's house. The dining room table was surrounded by ten high back chairs, as if heads of state routinely dined there. He imagined Fritz and Lisa eating with baby Adolf, dwarfed by a parliament of armchairs.

"Fritz is an editor at *Der Angriff* – Dr. Goebbels's newspaper here in Berlin. I wasn't sure if you knew." When Ernst didn't respond she continued. "You do know Goebbels, don't you?"

"Only what I've read, and by reputation among the Nationalists at Striegau. But being in gaol is rather like being abroad. One doesn't really know what's going on. There is no context."

Their eyes met again and lingered until Lisa lit another cigarette. "I sometimes think of the old days," she said, looking out the window. "Quite a lot actually. Too much."

She flicked the cigarette, stained with her red lip print. He yearned for the taste of her mouth.

"The old days are all I have," Ernst said. "I don't quite know how to start over."

She turned to him and earnestly asked, "Why did it have to be you, Ruby?"

"I don't like to think about it. Things would be very different... for you and me."

"It makes me so sad. I do love little Adi, but the rest of my life is... difficult. The Nazis have little use for intelligent women – strictly 'children, church, kitchen.'"

"You should have been able to do anything. You're smarter than any of us."

"Fritz has made his choice. His career has always been what mattered most. He says it's for our safety – our security as a family."

"Has he changed that much?"

"You'll have to judge for yourself. There is a price to pay for becoming a member of the Party. Fritz says we are revolutionaries. We follow the Party line and have to make sacrifices."

"You live quite well for a revolutionary. Nazis are not known for their opulence."

"My father..."

"He must be delighted about Fritz. Does he contribute to the Party?"

"Heavily."

Even before the front door opened, he heard Hans Gerd's distinctive laughter. Lisa jammed out her cigarette and fled the parlor with the incriminating ash tray. Fritz was already in the room as Lisa strode out. He stood in the doorway, a thin smile on his face, and quickly took in Lisa's retreat before turning to Ernst.

Fritz's close-shorn blond hair had thinned, and the black leather coat he peeled off his shoulders would soon be a size too small. On his left shirt-sleeve, the black spider swastika seemed to writhe in its white circle on the red armband of the Nazi party. Though Ernst had worn the same insignia on his helmet as a Freebooter, there was something ominous about seeing Fritz, a civilian, branded with the military mark.

"Hello, Fritz," Ernst said, and he heard his own hesitancy.

"I see you've already made yourself at home," Fritz said. "That's good. I trust the drive was satisfactory?"

"Yes, yes. Excellent. I didn't expect it. Thank you."

After shaking hands, Fritz continued to hold onto Ernst with both hands and smiled again. "My old friend. You are always welcome here. You know that, don't you? You look tired."

"Ernst!" Hans Gerd burst into the room, his eyes wide with joy, his red hair cut so short the curls only suggested themselves. He too wore the red Nazi armband. "Now everything will be all right." Hans Gerd reached out his left hand but was so overcome that he threw his arms around his brother. "Wait till you catch up." He rubbed his good hand against his one fingered hand. "We will have good times. Might I have a scotch, Fritz?"

Fritz still studied Ernst and called over his shoulder. "Lisa! Scotch for Hans Gerd." He pointed to Ernst's drink. "I see Lisa has taken good care of you." Fritz fingered a gold watch chain draped across his vest. "I instructed Heinrich to heat the water for a bath before dinner, if you would like. Casual dress. I asked Lisa to get you some new clothes. I hope they fit. Don't mind me with this cravat." His black cravat, perfectly knotted, was precisely centered though it was the end of the day. "Hans Gerd and I only just returned from the office. There are interminable meetings. So much to tell you. Such times we live in!" His eyes twinkled. "I am so pleased to see you a free man again. Dr. Goebbels himself asked about you."

He called into the empty dining room. "Lisa, Hans Gerd is still waiting for his drink. And an ashtray for Ernst." Ernst looked at his smoldering cigarette, red tipped with Lisa's lipstick. Fritz looked into Ernst's eyes. "I know she sneaks cigarettes," he winked. "It's entirely your fault – you addicted her when we were *Wandervogel*."

"This Strasser business is getting quite out of hand," Hans Gerd began even as he pulled a chair toward his brother. "Brüning has called the election for the fall, probably September. A critical moment for the Party – a time for unity. The Strasser brothers, the bastards, have their own agenda. Hitler will not abide them..."

Ernst listened for Lisa's movement in the pantry, the tinkle of glasses, her light step. When she returned she flashed a brief smile, for his eyes only. Hans Gerd continued as if talking was no different than breathing.

★　　★　　★　　★　　★　　★　　★　　★　　★　　★

Four months later, as the Linden trees bloomed, Ernst waited again among the columns of the National Gallery, watching for Lisa. War veterans and beggars still held out their caps for alms, as if the Great War had ended one year ago instead of twelve.

Ernst lived alone in a small flat on Pohlstrasse. He preferred it, he told his mother. He supplemented his meager income from the press room of Goebbels's weekly newspaper *Der Angriff* by providing high quality forgeries for selected customers still on his list from Striegau. Word of his talent spread, and the extra income allowed him to eat simply, but well, and to keep a bottle of reasonable schnapps.

He tried to re-engage Berlin, to feel the animation: the hum of the streets, Grünewald, the Havel with all its bright sailboats, real and toys, Wertheim's Department Store. He took nostalgic walks by the Moabit barracks and through the Tiergarten as spring unlocked the flora and fauna of the city. Red-breasted Rotkehlchen flitted from bushes, their distinctive 'tsi, tsi' an invitation to lust for life.

But it was futile. The city seemed to have revolted against him, or perhaps it was the other way around. What once delighted his eye now felt crowded and shocking. Animation became chaos. The tempo of downtown, of Kochstrasse – Newspaper Row – where *Der Angriff* was published, jolted his sensibility. He felt like an automobile trying to start after being on blocks for seven years, coughing, not quite catching.

Today was their third rendezvous at the museum, an innocent meeting place, public. He never asked if Fritz knew of their meetings. He presumed not, but he did not want to know. They savored the sanctuary of the galleries, consorting with the statues of Rodin, Brancusi's gleaming metal "Bird in Space", and, of course, the Impressionists.

In Striegau he had given up on her. The letters and visits stopped, and she was so utterly gone that it felt like her death. He had buried her and kept his grief inside. Striegau was no place to show emotion. But now, after seven years – only seven years – unexpected resurrection. From the moment he saw her again he felt her gravitational pull and was prepared to risk everything for her.

They sat on a bench in a deserted gallery room, and Ernst took her hand. It was the first time he had touched her in that way, and he felt her stiffen.

"The more I see you," Ernst said, "the more I want to see you. I feel like an opium addict."

Ernst saw the fear in her eyes, the way they averted from his, then sought him out again, pleading.

"We're old friends, that's all," she said. "I don't have any illusions – and neither should you."

Ernst felt her hand relax and settle on his thigh.

"We had a fight last week," she continued. "Fritz became more angry than I've ever seen him. A few days later he told me about his friend – a Party man, like himself. His wife was having an affair, and his friend had the man murdered."

"What does Fritz have to worry about? As you said, we're old friends, that's all."

"Fritz says nothing. Sometimes I worry."

"Are you afraid?"

Matter-of-factly she said, "I'm always afraid." Lisa pointed at the sculpted head in the center of the room, a plaster cast of Rodin's fierce Balzac. "He reminds me of Fritz."

"Do you ever think about us?" He had to look away.

"You know what I think. I haven't changed that much. What I lack is courage. These are dangerous times, especially for women, and with little Adi..."

An older couple entered the room, seemed lost and disagreed for a moment about which way to turn, then Ernst and Lisa were alone again.

"I can see that you want this," he said.

"I don't trust myself anymore. I've always been attracted to what's dangerous –hurtful."

"But you and I – we're different," he said.

"It always seems that way at first."

"Will you meet me again next week?"

"Of course," she smiled. "We're only at a museum. What's wrong with that?"

Two weeks later, in the early evening when Venus glittered between two tenement buildings across Pohlstrasse, Lisa came to Ernst's apartment for the first time. Fritz was speaking at a huge rally at the Sportspalast, and he would not return until after midnight. They both knew why she was there, and after a few moments of awkward conversation, she was in his arms.

He undid the buttons on her blouse, and she protested that this was not good, that she was afraid, then kissed him again, with more passion and circled her hands about his waist. She pulled his pelvis into hers. As he unfastened her skirt and kissed her soft belly she held his head against her and protested that she could not risk everything for this love. Their time had passed – she had Adi. Ernst tore a button off his shirt as he pulled it over his head, and she unhooked his belt whispering about their secret. She raised both arms to allow Ernst to lift her blouse over her head then held him tightly against her breasts. They rolled over each other in his bed, first Lisa straddling his hips, guiding him into her wetness, then turning again, still united and Ernst slowly dancing inside her. Writhing against each other, he deep inside, her mouth sweet and alive, convulsive with heavy breath. They climaxed together for what seemed like a suspended moment in eternity.

Afterwards, she leaned against his chest, and they shared a cigarette. The spring breeze lifted the curtains, dissipated the smoke, and it would have been enough just to smell her hair and listen to her breathe.

An unexpected tear spilled down Ernst's cheek and dropped into the stream of her own. They held each other more tightly, and Ernst could feel their passion turning somber.

"What will become of us, Ernst? I feel trapped."

"We always have free choice. Not even death can take that away. It's an oddly comforting thought."

"There are no good choices, and I'm afraid. Sometimes I want to hurt myself. I want to kill these feelings."

"You can choose love," Ernst said. "It may not make sense..."

"Luxurious choices." She stiffened. "I have to choose survival –- for Adi – for me."

"People do monstrous things when they're afraid."

"I'm not a monster – just afraid."

"I only know that I will always love you more than I should."

"I can't risk everything for this. For better or worse, Fritz and the Nazis are our future. They will roll over us. What choice do we have?"

"There is no future," Ernst said. "There is only this moment." He kissed her forehead.

"The Nazis are our future. Fritz says it will be a good one."

"But not for us," Ernst said.

"No, not for us."

"Love's unplanned course."

She turned her face up to his, and they kissed again, their wet cheeks pressed together. Their bodies glistened with sweat, and she rolled over on top of him. Her body slid without friction against his, and he was hard again. He could feel her heart pounding and wondered how much it was driven by passion, how much by fear, but their lovemaking was all the sweeter for the heaviness in their hearts, all the more sensual for the virtue of their desperation.

⋆ ⋆ ⋆ ⋆ ⋆ ⋆ ⋆ ⋆ ⋆ ⋆

After the stock market crash of 1929, the contagion of Depression spread worldwide and by 1931 in Germany, the Danat Bank, then the Dresdener Bank failed, followed in quick succession by others. Unemployment more than doubled. Unrest and membership in the Nazi party soared.

Six months after the market crash, Leo and Katherine moved into the flat on Heydenstrasse. His mother appealed to Ernst for help moving them, and Fritz insisted they use his Mercedes and chauffeur, though the scowl on Heinrich's face betrayed his contempt as he waited in the car. Their boxes and suitcases filled Ernst's former bedroom, and the only evidence that it was once Ernst's room was his favorite charcoal battleship drawing pinned to the wall. He wondered why Leo had not taken it down.

Katherine brought her most treasured items from the larger flat they could no longer afford – a large woven basket holding sheaths of dried reeds and a wall of photos: baby Katherine on a horse, Leo and Katherine as young children, Katherine and her father in his uniform, and a wedding portrait of Katherine and Leo, all framed in simple black.

When Ernst was alone with his mother, she told him the bank had fired Leo. The only work he could secure was with a pick and shovel, and that was none too regular. And, less than six months after her stillbirth, Katherine was pregnant again.

"Leo never mentioned... I didn't notice."

"No, of course, it's very early. Leo will tell you soon enough. Don't be so harsh with your brother. It's been difficult for them." She lifted the embroidered tea cozy and poured another cup for Ernst and herself. "It was good of Fritz to hire you at *Der Angriff*. Please, don't argue with Leo. You know how he feels about the Nazis."

"He'd better get used to them."

She seemed uncomfortable and picked at a stray thread on the embroidery. "I'm glad to have Leo and Katherine live here. Since Hans Gerd took a room at the Law Faculty I've been alone here."

"What do you make of Hans Gerd?"

"I think the Nazis have been good for Hans Gerd. How many law students get to work for Dr. Goebbels? What surprises me most is his behavior. He's a hard worker and does what he's told – at least in school. I would never have guessed. It's ironic and a little sad. I worry that he is a blind follower, but what do I know? Leo is unemployed, and Hans Gerd clerks for the most powerful man in Berlin. Who would have guessed?"

"I think it's a game for him," Ernst said. "But if it keeps him out of trouble... Is Uncle Erwin still helping out?"

She nodded and looked wistfully out the window. "Erwin does what he can, but the depression, it takes its toll. At least winter is over." She smiled. "Everything looks better with leaves on the trees, even if they only disguise the misery."

★　★　★　★　★　★　★　★　★　★

Later that evening, Leo invited Ernst for a few beers at Pauli's Rathskeller to thank him for his help moving. But as they sat across the table from each other an uneasy silence hung between them like fog on the morning of battle.

Ernst lifted his glass. "I suppose we should toast your new baby."

"Yes. The baby." Leo's glass touched his. "It was good of you to give us your room, Ernst. I don't know what we would have done."

Ernst finished his beer, feeling its effervescent relief. "I didn't give you my room, Leo. Mother gave you my room."

Leo sat forward. "Listen, Ernst. Can't we drop this petty jealousy? We got along so well as children. Will you shake my hand?"

Ernst thought of Kern's request for his hand the day before the assassination. He put his elbow on the table and held his hand open, a challenge to wrestle. Leo matched his arm, and their fingers clasped.

"You haven't a chance," Leo said. "I'm a worker now."

Their hands intertwined and tightened, matching each other force for force, their forearms beginning to tremble, and then the true struggle began. Slowly, Leo prevailed, and Ernst's forearm gave way, but he recovered before the point of no return and wrestled Leo back to a neutral stance. They grunted and gritted, stared over white-hot knuckles into each other's crimson faces, neck veins bulging. Little by little Ernst felt Leo's strength slacken, and he eased his arm slowly onto the wooden table without a sound.

"You let me win," Ernst said. He felt Leo steal the thunder of his victory, like a patriarchal brother making allowance for his weakness.

"Just like when we were kids."

Leo's enigmatic smile reminded Ernst of his brother leering at him across their bedroom on Wannseestrasse, daring him to cross the imaginary line on the floor.

"Fuck you, Leo. I was always stronger than you."

"No, you only got into more fights. Who was that – Heinrich Schliefen? – then Kern and OC."

"As righteous a cause as your Spartakists," Ernst said.

"I have no use for ideology any more. Katherine and the baby are my cause now." Leo signaled the waiter. "Another round!"

Ernst tried to gauge Leo as his flesh and blood, to peel away Leo the naval officer, the mutineer, the Spartakist, the bank clerk, the day laborer. He searched the man, for the boy across the line down their bedroom, the brother he wanted to love him, but who had nothing but contempt for his models and drawings.

"Will you keep my drawing on your wall?"

"It's quite good. Do you want it?"

"Only if you were going to take it down."

"I've already told Katherine. If all her photographs go on the wall, your drawing has to stay also."

Ernst tried to feel kindly towards Leo. It was what he wanted from him for all those years, across the line neither dared cross. But now that Leo seemed to offer kindness, Ernst didn't know what to do with it.

As far as Ernst knew, Leo's only childhood transgression was to smoke a cigarette when he was nine years old. Their father caught him behind the kitchen in the well of cement steps leading to the wine cellar. Even as he berated him, Leo stood erect and answered without shame. The forgiving tone of his father's reprimand was only more evidence of Leo's favored status, and Ernst had hated him for it.

"What about you?" Leo asked. "What will you do?"

"I have my work."

"*Der Angriff*? You don't believe that junk, do you?"

Ernst's spine stiffened, his skepticism verified. "I run the presses. I leave the editorials to Fritz and Herr Goebbels."

"I remember when you were Hans Gerd's hero. I was always a little jealous about that. Neither of you ever really respected me."

"Are you kidding? I thought you walked on water when you enlisted."

"I guess we never really knew each other very well."

They drank and avoided eye contact.

"Whatever happened to that woman – Lisa? Didn't she marry Fritz Sommers?" Leo leaned forward. "You loved her a lot, didn't you? Do you still?"

Ernst rubbed his palm on the laminated oak table. Maybe Leo did know him after all, or maybe he was fishing for trouble. "I trust you will keep my confidence. It would be disastrous..." Ernst looked squarely at Leo. "I think of her every day. I don't want to, or maybe I do, but she intrudes on my thoughts constantly."

"How often do you...?"

"Whenever we can. Sometimes once a week."

"Her husband... he's not your boss at *Der Angriff*, is he?"

"Not really. He's in the editorial department, with Goebbels. We're just old friends – or we were. Maybe we still are. He doesn't know. I feel terribly guilty. He and Lisa live on family money. He edits the 'Struggles in Berlin' section."

"A police blotter for fights between the SA and the Communists. Trash journalism."

"You have to understand. Fritz is brilliant. Editing is only a small piece of what he's involved with. I hear that Goebbels seeks his counsel frequently."

"I would guess that you and Fritz don't have port and cigars together." Leo laughed to himself.

Ernst finished his third beer and smiled. "No, but I'd like to run away with her."

"Be careful," Leo said. He was trying to be serious, but his eyes were unfocused. "Nazis don't like to be cuckolded."

"He treats her badly."

"So he's a bastard. Does that matter for anything?"

"You'll be a father soon. I'll wager that changes you."

Leo collapsed against the back of his chair. "I can't quite believe there will be a person in the world soon who will call me 'Father.'" His eyes sparkled in a way Ernst had never seen.

"You were always the good son. I hated you for it then, especially when Father praised you." Ernst deepened his voice in imitation, "'Why can't you be like Leo?'"

They both exploded with laughter.

Leo leaned in close to Ernst again and whispered. "What's Goebbels really like?"

Ernst looked over both shoulders and dropped his voice. "An asshole. Gives me the creeps. He's a little guy, weighs about a hundred pounds, limps, looks malnourished. But everyone is pretty much scared shitless of him. Even Lippert, the Editor-in-Chief, gets this gray look when Goebbels comes to an editorial meeting."

"What do you really think of the Nazis?"

"Really, I don't give a shit. Why shouldn't they go the way of every other party? There's so much shit between the Strasser brothers and Stennes and Goebbels, never enough money, preaching to the proletariat of the most left wing city in all of Germany. I wouldn't give you a pfennig on their future."

"So it's just a job?"

"Pretty much. No one asks my opinion, which is just fine."

Leo laughed again. "So what is your opinion?"

"I think you're getting stupid and drunk. One more round? I'm buying." Ernst signaled the waiter.

Leo yawned. "I have to admit, there's a part of me that wants to believe their promises, and if I thought they could actually make them happen... Don't you have to be some kind of Nazi to work at Der Angriff?" Leo asked.

"It helps."

"So what kind of Nazi are you?"

"How many different kinds are there?"

"I was certain you were," Leo said. "Mother says I should watch what I say – that soon everyone will be some kind of Nazi."

"You've had too much beer," Ernst said.

"True, but Mother has really become a believer," Leo said. "She reads Der Angriff, and she's even gone to some rallies. And you know how she hates crowds."

"I don't know, Leo. Maybe it's just because I work there. I know these people, warts and all. It takes something away from their charisma."

"You've become quite the cynic."

Ernst shrugged his shoulders.

Leo finished another beer. "Actually, I like you better confused. You were such a fucking bore when you were younger."

"Puck says..."

"Who's Puck?"

"A smart guy at Striegau. My cell-mate." Ernst missed his friend and teacher. "Puck would say things like 'confusion is the first step to wisdom' and 'doubt is necessary for faith.'"

"Is that why I feel so wise when I've had too many beers?" Leo's head bobbed. "You want wisdom? Don't get caught in the pants of an important Nazi's wife."

"I think I can handle myself."

"Just friendly advice."

"Up yours, Leo." They clinked glasses.

★   ★   ★   ★   ★   ★   ★   ★   ★   ★

Ernst's flat on Pohlstrasse was as small as two cells in Striegau and almost as dark. Two ineffectual windows faced the brick wall of the neighboring apartment building; the remaining two allowed him to consider Pohlstrasse's dull façade of tenement flats.

Puck was correct – forgery was lucrative, and Ernst earned at least as much from his freelance artistry as from his meager income at Der Angriff. He could afford quality inks, pens, magnifying lenses, drafting compasses and brushes, which littered the shelf hanging over his work-table. Pinned to the easel that sat on his desk was his current effort, drawings of a German exit visa and a Spanish transit visa stamp.

Ernst rode the Blankenstrasse trolley to work each day, and one day a man in a dreary coat, his face shadowed by a fedora pulled low on his forehead, maneuvered his way around the rush hour passengers. He stopped beside Ernst, studied his face and said, "Techow?"

Ernst looked warily at the man. "I beg your pardon."

Ernst could barely hear him. "You are Ernst Techow, aren't you?"

"Why do you ask?"

"Something from Puck."

His heart backfired. The evening trolley, crammed with workers, rocked back and forth; the steel wheels screeched.

"Give me your newspaper," he said. "I'll give you mine. A letter is tucked inside. I will find you again." They exchanged papers, and the man backed into the crowd and was gone.

Ernst's heart raced more than usual as he reached his third floor landing. Inside, he poured a glass of good scotch that he saved for special moments, like Lisa's visits, and inspected the letter, a long envelope with Puck's distinctive handwriting. He lit a Gauloise.

My dear Ernst,

I hope this letter finds you well. You have still been working for me, though I'm not sure you have known it. I have been enormously impressed by the quality of your workmanship. I am especially pleased by your artistic reproductions of official stamps – truly a great advance in the art.

I have been living in Corsica for almost four years, ever since some unpleasantness in Rostock that I needn't go into. God moves us (you and me) in mysterious ways. When the police closed in on me in Rostock, I was sick with thinking that the same rogue God that swept my brother Jacob into the sea was about to sweep me back into gaol. I learned all I care to from Striegau, and I would sooner die than return.

Little did I know God was simply changing my itinerary so I would come to this warm Mediterranean island where my particular skills, my unusual connections and discretion are appreciated. That I am a Jew is of no more consequence than that I am short or stout. Jacques, the undisputed ruler of the Corsican underworld, actually finds it amusing when I exclaim in Yiddish at predictable moments. Even more amusing is Jacques swearing in Yiddish now and again.

Corsica has much to recommend it. The only thing lacking is a Torah study group and a table large enough for me to sit under at my father's feet. But you know about that dream.

In the near future Jacques will be requiring German documents with official stamps for some project he is initiating in Germany. New territory for his organization. I will contact you in similar ways with the specifics. The mail is unreliable and, I fear, tampered with, so delivery will be via the tram. You will be instructed as to drop-off points and payment will, of course, be generous.

I think of you often, Ernst. Our years at Striegau were unique and unforgettable. I believe we have a deep connection that will not be lost, whether in the service of the underworld or the service of God, or both. I think of you

fondly and wish you well.
With abiding affection,
Puck

★   ★   ★   ★   ★   ★   ★   ★   ★   ★

Ernst was successful at *Der Angriff*, and in less than a year he had risen to Chief Pressman. He and Lisa continued their affair, but Lisa was more circumspect and sometimes weeks would go by before they met at Ernst's apartment. Ernst declined the few dinner invitations from Fritz, and he stopped asking. Lisa said no, they never spoke of Ernst at home. And yes, he might be spying on them.

Ernst had just returned from press #2, a bothersome antique that required as much care as a senile man, when he saw Dr. Goebbels waiting alone at the door to his small office. Right away he worried that it had to do with Lisa. The stench of lead fumes and hot ink from the typeset was somewhat heavier than usual, and the rhythmic whirring and thumping of the presses were at their loudest. Goebbels looked even shorter than his five and a half feet. He covered his mouth and nose with a white handkerchief.

Goebbels, the Gauleiter of Berlin, never visited the basement press room. He had neither regard nor concern for the tedium of printing what had recently become the Nazi daily. Polished jackboots showed under his trousers. Goebbels's coal black eyes burned, and his thin lips drew taut.

"Ernst Techow?" He clicked his heels and bowed imperceptibly.

Ernst invited him into his office and closed the door, muting the whoosh of the presses to the level of a heavy storm. In the guise of tidying his desk, Ernst shuffled a forged identity card under another folder. He adjusted his cravat and smoothed the wrinkles from his only suit.

"Herr Gauleiter," he said and bowed, briskly. "An unexpected honor. How may I help you?" He was relieved that Goebbels still did not actually know him.

Goebbels's handkerchief came away from his face. "Please, Herr Techow, sit down." Goebbels perched on the edge of the hard wooden chair, his spine erect, and peeled off black leather gloves one finger at a time. "Your friend, Herr Sommers, speaks highly of you. Even without such an eloquent friend, your past speaks volumes, and your performance at *Der Angriff* has been commendable. I hope your time in gaol was not too taxing?"

"Gaol is never pleasant, but I am unchanged." He felt shamed by his lie,

316

spoken like a toady, but Goebbels's intimidation was formidable.

"There are liable to be some changes in the editorial staff soon. When this Stennes unpleasantness blows over there may be an opening for you in the editorial offices, if you're interested. I wanted to speak with you in advance. Now that we are a daily, this press room is noisier, the air more noxious." Goebbels's mouth seemed overly large; his beefy tongue darted across his lips. "*Der Angriff* will be the premier German evening newspaper in Berlin. My ideas – our ideas – will bring National Socialism into every home in Berlin. I am considering presenting my novel, *Michael*, as the first serialized literature. Have you read it?"

Was this a test? "Yes, Herr Gauleiter. It is quite good, especially for a first novel." He lied easily, almost gratuitously. Although Ernst admired Goebbels' writing ability as a journalist and politician, sensing a talented, if restless and demonic genius at work on the pages of *Der Angriff*, Goebbels's fictional abilities were undistinguished. Ernst had read *Michael* as soon as he began his job and found it wanting at best, shrill and puerile at worst.

In that moment, Dr. Goebbels allowed his inflexible trunk to soften; perhaps he had even blushed waiting for Ernst's critique. "What did you like about my book?" He smiled and crossed his good leg.

Ernst urgently tried to remember something of value from the eminently forgettable excesses of cliché and juvenile writing that encumbered yet another tragic tale of a hero who returns from the Great War, goes to the university and meets a girl with whom he has long talks about the meaning of life. Dostoevsky and Christ had somehow become enmeshed in this tale, and the boy ultimately commits suicide, young and unfulfilled.

"I remember the scene where Michael goes to hear a speech by a powerful orator. I presume that is Herr Hitler?"

"Yes, it is. One writes best from one's own life. Did you like the book?"

Ernst felt his skin crawl. "Yes, yes. It is quite good."

"It has taken eight years to get it into print. The Jewish publishers, of course, would not touch it. I graduated from Heidelberg in 1921 – studied literature under Friedrich Gundolf, a Jew. He detested me – kept me from becoming part of Stefan George's circle. It was because I was poor – of low stock."

Was he drunk? Odd enough to see the publisher alone, without his SA body guards, and in the noise and stench of the press room. Joseph Goebbels did not trifle. He was on a mission, and Ernst's lips twitched with premonition.

"What do you think of Stennes' position?"

Goebbels's question invited guile, not honesty; surely this was something every prisoner learned, however short his time in gaol – to say what was expected. "Party unity is of critical importance. I try not to take sides, Herr Gauleiter." Truth be told, he didn't give a damn who signed his paycheck. But if he had to take sides, he would have chosen Stennes, the old Freebooter, over Hitler. Goebbels played both sides of the dispute. Although he spoke highly of Hitler, he was conciliatory towards Stennes, whose philosophy of revolution more closely approximated his own – for now.

The Gauleiter sat erect and reached into the breast pocket of his leather coat. "This is an article I will be publishing about the role of women and the raising of children in a National Socialist state. Please give me your editorial comments by next week." He laid it on the desk. "I know you appreciate German culture – literature, poetry, the arts –unlike most of the party faithful. I would like to see you advance."

"Thank you, Herr Goebbels. I am honored."

"Fritz Sommers's suggestion." He looked about, as if to confirm their privacy. "There is another matter I'd like to discuss with you. It is of a most delicate nature. I understand you are an artist – a particular kind of artist." Goebbels leaned forward and his tongue darted like a snake. "My party documents indicate that I joined the Nazi Party in February 1925. I distinctly remember that it was a year earlier. This 'paper problem' has become a sticking point in my struggle with the Strassers. I am certain it is a clerical error, but so difficult to adjust without drawing attention." He unfolded the official party papers on Ernst's desk. "Here," he pointed. "A simple matter of one year. This should say 1924, and here also."

"But, Herr Goebbels that is a relatively simple change to make. One could almost do that oneself."

"The official party stamp had changed. That is the difficult part. That is why I come to you. Here is a blank form – and here a document with the 1924 imprint. Can you reproduce it? Strasser will have the document examined by a forensics expert. It must be flawless."

"No forgery is flawless."

"But I understand you are the best." Goebbels regained his icy exterior and forced his small hands back into his black gloves. "I'm sure that your comments on my article and this minor correction will help you rise above the press room." He stood and clicked his heels together then thrust his black hand through the air. "Heil Hitler!"

Ernst hesitated a moment and then, for the first time in his life, extended his arm tentatively, in the Nazi salute. "Heil Hitler!"

★   ★   ★   ★   ★   ★   ★   ★   ★   ★

As a daily, Der Angriff was well enough endowed to afford a stable of talented writers, but the news was heavily slanted. A Nazi rally at the Hallesche Market on Gleimstrasse in the slums of northern Berlin was reported as a prodigious success. Unemployed workers lined the street to cheer the swastika flag, and when a rag-tag gang of Communists attacked, Nazis and workers alike were injured.

Hans Schweitzer's cartoon featured the hook-nosed deputy police commissioner Dr. Bernhard Weiss, a Jew, labeled as 'Isidor,' horns sprouting from his forehead, leading the Communists against the hapless Nazis and workers.

On his way home each evening, Ernst bought the Berliner Tageblatt, and they reported on the same rally:

> A band of thirty or thirty-five Nazis rallied at Hallesche Market and when they clashed with a band of Communists, the spectators cheered the red flag and stoned the Nazis.

But after the September 14th election, the two papers carried the same news. The Nazi vote had risen from 810,000 in 1928 to 6.5 million in 1930. The Nazis hoped for 50 Reichstag seats, they captured 107. Overnight, the Nazi party became the second largest in Germany. The Social Democrats, still the preeminent party, polled 143 seats, a loss of 10. The Communists, favored by rising unemployment, and proletarian unrest, also prospered, ending the day with 77 seats.

Ernst's first thought was that this surprise victory for the Nazi party – this momentum – was also an opportunity for him and Lisa. Fritz would be exhilarated, preoccupied. Ernst felt emboldened, knowing he had Lisa's heart, confident he could win her back, though he couldn't imagine how. His resurrected need for her felt like a glimpse of heaven; he felt lighter, inspired. But in that same moment of anticipation, of infatuation, he agonized that someday, something would go terribly wrong, as if they were Rodin's lovers in Hell, Paolo and Francesca, their lips never to touch.

Ernst returned to his flat and lit the gas for tea. He peered through a 30X lens at a stock ownership certificate with a new date and a forged postal stamp. Puck will be impressed, he thought, and smiled as he slid his work between two cardboards and into an envelope. 'Herr Trolley Car Man' had given him instruction on the handover.

The next morning he was in Neukölln, at the junction of Mittelweg and Thomasstrasse, where an island of green came to a point. In the shade of a Linden tree, a plain looking, middle-aged woman sat on a park bench reading a magazine, her blue beret tipped slightly over the left side of her forehead, a bag of knitting by her left leg. Ernst sat beside her and opened his copy of *Der Angriff*. After a few moments he placed the envelope containing his forgery between them on the bench. She placed an identical envelope, slightly fuller, on top of his. After a few moments, Ernst took the top envelope, with 1,000 Swiss francs and walked north towards Alexanderplatz and the Reich bank.

One did not walk alone in Neukölln at night. Neukölln, a devastated district of tenements, boarded up shops and rundown beer halls, had become fertile ground for the SA, who recruited and gathered for weekly "storm center" meetings. For men on the dole, who queued for hours for their semi-weekly government handout, Hitler's Nazis, with their brown uniforms and extravagant promises, restored a sense of fraternity, of self-respect. They were defeated men with hungry families. After more than a decade of lies and empty promises from the Communists, Neukölln's working class was ready to give the Nazis the benefit of their considerable doubts.

The 1,000 Swiss francs felt thick in his breast pocket, and he thought everyone he passed must know he carried a lot of cash. He felt the menace of three lean and hungry young men smoking around a lamppost, whose conversation ceased as he walked by. Ernst felt certain they followed him, could almost hear their footsteps and feel them with his neck hairs. But when he turned around they still watched him from the lamppost.

The crispness of autumn was in the air, and Neukölln's children would soon feel the bite of winter. At the next corner four men stood around a fire burning inside an oil drum. Two wore fraying trench coats, the only truly lasting gift of the Great War. Prostitutes were abundant and all too obvious, but the police generally left them alone for fear of dislocating one of Neukölln's few viable industries.

At the Reich bank two blocks further on, Ernst deposited the money into an account under the name of Ernest Tessier. His documents were in order, his nest egg beginning to grow, and the account untraceable; he left the bank with a jaunty step.

Before he reached the end of the block, he heard chanting, a pulsing sound around the corner, cadenced by the percussion of jackboots slapping cobblestones. Curiosity got the better of him, and he turned onto Mainzerstrasse where a ragged column of fifty to sixty Brown Shirts, led by an SA man carrying a Nazi flag, goose-stepped up the street in undisciplined ranks. A thin gauntlet of onlookers lined the sidewalks; some hissed and booed, others cheered. A vegetable fragment flew through the air, and a brown shirt snarled and barked an obscenity; another waved a black truncheon. Ernst watched from a gap among the spectators, curious that the Nazis would be so bold in a Communist stronghold.

"Ernst! Ernst!" Hans Gerd called from the brown clot of marchers, waving his good left arm with the swastika armband, his right hand jammed in his pocket. "Here Ernst. Over here!"

Ernst reluctantly acknowledged his brother and walked alongside him in the street. He would have preferred not to be recognized in this section of town.

"What are you doing here?" Hans Gerd asked.

"An errand for the paper."

"Isn't this remarkable?" Hans Gerd's eyes twinkled. "Last year we could never have set foot in Neukölln – the Communists would have beaten us to a pulp. Now look – there are twice as many of us, and some people are actually cheering us on. Look at these Brown Shirts – the Neukölln formation. They live right here. They call themselves The Band of Rogues."

They began to sing with gusto.

> Oh, raise the flag and close your ranks up tight!
> SA men march with bold, determined tread.
> Comrades felled by Reds and Ultras in fight
> March at our side in spirit never dead.
>
> For the last time the call to arms rings out...
> Soon the Hitler banners will fly over all the streets.

"Wessel's song," Hans Gerd said. "Our anthem."

"So, Goebbels has finally made Wessel a martyr."

"Like Kern and Fischer – heroes of the new Reich. You could have been one of those heroes."

"I heard Wessel was a pimp, and he was shot by Ali Höhler, another pimp

– some argument over a prostitute."

"Höhler was a Communist. Wessel was a Storm Troop leader."

"What's the difference. A pimp is a pimp." Ernst wanted to shake Hans Gerd, but the Brown Shirts surged forward chanting "Sieg Heil! Sieg Heil! Heil Hitler! Heil Hitler!" Hans Gerd's misshapen right hand sliced the air with each chant. Ernst was embarrassed for him and only walked with him out of pity.

One block further along, in front of the experimental Karl Marx School on Mainzerstrasse, the column of Brown Shirts came to an unruly halt. They were mostly young men, too young to have fought in the Great War fifteen years earlier, their hair shorn close to the skull. Most carried Gummiknüppel – black rubber truncheons more than a meter long.

At the head of the Nazi column the SA-Obersturmführer turned to the school. Children peeked through the windows. He raised a cardboard megaphone to his mouth.

"Children of the Karl Marx School! We are here to liberate you – to liberate Germany – from the grip of Weimar – from the lies of Communism. We are the party of the future – the party of a strong, proud and united Germany."

"Who's that?" Ernst asked.

"Ernst Röhm, head of the SA."

The largely silent spectators grew increasingly restless. An older man in a trench coat stepped onto the street shaking his fist. "Fascist dogs!" Cheers, boos and catcalls erupted, first singly, then spread until now it seemed as if half of Neukölln cheered, and the other half booed the Nazis.

Röhm continued. "The bourgeois state is approaching its end! A New Germany must be forged. Workers of Neukölln! In your hands lies the destiny of the German people."

"Ernst..." Hans Gerd began.

Suddenly a hail of rocks rained down from the corner across the street and a band of Communists, more numerous than the Brown Shirts, led by a red flag, burst across Mainzerstrasse, their fists raised. The Nazis turned to face their attackers, Gummiknüppel at the ready. Before Ernst could back away, the two groups meshed like medieval armies. Ernst saw the giant red flag beside him, then behind him, fists and truncheons flying, blood and spittle, cursing and the cries of pain. Ernst thought Hans Gerd smiled as his good hand flailed his Gummiknüppel over his head, his deformed hand a perfectly usable fist. The Nazis were swept backward by the mêlée, and Ernst stumbled over an unconscious Communist, abrading his knee on the asphalt. He rolled away from a Brown Shirt who mistook him for a Communist, his stick raised to strike.

From where he lay on the ground all he saw were worn boots, running and kicking, seemingly unconnected to the men above. They all looked the same. Ernst scrambled to his feet and sprinted for the curb where the crowd cheered for one side or the other, as if brawling was a sporting event. His knee ached, and there was blood behind the tear in his trousers.

A pistol shot cracked the chaos, and the cheers became screams as the onlookers turned to flee. A police whistle shrieked, and the determined frenzy of battle dissipated into panic. Brown Shirts lifted their wounded under their arms and dragged them away. Many more Communists lay on the blood-stained asphalt, one clearly dead, a black hole where his eye should have been.

Hans Gerd grabbed Ernst under the arm and dragged him along the street ahead of the police batons. A stream of dried blood clotted over Hans Gerd's cheek, and a walnut size bruise on the side of his head formed a lump. After they had run three more blocks, Hans Gerd coughing and wheezing, clearly short of breath, they ducked into an alleyway and leaned against the wall. He saw how exhausted Hans Gerd was. "Are you all right? You look terrible. You're wheezing."

"I'm fine. Couple of minutes – no problem." Cord-like muscles strained in his neck to lift his chest; his nostrils flared. "You know – that was a victory – don't you?" Hans Gerd coughed paroxysmally

"Are you crazy? They routed you. They broke up your march."

"But there was cheering. Last year – no one cheered. This is not – not just another street fight. The pendulum is swinging. The workers are losing patience with the Communists. Even Leo is disgusted – with the Communists. Who else can they turn to – except us?"

"You're delusional, Hans Gerd. Not enough oxygen."

"Time will bear me out, Ernst." When his wheezing had abated they walked down a narrow street leading out of Neukölln, and Hans Gerd resumed his diatribe against Communists and Jews. In mid-sentence he stopped and said, "Each time we speak you seem more and more cynical. Why do you still work for *Der Angriff*?"

"It pays fairly well."

"It's a newspaper to be proud of, Ernst. National Socialism must be made comprehensible – palatable for Germans – all Germans, even the Communists in Neukölln. When they understand it they'll join us."

"Tell me something, Hans Gerd. Are you terribly disappointed with me?"

Hans Gerd considered his brother. "No. Not disappointed. I just don't understand you. Something happened to you in gaol. But you'll come around. I know you will. You're still my hero."

They walked past a pair of prostitutes, the older of the two with a short skirt and black stockings and such thick cabaret makeup that Ernst thought of a circus clown. Her associate seemed no older than sixteen, and Hans Gerd turned to ogle her. She smiled and hailed the brothers, but Ernst gripped Hans Gerd's elbow and led him on.

"Not now, Hans Gerd." After another block Ernst said, "You know I'm not a member of the Party, don't you?"

"Oh, you'll get around to joining. Sooner or later every German will."

"Maybe I'm missing something, but I don't find Herr Hitler any different..."

"Of course you're missing something. You've been in prison for eight years, you've never been to a rally, never heard the Führer."

Hans Gerd stopped at the corner where they would part company. "I think you're getting old and frightened."

"Old? Not yet. Frightened? Perhaps. Goebbels frightens me. Hitler too." He paused. "And you, Hans Gerd – don't become as wicked as those around you."

★   ★   ★   ★   ★   ★   ★   ★   ★   ★

Katherine's baby, Alexander, was born on a snowy night in 1931, during a winter that had been longer and colder than all but the oldest Berliners could remember. Few had sufficient heat or hot water. Overcrowded apartments contributed to a particularly severe influenza epidemic, and the hospitals and morgues were full. The night Katherine went into labor a fierce snow storm blanketed Berlin, and the midwife stayed for almost two days. Neither trams nor automobiles drove that night or the next.

Wind rattled the thin glass in Ernst's flat sucking heat from the room. When he complained, the landlord said he was free to leave. He was sick of Ernst's complaining, and scores of families waited to replace him, probably for higher rent.

To compound the misery, after the 1929 collapse, depression and unemployment gripped Weimar like a polar storm, and recovery seemed less than a distant possibility. The economic collapse also took a heavy toll on Ernst's forgery business, and were it not for Puck's orders and prompt payment, he might not have been able to pay for rent and heat and to keep a bottle of cheap cognac. More of his clients defaulted on their payments or simply disappeared. Until the cold weather, Ernst had felt he was financially secure, but months of snow and cold cleansed him of that illusion.

He worked at his easel in the evenings, wearing gloves with the finger tips cut out, perfecting the German exit visa stamp for Jacques's son, Louis. On Corsica, Puck wrote that everybody knew Jacques. They all knew what he could do for them, or to them.

★   ★   ★   ★   ★   ★   ★   ★   ★   ★

Goebbels called an urgent staff meeting in March 1931. An air of crisis pervaded the glassed-in Editorial Room, and when Ernst took his seat behind Frau Weidemann, Goebbels had already begun to pace.

"How dare Stennes question my loyalty to the Party!" Goebbels spit as he talked. "National Socialism is not a debating society. We are a party of action! Need I question the loyalty of anyone in this room?" He looked in turn at each man, and then especially long at the lone woman, Melitta Weidemann.

"This is a critical moment for the party in Berlin, indeed, the entire future of National Socialism is at stake. Stennes and the Strasser brothers must be amputated, like a gangrenous limb, or the entire body dies." He stopped before Editor-in-Chief Lippert. "Don't you agree, Herr Lippert?"

The editor flushed crimson and bowed his head, unable to hold eye contact. "Yes, Dr. Goebbels. Completely."

"Goering thinks I am too close to Stennes. What sort of madness is that? Where would Goering hear such a rumor? From these offices?" He paused in front of the Economics editor, a close acquaintance of Stennes. "From you, Herr Weissauer?"

Weissauer demurred. "I only serve the people, Dr. Goebbels."

"A most delicate response, but under the circumstances inadequate."

Ernst felt little sympathy for Goebbels. Since providing him with the 'clerical correction' of his party documents, he had not heard from him. When they had passed in the hallway two days before, Goebbels did not even register a flicker of recognition.

After he finished with Melitta Weidemann, Goebbels looked through Ernst as if he was invisible, a slight that came as a relief. Fritz too was passed over. He had recently become Assistant Editor to Lippert, but it was well understood that editorial content was to be cleared with Fritz, who met frequently with Dr. Goebbels.

Ernst's personal animosity towards Goebbels was inseparable from the visceral mistrust he felt for Hitler's Munich wing of the Party. Whatever sympathy Ernst still felt for the Nationalist cause allied him with the rebellious Berlin SA and their supreme commander Stennes, whose style made him nostalgic for his old Free Corps comrades. A kinship endured – a sentimental affinity.

As the flushed Goebbels circled the room, nostrils flaring, Ernst feigned attention, but he allowed his thoughts to entertain the bottle of wine he had bought for that night. While Fritz and Goebbels debated at the evening's weekly party meeting at Hedemannstrasse, he and Lisa would share a fumé blanc in Ernst's bed.

★ ★ ★ ★ ★ ★ ★ ★ ★ ★

Katherine and Leo's baby, Alexander, was six weeks old and the Linden trees were speckled with March buds when the Nazi party fractured and nearly disintegrated.

Ernst arrived early at *Der Angriff* the morning after the Stennes Putsch on March 31st and had to walk through a cordon of insurgent SA Storm Troopers who inspected his identity card and work papers. A cordon of Stennes's mutineers surrounded the newspaper, occupied every floor and looked down from the flat roof, their rifles at the ready.

Stennes ordered the presses halted. Ernst waited in his office sharing coffee and cake with his chief type setter, Hans Fricke, an older man whose bald head rose over his green forehead visor like a desert island from a green ocean. His worn leather apron, scarred from hot lead, creaked like old shoes. An SA man stood guard at Ernst's office door; another marched up and down the catwalk to and from the presses.

Fricke cut another slice of cake with his pressman's knife. "Stennes is preoccupied with numerology. Storm troop 31 on March 31, 1931. Weissauer and that Weidemann woman are with him now. They're re-writing the editorial page."

Two days later, April 2, the first pro-Stennes edition of *Der Angriff* was printed. In a reconciliatory gesture, Stennes invited Goebbels to a meeting at the editorial office to discuss the future of the Gauleiter and his newspaper. If only he would endorse the mutineers, take a stand against Hitler and the

Munich party, all would be pardoned.

As the second edition of the paper was being set, Goebbels unexpectedly arrived at the shipping door and hobbled urgently up the few steps to Ernst's office, shadowed by two brawny SS men. As he reached the door, Ernst looked up from laying out an editorial ridiculing the 'declaration of rights' submitted by 'that dark skinned radical, Mr. Gandhi,' to the Congress in Karachi. Goebbels let himself in and slammed the door behind him, leaving his SS men to face down Stennes's SA troopers.

"Heil Hitler!" Goebbels's right arm dropped like a stone. "What is the meaning of this insubordination?" His face was pale, his lips tremored. "I order you to stop the presses immediately!"

Ernst looked up from the layout table and weighed his options. Pity for this misshapen man was impossible, and the urge for retribution powerful. How quickly the mighty fall, he thought, and, presently, that was vengeance enough.

"I'm sorry, Dr. Goebbels. Commander Stennes ordered –"

"Herr Stennes is an outlaw – a mutineer!" Spittle flew from Goebbels's thin lips. "You are bound to me. Berlin is *my* city!"

"I'm sorry, Dr. Goebbels."

Goebbels limped to the door. He wrenched it open and pulled a Luger from the holster of the nearest SS man. His hand shaking from the unaccustomed weight of the pistol, he advanced on Ernst again. "You are nothing to me, Herr Chekow. I order you to stop the presses!" He held the agitated Luger with both hands.

Ernst's pulse quickened, first with fear, then anger. "My name is Techow, Herr Gauleiter. There is nothing..."

The Luger flashed, kicked upwards and immediately the crack of its report stung his ears. He felt punched back into his chair, and a hot needle pierced his left shoulder.

"We are not having a discussion!" Goebbels's eyes narrowed to slits. He shrieked, "Stop the presses!"

Ernst's right hand clutched at his bleeding shoulder as if he could catch the pain. Hot blood seeped between his fingers down his left arm, the pain crescendoing second by second. His eyes would not blink. He saw only the trembling Luger.

At that moment the door burst open, and scuffling boots and shouted orders filled the office. The two men continued to stare at each other. Ernst could not remember who took the pistol from Goebbels, but suddenly the dark pit eyes were gone, and his office was full of brown-shirted SA storm troopers. Outside his office door a precise tramping of boots ceased, and Captain Walther Stennes advanced from the phalanx of SA officers. A tall, broad-shouldered man of fifty, his mustache gone gray, his head almost bald, Stennes towered over Goebbels.

"I understood that we had an agreement, Herr Goebbels. It seems you have chosen to violate our understanding and follow Herr Hitler and the bosses. It was the bosses that cheated us out of victory in 1918, 1920 and 1923. We will not be cheated again."

Goebbels's head dropped another few degrees.

"I have named Bruno Wetzel as the new Gauleiter of Berlin. Not that it will make a bit of difference to you." He turned to his SA commandant. "This man attempted to murder a worker. Take him out and have him shot."

"Sir," the Commander whispered. "I don't think we can just do that, sir..."

"I said, have him shot! If you cannot do it then order someone else to, but I will have him shot!"

"But, Herr Oberführer, this is Dr. Goebbels. We should consult..."

"Am I surrounded by cowards and crybabies?" Stennes's rogue hand gripped the butt of his Luger in its cracked leather holster, an old friend from the Great War. "This poor excuse for a man will bring us nothing but grief." He drew his revolver.

"Commandant Stennes! Please, hold your order!" Ludwig Weissauer, the associate editor, stood at the top of the landing. "We would have a word with Dr. Goebbels. In the editorial room, please."

Weissauer had Dr. Goebbels escorted by two SA men to a leather chair in the center of the editorial board room. Goebbels's wide eyes darted about the room, and he recognized each face. He seemed to become confused.

Ernst's wound was superficial, but there was a large blood stain over his shoulder and left chest. Melitta Weidemann bound it with gauze, and the bleeding stopped. Ernst insisted on taking his place in the circle of editors, feeling unnaturally mindful of the throbbing pain in his shoulder and his compelling anger. The only person missing was Fritz.

"The Führer demands an end to this pointless..." Goebbels began and looked around until he saw Melitta Weidemann, and he licked his lips. "Your future in the party depends upon..." His eyes turned further around the circle of glaring, accusing stares until they fell on Ernst. "An excellent forgery, Herr... What is your name?"

Ernst strode up to him and searched the black holes of his wild eyes. On a moment's impulse, as the publisher was about to speak again, Ernst slapped Goebbels' face, leaving the imprint of his hand.

"It wasn't for swine like you that we killed Rathenau."

He turned and walked out of the suddenly still room, his head airy, his balance unreliable. He had crossed a chasm from which there was no return. The pressroom looked alien, his office belonged to someone else, and there was nothing he needed from his desk save the photo of Lisa when she was eighteen, at Halle Municipal Park, a photo he kept face down in the top drawer and looked at every day.

★　★　★　★　★　★　★　★　★　★

Goebbels barely escaped Berlin with his life and retreated to Munich where he and Hitler organized countermeasures against the Stennes Putsch. An editorial in Hitler's *Völkischer Beobachter* denounced Stennes and his mutineers and expressed Hitler's fullest confidence in Goebbels. Financial concessions – bribes, some said – were made to the loyal Berlin SA, and most mutineers returned to the party. Goebbels delivered a moving appeal for loyalty, one of his best speeches, at a Sportpalast rally. The next day, loyal SA Brown Shirts expelled Stennes and his now isolated mutineers from the offices of *Der Angriff*. The editorial staff was purged, and Ernst was glad to have quit when he did.

He walked along the Havel the Sunday after Stennes's Putsch was quelled, pondering his narrow brush with death. His grazed shoulder still throbbed. Had he been shielded by a merciful God or thrust into harm's way by a vindictive deity? It was Puck's dilemma, compassion or justice, and like Puck he vacillated between gratitude and scorn.

His fists ached from clutching the metal bar separating him from the river. A few centimeters to the right, and Goebbels's bullet might have killed him. If his life hung in the balance of incident and chance, did that law of nature not also pertain to Hitler and his henchmen? Why was Goebbels spared? Was God the puppeteer or did he merely wind up the toys and watch them rattle and bang against each other? Hitler could as easily fall as prevail in the chaos that was Weimar.

Puck had embraced probability and chance as 'one of God's limbs – a particularly destructive and wanton extremity.' In Striegau, Puck used the story of the Norman Conquest as an exemplar. The French archers arced thousands of arrows into the air to rain upon the defending Anglo-Saxons. One arrow pierced the eye of King Harold of England, and his death caused panic among his men. They were routed, the battle was lost, and the Normans conquered. In the wake of the Stennes Putsch, Hitler was unopposed, and the Munich Nazi party reigned supreme.

Berlin's other newspapers made little of the Stennes Putsch – a family spat, mere sibling rivalry from a splinter party. But Ernst's mind could not stop retracing and analyzing the events of the week, feeling he alone saw the emperor naked. To escape his feverish preoccupation with Stennes, Hitler and Goebbels, he came to the Havel, where he expected to be pacified by the sight of sailboats skimming the water and children playing.

But the Havel was subdued and colorless, and Ernst wondered if it was his tainted vision. Children still played, though slower than he remembered, their gaiety forced, their parents and Kinderfräuleins burdened by a solemnity that seemed to exude from the city. Older boys swaggered in the brown shorts and shirt of the Hitler Jugend. Pre-pubescent girls of the Bund Deutsche Mädel – the BDM – still gossiped and giggled in twos and threes. But in their uniforms – black skirts, brown blouses, and black neck scarves – they were as indistinguishable as soldiers. Their parents, his post-war peers, brooded on benches or on newspapers spread under trees or in the sun, staring into the Havel as if deliverance might rise from the water.

An older woman with a craggy face leaned on her cane by a lamppost and watched Ernst. She was all in black, from her flaccid, wide-brimmed bonnet to ankle boots, a heavy skirt of ancient black in between. Her resemblance to Frau Rathenau was so striking Ernst had to look again, but on closer inspection her features were much too coarse, and that was when she scowled.

In that moment he knew he could not continue living from day to day, waiting like the unemployed along the Havel, waiting for the return of the sailboats, watching for the miracle in the center of the lake.

18

Loyalty

September 1932 – January 1934

year and a half after he left *Der Angriff*, Ernst's small photography shop, *Image in Nation*, was just beginning to turn a profit, though not from the sale of cameras or the developing of film. He invested in excellent optics, chemicals and a state of the art enlarger, which allowed for ordinary film processing and the production of high quality forgeries for his other clientele, principle among them Puck's 'colleague' Jacques, the Corsican 'sheep farmer.'

At Lisa's insistence they stopped meeting at the National Gallery. She could not be seen in public with him, but when it was possible, she came to the privacy of Ernst's flat. After making love on a crisp September morning when Fritz was in Munich and Adi in school, they drank tea and talked about the weeks since they had last seen each other – or rather, Lisa talked. Adi was spilling over with excitement at starting First Class. He was so clever and beautiful. Things were somewhat better with Fritz. He was more attentive, engaging, and he showed her a modicum of respect. As the Nazi party grew in stature, there were more official functions, concerts, and lectures for her to attend on her husband's arm, and she had to admit, she enjoyed the glitter and attention – the enthusiasm of party members. "This is a heady time," she confessed.

Their stolen moments and ecstatic lovemaking were all they had. Ironically, Ernst thought the illicit nature of their liaison kept it vibrant. At the moment of each meeting, the flash of desire and infatuation, the enchantment, still sent shudders through him. Where their relationship could possibly go was not something they discussed, and Ernst had to remind himself he had no right to expect anything more than this. Some days he had more hope, when Fritz had been particularly harsh with her, and then there were unhappy days like this. When he could speak again he reminded her of the new Picasso exhibit and wouldn't it be fun to go on the same day. Yes, she said, but not together.

"He's only being attentive because he suspects you," Ernst said. "And he needs you to be the perfect Nazi wife."

"I'm not proud to be deceiving him. Sometimes I feel sorry for Fritz." She considered Ernst's face and said, "You hate him, don't you."

"I don't know him. He's not the same Fritz we grew up with. You know what your life will be like. I don't think you can stand it."

"I will for Adi. Only for Adi."

"Would you leave if you could take Adi with you?"

Ernst could tell by her silence that he posed an impossible question – a dilemma she had not considered.

"I need more time."

"Sometimes I feel like kidnapping you."

She laughed. "Maybe you should. I love our secret nest here. I'd hate for anything to change. I can't leave Fritz, but I also need to see you, to be with you." She kissed him. "To make love, to be reminded what it is to be a woman, to be alive."

★ ★ ★ ★ ★ ★ ★ ★ ★ ★

At Christmas time in 1932, Uncle Erwin invited Ernst's mother and 'the children' to visit for a week at his estate in Jacobsdorf. A day before their arrival Hans Gerd cabled that he was unable to attend, due to Austria's unexpected release of Nazi prisoners who had been incriminated in the Königsberg assassinations. Hans Gerd ended his euphoric cable with "Heil Hitler!"

The day before Christmas, Ernst picked up Leo and Katherine at the Jacobsdorf station in Erwin's sedan. Leo seemed troubled. His greeting was remote, and he looked dispirited. Not so Little Alexander, who had never left Berlin in his two short years, never ridden on a train, never conceived of people living in such a large house. But before long the normally quiet and self-absorbed toddler found his courage and raced up and down long carpets from one overlarge room to another, accompanied by Uncle Erwin's snoozy dachshund Bijou, who shook off arthritis and sloth to befriend the tiny human.

Alexander wore his great uncle's bowler hat tilted low, covering one eye;

his feet still turned out like a clown and he walked with a wide-based gait.

"Rather looks like Charlie Chaplin, don't you think." Uncle Erwin laughed, coughed and puffed his pipe again.

Ernst's mother watched Alexander with more detachment. Her tuberculosis had been quiescent for a few years and she had gained back most of her lost weight, though her eyes cast dark shadows. Each time she coughed Ernst remembered that her disease was not cured. There was no cure; it only lurked like a tragic memory, or a spy. He wondered if she was afraid, and if that prevented her from delighting in Alexander's antics. And he wondered about the other fear, from the birth of his memories, that kept her from delighting in the antics of her own children?

Later that afternoon, under a cold solstice sun, while the Christmas goose and apple stuffing cooked, Uncle Erwin, Leo, Ernst and his mother walked about the estate, "to build an appetite," Erwin said. Alexander reluctantly took his nap with Katherine.

"I preferred the Stahlhelm," Uncle Erwin said as he led the family. "But, I suppose the Nazis will do. The nation could use a healthy dose of discipline. At least they're not afraid to take on the Reds. *Facta non verba*."

"The violence is vulgar," Frau Techow said. "Of course I prefer the Nazis over the Communists, but this fighting in the streets – it troubles me. I'm all for discipline, but let it be civil."

Ernst wondered what his mother thought of Hans Gerd, her crippled son, now a lawyer, hunched over his desk, doing whatever it was new lawyers did – researching, arguing cases, filling out dense legal forms. He wondered if she suspected that he was in the SA. She still knew nothing of the brawl Ernst had stumbled into when Hans Gerd fought the Communists two years before. And more than a year ago, Hans Gerd, dressed as one of the unemployed, participated in a 'demonstration' on the main shopping thoroughfare of Berlin, the Kurfürstendamm. The demonstration was organized by Goebbels and the Berlin SA leader Count Wolf-Heinrich von Helldorf and timed to coincide with the Jewish New Year. The disguised SA men abused, insulted and struck any person they concluded was Jewish. Hans Gerd eluded arrest after the two hour pogrom, though most of the other participants were apprehended, as was Count Helldorf himself. He made no effort to escape after he had prominently directed and encouraged his men from an open green Opel sedan driving up and down Ku'damm.

"Mustn't coddle the Communists," Erwin said, puffing vigorously. "Take the bull by the horns, eh. Takes a dose of strong medicine. And anyway,

Gertrude, you're hardly one to talk about discipline, the way you've spoiled your boys."

Uncle Erwin obviously thought it a joke, but Ernst saw his mother wither under his judgment.

They passed the shabby barracks that Uncle Erwin provided for his workers, wisps of smoke drifting up from regularly spaced stovepipes along the peak of the tin roof like teeth on a comb. Moisture fogged all the windows except one where a child had wiped a clear circle and peered out at the master and his entourage. Coming towards them on the dirt road, a laborer pushed a wheelbarrow in which slumped a youngster of perhaps five or six – it was difficult to tell. His limbs hung flaccid over the sides, while his head lolled about on a slender neck like a marionette whose only uncut string rotated his head in monotonous, unpredictable circles.

Erwin tipped his hat as the two approached. "Herr Sondheim. A good Christmas to you. How is young Christian?"

"Well, sir, thank you." He crushed his hat in his fist and bowed. "Frau Sondheim and I – we thank you for the generous Christmas bonus, sir."

"My pleasure. Please give Frau Sondheim my warm regards."

"Surely I will, sir. Thank you, sir, thank you." He bowed several times then bent to pick up the wheelbarrow tines.

"What's wrong with his child?" Leo asked when they were well past.

"Little's disease – born with it. Most distressing. Crumpled up thing. He will never walk. Soils himself. Lives in that wheel barrow. Barely comprehensible when he speaks – feeble minded. His feet are useless – his arms move in non-human ways."

"What's to become of him?" Ernst felt a deep discomfort about the boy and pity for his father.

"It will be a blessing when he dies." Erwin waved a greeting to a family with six children who crowded a doorway to see him passing by. "Unfortunates such as Christian should be euthanized. Resources are limited. We cannot save everybody, and the unproductive can scarcely be supported until natural death. If someone cannot work, cannot contribute, they will die – it's a biblical consequence – what with the Garden of Eden and all – you remember – 'by the sweat of your brow' and all that."

"Where does it end?" Ernst found himself saying, hardly knowing why. "Today the deformed. Tomorrow who? the sick? then the unproductive? then the racially impure?"

Erwin faced his nephew, a puzzled crease in his brow. "Really now, my boy. No need to be so dramatic. This is science – truth – not politics. No one is talking about killing normal people. We are not barbarians. Young Christian is an empty husk, a living creature, but not a human."

"Ernst," Leo said. "This is Germany, this is 1932, and we can scarcely feed the productive, let alone immigrants and mental defectives."

"Good God, Leo," Ernst said. "You sound like the Nazis."

"I'm tired of the chaos; there is no end to it. I was an Imperial naval officer – now I dig ditches when I'm lucky enough to find work. The Social Democrats are at their wits end. What have the Communists ever done for me? I agree with Erwin, a good dose of discipline. If the Nazis can provide a little order, conditions will improve."

"I don't really like Herr Hitler," Frau Techow said, "but our situation is frightening. How much worse can things get?"

Uncle Erwin lit his pipe, and the sweet aroma masked the stench of a latrine.

After a moment's silence she continued. "Something odd happened the other day while I was shopping. As you know, the butcher, Herr Gruenspecht, is a Jew. He is always friendly and has excellent meats for a reasonable price. I was with Frau Klaus, from downstairs. We often shop together – her stories are distracting. Several SA men loitered outside the shop when we arrived. They said we should shop elsewhere – we should not buy from a Jew. I ignored the Brown Shirts. They stunk of beer and tobacco, but Frau Klaus said she was afraid and perhaps we should go to Bleimer's, three blocks away. It was Friday, a busy day for a butcher, and Gruenspecht's was empty. He looked at me from the window as if I was to blame. The Brown Shirts started to shout about the Jews. They used foul language. People stared, as if we were Jews. I was embarrassed – self-conscious. I left with Frau Klaus and we went to Bleimer's. It was crowded and I recognized many of the women I usually see at Gruenspecht's. But I'm haunted by Herr Gruenspecht staring at me through the window. Now I wish I'd had more courage."

"What does courage have to do with it?" Erwin asked. "More like common sense. You are a German – your butcher is a Jew. Good God, why patronize a Jew when you have other choices? Bully for Herr Hitler. *Carpe diem*. Germany for Germans I always say. Squeeze them out. It's the decent thing to do. Jews are smart. They'll understand and leave. It's good for the Jews. They've never been wanted – should go back where they came from. They're Russia's problem, or Poland's problem."

"I understand what you say, brother, but I keep seeing Herr Gruenspecht's expression, as if I had betrayed him. It's quite distressing."

"You're a woman, Gertrude. It's understandable. But one cannot be squeamish about racial purity."

"What does Katherine think?" Ernst asked.

"She's a mother now," Leo said. "And times are hard. With all their faults, the Nazis offer hope. It's good to feel hopeful again."

Uncle Erwin and his mother walked ahead deep in conversation. Leo slowed his step and took Ernst by the arm. "I have to ask you something. I didn't want mother to become anxious. Yesterday a man – Herr Dieter – asked about you. Ring any bells? He showed me a very official Nazi identification card – SD. Wanted to know where you were on such and such a date. I said I didn't know, and he said if I wanted to keep finding work I would do well to find out."

Ernst felt exposed and afraid, not unlike the moment when Headmaster Kremer held up Ernst's cruel caricature of Herr Strauss and asked who drew it?

"It's about your little affair, isn't it?" Leo shook his head. "Nothing can come of it except trouble. These are not people to trifle with, Ernst. And now it menaces my family. It's got to stop."

Ernst twisted his elbow out of Leo's grip. "It's none of your business, Leo. You don't know anything. Is Herr Dieter part of the new discipline that everyone agrees will be good for Germany?"

By now many of the workers and their children had come out of their barracks to watch Erwin and his family. The children's clothes were ill-fitting and soiled, their hair in disarray. Many coughed or had mucous stained noses. Some of the men called to Uncle Erwin, "Holy Christmas, Herr Behrens!" and "Many thanks for the bonus!" Most clutched their hats and stared, open-mouthed like their children.

★　★　★　★　★　★　★　★　★　★

By the end of 1932 the Nazi party was in financial and electoral disarray. The economy had continued its relentless slide into ruin, and the army of unemployed had grown in one year from 4 million to over 5 million. In the November 6th election, Hitler's party had lost 2 million votes, and it drew scarcely 25% of the vote in Berlin. But, to the amazement of the pundits, they were still the largest party in the Reichstag. On December 2, President Hindenburg named his old friend and protégé General Kurt von Schleicher as the last Chancellor of the Weimar Republic. Schleicher tried to divide the virtually bankrupt Nazi party and deliver a 'coup de grace.' He was reputed to have said, "Hitler is yesterday's concern."

But, scarcely a month later, Schleicher admitted defeat in his maneuvers to split the Nazi party and was unable to win a Reichstag majority. On January 30, 1933, following constitutional process, Hindenburg named Hitler as Chancellor after being reassured that he would be kept under control and that the army was loyal. Most Germans thought Chancellor Hitler would not last six months.

But Hitler and the Nazis moved quickly to consolidate power. He gained control of the police and army. A month later, Goebbels's Storm Troopers secretly set fire to the Reichstag and blamed the Communists. In response to the fire, severe restrictions on freedom of the press and speech were imposed. Hitler called an election for March and won 44%, his highest vote count. He achieved a parliamentary majority by banning the Communist delegates and arresting their leaders.

When the legislature convened, Hitler demanded and received an 'Enabling Act' that empowered him to 'rule by decree.' On April 7th, the first anti-Semitic decree was issued eliminating Jews from the Civil Service and Schools. That same month Hitler appointed Goebbels as the head of the Ministry of Propaganda and Public Enlightenment. Less than a month later Goebbels extracted his pound of flesh from the Jewish intelligentsia who had scorned him and rejected his novel. On May 10, between the Opera House and the university on Unter den Linden, the first public book burnings commenced.

*   *   *   *   *   *   *   *   *   *

Under a hot July sun the green suburbs of Berlin sped by Ernst's railroad compartment, distracting him from the poetry of Heine in his lap. Morning mist had vaporized from wheat and barley fields ripe for a second cutting. He watched the countryside recede from him like memory, swift and vital when proximate, then a blur, always changing, becoming a still life as the perspective lengthened.

Across the train compartment, a gentleman in a bowler hat read the *Berliner Tageblatt*, now Goebbels's newspaper, which prophesied the banning of the Social Democratic party. On the wall behind him was a poster that read:

Germans!

Defend yourselves!
Don't buy from Jews!

Ernst had been surprised to receive a personal invitation from Captain Ehrhardt to join his former comrades in dedicating Kern and Fischer's monument in Saaleck on the anniversary of their deaths, July 17. He presumed Ehrhardt and Ernst's fellow defendants knew of his confrontation with Goebbels and his absence from Nationalist activity. He wondered how his former comrades and co-conspirators had aged. If nothing else, it would be good to see Baer, Norbert, and Heimler. But there was something else, something inexplicable that drew him to Kern's and Fischer's graves – perhaps a need to close a chapter in his life, or, perhaps more likely, to open it again and see it with new eyes.

After all these years, Ehrhardt continued to bear the standard of the Second Marine Brigade. Ehrhardt's invitation explained that, after long negotiations with Hitler, the Brigade was to be incorporated as an autonomous unit into the SS under Ehrhardt's command. Members of the Brigade were to retain their distinctive gray uniforms with the imperial crown on their buttons and a Viking ship on their sleeve, and they were to function as a special unit linking the Army and the police. Ehrhardt would be elevated to the rank of Brigade Commander.

At the Savoy Hotel in Saaleck, Ernst picked up a message at the front desk from von Salomon inviting him to dine on the veranda with some 'old friends.'

Ernst arrived for dinner wearing his khaki cotton suit, still creased after a year in a valise. Bright flat light from the setting sun bathed the crowded veranda. The fragrance of evening lulled Ernst's dread at this reunion until von Salomon's distinctive laughter floated above the other diners. He saw The Fat Man right away and then began to recognize his old colleagues around a table at the railing. Most men on the veranda wore the distinctive SS, SA or Party uniforms. Except for Ernst, Swastika armbands embellished virtually every man's left arm.

"Techow! My word, it's Ernst Techow!" Von Salomon fairly bounded from his seat and gripped Ernst's hand with both of his. Conversations all across the dining terrace stopped, and Ernst was uncomfortably aware of turning heads. There was a smattering of applause.

"By the way, best regards to your little brother," Von Salomon said. "He seems to be filling your boots." Von Salomon looked more than eleven years older; he had lost some hair, was still too thin, but retained his haughtiness and sarcasm. He escorted Ernst to the table. "Gentlemen," he proclaimed. "Our table is complete. The older Techow is here."

Ernst was not happy to see The Fat Man, Hellmut Plaas, who lifted one eyebrow and nodded in his direction. Tillessen rose stiffly and looked Ernst dead in the eye, the same small smile on his lips that Ernst remembered from the trial. Tillessen pumped his hand, then straightened his starched party uniform with swastika collar buttons and quickly sat again.

"This is Herr Ditmar." Von Salomon indicated the lanky man in a naval uniform beside Tillessen. "He's the war criminal we rescued from Naumberg prison and hid with Steinbeck right here in Saaleck Castle. Lieutenant Ditmar was the officer mentioned at our trial. Remember? The one we were to rescue from the French prison?" Von Salomon snickered.

Though he was much older than Ernst, Ditmar also rose deferentially, bowed succinctly and shook his hand, studying him with an openly curious expression.

Von Salomon continued around the table. "May I introduce Kurt Wende – Kern's brother-in-law." He too wore a uniform – that of the National Labor Service. "Ernst Werner Techow, I'm sure, needs no introduction." Von Salomon waved for the waiter. "I tried to see the graves today," he said, "but the SS guard wouldn't let me in without a special pass. What are you doing now, Ernst?"

Ernst said only that he had left *Der Angriff* to start his own photography shop.

Tillessen polished his fingernails. "It's been a long time since we've heard from you, Herr Techow, except of course that unfortunate incident with Dr. Goebbels. You've disappeared."

"I needed to take a rest from politics," Ernst said. He sat down and busied himself with his napkin.

Suddenly The Fat Man started to laugh, quietly at first, but then his shoulders shook. "I was remembering Günther." He suddenly stopped, and his smile vanished; the corners of his mouth drooped sadly. "That's when you disappeared. That's quite a long rest."

Tillessen inspected his water glass for stains. "Your friend Fritz Sommers is rising quickly with Dr. Goebbels. I believe you know his lovely wife, Lisa." Tillessen looked directly into Ernst's eyes, a piercing challenge. "You will be marching with us tomorrow at the graves, won't you?"

Lieutenant Ditmar attempted to start idle conversation with Wende, but everyone waited for Ernst to reply. His mouth went dry except for the acid in his throat.

After all these years, Tillessen still frightened him. "I'm here to pay my respects," he said.

"Hans!" Von Salomon summoned the nattily dressed waiter, a stout man with a bushy mustache and round wire spectacles, old enough to have fought in the Great War. "A beer for Ernst Techow! By the way, Hans, whatever happened to Herr Staube – the pastry chef? A true genius. I haven't seen him this year."

"He's in a concentration camp," the waiter said.

"Whatever for? He's a fine and patriotic man."

"He spoke against the National Socialists. That's all I know." He backed away. "If you will excuse me."

"Damn paranoia," von Salomon said. "People are so guarded. A nation of nobodies who know nothing." Von Salomon sat down besides Ernst and said privately, "Try not to take our solemnity too seriously."

Though the food was as good as its reputation, Ernst ate little. By the end of dinner he felt a tight pit in his stomach, and he had to wipe sweat from his forehead several times. Von Salomon seemed to be the only one unequivocally enjoying himself. The Fat Man was more interested in his private conversations with Tillessen and Wende. Lieutenant Ditmar sat stiffly and hardly spoke.

Von Salomon continued, returning to his schnitzel. "Ernst, word has it that Goebbels will be the next Reich Minister of Culture." Tillessen and The Fat Man looked up.

"It's of little concern to me," Ernst said.

"It must rankle you though, a Reich Minister of Culture who burns books. You do know that it was Goebbels who oversaw the bonfires at the University in May."

"An unfortunate night." Ernst wanted to say "shameful," but he felt fear spasm in his stomach.

He remembered the fires of May 10th and the midnight parade of right-wing students, drunk with power and rebellion, who gathered in the square on Unter den Linden opposite the University. Frenzied by the pounding of SS and SA drums, the students ransacked the library and university buildings and re-emerged to cast some 20,000 volumes onto the pyre like so much kindling. So tumultuous were the drums that few in Berlin slept, and the radiance of the flames lit the night sky as if the precious words themselves were written in petrol. Days later Ernst had read the roll-call of authors ravaged under Goebbels's approving eye.

There was a murmur around the table as von Salomon spoke. "That was a most unsettling spectacle."

"It was necessary," Tillessen said sharply. He sliced his pork roast and scraped the plate. "Surely, von Salomon, an intellectual such as yourself believes that the arts, radio, film, and the press are the lifeblood of a nation – for better or worse. The blood must serve the Reich, and it must be pure. Nothing kills an organism faster than toxic blood. You do agree, don't you?"

"One can make an argument..."

"When it comes to the survival of the nation there can be no argument. What may seem to you excess is, in fact, necessity."

"Necessary, perhaps," von Salomon continued, "but disgusting nevertheless. I suppose we should get used to that – necessary but disgusting."

Tillessen stopped chewing his meat and studied him. His cunning smile returned. "You are making a joke, of course, Herr von Salomon, are you not?"

"Yes, of course." He winked at Ernst.

"You know how mothers protect their newborns?" Kurt Wende asked. Coming from this granite quarry of a man the question seemed exotic. "A new mother would kill anything that threatens her young. It's not even a moral dilemma; it's instinct. We have birthed a new Reich, gentlemen, and we must protect it. We should not underestimate its fragility or its adversaries."

Ernst struggled with the impulse to protest. He remembered how he had marveled at Rathenau's books in Striegau, and they were surely on the pyre. "But to burn the poems of Heine?" Ernst stared at Kern's brother-in-law.

Wende articulated each word as if to freeze them in the air. "Heine. Was. A. Jew."

The Fat Man smiled and wiped his mouth with a linen napkin. "As were Mendelssohn and Einstein. Sacrifices are necessary." He helped himself to another potato and bathed it in thick gravy. "German culture is at war, and there will be casualties."

Ernst laid his utensils down. "Wherever they burn books, sooner or later they will burn human beings also."

"A bit dramatic," the Fat Man said. "Your words?"

"No, Heine's." Ernst pushed back from the table. "If you will excuse me."

★　★　★　★　★　★　★　★　★　★

Four hundred Marine Brigade members lined up on Saaleck Square the next day. Ernst arrived early to seek out Baer, Norbert and Heimler, but he was told they were no longer part of the Marine Brigade.

"I was with the three of them in Pomerania," another Freebooter volunteered. "We greased our guns and buried 'em – did some field work on this big estate. Mostly we waited. Didn't do nothin' – sat around, played checkers, '66'. Just waitin'. Made Baer crazy. He couldn't stay, and you know Norbert, he's nobody without Baer, so they took off together for God knows where. Heimler went along with 'em." Ernst was more disappointed than he had anticipated.

Captain Ehrhardt stood alone at attention before the gray uniformed Freebooter formation, sandwiched between columns of SS Blackshirts and SA Brownshirts. Behind Ehrhardt, flanked by the Marine Brigade flag and standard, Ernst stood between The Fat Man and bone-thin von Salomon, the only three without uniforms. Every other unit, SS and SA, carried swastika banners and standards. Each formation had its own brass band and drummers that played against each other like a fibrillating heart. The late morning sun glinted off horns and medals, flashed from silver buckles and buttons. Nazi party leaders Röhm, Himmler, Saukel and Tillessen lined up before the elite SS. In profile, Ernst could see where the bridge of Röhm's nose had been shot away during the Great War, accentuating his cruel features. Tillessen's slight smile threatened to spread. The bands suddenly stopped, and for a moment Ernst heard only the flapping of flags. A single drum began its tattoo, then was joined by two, then ten, then a hundred drums that launched a parade of solemn Hitler Jugend in their shorts and smiling Bund Deutsche Mädel in their identical skirts, waving and casting flower petals along the route.

As far as Ernst could see, they three were the only civilians in the entire parade, but it was more than the lack of a uniform that made him feel alien and awkward. There was no question – he had to be here. He easily remembered the thrill when, as a twenty year old, he had first marched with the Free Corps, a naive boy with a gun, a raw cadet in a new uniform, hungry for distinction, contentious, frightened. It was a brutality whose meaning and power lingered on, fermented over the years into an intoxicating reminiscence.

Now he was here, eleven years later, more puzzled than ever. There was no relief in reunion. It was more like a hangover. He stood at flaccid attention, feeling corrupt, adrift, in need of absolution's balm more than ever.

The asphalt baked in the midday sun as they marched past the old Jewish

Cemetery. He was glad when the pungent tar turned to dirt. These Jewish graves were surrounded by a cement wall, and the iron gate had rusted half shut. The headstones bore Stars of David, worn smooth. All together in death, the communists, the Nationalists, the Jews, the Protestants, the Catholics, the athiests, everybody dead together under the ground where there were no walls, no gates, no distinction. It was a baffling awareness that kept him off balance, one conflicting emotion jarring another. The sun beat down mercilessly. There was no distraction.

On the crumbling wall a hastily scrawled graffito in black paint warned:

'Soon all Jews will be here!'

Several hundred meters further, around a sharp bend, the dirt road ended at the Protestant Cemetery's freshly painted wrought iron gate garlanded with fresh flowers. An SS honor guard ceremonially parted the gates. The grass had been trimmed short for the ceremony, and floral ropes punctuated by wreaths lined the gravel avenue. The stage and speaker's platform stood across from the flower-bedecked graves of Kern and Fischer, buried side by side, just the way they had died in 1922.

Like a headboard for the departed, an ample square of black marble dominated their graves. The polished stone was inscribed with Kern's and Fischer's names, their dates of birth and their death on July 17, 1922, along with the inscription:

"Do what you must, conquer or die,
and leave the decision to God."

It was good to die young as a patriot, Ernst concluded. It spared one the awkward compromises required of old patriots. As revolutions aged, the atmosphere changed. Noble ideals, like stale air, became progressively more nuanced, then ambiguous, desperate, and finally cannibalistic. Better to die young. Ernst thought of his father, who would always be young and vigorous. Better for the nation, not for the son who waited so long for affection that would never come. Kern and Fischer would always be in the springtime of life, without grief, without loss, and the Nazis would spare no expense to mythologize their memory.

When they reached the reviewing stand opposite the graves, an SS band played *Siegfried's Rhine Journey* after which a 21-gun salute boomed over the walls. Himmler delivered a long and flowery eulogy over the microphone and concluded his remarks by saying, "Your spirit, Kern and Fischer, is the spirit of the SS, Hitler's Black Soldiers!"

Other speakers followed, emphasizing the sacrifice of Kern and Fischer and the dawn of the thousand year Reich. Each paid tribute to Adolf Hitler and ended his speech with a resounding "Heil Hitler!"

When it came his time, Captain Ehrhardt declined the stage and delivered his remarks without amplification, as a speech to his men. The Storm Troopers strained to hear, as did their leaders on the stage.

"Men of my brigade, you know that it was only after a very long time and after many and fierce struggles that we felt ourselves ready to join a formation of the new Germany. And I'm glad of that because it's only by fighting that you come to know your enemy – to respect him or to despise him, as the case may be. And in the future we shall continue to behave as we have done in the past."

This was not the same enigmatic Captain Ehrhardt, the brilliant tactician who had led the torpedo attack at Jutland, the mutineer who led a younger Ernst into battle with an army of Freebooters to "clean house" in Berlin, Bavaria and Upper Silesia. He had shrunk with age, and his uniform hung loosely enough that his belt wrinkled his tunic, much as time had furrowed his face. Ernst saw Röhm lean over and whisper in Tillessen's ear. Himmler chewed his lip and gripped his armchair with particular fury.

"Men of my brigade have asked me about the so-called German greeting. I have arranged that we shall greet one another in the manner to which as soldiers we are accustomed, that is to say by raising the right hand to the headpiece, if we are wearing a headpiece. Should we be bare-headed we shall give the German greeting. I hereby order the men of my brigade, whether on or off duty, at all times to wear a headpiece.

"One other thing. No Hurrahs! No Ahoys! Our cheer will no more be used. Instead the cheer is Heil!, to my Chancellor, to our Vaterland, for which we are ready to undertake any duty." In place of the outstretched arm, Ehrhardt crisply touched the brim of his officer's cap and saluted his troops. "Heil! Heil! Heil!"

The dignitaries on the speakers platform murmured to each other and shifted uneasily. Ernst Röhm stepped to the microphone and delivered the closing oration. Himmler laid the official wreath at the black marble tomb.

Ernst caught the late afternoon train back to Berlin, riding in one of the extra coaches added to accommodate the marchers. Von Salomon begged

Ernst to join him in first class "lest you be frightfully bored," and Ernst said he would consider it. But he preferred the sweat and discomfort of the coach, and he felt a growing certainty that he would never willingly be with von Salomon or his cronies again.

$$\star \quad \star \quad \star \quad \star \quad \star \quad \star \quad \star \quad \star \quad \star \quad \star$$

Two months later, at their mother's apartment, Hans Gerd urged Ernst to accompany him to a giant rally in Grünewald Stadium. Hitler was to speak to 120,000 people, and another 100,000 outside would hear his voice through powerful loudspeakers.

"Bring Alexander along," Hans Gerd said, knowing that Ernst was to spend the day with their nephew. "It will be wonderful. You've never heard der Führer."

"Go without us. Alexander and I have a date with a Schwarzwälder Kirschtorte mit Schlag. Isn't that right, little man?" Ernst knelt and guided his nephew's arm into his coat sleeve.

"What happened to you, Ernst? You used to be committed to this revolution."

Ernst buttoned the boy's coat. "This is no revolution. It's Hitler and Goebbels and Himmler's private vendetta. They want power and they hate Jews."

"You shouldn't speak like that, Ernst. I must warn you, as you once warned me. The SD knows everything."

The SD – Sicherheitsdienst – the intelligence branch of the SS – had been constituted by Himmler in 1932 under the direction of Heinrich Heydrich. Their stated function was to watch over party members and report suspicious activity.

"Why should I fear the SD?" Ernst asked. "I'm not a party member."

"Don't talk foolishness. You know it's much more than that. Informers are everywhere. Children report their parents, students their professors. . "

Ernst felt his anger rising and only by force of will continued tying the string of Alexander's knitted cap under his chin. "Do brothers betray their brothers?" he asked without looking.

"I have to warn you," Hans Gerd said. "I should have told you sooner. Fritz has made inquiries. I told him I didn't know anything about you, which is true. I don't really know you anymore."

Ernst snugged the bow under Alexander's chin, then stood slowly and faced his brother. "What kind of inquiries?"

"I'm not sure. There is talk. You should be more discreet."

"These people are thugs."

"Ernst!"

"I know these men. I fought with them. I worked with them. They'll stop at nothing to consolidate their power."

"This is dangerous talk."

"Will you report me? Are the walls thin enough to report my treason? Is there an SD microphone here? Maybe under here?" Ernst pushed over the end table between them, and it rattled onto its side. Alexander began to cry. Ernst stared into Hans Gerd's eyes and found a stranger there – ostensibly his brother, but someone fundamentally altered inside. Ernst was as disappointed as he was angry. He dropped his voice to a whisper. "What have they done to you?"

Ernst sank down to Alexander again. "I'm sorry, little man, Uncle Ernst was just angry with his stupid brother."

"Ernst! Don't be an ass. I've worked for Dr. Goebbels for four years now."

"I worked for him also. A deformed little man, with deformed ideas."

"Whatever you think of Goebbels, the Third Reich is born, and our only charge is to be patriotic." Hans Gerd strode to the door and gripped the knob. Without turning to his brother, he said, "Be careful, Ernst. Do not taunt the tiger. You will get hurt." He slammed the door behind him and rumbled down the stairs.

★　★　★　★　★　★　★　★　★

Though he was not yet three, Alexander spoke in paragraphs and read simple books. A curious but quiet toddler, he liked to watch people and study their ways. He liked to disassemble broken clocks and study their innards. As a baby he had been so overly quiet, absorbing the world with what appeared to be a dull stare, that Leo and Katherine had feared he was retarded. Their fears vanished at eighteen months when he recited the alphabet.

Ernst took Alexander for a walk to Blankenburgerstrasse where the cafés and shops still offered respite from the depression. They sat at a sidewalk café table at the Berliner Konditorei. Since the April decrees most restaurants and cafés carried warning signs that Jews would not be served. Heilige Nacht Café hung a sign warning **'Entry forbidden to Jews and dogs.'** In a conciliatory gesture, the Berliner Konditorei merely noted that:

"Jews may be asked to leave."

Alexander was explaining how elephants fly – he had seen one – when his first ever Schwarzwälder Kirschkuchen arrived, an extra dollop of whipped cream on the side. After his first taste, Alexander's eyes grew large; his imaginative commentary froze. His mouth hung open, and he followed each dollop of cake and cream proffered by Ernst and a dancing spoon. As Ernst had instructed, the waiter left a steaming glass of chocolate, mit Schlag and two spearmint leaves, the same as Ernst's father used to buy for him and Leo after a day at the museum, one of his fondest recollections.

Ernst had just spooned a taste of the hot chocolate into Alexander's eager mouth when there was a sudden commotion not twenty feet up the street. Four Brown Shirts encircled a frail, elderly man. The biggest of the SA men, heavy, broad shouldered, stubble faced, bumped his chest against the bent man, almost knocking him down. The other café patrons averted their attention.

"This is not your street, Isidor! You stink of garlic."

The old man bowed lower, trying to shrink and retreat, to change his direction, but he was bottled up by the other three SA men.

"What are you doing out on the street? There are women and children here." He pointed to Alexander, who gripped Ernst's cream laden finger midway to his mouth. "How can they enjoy the day when an old Jew bothers them?" The Brown Shirt bumped him again, and he staggered into the semi-circle of SA men. "You are a Jew, aren't you? Your papers say 'Jew.'" He waved papers in the air, but the old man's eyes had closed; his lips mouthed a prayer, perhaps the Shema, the Hebrew prayer Puck had taught.

The SA man scowled and pulled the Jew's shirt from his trousers, and his fringed undergarment spilled out.

Ernst stood up from the table and approached them. "Please, gentlemen. You're frightening my young nephew. Why don't you let Old Isidor go. He's harmless."

"Harmless? He's a Jew." Ernst smelled beer on the older SA man's breath.

"Come, friend, leave this relic alone."

The Brown Shirt looked quizzically through bloodshot eyes at Ernst until a dim flicker of recognition seemed to dawn. "Wait a minute. I know you." He probed Ernst's face and his own memory. "You're Techow, aren't you? Rathenau's murderer."

The old Jew slipped through the ring of distracted Nazis and staggered into the busy thoroughfare. A taxi screeched to a stop and blared its horn, then swerved around him. The SA men gathered about Ernst, tried to shake his hand and thumped his back as if he was their best friend. Ernst backed away from their enthusiasm, to the table where little Alexander's brow furrowed and his lips quivered. He reassured Alexander that "they are only clowns, like a circus," but he felt provoked – angry and afraid.

Across the thoroughfare a man in a dark suit folded his copy of *Der Angriff*. After the brown Shirts moved on, he crossed over and sat at the next table. Ernst spooned another sip of hot chocolate into Alexander's mouth. The boy was pacified again.

"A sweet boy." The man leaned over. "Your son?"

"My nephew." Ernst turned back to Alexander.

"You rescued that old Jew. His lucky day, don't you think?" The man reached into his breast pocket and removed a small card. "Herr Techow, I don't want to spoil your Sunday, but tomorrow morning I will need to speak with you at my office."

"What is this about?"

"It is a matter of utmost importance. It will be worth your while, I assure you."

"Herr..." Ernst squinted at the small print on the card. "Herr Dieter..."

"It involves Lisa Sommers. Be sure to come alone – nine o'clock. And tell no one of this meeting." He rose from the table and tipped his hat. "An honor to meet a man of your reputation." He stroked Alexander's cheek. "A lovely boy."

The following morning Ernst arrived at the unassuming office building on Hedemannstrasse, identified only by the initials "SD" on the doorpost. The next building further up the block was Dr. Goebbels's Gauleiter office, Nazi headquarters in Berlin. A squad of SA men lounged on the steps smoking cigarettes. One bored Brown Shirt leaned against a lamppost slapping his Gummiknüppel into his palm.

Ernst's identity papers were scrutinized by a formidable SS man in a black uniform who smelled of musk. He was led through a door with frosted glass into an empty office. Hans Gerd had warned him, and now it was beyond warning. He had cause to fear.

Herr Dieter came through an adjoining door in shirt-sleeves and suspenders. "Empty your pockets." His tone had changed since yesterday.

Ernst felt the way he did when he stood before his father in their Wannseestrasse dining room, about to be chastised for yet another outrage, another failure of character, another betrayal of family honor. He resisted saying, 'Yes, Sir.' A cold sweat condensed on his upper lip. Dieter sat at the desk and looked from Ernst's face to his identity card. He opened a folder and leafed through several pages, some typed, some handwritten.

"You come from an illustrious family, Herr Techow. You were a hero of the Nationalist cause. Strange you did not vote for the Nazis in the last election and, of course, there is your assault on Dr. Goebbels."

Herr Dieter adjusted both suspenders and pursed his lips as if trying to decide something of great import, then smiled. "I could let Herr Goering and the Gestapo handle your case, but they are preoccupied with eliminating traitors, whereas we serve more of an 'educational' role. Herr Goering can be so crude. He tends to see everything in black and white. And you are not a traitor, are you, Herr Techow?"

"I have done nothing wrong. I wish legal counsel."

He laughed. "Legal counsel?" He slowly walked around his desk until he stood so close that Ernst could smell peppermint on his breath. "Perhaps you have been asleep these last six months, but the Law of February 28th suspended those clauses of the constitution that sheltered people of criminal intent. We Nazis are scrupulously legal."

Ernst felt the weight of the Nazi system; the room seemed to shrink. He had heard about Schutzhaft – protective custody in the concentration camps that had sprung up less than a year after Hitler's rise to the Chancellorship. Rumors of beatings, sadistic guards, even murder, already hung over the Oranienburg Camp near Berlin. It was reported that the guards at Oranienburg were drawn from the Deaths Head Regiment, reputed to be the most brutal SS unit.

"Let me get right to the point, Herr Techow." Dieter fussed with his party ring to center the skull. "Fritz Sommers has asked me to speak to you. He has pressing business elsewhere and regrets he cannot be here."

"Fritz should do his own dirty work."

"Oh, no, no, no, Herr Techow. This is cleansing work." He smiled and returned to his side of the desk. Dieter gestured to a plain wooden chair for Ernst to sit. It was slightly lower than he expected, and he felt Dieter's menace magnified.

"Herr Sommers is most distressed about certain indiscretions concerning his wife, Lisa. It would not do for a bright young party man to be cuckolded by an old childhood friend who doesn't know when to stop."

Ernst's leg began to tremble. His chest tightened. He hoped Dieter didn't notice his agitation.

"Herr Sommers is even more concerned about certain criminal activity that may tempt you. There has been a brisk trade in forged documents – identity papers, exit visas, and the like. Herr Sommers is certain you have enough good sense to avoid becoming involved with such dangerous traffic."

He had no doubt that Fritz was grievously wounded by his affair with Lisa, but there was more to this than personal vengeance. As angry as Fritz must have been to discover their affair, could it be that Fritz was also warning Ernst? Was this loyalty to his old friend? Was he simply using his affair with Lisa as a pretext to alert him in a more dramatic fashion? The double standard was appalling. It was well known that party bosses routinely engaged in trysts with attractive women (and men) regardless of their marital status. If Fritz were here, his expression and manner could not have concealed his true feelings. By using Dieter he injected fear, made more potent by ambiguity, and preserved his distance and his virtue.

"If we find ourselves discussing this again," Dieter said as he slipped his party jacket on, "a few days at Oranienburg will be necessary. But Herr Sommers assures me you are an intelligent and reasonable man. Your file need not leave this office. There is no reason to run afoul of the Gestapo."

★　★　★　★　★　★　★　★　★　★

Three months later, after the first Christmas and New Year under Nazi rule, Ernst waited for Lisa at Anhalter Bahnhof station. It was more than an hour before the night train to Paris was scheduled to depart; he worried something would go wrong. Garish red swastika flags draped Berlin's central train station like a whore. Christmas wreaths turning brown still hung beneath each towering red flag. Remarkably, 1934 brought the first intimation of economic recovery and the station bustled with travelers, even at ten o'clock in the evening. Many were emigrating Jews. The cathedral-like main floor of the terminal glowed golden.

The giant Gothic clock hand ratcheted another tiny arc and struck ten o'clock as he passed through the SS checkpoint. He had dyed his hair brown to conform to the photograph and papers identifying him as Ernest Tessier from Ihringen, near Freiburg. The routine search of his valise revealed only his favorite Leica camera, a collection of pens, two ink bottles, some magnifying glasses, a draftsman's compass and several changes of clothing. It was the same valise he'd carried into and out of Striegau, the one he had been given by his mother on his fifteenth birthday, embossed with flaking gold leaf initials, **EWT.**

A steam whistle suddenly resounded from below him, from the platforms and tracks. His directions were specific. She was to be on Platform #12 by half past ten. Fritz was in Munich for several days, and Frau Staats was staying at the house with Adi, simplifying the deception.

Ernst turned up his coat collar and walked down a flight of stairs into the pool of cold air on the subterranean platform level. He found an empty bench on Platform #12 and opened his newspaper, *Der Angriff*, once his employer, now his masquerade.

At precisely 10:30 the overnight train to Paris backed into the platform and stopped with a sudden hiss of steam. Enthusiastic passengers clustered like bees around coach doors even before microphones blared that the Paris express was on time and would depart in thirty minutes. Still no sign of Lisa.

Ernst lit another cigarette. He knew he shouldn't smoke so much; it was the red flag of anxiety. The same SS man stood nearby, his hands folded behind his back, still looking in his direction. There was nothing to do but wait.

The '2300' left Berlin each evening at 11 o'clock. Popularly known as the "Red Eye Express," it was an express in name only. Once it crossed the frontier into France it became the milk train for the suburbs of Paris and finally crept into the French capital at eight the next morning. It was also the boat train for passengers disembarking to America, and the shuttle-carts full of valises, suitcases and steamer trunks suggested emigration, not the business trips that, until a year ago, had been the mainstay of the '2300.'

He searched the crowd for Lisa and was distressed to hear himself damn her under his breath. But time grew short. Now there were two SS men, uncomfortably close, surveying the crowds from behind the gate. Did he only imagine their suspicious glances?

Since Ernst's encounter with the SD, he and Lisa had stopped meeting at his apartment. There was no doubt that Fritz would have her followed, that phones would be tapped, letters opened. Fritz maintained his busy distance from Lisa and never mentioned the affair. In that first hectic year of dictatorship, of Nazification, talented Nazis were in demand at every level of government, and Fritz was nothing if not gifted. He was often away for days at a time, but Ernst and Lisa could not risk further discovery.

At their last meeting, in the Tiergarten, Lisa broke down and tearfully agreed to leave Germany with Ernst. They plotted their escape, but Lisa's ambivalence was unmistakable. In the preceding two months they communicated through notes delivered by Adi's Kinderfräulein, Marlis Staats, to Ernst's photo shop. Frau Staats was to leave with Adi the day after Ernst and Lisa and meet them over the frontier. They held each other in a copse of trees, and Ernst had kissed her eyes, tasted her tears.

"I was just remembering Margaret," he said, "in Halle, when we had to sneak you out of your father's house. Do you remember?"

She laughed. "I was afraid you would be more interested in Margaret."

"There was never anyone but you." He kissed her again.

To dull the pain and frustration of the last two months' separation, Ernst worked long hours, finishing a backlog of forgeries, including his own, and began transferring Ernest Tessier's account to Paris. Since the Enabling Acts of April decreed that only 'Aryans' could be employed in most official capacities, from street cleaner to Reichsbank employee, he began to serve a largely Jewish clientele seeking new documents proving they were 'Aryan.' Vital Statistics documents had to withstand closer scrutiny than exit visas. Remarkably, these Jews chose to stay, to abandon their faith, at least on paper, in order to work. When Ernst inquired, they gave three reasons. Where would they go? French anti-Semitism was only camouflaged and less officially sanctioned, and there was no returning to the pogroms they fled in Eastern Europe and Russia. Emigration was expensive, and as the depression wore on and Jews lost their jobs to 'Aryans', fewer and fewer had the resources to flee, even if there was a promised land. And finally, and most desperately, many believed Hitler and the Nazis were just another transient government. Germany would wake from its nightmare, and everything would be set right.

It would be different for Ernst and Lisa. When they left by train there would be no trace of them; their new documents were flawless, and Ernest Tessier's bank account was healthy enough to start over. He wondered how Fritz would react when he learned of her flight – when he learned that his son was gone as well. It was astounding to Ernst that he and Fritz, who loved each other so much, could have collided so catastrophically.

He felt for Lisa's ticket. Her papers, as Elsie Hoffmann, would pass any scrutiny. The monumental clock hand above the swastika banner cranked another minute. Somewhere across the station a locomotive backed into its coupling, locking hard with metallic finality. In the cool of the station, clouds of steam condensed into fine mist, a fog. The SS guards were harder to see.

His directions couldn't have been more explicit. Ernst felt the Walther PPK automatic pistol in his pocket. It was the perfect concealed weapon –

less than one and a half pounds with a seven round magazine. It was a reassurance well worth the three hundred and fifty Marks he had paid Jacques's Berlin agent in Neukölln two weeks before.

Suddenly, from behind him, Lisa whispered. "Ernst! Don't turn around! I'm just behind you – under the stairway. Do you see those SS men?"

"I've been watching them." He opened his newspaper.

"They're looking for you and me."

"What do they know?" His heart punched his chest from inside. In the mist, the SS men looked more menacing; one leaned to speak to the other, and he thought they both looked in his direction again.

"Frau Staats betrayed us. I found a note from the SD in Fritz's desk."

"You can't stay. You're not safe."

"I can't leave Adi." She was sobbing, quietly.

Ernst's breath came fast, squeezed out of his chest. He wanted to hold her, dissolve into the shadows, flee into the night as if neither had a history.

"I don't know what's right," she said. He turned and saw her shadow behind the bench, the brown raincoat hanging open, her light blue dress shimmering. "I can't come with you, Ernst. Go without me, please."

There were now two more SS men at the next platform. They would easily find them on the train.

"It's not what I want, Ernst."

He couldn't stop himself; he rose from the bench and stepped into the shadow where they embraced.

"Ernst, you must believe me. If I didn't have Adi it would be so easy, but..."

As they held each other, for perhaps the last time, Ernst saw one of the SS men point towards them and the two men started forward, pushing aside passengers as they strode briskly. The overhead microphone announced the imminent departure of the '2300'.

"Lisa! Take my hand." He grabbed his valise and pulled Lisa down the platform.

"Ernst, I can't..."

"They've seen you."

"Ernst..."

"No time. This car!" He pulled her through the surging crowd. "We'll get off just before it leaves."

Now all four SS men strode down the platform. Ernst jumped up onto the next car and pulled Lisa inside. Compartments were filling with passengers jockeying for overhead luggage space and seating. In the narrow corridor a conductor confronted them, an older man whose beer gut distended his uniform.

"Just a moment here. Let's have a look at your tickets."

Ernst looked over his shoulder; the corridor was packed. The conductor examined their documents and leered at Lisa, his yellow teeth crooked, overlapping. She pulled her coat closed. Passengers squeezed by, grumbling. He returned her papers and smiled.

"Frau Hoffmann." He bowed and touched the brim of his cap and smiled again. "Herr Tessier. Good trip."

They hurried on, cloaked by the confusion of departure, moving from car to car toward the front of the train until they came to the baggage car, locked and guarded by a young man with an overlarge uniform and severe acne.

"Excuse me," the boy said with a sweet smile, affable as a farm boy, "but it is forbidden to go further."

Ernst hardly slowed but continued up to the young man in the space between cars and thrust the barrel of his pistol against the boy's ribs. Color drained from his face, his eyes rolled upward, and he fainted.

"That was easy." Ernst pulled a key ring from the boy's pocket as he regained consciousness.

"Which key?" Ernst pressed the gun again.

He herded the boy into the baggage car and secured him to the rail inside the door with his own handcuffs. The dimly lit car was filled with trunks, suitcases, boxes and sacks of mail.

At the other end, the door opened onto the coal car. Ernst balanced on the coupling and helped Lisa through the door.

A deafening whistle suddenly whooshed and screeched, and a cloud of steam billowed over their heads. Ernst jumped onto the tracks between the cars and held Lisa by her waist as she followed. They ran across the adjacent tracks toward Platform #11.

"Halt!" More SS men ran down that platform as well, waving Lugers in the air.

For an instant Ernst thought of the fruit man chasing him with a stick that first day he had almost killed Fritz. "Quick, the other way!" They ran awkwardly along the track from one wooden tie to the next, gaining the darkness just as a pistol shot resonated and ricocheted off metal. The immense darkness engulfed them, save for the green and red dots of signal lights and murky light pools from overhead low wattage lamps.

"Halt! Halt!"

Across the vast dark yard of tracks, a whistle screeched and the '2300' began to move. Its cyclopic beam suddenly shifted diagonally across a switch, the screech of metal on metal, quickening piston strokes.

More pistol fire from too close. He pulled Lisa down a side track. Another train whistle shrieked behind them. He could hear Lisa's panting breath.

"Ernst... I can't!"

"Lisa... If you're caught... just say I forced you... I had a gun... The boy in the baggage car... he'll say the same."

Their breath puffed like piston stroked steam. Another discharge and ricochet. Bouncing pencil beams of hand-held torches searched along the track.

"I'm going to distract them. You go down the track that way. It should get you back to the other side of the station. Lisa, it's your only chance. You must do it."

"What about you?"

Her hair was plastered against her cheeks in strands of sweat. She pressed herself against his side, breathing hard.

"I'll contact you – somehow. Now go!"

"I love you." She kissed him hard on the lips, turned and ran onto the dark track.

Ernst spun back to the pursuing SS men and fired his pistol at the closest torch beam, then ran in the opposite direction that Lisa had gone, out toward the night sky and Paris. He fired again to draw them away from Lisa's escape. The dancing light points, now six instead of four, moved closer.

The '2300' whistled, and a bullet clanged off a girder. Another pistol crack and dirt spit up between the railroad ties at his feet. Ernst sprinted around two more signal light islands.

The pursuing torch beams began to form a half circle, creating a net from which he would not escape, backing him towards a sheer wall, blasted out of the bedrock of Berlin. Five more light beams joined the chase. The multitude of tracks leaving the station fused sequentially to a narrow waist of only four.

More electric torches beamed from the direction Lisa had gone. They were still at least 50 meters away, the net tightening; there was no place else to run – no recourse but surrender. He felt the track vibrate beneath his feet and saw the '2300', it's single luminous beam gathering speed from the station, billows of steam, pounding pistons.

"Halt! Halt!" More bullets ricocheted and burrowed into wooden ties. Ernst jumped from track to track, keeping to the dark, past signal lamps with numbers and letters.

He stopped and squinted at the closest SS man, not thirty meters away, a voice behind an electric torch, now the suggestion of a gray coat, legs pumping as he ran. Ernst leveled his Walther and fired once.

The man grunted and fired his Luger several times without aim. It must have been the only way he could scream. His torch fell, angling up to the track yard ceiling.

Ernst tried to predict which track the '2300' would follow. The single engine lamp came nearer, moving faster. He tried to gauge distance and speed, hoping the train would reach him before the SS men; more pistol shots. He thought a bullet whizzed close by his face, brushing his hair. His chest ached with each stroke of breath, white mist flashing in the murky light. The beacon of the '2300' zig-zagged onto another track; SS light beams danced like lethal fireflies. Which track? He stood between the two likeliest. Again the engine's beam swung sharply left over a switch and then left again. His decision was now irrevocable – it had to be the last switch or all was lost. He cleared the last track just as the engine thundered by, cutting off most of the SS men.

The roar of the train was everything. The baggage car thundered past, screeching over the switch track, rocking slightly, already moving too fast. Another pistol shot pinged off metal. As the first coach passed, he jumped up onto the side, grabbing a thin metal bar. In that instant of contact he felt as if his arm would be torn from its socket. The momentum of the train slammed his face against its metal skin. Only the pain in his shoulder kept him from losing consciousness. His feet scrambled for purchase until they found the lip of the boarding platform where he clung anticipating a bullet's impact.

The train moved rapidly out of the train yard. It would be death to jump off now. He groped for the chain that ran between cars, but it was too far. Only one chance – before he dropped from the train. Swinging back and forth to gain momentum, his shoulder aching with each arc, Ernst released the bar and felt himself airborne for an instant as the train surged forward, until his fingers felt and seized the chain. His feet momentarily dragged along the rail bed. In spite of the agony in his shoulder he pulled himself up, his good arm grabbing another metal rod. He rolled over the chain and fell to his knees on the metal platform between the cars, panting, a stab in his chest with each breath, a deep ache in his right shoulder. He felt the snub nosed Walther PPK still in his pocket.

Ernst propped himself beside the coach door, gasping for breath. He could not move, paralyzed by the darkness, the noise, the clatter of steel.

Suddenly, the connecting door opened and an older man, in his fifties, with a black top hat reminiscent of Dronsch's bowler, escorted a young woman from the golden glow of the train's interior. He gallantly led her high-heeled steps over the transom, across the grinding plates. Then he saw Ernst.

"What's this? Are you all right?" He stood back, more afraid than concerned.

The young woman gasped, her hand to her mouth.

Ernst clutched his stomach. "Motion sickness. I'll be all right. Happens all the time."

"You shouldn't travel," the man with the bowler hat scolded.

"Thank you. I'll be all right." He leaned over the chain as if he would vomit. They completed their perilous crossing and left Ernst in the dark again.

The cool air felt healing. His sweat evaporated, chilling his skin. He checked his identity papers, his ticket – he was now Ernest Tessier, from Alsace. His valise was gone, but the Bleiguss was still in his pocket and he laughed. Of all things to save. This lead ball that resembled Puck, this sacred relic of that first night he and Lisa slept together. If he left this life as Ernst Werner Techow with nothing more than this compelling amulet, then it was sufficient. From his inner breast pocket he removed a document, unsure as to what it was. But as soon as he saw it, he knew it was Frau Rathenau's letter.

An hour later Ernest Tessier slumped in the corner of his compartment, oblivious to the stares of his fellow travelers. After a few moments he was deaf to the chattering of an obese woman grumbling about the deplorable conditions in the dining car where men smoked cigars. In his twilight sleep her voice became the wind blowing over gently undulating sand dunes, stripping away the remnants of his life until only a desert remained, and there was nothing left except for sleep, which mercifully came quickly.

19

Legionnaire Tessier

1938

Mocha sand dunes, standing waves in a dry ocean, shimmered with heat. There was only a smeared horizon, the sky becoming granular and yellow as it seamlessly joined the desert. Ernst's gaze followed the azure sky's dome to the south over the dread emptiness of the Tanezrouft paletted in shades of yellow and brown. Past the Tanezrouft stretched the Téneré, which literally meant 'nothing' in Tamashek, the Tuareg language. The horizon was so distant and featureless that demonstrably, the earth was flat. It was the season of the hot, dry sirocco, a continental wind that sculpted the desert, chiseling with blown sand. Moulay Bassim said he could tell from which part of the Sahara the sand had originated by its taste and texture on his teeth. The sirocco signaled the end of the North African winter, and, after four years posted at Fort Flatters, Ernst knew well the gritty taste of the Tanezrouft. Its bitterness invoked Moulay Bassim's first admonition about the Sahara.

"Submit to the desert. Confess your frailty," Moulay Bassim advised, "or the Tanezrouft will break you." Counsel from one designated as Moulay, a title of respect indicating descent from the prophet, was not to be taken lightly.

The pneumatic blasting of a compressed air jackhammer startled Ernst. In this void he was Capitaine Tessier, Commandant of Fort Flatters, the French Foreign Legion Bordj in the most desolate Legion posting, between the oceanic dunes of the Grand Erg Oriental to the north and west, and the nothingness of the Téneré, due south in the Algerian Sahara. Ernst walked the gravel road alone, tapping a riding crop against his thigh. Pink-skinned Legionnaires swinging picks on the roadside, all newer recruits, wrapped their cotton blouses about their heads with a slit left open for their eyes, in the fashion of the Tuareg's ceremonial headgear, the tagelmus. Neither Arab nor Negro, the Tuareg – tall Berber tribesmen, Muslim, copper-skinned and dark-haired – had occupied the mountainous regions of the Sahara long before the colonial Romans named them Berbers. These once ferocious warriors of the Sahara, barbarians to the Romans, made their tagelmus of cloth with indigo dye beaten into the fabric until it was saturated. Blue dye sweated into the warriors' skins, and they were known and feared as the 'blue men of the desert.'

Working alongside the Legionnaires were the meharistes, the camel drivers of the Shamba tribe, traditional enemies of the Tuareg. Unlike the Tuareg, the Shamba men wore turbans, leaving their faces unmasked.

When they saw their Capitaine, the Legionnaires discarded their cigarettes and resumed picking and shoveling, preparing the roadway for packing. Tar was useless, melting in the 120 degree heat; stones were only found hundreds of kilometers away. But gravel could be packed and desert grasses planted to restrain the shifting sands.

It would be another six months before the road reached Tamanrasset, but already the rattle of the drill and the quake of dynamite regularly disturbed the silence of the desert city, a mile high in the Hoggar Massif. Such was the pervasive reach of sound in the desert, huge like the sirocco. Mount Garet el Jenoum, the highest peak in the Hoggar range, towered over the severe landscape, its sandstone cliffs carved by the wind into fantastic shapes out of the Arabian Nights.

Occasionally the road builders gave in to humorous fancy with road signs: **"Timbuktu, 3,000 kilometers and turn right"** or **"It's a long way to In-Salah, but if you survive you'll get there."** Remnants of desert disasters adorned the signs, a steering wheel planted in the sand or a radiator spiked on a pole. Some of the signs carried grimmer warnings: **"Attention! Next 250 Kilometers – No Water."**

Every two or three kilometers a whitewashed stone marked the route, and every ten kilometers a conical marker of metal, about a meter high, served as a landmark for airplanes. In the fierce glare of the Sahara sun the shadow of this cone could be seen easily from the air even at great altitude.

Capitaine Ernest Tessier supervised the last extension of the Trans-Sahara road approaching Tamanrasset, the 'mountain city, the smuggler's city.' Fort Flatters was not the nearest Legion garrison or Bordj, but Ernst had convinced his superiors at Sidi-bel-Abbès to allow him to complete the desert construction. He was passionate about the road only because it gave meaning to each arid day, each tiresome week, each inconsequential month. It was his road; it kept suicidal thoughts at bay.

Ernst's road had reached the Arak gorge, the final approach to Tamanrasset. The Arak was an imitation of Hell, a narrow pass fifteen kilometers long and two hundred meters wide that snaked between sheer rock face walls, atop which square columns of basaltic rock towered like trunks in a decapitated forest. The Trans-Saharan would gravel over Wadi Takumbaret at the base of the gorge, leaving a generous drainage channel for the seasonal floods. The road would then wander upwards toward the central massif, which the Tuareg called Atakor, the knot, and finally end in Tamanrasset.

Morale flagged as the Legionnaire road crews entered the gorge, for though its sheer walls shaded the direct sun, the narrow confines caused the Arak to heat like an oven. Thunderous explosions of dynamite reverberated off the walls, jostling Tamanrasset's adobe huts. Blasting and drilling began at six in the morning and did not cease until eight o'clock at night. Almost a hundred Legionnaires toiled beside dark skinned Shambas, pressing to clear the Arak. Newer recruits fainted; there were occasional deaths from heat exhaustion. The veterans, though acclimatized to the desert, suffered in the Arak as mightily as the new recruits.

A topographic map lay on a plywood board over two saw horses, three corners held down by hand grenades, the fourth by a flare pistol, shaded by a tarpaulin stretched between two armored cars.

"Sous-lieutenant Rocque." Ernst returned the salute of the sous-officier in charge of the shift. "Your unit was to be in the gorge by now."

"Mon Commandant, the men have been overworked. The pace is too much."

Ernst studied the map for a few moments, then looked south to the precipitous rise of the Hoggar Mountains. "They are Legionnaires," he said softly. "They will do it. It is a problem of leadership." Ernst studied the map again, then snapped back up to attention. He slapped the loop of his riding crop into his palm. "I have another concern, Sous-lieutenant – more pressing. Tuareg women are being harassed by some of the men in the market. See to it that I never hear another such report. Though they wear no veils, the Tuareg are not like the whores of the north. The market is a privilege. Not one more incident, do you understand? If there is, that man will be whipped, you will lose your commission, and no man will leave this construction site." His eyes slitted as if still in the sun's blaze. "Do I make myself perfectly clear?"

"Yes, Mon Capitaine, perfectly clear."

"Add a third shift."

* * * * * * * * * *

He thought of Lisa every day. After two years, she was a muted but persistent ache. Growing old must feel this way, he considered – an accrual of dazed and persistent aches, body and soul. And, he reasoned, it must be the accumulated weight of it all that finally kills us. Indeed, Lisa's memory brought him another step closer to death. The desert was his last effort to scorch clean the crucible of his losses.

However, in his dreams, Lisa was anything but a dull and persistent ache. She was palpable, she was corporeal: her face, her neck, her breasts. Sometimes he could smell her perfume. She was so real that his grief upon waking pierced like a spear.

And then there were her letters, kindling to his desire, which would never become dull. Several weeks after Ernst's escape, Leo had taken it upon himself to meet Lisa in church one Sunday. She recognized him and was about to speak, but Fritz stood beside her, and Leo raised a finger to his lips. He stood behind her and pressed a note into her hand, then disappeared. The note gave instructions for how she and Ernst could communicate. On the first Sunday of every month Leo would find Lisa in church and exchange hymnals containing letters for and from Ernst. It was the only safe way; she could not know where Ernst was for fear the Gestapo would hunt him down. With each change of address Ernst sent a letter to Leo with a sketch of a warship, a drawing that only Leo would recognize as Ernst's. His new address was woven into the lines of the ship's wake.

In her first letter Lisa described her virtual house arrest, supervised by Marlis, who, she suspected, was sleeping with Fritz.

> *... After you fled everything went wrong with Fritz and me. He treats me much the way Father did, the one thing I swore I would never abide. Fritz identified you as the murderer of the Gestapo agent at the train station. Since then he never speaks of you, as if you were dead – or had never lived. He has never asked how long we had been sleeping together, although I am certain he knows everything. It's as if you are a Jew, that's how unspeakable to Fritz is the very thought of our relationship.*
>
> *For the first few weeks after your escape Fritz was silent and sad, the deep-*

361

ly injured but understanding husband. One day he finally saw how unhappy I was, and he became enraged. I'd never seen that side of Fritz. It must have been obstructed, confined for a long time, and it finally erupted with a fury. He struck me in the face – just once – but that has changed everything.

Adi, who has been my only joy, is twelve years old, and he prefers to spend his time with the Hitler Jugend. His friends all belong. Every boy is fascinated by their uniforms, and the leaders carry real Luger pistols in shiny black holsters. He is eager for another war against the French. The Hitler Jugend is parent and teacher. Adi hardly needs me anymore. I am afraid for my own safety.

Escape? It becomes more and more complex and expensive, and Fritz has severely restricted my access to money. He holds my passport and Reich bank identity card. I am required to put on gowns and jewels for formal obligations – state dinners and receptions. I've met Hitler on several occasions. His hands are small and cold.

In sum, my life is that of a prisoner in Berlin, my jeweled cage. I would give it up in a moment to be with you. If only I had known that when we could have fled in January. Not a day goes by that I do not think of you and imagine our life together...

Lisa's last letter, dated July 1937, was almost two years ago, the same month Leo had been mobilized into the Wehrmacht. He was sent to the Belgian frontier, and just before the first snow Leo had written to say that everything was 'All boring on the Western front.' He was sorry he could no longer act as courier for Lisa's letters. He knew that Ernst would miss them, he wrote, adding,

Besides, it was an exciting game and I enjoyed the thrill of it.

I do so miss my darling boy. Alexander thinks it completely magnificent that you, his favorite uncle, are an officer of the Foreign Legion.

Ernst's mother's letters were delivered about a month after they were posted, addressed to Capitaine Tessier, Fort Flatters, Algeria. Ernst wondered if the Gestapo intercepted her letters and knew of his new identity. She wrote glowingly of the cession of the Sudetenland after the Munich Pact in September of 1938. She believed, she prayed, there would indeed be 'peace for our time.'

In his last letter, Leo wrote of the return of prosperity to the Vaterland

and his excitement about the rush of history. Everything was turned on its head. After all, wasn't it ironic that Hans Gerd was now a prominent lawyer on Reinhard Heydrich's Security Service staff. Hans Gerd had become the most successful of the three brothers. He worked long hours and found that Gestapo police work suited his temperament far better than Goebbels's propaganda ministry. Leo described the prosthetic hand that had been made for Hans Gerd so that his 'Sieg Heil' salute would be normal, more Aryan. Ernst sadly concluded that the Party had made Hans Gerd whole; they had become his family.

Hans Gerd's prosthesis took on yet another meaning in the Foreign Legion. A Legion hero, Captain Jean Danjou, had lost his hand in the Crimea and was fitted with a wooden prosthesis. Years later he became one of the martyred heroes of The Camerone, a Mexican battle in which all but three legionnaires perished after a heroic defense against staggering odds. Captain Danjou's wooden hand, encased at the Legion Headquarters at Sidi-bel-Abbès, had become the most treasured icon, and the Battle for The Camerone the mythic battle of Legion history.

Ernst had such turbulent feeling about Hans Gerd. He loved him as his nest-mate, a comrade in the army of family. And he hated who he had become. It was more than the sibling bickering and tussle. Those things about Hans Gerd that bothered Ernst had transformed and calcified into something demonic. There was a game that Ernst had played with Leo and Hans Gerd – Rock, Paper, Scissors. He thought of the Heil Hitler salute not as the knife edge that was intended, but the flat hand of paper, with the fisted Communist salute the rock, and Winston Churchill's 'V' for victory the scissors. None conquered all; each was susceptible to another. But it had only been a game. Who would have guessed that in 1938, Hans Gerd's wooden hand thrust in a "Sieg Heil!" would prevail over rocks and scissors.

⋆   ⋆   ⋆   ⋆   ⋆   ⋆   ⋆   ⋆   ⋆   ⋆

In Tamanrasset, the Shamba and the Tuareg lived in segregated communities. Mud-bricked houses the color of the earth lined the oued, the dry riverbed. Shamba women, veiled and secretive, rarely left home – and then only with other women or a male relative – to shop in the souq, the market, or draw water in the dusty square outside the Hotel Imperial. Shamba women were subject to absolute male authority. When a man walked towards them in the souq, veiled Shamba women ducked out of sight.

Tuareg women, tall and stately, were subject to no man's authority. They exhibited their beauty free of veils and walked arm in arm through the souq with their heads high. Anywhere else in the Sahara a woman without a veil would be clearly identified as a prostitute. But the Tuareg turned stereotype on its head: the blue warriors veiled, secured by anonymity, and the women, who wielded much authority in the home, souq and water hole, exposed and dignified.

Ernst trained his binoculars on the smudged southern horizon. Spotting a convoy of Peugeots or Berliets was not difficult; the trucks threw off tall columns of dust that moved quickly, but Moulay Bassim's camels required a devoted gaze. He knew exactly where on the horizon the caravan from Tessalit would appear, and he kept his glass focused resolutely on the unchanging heat waves.

Charbonneau, the French administrator, predicted that soon enough the Peugeots and Berliets would replace camels, and Ernst agreed, but Moulay Bassim thought otherwise.

"Camels are dependable," Bassim had argued when they first met four years earlier. "Thirty days on a little hay, a little water. Peugeots break down, their tires sink in the sand."

In some ways Moulay Bassim reminded Ernst of Puck, and their animated arguments lifted Ernst's spirits, if only briefly. Whenever he remembered Puck, it was with a warm sense of having an older sibling, a beloved uncle, someone who cared deeply for Ernst during those critical years in Striegau. Someone who felt like a mechanic of the soul. Or maybe it was just a coincidence, and Ernst would have begun to transform on his own, though that seemed unlikely. And he might just have killed himself. The thought certainly crossed his mind with regularity. And maybe it was nothing more than growing older, the flame less intense. But when it came to Nazi Germany, so many kilometers and so many years away, the flame was extinguished. He thought only of Lisa and his family, and worried for them all.

But now he was on another planet – a hot, dry world where the horizon of concern was only as far as the eye could see. Ernst peered beyond that horizon by training his binoculars onto the pass through which he would first see Moulay Bassim's camel caravan.

The telltale smudge appeared and disappeared, then appeared again. The caravan would camp at the edge of visibility tonight and resume their journey before dawn the next day, traverse the Arak gorge by midday and lay down their camels in the souq before sunset.

After a hiatus of almost five years, Ernst had visited with Puck six months earlier in In-Shalah. Since fleeing Germany in 1934, Ernst had met Puck only that one time, at the northern rim of the desert. It was at the conclusion of Ramadan, under the cover of feasting and celebration in the spring of 1938. Puck had just arrived from Southern France and summoned Ernst with a sense of urgency. When they met, Puck had only an hour to spare. He was preoccupied, nervous; he needed maps of the desert as far south as the Niger River. Years in the Corsican sun had browned Puck's balding head. He looked much older, his beard still wild.

He asked questions about smuggling and Tamanrasset. Who were the smugglers, could Ernst connect Puck for an important transaction, what was the exchange rate for 'human services,' what communication links existed – cables, telegraphs, radios? Finally, Ernst pulled him aside from his turbaned interpreter.

"First of all," he hissed at his old friend, "never hire a Shamba as an interpreter. They tell you what you want to hear. If you want the truth, hire a Tuareg. The smugglers? Tuareg. If you have business with the Tuareg let me be your intermediary. It's horribly confusing and not a little dangerous."

It was disturbing to see Puck desperate, floundering out of his element, making mistakes. For the first time Ernst felt a disquieting equality with Puck. No longer mentor and student, Puck was a colleague, a dear lost brother who had unexpectedly reappeared in need of what? He would not say.

"I would tell you, if I could," Puck said. "You have my unconditional trust. But this is too big. I almost don't believe it myself."

Ernst laid his arm on Puck's shoulder. "I'm confident your latest scam, whatever it is, will be successful. If I can be of assistance... But now tell me about you. Where have you been, you old fool!" Puck smiled and blushed. Then they finally embraced, and Ernst felt the relief of reunion.

Shortly after that meeting Puck sent Ernst a package containing three black slips of a flexible, hard plastic and a letter.

My dear Ernst,

I was glad to reunite with you recently in In-Shalah. I'm sorry it was so short and, I would guess, not satisfying for either of us. But circumstances dictated the truncated nature of my time. The main thing is that we have resumed a broken connection.

I hope you are well, Ernst. My friends and business contacts in the Legion and in the desert give me periodic reports on your progress. I understand that you are a respected Legion officer with a hard reputation. I hope you are still drawing and using those skills that you perfected in Striegau.

I cannot tell you where I am or what I am doing for fear this communication will be intercepted. Nevertheless, I must take some risks, because the possible harm is great.

In the next little while, I don't know when, you will receive rocks and you will determine if they are special rocks – radioactive rocks – Uranium. With this letter are a few strips of roentgen paper used for medical radiographs. If a substance is radioactive, it gives off invisible radiation that will develop this special film and turn it white. If that is the case, it means that a very powerful, destructive new force will be in the hands of whoever finds it first. Certain German officers and geologists are seeking this ore in your neighborhood of the desert. If the rocks are what I think they are, there is no time to waste. Something must be done immediately. I will tell you what you need to know, when you need to know it. I appeal to you from my heart. I need you as much as you needed me once.

I miss our time together and think of you often with tenderness. I know your journey is hard and long. And I know you are lonely for that girl – the one and only love of your life. I understand your grief, for I too have lost someone so singular. I think life is about gain and loss, and always there is a tenuous balance of the two. I miss our long talks. I trust we will meet yet again as I am not very far away. I cannot tell you where, but we'll see. The world is changing rapidly and one never knows from day to day what is required. Moulay Bassim would say it is all pre-ordained. I respectfully disagree, believing as I do that we are responsible for this world, each in our own small way.

If you were with me now, I would grasp your shoulders and look into your eyes. And I would tell you "to thine own self be true." You know the rest.

Much love to you, Ernst. May our paths cross again.

Puck

Since then, nothing. Then, a few days before Bassim's imminent arrival Ernst received an urgent cable from Puck, sent from Oran a few days earlier. It was brief.

Bassim arrives – few days. See him for important parcel. Puck

★   ★   ★   ★   ★   ★   ★   ★   ★   ★

The day after Bassim's caravan arrived, Ernst left the road crew at twilight and drove the squad car up the unfinished road to Tamanrasset. He crossed the water pump square to the flickering incandescent entrance at the Hotel Imperial. Legionnaires lingered at the Cote d'Azur Café, three round tables in front of the hotel serviced by a tall, thin Tuareg. The pied noir, black booted Legionnaires, came to tipsy attention and saluted their commandant.

Inside, at the bar under a sluggish ceiling fan, Ernst saw three European guests, too hot to speak, but still drinking and smoking. The lounge at the Cote d'Azur was the only place in Tamanrasset where alcohol was legally served. However, the souq-noir also offered a variety of beverages and drugs at competitive prices, in addition to other hard-to-find items like tires and radiators. In fact, the souq-noir was the not-so-secret heart of Tamanrasset, and its blood flowed through Tuareg, Shamba, and European alike.

Moulay Bassim sat alone in an ancient overstuffed chair in the lobby. When he saw Ernst he pushed up his ample body to stand and greet him. "As-salaam 'alaykum." Bassim bowed slightly.

"Wa 'alaykum as-salaam." Ernst touched his forehead, lips and heart.

They exchanged pleasantries. Ernst knew to allow Bassim his own time to reveal his message from Puck. He ordered a whiskey from the Tuareg waiter and then inquired about Bassim's caravan journey. Their old argument resumed about Peugot vs. camel. "It's a question of commerce," Ernst said. "The Peugeots can cross the Erg in five days instead of thirty."

Moulay Bassim paused, then said, "You Europeans are obsessed with time, as if it is real. Time is elastic in the Tanezrouft – the rhythm of the desert is the swaying of the camel, the brass bell beating out the camels' footfall. I don't expect you to understand. Your way has consequences you cannot imagine. Our way has been tested by untold thousands of years."

Bassim had grown up under the French conquerors who, after defeating the Tuareg nomads, became the only protectors they ever knew. He was consigned to the "nomad" school to learn French language and history, at which he excelled. But he also prowled the souq and learned the particular ways of his people, the Hoggar Tuareg, who referred to their race as Ihaggaren – the Nobles.

But, Bassim had explained to Ernst, the Tuareg surrendered their nobility to the French, who required them to abandon their caravan raiding and relinquish their Haratin slaves. A small tax was levied, more as a token of vanquishment and allegiance than as a source of income. The older men in the souq, once proud warriors of the desert, now the last witnesses to a dying culture, filled young Bassim's head with tales of glory.

Most Muslims despised the French twice, once as colonial masters, and again as Christians. But not Bassim, whose name meant 'the smiling one' in Tamashek. "Your Peugots will come and go, Ernst. We will wait." He smiled to himself. "We were once the feared blue men of the desert." Bassim sipped his strong tea. "But you pied noir have reduced us to desert merchants. So now we are smugglers. We adapt. To our mutual benefit."

There was a long silence during which Ernst finished another whiskey and smoked a Gauloise. There was nothing to do but wait. It was the old way, he told himself, only half in jest, tested by thousands of years. Maybe Bassim was correct and this road Ernst was building would bring nothing but more misery to people who had learned to live with adversity and did well enough. The Tuareg had slaves, the Europeans had the Great War. Who was to say which was the more civilized?

Bassim reached into a goatskin sack that he always carried over his shoulder and found two smaller sacks cinched with leather drawstrings.

"These are Puck's precious rocks. He said you must have them. He said you would know what to do with them."

Ernst felt the weight of each pouch in which hung a rock the size of an ostrich egg. When he asked Bassim if he knew what the samples were, the older man shrugged his shoulders.

"What you Europeans value often makes little sense, but these rocks are good business; 50,000 dinar and a two-year-old Peugeot for rocks. That's what Puck said he paid for them."

As was their custom, Ernst and Bassim played a game of Mancala that Bassim won, the usual outcome. They made their obligate Arabic goodbyes, and Ernst retired to a room he kept at the Hotel. In his small closet he rummaged through his leather document case until he found the three rectangles of black radiograph film. In accord with Puck's instructions, he cut the rectangle into two squares, noted the time and carefully placed one square into each bag with the rock, cinched the leather thong, then hung it on a nail near the window. He tried to read but was distracted by thoughts of Puck and what hung in the bags that swung back and forth for some time, as if they contained creatures squirming to escape.

In Tamanrasset Ernst felt altered – a hybrid – half Legionnaire, half Berber. The Romans with the dismissive Barbarus, 'foreign and uncivilized', had named these beautiful people. Their mountain adobe city deep in the

Sahara, a junction for smuggling, was that most unusual of places where the Sahara met the modern world on the desert's terms. Ernst liked the rich uncertainty of this boundary. It was a place where Ernst could feel with intensity the heat, the isolation, the explosives, the road project, yet be in suspended animation at the same time. Ernst knew it would not always be so. He knew Tamanrasset was Striegau by a different name, one in which he had respect and dignity, if not integrity. And this road was now the focus for every stray feeling or need. It sufficed.

Indeed, his road, the Trans-Sahara, altered not only Ernst, but everything it touched. Approaching Tamanrasset from the north it would continue south to Agadez, Dogondoutchi and finally Niamey, on the Niger River. The region's riches would be available to the colonial interests of France, and Central Africa would never be the same. For thousands of years the holy trinity of desert commerce was gold, salt and slaves. Over the millennia, only gold had endured. In less than a generation the deities had mutated into gold, oil and now, Uranium. It was that strange element, Uranium, perhaps in the ore sample hanging on the nail, that reunited Ernst with Puck, that made this road through the desert more than just another caravan route opened to motor vehicles by the Colonials.

Ernst wondered if these rocks would bring Puck back to the desert. The sirocco and the whiskey lulled Ernst into twilight sleep, dreams on the edge of waking – a mulatto woman on a train, smiling at him, reciting a sensuous poem in a Tuareg dialect, her tongue sliding over ruby lips, inviting; he drifted close to kiss her and her lips were etched with tiny cracks, her mouth filled with sand...

The next morning Bassim's nephew Ameur, a brown Tuareg boy not yet in his teens, hand delivered a cable from Puck instructing Ernst how to record the proportion of each black square of film that had turned transparent overnight. Ernst was to give Ameur the two sacks with Bassim's rocks. The first square was so completely bleached that Ernst could read a newspaper headline through it – the second only slightly less developed.

Before relinquishing the two rocks in their goatskin sacks he marveled at how much in the universe was hidden from view. Two rocks worth 50,000 dinars and an almost new Peugeot. Two rocks that told an enigmatic story that only the roentgen film understood and recorded as a footprint of an invisible, inevitable force that so unsettled Puck. And now Ernst felt himself drawn into a perplexing disturbance, a maelstrom. Though he did not share Puck's angst, his interest and curiosity were piqued. He would assist his old friend, at the very least out of loyalty. After all these years, he still had complete trust in Puck, though he did not exactly know why he should.

★   ★   ★   ★   ★   ★   ★   ★   ★   ★

Ernst waited for Bassim at the edge of the mountain city in the blast of heat just before sundown. Ordinarily drab and colorless, Tamanrasset's earth brown adobe fluoresced with the flat harsh light and sharp contrasts painted by the setting sun. The sirocco would gust for forty more days, blowing sand into every crevice, every skin pore, every breath. Just before the horizon claimed the sun, he felt illuminated by the last rays and marveled anew at the vast Tanezrouft. The sirocco swept over him like loneliness, the bittersweet breath of a world so manifestly terrible and beautiful.

Ernst's friendship with Bassim was grounded in shared commercial interests and sweetened by genuine affection. Bassim, as Little Amenokal, the secular Tuareg leader of Tamanrasset, provided Tuareg labor for the French road builders, and Ernst provided him with access to automotive parts for his smuggler's network. A Michelin tire in the desert fetched three to four times its actual value in France, a radiator as much as ten times.

Their meeting tonight had been urgently arranged by Bassim, a week before their regular 'business meeting.' Ernst was purposefully early, grateful for some quiet reflection. Bassim had taught him that beneath the Tanezrouft, the driest place on Earth, there was water, deep and strong in some places, merely molecules in others. Invisible like the rays from Puck's rocks. Only in the Sahara was the Earth quiet enough, bitterly desolate enough, that one could feel the current beneath one's feet. His black boots scratched the dry ground, and the sirocco sucked away the dust. He breathed the desert's empty sadness deep inside, and it occurred to him that Bassim's water beneath the desert was like hope, buried deep underground. He could not access it, could not feel its cooling relief, but he could choose to believe in an aquifer of desire, of expectation that might surface in an oasis somewhere or sometime. He dared not name it, or give it any more substance, for fear the sirocco would scatter it like so much sand.

After sunset, the sky darkened to hues of blue, indigo, and violet. Ernst crouched behind his staff car in the lee of the wind. He set a lantern and prepared their customary Mancala game, digging shallow depressions in the sand, two lines of six each, with a larger depression flanking them on either end. He lit a small coal fire against the rapidly chilling night air and soon had a bed of red embers. Perhaps tonight, if Bassim felt in the mood, he would finally teach Ernst how to bake the tagela, desert bread. These coals would be the oven.

In the sustained wind Ernst tasted the saline sand of Gao, where Bassim had obtained the film-bleaching ore. For an aching but tender moment, he felt for Lisa in the sirocco, tried to imagine her scent, her taste, but she was no more substantial than an elusive dream. A sudden gust blew with demonic purpose, darkening the twilight sky with sand, and it seemed impossible to associate it with nostalgia or mourning, certainly not tenderness. Like their red kite so many years ago, so many lifetimes ago, she was in the wind and she was irrevocably gone.

"As-salaam 'alaykum." Bassim appeared out of the darkness and squatted before the fire, a ghostly apparition in his desert robes and indigo tagelmus.

"Wa 'alaykum as-salaam." Ernst touched his forehead, lips and heart. "Ameur said you had important business."

Bassim gave no intimation of the urgency of this meeting, only sighed. "There is much to occupy me these days, Nasareh." He called Ernst by the Arabic name for 'Christian,' part jest, part historical enmity. "Your Legionnaires must be more civilized in the souq, lest one forfeit his life."

"I am aware of the misbehavior. I will deal harshly with the guilty, Moulay Bassim. I have already spoken to my officers. I depend on your patience and your mercy."

"Mercy is a question of good manners. I know we will not have this discussion again. Come, let us play a Mancala. "He emptied a goatskin of black pebbles into his palm. "I trust you to correct the behavior of your pied noir."

"The Legion is not a tribe. Loyalty is sometimes cheap – discipline a challenge."

The light skinned Tuareg began distributing six stones in each well. "Neither of us owns any of these pebbles, Nasareh. What matters is how we move them. You are the Moulay of the pied noir. It is only for you to move them correctly."

Ernst tried to see through the slit in Bassim's tagelmus, felt more than saw the black fixity of his gaze. He envied the order in Bassim's world, the predictable behavior of his people. Bassim could never understand that, no matter how brutal Ernst's discipline, the Légion d'Etranger, the Legion of Strangers, was just that.

"Do not be troubled, Nasareh." Bassim said. "In Mancala, as in life, there is no such thing as chance. All is preordained; one has only to move correctly." He laughed.

Half an hour later Bassim plucked the winning pebble from the last well. "You have asked several times how to bake the tagela," Bassim said as he returned the stones to their bag. "I have never been asked by a pied noir how to bake our bread. Flat bread is for nomads – Arabs." Bassim unhooked a goatskin of water from his donkey's pack and unknotted the neck of a flour bag. "Your fire is good – the coals are ready. Baking the tagela is a lesson every Tuareg child learns – every child, not just young girls. It is necessary – to survive in the desert."

He chanted under his breath, under the sirocco, as he mixed just enough water with flour in a shallow bowl to form a dough that he kneaded and formed into a flattened sphere. "Each tagela is round – complete." He drew his curved dagger from its secret scabbard and inscribed a deep cross in the center of the dough. "It is not a Christian symbol, Nasareh, though I understand the importance of bread in your rituals. Tin Hinam, our grandmother, our original ancestor, gave us the symbol of the cross. It forms the pommel of our great saddles – the rahla; it decorates our warrior's shields, the handles of our swords." He dug a pit beside the fire and laid the dough inside, then moved the fire, pushing the glowing embers, to cover the bread. "It will bake in one hour. Let us play another Mancala. Perhaps you will finally win a game."

The night was cool and refreshing. Strange shadows danced from the fire. The black Mancala pebbles clicked against each other; Ernst lost two more games before he felt the time right to discuss commerce. He passed a list of automotive parts to Bassim who made marks with the stump of a pencil.

An hour later Bassim's curved dagger unearthed the loaf and began the slow process of scraping and tapping sand from the tagela crust. "One can never remove all the sand. Baking the tagela marks time like a slow clock. We Tuareg take pride in what the desert does to us, not what we do to the desert. In that way you and I are essentially different."

"I understand that. You Tuareg have perfected waiting, like those tiny yellow flowers that bloom when it rains."

"No, Nasareh. It is not a question of waiting. A Tuareg knows it will come, Insh'Allah."

"But their roots are twenty feet long."

"God favors the prepared mind."

"You have it wrong, Bassim. It is chance that favors the prepared mind. I believe it was Louis Pasteur who said this – a great scientist – sure of the world."

"To Europeans it is chance. To Muslims, God. Perhaps it is all the same thing. No one can know. There is no faith without doubt."

Ernst was struck dumb. Puck has said these exact words to him in Striegau. He would not have been surprised for Bassim to unwrap his tagelmus and reveal himself to be Puck.

"You look as if you've seen a ghost. Come, let us walk. My old bones cannot remain still for too long."

The desert gravel crackled under their boots as they walked. The dome of the sky bowed over them, the Milky Way like pulverized light, luminous grains immune to the sirocco. Mahogany night slowly extinguished the last trace of amber twilight.

"Normally I do not care a fig about you pied noir. But you and I have become friends, and as such I am curious to know more about you. I do not even know how it is you came to be here in the Sahara?"

Ernst spoke quietly. "It was an unfortunate police matter in Berlin four years ago. You might say the Sahara is a suitable hideout." Even as he spoke, Ernst knew his story to be a lie. He had fled to the desert to forget her, and, depending on his disposition, to begin his life anew or to court death. Harsh Legion discipline, painful and difficult, was a relief, a distraction. He remembered Lisa explaining how she pricked herself with a pin to block out the pain after her mother had died. Now he understood how that could be, how one pain could numb a much larger pain.

And, on a much less complicated level, one that perhaps applied to most of his men, the Legion obliterated the tyranny of choice – a relief for those injured by a complex and cold world or fleeing some injustice, real or imagined. But as one year baked into another, even that had become perverted, and he understood this "relief" to be yet another little death in life.

"When I first joined the Legion I was stationed in Syria," Ernst said. "I met a Quaker – a British diplomat named Jameson. We kept meeting by chance at the Euro Café in the evening. Though I thought him a fool, a pacifist, I enjoyed our philosophical discussions. There was no one else within a thousand miles as erudite."

"One makes do with what one finds in the desert."

"He insisted that, like water in the desert, there is that of God in every man. Those were the words he used, over and over: 'there is that of God in every man.' I dismissed his theory, having just escaped the Nazis. I was depressed, angry. I did not want to believe there could be water in the desert, except for a few oases. His analogy, so obviously wrong, only strengthened my skepticism."

"You have much pain, Tessier, if that is your name. Another curiosity of you Europeans," Bassim said. "You strive to conceal yourselves in the desert, hiding from yourselves. The desert is, of course, the exact incorrect place to do that. But you are burdened by shame. You may see us as ignorant and brutal, but we are plain and direct. And, in turn, we see you as merciless in your self-delusion – another kind of brutality."

"Yet we are friends," Ernst said. "I have known you long enough to realize your, shall we say, curiosity extends beyond the Hoggar Mountains, beyond the Tanezrouft."

They returned to the fire and Bassim scattered the embers with his boot. "Our collaboration suits my interests. Allah is generous. I care little for what occurs in Europe. You foul your nest – it is nothing to me. But when you burden us with your rivalries, when you shit in the Sahara, it is indecent. You are different, Nasareh. As your Quaker friend observed, a little too broadly, there is that of God in you. You are respectful. You learn to bake the Tagela."

Ernst crushed a live coal. "The world is changing, Bassim. I fear the Tuareg will be blown away, like so much sand in these devilish winds."

Bassim laughed. "And are you the wind or the sand, Nasareh? Let me tell you about sand. My town, In-Salah, has been moved by the sands three times in living memory. When the sand invades our town we remove the windows and doors to our homes and let it drift in, fill our shells. But like the sand, you Europeans will not last forever, and when you recede, our houses will still be standing. It is fate and we trust in Allah. For every man there are two moments in life that are inescapable, preordained – birth and death. If our way of life is to die, Insh'Allah – it is the will of God."

The crags of the Hoggar Mountains fell away on Ernst's left, several thousand feet onto the Tanezrouft. The last light played tricks with his eyes; in the basaltic rock, carved by eons of sirocco, a woman's face suggested itself. His heart felt as dry and cracked as the Tanezrouft.

Bassim had been quiet for long moments, then shared his concern, the reason he had urgently summoned Ernst.

"A certain fat German, Herr Lauber, recently arrived in Algeria. My nephew works at the Prefecture of Police in Oran. He sees every transit visa. Herr Lauber is a geologist from the Kaiser Wilhelm Institute in Berlin who seeks unusual rocks, perhaps the rock I gave you, from Gao. Puck will want to know. I do not understand the details, but I feel in my bones the importance of this, Nasareh. You and Puck are my friends. I keep this burden of knowledge under my litham and share it with no one except you and Puck. I hope you will see this as more than a returned favor. I will help you in any way I can. Now, I must be returning to my brother's house." He tore apart the desert bread and gave half to Ernst. "The tagela – it is quite simple to bake, is it not?"

*　*　*　*　*　*　*　*　*　*

Thanks to the Legion road, Puck raced from Algiers to Tamanrasset in two days after Ernst's cable informed him of Herr Lauber's arrival in Oran. Bassim's nephew could create several 'bureaucratic inconveniences' for the eager German and his two assistants, but they were determined, and Gao was their destination.

Puck's car, a battered Peugeot, stopped at the end of the road construction in the Arak gorge, and Ernst was urgently called. Puck paced nervously, limping slightly with a walking cane, and when he saw Ernst he walked quickly to him with obvious pain. He looked exhausted, his eyes red and heavy from too little sleep.

He took Ernst by the elbow, his grip urgent, and led him up the unfinished portion of the road into the roasting shadow, a slit of cool blue a hundred meters overhead. In the scant six months since their last meeting, the gray of Puck's hair and beard had gone white, and that alone aged him more than his years. Puck began to cough, and his breath was short. He sat on the dirt leaning back against a boulder, his nostrils flaring with each breath, and wiped his head again with a wet handkerchief. Ernst crouched down and took away the black Turkish cigarette that trembled between Puck's fingers.

"You may not believe everything I say, Ernst, but you must trust me. Two months ago, Hahn and Strassman at the Kaiser Wilhelm Institute in Berlin used an element called Uranium to produce something incredible. It's called nuclear fission. It seems that a certain Belgian, Edgar Sengier, president of the Union Minière du Haut-Katanga in the Belgian Congo, has stockpiled some 1200 tons of Uranium ore, presumably available to the highest bidder. The search is on for large quantities of this unusual ore."

"Why are you telling me this?" Ernst said. "I have a road to build and little interest in geology."

"Have you played billiards or Snooker?" Puck asked.

"Occasionally," Ernst said, "though the French are not fond of it."

"Imagine what would happen if when you break with the cue ball each ball in the rack jumps to another table and breaks another rack and so on, and so on, and indefinitely."

"It would make a hell of racket."

"Yes, a hell of a racket. Now imagine that every time one ball struck another it exploded, like a bomb." He rapped his walking stick against a rock. "One Uranium bomb the size of a pineapple could destroy Berlin or London." He pulled a brandy flask from his pocket and drank from it. Ernst declined his offer.

"What's the point?" Ernst asked. For a moment, he wished they could be back in Striegau where life was predictable and extraordinary stories had no consequences.

Puck leaned forward, suddenly grave. "A few months ago a Belgian prospector was rumored to have found Uranium near Gao, on the Niger River. Those x-rays from Bassim's rocks confirm it. For now it is mere gossip among geologists, but it won't remain gossip for long. If the Germans cannot obtain Monsieur Sangier's ore, they will try for Gao – over your road. It is essential that the Germans are denied this knowledge for as long as possible – by whatever means necessary." Puck coughed. The Arak's deep canyon walls augmented what the unrelenting heat muffled, and his cough echoed like two rocks banging together. "I must stress, Ernst that very few people know of this, and that is how it must stay."

"I've never seen you so tense. What's in it for you?"

"This is not about business. If you would like, I can arrange payment for your services, but I could have offered that to any number of desperate men in North Africa."

"Then why come to me?"

"This must not become an incident. Our friend Moulay Bassim is fond of saying of his fellow Saharans, 'they have long ears and a long tongue between them.' I thought you might do it for the same reason I do."

"And that is...?"

"It is correct and necessary. If the Nazis obtain this Uranium the Third Reich will dominate all of Europe, Africa and Asia. I don't know why you are here, Ernst, but you can perform a deed of penitence by depriving the German war machine of this ore."

"Penitence? For what?"

"For Rathenau. Ultimately, that's why you're at Fort Flatters. It was his assassination that set your life on its course. I have long believed that in your heart you feel shame for your part in his murder. You can't undo the shame so you flee as far as you can from your old life. The goodness in you tries to atone by sadness, but that is self-indulgence, not penitence." Puck drank from his brandy flask. "I don't presume to know your mind, Ernst. I'm sure you have other compelling reasons to be here. I only ask for your help, should it become necessary. It is plain to me that life continues to be unkind to you. The Legion is an outpost, a hideout – another disguise. Maybe you hope it will be your last. I don't know."

"At Fort Flatters life is defined by four cement walls," Ernst said. "Expectations are clear. Choices are not required." He drew his Lebel service revolver and laid it on the ground between them. "My life is over, Puck. I cannot go home, I have forever lost the only woman I love, and I am too much of a coward to use this. As for penitence, it is a luxurious concept – one I can ill afford. You will forgive me if I am indifferent to your mission."

Puck stared at the Lebel. "It was a long time ago, but do you remember we discussed redemption at Striegau?"

Ernst nodded but could only barely recall their spirited prison arguments. "Puck. To be philosophical in gaol was effortless. Words, only words. You called them butterflies. I fear redemption is only conceivable in prison and in the mind, nowhere else."

Puck passed the dented flask to Ernst, and now he took it. "Pessimism does not absolve you from responsibility. Neither does cynicism."

"Responsibility?" Ernst laughed and drank again. "I take orders. I give orders. For amusement I build a road. I work with Bassim's scams, forge a document now and then. But I am committed to nothing, attached to no one. It is not a happy life, but I anticipate nothing, and so I am not disappointed."

Puck examined the Lebel, turned it over from one hand to the other, and extended it to Ernst. "If your life is nothing more than senseless anguish and boredom, then I urge you to use this." Ernst laid his hand on the Lebel, but Puck held it fast. "There is another choice. If you give meaning to your distress, the doors of possibility open. In Striegau I appealed to you as a teacher, now I appeal to you as a friend. I need your help, Ernst. I don't care why you do it, I only ask – no, beg – for your help."

Ernst felt his eyes drawn irresistibly to Puck's. Something cold and hard inside begin to melt. "You are my friend, Puck. I give you the benefit of my doubt." A hot draft of sirocco funneled up the canyon, and he tasted the Tanezrouft. Ernst stood and holstered his revolver. He looked down on Puck and felt sad that he had grown so old.

20

Confession

November 1938 – June, 1940

A small trumpet sounded retreat, and Ernst saluted as the French tricolor fluttered down the mast at Fort Flatters, deep in the Tanezrouft, what the Tuareg called the Téneré, or Nothing. Long shadows advanced to the east, spreading from the squat towers at each corner of the four parapeted walls. Empty desert surrounded the fort, as if a child had dropped his toy onto a sandy beach whose ocean had baked dry. Even in March, the heat lingered through twilight until it evaporated into the Milky Way's chill. Snakes and scorpions came to the surface, as they had for hundreds of millions of years, to hunt and absorb the waning warmth of the sand.

Among the new recruits at Fort Flatters an unusual number were German Jews, many of whom had fled after Kristallnacht, in early November of 1938. When Ernst interviewed them, they were surprised to hear him ask, in fluent German, if they were not uncomfortable betraying their own country. "Dante," he noted, "consigned that sort of traitor to the lowest circle of Hell."

Most had no response, but one recruit, Conrad Ullmann, a former lecturer in Philology at Heidelberg, replied that although Fort Flatters might very well be an outpost of that circle of Hell, he preferred the desert to Dachau, preferred Algeria to Germany.

"A measure of your animosity?" Ernst had asked.

"Animosity is far too benign a word."

Ernst's conversation with Puck in the Arak Gorge was still fresh in his mind when he received an urgent cable from Puck to meet him the next morning in the souq at Ali's date stand. The souq had been buzzing with rumors about Hitler annexing the Sudetenland from Czechoslovakia, about German troops occupying Prague. Newspapers that arrived a month after the event reported Prime Minister Neville Chamberlain's pronouncement after meeting with Hitler:

> *My good friends, for the second time in our history, a British Prime Minister has returned from Germany bringing peace with honor. I believe it is peace for our time. We thank you from the bottom of our hearts. Go home and get a nice quiet sleep.*

Ali, a stout and dark Shamba, his brown teeth rotten from eating too many of his own dates, smiled when he saw Ernst approaching his stand. Ali was unusual among the Shamba – he spoke serviceable French and was a trusted friend to Shamba and Tuareg alike. As was the custom, Ernst made polite inquiries about Ali's family and his various businesses. The date harvest was mediocre, but hashish was fetching premium prices. No, he had not yet seen Puck. Yes, Puck had arrived in Tamanrasset the day before in a new Citroën with three Germans.

"Created quite a stir in the souq," Ali said. "Milhoud Sassi is the driver. Do you know him? A nephew of Moulay Bassim's cousin's uncle – from Oran. Your ears should have been ringing. Milhoud paid tribute to your road, Nasareh. The Citroën remained clean until the last ten kilometers in the Arak. Now it is the color of the Great Eastern Erg."

After a few more requisite inquiries about the health of Ali's family, Ernst said, "I understood Puck was to meet me here."

Ali surveilled his little corner of the souq then, beneath his breath he whispered, "Under my stool is a Litham. Put it on. Stand with those two Tuareg across the way. Monsieur Puck will be along shortly. The Germans – they avoid French authorities."

Minutes later Ernst was swathed in the wide blue desert cloak of the Tuareg, sweating heavily. He searched the crowded souq through the slit of his Tagelmus. Puck suddenly appeared at Ali's stand, and Ernst saw the date merchant tilt his head in Ernst's direction. It was not unusual for Tuareg to stand ramrod straight, lithe, yet unmoving. Puck greeted them with his right hand to his forehead, his lips and heart. The two Tuareg responded in kind.

"Ma-t-toulid?"

"Hello, Puck," Ernst whispered. He was momentarily cheered to see his old friend, but also wary. He could not muster the energy for an encounter with Puck. He did not want to be roused from his certainty that nothing good would ever occur again. The predictability of the desert was the stupor from which he did not wish to be awakened. "I hate this Litham. Speak quickly."

Puck tried to suppress his smile. "I am sorry, Ernst. But I am almost certainly being watched. Do you remember our conversation some months ago about Uranium?"

"The pineapple bomb – Snooker?"

"Yes. I believe Bassim told you of our 'friend' Professor Lauber. He is preparing to prospect in Gao, and he seeks a reliable guide to take him south."

"How did he find you?"

"Moulay Bassim. Herr Lauber is well financed; his francs and dinars are crisp and new. He hired me to guide him this far. He is traveling with two 'students,' powerful men of few words. They don't seem the academic type. I helped him make arrangements in Oran. He appreciates a smuggler who speaks fluent German, and he believes my sympathies lie with Herr Hitler.

"Herr Lauber has hired a second automobile, a battered desert Peugeot, as well as picks, shovels, and dynamite. He can hardly believe everything has gone so smoothly. I've even secured several bottles of fine Schnapps. The most frequent warning he had heard before coming to Algeria was to beware of the cunning Arabs. He is grateful to have me as a civilized intermediary."

"What does this have to do with me?"

"Herr Lauber will proceed south on his own. It seems his trust only goes so far. He will be accompanied by Milhoud Sassi, as driver and guide."

Ernst saw the hot dusty market through the dark slit of his Tagelmus. "I don't understand. What do you require of me?"

"If Herr Lauber finds Uranium, no one must ever know. He and his two 'students' must never leave the desert. Be ready to act on a moment's notice." He gripped Ernst's arm through his Tuareg gown. Puck's gaze penetrated the narrow slit of his Litham. "This is the moment I feared. I can say with certainty that the future of the world hangs in the balance."

Ernst retreated through the alleys muttering obscenities about Puck, wishing him dead. Did he think he could move Ernst about, have him do his every bidding? He stripped off the suffocating Tagelmus. At the Hotel Imperial he ordered two glasses of whiskey and drank them both.

*   *   *   *   *   *   *   *   *   *

A month later, the two friends met again at Ali's date stall. Puck was conspicuous in the souq among the noble, shrouded Tuareg, who towered over wiry Shamba and jet black Haratin. This time Ernst made no effort at disguise. Several other Europeans, soaked in sweat, walked slowly through the narrow winding streets of the Tamanrasset bazaar.

Puck bit into one of Ali's dates; he argued with the merchant about the new Prefect of Tamanrasset, Inspector Rheume, a somber young police lieutenant from Oran who took his responsibilities entirely too seriously.

When Puck mentioned the new Inspector, Ali waved him off. "The man has much to learn. And he'd better learn quickly before he ends up with a curved knife in his gut. He demanded to see my license. Do you hear me, Puck? My license!" He returned to his thick sweet coffee. "Young fool!"

Puck disengaged from Ali and walked Ernst through the narrow streets of the camel market. "Have you seen a newspaper? Things are going from bad to worse on the continent. I fear for France."

"I try to disregard the continent. After all, I left to disappear; the least I can do is ignore the news. But, yes, I have read accounts – and there have been cables."

Puck steered Ernst into a side street of the souq. When they were alone Puck's tone suddenly turned pressing. "Herr Lauber found Uranium. Gao has no radio transmitter, so he will send a cable from Tamanrasset. A courier arrived today with Herr Lauber's cable and a note from Milhoud. The Germans are collecting ore samples and will leave Gao in a day or two. They will arrive at Bidon Cinq a day later." Puck wiped his forehead. He reached into his pocket and pulled out two folded cables.

U-238 plentiful. Shallow mine potential, thousands of metric tons.
–Lauber

"Here is the cable I sent on to Berlin."

No U-238. Failure.

–Lauber

Puck linked his arm through Ernst's elbow, but it was urgency, not intimacy that drew him close. "Hitler must never learn of the uranium at Gao. Herr Lauber must never return from the Tanezrouft."

Ernst frowned. "Why not hire a Tuareg?"

Puck's grip on Ernst's elbow tightened. "There can be no mistake about this. As soon as Herr Lauber returns to Tamanrasset with the Uranium, he will send his own radio message to Berlin, and then we are defeated." A donkey brayed in the dirt, and they turned into an alley, dark with shadows like the Arak.

Ernst felt something kindled. Something not unlike the spark of a new military mission, something he did not want, something rousing, something compelling. "Bidon Cinq?" Ernst calculated the timing. Tessalit, in the French Sudan, more than 400 kilometers southwest of Tamanrasset, was the last French fort, the last petrol, the final outpost of civilization. The caravan route continued on from Tessalit, southwest. Drums of petrol were dumped along the ancient route at strategic intervals where the long distance trucks, Berliets and Peugeots that had roamed the desert for almost ten years now, could refuel. Each petrol dump was colorfully named Can No. 1, Can No. 2, etc.

The midpoint in this bitter expanse of sand, wind and heat was Bidon-Cinq. Can No. 5 boasted a perpetually full windsock beside an airstrip and a skeletal lighthouse from which a self-turning beacon was visible for over a hundred kilometers. From either the north or south the approach to this sanctuary was a particularly forbidding stretch of desert where unwary travelers were most likely to stray from the rudimentary road and become disoriented in the vastness and heat. Before succumbing to dehydration and exposure, they would finish the water from their Jerri cans, drink their radiator water and finally, in desperation, their gasoline, and die in the shade of their Citroëns and Renaults, their bodies desiccating and mummifying or served up as a providential feast for a lucky jackal. The lighthouse improved the odds tremendously, and like sailors on a pitiless ocean, those daring to cross the Tanezrouft sought the flickering guide of Bidon Cinq.

The proprietor of Bidon Cinq changed frequently – no one could suffer the isolation and blistering heat for long. At least two had had to be taken away, driven mad by the constant stinging wind. Another simply wandered off into the geographic nothingness and was never seen again.

"I must return to Paris," Puck said, "where I am living with a good friend. Cable me there when this task is complete. His name is Bill Freier, and his address," he stuffed a paper into Ernst's breast pocket, "Rue d'Alsace."

The narrow alley returned them to the souq's main square. At a dusty well several Tuareg women pumped water into rubber bags and clay pots. They laughed and joked. A donkey with empty saddlebags and a white muzzle swayed his head and swished his tail to dislodge flies.

Ernst dismissed his doubts. He certainly had no more loyalty to Germany, and he despised the Nazi regime. He thought of Dante again and this circle of Hell. Hans Gerd would condemn him as a traitor. Leo and his mother would at the very least be mortified and saddened by his betrayal. Lisa – he had no way of knowing anything about Lisa. She was a mirage, a memory, a ghost.

Redemption? Puck used that enigmatic word when they last met. What exactly did any of this have to do with redemption? Absolution for his crimes – all his crimes, all the killing he had perpetrated to advance the Nazi cause – the assassination of Rathenau being certainly the most notable. Had not Frau Rathenau already forgiven him? What were her conditions? Confess before an earthly judge, repent before the court of Heaven. It was bewildering then, when he first heard the letter read in court. Now it was simply mysterious, even benign. An unfamiliar kind of blessing. He kept her letter in his leather pouch because it was powerful, and up until now, easy to carry.

What Puck required of him was not redemption; it was murder, pure and simple. There was no question it had to be done, quickly, quietly. Necessary, but hardly redemptive.

Necessary murders were elementary in the desert.

★   ★   ★   ★   ★   ★   ★   ★   ★   ★

There was no time to lose. Ernst sought a German speaking driver, a refugee whose background guaranteed an extreme dislike for the Third Reich. As he read the roster of new recruits one name sprung from the page – Wilhelm Rathenau.

Legionnaire Rathenau was relieved from the Arak road crew, and Ernst queried him about his past. He found him suitable for the mission. He could have chosen any number of recruits as a driver, but Ernst felt an amorphous temptation, almost compulsion, to choose this one. He could see right away the family resemblance. A handsome young man, clear eyed and eager, he sported the same mustache and goatee that Ernst saw in his nightmares – Foreign Minister Rathenau, as the murder car drew abreast, smiling at him, touching his cane to his hat on Königsallee seventeen years ago.

Ernst and Legionnaire Rathenau left immediately and drove southwest, through the Tanezrouft in the day's heat. As Rathenau drove over the rutted road south from Tamanrasset, Ernst cleaned his Lebel and tried to ignore the awkward silence between juvenile recruit and hardened Commandant. They pounded over the rough caravan track towards Bidon Cinq in a Foreign Legion Renault with two steel tracks strapped to the roof, each three meters long. Not only did the tread provide shade over the windscreen, but when they became mired in fesh-fesh, what Saharans called shifting sand, they would dig, roll ten feet on the tread, then dig again. It was the way of the Sahara.

After driving for an hour, Rathenau volunteered that he was glad for the chance to trade his pick axe for the steering wheel and an adventure. He had to almost shout to be heard over the road-noise and the air blowing through the windows.

"This is not an adventure," Ernst admonished as the Hoggar mountain range receded behind them. "It is a military mission; there may be danger involved."

Several hours further into the Tanezrouft, when all recognizable landmarks had disappeared in haze, when they were deep into the Ténéré, the nothingness, Ernst turned to Rathenau, and though he knew the answer, he asked in a loud and unnatural voice, "Are you by chance a relative of the late German statesman?"

"He was my uncle, Sir," he answered, his doe eyes unmoved from the road.

After another lapse, Ernst said loudly. "Rathenau, I have to tell you something. I am one of the assassins of your uncle."

Rathenau braked hard. The Renault side-slipped and skidded to a stop, and the engine stalled. He looked at Ernst, brow furrowed. It was silent and he could speak normally. "I beg your pardon, Mon Commandant?"

"I was one of the three men who killed your uncle on June 24, 1922, on the Königsallee in Berlin. In Germany my name was Ernst Werner Techow."

Ernst was astounded at his words, as if he had just listened to someone else deliver them. Though he had thought it possible, it was not his intention to have this conversation. But he could not stop his tongue.

Rathenau's brow furrowed and he looked suddenly pale, as though he might vomit. Ernst reached into his document case for Frau Rathenau's yellowed letter. He held it reverently, carefully, as if he might crush it, or it might be blown away in a breeze. He offered it to the stunned young man.

Rathenau unfolded the brittle yellowed paper. He read his grandmother's words for the first time and read them again, and then once more. "My family spoke of this letter often," he said, "but I've never wanted to read it. My father could not understand how my Oma could write such a thing. He called you a monster." The radio antenna vibrated in the wind.

Ernst had to turn away from Rathenau's glare. Beyond their steel cage, through the dusty wind screen, the Tanezrouft was everything and nothing.

"Why did you choose me, Sir?"

"Because I know exactly why you are here. Your name is Rathenau. You are a Jew, you fled Germany." Rathenau refused Ernst's proffered cigarette; Ernst lit it for himself.

Rathenau's hand suddenly, impulsively, moved to his leather holster cover.

"Go ahead," Ernst said. "You would relieve me of my burden."

The catch of the holster was already undone, but his hand lay still. Ernst felt strangely calm; he sat back and drew long on his Gauloise.

"You bastard! I grew up hating you."

"You have the opportunity for vengeance." Dust devils swirled in the Sirocco. "Fate seems to have brought us together. Like you, I was once a driver. It's how I got my start." Ernst felt desiccated. Hot wind blew through the Renault; fiery smoke filled his lungs. "I wish that was all that connected us. Your family has suffered mightily. I am deeply, deeply sorry. I wish with all my heart and soul that I could take back what I have done."

They sat, each with their thoughts. A fly buzzed against the windscreen glass. Rathenau stared forward, turning to look at Ernst now and again. Ernst felt lighter, as if a small stone had been removed from his heart. He hadn't planned on apologizing. He hadn't planned anything; it had just come out, perhaps because it had to.

"Legionnaire Rathenau. Continue driving." He pointed up the road.

Rathenau started the stalled engine, and the Renault continued rattling along the rock-strewn path. He drove faster, and a dust cloud expanded behind them.

There was a long period of silence as they crossed the unchanging Ténéré. After a few hours, they began to exchange small talk, as much to manage the boredom as to communicate after Ernst's revelation and apology. Small talk became more consequential as Ernst told Rathenau of Striegau, then Berlin, and escaping to France. The hum of the Renault motor propelled his recollections. Such was his relief that Ernst could not stop recounting the details as memories returned with photographic vividness. His recollections became more specific – his first day in Striegau, first month in Puck's print shop with his forgeries, each specific day of epiphany, Günther's murder. He told Rathenau Puck's stories – of losing his brother, of sitting at his father's feet while he argued Torah, Jonah and the Whale; he recounted details about his four years in Germany with Der Angriff, losing Lisa, slapping Goebbels. One story fed the next.

Rathenau interrupted. "Excuse me, Mon Commandant. But why did you do it?"

"I was young. I was angry. I felt impotent. At the time it seemed the necessary thing to do."

They lapsed into silence again. Ernst tried to reconstruct his state of mind, but all he conjured was increasing estrangement from his twenty-year-old self – shame at having inhabited that skin.

A few kilometers further Rathenau said, "You have explained about Herr Lauber. But it would be murder."

"It seems the necessary thing to do." Ernst's words came out before he could consider them. How baffling, he thought, that murder could become so ordinary, sanctioned. But war altered the verb from 'murder' to 'kill,' and it was sanitized, scrubbed of moral injunction. And every sentient being knew this to be true. He wondered at the burden all humanity shared, of holding these two opposing fundamental ideas in their heads and sometimes in their hearts.

They rolled out their sleeping mats under a star-strewn sky. On the distant horizon, bright as a planet, he could just make out the blinking lighthouse at Bidon Cinq. Ernst explained the connections between their two families – the Techows and the Rathenaus, the friendship between his father and Minister Rathenau's father, his visits to Ernst's childhood home on Wannseestrasse. Under the star-strewn sky this too, felt like a confession.

"But you see, Rathenau," Ernst continued as they warmed their hands over hot coals. "Of what little remains for me, my most precious possession – and my heaviest burden – is your grandmother's letter. For many years I simply could not understand it. I'm not sure why I didn't discard it. But there was something mysterious and animated about the letter, like a warning sign, a 'do not disturb' sign. I read it again in Striegau under the mentorship of Puck, that funny little man I told you about. The combination of the letter and Puck's wisdom opened a new world to me. In Striegau I began to read the works of your uncle, one after the other. Later, in the Legion, I studied the Jewish faith. I learned Hebrew in Syria. I have long known how the Nazis had lied about the Jews to rationalize their excesses, yet not even my family could see that. I know how strong Nazi barbarian impulses are, as I too, was once possessed of them. For eighteen years my life has been a struggle to suppress the evil in my soul. I have struggled to understand your grandmother's words to my mother – to be worthy of her pardon. Just as she conquered her anguish when she wrote this letter, I have tried to master myself... and I have failed. I don't know how to be worthy of her forgiveness. I only wish I had an opportunity to right the wrong I've done. It is in that spirit that I volunteered for this mission. And it is in that spirit that I offer you, again, my apology."

Rathenau sat silently, a shadow in the dark. He dragged his sleeve across his eyes, but Ernst could not be sure if he was weeping or if it was the campfire smoke. Finally, he cleared his throat and said, "Mon Capitaine, I am at a loss for words."

Ernst felt a peculiar warmth deep inside, perhaps the cognac they shared, perhaps the dying coals. "For now there is nothing more to be said. Bury the coals."

They settled into their sleeping rolls, the silence so complete, the sky so black and huge, that it pressed down upon them.

After many more empty moments Rathenau asked if Ernst was still awake. "Mon Capitaine. Your apology – I accept it. Thank you."

★ ★ ★ ★ ★ ★ ★ ★ ★ ★

Ernst roused young Rathenau as dawn blushed the horizon. The world was still cold enough for their breath to steam, and they blew the buried coals to life to heat tea and their hands. They set out as the sun rose, and they and the desert quickly thawed then heated. They crested a small rise, and Bidon Cinq appeared through the shimmering heat waves, its orange windsock flapping like a flag. At that moment Ernst heard the first faint drone of an airplane, its motor amplified by the desolation.

Ernst brought his fist down hard on the dashboard. Rathenau swerved, then recovered the road. "Damn! They're going to leave by air! Faster, Rathenau, faster!" He watched the Fokker T-2 lose altitude as it prepared to land on the desert airstrip.

Nearly two hours later they raced into Bidon Cinq. Ernst swung out the cylinder of his Lebel and counted five rounds. The Renault raced down the road and onto the runway where the Fokker idled as it took on fuel near the dancing windsock. Herr Lauber's dust-covered Citroën and the old Peugeot stood nearby, doors and boots wide open. Canvas sacks, tied with drawstrings and heavy with rocks, were being transferred from car to plane by three foreign men in khaki. One of them was clearly the portly Herr Lauber, who grunted and wheezed, wiping his balding head frequently with a white handkerchief. Milhoud carried their suitcases from boot to luggage compartment.

Rathenau skidded to a stop near the two cars. Ernst adjusted his képi blanc and straightened his dusty uniform, then came to attention by the front fender. Herr Lauber argued in whispers with one of his two associates as they came to meet him.

Ernst saluted. "Good day, Monsieur. I am Capitaine Tessier. At your service."

"What a surprise," Herr Lauber said in stilted French, then wiped his head again. His white cotton shirt, discolored by yellow sweat stains, overflowed his belt. His cravat, pulled off to one side, but still tight, defined his brief, fleshy neck. He regularly reset thick glasses that slipped down his glistening nose. Ernst ignored the hand extended in greeting. "Seeing anyone out here," Herr Lauber said. "It's quite unexpected."

"And you are...?"

"Professor Lauber, and these are my associates." He produced his identity papers, transit and exit visa. "All properly stamped and in order."

"What is your cargo?"

"Samples of ore. I am a geologist at the Kaiser Wilhelm Institute in Berlin." Ernst looked up in time to see the caretaker finish fueling the Fokker and pocket a generous gratuity. The pilot gunned one engine, then the other.

"Is the ore high grade, Herr Lauber?"

"Well," he stammered, "it's... it's really quite technical and somewhat arcane, but yes, I am very pleased with the samples. Now, if you will excuse me, we are already quite late in leaving. Our pilot is eager..."

"Herr Lauber. You found quite a lot of Uranium in Gao, didn't you?"

Herr Lauber lost his composure for a moment, then smiled. "You know more than most Legionnaires, Herr... Messier?"

"Tessier. I'm afraid it will be impossible for you to leave just yet."

"But Monsieur Capitaine. I must protest. We are honest citizens of the Third Reich. It will create quite a diplomatic tempest if you interfere with our passage."

Ernst produced a forged letter. "This warrant is from the Prefecture of Police in Oran requesting your detention for now." He offered it to Herr Lauber.

One of Lauber's 'students' advised him in German to "ignore this shithead. It is time to go." Ernst did not evince understanding, but stood at attention as did Rathenau at the driver's door. The attendant returned from the petrol shed with a clipboard and an invoice that flapped in the wind. The loyal sirocco blew sand across the dirt runway only to have it swirled up and swept back by the exhaust of the two Fokker engines. The pilot tested ailerons, flaps and rudder in preparation for take off.

"I am sorry to delay you, but in the desert..." Ernst reached for his Lebel.

Suddenly one of Herr Lauber's companions flanked Ernst, his revolver already drawn. Herr Lauber sighed and produced his own Luger. The third man continued to load the last bags into the airplane and stood at the door to the passenger compartment. He waved and called to them over the roar of the engines. Slowly, the monoplane began to taxi forward.

Ernst felt his pulse quicken; acid fear seethed up from his stomach, but he hardly moved. "Now it is you who will create the international incident. It is a serious offense to harm a Legionnaire. The Prefecture knows I am here serving this warrant."

"Your pistols, please." Herr Lauber pointed with the Luger's barrel. "On the ground. Thank you."

Ernst and Rathenau dropped their ancient Lebels on the dirt, and Herr Lauber's associate retrieved them. He directed the two Legionnaires, Milhoud and the caretaker, to sit on the bench in the shade of the caretaker's tent.

"My associate has already removed your field radio from inside and we will, of course, take your pistols. By the time you return to Tamanrasset we will be long gone. Your story will sound fantastic, but," he wiped his head with a limp handkerchief, "hardly an international incident." He sniggered and backed away, then laughed out loud. "Perhaps you will be court-martialed for diverting pistols and radios to the black market."

Herr Lauber jammed his Lugar into his belt, then ran as fast as his stout legs would carry him to the taxiing aircraft, its engines throttled up, gray exhaust and heat blasting from its engines.

As he closed the door the engines roared, blasting dust and exhaust. The plane fish-tailed as it gathered speed and finally straightened.

The Tuareg caretaker was already counting his gratuity, implacable behind his litham and desert trousers. Ernst tore off the man's head scarf and ordered Rathenau to the car. He jumped into the back seat of the Renault as the motor roared to life.

"Catch them!" Ernst yelled over the roar of the Fokker. He spun the Tuareg's desert shroud into a long thin roll and laid it at his feet.

"Shall we throw rocks at them?" Rathenau said as the Renault gained on the Fokker.

"In a manner of speaking, yes. You just catch them. Faster, dammit. Faster!"

The distance between the car and the plane shortened as the powerful Renault engine carried them forward. Ernst could see the approaching rocks and debris at the end of the runway. The Fokker gathered speed as the Renault drew closer, almost abreast of the tail wheel. For a brief moment Ernst saw Herr Lauber turn to him at the passenger's window and wipe his head. The nose of the Fokker jerked up slightly, its engines screaming at full throttle.

Ernst aimed the flare gun that each Legion vehicle carried and fired. The flare rocketed over the wing and smashed against the pilot's window. It ignited and burned for a moment then fell away. He could not be sure if he heard the shriek of the pilot being burned with white-hot phosphorous over the scream of the engines, but the airplane's nose lifted steadily. Two wheels left the ground and it was airborne, drawing away from them.

"The runway is ending!" Rathenau screamed.

"Faster! Faster!" Ernst reached under the seat cushion for the hand grenade he kept hidden there and pulled the pin with his teeth. He dropped it into the rolled up Litham and leaned out the window counting slowly to himself. For a moment he thought of the pigeons outside Mariakirche and his slingshot. The Fokker moved quickly away from the Renault in a steep climb. On his third count Ernst catapulted the sling, hurling the grenade over the plane's left wing.

The explosion occurred just above the left engine, shattering the propeller. The engine spluttered, then sparked and black smoke exhaust turned to flame. The steeply climbing airplane slowly rolled left. The pilot tried to feather the remaining engine but there was insufficient air speed or lift and the Fokker continued to bank and slowly settle. The left wingtip caught the ground first and cartwheeled the plane once before it exploded in a brilliant orange ball.

The moment Ernst released the grenade, the Renault's front tires hit gravel and debris at the end of the runway, and its speed suddenly fell by half. Momentum threw Ernst against the front seat and bounced him back and forth inside. He heard the tires explode one after another; there was a flash and a shock wave, and immediately a deafening roar. He thought the Renault had exploded. Intense heat seared him for a moment, rolled over him and threatened his consciousness. Rathenau yelled something incomprehensible in German. A moment later the car clattered to an abrupt halt, the engine stalled, and steam billowed from under the bonnet.

Ernst slowly recovered from a crashed position on the floor to the back seat. Focus slowly returned, and he recognized Rathenau lying across the steering wheel, blood running down his face. He sat dazed and wondered, is Rathenau dead? Did I kill him too? A far away hum grew suddenly loud, and he realized it was their own blaring auto-horn, and he was back at Bidon Cinq. A moment later, another flash of light was followed immediately by a blast wave as the Fokker's spare fuel tank exploded.

Ernst eased the groaning Rathenau back from the wheel, and the horn stopped. His scalp bled freely from somewhere over his eye, his face awash in blood. His goggles had fallen around his nose and mouth. Ernst pulled them down around his neck, and Rathenau started to rouse. The burning Fokker crackled like kindling. The attendant and Milhoud ran towards them with easy loping strides. As far as they are concerned, Ernst thought, Insh'Allah, so why hurry?

Rathenau seemed free of other injuries and, with Ernst's arm around him, the two walked back down the runway, Rathenau leaning against him. Ernst looked over his shoulder at the burning pyre that was once a Fokker T-2 with enough fuel to fly non-stop to Oran.

Except for the flapping of a sirocco-full windsock, stillness returned to strange and lonely Bidon Cinq. Four men walked down the runway, behind them the smoking remains of an aircraft, its landing gear up in the air like a dead crow.

Ernst gave the caretaker, a distant relative of Moulay Bassim, a generous second gratuity to corroborate Ernst and Rathenau's account of the tragic crash and explosion of Herr Lauber's airplane. Ernst's report noted a brisk sirocco, that day, adding to the hazard. He had warned Herr Lauber to delay, but he would not. Milhoud, who had driven the men (he called them 'the condemned') from Gao to Bidon Cinq, remembered to tell the authorities, French and German, that Herr Lauber was despondent because his mission in Gao had been unsuccessful, though he did not elaborate on the nature of that mission.

The officials seemed satisfied, and the matter was quickly closed. The Germans seemed pre-occupied when Ernst made his official report in In-Salah, and only later, in the café of the Hotel Imperial, as he finished his second whiskey, did he hear the news of the German invasion of Poland. All diplomatic personnel were recalled home for consultation. Though they were all "civilians," merchants and engineers, most of the Hotel Imperial's guests left within a day. The tragedy at Bidon Cinq was left to the Algerian authorities to sort out.

* * * * * * * * * *

Within days of the German invasion of Poland on September 1, 1939, Britain and France were officially at war with the Third Reich. For the next six months a "Twilight War" simmered as each side maneuvered for position and considered their next gambit on the European chessboard. Ernst received urgent orders redeploying most of his unit to Legion HQ in Algeria at Sidi-bel-Abbès for training. A small detachment of Legionnaires, mostly Spanish expatriates from the Fascist war in Spain whose command of French was still primitive, would remain to defend Fort Flatters. Ernst's great disappointment was that the Trans-Sahara road still ended in the Arak, three hundred kilometers short of Tamanrasset.

The next morning, Monday, September fourth, Ernst was surprised to find Puck at the Hotel. He sat at the bar where a short-wave radio crackled BBC coverage of the Polish invasion and the British and French declarations of war.

Ernst clapped him on the back, and Puck smiled when he turned and recognized him.

"I was going to look you up," Puck said. "You've saved me the trouble." They embraced, and the Tuareg stared.

"What are you doing here?" Ernst asked.

He winked at Ernst. "I have business with Moulay Bassim."

An excited reporter interrupted the droning radio announcer:

"The British liner Athenia, with some 1,400 passengers, has been torpedoed and sunk 200 miles west of the Hebrides en route from Liverpool to Montreal. Rescue efforts are continuing. Great loss of life is feared."

The few other Europeans in the lounge collectively gasped and clustered together, bonded by the radio's electromagnetism and the curious community galvanized by disaster. The Tuareg hotel workers gathered in their own flock, as if they sensed that the Colonials' European cesspool would overflow and inundate even the Sahara.

"Come Ernst, let us sit on the veranda. It's a bit more private." Puck led him to a warped table with a vista overlooking the Tanezrouft. To their right, the souq still seemed unchanged, untouched by the news from over the sea.

"I heard of your re-deployment," Puck said. "After I conclude my business with Bassim, I must hurry back to France. I may not see you for some time. The chaos of war makes everything uncertain and difficult. You can still reach me at Bill Freier's, in Paris. It may take some time, but I will respond."

Ernst saw a tear glisten in Puck's eye and felt the joy of their reunion chilled by gloom. He felt an unanticipated sensation of foreboding, of superstition. He wanted to say how much he loved Puck, but other words came out. "There's something I must know, Puck – before you go. A week ago, at your request, I killed four men at Bidon Cinq. Am I still nothing more than an assassin?"

Somewhere in the souq a Tuareg woman called in Tamashek for her children. Puck laid his hand on Ernst's shoulder and looked into his eyes. "You have a burden, Ernst. You have carried it for almost twenty years. Last week you added to and subtracted from that burden. All of us carry burdens – and we have only flawed choices. You are no more, no less, an assassin than a saint."

Ernst unbuttoned the collar of his tunic. "That doesn't help. I want to be rid of it. I want the ordinary cares of ordinary men."

Puck's gaze remained steady. "My grandmother, may she rest in peace, used to say in Yiddish, *As mi laght di tsuris offin tish, nemt men di agenin tsuris tsurick.* 'If a group of men sat down and each put their troubles on the table to exchange, when they saw those of their fellows, each would reclaim his own.'"

★ ★ ★ ★ ★ ★ ★ ★ ★ ★

On the day before the mobilization, Ernst called Rathenau into his cabin.

"At ease, Caporal Rathenau." Ernst proffered Rathenau's new bars and shook his hand. "I cannot give you a medal for your bravery at Bidon Cinq. After all you were but a witness to a tragic accident. But I can promote you – even two ranks."

Rathenau smiled tentatively. "Thank you, Mon Capitaine. It is a great honor."

Ernst saluted, then sat again at his desk and opened a folder to avoid Rathenau's eyes. "You will be remaining at Fort Flatters, Caporal Rathenau."

Rathenau's smile melted. "But, Sir, the unit is being called up. We will finally get to fight. You cannot..."

"I can do anything I damn well please, Rathenau." Ernst's eyes burned. "You will exact your revenge on the Third Reich by surviving, by having children, by championing your uncle's life and work."

"With all due respect, Sir, I joined the Legion to fight against the Nazis, not to cower in the desert and merely survive."

"This is an order, not a discussion, Caporal. You cannot refuse my gift. Dismissed!"

War fever infected Ernst, replacing his deep and persistent depression with a sense of mission, of possibility, resurrecting long dead fervor. The same passionate intensity he once knew in Kiel before the mutiny surged through him, waking dormant meaning. He remembered the Free Corps, his boyish excitement at being able "to clean house" with an inexorable sense of moral certitude, the intensity of that youthful zeal incited by vengeance for everything that had been taken from him, for every deceit. Moulay Bassim said more than once that the Sahara taught by taking things away, by threatening life itself. He often ended his philosophical musings with a caution.

"Make peace with your anguish instead of waging war."

Ernst had been a student of the Sahara for more than five years, and he was finished with its harsh lessons, felt released from the clutch of the desert. All at once he felt powerful again, felt that nothing could subvert victory. He felt released from the clutch of the desert. It was bliss and arrogance entangled with deep-rooted need. Perhaps he would feel this way if he met Lisa again, that was how powerful the impulse. His devotion to the Trans-Sahara highway paled by comparison. A surging life force came from beneath the sand, like the little yellow flowers that bloomed every twenty years, like the aquifer of water that surfaced at the oasis of Tamanrasset. Once it was the Trans-Sahara that kept suicidal thoughts at bay, now it was the prospect of war.

In November 1939, Ernst's unit embarked from Sidi-bel-Abbès for France. A sense of expectation inspired the Legionnaires and, as they packed lorries for redeployment to Barcarès, a crude solidarity amongst the various ethnic groups was in evidence. As they sailed from North Africa, Ernst stood at the stern of the troop transport watching the receding continent. Though still filled with anticipation for the coming fight, he could not ignore a premonition of disaster, the same foreboding he had felt when he last saw Puck, and that in itself was an awakening. After five years underground, that dead and defeated piece of him that he barely recognized as his soul felt fear as well as exhilaration. Bassim was right. The desert always played the last hand, always moved the Mancala stones. Everything was preordained, and any affectation of control was just that, pretense.

Waking up that first day on French soil again, in Barcarès, Ernst felt the whole pace of his life quicken, as if transfused with young blood. Sitting on the hill called Mont Sacre Couer beside the cemetery overlooking the encampment, he inhaled deeply the morning fog and suddenly realized how he had longed for rain or snow or any form that water could manifest.

After mobilization from Fort Flatters, Ernst became Capitaine to the newly created 22nd Régiments de Marche des Volontaires Étrangers (RMVE) of the 10th French Army. From November 1939 to May 1940 they trained and waited at Barcarès in Southern France to fight in the fields and forests of Europe.

It was late spring, May 1940, when Ernst returned from a twenty kilometer training march to find Lisa's letter amongst the day's dispatches. Right away he recognized her distinctive back-slanted script, and his heart palpitated with excitement.

The letter, post marked 5 March 1940, Zurich, finally arrived after a journey of two months, first to Sidi-bel-Abbès, then to Barcarès.

Dear Ernst,

Margaret posted this letter in Zurich. She said she knew someone who knew where to find you in Algeria. She's so clever.

Since Leo was mobilized into the Wehrmacht I haven't known how to get a letter to you. Fritz has isolated me. It's his revenge. I try to live day to day. I am surrounded by Fritz's friends who are so excited by Hitler's progress. Everyone feels as if Germany's honor has been restored. It is a difficult tide to swim against, so I float and try to keep my head above water. I really don't know what to think anymore. I only know that I hate my life here.

I am watched all the time. Fritz seems intent on making me as miserable as possible – a form of house arrest, not unlike what my father did. Good days are barely tolerable – on others I sit in a daze, immobilized. On bad days I think of poison.

You remember Margaret, of course. She's divorced. Her only child died of pleurisy as an infant. One day she just appeared at our house – a very dramatic entry, as only Margaret can do. She wore a very tight dress with too much bosom and charmed Fritz anew as we relived old days in Halle and Berlin. I so felt your absence.

Margaret later told me that she is the mistress of Assistant Finance Minister von Greuning. So much more exciting than marriage, she said. She took me to the Französische Café and we caught up on fifteen years. How can that be? There is no one I can talk to honestly, no one I can call a trusted friend and confidant, so by the time I finished my story I was in tears.

Why am I writing now, after almost two years? I had all but despaired of anything changing until Margaret said there still are ways out. These were her first words when we sat down alone at the café. She could tell, from the very first moment, that I was unhappy, resigned to my fate. She said she still saw a light in my eyes – dim, but still burning.

I trust Margaret. There is no one else. Isolation is a helpless feeling, frightening. All the more remarkable that Margaret has returned to my life, like a guardian angel, when I need her the most. After our first lunch, Margaret reassured me about this letter – that she would post it in Switzerland. I feel as if I have sealed a message in a bottle and thrown it into the sea hoping it would find you.

In any case, I have decided to escape. Adi is the only reason I stayed five years ago and he has no use for me now. He seems angry with me all the time. He secretly smokes cigarettes. I smell it on his uniform. His life is the Hitler Jugend – nothing else matters. He is Fritz's boy. He adores his father and is fascinated by guns. That wasn't supposed to happen. My boy was to learn music and love literature.

What I feel is despair, and all I have to counter it is pain. I prick needles into my flesh again. When I am alone I sometimes cut the inside of my leg with a needle – just to feel something.

The only thing that has kept me here is fear, but now I have Margaret's help. I don't feel so afraid or alone.

The borders have been sealed and escape is hazardous. Fritz has made it clear that if I attempt to flee he will track me down "like a common dog."

Margaret met "a funny little man who quotes the Hebrew sages" who has promised to help me escape. I don't know how much she paid him, but she has more money than she knows what to do with. She trusts this funny little man and so must I. Over the next few months Margaret will put me in touch with someone who can escort me over the border in the spring. She alluded to contacts, 'safe houses,' 'drop-offs.' As I said before, Margaret loves a good intrigue.

If I am successful I will go to Marseille where, apparently, I have a cousin, Gabriele. It seems an impossible dream, but I would rather die trying to flee than live a life in death. I don't even know if you will receive this letter, but if you do, and if we both survive (how strange to write that), meet me in Marseille, at Eglise St-Laurent, a small romanesque church on the old quay, opposite the Legion Fort St. Jean at sunrise. I will wait there the first Sunday of each month, the way Leo met me at church and we exchanged letters. I will wait for you there on Sunday – the first Sunday – sunrise. Be there, Ernst!

Not a day goes by that I do not relive the last time we were together. I can almost feel the train ticket and my new identity papers — Elsie Hoffmann. I have made many mistakes in my life. That one I grieve the most.

Do you recall the Cabaret song "Peter, Peter"? You, I, and Fritz heard it that night so long ago, at the Megalomania Club, before our dreams became nightmares.

Peter, Peter, may I have this dance
Peter, Peter, give me one more chance
Peter, Peter, tell me what to do
Peter, Peter, I'm still in love with you.

Sur le Vieux Quay — en Port de Marseille
Much Love, Your Lisa

Ernst bundled Lisa's letter with Frau Rathenau's and felt as if they complemented each other. One only had meaning because of the other, and Ernst felt suspended in a temporary state of grace between the enigmatic gravity of Frau Rathenau's forgiveness and the soaring possibility of sunrise in Marseille.

★ ★ ★ ★ ★ ★ ★ ★ ★ ★

After the German Blitzkrieg into Belgium and Holland, the 22nd RMVE left Barcarès precipitously on May 6th for the Alsace sector. So rapid was the German mechanized advance, supported by the virtually unopposed Luftwaffe, that every available French unit was thrown into the fight. Legionnaires jammed into railcars and army trucks, then marched for six days to take up positions on the Somme River as part of the 10th French Army, facing overwhelming German forces.

On the road north the Legionnaires marched against the current of refugees streaming towards Paris. An occasional automobile sped south, down the center of the dirt road, its horn blaring importance, but most refugees walked without noticing.

The refugees carried what little they could with the vacant look of castaways, most still astounded that their world could collapse so quickly and completely. In a wheelbarrow pushed by an old man with a grizzled beard, a crying baby flailed in a goose down quilt nest. The child's mother, milk stains around each breast, pushed a perambulator piled taller than she with books, clothing, an end table lashed with rope. It swayed precariously on four white rubber wheels.

An old farm horse, gray muzzled head bent low, its sway back yoked to a wagon, trudged beside its master, whose creased face seemed no longer capable of emotion. Though it was neither raining nor hot, an older woman dressed in peasant black held an umbrella and pulled a child's wagon. By the third day the Legionnaire's nervous jokes were used up and their small talk dwindled, until only the most shameless spoke.

Ernst struggled against the impulse to think of Leo as part of the German Blitz. Once again the brothers were on opposite sides of the barricades, a long way from Kiel, from the *Vorwärts*, from Wannseestrasse and the line down the center of their bedroom.

The first Stuka dive bomber attack came on that third day, out of a sky half full with cottonball clouds. It began as no more than a distant buzz, but it grew rapidly. The refugees, who had heard this before, looked up as one and abandoned the road; the mother with milk stains grabbed her crying baby as if it were a sack of onions. The old horse just stopped, appreciative of the respite, and hung its head lower, suddenly alone on the road. Ernst's unit took up positions in the line of oak and cypress along the shoulder. The buzz crescendoed into a shriek, and from the roadside foliage, Ernst wondered that so demonic a sound came from something small as a sparrow, angular wings delicate as a dragonfly's. The Stuka swooped low and released two bombs that whistled. The ground shook with two deafening explosions. Another Stuka, a wailing twin, followed the first, spitting bullets, a double line racing up the road like an army of demons, in perfect marching order.

There was little panic. The civilians watched with numbed, perhaps resigned dismay. A woman in a dark dress and white crocheted cap gathered her two children near her; an old man who had lost his cane was steadied by two women.

At first Ernst could see no casualties, and the weary refugees reassembled and resumed their dirge-like procession. Then he noticed the wagon was still and refugees flowed around it like river water around a boulder. The horse lay in the dust, several bullet wounds in its flank, but still breathing, trying to raise its head, issuing an anguished sound, part moan, part wheeze. A Legionnaire crossed the road, his revolver already drawn, and delivered the coup de grace. Ernst helped him cut the horse free and the old man, who had probably worked his fields with this horse since it was a sprightly colt, took its place under the yoke. His arms straddling each pole, his gray stubbled head hanging low, he leaned his sway back into the load. Another man pushed from behind, and the wagon creaked and joined the retreat. Only the babies and the goats cried.

★ ★ ★ ★ ★ ★ ★ ★ ★ ★

Four weeks later, Ernst trudged south along with the refugees and wondered why he was one of the few to survive. It had been a suicidal mission – to stop the juggernaut German advance with nothing more than Great War vintage rifles, mortars, anti-tank guns, and a few machine guns. Their mortars lacked sights and had to be aimed with a weight on the end of a string; his men had only trained once with 25 mm antitank guns. For more than three weeks they had fought valiantly and still held their sector at Villers-Carbonnel near Marchèlepot. Was it June 5th or 6th when all order had broken down – when the chaos of battle made a mockery of military sense? That was when the French Lieutenant came.

Ernst could only remember the French officer's pallor and how his hands shook as he stepped down from the German command car with the white flag tied to its radio antenna. In a halting voice he explained how his car had been ambushed and he himself captured while en route to Legion Headquarters. Now he stood before the Commandant and said, "My captors have instructed me to tell you that either the 22nd surrenders," his voice strained and he cleared his throat, "or 300 prisoners will be shot."

Lieutenant-Colonel Faunier had saluted the Lieutenant and said, with only a moment's hesitation, "We are a regiment that knows how to faire Camerone! Vive la mort! We will never surrender."

The captive Lieutenant snapped to attention, a crisp but still trembling hand at the brim of his képi blanc. "Oui, Mon Commandant." Ernst thought he smiled as the German driver backed away from the cellar of the chateau of Fresnes-Mazancourt, now the regimental command post.

An hour later the German line erupted with artillery, tanks, mortars, heavy machine guns and a sea of infantry. Lieutenant-Colonel Faunier ordered the retreat just as the Panzers overran Ernst's position. Many of his men lay dead or dying. A few had committed suicide rather than be captured by the Germans. Ernst spent his last rounds and threw his last grenade. Both French antitank guns were long silent. He had seen Ullmann blown apart after a shell demolished the barn he fired from. Ullmann had taught him the first lines of the Jewish prayer for the dead, the Mourner's Kaddish, the prayer that never mentioned death. Ernst mumbled the words to honor him.

What was the use of it? He wondered how many Sunday mornings in Marseille would go by before Lisa learned of his death. Ernst fumbled in his pocket for his last .38 cartridge, the one he saved for himself, and loaded his Lebel. Before Lisa's letter, when he had put that bullet aside, he thought it would not be difficult to use, but now his hand shook.

His last memory was a blinding light and a concussion knocking the wind from him. When he regained consciousness he lay in a debris-strewn cellar hole looking up at a smoke stained sky. Distant artillery percussed in his ears, but his hearing was muffled. He crawled up a splintered staircase and crouched behind the remains of a stone foundation. He watched the smoldering remnants of Villers-Carbonnel for any sign of life. Two sparrows bickered in a maimed oak that had lost half its trunk.

The hum of an automobile engine gradually swelled until the sparrows fled and an open German Staff car with only a driver turned the rubble littered corner and tried to pass a smoking Panzer. The car swerved off the road and bogged down in mud and debris, its rear tires spinning uselessly. The driver turned off the engine and circled the disabled automobile, shaking his head; finally he swore and kicked a tire.

Ernst called to him in perfect German, "Corporal! Come immediately! Help me with a wounded officer."

The driver swore again and abandoned his vehicle. As the Corporal peered over the crumbled wall Ernst fired his last bullet into the driver's forehead and he slumped onto the rubble. Ernst dragged the body into the cellar and changed into his Wehrmacht uniform, stuffing his Legion identity papers into one boot, the two letters in the other. The Corporal was a smaller man, and his trousers chafed as Ernst sprinted for the staff car.

Perhaps it was the concussion and loss of consciousness that cleared his suicidal intent. He was alone, alive, unhurt. Lisa. Her voice, her hair, the feel of her lips – that was all he could remember, all he could consider. It was not hopefulness, or even intent, but a force like destiny that gripped his attention. He would find a way to Marseille – find a way to Lisa.

What brought him back to the moment was how tightly his disguise fit, the dead man's medals, the enemy's epaulettes.

Freeing vehicles from desert sand was infinitely more difficult than rocking the mired staff car from the mud. Ernst drove south, eventually catching up with the leading edge of the Blitz. He wove in and out of a column of Panzers and infantry, leaning on his horn and shouting in German to clear the road. A few kilometers past the knife-edge of the Panzer attack the engine sputtered and died, the fuel gauge on empty. Ernst abandoned the car and melted into the woods. His Wehrmacht uniform would not protect him now. Just off the main road he stumbled over the body of a dead farmer and took the blood-stained clothes – his next disguise. He kept his own mud caked boots and marveled that they had ever been called pied noir by the Algerians. How had Puck put it? Wear your disguise as long as it fits.

It was only the thought of Lisa that drove him on. He repeated Bill Freier's Paris address to himself as if it were a mantra. Crossing a field of barley and wheat he came upon a deserted farmhouse where he found the remains of a sack of flour in the barn. The family cow had died in her stall, unmilked for days, her carcass bloated and foul, covered with flies. How close he had come to the non-being of the cow, released from the pain of life. Death only smelled rancid for the living.

The next day the advance columns of the Blitz overtook the refugees Ernst walked amongst: the stragglers, the old and infirm who could not believe that their world was finished. To resemble them he had learned to slouch, and pulled the dead man's cap low over his forehead. He mumbled through his new beard to other refugees, seeking direction, but it was only partially an act. Now he also felt the shame of surviving and fleeing the battle, a disgrace that weighed heavily. The smell of smoke, cordite and blood taunted him.

That night, Ernst slipped into a wooded area where he kindled a small, smokeless fire in a pit of sandy soil. When the embers were hot he made a dough of the flour in his sack with muddy water from a rivulet and baked the tagela the way Bassim had taught him. His hunger temporarily slaked, he lay down, exhausted. He remembered the Sahara, longed to return to the brutal simplicity of the desert, the denial and forgetfulness that fogged and soothed his mind like opium, the predictable constancy of the Sirocco. He slept for a few restive hours.

Before dawn he rejoined the funereal column of refugees moving south. Towards noon he noticed a motorcycle moving slowly down the refugee column with a German officer in the side car scanning the line of refugees. Ernst slowed his walk and edged towards the woods at the side of the road. A young woman, a dark eyed beauty whose black hair hung in clumped strands, her delicate skin still radiant under sweat and dirt, caught his arm.

"You have reason to fear les Boches?" She pushed a package into his hands, bread and cheese wrapped in an old copy of Le Monde. "Anyone who is afraid of les Boches is a friend of France. There is a dirt road several kilometers due west of here. Stay with it until you get to Franceur, then you are already in the suburbs of Paris."

He stammered his thanks, spellbound by her dark brown eyes and the way she coyly tipped her head.

"I don't even know your name... I mean, I want to thank you."

"I am Marie...Marie Bonvoleur." She looked up the line at the German checkpoint. "Monsieur, you must hurry. I have seen them shoot people only on suspicion. Go! Bon Chance. God be with you."

★　★　★　★　★　★　★　★　★　★

After walking two more days, Ernst arrived at Bill Freier's flat as first light stained Paris. These final twelve hours he had lurched along, one foot before another, following the light atop the Eiffel Tower as if it were the beacon from Bidon Cinq.

Paris's streets bustled and droned with the commotion and chaos of flight. Two men argued on the corner of Rue d'Alsace, their hands flying, their faces red. Artillery shells, German 88's, resounded in the distance. An automobile packed tight, a mattress and chest of drawers lashed onto its roof, drove too fast through the street.

He crossed Rue d'Alsace in the ghostly light and checked the address again under the streetlamp before passing through the gate into the courtyard. Shadows silhouetted across several windows.

After Ernst's third knock Bill Freier opened the door a crack. He was still in his bed clothes,

"I'm a friend of Puck," Ernst said.

"Tessier?"

Ernst nodded, and a moment later the chain came down, and the door opened again. "Come in." Freier looked up and down the hallway behind Ernst, then locked and chained the door again. The small garret was being dismantled, stripped almost bare. Two suitcases stood near the door, and a rucksack hung open, probably for the coffee pot on the stove. "Puck said I might expect you."

Ernst smiled as he remembered Puck's description of Freier. "A small dark man with coal eyes and a large head covered with unruly black curls. He looks like an adolescent." Freier's Viennese accent was unexpected.

He served Ernst stale bread and jam, which Ernst devoured with gusto. While eating he tried to recount his last few months, his last two days, but he was so tired he made no sense.

"I never thought I would live to see this day." Freier yawned and shuffled into the small kitchen where he emptied a bag of coffee into a pot and lit the gas. "France overrun by les Boches, Pétain negotiating with the Nazis – the bastard!"

"Where is Puck?"

"Marseille. He left two weeks ago."

"I too must get to Marseille, Monsieur Freier. You and Puck are the only people I know in France. It is vital."

Freier laughed. "Vital to whom? Look." He pulled back the curtains on the quickening flood of Parisian refugees. "Look out there. Everyone 'must get to Marseille.' It's the only way out of France. What is so important about you?"

Ernst began to explain about Lisa, when a German artillery round fell closer.

"The Legion is to regroup," he lied, "at Fort St-Jean in Marseille." Regroup for what, Ernst thought. The Legion is finished, and the devil take them anyway. If Lisa were dead, the final catastrophe, he would return to Tamanrasset to die, a place where this madness would have no meaning. He would rather lose his life in the perennial desert than be a victim of the madness of 1940 Europe. It made him wonder which culture, which civilization, was more advanced. His return to the desert would be cowardly, empty, suicidal, and perhaps he had left Willi Rathenau at Fort Flatters as insurance against his return.

"You want to fight again?" Freier said. "I'm afraid you are too late. Nothing stands in the way of the Nazis. Some say they will march through the Arc de Triomphe in a day or two. As you can see, I myself am leaving." He held up the coffee pot. "Coffee? It may be quite some time before you have any more."

Exhaustion overwhelmed Ernst, and his eyes drooped shut.

"You don't even have papers, do you?" Freier said.

Ernst jerked awake. "No, no papers." The commotion from the street intensified and Ernst felt his pulse quicken. "Puck gave me your address – said you would help."

Freier unlatched one of his battered suitcases. "Puck told me all about you. He said you are a gifted forger." He laid a blank identity card on the table. "Copy that seal."

Ernst was more tired than he had ever been. He drank two cups of strong coffee and set about reproducing the seal of the Prefecture of Police of Paris.

Freier smoked one cigarette after another and watched Ernst's work. After two hours it was complete.

Freier examined his work through a 20X lens. "Remarkable."

"I need money, sleep... I haven't eaten."

Freier offered him more bread and cheese, which he wolfed down, after which he fell back on the sofa to sleep. He awoke an hour later, Freier pushing on his shoulder.

"It's time to go," Freier said. "Have another cup of coffee. Puck specifically said to help you if you ever came. He said there was something important you had to do in Marseille, but he would not say what that was."

Ernst rubbed sleep from his eyes but could not imagine what Puck meant.

"You'll come with me. I have already arranged my passage through a series of safe houses. You see, I am already wanted by the Nazis for my cartoons and soon enough, I will be wanted by Pétain's collaborationists."

Freier shook him again. "Here are your papers. I finished them while you slept. You are Ernest Toussaint, a dock-worker in Marseille. Grab that suitcase – it's time to go. The others are waiting."

Ernst's eyelids grew heavy again. "Bikher, al-Hamdu lillah."

"French, Toussaint, French."

21

Marseille

June – August, 1940

L ong before the Germans occupied Paris, the banks had closed. Ernst's carefully stashed French account, now in a shuttered Paris bank, was frozen and he was penniless.

"Not to worry," Bill Freier said. "We have the most valuable asset of all – reputations as master forgers. I assure you, we won't go hungry."

French resistance crumbled daily against the German Blitz, and there was little doubt that all of France would fall in short order. In their two days together before leaving Paris, Freier filled Ernst's head with speculation and hearsay about Marseille – the city of hope, the city of rumor – from which escape, though difficult, was still possible.

"I have it on good authority," Freier said, as he and Ernst left his apartment for the last time, "that in Marseille everything is for sale, with the proper connections or tangibles – jewelry, furs, foreign exchange, gold." Freier began to lock the door, then laughed at his futile gesture and left the key in the lock. "I'd hate for les Boches to break down my door."

Freier was at least a head shorter, and Ernst had to remind himself that he was with an adult, not an adolescent. He learned to assess the little Austrian's anxiety by how much he talked; the more nervous he became, the more he talked about food. As they reached the teeming street, everyone alert to a worrisome barrage of German 88's concussing the suburbs, Freier described how his mother fried chicken skin into crisp Grieben. Ernst stopped at a pissotière and Freier complained about missing breakfast, then continued his saga, 'How I Met my beloved Mina.' As he tended to his business, Ernst watched Freier's little shoes under the metal barrier, pacing as close to the street latrine as he could get, and he was temped to tell him to shut up. When Ernst came out, Freier told him again about the warning his editor had passed along about the Gestapo list his name was on. "For treason," he said.

"Can you imagine that? My cartoons undermining the Nazi empire? It's too bizarre. Are you sure you still want to accompany me? I would understand."

A few blocks and a dissertation on linzertorte later, Freier came around to Marseille again. "A clever person, or more to the point, a rich person, can still obtain a visa for Portugal, Oran, or Casablanca. A king's ransom may get you to Cuba. One can flee over the Pyrenees with the proper guides. You're not rich, Ernest, or whoever you are. But you are clever. That much Puck has told me and you have demonstrated."

"Is that why you are helping me? For Puck?"

Freier set a fast pace, to match that of their fellow Parisiens. "Puck is not much help to us now. And my help is neither free nor without risk, more collaboration than aid." Each carried a valise, and Freier had a rucksack on his shoulders as well. "Throwing your lot in with me may not be the wisest strategy."

"I'm afraid it's my only strategy. I no longer believe in miracles, Monsieur Freier, I depend on them." Ernst wondered if Hans Gerd had a Gestapo list with Bill Freier's name on it. Maybe he had a list with Ernst's name on it. His mother, Hans Gerd, and Leo, they would win this short, brutal war and then what? Did they even think of him? Did they wonder if he was alive or dead? Did his treason condemn him in their eyes as well as those of the Gestapo? "I've been wanted by the Gestapo for years, Monsieur Freier. Or should I say Herr Freier? It's hard to know who we are anymore. Now I am Toussaint, a Marseille dock worker. This is my third name, my third identity card. Perhaps more accurately, we are nothing more than two frightened rabbits fleeing the dogs. It doesn't matter who we are, only that we get away."

★ ★ ★ ★ ★ ★ ★ ★ ★ ★

A few blocks further from his apartment an automobile idled at the curb and when they approached, the door opened, and a young man in a beret hustled them into the back seat. Once out of Paris they were passed to another automobile, from one safe house to another, from one ragtag band of leftists dreaming of resistance to another mourning the death of possibility. As they moved south there was always someone who knew Freier, and he was handled like a national treasure. At each stop they learned the details of Hitler's lightning advance through France. Several days out of Paris, the Dijon Gazette reported that on June 14th General von Kuechler's Eighteenth Army occupied the city of light. The photograph of a swastika banner hanging from the Arc de Triomphe brought tears to Freier's eyes. On the evening of June 18 in the village of La Vacherie, two families gathered around a short wave radio straining to hear the voice of exiled General Charles De Gaulle through the static of the BBC.

> "It is quite true that we were and still are, overwhelmed by enemy mechanized forces, both on the ground and in the air... Must we abandon all hope? Is our defeat final and irremediable? To those questions I answer – No!"

De Gaulle exhorted his countrymen to work for their own liberation. He reminded them that France's overseas empire was still free and that other powers, Great Britain and the United States, had not yet been brought into the fray.

> "Whatever happens, the flame of French resistance must not and shall not be extinguished."

Four days later in a mountain cabin near Chambry, Ernst and Freier's hosts, leaders of the local Socialist club, told them that Premier Reynaud had resigned and been replaced by Marshall Pétain who asked the Germans for an armistice.

A week later in Banon, a young man, not yet twenty, his beret at a jaunty angle over his clean shaven face, delivered a soiled copy of Le Monde which carried the headline "**Armistice!**" over a photograph of the clearing in the woods at Compiegne and the railroad car where Germany had been humiliated in its surrender to France on November 11, 1918. Twenty-one years later Hitler's face radiated revenge, and according to the reporter, he danced a jig.

Among the terms of the armistice was **Article 19**, which the French delegation strenuously resisted, to no avail, and which the refugees feared more than any other.

> The French government is obliged to **surrender upon demand** all Germans named by the German Government in France, as well as in French possessions, Colonies, Protectorate Territories and Mandates.

As the newspaper pointed out, "Germans" in Article 19 included all inhabitants of the Greater Reich, including Austrians, Czechs, and Poles. Refugees from occupied countries, so-called apatrides, stateless persons, were subject to arrest and internment.

Monsieur Palmier, a blacksmith with massive arms and hands, drove them through the night on serpentine back roads from Banon to Toulon, as close to Marseille as he dared come, fearing he was already on several police lists. "Everything from petty larceny to Grand Treason." He left them at a bus station, where Ernst and Freier waited until sunrise, at which point they joined workers commuting by bus to Aubagne and, from there by tram line, into Marseille. All that distinguished them from the workers with their daily satchels were their valises.

As the tram approached Marseille, Freier became uncharacteristically quiet, somber. Ernst tried to remember: what was it Bassim had said in the desert, about fear being the handmaiden of courage? Freier once had a mission – articulated by his anti-fascist cartoons – a way of employing humor to both defuse fear and ignite anger. His anxious chatter no doubt also defused his fear, but it seemed even Freier had reached his exhaustion point, and he looked to Ernst like a ghost – a shadow of the Bill Freier who fled Paris.

Ernst saw his own emaciated form reflected in a shop window. He had lost so much weight that he had discarded his belt in favor of a length of knotted rope. They had not eaten since the night before, and hunger pitted his stomach. Their stubbled, soiled faces blended well with the laborers, those phantoms of men, defeated shadows. What sustained Ernst day after grinding day was his anticipation of Sunday, August 3rd, only eighteen days away, "Sur le Vieux Quay – en Port de Marseille." Thinking of Lisa uplifted his mood, as if he had captured the secret that eluded everyone else on the tram and only by force of will did he suppress a smile. Perhaps he would meet her by chance in the street, and a deranged part of him kept a vigil for her face, became aroused by every blond woman he saw from behind. He remembered miraculous stories, even in Berlin, of accidental meetings in the crowded downtown. He hungered for her, readily conjured their first time making love, tasted her warm mouth like the first taste of a sugar frosted sweet cake.

In Gare de Noailles, at the identity checkpoint, their papers were scrutinized and it was a wonder that Freier's heavy sweating did not betray them. His head shook with a fine tremor until their papers were returned and they passed through. As they walked away, Freier regained his courage and explained how his grandmother fried Schnitzel, his words spilling out swift and luscious, and Ernst could almost taste Frau Stimmel's Schnitzel. Ocean scents from the harbor, a stew of sea air and rotting fish, stimulated Ernst. He and Freier walked at a fast clip down the broad Boulevard D'Athenes and onto La Canebière. Freier wiped sweat from his forehead and rattled on about his scheme, after the war, to counterfeit masterpieces – Rembrandt, Michelangelo, Velasquez – and sell them for handsome profit.

Place Victor Hugo bustled with travelers, most of them obviously refugees, streaming down Gare St. Charles's white steps. Every foreigner, displaced person, refugee or fleeing Jew, came to Marseille to wait. They waited for those most valuable and elusive of commodities: an exit visa, a foreign passport, an affidavit in lieu of passport. But for every one who escaped on a freighter to Lisbon or the ferry to Oran or Casablanca, ten more arrived, and the port swelled with a complex and urgent human commerce. Prices soared; the black market flourished.

By and large the refugees were easy to distinguish. Parents argued in whispers while their children clung to them. The well-to-do wore what they could not carry: layers of coats, suits and dresses, and bizarre layers of jewelry – strings of pearls, multiple brooches, rings on every finger, two wristwatches. Refugees displayed a distinctive countenance, stiff with apprehension and discomfort, easily distinguished from the exhilaration of a traveler, the lassitude of the work-a-day commuter, or the exhaustion of the day laborer.

At the base of the rail station's stairway they passed a mammoth pedestal atop which a bronze lion mauled a doe. Someone had painted a black graffiti 'V' on the cement plinth. Freier acknowledged it with a tilt of his head. "Oh, the cartoons I could create!"

The 'V' was ubiquitous, scratched in cement, painted on walls, defacing German propaganda posters. On the Rue de Prison side of the seventeenth century Hotel de Ville hung a poster of a German soldier holding a smiling French boy, urging Frenchmen to be confident that German soldiers protected French children. A citizen had smeared a 'V' beside the soldier's face and scrawled, "He replaces the father he killed." Collaborationists had retaliated by turning the 'V' into a Star of David and writing '**Morte**' across it.

*   *   *   *   *   *   *   *   *   *

Freier led Ernst through the old section of Marseille, Le Panier, navigating serpentine streets and alleys without names, never consulting a street map. Though winded, the short Austrian chronicled the story of a family reunion and picnic when he was eight years old, where everyone suffered food poisoning; he saw his entire family in pain, vomiting and holding their abdomens. Somehow he wasn't affected and for a long time thereafter he thought that he was magically endowed with immunity to poisons. Each time he met a relation after that, he immediately remembered them from that disastrous gathering, and it was hard to see them in any other way. Freier laughed out loud as he related his tale, a nervous cackling that he almost could not stop, and Ernst wondered if he had not become a little unhinged.

When they turned the corner onto Rue Ste. Françoise, Freier ducked into the Café Pelican. He informed the maitre'd that he was "Monsieur Durand from Cerbère".

A waiter seated them immediately and brought two small snifters of cognac. Under Freier's was a folded note that the waiter tapped with his forefinger and said, "Thomas Carlyle is a gifted author, don't you agree, Monsieur?" He stooped as if retrieving something from the ground. "You dropped your key, Monsieur." He bowed slightly and left.

Ernst emptied his glass. As it went down, the cognac burned, bracing and restorative. "Who sent the cognac?"

"An admirer of Carlyle." Freier pocketed the key and sipped his cognac. "Prosit, Monsieur Toussaint."

His new name became more familiar as he practiced it, felt it inside. When Freier had presented Ernst with his new name, identity papers, and forged work permit in Paris, he had explained, "I'm a cartoonist – I can't help but make a joke. Toussaint was the liberator of Haiti one hundred and fifty years ago. It is our little joke on les Boches, n'est-ce pas?"

"What's all this about Carlyle?"

"A code. I'll show you at the flat." Freier finished his cognac. "There may not be much of this after a while, Ernest, what with the British blockade. Savor it and remember."

A few blocks into the Vielle Ville Freier used the waiter's key to unlock a stifling one-bedroom flat just off Rue du Thier. He opened a window and started the tabletop Vornado fan, its black blades hooked like a three-armed swastika. The fan's cage rattled, then vibrated and gradually settled into an eccentric hum. Torpid flies roused and settled again; steamy air circulated, hardly cooling.

"This is where Mina and I will live for now. I'd offer you tea, but the cupboards are bare." He motioned for Ernst to sit at the spare table. "Let's have a look at this note." Freier flattened the typed message from the waiter, a string of numbers separated by dashes. In his valise he found a well-thumbed copy of Carlyle's French Revolution, Volume 1, and opened to a passage on page 195 marked with a blue dot.

"The first three numbers tell me the page – 195. The passage starts here with 'Cardinal Mazarin…'" Freier laid his pens out on the flat table with the care of a Zen calligrapher and transcribed the passage in large letters. He returned to the beginning and numbered each letter in turn starting with the number 7. Then, in small letters, he wrote the whole alphabet in a vertical row down the left side of the page. Opposite each letter he wrote all the numbers that corresponded to that letter in the passage.

"The code is elegant – simple but complex. One writes down all the numbers for each letter, never the same one twice in succession, and separates each group of numbers by a dash. Never indicate where one word ends and the next begins. To decode, one simply runs the eye down the passage from Carlyle until you come to the number you are looking for, then write the corresponding letter down on a sheet of paper. It's a bit convoluted but extremely hard to crack. The greatest difficulty is finding passages that use all the letters of the alphabet several times – hence, Carlyle."

Ernst watched as the letters appeared one by one out of the potpourri of numbers: "sept petits pecheurs tuesday seven AM"

"Our next contact – Sept Petits Pêcheurs, 7 AM. What do you think of this playing spies?"

Freier's words, 'playing spies,' brought Ernst up short. Not since Organization C had he felt enough loyalty to either cause or country to put his self interest aside or put himself in harm's way. Did Freier assume Ernst's complicity? For all of Freier's talk about his girlfriend, Mina, Ernst had said nothing about Lisa. She was his secret, the decoding scheme to his heart, to what remained of his existence. He didn't owe Freier, or Puck for that matter, anything. He had come back for Lisa – for the first Sunday of the month. He liked Freier, was grateful for his help. Maybe he had even saved Ernst's life and certainly Freier had been instrumental in getting him to Marseille. So he said only, "I don't know what to think. It's all a bit of a blur."

That evening they walked toward the Vieux Port, the old harbor, to meet Freier's fiancée, Mina, about whom Ernst had heard from Paris to Marseille. The scent of the harbor air thickened as they descended into the bowl of the Vieux Port. Twice, caped Agents de Police stopped them to check their identity cards, shone electric torches in their faces, and moved them on.

The Vieux Port nestled between parallel arms of land, each ending in a fort. This Mediterranean harbor, which had once served the commerce of the Greeks and Phoenicians, now only harbored the Marseille fishing fleet. Along the quay, every 25 meters, a low wattage electric bulb hung from a wooden pole, spotlighting a small craft bobbing on summer swells. Bisecting the harbor channel, the gothic Transbordeur, the transporter bridge, cut the harbor off from the sea. To his left, the southern arm ended in Fort St. Nicholas, a massive military prison that dominated the entrance to the harbor. Across the Transbordeur at the northern arm, Fort St. Jean, the first depot of the French Foreign Legion in France, loomed in the twilight. Ernst felt a pang of guilt, knowing his surviving Legion comrades were still confined to Fort St. Jean, their fate debated by German occupiers in Paris and French collaborators in Vichy.

It was near dark when they reached the Quai du Port. Suddenly, out from the shadows, a small, waif-like woman came running at them. It was Mina, materializing from the ramparts of Fort St. Jean, running into Freier's open arms. They looked like children in the First Class, locked in a startlingly adult embrace. It was too painful to watch. Ernst turned away and found himself directly in front of the Eglise St. Laurent, where on some joyous Sunday morning at sunrise he would meet Lisa, the way Freier met Mina. He whispered a prayer to the dark rounded Romanesque church, hoping that God was inside.

By now, the Legion would have designated Ernest Tessier as missing in action and presumed dead, or a deserter. Ernest Toussaint, a French laborer, leaned his back against the wall of the Eglise St. Laurent and lit a cigarette. In the match-light he saw graffiti on the wall of the Romanesque church:

Victory — Vengeance

★   ★   ★   ★   ★   ★   ★   ★   ★   ★

Ernst woke in the night to hear Mina and Freier making love in the small apartment. He was an aural voyeur, experiencing a mixture of joy and envy, a bittersweet reminder of the unquenchable force he knew only too well. It was the water beneath the desert, the long dormant seed awakening and seeking the light. It was hope itself.

Mina left at dawn, shortly after the curfew expired. Ernst and Freier left an hour later, indistinguishable from the workingmen of the port, shuffling through the narrow streets of Le Panier.

Sept Petits Pècheurs, owned by Robert Guerini, a Corsican boss, was one of two respectable restaurants in Marseille. When Ernst and Freier arrived, the odor of beer and wine still hung like dew. A waiter was sweeping up last night's cigarettes and napkins, rousing flies from their drunken stupor. Freier asked the waiter for "Monsieur Durand" and was immediately seated in a dark corner near the back where no breeze reached. July nights were only marginally less hot than the days.

Before Ernst could light a cigarette, a small man seemed to materialize out of the torpid air; he settled onto the third chair like a dragonfly on a lily pad. He was less than five and a half feet tall, slight, but with a wide face and narrow eyes, his black hair slicked down flat. His smile flashed momentarily, his teeth luminous, one gold, his handshake limp and brief.

"I am Dimitru," he said. "You are new in Marseille, n'est-ce pas? If you need to make arrangements – of any kind – let me offer my services. I can be found here most days, or ask the proprietor, Robert." He indicated the man behind the cash register, who was speaking on the telephone and stirring a bicarbonate of soda.

Ernst felt an instinctive antipathy for the imp at whose signal three cups of excellent coffee appeared. The rich aroma, a dark roast, woke a thousand pleasure nerves in his nose, and Ernst's eyes automatically closed and he smiled.

"The ports are blockaded," Dimitru continued, "and les Boches have yet to open the Unoccupied Zone to normal trade. It makes one appreciate special favors, n'est-ce pas?" Dimitru sipped his coffee; on his erect pinky finger a diamond glinted.

Freier set down his cup and very quietly said, "I would like to change 57 francs, Monsieur Dimitru."

"Ah," his face lit up for an instant, then returned to rueful complacency. "You are Monsieur Freier and..." He looked expectantly at Ernst.

"Ernest Toussaint."

"Enchanté." He offered his limp handshake again, then he was gone.

Before they could sip more of the strong coffee, a heavy shadow slipped from the curtain behind them, and Puck sat in the chair Dimitru had just vacated. Puck had his finger to his lips. His beard had gone white and Ernst thought he looked shrunken, having lost considerable weight and most of the hairs from his head.

"Hush! Do not react! Marseille is full of informers and spies." He smiled. "It is good to see you, my friends." He held out one hand to each of them. "Ernst. I had to be sure it was you. That is Robert Guerini at the cash register. He and Dimitru are trusted friends. But this is too public a place to speak."

Freier patted Ernst's shoulder. "I've made my delivery." He drained his cup and got up to leave. "Give me a few days, Puck, to settle in with Mina, then I will be ready to work. I'll wait to hear from you." He turned to Ernst again. "I hope I haven't bored you too much with my stories. Mina says I talk too much. I look forward to our artistic collaboration. Good luck, my friend."

Puck led Ernst through the narrow streets and alleys of Vielle Ville under laundry hung from one tenement to another. Before they turned onto Rue Ste-Françoise he stopped and surveilled the street.

Puck explained Marseille in its simplest terms. Robert Guerini parlayed his anti-Vichy persuasion into lucrative smuggling of refugees who could pay, which handsomely augmented his income from the black market for food, prostitution, and gambling. Across La Canebière, the boulevard running down to the Vieux Port, the collaborationist Sabiani, Guerini's nemesis, and a powerful Corsican gangster in his own right, held court from Le Beauvau. Marshall Pétain's portrait hung in Sabiani's restaurant's window surrounded by bright bunting and a sign declaring *"Viva Pétain! Viva La Revolution Nationale!"* Sabiani enjoyed the advantages of collaboration. At Le Beauvau one could eat a gourmet meal even at the worst of times, with aromatic coffees and freshly baked bread. "Sabiani has it in for me," Puck said. "An old grudge. Corsica. Last week I was almost certainly followed by one of Sabiani's thugs."

They emerged again on La Canebière. "Marseille is a frightfully complex city just now. Smuggling human beings has always been good business, but don't try to do it alone," Puck said. "As every child knows, foreigners picked up without safe conduct documents or identity papers are treated like apatrides and sent to a concentration camp – Millia, le Vernet or Gurs – or they simply disappear. Those who assist them suffer the same fate."

Though it was early on a weekday, the streets were crowded. "These people passing us – one in five is a refugee hiding somewhere in Le Panier's labyrinth." Puck's hand waved in the direction of the winding side streets. "A very interesting clot of political refugees, Communists, Jews, artists, intellectuals. Café talk is suddenly interesting. Everybody has an edge, an agenda – everybody is preoccupied."

They passed three crow-like Agents de Police, eerie in their spiked Kaiser Wilhelm helmets, rifles and dark cloaks. "They know enough to keep together," Puck said. He explained that rafles, roundups, were conducted only with reinforcements, and not very often. Though rafles were unpredictable, inside information was available with the right connections and appropriate payment or 'gifts.'

And Puck had cultivated many connections. He explained that his finest forgeries were rendered in service to an American journalist, Varian Fry, director of the Emergency Rescue Committee. "He smuggles artists and intellectuals out of France," Puck said. "His list reads like a Who's Who. It's quite an honor to be one of Fry's clients. I also provide forged documents to a network of Jews – legal organizations for now." Puck explained how he lent his services to The Jewish Committee for Children from Germany and Central Europe and the EIF, Éclaireurs Israélites de France, the Jewish scouting movement.

Ernst's valise felt heavy as he walked with Puck. In this time of disorder and dread he had been seamlessly shuttled from Paris, to Marseille to Puck. It was bewildering, more than good fortune. Halfway up Rue d'Epice, across from a vacant lot that hosted a scrappy willow tree, Puck signaled his address, a nondescript three-story tenement. By the time they reached the third floor, Puck wheezed audibly. He leaned against the door to his flat, shoulders heaving with each breath.

"You're not well," Ernst said as Puck fumbled with his key in the door.

"Too much... talking." He coughed hard and the lock surrendered. Ernst smelled dust and mold; floorboards creaked as Puck crossed the room to turn on a bare bulb. Atop a bookshelf he noticed a small phonograph with one record leaning against it.

"Is this the best Jacques could do for you?" Ernst asked.

"I don't work for Jacques any more. And I don't attract attention living here. It's quite expensive to live in Marseille these days." He pointed to the sofa. "Your bunk for now, Ernst. It's not too bad." As if it were already agreed, Puck explained, "an empty bed is almost impossible to find these days."

Ernst set his valise down by the table. So many coincidences, like synchronized cogs and wheels – Lisa, Puck, Bill Freier. What he had regarded as good fortune suddenly became abnormal, suspect. "Did you arrange it with Freier that I would come to Marseille?"

Still breathing hard, Puck opened the shades. He sat down hard on a plain wooden chair and contemplated Ernst in the scant light. "You look older. Perhaps it's the beard. And you've lost weight. I could afford to lose weight, but not you. Tea?"

Ernst scrutinized his old cellmate. He felt played – the fool. "You knew about Lisa?" He didn't want to believe it; he was still trying out the words.

Puck tied on a soiled white apron. He shrugged his shoulders and tipped his head as if Ernst's sharp tone was inconsequential. "Ernst. She's the wife of an important Nazi. Easy to find."

Another puzzle piece tumbled into place. "I remember. Margaret talked about you. You are 'that funny little man who quoted Jewish sages.' You arranged it all, didn't you?" Ernst's fists balled so tightly his nails cut his palm. "Lisa's escape – her coming to Marseille..." Only his need to know kept him still. "Was it my foolishness, or simply for your own entertainment? 'What fools these mortals be,' isn't that what Shakespeare's Puck said?"

Puck poured dry tea into a strainer. "It was all for a good cause, I assure you."

Ernst felt his bile rising. "Listen, you scheming bastard. I came to Marseille for Lisa, not for you. I don't give a damn about whatever diabolical scheme you're playing at or whatever mission you're on. I'm here for me, not for you."

"I don't care why you're here." Puck spoke softly. He pulled out a wooden chair and signaled for him to sit. Ernst's eyes narrowed to slits and he remained resolutely standing. Puck shrugged. He lit the primus and set a dented kettle to boil. "I need your help, Ernst. The entire world needs your help. Does that sound grandiose? Does that sound completely mad? Pretentious? The Talmud – you remember I spoke about the Talmud in Striegau? The Talmud teaches 'Who saves a life, saves the world entire.' That's what I'm asking of you. To help me save a life, to help me save the world.

"This man I told you about – Varian Fry. Bill Freier and I are part of his rescue network. Fry has changed me. I believe in something larger than myself. At first I saw this as a way to make money – a good business opportunity. But then, slowly, forgery became rescue. And that has purified my motives. I don't expect you to understand this. I certainly didn't at first."

Ernst felt his face flush. "You're a fucking madman, Puck. You're playing a dangerous game. And you've dragged Lisa and me into it. Whatever happened to the Puck I knew at Striegau – the entrepreneur who was only in it for the game? Yes, the game – it was always a game – and you were only in the game for yourself." He grabbed his valise and made for the door.

Puck was on his feet. "Please, Ernst. Wait! Let me explain."

Ernst stopped but did not turn to him. He walked two paces more to the door, one hand on the doorknob. "What do you want of me?"

"Only your forgery prowess. You are a gifted artist. Your skill will keep you fed and housed while you pursue your beloved. Both our needs are met."

Ernst turned to Puck. "Why shouldn't Lisa and I just flee, like everybody else? You're using me. Lisa and I are nothing more than pawns in your chess game."

Puck winced as if Ernst had dealt him a glancing blow. "A harsh judgment, Ernst. Perhaps you could think of it as encouragement, or maybe I could be your muse or your patron. Every artist needs a patron."

Ernst dropped his valise and lunged at Puck. "You self-important bastard!" There was no stopping. His hands groped at his throat. Puck staggered back and fell to the floor. Ernst stood over him, fists at the ready.

Puck slowly, painfully, got to his knees and looked up at Ernst without fear. "Our interests coincide. Always the best of circumstances, don't you think?" He smiled.

Ernst pointed to his own chest. "The ache in my heart is your business opportunity? I hate you!"

Puck pulled himself onto the chair and waved his hand at Ernst. "Oh, piffle. It's the way of the world. Call it what you will. Everything has a mechanism – even the human heart."

"You cynical bastard!"

"Calm down, Ernst. I simply use the spiritual in service of reality. Your 'Sunday at sunrise' rendezvous? I suggested it. I thought it would appeal to your romantic persuasion. I should think you would be grateful." Puck gestured at the empty chair for Ernst to sit.

"Thank you and fuck you." Ernst sat down hard. He was too tired to sustain his homicidal rage.

"I understand," Puck said. "You'll get over it."

"How did you do it?"

"In church – like your brother Leo – where she was accessible."

"But she doesn't know you."

"The Sommers's Lutheran minister has a lovely custom. Angelic altar boys choose parishioners, seemingly at random, to accompany them to light holy candles. An altar boy – I gave him cigarettes – chose Lisa to light his candle and whispered that she should take his note – that it had to do with you."

"And the note?"

"The note said that it was important for you, Ernst, to come to Marseille. Margaret could help her get there as well. I urged her to write you and invented her fictional cousin, Gabriele. I was in contact with Margaret, and she did the rest. I thought it prudent that Lisa not know too much about me."

"And the part about sunrise?"

"A nice touch, don't you think? I merely planted the seed and left it to her.

I think she must care about you a great deal." Puck got up from the table and dropped the tea ball into the boiling kettle. "Tea is ready soon."

"You did it for the money?"

"On the most primitive level, it was about the money – at first. I must pay for this flat, and food is quite dear. There's only so much one can charge desperately poor refugees for papers. Forgery has become a volume trade. I need your help for the extra income you can bring. And so do you."

Ernst scrutinized Puck as he poured the tea. "And on a less primitive level?"

"Yes, Ernst. There is more. I've missed you." Puck's voice hoarsened to choke back tears. "I didn't want you to die. I would have done anything to save you."

Ernst cradled his hot teacup, smelled steaming chamomile. This was unexpected, and it melted a portion of his wrath. "Don't expect my gratitude."

"Well, at the very least I hope you choose to stay here with me – share this slightly more extravagant cell with me again. And let me remind you, your freedom – your life – is still precarious. As a Legionnaire you are a deserter – you could be shot. Your colleagues in Fort St. Jean have only two options, joining the Wehrmacht or remaining in the Legion and returning to Africa."

"What coward would join the army that defeated him?" Ernst said.

"You would be dismayed to learn how many Frenchmen are like Sabiani, glad for this revolution from the right. Pétain's portrait hangs in many shops. 'A blessing in disguise,' they call it. 'A common front against Communism.' People's worst excesses are being aired."

"And those who follow de Gaulle?"

"Like the Jews, they must find a way to escape. Until recently one could easily take the public ferry to Oran – with the proper papers – and I could produce those in an afternoon. But, like every other window of escape, this one is closing. There have been more arrests. The Germans want their nationals and other fugitives. Les Boches are becoming expert at detecting our forgeries. The Armistice Commission is demanding access to Fort St. Jean. Marshall Pétain doesn't want to lose a potential fighting force. What the Germans don't know is that there are British soldiers in the fort – several hundred. They must escape."

"What does this have to do with me?"

"Do you think the Germans know who you really are?"

"Perhaps, as Ernest Tessier. Not as Techow, or I would have been arrested long ago." Ernst laid his identity card on the table. "My new papers – complements of Freier. Ernest Toussaint – dockworker. Freier said I could get work on the docks."

"Done. I've been in Corsica for ten years. I know all the gangsters – good and bad. You'll work alongside Corsicans at Bassin de la Joliette where Sabiani has a stranglehold. I fear there are just as many collaborationists as there are resisters." Puck rubbed his mouth as if it was chafed by a muzzle. He poured his own tea.

In spite of the heat Ernst savored the flavorful warmth as he appraised the spare commodities on Puck's shelf over the stove – sugar, a nearly empty flour bag, and a small bottle of oil. Near the open window stood another table with documents flanked by two pens and a magnifying glass.

"Where will you go – after you meet Lisa?" Puck asked.

Ernst shrugged his shoulders. "Cuba or Mexico." Ernst thought Puck gave him a disapproving glance. His resentment returned with swift sarcasm. "Do you find that disturbing? Everybody in Marseille is trying to leave. Why should I be any different?"

"You will disappear?"

Ernst felt an unexpected prick of guilt. "Something like that."

"I wondered how the desert had changed you. Perhaps not much." Puck sipped his tea and seemed to condemn Ernst over the cup's rim. "You've seen the refugees. Vichy is refusing to issue exit visas, so everyone is stuck here. Some are in mortal danger – Article 19 – Surrender on Demand. Their only hope is to be spirited out of France quickly. Then there is the matter of the British soldiers trapped in Fort St. Jean. Everyone is stuck in Marseille – writers, artists, political figures who have been critical of the Nazis, all due to be arrested. I have a friend at the Prefecture of Police who has given me a copy of the list. There is a certain distinction, a vote of intellectual excellence, to being on the roster. Would you like to see it?"

Ernst browsed the list of over two hundred of the most prominent cultural, artistic, and political figures of Europe.

"My employer, this Varian Fry fellow, is always looking for talented artists," Puck said. "No one can forge a document like you. You have a gift – some would say an obligation. Lives depend on it."

Ernst felt on guard again. "You don't give a shit about me, Puck. This is all about what I can do for you."

Puck closed his eyes and took a deep breath, as if containing his own exasperation or annoyance. "Our needs and opportunities coincide. I'm offering you the possibility to save lives and repair the rent you have created in the world."

"I'm not interested. In any case, I don't share your zeal."

"Neither did Jonah – even after he re-emerged from the belly of the whale."

"God doesn't talk to me."

"God talks to each of us – all the time – often in baffling ways. We are all equipped to hear God talking; the question is, do we listen?"

The image of Frau Rathenau leapt to Ernst's mind, in black, perched in the balcony of the courtroom, her raptor gaze boring down upon him. "Why do you torment me with this?" Ernst fought the urge to leave and never return. "You're referring to Frau Rathenau's letter, aren't you?" Ernst felt a tug of war inside, as if the two letters he kept battled for his soul – Lisa's invitation to meet in Marseille, sur le quay, and Frau Rathenau's invitation to forgiveness, to repentance. They could not coexist. He felt impotent to disentangle himself from the indelible apprehension that he had never left that Leipzig courtroom, that he had never ceased standing before the court of Heaven.

Puck laid his hand on Ernst's shoulder. "Drink your tea. It may be the best you can do right now. No need to answer the question. Just drink your tea."

Ernst felt his eyes water – shame and exhaustion conspiring with confusion and longing. There was no untying this Gordian knot. "I feel as if I have no choice."

"You always have a choice, Ernst. Maybe you cannot make a choice right now, but you always have free will."

Almost in a whisper, deflated, he said, "All right. Until I leave Marseille, I'll do what I can for you." He did not want Puck to see his tears, so he busied himself with the Vichy police list. "And you should be glad for it. It's for the rent, for my food, for getting me here with Freier. And perhaps I feel guilty... I don't even know anymore."

"You don't have to explain why you do it. And, in any case, guilt is a strong but useless emotion. Guilt heals nothing, though it may allow you to continue sinning. You can move beyond guilt."

"Yes, 5,000 kilometers beyond guilt – to Cuba or Mexico."

"I must warn you, in Vichy France, forgery puts you at great peril."

"I'm not leaving Marseille without Lisa. And besides," Ernst said, "I'm a small fish." (A Kiel sprat, he wanted to say, but only Leo would understand.) "I'm a garden-variety deserter. I'm not even on this list. I suspect my crimes are old news to the Germans and uninteresting to the French. I will stay and draw pretty documents and seals for your precious refugees. We will be cell-mates again."

Puck sat back and chuckled, rubbing his hands together. "Excellent. It will be an adventure. Les Boches don't know who they are dealing with, eh?"

"I give up, Puck. I'm exhausted. You've brought me here as if I'm still a prisoner, except now you're the jailor. But I owe your refugees nothing." Only now he was not so sure.

★   ★   ★   ★   ★   ★   ★   ★   ★   ★

On the first Sunday in August, Ernst waited in the shadow of Eglise St. Laurent; he was so eager for the dawn that he defied the curfew and sneaked through the alleys of Le Panier to the quay of the harbor in darkness. Each night before he fell asleep Ernst had imagined this Sunday, and she was always there, waiting in the shadows of Eglise St. Laurent's rounded arch-way. His own exit visa was a masterpiece and it would take no more than two hours to finish Lisa's, leave a note for Puck, and they could be gone.

Fishermen readied their boats for the morning catch. A freshening south wind, ripe with the scent of rain, whistled through the arches of the Transbordeur Bridge. One by one, cabin lanterns flickered on and bobbed with the boats in the predawn. There was a chop on the water, and soon the harbor glittered as if with fireflies. The sky lightened enough for Ernst to see the silhouette of the l'Etoile Mountains east of Marseille. Three Gendarmes walked the Quai, questioning fishermen, inspecting curfew exemptions. Near the church a plainclothesman looked more menacing still, his dark hat pulled low, black trench coat tightly belted, hands deep in his pockets. Ernst felt invisible in the shadows as the detective walked by him. The cabin lantern and white wake of the first fishing boat passed under the Transbordeur.

This matter of the refugees troubled Ernst. What were they to Puck? What transformed Puck from an opportunist who argued with God to an altruistic rescuer? Ernst hated the refugees, disdained their helplessness, cursed them for their painful reminder of every defeat, every abandonment. And they put him at great risk, as if they carried a lethal infection he would contract by his association with them. His new lease on life suddenly felt tenuous, as fragile as the first light of dawn.

Ernst blew into his hands and turned up his collar, trying to quell the circus of emotions that picked at his heart like crows at carrion. He knew the pain of losing her once in Striegau, again in Berlin. He could not endure that pain again. As the sky lightened and the curfew lifted, his heart quickened and he scrutinized the cul-de-sac of the harbor, then swept his gaze back to the shadows of Eglise St. Laurent. Desire played tricks in the illusory light and he produced a mirage – Lisa in the shadow of the Romanesque church. His heart upended in his chest. In a moment she would step into the yellow light of the quay and recognize him, wave and run into his arms. Their embrace would linger for long minutes; he anticipated the feelings of relief, joy, arousal. In less than a day they would flee over the Pyrenees, then on to Lisbon and passage to Cuba or Mexico where they would start their new life, oblivious to the European insanity. With almost no effort, Ernst imagined their cottage set back from the beach, the twinkling lights of Havana far enough away for anonymity. Their first son, Alfred, named for Ernst's father, nestled against Lisa's chest as she waited in the darkened doorway. How would they explain to him about Rathenau?

A bell buoy rang again, its mournful warning a distraction; his thoughts jumbled, his mirage disintegrated. Time slowed as if dawn could not bring herself to give way to morning, to sweep away the shadows of Eglise St. Laurent. A priest arrived and soon altar boys came, some holding the hand of a younger sibling, some on bicycles. Ernst had reasoned that this first rendezvous was the most likely to be successful; surely Lisa was already in Marseille, perhaps she had already waited for months.

When the first dagger of sun crested the Chaine de l'Etoile, the Quai Du Port already bustled with the fish market, and he worried he would miss her in the growing crowd. He stood in the center of the square before the church, as conspicuous as possible. He stretched 'sunrise' out as long as he could until the church bell rang twelve times.

In that moment of disappointment, when he could not deny the day's failure, the thought that crystallized, that made Ernst shudder, was that he too was a refugee.

When Ernst returned to their flat, Puck was already at work with his brush, his pens, inspecting his work through the 30X lens. Without looking up he said, "I'm sorry, Ernst. Perhaps next month."

He felt dead. Exhaustion was too kind an explanation. "Perhaps."

"I felt your anticipation all week – you seemed alive, electric."

Ernst threw his jacket on the sofa. "What of it?"

"I know that today's pain is greater than you could imagine. But what did you expect? You are no different than the rest of us. It is aberrant for anyone to get what he wants."

22

Varian Fry

September – November 1940

S eptember's harvest moon hung over the mountains east of Marseille. Playing tag with the moon, Ernst strode through the twisting streets of the Vieux Ville, catching a glimpse of it between rooftops, at crooked intersections, reflected in a pool of rancid water where cobblestones had been washed away.

He was weary from his day on the docks, carrying 40 kilo bags of rice from the oven-like hold of a rusted freighter registered in Siam. Physical labor exhausted him, but it also calmed him, purged his consciousness, if only for a short time, of the chronic ache of longing and despair. And when the anodyne of hard labor and too much wine failed, he transmogrified his longing into the opium of renewed anticipation and hope. With the surety born of love's blindness, a force of life, he told himself: *next month at sunrise... next month at sunrise.* And they would finally leave this suburb of Hell behind.

Ernst had accepted a dinner invitation from his one friend on the docks, Henri, who lived in an apartment in the Vielle Ville with his wife and five children. Henri groomed their friendship, sought Ernst out, secured him a preferred assignment on the docks. Tall and thin, Henri had a larynx that protruded from his long neck and bobbed up and down when he spoke. He towered over his petite wife, Marie, who looked completely depleted, breast milk stains on her blouse. Ernst wondered how they made love; in any case they were far too young to have five children. The youngest, Genevieve, only a few months old, lay in a bassinette staring dully. She did not react to Ernst when he tried to engage her, except to blink her eyes, dark circles underneath, her cheeks flat. The other four fought over a half loaf of bread Ernst brought with him and devoured it, then tumbled back out into the street.

"The streets are safer now," Henri said. "It's a small benefit of the armistice – and Pétain." Ernst could not hide his disapproval. "Don't get me wrong, Ernest. I hate the fascists as much as anyone. Viva De Gaulle! But there are certain unmistakable advantages to a fascist state."

Marie brought a pot of thin stew to the table. Without so much as a thought, she picked up the baby and lifted her blouse to nurse her, though she did not cry for her. Her flaccid breasts hung like empty sacks. She rocked in her chair, staring sullenly at her lap as if her world had shrunk to the space between Genevieve and herself.

There were not many advantages to being independent on the docks, Henri was saying. He worked for whoever had jobs and paid the best. Currently, that was Sabiani, who distributed a "stipend" in addition to a paycheck. He was guaranteed work. Still, it was hard to feed a family of six and pay for their small flat. Henri wore the small blue bar of Sabiani's organization on his beret.

"You don't have to agree with his politics. I myself don't. It pays the bills. I am always chosen for the work gangs. Some of the newcomers, like you, try to stay aloof – they don't get much work. You need someone like me to help you."

"You hardly know me. Why would you do that?"

"I like you. I liked you the first day you came to the docks. I have a feeling about people. I'm rarely wrong."

It had been an unexpectedly happy evening, drinking cognac stolen from a smuggled shipment, smoking Gauloises on Henri's small veranda overlooking the street, the children rollicking below. After a few shots of cognac he could easily envision them sitting on a terrace in Paris, overlooking the Seine. The moon rose over a tenement further up the hill, silvering the evening sky, fluorescing a swath of cobblestones.

Henri leaned back in his chair and let the moon reflect in his eyes. "One thing the Sisters of St. Germaine did, besides beating me till I was bruised, was to teach me to read. Not many on the docks share my enthusiasm for Heine or André Gide." Marie brought two cups of coffee, a remarkable surprise, to the veranda. Ernst delighted in the aroma. Most days there was only acorn coffee to drink, or stale bean coffee, or none at all.

"Real coffee?" How like a drug, Ernst thought, and he understood the risks people took to obtain it. "Where did you get it?"

"Sabiani. Stolen from the docks. Another "stipend" at no cost to himself. He regulates the thievery. I depend on it. Rationing will worsen. Half a pound of pasta and six ounces of rice a month? Ten ounces of meat a week?"

Ernst nodded and savored the coffee. "Did you know Heine was a Jew?" Ernst watched for his response.

Henri smiled. "Yes, he was born a Jew, then became a Protestant, and then married his Catholic mistress. Heine died a Catholic. The nuns never tired of reminding us of Heine's sordid allegiances – they delighted in the details of his journey to Hell. Sister Francouer called his love poems pornography. I mean, I was only twelve years old, but Heine became forbidden fruit. Such passion. I fancied myself a writer in those days, and my heart burned with jealousy and amazement, in equal measure, that a mortal could string together ordinary words and set them on fire."

"Rumor has it that Gide is hiding in the Vielle Ville," Ernst said. "Feuchtwanger and Franz Werfel, too. Have you read *The Forty Days of Musa Dagh?*"

Henri nodded vigorously. "Spectacular. I tried to get my wife to read it, but she could barely get through the first chapter. Don't have too many children, Ernest. If I didn't have so many responsibilities, I might have chosen to avoid Sabiani, but, alas, I have made my bed and slept in it, literally. Trust me, Ernest. You can make some real money with Sabiani, in spite of his politics. One does what one must. After the first time it's not so difficult."

★   ★   ★   ★   ★   ★   ★   ★   ★   ★

Wary of Sabiani, Ernst made no commitment to Henri, but since their dinner Ernst had been regularly chosen for work and received a bonus of Brazilian coffee beans. Puck refused the coffee. He would rather drink acorn coffee, he said, than be obligated to a swine like Sabiani. Puck stormed out of the apartment, and they didn't speak for days. Ernst brewed the coffee, filling their flat with its rich aroma. But his joy in drinking it was diminished by Puck's disdain.

Two or three evenings a week Ernst forged identity papers and visas for Puck's employer, Varian Fry, and the Emergency Rescue Committee. The work brought in some additional money and that was enough reason for Ernst. It was well known that the police watched and listened to all that went on with the man the Vichy press called 'that repugnant American journalist.' He made forgeries for Puck as well, as he required them, but more than once he reasserted that he didn't share Puck's love or concern for the refugees and that he put himself at great risk.

One night Ernst refused to complete an extra pile of documents that Puck said were urgently needed. "I do enough for you. I don't care about this. I have my own life to live." He stormed out of the flat and spent the evening drinking with Henri.

After three days of hardly speaking, Ernst returned from the docks with a pulled muscle in his back. He groaned as he lay back on the sofa. Without even looking at Ernst, Puck lit the primus and began heating water for a hot water bottle and a pot of soup.

Puck wore his soiled cotton apron, ridiculously small, tied up high on his stomach. His wooden spoon scraped angrily at the tomato soup on the primus. Puck poured a glass of cheap burgundy and put it on the floor beside Ernst.

"It's not my nature to be silent," Puck finally said. "I much preferred Striegau – at least we talked. Have you heard there is a war?"

Ernst drank the burgundy in one mouthful, then lay back and covered his eyes. "Get off your fucking pedestal! I do what I can, and you should be glad for it."

Puck tasted the soup from the wooden spoon, then wiped his hands on his apron. He picked up a card from the table. "This identity card you completed yesterday," he waved it in front of Ernst. "Oh, it's quite good. But do you know who it's for? Hans Sahl – a poet. Real flesh. Real blood. He sits and waits every day at the Hotel Splendide. Here." He laid a paper on Ernst's chest. "Read this."

Marseille IV

Without thought or feeling, we wait.
We ball our restlessness up tight.
We spend days in front of consulate doors.
We have our skins to pay with
As we pursue papers, stamps, permit, from morning to night.
And we are still here.

Neither living nor dying, we wait.
It's a race with death.
We know the best we can do is wait.
Perhaps we know we have waited too long.
And so we juggle with our feelings.
Swallow every rumor,
Book seats on phantom boats.
We face our destiny
And don't die.

"Here is another – Walter Mehring." Puck dropped another page onto Ernst's chest. "Written in the concentration camp at St. Cyprien. Fry arranged his escape."

> I grope about within the clammy fold
> Among the bodies strewn on hay and mold...
> The starved flesh fevers and exudes a sweat;
> This human mist, aciduously wet...
>
> We fret and squabble over sticky stew;
> We sleep with plagues; and those who will not brew
> The rancid water, yield to thirst instead...
> And in the dawn these lie among the dead...

Ernst read the poems, then let them slide off his chest onto the floor. He lit one of Sabiani's Gauloises, knowing it burned as an insult, an affront. "As you are so fond of pointing out, I too, am a refugee."

"You built a road through the desert," Puck said. "Why not bring that same enthusiasm to your forgeries?"

Ernst sat up and glowered at Puck. "They're not my forgeries – they're yours." He crushed the cigarette under his heel and walked over to stare out the window at the brick wall across the alley. "I don't want to care about these people. Does that surprise you?"

"The truth of the matter is, my friend, you do care. And that baffles and bothers you." Puck returned to his soup and stirred until the silence was unbearable again. "No matter how many identities you assume, Ernst, you always come face to face with yourself – with the hole in your heart. You will always be Techow – not Tessier, not Toussaint."

It was more and more difficult for Ernst to wear Puck down, to push him away. Puck had the uncanny, and unpleasant ability to see deep within Ernst's core, almost to read his mind. There was no deceiving Puck.

"I'm not responsible for this insane asylum!"

"You and I know that's not true, Ernst. In no small measure you are responsible. But you are correct; there are other pains and sorrows for which you bear no guilt. I wonder what they are? Will you ever share that with me – or even with yourself?" Puck stirred the red puree, and the fragrance of basil and oregano began to scent the air. "I would guess you would do anything to fill that hole – lie, cheat, steal; killing is old hat."

He hated it when Puck spoke like that. "There is no hole in my heart."

"Then why do you keep people at arm's length? To prove to yourself that you are still unworthy? To pretend you are whole?"

"You're talking rubbish – sentimental garbage."

"What happened to you?"

"Nothing happened to me. And everything. My family, Versailles, Bolshevism, depression, war..."

"No, Ernst. I know what happened to us. What I want to know is what happened to you? To you personally, Ernst Werner Techow, son of Alfred and Gertrude. If you let someone get too close what awful thing will they discover? That you are an impostor, like your forgeries?"

"You sound like that lunatic Freud!"

Puck tasted the soup and continued to stir. "Why do you think Freud is reviled by the Nazis? He struck too close to home – scared the shit out of Hitler and Goebbels and Himmler and Röhmer, because they would have had to look at what happened to them – what it was that turned them into monsters."

"I'm not a monster."

"We all have a monster inside us." Puck sipped from the spoon again.

"You're going senile, old man."

"That's what you said when you first met me. Do you remember? Come, the soup is ready. You'll feel better."

"When I first met you, you were a funny little man." Ernst sat at the round table and smiled at Puck for the first time in three days as he remembered their awkward first day together. "You're still a funny little man."

Puck eased the hot water bottle between the small of Ernst's back and the chair. Then he brought over the soup and poured it, steamy and red, into Ernst's bowl. Ernst felt the fragrant mist warm his face, and he inhaled the sultry savor. It spread deeply where other essential but buried memories of care lay in wait, and it pacified him. In the failing light, the tomato soup shadowed to dark burgundy, the cheap wine to black.

Puck broke off a piece of baguette and dipped it into the soup. "Do you know what I find so ironic about Frau Rathenau's letter?"

Ernst did not want to hear this again from Puck. But the soup allowed for his patience. Puck had arranged the moment well, he decided.

"Her forgiveness was costly, both to her as a grieving mother, and to you – a confession in an earthly court, repentance before the court of Heaven. But, don't you see? Ultimately, your forgiveness is free. If you choose in your heart to be worthy of love, of redemption, it is yours." He dipped his bread again. "Do you like the soup?"

Ernst felt Puck's care. "It's remarkably good."

"I'm glad." He wiped his bearded lips and sat back, contemplating Ernst. After a long pause he continued. "Whatever it was that happened to that young boy inside you, Ernst, you must let it go. Everybody carries disappointments and betrayals from childhood. How heavy the burden is your choice."

Ernst saw the Striegau twinkle in Puck's eyes, heard his delight at playing the mentor, the philosopher, the wizard. "Why are you so concerned with my soul?"

There was another long moment of silence. Puck tipped his head one way then the other, as if engaged in an internal conversation. Finally, he looked up, his eyes gleaming, and said, "Because I love you like a brother and a father." He cleared his throat and waved a finger at Ernst. "Eat your soup before it gets cold."

Later that evening, just before curfew, Ernst leaned against the willow tree across Rue d'Epice, smoking a cigarette and trying to calm himself with thoughts of Lisa. The sole tree on a block of empty lots and run-down tenements, the willow hung its head over a rubble strewn lot that scrub-grass slowly reclaimed. It was one of the few places in Marseille where he could be alone, feeling an open space in the city, rare silence, a pleasurable vacuum. In the night ocean he felt the tidal pull of the willow's sadness, its radiant solitude, an island of reprieve amidst rubble and fear. Puck's words intruded. What was Ernst prepared to forgive?

*　*　*　*　*　*　*　*　*　*

Several weeks later, weary after another particularly strenuous day on the docks, Ernst climbed the stairs of the tenement, eager for the hot water bottle. As he reached the third floor landing he heard low chanting from inside the flat. He let himself in as quietly as possible and saw strange flickering shadows rocking rhythmically in candlelight coming from Puck's bedroom. A floorboard creaked as Ernst crossed the floor and looked in.

Puck and two dark shadows of men stood in their stocking feet facing the grimy window overlooking Rue d'Epice, mumbling and bobbing forward and back, their heads covered with Hebrew prayer shawls, faded white with black stripes and white fringes.

Puck whispered to the two men, who continued swaying in time to some internal rhythm. He lowered the prayer shawl onto his shoulders like a scarf and led Ernst from the room.

"What's going on?" Ernst whispered. "Who are they?"

"Two Jews. Men without names."

"Why are they here?"

There was a mystical twinkle in Puck's eyes, a mesmerized look. "Yom Kippur." They stood face to face for a long moment. "Would you join us?"

"I'm not a Jew." Ernst turned his back on Puck, feeling cross. "And I have a bottle of wine to drink."

"Indulge me for a brief moment. Please. Stand beside me, Ernst, before the gates of heaven close for another year."

Reluctantly, Ernst followed him into the bedroom where Puck draped his prayer shawl over both their heads. Puck thumbed through the yellowed pages of a Hebrew-German prayer book whose leather cover curled with the softness of age. He pointed to the text. His finger trembled as he whispered the start of a new prayer.

Puck signaled for Ernst to remove his shoes. "No leather today," he whispered.

The undulating Hebrew chant, a simple melody, and the flickering shadows worked some unexpected enchantment on Ernst. He experienced a rare moment when he became a spectator of his own life, saw himself as if from above, mindful of each detail. After a brief pause, the prayer repeated, this time louder, and Ernst tried to follow the German text, but meaning was elusive. Finally, there came a third time the same few sentences, this time with conviction, in a clear chant, so loud he worried about alerting attention from the street or the neighbors.

> All vows and oaths we take, all promises and obligations we make to God between this Yom Kippur and the next we hereby publicly retract in the event that we should forget them, and hereby declare our intention to be absolved of them.
>
> And all the congregation of the people Israel shall be forgiven, as well as the stranger who dwells among them, for all the people Israel acted in error.

Ernst's knees buckled and he remembered he had not eaten since morning, but there was something compelling in the repetition of this prayer that was dizzying. He grasped Puck's elbow. The fringes of the prayer shawl quivered against his cheek like rain.

At the conclusion of the chant, the two bearded men muttered the same Hebrew phrase and shook Puck's hand. "Gemar Hatimah tovah," and then in German to Ernst, "May you be finally sealed for good in the Book of Life."

As they left the apartment, each Jew placed a miniature purse, a small square of cloth cinched with twine, on the table. When they were alone again Puck lifted one of the bags, which appeared to be empty. "Tzedakhah – literally it means Justice, but one can think of it as charity. It is customary on Yom Kippur to perform an act of justice, of humanity. These two old men, who have nothing, who are hiding somewhere in the Vielle Ville with their families, leave a promissory note in a coin purse for a few precious coins, as do I. It is forbidden to handle money on Yom Kippur, but after sundown tomorrow, when the fast day is over, they will redeem their notes and I will bring their offering to the Hotel Splendide, to Varian Fry's office. Fry will do nothing for these men, perhaps their days on Earth are numbered, but they give as an act of Tzedakhah."

"What was that last prayer?"

"Kol Nidre – one of the most enigmatic of Jewish prayers. Kol Nidre is the prayer concerning the court of Heaven."

Ernst felt the words like an icicle in his heart. He took a small block of Gruyére from the ice chest and, with his Free Corps dagger, cut off a slice and tore a piece of baguette. "Have you eaten?" he asked Puck.

He shook his head. "Yom Kippur is a fast day."

"I never knew you to fast in Striegau. Why now?"

"The war – the occupation – I'm getting older. Choices become more clear. One hardly has the luxury of philosophical confusion, or even ordinary cowardice. In Striegau I could afford to indulge my long standing complaint against God." Puck paced the floor, his hands behind his back, his face lifted to the cracked ceiling. "This prayer, the Kol Nidre, when I was a boy this terrified me. Kol Nidre. It is more than a prayer, it is a courtroom drama deciding who lives and who dies. Each participant is the defendant." Puck leaned against the wall with his eyes closed and stroked his white beard. "Like you, I was a most troublesome child, and on this night my father said 'all the chickens will come home to roost.' Those were his exact words. It didn't correct my behavior, but it did frighten me."

"What makes you think I'd be interested in this voodoo?" Ernst carved another sliver of cheese. "I was only concerned lest you be overheard. The Gendarmes. It was quite loud."

"Do you think it an accident that you came in tonight when you did?"

"Your prayer doesn't make sense – the court of Heaven doesn't make sense."

"What you don't understand doesn't make sense." Puck opened the ancient prayer book again and laid it beside the Gruyére. "Kol Nidre is chanted three times. First timidly, as if a child approaching the judge, louder the second time with more confidence, and finally the third time, as if we are completely at ease in the presence of God – face to face."

Ernst read the prayer again as he drank his wine. "From what you have told me, Yom Kippur is an annulment of vows from the year just past," he said. "But this Kol Nidre prayer annuls vows for the year to come."

"Those two men will be secret Jews again this year, until they escape or die. I will continue my secret work for Fry and his associates. We will break vows this year. Kol Nidre, this court, frees us from having to act out of a promise. We are challenged to act from free and mindful choices of what is good. Kol Nidre invites us to be decent by choice, not by guilt or obligation to an oath or the law. Sometimes you have to break earthly laws to satisfy the laws of Heaven."

"How does one chose?"

"Precisely. These men have already violated their oath. Jewish law requires a minion of ten Jewish men be present to pray. But it is too risky."

Ernst felt a question burning in his heart. "The court of Heaven will not absolve me, will it, Puck?"

"No, my dear Ernst. It will not." He shook his head sadly. "That is not the point of Kol Nidre. These are the proceedings of acts yet to come, of imperfect choices in a flawed world. It is not for the court of Heaven to absolve you. Only you can absolve yourself – and only by your acts."

The cheese had a bad taste. There was no more to be said. Puck retired to his bedroom. After a few minutes Ernst had blown out the candle and it was dark. He stayed up for hours with his wine and Gauloises.

★ ★ ★ ★ ★ ★ ★ ★ ★ ★

Each monthly rendezvous with Lisa approached like sexual anticipation and ended with the self-loathing and despair of impotence. In November, after the fourth failed encounter, the first scent of winter spilled over the Chaine L'Etoile before sunrise, the smell of snow closing mountain passes to Switzerland, and he knew there might be no escape for her until spring. He left the square after the eleven bell, as Sunday mass at St. Laurent ended.

The Quai approximated normality, bustling with parishioners, fish stall customers, merchants, Agents de Police, and Gendarmes. The refugees were conspicuous for their dress or furtive glances, and he wondered that the Gendarmes left them alone. Seagulls and pigeons competed for scraps and crumbs.

Because Ernst declined to make a commitment to Sabiani, to wear the blue bar on his beret, work on the docks grew unpredictable and scarce. He spent more of his empty hours with Puck's forgeries. To Ernst's relief, the delicate, close work, like the heavy lifting on the docks, became a narcotic for his pain, filling Ernst's expectant days from one month to the next, convincing him, against all reason, that she would be there at sunrise.

The first time he felt delight in his forgeries for Puck he dismissed it as an aberration, but he worked into the night and found himself eager to pick up his pens and magnifying lenses again the next morning. When Puck first pinned the verses of Sahl and Mehring over his desk, Ernst fought the impulse to tear them down. He felt their animation, how they watched him, pleaded with him, argued, growled at him, and inexplicably, he began to feel pleasure in contemplating their rescue. He read the poems again and again, and by now they were like childhood verses whose memorized words, whose rhythm and rhyme, comforted.

In early November, on an unusually hot day, Puck asked Ernst to accompany him to meet Varian Fry at the Hotel Splendide. "You could use some fresh air and sun," Puck said. "Your skin is beginning to look as sallow as mine. And it's high time you met Fry."

At the hotel, Puck left Ernst alone in the lobby. After a few moments he was approached by a trim young man, tall with an angular face and blue eyes, blond hair slicked back, an expensive blue suit well pressed.

"Monsieur Toussaint? I am Franzi." They shook hands, and he bowed. "So good to meet you. We at the Committee very much admire your work. Varian... Mr. Fry is eager to meet you. Please, come with me."

Ernst could see Franzi did not smoke, his teeth shining as white as his crisp, new dress shirt. Franzi was as singular in Marseille as an elegant woman in the fish market.

In the richly carpeted hallway on the third floor of the Hotel, it was dark and hot enough to cause candles to bend. The ten or twelve refugees who sweated in a haphazard queue talked amongst themselves, but quieted when Ernst and Franzi walked by. Inside suite 311 a jalousie hung over the window, partially closed to admit what little air moved outside and still shade the afternoon sun that beat down on the hotel's western exposure overlooking the Vieux Port. Across the Boulevard d'Athènes atop the six story Hotel Marseille, the huge electric 'CINZANO' sign, skeletal in the daylight, had been dark since the armistice. Despite two Vornado fans, each thumping to its own internal cadence, hot air sloshed about the room like swamp water. Two seated men with sweat stained underarms, their shirt sleeves rolled up, ties loosened, wiped their foreheads frequently. One sat at a writing desk and scribbled on a form as he spoke in pressured whispers to an old man with tousled white hair. The other sat across from a young woman, a mirror turned flat serving as a makeshift desk between their knees. Across the crowded room an older woman sat behind a typewriter, her salt and pepper hair already matted and damp. She whispered directions to a young blond boy who looked no more than twelve or thirteen.

"That's Gussie," Franzi pointed to the boy. "He's from Danzig – speaks fluent German. His parents sent him to Paris to avoid the Nazis. He came south on his own and now works for us. Can you believe he's eighteen? His baby face is very useful."

The bedroom door opened, and a square-shouldered man strode out, slightly shorter than Ernst, with dark rimmed glasses and green eyes, his tie knotted just so. He adjusted his boiled white shirt so the cuffs bordered his suit precisely.

Franzi stopped him. "Varian. May I present Monsieur Toussaint."

Fry studied Ernst for a moment, thoughtful as if going through a mental card file, then his face appeared to register the name, but not with a smile. He shook Ernst's hand once, with a strong grip.

"Come with me, please." He returned to the bedroom and indicated for Ernst to follow him into the bathroom where he closed the door and turned on the taps in the sink and bathtub full force. "I am certain the Gestapo have listening devices. One never knows who is in the office, perhaps an undercover Gendarme, a Gestapo agent, a citizen eager for a reward. So many incentives for treason these days. You see the parade of people in the hallway? We don't know anything about them. The bathroom is safe. It's where we have all our meetings." He sat on the closed toilet and proffered the edge of the tub to Ernst.

"Your work is excellent, Monsieur Toussaint." He spoke slowly, choosing his words with care. "Puck speaks highly of you. He says you have extra time on your hands. As you can see, we are somewhat overwhelmed with clientele. And I'm sorry that we cannot pay more."

He opened a manila folder and passed a crudely drawn map to Ernst. "This is the map of a footpath over the Pyrenees from Banyuls to Cerbère and Port Bou."

The map was titled "Early Autumn Tour in the Pyrenees: recommended to illegal tourists."

"I hope we can call on you to be of assistance in some capacity, other than your artistic skills. Franzi will tell you more. I wish we could speak more, but time is short. Good to meet you, Monsieur Toussaint. And... thank you." He shut the taps and left the bathroom.

★   ★   ★   ★   ★   ★   ★   ★   ★   ★

Mary Jayne Gold was even more beautiful than rumored. Her flaxen hair, not quite shoulder length with a bit of curl at the edges, glowed in the shadows under the awning of Sept Petite Pècheurs. She watched him as he crossed Rue Dominicaine and leaned over to scratch the ears of her black miniature poodle. Afternoon rain steamed off the hot pavement with a sweet and sour scent. Ernst wondered just what kind of underground network Mr. Fry directed; like Franzi, this woman did not blend.

He introduced himself and she smiled coyly from her seat. Her insistent grey eyes sought his. Her perfect lips pursed slightly. She presented her dog, Dagobert, as if he were an old friend, but the poodle growled as Ernst sat down.

"Hush, Dago darling." Then to Ernst, "You're not a Vichy agent, or a Gestapo man, are you, Monsieur Toussaint? Dagobert hates collaborators and Nazis."

"Monsieur Fry prefers geraniums." He mumbled the predetermined phrase, then offered her a cigarette. "Enchanté, Madame."

"Mademoiselle. And please, call me Mary Jayne. May I buy you a drink? Robert will pour the good stuff for me." She waved at the waiter.

"I will be seeing Monsieur Solomon soon," Ernst said as soon as the waiter left. "He requires funds."

"Yes, of course. I have something for Monsieur Solomon." She sat forward inches from Ernst's face. "But First – tell me about yourself. You're not from Marseille. You have an intriguing accent."

Did she think this was one of her cocktail parties, that she was grilling the guests for their social and genetic pedigree? Or was this something more physical. "Near Freiburg originally, but I've been in Marseille since the occupation. I work on the docks. And you?"

"I'm an American, if you couldn't already guess." The waiter brought two glasses of her usual, which turned out to be dry vermouth. "I met Miriam in Toulouse, and she introduced me to Varian – Mr. Fry. You do know Miriam Davenport, don't you? A Smith girl. Fabulous! Speaks German and French like a native." She lifted her glass to Ernst. "Prosit, monsieur Ernest."

She watched him over the rim of her glass as they sipped. "I had my schooling in Italy and lived in Paris up until the war. I'm also a pilot, you know. Strictly for fun. Owned my own monoplane. I would fly to Switzerland one day to go skiing, and to the Riviera the next week to lie on the beach. All in all a rather decadent existence. Now and then I miss it." She slumped a little and looked off into the distance over Ernst's shoulder. She forced a smile.

Ernst noticed three men who sat down at the table behind them. Marseille was rife with Gestapo agents, and this American woman's bluster made him nervous.

Before he could say anything, she finished her Cinzano and said, "Would you accompany Dagobert and me about the Vieux Port, Monsieur?"

"I would be honored, Mademoiselle." He pulled her chair back as she got up and little Dagobert led them down Rue Mery through the twisted streets to the port, his little nose twitching this way and that, sampling the rich fare.

As soon as they disappeared into the narrow streets of the Vielle Ville, her flirty nature transformed, took on substance and intention. She began speaking quickly, in hushed tones.

"Herr Solomon must leave France in the next two weeks. The new Jewish laws – he will almost certainly be arrested. There is nothing Varian can do for him – he is not on the list. There will be no American visa, no passport – nothing."

"But he gets money. What is so different about Herr Solomon?"

She was as serious now as she had been flippant and ditsy before. "Unfortunately, nothing. He came forward to ask for help at the right moment. There are thousands like him. Winter is coming. It won't be easy in the camps, and the passage through the Pyrenees will be awful once the snow flies. It's all a matter of luck, of timing. A poor excuse for deciding who to save and who to leave behind, n'est-ce pas, Monsieur Ernest?"

They walked on in silence for a few more blocks. "Do you see that boy walking this way? The one with the black beret?"

A boy of perhaps twelve or thirteen sauntered toward them, a string bag with groceries and a baguette hanging from his left arm.

"The baguette is on his left arm. That means we haven't been followed." She opened her handbag and removed an envelope. "Three thousand francs." She passed it to Ernst. "Also three pieces of green paper, cut in an erratic fashion through the word 'Constantinople'. Your guides in Banyuls have the matching halves. Varian gave you the map – for Autumn Tourists? You will accompany Herr Solomon and his companion across the Pyrenees on the 'F' route. Listen very carefully; there is no itinerary for this journey." She explained the escape in clipped details, then quizzed him about names and places. "I hope you return, but I'll understand if you decide to high tail it for Lisbon."

Ernst thought her most attractive and not a little baffling. "Why do you do this, Mademoiselle? You need not be here."

"I'm rich. I'm bored. It's one of those rare opportunities to do the right thing." She smiled and, like a school girl, giggled. "And a ripping good story to tell at parties." After a block of silence she said, "And you, Monsieur Ernest?"

Ernst deliberated most of a block. He wanted to say 'I'm waiting for the love of my life, without whom there is no reason to go on,' but felt ashamed and stumbled for words, which came together mysteriously from a dark district of emotion and intuition. "A debt. I have a debt to pay."

"It must be quite weighty if it keeps you here."

She squinted at him, the oblique incline of her head at once puzzled and coquettish. "Most of the others simply shrug their shoulders and say something like, 'I hate Les Boches.' I could feel that you were different." She smiled and looked down with some embarrassment.

"Sometimes it surprises even me," Ernst said.

"Yes, I know exactly what you mean. I'm sure we will meet again, Monsieur Ernest." She offered her hand. He kissed its perfumed softness and felt something good, deep inside, that he could not explain.

* * * * * * * * * *

A week later, after the first brief cold snap, a middle-aged man came to the apartment two hours before curfew and asked for Monsieur Toussaint. "I have his copy of Carlyle," he said through the chain lock, and Ernst let him in.

"Emil Solomon?" Ernst asked.

"Yes." He took off his hat and passed it from hand to hand. "Mr. Fry said you could help me."

"You're late." Ernst directed him to the cleared kitchen table. "Sit down. You have your papers?"

The little man sat slowly as if his knees would give out, and put a green accordion-folded refugee passport, his titres de voyage, on the table.

"If the Gestapo truly wants you, this document is your death warrant." Ernst slid the pass back at Solomon. "The Spanish won't recognize it."

"That's why I was sent to you. I'm sure the Gestapo would arrest me if they could. Not only am I a Jew, but I was on the editorial staff of the Berliner Tageblatt for eight years, assistant to the editor, Theodore Wolff. It would not surprise me if he has already been arrested. I myself had a close call with the Gestapo in Berlin. I fled with the shirt on my back. My wife is with me."

"Are you willing to chance going through Spain under your name?" He had done this often enough that his queries were routine, but he knew that each question burned for Emil Solomon.

His hat shook from tremor. "Mr. Fry discouraged that. We had been waiting for an affidavit in lieu of passport."

"Do you want to find out how badly the Gestapo wants you? And if you do get to Spain? German fascists and Spanish fascists only speak a different language. You need a new identity, Herr Solomon. That is why Mr. Fry sent you to me."

"And my wife. I won't go without her."

Ernst thought of Lisa, and he was disconcerted at how quickly his tears threatened. It was a relief to sort through Herr Solomon's papers and regain his composure and voice. "Czech passports are obtainable, but then you become apatrides. French exit visas are never available for foreign refugees. If the French arrest you and see you are apatrides, you are sure to end up in some hell-hole, le Vernet or St. Cyprien."

"We are aware of the risks. But it is now or never."

"Escape over the border itself is difficult, although you seem to be fit. Your wife?"

There was a long pause. "She is seven months pregnant. But she is strong."

"She had better be." Ernst opened the drawer of the desk and removed Mary Jayne Gold's envelope. "If you return next Tuesday evening, the same time, I will have made progress. In the meantime, some funds on your behalf. Don't ask from where." He pushed the envelope across the table. "It's not much, but you and your wife should eat well for a week – strengthen her for the crossing. I will, of course, need more information about you and…"

"Sarah. Sarah Solomon. Yes." He fumbled in his jacket pocket. "Here. Our photographs and physical information." He laid out documents and ration coupons like cards in a high stakes gamble. "Sarah and I have been married for eight years. We've never been able to conceive. We thought we never would. While we were in hiding, in Belgium, we made love one night. Wouldn't you know it," he laughed and it was almost a sob, "this time it worked." He sat up and became suddenly serious. "We want this baby, Monsieur Toussaint. I would gladly send Sarah out alone if it would improve her chances of survival. We had all but given up. You don't know what hell it has been since June." He looked down again, into his lap, his hat passing from hand to hand. "It is for Sarah and our child. Monsieur Toussaint, I cannot thank you enough."

A single tear spilled down Solomon's cheek, and Ernst had to look away. "I understand, Herr Solomon. I understand."

*   *   *   *   *   *   *   *   *   *

As Ernst left the docks the next evening, Dimitru materialized from an alley and fell in step with him. "Please. You will carry this package to Puck?" He pushed a file folder taped shut, under Ernst's arm. Dimitru was far too short and slight to blend with the other dock workers streaming to and from Bassin de la Joliette. "Blank ration cards. Identity papers – for children. Do not be caught with these. I am followed by les flics." He disappeared as quickly as he had appeared, into a tobacconist's shop.

When Ernst let himself into their flat, Puck was fussing with the record player and only grunted a greeting. He lifted the turntable off the machine, unraveled the wires beneath it and fixed a crude headset to his ears, then marked the time in a pocket journal.

"The Gendarmes staged another rafle today," Puck said. "They bagged Basante and Georges." He inserted two vacuum tubes and turned on the power.

"Bo Peep with her flock," he said into a small microphone. "The second bar – Lord Byron's day." He repeated the code twice. Ernst could hear static crackle in Puck's ears. He scribbled numbers and letters onto a paper, then disconnected the wiring and tubes and slid the turntable back in place. He put on the only record – The Magic Flute.

Ernst dropped the folder of identity papers on the table. "From Dimitru.

He found me near the docks – said he was being followed. What a nervous little man. And I have something else to brighten your day." Ernst reached into his rucksack and found a thick envelope. "From our lovely American friend – Mary Jayne Gold."

Puck slit open the envelope and fondled a stack of postal orders. He licked his forefinger and began counting. "Forty Thousand francs? That's very generous. "

Ernst smiled as he recalled their meeting. "A donation, she said."

"If it weren't for her American passport and her cheek she would be in a concentration camp. You know, Ernst. Giving this to you – it's her way of flirting. You must have charmed her."

Ernst poured himself a glass of wine. "Who's Bo Peep?"

"Captain Fitch, British Expeditionary Force – in Fort St. Jean. There are still over a hundred Brits left. We finally secured a boat for about sixty to escape on Thursday. Fantastic prices – two hundred thousand francs for a single trip to Gibraltar. That just about breaks the Committee's bank account."

"My friend Henri tells me that Sabiani and Robert own capable boats. Sabiani will smuggle refugees, maybe even the Brits, for money. Robert also for the money, and the chance to stick it to les Boches."

Puck finished his glass and stared at the bottle. "Is Henri trustworthy?"

"An opportunist, maybe, but not a collaborator, if that's what you mean. Sabiani gives him work, cognac, coffee. He has five children to feed."

"One can never be too careful," Puck said and finished his wine. "The British want their men back. Fry has been spiriting two or three at a time over the frontier to Spain, but time is running out. Luckily, the French Officer in charge at the Fort only counts noses every day. Civilians take the place of the escaped Brits each day for role call. But the money is running out. Hence," he held up the postal orders, "manna not quite from heaven, but from a cheeky angel. Vichy is cracking down. Dimitru says that the Gestapo will 'inspect' the Fort soon."

"Dimitru knows too much about the Gestapo," Ernst said. "Do you trust him?"

"One hears that question so often it's become rhetorical." Puck spread a thin grape preserve on a piece of baguette. "Keep your ears open. Any boat will do."

Ernst said, in a quiet voice, "I'll be going to the frontier for a few days next week. Mary Jayne asked me to escort two refugees over the border."

Puck giggled. "And you couldn't say no to Mary Jayne, could you? She's quite persuasive in an American kind of way, and very attractive."

"Has nothing to do with it."

"So you're doing it for... for what?"

"She asked me the same question. I said I felt strangely compelled. How well do you know Mary Jayne?"

"She's rich and beautiful. What else is there to know? You didn't tell her about Lisa and she didn't tell you about 'Killer,' her lover. Jacques Daunis, a Frenchman – ex-Legionnaire, like yourself. He calls himself 'Killer' – watched too many Hollywood movies. He's been in prison in Fort St. Nicholas for a month or so. Desertion or some such thing." Puck tore off a piece of baguette. "You seem lighter," he said.

Ernst snorted and poured another glass of wine. "It will be good to get out of Marseille – fresh air, hiking in the mountains."

Puck nodded and ate his bread. "Hmm."

★   ★   ★   ★   ★   ★   ★   ★   ★   ★

Sarah Solomon sat across from Ernst on the Perpignan train as it rattled first west, then south, toward the Pyrenees. She caressed her womb as if it were a sleeping cat and stared absently at the Étang de l'Ayrolle wetlands. Lit by the glaring sun her pale face seemed baked and hardened like clay. For a moment Ernst glimpsed his own pregnant mother, so long ago, sitting in the dark parlor.

Before they left Marseille, Ernst had given Herr Solomon and Sarah each a tube of 'toothpaste' containing messages and lists, inserted into a rubber finger and tied off, then pushed into the toothpaste tube from the bottom and resealed. Fry's refugees carried at least one tube across the border, and they were instructed to mail them to the Emergency Rescue Committee in New York.

At Perpignan they waited on the platform, Emil Solomon and his pale wife flanking Ernst, who lit a cigarette. He let a crumpled blue Gauloises pack fall at his feet, indicating nothing was amiss. Almost at once, a young man with a white boutonniere appeared and asked if he could help them with their bags. Had he not appeared, Ernst would have taken his charges directly back to Marseille on the next train. 'Paul' helped carry their bags to the Café Perpignan in the station and led them to a table at the rear of the restaurant where he ordered coffee for all three, though Sarah protested she could not stand the smell. It was necessary, he said, please do not question. Once the three steaming cups sat on the table, Paul left and a young woman approached.

"Would you like to see my new Opel?" she said.

She was dark haired and, as most adolescents, alluringly attractive even with too much lipstick on her smooth lips. Ernst faltered, then remembered. "My Opel has five tires."

Her shoulders relaxed. "My name is Anya."

She embraced him mechanically. He felt her arms around his neck, smelled her freshly washed hair, a strange perfume – not Lillé. He imagined Lisa – another Sunday sunrise less than two weeks away – maybe this time. He almost conjured her breath entering him, her breasts and pelvis pressing hard. But Anya held her body back from Ernst; their cheeks touched and anyone watching saw an affectionate but cool greeting.

Anya whispered in his ear. "The way is clear, Monsieur Toussaint."

Though their script was complete, Ernst could not let her go. "You smell heavenly, Anya."

"I should slap your face," she whispered and pulled back. She tilted her head and smiled coyly. "But thank you."

The train to Banyuls was delayed almost an hour. Their papers were inspected on the platform by a Captain of the Agents de police who studied Solomon and his wife, then their papers. Ernst thought the policeman sensed a problem, but was too tired, bored or cynical to pursue his doubts. He could almost hear the captain's brief internal debate over the relative merits of compassion vs. justice, and why he should care. A Gendarme would not have suffered this ambivalence, and if he did, would have quickly erred on the side of justice.

No one spoke during the short ride from Perpignan to Banyuls. Ernst now sat across the compartment from Anya, and each time their eyes met she looked away with schoolgirl embarrassment. It was her supple body and coy face that first aroused him. Her flirtatious attention delighted him. Then he fathomed the enormity of the risk she undertook, and he could no longer take her innocence for granted. She couldn't have been more than twenty; young people were so foolish, as he had once been. Youthful indiscretions had a disturbing way of masquerading as courage, as he knew only too well. He wondered how today's rescue would look to Anya twenty years from today – in 1960. This young girl put her life in grave jeopardy for people she did not know. What kind of courage was that?

Monsieur Hans Fittko and his wife Eva met them in Banyuls near the train station at the bottom of a dry riverbed leading to the mountains. They matched their green paper 'Constantinople' cut-outs and immediately began their climb. Bill Freier had provided the Fittkos, German Socialists, with French Identity Cards that showed them to be citizens of the Forbidden Zone in northeastern France to which they could not return. The Fittkos worked in the vineyards, as did almost everyone in Banyuls, often taking jobs near the border. Monsieur Fittko explained to his neighbors that many friends, also from the Forbidden Zone, would visit from time to time. At the Fittkos' home these "friends" changed into the trousers and blouses of farm laborers or country people on holiday and climbed up the riverbed, never to return.

During their ascent Anya walked with Ernst. "I'm not as young as I look," she said, as if anticipating his question. "I'm training to be a mountain guide and counselor for EIF – The Jewish Scouting Organization. We lead mountain climbing and hiking trips for Jewish teenagers. Rugged terrain. This is nothing."

They walked in silence until Anya said, "After the war we'll do that again." There was swagger in her tone. "Ours were the first evacuation centers for children in the Southeast. In '39 and '40, after the men were mobilized, we women took over EIF. At first it was all legal. But now... "

They left the dry riverbed at a well and climbed through a vineyard, keeping an ancient Norman tower directly before them. They reached the tower after sunset and stopped to marvel at their first view over the border at a few specks of light from Cerbère and Port Bou on the Spanish side.

"They say we Jews are victims." Anya spoke gently and it surprised Ernst. "It's not true. Some say we should cooperate. They say it will go better for us if we are not troublesome." She sighed. A sunset rim of gold, orange and purple back-lit the jagged Pyrenees to the west. "I think the Nazis have murderous designs on us Jews, not simply deportation. To my way of thinking it is far more dangerous to cooperate. At least if we defy them we have the chance of escape and survival."

"Ten deported for every one rescued? A complex mathematics, Anya."

"Not complicated, Monsieur Ernest. Necessary."

Fittko and Eva reviewed the rest of the trip and the timing for crossing, then bade them farewell and headed back to Banyuls and the vineyards. They left the hand-drawn map. The mountain path had been steep and there was more climbing ahead. Sarah had vomited several times and was limping badly; Ernst and Anya took turns with her husband steadying her during the ascent. The evening star shone over the mountains when they reached the abandoned barn where they would spend the night.

The remains of the day silhouetted the Pyrenees in darkening shades of blue. Anya and Ernst sat close together reclining on old bales of hay in a barn so long abandoned that the chill wind blew almost unimpeded through gaps in the boards. Anya shivered, and Ernst wrapped a blanket around her shoulders. She leaned against his side. The thrill of her touch excited long buried desire, and he was powerfully tempted to put his arm around her.

"What was it like, growing up in Berlin?" Anya sounded dreamy.

"Before the war or after?" he said. "Everything changed."

"I mean as a child."

"It was a difficult time, and I was a difficult child. When I remember my father, the man who comes to mind is angry or cold. He is arguing with my mother about things I don't understand, or disciplining me. Mostly, he ignored me. Except for some rare moments alone with him in the National Gallery – with the Impressionists. He loved these new paintings and I saw a piece of him I otherwise never saw. I remember it so well, his enchanted expression as he contemplated each painting. He didn't look at me, he didn't touch me, but his words were soft and tender. He called it 'the painting of the light' and wanted me to understand it as if it was the most important lesson he could transmit. I cherish that memory more than any other. Father died when I was 16. It was 1918, during the War."

"And your mother?"

"Until her stillbirth, Mother argued right back at Father, and I couldn't understand her either. She favored my older brother Leo and felt sorry for my little brother, Hans Gerd, because of his deformed hand. I always had the feeling that she and Father were angry at me – all the time – and I thought it was because I misbehaved so and brought shame on our family. But not more than Hans Gerd. I suspected there was something especially bad I had done – something unforgivable. I still don't know what that was."

Through an opening in the hayloft Anya pointed out the constellation Orion, and she told Ernst how she and her sisters always wished on the middle star in Orion's belt.

"Now it's your turn," she said. "What will you wish for?"

He felt completely at ease with Anya, as if she was his sister. "Can I say it out loud?" he said.

"If you're this close to another person it's allowed. And we are so high up – so close to the stars – that the magic is very strong."

444

"I wish I could live one day in my life over again."

"Why that day?"

"I helped kill a man – long ago."

"Only one?"

"My real name is Ernst Werner Techow." He felt a curious relief as he told her of Rathenau's murder, the trial and Frau Rathenau's letter. Anya shivered under the blanket.

"I was born a month before the trial," she said, "Over the years, I recall my family talking about Rathenau. They loved him. It was like a death in the family, and they remembered exactly where they were when they heard of his assassination. My father called it the first Nazi murder." She sat up and looked at Ernst in a troubled way. "You were a fascist assassin and now you rescue Jews? Why?"

Ernst still was not sure – it had been only a few weeks since he had argued with Puck that he didn't care about the refugees. Then he chose to do this. "I suppose it's because I cannot live that one day over. This is my penance."

She was quiet for long minutes, then asked, "Do you have a special some-one?"

Ernst nodded in the dark. "Her name is Lisa."

"Tell me about her."

"She's married to my childhood friend, Fritz – a powerful Nazi. They have a son."

"Sounds very complicated."

"She's trying to escape – to meet me in Marseille." After a pause he added, "Maybe that's another reason why I'm here. I hope she has someone as brave as you to help her escape."

Ernst began with simple stories of how they met, of their time together as *Wandervogel*, falling in love. By the time the waxing moon shone through a roofless corner, Ernst had progressed from his longing for Lisa, to the Free Corps, Organization C, his time in Striegau, each episode another rosary bead of confession. Perhaps it was the clarity of the mountain air, or Anya's innocence, but he recalled with heaviness the shame in his heart for all his failures. By the time he described his years in the Sahara and his escape to Marseille, silver-lined clouds obscured the gibbous moon, darkening the barn further.

"You are ashamed of your whole life?" she asked.

"Not of today," he said. "And not of Lisa. But everything else... "

She sighed. "I'm sad for you."

Anya laid her head down in Ernst's lap; he drew the blanket about her and stroked her hair. She smelled like a woman, but she was slight and smooth skinned, like a girl.

"Whenever my sisters or I misbehaved, my father always said the same thing. 'To redeem your error you must alter the future.'" The wind's caprice rattled the barn's wooden bones. "Do you still have Frau Rathenau's letter?"

"Yes."

"That's a long time. The letter is as old as me."

Ernst felt uneasy, as if he was a fugitive and she had picked up his scent. "And what would you wish for?" he asked.

"When I was a little girl I would wish for a brother," she said. "I am one of four girls. In a Jewish home it is good to have at least one boy – to study Torah – to go to Yeshiva – to carry on the name."

"Your father was blessed to have you. Did he ever tell you?"

"I'm the youngest. Just after I was born, my oldest sister Hannah remembers one night coming upon my father praying, after everyone was asleep. She describes it more as my father bargaining with God. He gave thanks, said prayers for his newest daughter and then said he didn't understand. Would it be so much trouble to give a son? Hannah was about to step from the shadows and scold him. Hannah is like that – she always speaks her mind. But then my father said to God that he must have a very special reason for Anya to be on the Earth so he would take special care of me. Hannah told me that story when I was five years old and every year on my birthday she tells me again."

Ernst inhaled the sweet musk of her hair and lay down beside her. She turned away from him onto her side and they lay under the blanket like nesting spoons. Neither sought more intimacy, each content with the other's scent, embrace, warmth.

"You are so brave, Anya."

"No. It's not courage. I don't choose it. Neither can I run away from it. It is simply my life. I try not to think about it too much for fear I would go mad."

"I think your father must be afraid for you, but also proud."

"My father died last year at le Vernet – typhoid." She said it matter-of-factly.

"Is that what spurs you on?"

"It's nothing noble. I need something to do with my rage."

⋆   ⋆   ⋆   ⋆   ⋆   ⋆   ⋆   ⋆   ⋆   ⋆

The next morning before sunrise the ragtag troupe completed their climb and several hours later passed the crossroads before the French mountain troop's first patrol. They skirted the obvious intersection and cut across the road half a kilometer further west.

Anya led them down no discernible trail and by late afternoon they saw the sun's reflection on a Spanish guard tower below. From here they were on their own, Anya said, and she hugged the Solomons goodbye. She welcomed Ernst's embrace and this time she held him tightly and passed her hands under his shirt, across his bare back. She kissed his cheek and whispered, "I forgive you, Ernst Werner Techow." Then, as if an afterthought, she kissed him full on the lips and he felt her hot breath. Just as suddenly, she pushed away and bounded up the hill where she turned and waved, then disappeared over the crest.

They approached the Spanish guard house singing a Castillian folk song so the guards would not be startled. Sarah looked gray and staggered down the path leaning on her husband's shoulder. One of the guards helped her into the hut where she was given hot tea and bread. After she revived, her husband presented the guards with several packs of Gauloises and Gitanes. This was a plum posting, productive of many gifts, and the guards were friendly and eager to please. Only a fool would have taken the three hiker's story at face value; a picnic in the mountains and "my very pregnant wife suddenly became ill. At this stage of pregnancy anything can happen." The pregnant woman's distress sparked effusive, even gallant, interest on the part of the guards. After an hour, their gushing hospitality manifested as a taxi that bumped up the rough road from Cerbère to take the ailing Frau Solomon down the mountain.

The next day, after crossing into France again, Ernst sat back in the train compartment exhausted, yet filled with an unusual sense of excitement, a lingering euphoria from the adrenaline of risk. He relived Anya's kiss, felt the rare blush of their daring adventure, deeply satisfied, curiously invigorated.

In Perpignan he picked up a newspaper that headlined a new Vichy decree that forbade listening to English or Free French Gaullist radio broadcasts. In Ernst's compartment a wine merchant from Perpignan, Monsieur Lariotte, grumbled over rumors of a possible Nazi occupation of the Free Zone.

"If we don't cooperate, they will invade," he said and gruffly turned the page for the soccer scores. His fists crushed the edges of the newspaper and shook. "The economy will go to Hell. So what if they hate Jews? Hating Jews is as old as dirt. They want to take the Jews off our hands? Good riddance, I say!" He looked ready and willing to rage on until his spleen was all used up.

Ernst grunted weary agreement, then sunk back and let his beret fall over his eyes. It was the best way to shut the man up. Soon enough he felt sleep darkening.

As the train left the Montpellier station he awoke and saw that he was alone in the compartment. He drifted in and out of twilight consciousness. For a while there was only the sound of the wheels and then he dreamed his mother sitting by the Wannseestrasse parlor window again, stroking her womb, her water world. It seemed perfectly normal to feel himself as a child, sitting on his bare knees by the door, driving his dreadnought *Brandenburg* to its battle station in the parlor, its massive 280 mm guns raised for a broadside. Was she crying, or only sighing? She rubbed her womb, her hands circling faster and faster. Imperceptibly, and maybe this was why he had not remembered, first one open hand curled into a fist, and then the other. The circular rhythm of fists turned inward, keeping time with her moans, first lightly, then more agitated, pummeling, aiming for the core, raining blow after blow with frenzied ferocity. Ernst trained his finger binoculars on her until, all at once, she shrieked. Suddenly Frau Stimmel grabbed him under the arms and dragged him away. He looked back at the *Brandenburg*, dead in the water; a rivulet of bright red blood pooled at the leg of his mother's chair, and then he was in Eric's garage. Eric sat him on his lap and they drove to the dairy for a slab of Weisskäse and then magically, they were at the butcher for a slice of bratwurst. Behind the counter, instead of Herr Gruenspecht, Dr. Katzenstein wrapped something the size of a baby in brown paper. Dr. Katzenstein glared at him and said, "This is your fault, you nasty child. Your mother is asleep. She may never wake up."

Ernst woke with a start, soaked with sweat, mumbling his defense. It took some time to regain his normal breath and even longer for his heart to slow; it was more than a fantastic dream and he was disturbed by its reality.

Two hours later, when the train pulled into the Marseille station, Puck met him on the platform.

"You look tired," Puck said.

"Bad dreams."

"It's near curfew. I thought it best you not walk alone." He patted him on the shoulder. "You did well, Ernst."

They passed through the Gendarmes at Customs Control, who carefully checked each passenger against a list.

"I'm afraid I have some bad news," Puck said as they descended the grand stairway to Boulevard D'Athenes. "Freier was arrested with all his paraphernalia. Mina is beside herself. Charlie Fawcett was also arrested, in Spain, thank God. He was carrying all sorts of lists and communications, but Mary Jayne thinks they were all safely hidden – in a plaster bust and in the third valve of his trumpet.

"We have a new Intendant de la Police, le Capitaine de Rodellec du Porzic. Not an easy man – a Breton naval officer – a friend of Admiral Darlan. The Gendarmes are his thugs. He is interested in neither money nor women. Mary Jayne will try her charms, but word is that he's incapable of normal sexual feelings.

"You remember last month when Vichy decreed that Prefects could intern anyone, French or otherwise? It seems our new Intendant, unlike his predecessor, is taking the order quite literally, and has already sent several hundred to Les Milles without trial. According to today's newspaper they were 'dangerous to public safety' – women and small children. Last night there was another rafle of foreign-born Jews. I heard one hundred arrested. No appeals, no lawyers. They were simply thrown into the camps. Freier was one of them."

He talked fast and hustled Ernst along the Boulevard d'Athènes. "There is a sudden clamor for escape. Fry is inundated. There is so much commotion at the Hotel Splendide that the Committee will have to leave. They'll open a new office on Rue Garibaldi. Fry and Danny Bénédite have gone to Vichy to plead Freier's case with the police Commissaire. Theo is out of her mind with worry and rage at Danny for traveling 'into the lion's throat' as she put it. She is convinced that the Sûreté will arrest him when he gets there. It seems the American Consulate turned Fry and Danny down. Warned Fry to mind his 'p's and 'q's. Can you imagine? The bastion of freedom will not take a stand, even though many of these Jews have immigration visas for the United States. They have sponsors waiting for them. Mind his 'p's and 'q's? It's shameful.

"And, if that weren't enough bad news, Pétain will visit Marseille – in December. De Porzic will try to make Marseille clean enough for the doddering idiot to lick, like he does the assholes of the Nazis. I expect we will find out just how much the Marseille police know about us in the next few days, Ernst."

"You think we'll be arrested?"

"If the Sûreté Nationale knows us, we will be arrested. It will be a test. I suggest you destroy any papers you would not like to have found, such as your tourist map of the frontier."

"And the boat. Did Fitch get out?"

"Fry paid 225,000 francs. The boat never appeared. Brits, the Bernhards, Walter Mehring, and a few others, they waited all night in the cold for nothing. Now Mehring is sick and Fry's visa has expired. De Porzic wants Fry to leave, as do the Americans. The easy days are over."

23

Rescue
December 1940 – February 1943

It was cold enough in the flat for Ernst to see his breath. His eyes burned after eight hours of squinting at forgeries under a harsh lamp that only partially warmed his fingers. Because Ernst would not submit to his enticements, Sabiani had punished him by restricting his access to dock jobs, thus work was scarce. His income dropped, but his back improved. He filled his hours with Puck's forgery. He could have continued for another eight hours and it wouldn't have made a dent in the stack of documents that Gussie had delivered from Varian Fry's new office on Rue Garibaldi. Ernst switched off the lamp and laid a wet cloth over his eyes.

It was unusually cold even for December, and the dark flat reminded him of winter nights in Berlin on Pohlstrasse, in the back of his photography shop, forging documents in gloves with the fingertips cut out, hearing only the scratch of his pen and the wind-rattled windowpanes. At least on Pohlstrasse he had the sweet anticipation of illicit trysts with Lisa. When she came to his bed they burned candles with pirouetting flames, and they burned each other with passion, although he also well remembered the crushing sadness, the vast emptiness that remained when she was gone and the lamp was out, as it was now.

Darkness came early, long before curfew, and he crossed Rue d'Epice to stretch his back. He drew a deep breath and felt cobwebs break in his chest. He leaned against the willow that had become his friend and companion. At first he had done "Puck's forgeries" as a favor to his friend and to fill the time between dock shifts. But over the past few weeks he felt a growing empathy with each masterpiece. He reveled in the craft of reproduction – a reawakening of the innate joy he felt when exercising his artistic skills. Memories of Striegau and of Puck's patient tutoring returned with the potency of family warmth from childhood, a feeling he rarely obtained from his natural family. The precise requirements of forgery kept his mind focused, a mindfulness that prohibited formidable sensations of despair, longing, and failure, which were constant attendants at other times. He studied each identity photograph of the Jews whose identity papers he created. He learned to see beyond the lack of expression, to understand that each carried his own despair, longing and failure. He would supply the hope, and it left him feeling generous and potent, feelings not otherwise extant in Marseille.

He was about to light a cigarette when, suddenly, in the faint street light, Ernst noticed two shadows moving in tandem, and he froze against the willow until they separated. The one disappeared into a narrow alley near their tenement, the other crossed Rue d'Epice towards him. He thought the shadow stopped to look at their third floor apartment, then pulled up its dark collar and disappeared into the dark.

Puck was in an agitated state when he returned just before curfew, wheezing harder than usual. "Light the stove!" He coughed paroxysmally as he pried up floor boards beneath the dining table and extracted papers, lists, identity cards, baptismal records, ration coupons, passports. "Captain Dubois... .went out of his way to find me today... before I went to Fry's office. He told Fry... an hour before he was arrested." Breathless, he rummaged through his desk for more documents. "Marshall Pétain will visit Marseille in two days. Dubois says the Vichy Gendarmes will stage a major rafle... tonight to clear Marseille of 'troublemakers.'"

Puck considered the record player, then resumed ransacking his dresser for other precious papers. "Damn it, Ernst, light the stove!"

Ernst considered his stack of forgeries, a week's effort all for naught, each a masterpiece of deception, a rescue from death. He fed them to the fire, watching placid faces curl and darken, then combust. There were rumors about crematoria at camps – Auschwitz, Belzec, Dachau. As unfathomable as it seemed to Ernst, they burned Jews like so many photographs. Everything burned – their efforts no more than smoke.

"If they find these," Puck said, "we'll spend the winter at Gurs or le Vernet. I would kill myself first." Pungent fumes of burning paper filled the apartment. "If only the doddering old fool would die. One well placed bullet."

"It would be justice," Ernst said, "but nothing would change."

"According to Dubois, Fry and his associates have only been 'detained.' He doesn't want us to think badly of Frenchmen." Puck laughed his impish squeal and coughed again. "I would be sorely disappointed, slighted, not to be 'detained'. Rather like an artist or writer excluded from Mr. Fry's list."

The Vornado fan blew most of the smoke out the window and a chill slipped in behind it. Puck pulled the two poems off the wall and they, too, perished in the fire.

★ ★ ★ ★ ★ ★ ★ ★ ★ ★

Several hours later Ernst woke from a troubled sleep to the undulating wail of sirens and the rising rumble of boots on the stairs. A police inspector pounded on their door and threatened to break it down if they didn't open at once. Ernst and Puck stood in their nightclothes near the cold primus as Sûreté Inspector Martigne reviewed their papers. Two plainclothesmen scoured the apartment, emptying drawers, scattering papers and books. The only 'evidence' of any value to the Gendarmes was Puck's typewriter, which they confiscated. Inspector Martigne assured them, their papers were completely in order, and he regretted any inconvenience. They would be released in no time, probably by afternoon, but it was necessary to be 'interviewed'; he was sorry for the annoyance, but if they were innocent, which he did not doubt, they had nothing to fear.

In the street Ernst noticed that Martigne's police car bore Vichy license plates. He and Puck were led down the block to a Black Maria – the police paddy wagon – already half full with men and women who had dressed rapidly, their hair still in sleep's disarray. Under a lamppost a child's single black boot lay on its side. Sirens moaned in the distance. Whistles shrilled over rooftops. A single pistol shot reverberated from down the block.

Instead of the Prefecture of Police, they were interrogated at the Evéché, the temporary police station housed in the former Bishopric. Crucifixes and other Catholic icons embellished the walls and dark hallways, but the sanctity and solitude of the house was betrayed by police bootsteps and the stench of too many people in too small a space. Ernst sat alone on a wooden chair in a hallway with vermilion wallpaper, drawing in his knees each time a Gendarme strode by. A door opened at the far end of the corridor; he thought he heard whimpering. Moments later the faint scent of urine passed him like an apparition.

His interrogator, SS Untersturmführer Schenck, a portly man with a large, almost bald head, spoke French badly. Ernst found his eyes incessantly drawn to the abraded skin on Schenck's neck, where his starched white shirt chafed. Schenck squirmed like a turtle, trying to change the friction point,

453

his finger prying first one side then the other. He reviewed Ernst's military and demobilization records, once those of Legionnaire Ernest Tessier, now washed and rewritten for dock-worker Ernest Toussaint.

At one point in the questioning, Schenck, who referred to himself as "an assistant to the patriotic Sûreté Nationale," leaned forward, his breath foul with tobacco and rot. "Do you know an apatrides, named Ernst Werner Techow? He is a German fugitive."

Sweat beaded up on Ernst's forehead and he was afraid his quivering lip or strained voice might unmask him. But Schenck was more concerned with his own neck and, in any case, the outcome was never in doubt. Until Pétain left Marseille, they would all be 'detained.'

By mid-afternoon he was reunited with Puck in the hold of an old merchant ship, the Sinaïa, with over six hundred other 'usual suspects' rounded up in the early morning rafle. Varian Fry and some of his entourage sat nearby. Oddly, they seemed in good spirits. Danny Bénédite, a thin, intense man with dark hair and heavily framed glasses exclaimed, "Tiens, Fry. Vive le President Veelsson!"

Puck leaned over to Ernst. "What does he mean?"

"We're moored at one of the new docks – Mole G, Bassin Président Wilson."

Fry described Harry Bingham, the American Vice-Consul in charge of visas, as the only decent representative of the State Department in Vichy, France, the only one who could see beyond his narrow diplomatic duty and intervene on behalf of the Jews. Bingham had already participated in the rescue of one of Fry's clients, the novelist Lion Feuchtwanger, from the concentration camp at St. Nicholas. The Vice-Consul had driven to a spot where inmates were allowed to bathe in the river. He brought some women's clothes along, and Feuchtwanger changed into them and escaped in the diplomat's car. For weeks he was hidden in Bingham's villa, until Fry's rescue team was able to assist him over the border.

That night they slept on burlap bags filled with straw under thin blankets, inadequate to the cold. Ernst felt an unexpected solidarity with the ordinary men and women with whom he was detained, each one a threat to the security of Occupied France and Marshall Pétain. Each alone had chipped away at the Nazi occupation, snatched victims from the jaws of death with myriad schemes. But all together, packed in the hold of this stinking freighter, they were a motley army.

After two days, during which they were fed only hard bread and thin soup, 'brief detention' became cramped and restless, worse than Striegau. Ideology fell by the wayside, and conversations that on the first day of this non-voyage sizzled with righteous indignation and spirited debate about the virtues of Socialism vs. Communism, the failure of the Third Republic and de Gaulle's Free French, gave way to reminiscences of food, recipe debates, rambling narratives of delicacies from childhood remembered to the point of tasting.

By the third day, even this bit of mental gymnastics proved ineffectual. Ernst found the memory of Frau Stimmel's schnitzel as diaphanous as smoke, the taste of his father's hot chocolate at the National Gallery unimaginable. Arguments erupted over trivial indignities, inopportune glances. Fry became increasingly irate about their unlawful detention. He stood at the bulkhead door and demanded to see the American Consul. Did their captors know that he and Mary Jayne Gold were Americans? There would be repercussions – international consequences.

The police guard, Vichy Gendarmes, seemed unimpressed and not a little amused until singing began below the foredeck. A chorus of hungry prisoners sang La Marseilles and Die Moor Soldaten and even the German Communist song Die Thälmann Brigade because it ended with a shout of "Freiheit – Freedom!" Their morale and tumult swelled as more detainees found their voices. The police rapped their clubs on the grates overhead. The captive chorus only sang with more gusto.

Finally, on the morning of the fourth day, Harry Bingham appeared on the dock with an American delegation, and after vigorous argument, debates and threats, Fry and his associates were released. A day later, after Pétain had left Marseille, Ernst and Puck were released and returned to the business of forgery.

But a chill was in the air.

* * * * * * * * * *

By March of 1941 the Agents de Police were no longer good-natured. After Marshall Pétain's visit to Marseille, Captain Dubois suddenly found himself transferred to Rabat, in French Morocco. Du Porzic named Charles Courbet, the former director of Vichy's fascist youth organization, the Jeunesse de France et d'Outre Mer to replace him. Courbet's greatest assets to Vichy were his slavish devotion to precise record keeping and his unflinching use of savage enforcers.

Freier was released by the Marseille court in March and immediately apprehended again by de Porzic's Gendarmes and interned at the concentration camp at le Vernet. Lena Fishman, Fry's secretary and courier, left France in February and was promptly arrested in Spain at Cerbère. When a strip search revealed nothing she was allowed to proceed.

After his arrest, there was no more work for Ernst on Sabiani's docks. After three weeks, money was tight, and he and Puck were forced to eat simply. Pleasures were few and even cheap burgundy became a luxury. Except for Henri and Puck, Ernst had no friends and devoted himself to forging documents – and, every few weeks, escorting Fry's clients over the Pyrenees. He looked forward to these mountain trips, a welcome relief from the collaborative threat and deadly tedium that marked his life in Marseille. On his last expedition he inquired about Anya, as he often did, but this time his escort had heard about her – had received a letter. After her last rescue, she had escaped with her refugees to Lisbon and emigrated to Palestine, where she lived in relative safety on a Kibbutz. Ernst felt the warm flush of relief and vicarious pleasure he presumed her father might have felt had he survived. What Ernst might have felt if he were her father.

There were other pleasures. Some quiet, like the satisfaction he derived from his forgeries, others more intense, like the exhilaration in the mountains, as close to pleasure as danger could bring him. His other delight, more cerebral, was at Henri's home where the two drank acceptable coffee and Sabiani's cognac, played cards, and argued about Faust and Heine.

The British blockade tightened and coffee disappeared, except at Henri's apartment and Sabiani's cafés. It was replaced by 'acorn coffee' sweetened with grapo. One night, after a few cognacs, Ernst mentioned his gift for copying documents and official seals for Fry. Henri was impressed and sympathetic. It was no secret in Marseille that the American with green eyes spirited Jews and anti-Nazi refugees out of the country. Henri laughed heartily when Ernst copied his signature perfectly after a few minutes of practice. Ernst stressed the need for confidentiality and discretion, and Henri was insulted. Ernst was his friend, Henri insisted, and loyalty to friends was unconditional.

Ernst's visits were a welcome relief for Henri also. The baby had been ill for two months – whooping cough, according to the doctor. She coughed until she lost her breath and her face turned purple. Her medicine was expensive. She was only now slowly improving, but Henri had not slept well for months, and he looked it. Deep crevasses lined his youthful face, dark shrouds hung beneath his eyes.

"I heard today on the docks," Henri said after dinner, "that a gold dollar is selling for 268 francs. What a killing one could make with some gold, eh?"

Ernst nodded but felt himself go on guard. Just the other day, Dimitru had offered a gold-for-francs deal to Fry. "There are always opportunities in war," Ernst said.

"This funny little Greek, Dimitru, told me about this," Henri said. "I have made deals with him before. Do you know him?"

Ernst's mind raced. Was he being tested or was Henri trying to do a good turn for an unemployed friend? "I don't know that name," he lied.

"A businessman, through and through. Dependable in that way. He always follows the best deal. One never has to worry that Dimitru will be seduced by patriotism or morality. It's weirdly reassuring."

The next day Ernst discussed Dimitru's opportunity with Fry at the Committee's office on Rue Garibaldi. Fry wiped a silk handkerchief with a 'VF' monogram across his lips and seemed to be weighing the risks and rewards. Danny Bénédite, thin and tall, his expression severe, and Danny's wife Theo listened to the gold-for-francs deal.

"If anyone can do this, it's Dimitru," Danny said.

Theo shot a hard look at Danny. "I don't trust him."

"We have no money!" Danny said. "Let me try a test exchange."

"Don't you dare!" Theo turned, hands on her hips.

"Ernest? Would you do it?" Fry said as he carefully rearranged the handkerchief in the pocket of his Brooks Brothers suit.

"I would."

"No!" Danny leapt up from the table. "Dimitru has to know he is dealing with the Committee. We have clout with him, and he knows there will be more business. I'll do it. It's too important to leave to an unknown."

"I'd hardly call Ernest Toussaint an unknown," Fry said and smiled at Ernst.

Ernst felt first hurt, then angry with Danny. At least Fry believed in him.

"OK, Danny, you make the test exchange," Fry said. "But Ernest, I want you to shadow Danny, in case something goes awry. I trust both of you implicitly."

The first exchange went flawlessly. Danny delivered $200 in gold to the designated corner in Le Panier and returned with almost 54,000 francs. A few days later Danny was on his way to Dimitru's hotel with a larger parcel of gold coins in a briefcase. Ernst followed thirty meters behind. As they neared the hotel Ernst caught a glimpse of a man with dark glasses who backed around a corner. Dimitru waited on the hotel steps as arranged. Across the boulevard three men loitered near a pharmacy. Ernst quickened his pace and had almost caught up with Danny at the Hotel entrance when he noticed the three men striding, almost running across the street.

Ernst turned abruptly into a kiosk and bought a newspaper. Danny saw the situation now and walked by Dimitru without recognition, but a few steps later the three men surrounded him and showed their badges. One inspected his briefcase. From around the corner where the man with the dark glasses had disappeared, a Black Maria turned and Danny was taken away.

Theo was furious. Everything stopped at the Committee while Fry tried any maneuver, legal and otherwise, to bring about the release of his friend. He finally prevailed again on Harry Bingham, the American Vice Consul, to present falsified papers to the douane at Prison Chave where Danny was detained. The papers, created by Ernst, showed Danny to be an employee of an American relief organization. Bingham prevailed upon the douane to bring Danny's matter before a magistrate promptly and, to everyone's surprise, the douane complied. Danny was charged with illegal possession of gold, transporting gold, intention to sell gold illegally, and presumptive intention of diverting funds to illegal use.

Miraculously, the court released Danny on bail pending trial. When a police car delivered him to the lawyer's office, where they all waited, Ernst saw Fry's cool façade fall away. He was so relieved to see his friend and co-conspirator that he threw his arms around him even before Theo could embrace him. She chastised all three of them for 'stupid recklessness.'

Ernst felt heavy with blame for Danny's arrest; he should have known Dimitru's offer was too good to be true.

Several days after Danny's release, Robert confirmed that Dimitru was indeed a Gestapo agent. He was almost certainly responsible for the disappearance of Captain Murphy's money and now the gold, which was never recovered. Long into that night they discussed Dimitru's betrayal and wondered how much else was at risk. Did he know of the British troops smuggled out? It was no secret about the refugees. Everyone in the Committee felt exposed.

A week later three detectives from the Prefecture burst into the Committee's office with a warrant to search for 'false passports, visas, identity cards and any machines or material for fabricating them.' They ransacked the office and even inspected the inside of the chimney, where they found a supply of dollar bills hidden for emergencies. Only Dimitru could have told them this. They found nothing else, since, at Fry's insistence, neither documents nor the apparatus to create them, were ever kept in the office.

As Fry had predicted, two days later, the Gendarmes came to Villa Air-Bel where Fry was staying and searched for the remaining gold coins that only Dimitru knew they had. Fortunately they were buried in the overgrown back yard, but again the unmistakable touch of Dimitru sent shivers through the Committee.

Fry wondered aloud to Ernst about Dimitru's 'elimination.' Robert, at Sept Petit Pècheurs, leaned over the bar and whispered near Ernst's ear that his price for murdering a man was a mere 5,000 francs. "I give a 20% discount if the victim is a policeman. Within reason, I will extend that to the Gestapo, of course."

But Dimitru disappeared. When one of Robert's men finally found him, he was in Cavallaire, on the Cote d'Azur, well protected by Nazi thugs.

"His murder would be extremely dangerous," Robert reported to Ernst. "I would do it for nothing, but now that word is out about Dimitru, we have to pay a specialist. Possibly 100,000 francs."

"Too steep." Ernst shook his head. "But perhaps you could put out word that he is a condemned man. If he cannot be murdered, he should at least live in constant fear."

★   ★   ★   ★   ★   ★   ★   ★   ★   ★

Sunrise, on the first Sunday in August 1942, came and went as twenty-four other dawns had come and gone. Waiting for Lisa at Eglise St. Laurent was by now more a ritual or a sacrament than a possibility. Though he expected less and less from each Sunday vigil, he also depended on the grace invoked by his faith in her. If she were still alive she would find her way to Marseille.

As he rounded the corner onto Quai du Port he played his foolish game of envisioning her on the wharf in her blue dress; it was the blue that anchored his hallucination and through his half closed eyes she smiled and waved. If only – he would disappear with her like sugar in tea.

But, once again, the sun cleared the mountain on this second anniversary, dawn simmered into morning, and the fishing fleet returned under the Transbordeur. Ernst's letdown felt particularly bitter, more than previous disappointments, though he could not fathom what was different now.

Puck was always solicitous on those Sundays, though they never discussed details, or even named Ernst's despondency. Puck had prepared a thick soup from what little produce was still available, thickened with an au gratin starch. On this August day their flat smelled of garlic and bay leaves, and a bottle of burgundy sat open on the table.

It had been a year since Varian Fry's expulsion from France and the Committee being closed down by the French Prefecture of Police for subversive activities in June. Danny and Theo Bénédite and Charles Wolff tried to continue Fry's work, but now they, too, were in hiding. Puck squinted at a sewing needle he held up to the bare bulb and passed the black thread through its tiny pore. "Danny will surely join the resistance, if he is not already a member. Theo will be furious, especially with baby Caroline only four months old."

A new stamp was required that made passport and identity card forgery more challenging. All Jews in France, whether refugees or citizens, were required to have a 'Juif' stamped on their passports. Since June 1, Jews in the northern Occupied Zone were required to wear the yellow star. Rumors were rife that SS Captain Theodor Danneker had leaned heavily on René Bousquet at the Ministry of the Interior to implement the same order in the Unoccupied South.

Ernst leaned over his drawing board studying an identity card with a magnifying lens. "Last night after dinner, Henri told me the strangest thing." Ernst studied the official signature, preparing to imitate it. "He heard a rumor regarding an order from Bousquet to the regional prefects about a monumental rafle. Exemptions for children under the age of sixteen have been suspended. They will all be deported with their parents."

"It wouldn't surprise me." Puck began to darn his socks. "Not after last month's 'Vel d'Hiv' roundup in Paris. I heard they deported over twelve thousand. I have no doubt your friend Henri is correct."

"You know something more?"

"It seems this rafle is suddenly a poorly kept secret. Just today I heard the same rumor from other sources – a coded message from Monsieur Gutman of the EIF. You've heard of them?"

"The EIF? Yes. My guide for that first rescue over the 'F' route – Anya – a lovely young lady from EIF."

"Today, just before you came home, Gutman was here begging for immediate help at Vénissieux. They expect the rafle soon and want to smuggle out as many children as possible. Foster families have been found. They require new identities, forged documents."

"What will become of the children?" Ernst asked.

"Those rounded up will go to Drancy and from there to concentration camps in Poland." Puck flinched as he pricked his finger and then sucked the blood dry. "There are reports – or maybe just rumors – of killing camps – of crematoria to burn the bodies."

"And if EIF gets them?"

"According to Gutman, they will be separated from their relatives – a necessary cruelty – and dispersed in the countryside. EIF cannot disclose their location – even to their parents, especially not to their parents. There have been incidents, unfortunate incidents – in Lyons. The parents of three children who were placed in foster homes managed to escape deportation. They knew where one of their children was placed. Two days after their reunion they were denounced. The Gestapo, Klaus Barbie, was alerted to their presence. They have all been arrested and deported."

Through his 10X lens, Ernst practiced the signature he had perfected, easing his pen over and over on scrap paper, rehearsing the fiction of Monsieur Manalle's hand until his eyes lost their focus and the undulating line became the profile of mountains and valleys. Lost in the magnified texture of the paper, fibers took on shapes and faces; he thought of his nephew, Little Alexander, almost eight years old, and tried to imagine him in le Vernet or Gurs or St. Cyprien – Alexander staring through barbed wire, hungry, thin, past tears.

When Ernst was satisfied, he applied Monsieur Manalle's signature to the identity paper of another Jew who would try his luck over the Pyrenees. Each rescue was unique, each refugee grateful in his or her own way, but for Ernst it was always the same. A brief moment of pride and satisfaction, a little embarrassment for their effusive gratitude, sometimes tears. It was all over in a very few moments, and then came disappointment, a curious emptiness.

"You know," Puck explained, "sometimes, when women give birth, afterwards, they feel a deep depression. They've done something magnificent, yet grief overwhelms them. In our work, too. Maybe in some way we are midwives to another kind of birth. Perhaps rescue is like that."

What countered the letdown was the relentless compulsion to start again. When he began forging for Puck, he was somewhat reluctant, and he produced documents mechanically. But as he devoted more and more hours to the task, he marinated in each document that he created – a new identity to save an otherwise doomed human being. It was heady work, a balm for his depression that finally became all consuming, a compulsion to which he happily surrendered. It eroded his sleep.

Ernst felt Puck's silent anticipation, his unspoken query at Ernst's most vulnerable moments. "Ernst. will you help with these children at Vénissieux? This will be a level of risk higher than simple forgery from the relative safety of our flat. This will be more perilous than mountain escapes. We would be in the belly of the beast."

In his mind, Ernst waged the now familiar tug of war between fear of apprehension and his compulsion to create the finest documents. When it was not deadly serious business, it took on the qualities of a grotesque game he played with the Nazis and Vichy France – a game to humiliate them, to degrade them in his mind, to nullify their evil. And, he had to confess, it was a personal contest as well: to triumph over Hans Gerd, to disgrace Fritz, to redeem some small measure of goodness for himself. But even that explanation was too facile, for it was much more than an amusement. It was a calling – an imperative he possessed neither the thoughts nor the words to examine or question. Neither could he refuse.

Hunched over his drawing board, beginning yet another exit visa, Ernst said, "This rescue business – it's a compulsion, rather like building my road to Tamanrasset. I don't ever want it to end – it occupies me, gives me purpose, keeps despair at arm's length."

"I would have thought it more a distraction." Puck cut the darning thread, re-knotted the end and picked up another sock. "Distraction from each month's vigil. Each Sunday that goes by I feel your disappointment – your rootlessness – as if nothing gives you what you truly need."

Ernst continued with his pen on a baptismal certificate. "And what is it I need?"

"The same thing you've needed ever since I met you. The same thing Frau Rathenau offered you in her letter – pardon, forgiveness, redemption – call it what you will."

A slight tremor began in his pen hand and Ernst had to stop his drawing. "Yes, I would like that. Wouldn't we all. But I don't expect it."

"I think you need it on such a profound, instinctive level that you cannot stop your work with these documents, with escorting people over the Pyrenees."

"I fear there is no pardon for me on Earth. I will live with my past until I die. We all do."

"Pardon does not erase your past. Deeds cannot be subtracted. And why would you presume that rescues and forgeries would secure you that pardon? My dear Ernst," Puck looked solemn, "here on Earth your crimes are beyond redemption; they cannot – should not – be forgotten or forgiven. But before a heavenly judge..." Puck re-threaded his needle. The silence swelled. "You still think forgiveness is an indulgence – a preposterous act of grace, like Frau Rathenau's letter – something conferred upon you by someone, or by the entire world, it doesn't matter, after some arbitrary number of redemptive acts. But you still have not forgiven yourself, and that must come first."

Ernst steadied his hand and resumed his drawing. The official seal began to emerge with photographic perfection. "I'll go with you," he said.

"I just want to be sure," Puck said, "that you do it for yourself. Not for me, not for distraction, not for absolution, but for yourself."

★   ★   ★   ★   ★   ★   ★   ★   ★   ★

They arrived in Lyons on Wednesday evening, August 26, as the mass arrests began. He and Puck traveled by train in separate compartments. In each valise's false bottom lay the bare minimum of forging supplies needed for the operation.

When they arrived at the Perrache railway station two men met them with urgent, whispered introductions.

"Charles Lederman – OSE, l'Oeuvre de secours aux enfants."

"Claude Gutman – EIF."

They bowed and shook hands.

"It was good of you to come so quickly." Gutman, an ardent young man in his twenties, wet his lips after each sentence. His haggard face suggested a meager body lost inside an overly large storm coat. The black hat pulled low over his forehead mimicked a mobster or a detective, except that he still looked like a school boy. "There is not a moment to lose. We may be too late already." He spoke quickly and hustled them along the platform.

Lederman lifted the lapel of his storm coat to block out the humid wind. "In the Northern Zone the deportations began ten days ago. Thousands are being sent east from Drancy."

Gutman spit onto the tracks. "They mean to kill us all."

Through the glass doorway to the station Ernst could see the stippling of rain in the streetlight. They hurried across the boulevard to a waiting automobile, a black Citroën with bright yellow wheels. Even before the door closed, the car sped from the curb, its tires spinning on the wet pavement.

In the front seat a tall man, older than Ernst, turned to face them with weary eyes. His white clerical collar glowed in the radiance of following headlights. The cleric forced his lips to smile.

"I am Father Glasberg – Christian Friendship. The arrests and deportations have begun."

"It's hardly surprising," Puck said. "After last month, in the Northern Zone..." There was little need to complete his thought.

Gutman's words ran so fast they tripped over his busy tongue. "I was just commenting to Father Glasberg that even Lambert and his UGIF-South have been helpful. It is a thin line they walk, between collaboration and rescue..."

"What would you have them do, Claude?" Lederman interrupted. "Take up arms?"

"The time will come, Charles." He took off his hat and finger-combed his thick brown hair.

Father Glasberg lit a cigarette. The smoke swept out the crack of his window. It was good to feel the cool air. "It is a dilemma, n'est ce pas?"

"Yes," Gutman interjected. "For every one we save, the police have to arrest another. They have quotas. And once the deportations start... The Nazis keep impeccable records."

"Things have gotten very bad here in Lyons," Gutman continued. "That's why we had to get help from afar. We will do everything to ensure your safety, but..." He looked from Puck to Ernst. "The UGIF committees cannot even screen detainees at the camps anymore. They go straight to Drancy. And from there," he drew his finger across his throat, "deportation!"

"It's Bousquet and Laval," Lederman said. "Traitors – monsters – SS Captain Dannecker's whores."

"Attention, please," the driver said. "Check point."

"Gentlemen." Father Glasberg threw his cigarette out the window and faced forward. "If you will just sit quietly and say nothing."

The vehicle drew up to the checkpoint across Rue La Croix and slowly rolled by the Gendarmes who came to attention and saluted briskly. Father Glasberg tipped his head and waved with Papal confidence and they were motioned on.

"How did you manage...?" Ernst looked out the back window.

"This automobile," Father Glasberg said. "It is an exact replica of the Prefect's Citroën. Our police chief has extravagant taste. Tonight is the first we have used it. Hopefully, it will be several days before the ruse is detected."

The car rolled further on and the blast of a police whistle suddenly shrieked from one side. Ernst felt his pulse sprint, but the others seemed unconcerned. Vichy Gendarmes ran across Rue La Croix in front of the car, first singly, then a whole unit. Another whistle erupted from the other side of the street. How could the others in the car not be afraid? Or perhaps their fear had been dulled over time, as it had for him in the Free Corps. A cluster of men, women and children huddled together at one corner under the rifle of a Vichy Gendarme. A few were manacled. Children cried. On the next block the Black Maria swallowed a mother and her small child; then it took an old woman and her husband, who managed to bring along his cane but little else. The Black Maria shark advanced on the corralled Jews under the light in the rain.

"This is only the beginning." Father Glasberg said without turning his head. "And we are only at the outskirts. We will drop you two off at Vénissieux, with the social workers." Now he turned and looked back and forth between Puck and Ernst. "Are you sure you want to do this? You could be arrested and deported – even executed on the spot."

"Like these two men," Puck indicated Gutman and Lederman, "I am a Jew. It is reason enough."

"I too," Ernst said, "have my reasons."

Puck gripped Ernst's hand and squeezed once.

"I have learned some Hebrew from these two," said Father Glasberg. "If you want to 'repair the world,' Tikkun Olam in Hebrew, this is a good place to be. We expect there will be over one hundred children rounded up tonight. We need bifs for each child." He picked up a satchel and handed it over the seat to Puck. "Here are the forms."

Ernst was relieved to hear that only bifs would be required. He had worried that they could not possibly compose the more complex, but reliable, synthés for so many children in such a short time. Father Glasberg explained how the children were to be placed in the countryside with "Aryan" families, their own identities "Aryanized" with baptismal records and rewritten ration cards. Some of the adults slated for escape, those who would continue in the resistance, needed far more complex synthés, so called because these counterfeit forms "synthesized" an Aryanized Jew with an authentic Aryan whose identity could not be traced by suspicious Gendarmes or administrators. Often they were the birth certificate and identity card of a prisoner of war or an Aryan recently deceased but not yet recorded in the civil records. Synthés required complicity from officials at the level of Mayoralty offices and small Prefectures of Police. There was always the risk of betrayal, but the disguise was impeccable.

"How many forgers are already in the camp?" Ernst asked.

"Twelve," Lederman said. "I was hoping for more, but many have been arrested. The photography workshop is already up and running. It's actually quite amazing."

"Any word about Freier?" Father Glasberg asked.

"Still in le Vernet." Puck shook his head. "It's been almost a year and a half. His wife, Mina, had a baby, his name is Francois. They let him out for a few hours to see the child, but we fear he may be deported. All because he draws cartoons."

"It is a great pity," Father Glasberg said. "So many are gone. Things will get worse now. Laval is more rabid than Pétain. Six weeks ago all the Jews in Drancy, Pithiviers, and Beaune-la-Rolande were deported. I have heard from more than one source that they are being systematically murdered in Poland, in the camps."

Under Gutman's flashlight Ernst examined his new papers identifying Ernest Toussaint as a Jewish social worker employed by the Vichy-sponsored UGIF, the General Union of French Jews. It was a bold gamble, dependent upon confusion during the roundup and the good will of sympathetic guards and officials.

The silver glow of flood-lights illuminated the night sky and silhouetted trees as they approached Vénissieux. At the sentinel gate Ernst first detected a faint sewer odor in the muggy air, as if rot and decay could be contained by the camp's triple-barbed wire. Again the Citroën rolled through the checkpoint unchallenged. The driver navigated the narrow access between ancient barracks. Silver smoke spiraled out of tube-like chimneys that sprouted irregularly from corrugated tin roofs. According to Gutman, the fires were meager stoves heating water for dilute tea and gruel made of cabbage, potato, and water. Horses that died in the southern zone and were unfit to eat were routinely sent to the camps for meat, if they were not first diverted to the soup pots of ordinary Frenchmen. Rat meat was a delicacy in Vénissieux. In the men's compounds, inmates slept on sand. The few windows let in meager light and no ventilation, even when fully opened. As the Citroën neared the center of the camp flies were everywhere, and the faint sewer odor had grown to a fecal stench.

The Citroën slowed to a halt in a dark alley behind the administrative building, and Father Glasberg left the car. After several minutes he opened a side door of a darkened building and signaled them to come one by one.

Inside, in a barely lit stairwell, Ernst and Puck met Trudel, a short, angular woman, her dark hair pulled back severely, who introduced herself as "an irritable baby, born in St. Petersburg on 'Bloody Sunday', January 22, 1905."

Ernst thought she had a mad look about her. "I was born and the revolution began. This time they will remember me." Half her mouth smiled. "Watch your heads. Bring your bags with you, down these steps."

Ernst saw no stairway. She pushed aside a rug and lifted a concealed trap door. Rough wooden planks creaked when Puck descended behind her. Ernst felt himself immersed in damp blackness as he followed Puck until Trudel screwed in a light bulb and he saw shelves packed with linen and suitcases, a sand floor and a stone foundation. Crates and barrels cast shadows; cobwebs hung from the low ceiling like an insane crochet pattern. Trudel pulled on the middle shelf and it swung open just enough to allow entry through a dark crack. Inside she pulled back a blanket that hung from a wire, and another half of the basement appeared, dimly lit by bare bulbs. Under each light, faces looked up from close work at individual desks, and in the farthest recess a red lamp glowed through a curtain – the photography lab.

"This is your workshop," Trudel said. "The warning is two taps, three taps, two taps – like this." She struck a wooden post. "You won't miss it. When you hear it, unscrew your light bulb and pray quietly. The children have started to arrive this evening. Time is short. I hope you are well rested. Joachim will bring the first batch for you as soon as you are settled. Toilets are upstairs. If the trap door is locked it is unsafe to leave." She pointed to a dark corner. "Chamber pots."

"And if we are challenged by guards, administrators, or the like?"

"You are social workers," Trudel said, "assisting in the screening of the children for transfer. In fact, they live on borrowed time. Vichy revoked the exemptions that favored children about ten days ago, but the superintendent of the camp is unaware. A sympathetic radio operator intercepted the cable. Thus we are operating under the governmental instructions from the chief of service of the SSE, Gilbert Lesage."

"Lesage, the Quaker?" Puck said. He untied and unrolled a soft cloth containing his pens and magnifying lenses.

"The same." Trudel screwed in another light bulb that suddenly spotlit her. "When Bousquet transmitted instructions regarding the rafle Lesage tipped off Édouard Simon of the EIF. This time we were lucky, maybe for the last time. After this rafle, Lesage, the Quakers, the Unitarians, the Jews – no one can help. The noose is tightening. Time is short." She clicked her heels and bowed curtly. "I am at your service, as are the young people from EIF. Good evening."

They worked into the small hours of the night. Ernst had been unable to sleep on the train, and exhaustion overtook him. After an hour on a cot he was awakened by Puck shaking him. Muffled footfalls drummed overhead on the hardwood floor.

"Come on, wake up, Ernst. This one needs to be done immediately. Wake up!"

Behind Puck a teenage girl swayed with a baby clinging to her neck like a chimpanzee, sobbing for breath, her little shoulders heaving up and down. The swaying teen sang Puck's Yiddish lullaby, *Oyfn Pripetshok*. Ernst knew the verse she sang:

> When you will grow older, children
> you will understand,
> how many tears lie in these letters
> and how much weeping.

In Striegau the words had made little sense, but now he grasped the heartbreaking weight of letters scratched out and rewritten, of names obliterated, of names conferred. Still they sang this song to their babies. There is no justice on Earth, he thought – they will sing for eternity for the justice of heaven.

The young woman stopped singing and laid papers on Ernst's desk. "Monsieur Gutman asks that you complete this one immediately so Hannah may leave with Father Glasberg. The doctors will give her something to make her sleep. My name is Edith."

"Ernest," he said and stood briefly to bow. She was young, perhaps seventeen, her dark hair bobbed just over her shoulders in awkward tangles and disarray. "Edith what?"

"Only Edith, Monsieur Ernest." Her chin thrust upward, trying to look haughty. "Hannah's new name is Hannah Loiseaux." Hannah buried her face again into Edith's shoulder. "At least we don't have to teach her how to make the sign of the cross or recite her Hail Marys. Sometimes I think I'm in a Christian seminary. All the children are praying and crossing themselves." She laughed. "Then they say the Shema." She laid the toddler's photo on the documents. "As soon as possible, Monsieur Ernest."

Ernst rubbed sleep from his eyes and fought the urge to lie down again. Hannah Liebowitz's papers identified her as an immigrant Jew, born eighteen months before. She had fled Belgium in her mother's womb just before the woman was arrested in Lyons and subsequently gave birth in Vénissieux.

He studied the most recent photo of the child, a toddler without cheeks wearing an expression as threadbare as the scarf over her head. His task was relatively simple – a bif. He dipped his brush in hydrogen peroxide and brushed over Hannah's last name, watching under his 20X glass as the ink bleached and flaked off – the opposite of painting. At places he had to interrupt the line of the official stamp. Incrementally, the yellow 'Juif' vanished.

He wrote her new name with bureaucratic black ink and painted over the interruptions in the stamp in burgundy. Her birthplace changed to Banon, the small mountain town in which Ernst and Freier had stayed on their way south from Paris to Marseille two years before. Ernst learned that the mayor of Banon had arranged for documentation in the village records for Hannah, and a baptismal record in St. Mary's Church. Her ration card was next, and it too had to be washed, then painted. The intricate lines of the ration card were more difficult to reproduce and his eyes teared. An hour later the papers were complete, spread out before Ernst. Hannah Loiseaux, "the little bird." Ernst imagined her flying over the triple barbed wire fence, into freedom.

Edith reappeared holding the sleeping toddler over her shoulder. She laid Hannah on a blanket spread on Ernst's work table and the little girl's head lolled to one side, eyes almost closed. "Barbital," Edith said and tied the baby's white cotton hat into a bow under her chin. She gathered up the new papers.

The drugged toddler resembled the photograph of Hannah Liebowitz except that her cheeks were more gaunt. Her breathing was deep and slow.

"Father Glasberg will be taking her out any moment now," Edith said. "I'll hold her if you would please fasten the tag around her neck."

The tag identified Hannah Loiseaux, born 25 November 1940 in Banon, child of Paul and Anna Loiseaux. Edith lifted a large picnic basket onto the table and folded the sedated child inside, then closed the wicker top.

"Your work is very good, Monsieur Ernest." She smiled at him.

"Thank you Edith." He watched her trying to assure Hannah's comfort. "What will become of Hannah?"

She shrugged with adolescent nonchalance. "Hannah will grow up with the Loiseaux family – the daughter of a pharmacist. Perhaps she will never know that her mother died two days after childbirth of the fever here in the camp, or that her father was taken by transport to Drancy for deportation east." Edith arranged a small wool blanket around Hannah so she would not shift in the basket. "Maybe she will be a Catholic all her life and never know anything of this. It is the cruelest fate of all, I think. Like being born without a name."

"Her father – ?"

"They took him yesterday." She caught her breath. "But before they took him, when he brought Hannah last night, he touched her face with his fingertips, memorizing her. He cried without making a sound. I have seen it before, at other separations. They give up their children to save them. Desperate acts of love."

Without knowing why, Ernst kissed the tips of his fingers and reached into the basket to touch Hannah's cheek. He wanted to bless her, but he was not a priest.

Edith closed the wicker lid and carried Hannah out past the askew shelves. Ernst followed her up the stairs slowly, needing relief for his tired eyes, craving the freshness of night air.

Upstairs the septic odor of the camp swamped the basement's mold, and Ernst could sense threat and confusion. He watched Edith leave the building, past a police guard at the door who stopped her briefly to check her identity card but did not open her basket. She smiled at him and he let her proceed. The duplicate of Prefect Angeli's car, black with yellow wheels, waited at the curb and she was escorted through the misty rain into the back seat. Another young woman, in a nurse's uniform with Swiss Red Cross markings, joined them at the last minute. The door closed and yellow wheels spit mud and dirt and drove out of Vénissieux.

Behind him Ernst became suddenly aware of bustle and commotion, the noise of the reception center. He passed a woman sitting on a low foot-stool, crying. A man startled him by pleading, "No baptism. You must promise. No baptism!" It was a relief when the trapdoor closed and he submerged again into the moldy air, the percussion of feet above his head, muted.

Puck leaned over his next document, magnifier poised. His knife flicked off truth – his pen painted lies. "Ernst," Puck said without looking up. "Do you remember what the Talmud says about saving a life?"

Ernst washed the identity card of a thirteen-year-old boy, Haim Feldstein. He blew over the document to evaporate the solvent then answered, "Who saves one life, saves the universe whole. We will save many universes, eh Puck?"

"Only this one, I'm afraid." Puck's eyes danced and Ernst thought he smiled beneath his beard. "It seems endlessly in need of repair. Fix it here, it breaks there. Maybe that's what we're here for."

"I just hope Haim learns to answer to Charles."

★ ★ ★ ★ ★ ★ ★ ★ ★ ★

Two days later Ernst completed his twelfth set of papers and laid his head down on the table. As he drifted into sleep, the danger signal knocks sounded. He sat bolt upright, eyes wide, heart pounding. One by one, the lights over each desk went out and the basement went dark. A powerful man stormed about overhead, his sharp boot-falls distinct from the shuffling gait of the Jews, his words muffled but discernible. He railed about missing prisoners.

"How dare you exempt them! The order went out on August 14. You are in violation of the law. Every child is to accompany their parent. You separate the children from their families? What kind of cruelty is this?"

For several hours the forgers sat in darkness as Wehrmacht boots tramped overhead. The trap door opened once, and soldiers rifled the shelves that separated Ernst and the others from prison or a firing squad, depending on SS Captain Dannecker's mood.

After another hour of searching, Captain Dannecker stopped directly overhead. "One hundred and nine are missing. One hundred and nine more will be arrested. Either way, you will deliver one hundred and nine children to the next transport." There was silence. "Are you idiots? I can have you all executed on the spot. Do not tempt me. This little charade of Jewish relief workers helping refugees, so-called social workers. Don't you think I know what your little game of hide and seek is all about? It will gain you nothing. One hundred and nine children will leave Vénissieux by tomorrow night, if I have to round them up myself." His boots tromped across the floor. A door slammed, and an engine roared to life.

"Where do the children go from here?" a young woman whispered from the next desk.

"Croix-Rousse," answered another disembodied voice. "EIF has its center there, on the Mount of the Carmelites. But they don't stay long. I've done this before. EIF disperses them to their new Aryan homes as soon as possible."

Two knocks over the door sounded the all clear. The incandescent lights flickered on, fourteen in a row, one by one, streetlights winking on in an underground city.

Earlier in the evening, several hours before the SS officer's tirade, the last bus had left Vénissieux, its driver wearing a poorly fitting Vichy Gendarme's uniform, following the black Citroën with yellow wheels through the gate. They had done all they could. It was time to leave before the Gestapo arrived.

Seemingly by magic, for he did not come through the bookcase, Gutman was in the room looking haggard. Two days' growth of beard stippled his jaw and upper lip; sweat matted his hair. The forgers clustered around him. He spoke fast and low, his tone urgent, intimate.

"Word is up. The Sentinel's gate is blocked. Superintendent Cussonac and Prefect Angeli are demanding to know where the children have gone. We, of course, know nothing, but you must not be apprehended. If the Gestapo gets hold of you... well, it would not be good for any of us. I don't worry so much about Cussonac – a witless bureaucrat. And Angeli may be corrupt, but he, in his own way, is simple-minded. But Dannecker is aroused and he is truly a monster. Behind barracks 36 we have arranged an escape through the barbed wire. There are no mines in the perimeter, although a sympathetic guard told me that, as of next week, there will be." He cleared his throat. "Gather your materials. I hope you don't get too muddy. Thank you again, ladies and gentlemen. You have saved 109 children. Five hundred adults have fled the camp, either through exemptions that are no longer permissible, or escape pure and simple. I would say a good few days' work. Thank you. Shalom."

They crawled on their bellies under the first wire and across the narrow dirt strip between fences, under machine guns in dark watchtowers. Ernst forced his thoughts elsewhere to banish the terror that suddenly the searchlights would come on and the machine guns spit at them and it would be over.

As the second wire passed over his head he considered, of all things, blessings. In the basement, waiting to leave, Puck had related how his grandmother had made the priestly blessing on his head any time the spirit moved her, but especially every Friday evening before lighting the Sabbath candles. "The Lord bless you and keep you. The Lord make his face to shine upon you and be gracious unto you. The Lord turn his face unto you, and give you peace." Puck repeated the prayer in Hebrew. "We can bless each other," Puck said, and Ernst could scarcely make sense of it.

He craned his neck and the last string of wire passed over him. "Blessings on our heads." Ernst remembered reaching into the basket to touch Hannah Loiseaux's cheeks, and that too was a blessing – a moment of grace. The third strand passed over his head and they were at the edge of a field of rye grass overdue for cutting. From here escape was effortless. The woods were near and then the main road.

*   *   *   *   *   *   *   *   *   *

472

Heavy fog settled over the Vielle Ville the night Ernst assisted the Weintraub family in their escape. Since the Nazi invasion of the Southern Zone ten days before, the luxury of careful preparation was a memory. He first met the Weintraubs in Sept Petit Pècheurs on the very night of their flight. Marseille was overrun with German troops and the Gestapo zealously assumed the duties of the more ambivalent Marseille police.

Puck was outraged to learn that the same day the Germans completed their occupation of France, November 10, 1942, Mussolini invaded Corsica. Marseille ceased its commercial function but the shipyards had never been busier, and Ernst had some work on the docks again. He loaded German tanks, munitions and supplies onto every available freighter and troop ship and watched them sail for Tunisia. Three shifts worked around the clock to service the convoys. Formations of heavy bombers flew south; the stench of diesel fumes and gasoline displaced the pungent saltwater scent of the harbor.

The skin on Herr Weintraub's face sagged and his overcoat, sized for a heavy man, hung loose. His wife's hair was poorly done up in a bun, and she wore heavy diamond earrings. The neckline of her dress sagged with the weight of three bejeweled brooches that she gave Ernst in payment. Despite their former wealth in Munich, they had few Swiss francs, and their Deutsche marks were useless. It must have been humiliating for Herr Weintraub to struggle with his wedding ring. When Frau Weintraub began to twist her own ring off her finger, Ernst covered her hand with his own.

"That won't be necessary," he said.

The two Weintraub boys, six and ten, could hardly miss the desperation in their parents' faces. Herr Weintraub pushed his watch across the table. "Klug-Baumen," he said. "Very valuable." Ernst wondered if Hans Gerd still wore his Klug-Baumen, inscribed *To My Angel*. What irony that Hans Gerd might be one of the Gestapo agents seeking spies and forgers such as himself and Puck. Perhaps he was even in Vichy, or Marseille. Since the occupation, this was probably a hardship post, and Hans Gerd might well have been sent here as punishment for some impropriety or impulsive stunt. Ernst felt angry at his younger brother, the Nazi lawyer with the wooden hand. But he also pitied and missed the hyperactive Hans Gerd, good-intentioned, but at the mercy of his impulsive brain.

When it was time to go, Ernst walked a block ahead of the Weintraubs, who kept to the shadows. They were between patrols, but as he passed Rue Duvalier, a motorcycle cranked to life. The unexpected headlight swept a wide arc across the street as it turned behind Ernst. His heart pounded. He stopped and lit a cigarette, the signal for the Weintraubs to melt into the nearest dark doorway. The Wehrmacht driver slowed as he passed Ernst. He heard the officer in the side-car bark an order, and the motorcycle squealed to a stop; the driver unfastened the strap on his pistol but left it holstered. The drunken officer in the side-car tried to stand but fell back, his peaked cap askew. Under the Eagle and its entaloned swastika shone the silver Death's Head Skull, the skull of the Hussaren Death's Head Regiment with whom the Free Corps had laid siege to the Royal Palace and the Marstall almost twenty-five years before. The officer tried again, and this time managed his feet but swayed. He brought his peaked cap back into alignment and fastened his collar, stiff with the twin lightning bolts of the SS. The drunken boor became a cruel conqueror again.

"Papers!" His voice sputtered.

Ernst reached into his pea coat, felt the envelope of money and his papers.

The Death's Head Skull officer shone his electric torch into Ernst's face, then back onto his documents. "Toussaint," he mocked.

Ernst's right hand retreated to his jacket pocket. His fingers wrapped the shank of his Free Corps dagger.

"It is close to curfew. Where are you going?"

"Home."

"Why so late?"

"I was at a young lady's flat."

The officer laughed and said, "So was I." He listed and steadied himself with a gloved hand on the side-car, then put on a stern face. "But I had to pay her. The burden of conquest. Don't you agree?"

Ernst averted his eyes. "If you say so."

"Go home!" The officer dropped Ernst's papers at his feet. He sat down hard in the side-car. His driver snapped his pistol strap closed and mounted the motorcycle. "Half an hour to curfew, Monsieur Toussaint." As they rumbled off into the night Ernst wondered about this young Nazi, barely born when Rathenau was assassinated. If only he knew whom he had challenged. If only he knew the genealogy of hatred and fear immortalized in that Death's Head Skull, and Ernst's role in its propagation.

When they reached the wharf Ernst shook Herr Weintraub's hand, and though it was hard to see in the murkiness, Ernst thought there were tears in the other man's eyes. He urged the family onto the freighter's gangplank. Their steps echoed in the dock's silence. As each family member reached the steel deck, a dark figure appeared, pulled them up one by one and pushed them through a hatchway into the ship's hold. The shadow of Mr. Weintraub, last of the family, waved to Ernst and disappeared It was always the same at the moment of departure, tears of gratitude for their lives, Ernst already feeling the letdown, feeling his impatience, contemplating the next rescue.

The next night, before curfew, Ernst walked up a dark street toward Sept Petit Pècheurs, the only glowing doorway on the street. Lilting accordion music leaked from the café. The wine bottle in the window was a merlot – Robert's signal that there were no Germans inside. A drunken merchant marine stumbled out of the bar and tippled up the street humming to himself.

Ernst peered through the window and satisfied himself that all was in order. He sat at one end of the bar at the cash register, and removed his beret.

A young dark-haired girl who couldn't have been more than fifteen, her black skirt too far up her thighs, sat stiffly on a bar stool in the far corner singing with a small squeeze box that overpowered her reedy voice. But it was music – a traditional Provence folk song. Clouds of smoke hung in the air, pungent with the aroma of homespun cigarettes made of eucalyptus and sage, sprayed with gardener's nicotine. Sawdust covered the floor.

"One hour to curfew!" Alexi, the barman, declared. A Russian exile from the Revolution, he nodded at Ernst and continued to dry wine glasses. In the mirror Ernst flattened his unruly hair; Puck would have to cut it soon. He remembered how Frau Stimmel applied greasy hair lotion and combed a part down the middle. Unlike in Striegau, where his beard bristled like a scrub brush, the few days of his neglected cheeks, neck and chin felt soft, almost downy.

Moments later Robert came from the back room and stood across the bar from Ernst. He prepared a bicarbonate, stirring the fizzing water.

"The allies landed an invasion force in North Africa," Robert said. "Casablanca, Rabat, Algiers." Robert lifted one eyebrow and looked askance at Ernst. "Still, Sabiani is very happy. All these Nazis in Marseille – the brass spend a lot of money at Le Beauvau. My principles are costly."

"It's amazing the bastard is still alive."

"No more amazing than that I am, especially with friends like you. Passions run high in le Vielle Ville."

A few stools down the bar, two old men argued and laughed, their words clumsy and thick with drink.

Robert finished the bicarbonate and prepared another. A black arm garter held his cotton sleeves above muscular forearms. "The doctor said my stomach would be better if I stopped all alcohol." He poured cognac into two glasses. "From Corsica." He pushed one snifter to Ernst. "The last of it before the Italians invaded. Prosit! On the house."

Ernst laid five hundred francs on the bar. "For your services with the Weintraubs. They left on the *Gibraltar* last night."

Robert covered the bills with his big hand. "Good. They made me nervous. A fat man and his fat children – had money written all over them." He counted the bills. "They paid you well?"

Ernst sipped his cognac and lit a rare Gitane that Robert produced from under the bar. "Yes, they paid me well."

"The fleet is at Toulon." Robert held another glass up to the light. "It wouldn't do for les Boches to get their hands on our battleships and submarines."

Ernst sensed that Robert was about to solicit his help for a hazardous purpose. Rescuing refugees was one thing. Spying for the Allies was completely different, though he suspected Puck was neck-deep in the intrigue. Before Robert could continue, Ernst said, "I'm not sure I want to discuss this."

"Just keep your eyes and ears open. Tell me what you learn."

Ernst told Robert more about the Weintraubs, finished his cognac and then left Sept Petit Pècheurs. Best to return home quickly, he thought, especially since he still carried several thousand Swiss francs, a currency violation. He turned up his collar and blew into his hands for warmth. Though it was still before curfew, Ernst waited until the next patrol drove by, then sprinted across Quai de La Tourette and didn't stop running until he reached the end of Rue St. Laurent and leaned against Eglise St. Laurent's ancient stone to catch his breath. Incandescent bulbs cast vaporous spotlights on the dark wharves, while ghost-like fishing boats, almost invisible in mist, swayed at anchor.

The church courtyard was deserted, the shadows especially cold. The damp mist, like an empty slate for his mind to draw upon, played tricks on his senses, made him see things he should not allow himself to see. He ached anew wondering if Lisa was alive, still suffering with Fritz, or if she lay dying in drifting snow on the Swiss frontier, willing her last thoughts to him. Or maybe she was long dead. Another wave of heat left his body and he shivered. He turned his face into the church's dark corner seeking relief from the provocative mist, leaned his forehead against the cold stones and inexplicably found himself weeping. The entire quay was deserted. No one to interrupt or disturb, no one to inhibit this deluge of sadness. It was the gently persistent lapping of water against rotting piers that finally anchored his anguish again. A foghorn sounded far out past the dark harbor. A bell buoy clanged. The gulls slept.

Ernst crossed Rue St. Laurent and turned onto Avenue St. Jean where he slipped into a narrow alley and disappeared into the darkness. A dog barked. The alleys of Le Panier, a labyrinth Ernst knew well after two years, served the underworld and the underground alike. They were far safer than the streets.

He and Puck could live for several weeks on Herr Weintraub's fare and still have money left over to assist a few more desperate families. But generosity was becoming more difficult. After their arrest and detention on the *Sinaïa*, they were more careful with refugees at their apartment. The German command offered generous rewards for denouncing spies, and their neighbors were poor and hungry. Puck's transmissions were quite regular now, ripe with details of the embarkation of the Wehrmacht for North Africa: numbers of tanks, unit identification numbers, freighter departures.

A week after the Weintraubs' escape, Puck returned to their flat churning with news. The Germans were about to seize the fleet at Toulon. One of Robert's informers, a waiter at Sabiani's *Le Beauvau*, had learned the date from a drunk and indiscrete Nazi officer two days before the attack. Once Robert heard, it required only six hours for news to reach loyal sailors at Toulon.

"They scuttled the fleet!" Puck's eyes lit up as they once did, and he poured a glass of burgundy for both of them. "At Toulon. I heard seventy-five ships sank. Hitler will be furious." He held up his glass. "Prosit, Ernst. We will win this. I can feel it."

24

Before the Court of Heaven

February 1943 – April 1943

several months later, in February of 1943, the trauma of German occupation had become routine, though no less odious. The Port of Marseille became a regular and predictable military port, trans-shipping every form of weapon from Panzers to pistols, along with enough food and supplies to sustain Germany's North African army. At the evening change of shift on the docks, Ernst lingered at the railing of a bridge over the railroad tracks to Gare Maritime. A sea of dockworkers in dark coats flowed both ways over the bridge – opposing currents of gray and black interweaving like coarse yarn on a loom. Ernst felt the man's presence before he saw him, leaning over the railing beside him.

"Monsieur Toussaint? I am Herr Moscowitz." He spoke to the railroad tracks below. Ernst could barely make out his feeble voice.

Ernst thought he looked not only exhausted, but also ill. He was days away from his last shave and perhaps his last meal. His eyes recessed deeply under the shade of a bruised fedora. "Two thousand Swiss Francs for each adult, nine hundred for each child." Ernst rattled off the fare automatically. "At the current exchange rate that would be approximately..."

"We have nothing," the man mumbled, letting the last word fall. "Monsieur Robert said you would help us."

Ernst felt annoyance rising. "Monsieur Robert is very generous, but he runs a café, not a rescue service."

"Monsieur Robert said you are a good man."

Ernst chewed his lower lip and squinted into the late afternoon sun going down between a dock crane and a warehouse. This is the way it will be from now on, he thought. No one will have anything. Ernst noted a steam locomotive coming into the station, pulling flat cars loaded with Panzer tanks of the

Second Armored Division. It was the fourth day in a row that so many Panzers had moved along this line. He began to count. The plume of steam from the locomotive engulfed them, and Herr Moscowitz sagged a little more.

"We have nothing." Moscowitz's voice trembled. "We know no one. You are our last hope."

"How many?"

Moscowitz slumped further on the rail and began sobbing. The train whistle smothered his weeping.

Ernst reached into his pocket and put a chunk of dark chocolate into Moscowitz's hand. "Eat this," he said.

A frail smile spread over Moscowitz's face as he looked from the chocolate to Ernst and back. "My children will appreciate this." The orange sun flashed red in his eyes and cast sharp shadows on his cheeks.

"Eat it. You can barely stand. I cannot have you calling attention to me." Ernst pulled him upright by his arm. Though the bustle of workers changing shifts on the docks was always a good cover, he looked both ways for the Gestapo. One never knew where they might appear. And he suspected that he was on their "watch" list, in any case.

"How many?" he asked again.

"My wife and our two children, Heinz and Greta. And my sister and her five-year-old daughter and my cousin with her two children."

"Nine? Where are the men?"

"Dead." Moscowitz began to explain.

Ernst cut him off. "No details. Where are you from?"

"Mainz. We've been in hiding for four years, since Kristallnacht. First on the Moselle, then the Rhone..."

"I told you I wasn't interested in details." Ernst looked out over the train yard. "How old are your children?"

"A four-year-old girl and six-year-old boy."

"They can be quiet?"

"Yes. They cry silently. Children who cry aloud are in the camps."

"Meet me at 15 Rue D'Epice at six tomorrow night. Do you know where that is?"

He nodded. "Do I come alone?"

"Come with your wife. Bring photos and identity cards."

"Only German identity papers and ration coupons..."

"That will do. Bring them with you – six, tomorrow night. For the time being I may be able to move your family to Monte Carlo – just for the winter.

Two Scottish ladies, the Misses Trenchard, run a tea shop there. You'll be safe with them. I'll make you new papers, and in the spring we'll see. You must be ready at any moment to leave. It's the best I can do."

"If I could pay the price we could escape now, couldn't we? I was only a teacher in Mainz. Perhaps the stockbrokers are all getting away."

Ernst felt the weight of Moscowitz's judgment and almost reconsidered. But in a more lucid moment, he weighed the risks that counter-balanced the judgment and the scale tipped undeniably. This was not a time to take chances, not a time to go soft. "It's the best I can do, Herr Moscowitz."

★   ★   ★   ★   ★   ★   ★   ★   ★   ★

The fate of the Moscowitz family haunted him. For two months they hid in Monte Carlo, suspended between deliverance and catastrophe. For those who could not be rescued or hidden, there were the camps, and they filled rapidly. Rumors of gas chambers and crematoria were becoming a near certainty. Ghettos throughout Eastern Europe had been liquidated, and reports of mass murder had spread through the underground and resistance. The reports were too appalling to believe, but came from so many disparate sources that they became incontrovertible. The deportations could not keep up, and the transit camps in France exceeded capacity, but still rafles occurred with increasing frequency.

Ernst could do nothing about mass murder, but he could do something for the Moscowitz family, and they became his mission. It was a sea anchor in the storm of hardship, threat, and failure that stalked those in hiding and all rescue efforts still operating in Marseille. He had little doubt that the Germans would ultimately prevail, that the last flicker of civilization, of decency, would be extinguished. It was just a matter of time, during which Nazi barbarity would obliterate everything he held dear.

The mechanics of life in Marseille became more taxing. Ernst's well paying shifts on the docks were a thing of the past, and he and Puck had to make do with considerably less. Food was more expensive and less available. Between German occupation and Black Market usurpation, it was time to get out if one could. Puck stayed for his own reasons, and Ernst stayed for Lisa. He waited for the first Sunday in March, and he would wait for April and May and June, until he knew for certain if she was alive, if she was trying to reach him.

The Talmudic injunction that 'to save one life was to save the universe whole,' emboldened Puck. Ernst considered the obverse, and he conferred carte blanche truth on it as well, that 'to save one family was to crush the Nazis whole.' He delivered the Moscowitzes' forged documents to the Trenchard sisters in Monte Carlo, and while he was there he reassured Herr Moscowitz about his efforts. Four-year-old Greta stayed near Ernst during his visit, perhaps because of the chocolate he brought.

Ernst received periodic postcards from the Trenchard sisters saying how much they enjoyed having the children stay in Monte Carlo. Finally, the postcard he hoped for reported "unfortunate illness in the family. Please pray for my niece. Luke, chapter 17:6 is especially beautiful."

At Eglise St. Laurent Ernst found the seventeenth pew and walked in six places. In the hymnal was a piece of paper with the Carlyle code. At the apartment he deciphered the message:

"Two blue shirts and one toothbrush – Sept Petit Pêcheurs – breakfast Tuesday."

Two children over six, and one between three and five. Herr Moscowitz's children, four-year-old Greta and six-year-old Heinz, could escape.

Ernst exchanged coded greetings with M. Giraud from EIF in the crowded café where Robert had put out the bottle of merlot. A broad-shouldered handsome man, Giraud had grown up in Annemasse and knew the Swiss frontier better than most. There was little time to spare, Giraud said. The Gestapo were in Monte Carlo; it was no longer safe.

"There are places on a transport crossing at Annemasse for two, maybe three, children. Another family was to come through Annemasse with EIF but they became nervous and left early – paid an unknown guide to escape over Col de la Givrine. There was a spring blizzard. They never met their contacts in Switzerland."

"Dead?" He winced to think of Lisa trying to escape over the Alps, or Greta freezing to death in a Swiss mountain pass.

"Probably. Swiss crossings are hazardous." Giraud shrugged. "People die. I try not to think of it too much. We can take three more children."

"And their parents?"

"Impossible for now – maybe later this spring or summer. You know how it is, Monsieur Toussaint. We rescue from day to day and count on nothing."

"Do you need me to come – for papers?"

"Of course. Time is short."

"Time is always short."

"We're bringing twice as many over – we can't make their papers fast enough."

Ernst folded his hands on the bar. "Do you ever wonder if we're crazy?"

"Crazy?"

"For saving people we don't know – and for not saving ourselves."

"As I said, I try not to think about it. It's what allows me to continue." Giraud looked up at Ernst with a curious, expectant expression. "And you, Monsieur?"

"I think about it all the time. It's what compels me to continue."

★   ★   ★   ★   ★   ★   ★   ★   ★   ★

In the gray light of dawn at a farm outside Villars-Sur-Var on the Var River north of Nice, Danny Bénédite and five other Maquis delivered Greta and Heinz to Ernst. The children remembered 'Uncle Ernest' from Monte Carlo and he gave them each a small piece of chocolate. Though only four and six, they knew how to be fugitives – how to play the silence game and do exactly as they were told.

In the barn Ernst and Danny shook hands warmly, then embraced, their breath condensing behind each other in the chill air. A five-day beard darkened Danny's bony face, but he smiled when he told Ernst of his baby, Caroline, now a year old. Theo and Caroline had joined him in the Haut Var with other Maquis, resistance fighters named for the prickly scrub bushes that grew on Corsica. They were part of the Katanga network of de Gaulle's Mouvement de la Libération Nationale. Danny couldn't stay long. One of his comrades signaled urgently from the edge of the woods.

"The countryside is thick with Boches," he said. "And besides, traveling with young children frightens me more than anything. They understand only their own comfort and they miss their parents. It's unnerving. I'm glad to be rid of them."

He was already out of the barn when he stopped and turned back. "You know, I never completely trusted you, Toussaint," Danny said. "You look too damn Teutonic. But I hear about you, through the Garel network, Jean Gemähling, Charles Wolff – even Rafarrin, that fat chef on the Paris-Marseille express. And Jean from EIF – he says you and Puck are practically a two-man rescue committee in Marseille." Danny began to turn from Ernst to join his fellows but stopped. "One never knows how long one has these days. Theo says it is best to tell people what you need to say while you can." Danny licked his lips and looked at his boots. "I doubted you, Monsieur Ernest. It was a mistake and I beg your pardon. Bon chance." They embraced again, and he slipped out of the barn and disappeared while the dawn was still dark.

On the train northeast to Annemasse, with the two children and Jean from the EIF, Ernst thought back to his first rescue over the Pyrenees two years earlier with the Solomons and Anya. He stroked his freshly shaved face, which matched the photo on his Swiss passport. Those were the easy days; his greatest fear had been that Frau Solomon would go into labor and he would have to deliver the baby. It was warm and the passage over the mountains had been almost an adventure outing. Not so, now. The older boy, Heinz, would cross with his 'older brother,' Jean, and four-year-old Greta would cross with him, her 'Papa,' Ernest Schoenfelt, a Swiss national. They practiced their rosary and Hail Marys.

In Annemasse, at the reception center of the SNCF, the National Railroad Company, a stout man in a black leather coat with a swastika lapel pin scrutinized their papers. Behind him stood two German soldiers with automatic weapons. He studied Ernst's papers and train tickets with particular attention, and then studied his face.

"Monsieur Schoenfelt, you are this little girl's father?"

"Yes, of course. Our papers are in order."

"Perhaps." He looked at Greta who, as instructed, clung to Ernst's pants leg. Her eyes were large, and Ernst could feel her hand trembling.

The Gestapo man knelt before the child. Ernst heard his leather coat creak and his knees click. "You are a beautiful little girl." He smiled briefly and touched her cheek. "Why are you here in France?"

"To visit my Opi," she said in a practiced singsong. The Gestapo man's left eyebrow arched.

"Do you go to church?"

She nodded and clung tighter.

"What do you do in church?"

"I pray to Jesus."

"And you make the sign of the cross?"

She nodded, averting her eyes from his.

"Show me."

Haltingly, she began to raise her left hand. Ernst quickly took her hand and knelt beside her. "Show the nice man how you make the sign of the cross, Greta."

She raised her free right hand and completed the ritual.

"And who are you meeting here, Fraulein?"

"My mommy," she recited.

"And where is your mommy?"

She bit her lip. "I don't see her anywhere," she said and gripped Ernst's trouser again.

The Gestapo man rose and looked hard at Ernst. He handed back his Swiss identity papers. "Your ticket is for two adults and one child. Your wife is waiting here? Perhaps you would point her out to me."

Beads of sweat ran down his sides. He scanned the people waiting across the customs desk and suddenly heard, "Greta! Oh, Greta!" A woman in a full-length coat with a sable collar waved, her face radiant with a smile. In her hand she held the children's book *Struwwelpeter*.

Greta saw the book and immediately waved her hand and called out "Mommy! Mommy!"

The Gestapo man seemed disappointed. He backed away, and Ernst laid their suitcases on the customs table. Greta's "Mommy" pushed through the waiting crowd to the front.

Suddenly, Ernst saw that it was Margaret. At the same moment she recognized him, and her staged smile became authentic.

"Ernest!" She moved forward with determination. "Greta!"

The Gestapo man watched from the periphery as they fell into each other's arms in a convincing embrace.

"Margaret?" He whispered as they held each other close. "Are you supposed to be my wife?" He wasn't sure if she was laughing or crying on his shoulder.

"Ernst – it's really you. I can't believe it."

"Lisa," he said, still holding her. "Do you know anything...?"

"Shh," she said. "Lisa's alive. I have news, but not here."

Ernst quivered with anticipation. He thought he might weep, or laugh uncontrollably with relief, the dam of memories, of longing suddenly breached. The three of them boarded the train for Geneva. Astounded, Ernst, stared out the window, mesmerizing himself with the unfocused motion of passengers, the police, German troops, porters. In an echo-chamber he heard Margaret reading *Struwwelpeter* to Greta on her lap. A German soldier entered their compartment, a young recruit in a crisp uniform adorned with untarnished leather, snapped his heels and bowed perfunctorily.

He held out his unblemished hand, palm up. "Madam's papers, if you please." He recognized *Struwwelpeter* immediately and smiled to see "The Story of Augustus Who Would Not Have Any Soup."

"How wonderful," he said. "I myself grew up with this book." From memory he recited the last line of the cautionary poem:

"Look at him, now the fourth day's come!
He scarcely weighs a sugar-plum;
He's like a little bit of thread,
And on the fifth day, he was – dead!"

★   ★   ★   ★   ★   ★   ★   ★   ★   ★

"En voiture!" The conductor's cry carried through the open window and the train lurched forward. They were alone in their compartment, and as the train cleared the platform Ernst leaned forward, his eyes wide.

"Margaret. Tell me everything."

"She escaped – eight months ago. It was just before winter, across the Bodensee to Arbon where I met her. She had to go to Marseille – it was the first thing she said to me in Arbon – to meet you. She was confused, exhausted, sick. She said something about a cousin, but it was to meet you." Margaret paused and caught his eye again. "At sunrise? You're such a romantic." She smiled and touched his arm affectionately. "Ernst. You must understand. She was weak and sick. I convinced her to stay, at least until she could regain her strength. She was finally free in Switzerland. Why would she want to escape right back into an occupied zone? She was bitterly disappointed – said it was impossible to contact you, she didn't even know what name you were using. I brought her back to Geneva and that's where she is now." Margaret's face darkened and her eyes fell.

Ernst could feel the pulse in his neck, his skin tingling with expectancy and trepidation. He perched at the edge of the hard seat, both his hands gripping. "What's happened?"

"As I said, she was not well – sick, exhausted, depressed. She had a nervous breakdown – hospitalized for a few weeks, sedated. She's staying with me at the reception center."

So many questions. Where to begin? "You live in Geneva?"

"For about a year. I came after my defection. I was with my lover, von Greuning, at a meeting in Basel. I simply went to the Police station and requested amnesty. It wasn't so easy for Lisa. She spent ten days on the run, through the woods, in the mountains, sleeping in rain, hiking through snow."

"But how is she now? I mean the breakdown."

"Better, but still quite fragile. She helps at the center with the children

485

who come across. There is so much to do once they arrive. It keeps her mind off Adi, she says." Margaret's voice dropped, and she cast her eyes down. "She'll be overjoyed to see you."

Margaret had nothing more to add and Ernst discerned sadness in her reply. She resumed her preoccupation with Greta and he leaned his head against the glass, allowing the countryside to hypnotize him – to calm his tremoring heart. Visions of Lisa, naked in his arms, her breasts against his chest, her eyes pulling him deeply inside. He dared not indulge but neither could he restrain these resurrected remembrances. He ached for her.

The town of Annemasse receded and the train descended toward Geneva, a dark tunnel of pines arched across the track.

At the Swiss border their papers were scrutinized again, this time by Swiss border guards, before the train continued down the valley of the Arve. An older man and his wife came into their compartment at the border and before the train had gathered speed, their sleeping heads tipped against each other and the man snored. Ernst leaned back, drunk with anticipation; he couldn't help but laugh at the miracle of meeting Margaret, at the imminent actuality of reuniting with Lisa. He covered his excited laughter with a handkerchief, but couldn't contain himself, until he realized he was weeping.

Greta had fallen asleep in Margaret's lap. She stroked the young girl's hair and smiled at Ernst across the compartment as if to say, *I understand, it's overwhelming.* Margaret's face carried fresh lines of worry and care, but her dark brown eyes, though sad, still shimmered with the dignity and confidence he remembered from more than twenty years ago. Somehow her cheeks had preserved a peach glow, but when she smiled there was too much bone. She reached her slender hand across the compartment. "An ocean of time has passed," she said.

Ernst inhaled deeply to dispel his tears and ease his breathing. He took her hand as if to greet a gentleman, but slowly and gently, more an embrace, not letting go for many moments. "I was remembering the first time we met," Ernst said. "You were a spy for Lisa. You spirited her from her father's house to meet Fritz and me at the park in Halle."

"It's my nature to be disobedient." Their eyes touched again and each had to look away. Everyone carried sadness; everyone carried a remarkable tale of courage or cowardice, or both. By 1943 everyone understood that only the charmed survived to tell their tales and neither rhyme nor reason distinguished the lucky from the dead.

By the time they left the station in Geneva it was dark, and a light rain fell. The bustle of Geneva returned Ernst to present verisimilitude: a sea of umbrellas, automobiles, animated citizens, a sense of hope, of normality. Greta clung to his neck, and the three of them huddled under Ernst's umbrella waiting for the next taxi.

The Reception Center was a private house set back from Jungfraustrasse in a quiet residential suburb of the city. In the entryway Margaret shook rain from the umbrella. A woman whom Margaret introduced as Simone came to take the sleeping Greta from Ernst's shoulder, but he waved her off.

"Greta doesn't know you," he whispered. "I'll bring her to her bed. Show me the way." Margaret nodded her approval. He followed Simone to the stairway at the end of the hall.

Overhead, on the floor above, he heard the feeble shuffling of bare feet, then someone's slow footfalls, a somber procession.

Ernst saw her bare feet first, pale and slight, one step at a time, as if a toddler learning the complexity of stairs. He knew it was her. The hem of her white cotton robe fluttered and trembled with each step. One arm, bare from her elbow, clutched at the handrail, her other lay across her chest, held her robe closed. Now her shoulders, her hectic hair, untended, frizzed like corn silk. Then her face – the face he held most dear, most magical, evocative, compelling. Her face had aged, her eyes half closed. But the years and the exhaustion could not alter her essence – a singularity that would ignite his deepest visceral soulfulness until the last moment of his life. She turned and looked at him in the dim light; she appeared to have trouble seeing, focusing. Her brow wrinkled as recognition slowly dawned.

"Ernst?" She tipped her head. "Ernst?" She stopped on the last step still clutching her robe, remembrance dawning. "Ernst? Ernst." Now she knew and her eyes widened. Her spine stiffened and she was tall again, electrified. She strode across the space between them, her arms unfolding, her white robe starting to fall open. "Ernst. Ernst."

Greta awoke confused, her weak arms pushing Ernst away and she started to whimper. Simone took her from Ernst's shoulder, and a moment later Lisa was in his arms, her embrace firm about his neck, her cheek against his own. Her breath came in short bursts, sobbing, exhausted as if she had just run a race. Time suspended, her face buried in his shoulder. Lillé perfume, the scent of her hair. Though she held him tightly, he felt the weight of her exhaustion, felt her short breath. She hung heavy on his neck, as if slipping underwater. Greta's cries subsided as she was carried up the carpeted steps. He heard the tick of the wall clock, the deliberate pulse of the house. Lisa sobbed on his shoulder. She could not catch her breath – her shoulders rose and fell with hitching gasps. Finally, her breathing slowed and became even. She rested her cheek against his; her hand stroked the back of his head. He felt her trembling as she tried to hold him closer. Her tears mingled with his. Her fingers dug into his back. Through the tangle of Lisa's hair he saw Margaret watching from behind, a desolate set to her mouth.

Slowly, ever so tenderly, he eased Lisa down onto the boot chest in the hallway. They sat cheek to cheek for several minutes until she was able to pull back and look at Ernst. Margaret had gone. They were alone in the hall under a single bulb casting long shadows.

She wiped her eyes on the sleeve of her robe. "I thought I would never see you again."

"Margaret told me about your escape and about... about the hospital. I'm sorry."

"Meg has been wonderful – a life saver. We've become very close." She leaned against Ernst's shoulder and wiped her eyes again. Ernst took a deep breath and tried to dry his own.

She smiled and dabbed at his eyes with the sleeve of her bathrobe. "We seem to make each other cry all the time."

Ernst held her face between his hands, searched her weary eyes, found the ember of better days, and kissed her, gently at first. Her eyes closed and her lips remembered; her mouth, warm and wet with tears, rivaled his passion. He felt her surrender, as their arms entwined. They could not stop their lips, their fingers, frenzied as if to breach the boundary of skin and merge into one.

Lisa eased back from Ernst, her half-lidded eyes seeking focus. She held his cheeks, held his gaze. "You're not a dream, are you?" Her hair was wild. "I wanted to come – sunrise – sur le Quai." She kissed him again.

"I waited – every month." She was more beautiful than he remembered.

She stroked his face. "You're safe here. We're safe." Her mouth twitched and tears welled up again; she slumped against his chest.

"Shhhh," he whispered. "It's all right. Everything will be all right."

She shook her head against his chest. "Nothing will ever be all right again."

He felt completely protective of her, as if he cradled a daughter. "It's good you didn't come to Marseille. Things are very bad now. Food is scarce, escape is difficult and more and more dangerous. There are roundups, concentration camps. I don't know what would have become of us."

She led him into the parlor, a comfortable room of throw rugs, two over-stuffed chairs, and a well-used sofa strewn with pillows and an afghan.

"Do you know anything of my mother, my brothers, Uncle Erwin?" Ernst was bewildered to have included Erwin – another manifestation of his evolution.

He thought Lisa stiffened, and he was afraid to hear what she might say. "Your mother still works at the Charité Hospital. A week before I left Berlin I visited her. The bombing... It was very bad. Many houses had been hit – not yours. She gave me something for you, in case we met." Lisa went upstairs and returned with an envelope. He recognized his mother's elegant script:

Ernst

In the envelope he found a brief note and three photographs, the ones from their Wanseestrasse parlor. One each of the three brothers on their first day of First Class, posing with their cone shaped Schultüte. They each bore the same posed, opaque expression demanded by the photographer, but Ernst could see inside each child and knew with God-like surety the arc of their histories. He glimpsed their innocent souls, including his own, and he felt an overwhelming tenderness for the boy he had been. The tenderness of a father for his son.

> "Dear Ernst,
>
> I didn't know how to keep these safe from the bombing. Uncle Erwin has most of our valuables, but I wanted you to have these. I don't exactly know why, but when Lisa came to visit I knew she would see you again.
>
> In the hospital I help many people who cannot be helped. I have seen many die. It changes one to watch a life slip away and to be helpless to do anything. Those who die want only absolution and the priest grants it when he can. Sometimes, I am the only one present at the moment of death and so I give his blessing.
>
> I don't know how to heal our wounds – or even what these wounds are – but I hope you know that I love you with all my heart and forgive that which can be forgiven between a mother and her son.
>
> Love, Mother

He studied each photograph. Five-year-old Leo, the eldest, smiling confidently with equal parts of entitlement and responsibility. Hans Gerd's face looking ever so slightly mischievous, but Ernst could not be sure. He was reminded of Shakespeare's description of young Richard III, "born with teeth, as if to bite the world." And then he met his own image, five-year-old Ernst, staring out across a gulf of almost forty years, wearing his first disguise: a smile that was mechanical, incomplete – a smile that degraded the sweetness of his face.

Lisa took hold of Ernst's hand and looked into his eyes. "Leo is in Stalingrad," she whispered, as if she didn't want to say those words. "Your mother had not heard from him for over three months. Katherine and Alexander are in Jacobsdorf with your Uncle Erwin."

"And Hans Gerd?"

She looked down. "What can one say? Your mother said 'Hans Gerd is Hans Gerd,' and he has found his own kind in the Nazi party. They reward him and he's happy. But she's afraid for him – afraid for everyone in Germany."

"But she is well?"

She looked into his eyes again. "Her cough is back, but taking care of patients helps her – she says it gives meaning to a life of bombs, disease and death." Lisa paused, weighing her words. "She misses you terribly. I'm sorry I don't have more cheery news." She looked down again at Ernst's hand. "But now you're here, you're safe – that's reason enough to be glad. Come, let's have some tea. There are so many stories to tell."

The tea thawed a glacier of sedation and depression. Lisa became more animated. "Alexander is quite gifted in mathematics," she said. "Your mother said he asks about his Uncle Ernst. He misses you. He likes to hear stories of how you and his father grew up together in the same bedroom."

They sat side by side in the parlor, drinking tea, trading fragments of their lives apart from each other. As a worker for the Emergency Relocation Service, Lisa lived in the reception home caring for the newly rescued children until their 'foster families' arrived. She still missed Adi terribly. It was excruciating not knowing where he was, what he was doing, even if his activities were wrapped up in the Hitler Jugend. Fritz had risen through the ranks and was now an assistant to Eichmann, Chief of the Gestapo's Jewish Section.

"He was finally too busy to keep track of me," Lisa said. "And he didn't care. He was beyond wanting to punish me. He had Adi. He had a mission, power, prestige. I was nothing. Long before I escaped I had already disappeared."

Her robe parted just enough for Ernst to see the cleavage of her breasts; a familiar ache swelled inside him. She seemed to sense his hunger, and her smile was coy. She pulled her robe tight again.

They spoke for hours, into the night, their stories navigating the world like those of the Arabian Nights – about Halle, the journey across the Bodensee, the forbidding Tanezrouft, Tamanrasset, Moulay Bassim, and Puck. They spilled the contents of their lives with abandon. Nothing was redacted – as if undressing, they bared all. Each had known despair and emptiness – there were days when each thought of death and days when each said in their way, 'I missed you more than I thought possible,' and 'everyday I thought of you.' Ernst recalled the night they poured Bleiguss, the night they first made love, and Lisa put her finger across his lips.

"Wait," she whispered. She returned cradling her Bleiguss horse and sang the song, *Mi Caballo Blanco*. The last verse brought tears to Ernst's eyes.

> *My white horse is as white as the dawn.*
> *We always travel together.*
> *He is my best friend.*
> *On the wings of happiness my horse races on.*
> *And in the arms of sorrow he bears me as well.*

He told her about Vénissieux and Mary Jayne Gold.

"Did you sleep with her?"

"No, she had a boyfriend, 'Killer'...."

Ernst leaned his head back against the couch and closed his eyes. "You and Puck are the only people who know me without my disguises."

"But I don't really know you at all. We shall have to start all over again." She laid her head against his shoulder. "Ernst? You must have been afraid so often."

"Sometimes."

"Here in Geneva there is nothing to fear, yet I am afraid all the time. I feel saturated with fear – immobilized. I understand why people choose death."

"I felt that way in the desert," he said. "One is never the same after courting death."

"What I wouldn't give to have my childhood fears back – the ones that could be banished by a light in the hall or Mother lying in bed with me."

They fell asleep leaning against each other on the sofa, Ernst still in his jacket and tie, Lisa in her robe. Early the next morning rose-petal light blushed the sky. She had finally lain across his lap, and he stroked her hair thinking of how he could paint this rare light, this evanescent tint. Lisa's arms embraced Ernst's hips. She sighed and drew herself closer. She looked up at him, sat up and wrapped her arms about his neck and kissed him tenderly. Without a word she slipped off the sofa and took off his shoes.

"My darling. You must be so tired. Lie down and sleep." She kissed his forehead and walked lightly upstairs.

It had been a long night of wakefulness and broken sleep. He was grateful for the opportunity to lie weightless on the couch and quickly fell into deep slumber.

When Ernst awoke to the faint clatter of dishes and spoons, sunlight streamed through gauzy curtains. Through slitted eyes he watched Margaret carry a tray into the dining room and stop behind Lisa, who stood at the table. She put down the tray and her arms circled Lisa's waist. She kissed the back of Lisa's neck and stroked her hair, now well groomed. Lisa leaned her head back, eyes closed, to rest against Margaret. After a few moments Lisa disengaged and looked at Ernst, who feigned sleep. A toddler cried upstairs.

She left the dining room and Margaret retreated to the kitchen. The house was quiet again. Ernst propped his head on the sofa's arm-rest and puzzled over what he had seen. In the upstairs bathroom, he splashed cold water on his face and rubbed hard. Had they been reunited only for him to lose her again? So many reversals – his heart was a roller coaster, rising with hope, plunging into despair. In the full length mirror he caught an unexpected view of his body. The undershirt that had once been snug against his torso hung loose, his upper arms thin with the barest definition of muscles. He fingered the scar from Goebbels's bullet in his left shoulder; there was no sensation in the scar. He was about to pick up his razor to shave when there was a knock on the door.

"Ernst!" It was Margaret. "A Herr Gersing would like a word with you. He says it is quite urgent."

He washed off the shaving soap and dressed again, his belt tightening one more hole. Before the stairs he passed Margaret's bedroom. The door was partially ajar, enough for him to see Lisa in bed, asleep, half under the covers. His mind mutinied at the obvious.

"Monsieur Toussaint." Herr Gersing greeted him from the bottom of the stairs, distracting him. "I would have only a moment of your time. If you would follow me. There is some urgency." Herr Gersing looked every bit the Geneva banker, with pin-striped suit, top hat and cane in hand, his generous stomach pressing against a tight vest. Indeed, he explained, he had only stopped at the Relocation Home en route to a branch office of the National Bank of Switzerland. "Please, come with me." He tapped his bowler hat into place, turned on his heels and strode toward a shiny black Mercedes, his umbrella a walking stick. When they had settled in the back seat, the glass partition closed to the driver, Herr Gersing opened his briefcase and found an envelope. First he asked to see Ernst's 'paper.' Just as he had with the 'F' route into Spain, Ernst produced a cut piece of colored paper that exactly complemented that of Herr Gersing.

"Good. We can speak frankly." He handed the envelope to Ernst. "This is the Gestapo list of most wanted 'criminals' in Provence."

Ernst unfolded the two pages. He recognized many of Varian Fry's associates, ironic recognition for those who had rescued artists and intellectuals from the Gestapo list in Vichy, France. The new compilation cited fewer refugees and more resistance suspects.

"We obtained this from the Milice. We have spies. I direct your eyes to the next page, half way down."

Two names were underlined:

* Julius Isaacs, a.k.a. 'Puck' – Jew, espionage, extortion, forgery, currency manipulation, Communist

* Ernest Toussaint, a.k.a. Ernest Tessier – desertion, espionage, forgery, suspected Communist

Asterisks marked Varian Fry's co-conspirators, Danny and Theodora Bénédite, Jean Gemähling, Charles Wolff, "Franzi" von Hildebrand. At the bottom of the list, after a space, almost an afterthought, was Justus "Gussie" Rosenberg, a.k.a. Jean-Paul Guiton. Gussie, everyone's favorite, the blond haired, sneaker clad 'office boy' at the Committee who, in short pants, looked ten years younger.

"In exactly three days," Herr Gersing continued, "on April 26th, there will be a grand rafle throughout Provence. The Milice have to prove their worth to the Nazis. Joseph Darnand himself will be in charge. It will be brutal." Herr Gersing sat back and lit a black Turkish cigarillo. He inhaled deeply. "I don't know if you've heard. Leon Blum has been deported. This is how badly things have gone. Frenchmen are sending their former prime minister to be murdered by les Boches. It is a sad time. When is your return train?"

Ernst felt the blood drain from his face. The events of the last 12 hours dizzied him, now this. Another letter, though hardly a rival of Frau Rathenau's missive. Yet this simple list unveiled again her two decades old letter – yellowed, brittle, the ink fading but not its dominion, not its leverage. After all that had transpired, it still left him baffled, conferring as it did her unfathomable challenge, her conditions for absolution – "...and before a heavenly one repent." He carried her letter always, and held it in his heart, occasionally conscious of its force, its burden, more often not. He felt it pulling and pushing, prodding and persuading, sometimes an embrace, often a barb, an enigmatic shadow that grew larger as the world plunged into darkness, surfaced before sleep and on first awakening, never entirely banished.

Herr Gersing's list blurred in his hands. How could they ever be warned in time? He felt lightheaded. Overnight he had resolved to remain in Geneva, with Lisa. Then he had walked past Margaret's bedroom and seen Lisa in her bed. Now came Herr Gersing and this intrusion of the world of April 1943. This moment, every moment, was time at a crossroads, every decision irrevocable. He feared that if he left Lisa now, he would never see her again.

"Monsieur Toussaint. Your train – when is it?"

Ernst's attention returned. "This afternoon, Herr Gersing. I was to cross the border past Vernier and proceed to Bellegarde."

"You *were* to?" One eyebrow lifted. "I would completely understand if you decide to stay. You've already risked your life many times over. One must know when to stop." Gersing's harsh smoke drifted gently out the window, drawn by the spring breeze. "This list means life or death. It must reach Marseille quickly. You already have a ticket, visa, papers. No one can get in sooner. I must know if you can take it across."

Ernst folded the list again and had difficulty fitting it back into the envelope. He could see the faces of those he knew. Puck had said he would die before being imprisoned again, and had taken to carrying cyanide capsules with him at all times.

"I will do it." When he spoke it was as if someone else articulated his decision, or that he simply surrendered from exhaustion and despair. As the words left his mouth, he felt the springing of a steel trap – as irrevocable as leaping from a bridge – this unthinkable decision. He felt like a spectator to his own consciousness, his own choice, and he wondered about the source.

Herr Gersing continued to speak quickly and Ernst had to force his attention. "Here is a second copy of the list and a thousand Swiss francs for expenses. In Lyon, stay one night at the Hotel Internationale. Your reserva-

494

tion is already made. Be at the piano bar at ten o'clock, drink in your left hand. You will be approached by a young lady who will mention a 'French martini.' She will have an identical envelope with bank transactions inside. Exchange envelopes, keep one list for yourself. Give it to Robert at Sept Petits Pêcheurs, whom you already know."

They shook hands. "Time is of the essence, Monsieur Toussaint."

Ernst left the Mercedes feeling dizzy. As he recovered his equilibrium, he felt cheated – as if God had played him like a cat tormenting a disabled mouse. It would not be the first time. His decision was a fatalistic impulse, and it baffled him to freely give his consent to be moved by fate. Free will, fate, it was a contradiction that had the force of inevitability. Moulay Bassim would smile and nod his head, say something about The Prophet, as if this was just another preordained move in a desert game of Mancala.

*   *   *   *   *   *   *   *   *   *

After his discussion with Herr Gersing Ernst went to Margaret's bedroom to tell Lisa. A bottle of pills sat on the bed-stand beside a half-empty water glass. She awoke slowly, groggy, barely able to open her eyes. With his assistance she sat up, her arms draped about his shoulders, her head heavy on his neck. He rubbed her back and whispered that he was returning to France.

"Oh, no Ernst," a torpid, pained sigh, through the fog of sleep and barbiturate. She lifted her head and their eyes coupled, her cheeks already wet with tears.

"I knew you would go," she said, her words thick and slow. "As soon as I saw you, I knew you would go. It was as if you were a ghost visiting one last time."

"I have every intention of returning," he said. "Puck is in danger. I owe him my life, my soul."

"Is that why you do it – for Puck?"

"Yes, for Puck." Almost as an afterthought he added, "I have rescued complete strangers. Why would I not try to rescue Puck? And I do it for myself. If it was you, I'd go back for you."

Her eyes hung heavy and wet, fresh tears like dew on her eyelashes. She studied Ernst, looking from his eyes to his mouth and neck, then to his eyes again. "We can't ever get it right, can we, Ernst? We really are Paolo and Francesca in 'The Kiss.' We will never complete that kiss. How utterly sad."

He kissed her forehead and embraced her for a long and tender moment.

"Every kiss, my love, is the completion of that kiss. We have only one life, and it will end one day. I suppose, in some way, every pair of lovers are Paolo and Francesca." He said a prayer for them both. "I'll return my darling – I swear it."

She wept on his shoulder. His own tears now flowing freely.

After many minutes she was able to speak again. "I'll say good-bye here, Ernst. It's difficult, but I try not to weep in public."

★   ★   ★   ★   ★   ★   ★   ★   ★   ★

Margaret called for a taxi and insisted on accompanying Ernst to the station. As they drove from the house, Ernst gave Margaret the two letters he always carried – Frau Rathenau's and Lisa's last letter explaining how Margaret would help her flee Germany and how they would meet in Marseille.

"For safe keeping," he said. "I wonder why I carry such incriminating evidence at all."

Margaret read Frau Rathenau's letter. "I remember this. It was in all the newspapers during your trial. I wondered then what it might mean to you." She looked at Ernst, a studious look, the kind of surprised regard of seeing something for the first time. "You've carried it for twenty years?"

"Yes. Twenty years. It still baffles me, but it has also comforted and instructed me in unexpected ways."

"A sort of talisman?"

"I suppose. Please give it to Lisa."

She took the letters and slipped her hand into his. "Come back quickly, Ernst." He had never seen Margaret weep, but now a solitary tear coursed her cheek. "You know, of course, that she prefers you."

"It doesn't matter." His throat swelled. It did matter, but he had already ceded his control. Perhaps Bassim was correct and it was all in the hands of a greater force. That it was either benevolent or cruel, or neither, or both, was an inconceivable distinction, one that only had meaning for humans. "I'm glad to know she is safe and loved. If I don't return..."

"Hush! I can't abide such talk."

"You love her very much, don't you?" Ernst said.

Margaret looked away. "Yes. But like you, enough to let her go."

"Then we can rest more easily, you and I."

The taxi stopped in front of the train station and they sat quietly, staring ahead. Finally, Ernst said, "I should be leaving."

She leaned over and kissed his cheek. "Come home safely, Ernst. I want to dance at your wedding."

★　★　★　★　★　★　★　★　★　★

As Ernst's train approached the border, he rested his forehead against the window, each breath lightly fogging the glass. His pale reflection, ghost-like, hung outside the rail car as the spring valley rushed by. He had barely recognized himself in the photograph his mother sent – the Schultüte photo – bewildered, sad. He wondered again why he had left the safety of Switzerland. His pulse beat a duet of fear and heartache. Monstrous evil was afoot, Puck's life hung in the balance, and Herr Gersing had burdened him with the choice of being David to the Gestapo's Goliath.

Ernst re-entered France as he had left, as Ernest Schoenfelt, bank officer and assessor for the National Bank of Switzerland. His Swiss exit visa and French transit visa were in order. He carried a forged letter from the Reich Minister of Finance that stressed his requirement for free movement. Margaret had purloined the stationery and official letterhead from her Reich Finance Minister lover before she defected.

In Lyon, Ernst felt the hammer-pulse of Nazi occupation. Wehrmacht units goose-stepped through the city with their drums and standards, swastika banners hung from every lamppost and draped government buildings. At the train station, SS officers in long gray coats and peaked caps clustered like raptors seeking carrion.

He checked into the Hotel Internationale as Herr Gersing had instructed. From a balcony overlooking the lobby he watched the green-coated German soldiers moving about like greedy insects and he could see why the occupiers were derisively called doryphores, potato bugs. In the lobby that evening, he stood by the baby grand piano with a drink in his left hand, and at precisely ten o'clock a young woman in a long black dress, with a black Spanish vest over a white blouse, approached him and leaned against the piano. She greeted him with flirty hello and Ernst asked if he could buy her a drink. She replied, as Ernst anticipated, "a French martini." Ernst laid an envelope with the list for the grand rafle on the piano and she covered it with her sequin studded black handbag. He left for the bar and when he returned he picked up her identical envelope with bank transactions.

At eight the next evening his train from Lyon arrived in Marseille at Gare St. Charles. As soon as he left the security check-point, Ernst was aware of being followed. He hailed a taxi for the Hotel Splendide, and once inside the lobby he ducked into the men's room, where a doryphore was just finishing his business at the urinal. After he left, Ernst opened the heavy iron window over the wash basins and climbed out into the dark bushes that surrounded the hotel. Moments later he was running through the alleys of Le Panier, then walking quickly, glancing behind, ducking into doorways and waiting, then moving on.

It was near curfew when he knocked three times, twice, then three times again at the back door to Sept Pet Pècheurs. He inquired for Robert. It was most urgent and personal, he said. Two muscular men accompanied him to a dark office where Robert sat at a spot-lit desk with his bicarbonate of soda.

"Herr Gersing sends his regards and this." Ernst laid the list on the table. "A grand rafle – tomorrow. Look at these names."

Robert studied it briefly. "You brought this back into France from Switzerland? Are you mad? Suicidal? Your name is on this list."

"I must warn Puck." Ernst heard the café's metal shutter clattering down. "And Danny and Theo."

"Do you know where Danny is? He and Jean Gemähling disappeared a few weeks ago. Everyone seems interested in their whereabouts; some would pay generously to know."

Ernst paused. Could anyone be trusted? Robert drank his bicarbonate and continued to scan the list, one eyebrow rising now and then.

"It would not surprise me to learn that Sabiani has this very same list. Be careful, Ernest." He opened a locked desk drawer and rummaged about the bottom.

"Take this." He handed him a Walther P-38 pistol wrapped in a cloth. "Compliments of a dead German spy." Robert ejected the eight-round magazine. It was full and he locked it back in place. "You may need it. I have a bad feeling that this will not be the usual rafle," Robert continued. "Those caught in the Milice dragnet will be deported, if they survive the day. Leave out the back, through my office. It's past curfew. Be careful."

They shook hands. "You have been a good friend, Robert. A true son of France. Bon chance!"

★ ★ ★ ★ ★ ★ ★ ★ ★ ★

It was an hour past curfew and the stretch of deserted streets felt ominous. Rain on asphalt liberated the scent of moldering earth, a light mist hanging in the narrow alleys. Ernst ran through the maze that he knew so well. He splashed through puddles, evaded obstacles, trashcans, bricks, almost tripped over a body that smelled drunk, not dead. He reached Rue de L'Evéche, a major thoroughfare in the Vielle Ville, and waited against a dark wall, listening. Every sound magnified in the dark. A motorcycle raced by followed by a squad car and a lorry from which rifle barrels protruded like porcupine quills. As their mechanical rumble subsided, Ernst heard the tiny sound of a child's footsteps racing towards him down Rue de L'Eveche. In the dim street-light he saw the shadow of a boy, no more than twelve. As he ran directly by, Ernst grabbed his collar and pulled him into the dark alley.

He gasped and stumbled, clawing at his neck, his eyes wide.

"You fool!" Ernst hissed at the boy and shifted his hold to grasp both his arms. "Where do you think you're going? The curfew!"

Color returned to the boy's face. "Rafle!" he rasped.

He squirmed in Ernst's grip like a hooked fish.

"Quiet, boy! Quiet! It's not until tomorrow." Ernst could feel the wiry child tiring, his spasms slowing to the point where Ernst could ease his grip. Ernst knelt before him and looked into his fierce eyes. "If you are caught it will go badly for you... and your family. Do they know you're out?"

He shook his head.

"You don't even have papers, do you?"

He shook his head again. "I have to warn my... my friend."

"Does your friend know you're taking this awful risk? I'm sure he would not want it. What's your name?"

"Leo."

"I have a brother named Leo." He thought the boy relaxed a little more.

Ernst looked out onto the street just as a motorcycle, this one with a side-car, snarled around a corner and came toward them. Its determined headlight pierced the mist, a jousting lance of light that lit Leo's face for a moment. Ernst pulled him back into the shadows of the alley.

In that flash of light, Ernst saw the boy clearly but briefly – a photograph with motion – a sullen, angry face, petulant red lips, dark brown hair escaping from an all too ample beret. Smudged dirt sullied each cheek, perhaps where he had squeezed through an alleyway between grimy tenements. Ernst thought his eyes were green, the same green as Varian Fry, but bloodshot: the eyes of a spirited boy, not yet defeated.

A pair of brighter lights turned the same corner and illuminated Rue de L'Evéche. Then another. And another. Three trucks, covered in canvas, rumbled down the street. Ernst's heart began to pound. The boy was right! The rafle had begun, a day early.

The motorcycle and three lorries screeched to a halt only a block further down. Wehrmacht soldiers clattered down, rifles in hand, and sprinted down Rue du Thier. The motorcycle that had led them roared to life again and continued on.

An officer barked orders that were repeated by two and three others, adamant, urgent. Rifle butts pounded doors, glass splintered, a high-pitched scream rose from a distant tenement up the steep slope of Le Panier.

"We can't stay here," Ernst said and they retreated into the blackness of the alley.

The boy shivered. "I've got to warn my girlfriend."

"Oh, it's your girlfriend."

"Why should I trust you?"

"You shouldn't. My name is Ernest. I too, came to warn a friend. It may be too late. Where does your girl live?"

Leo pointed to the street where the troops had just deployed. The corners of his mouth twitched down and his breath caught.

"Listen, Leo. There's nothing you can do here. You can't stay out on the street. My friend and I live close by. Come with me."

Leo's brow furrowed and Ernst could feel his anxiety and suspicion. They were about to leave the alley's sanctuary, when a flashlight suddenly blinded them.

"Halt! Stop immediately! Hands high! Come out of the alley."

They stood side by side; a single electric torch floated in the hands of a ghost. "Your papers! You, child, your papers!"

Leo slipped his hand into Ernst's and he could feel the boy trembling.

"He's just a boy," Ernst said. "He's scared. Let me help him."

The soldier unfastened the leather strap of his holster and motioned for Ernst to be quick about it with his flashlight. As Ernst bent over Leo, his other hand found the Walther P-38 in his pocket. The guard's hand moved to his holster, perhaps remembering something from his training. His Luger was half way out when Ernst fired the first round into the soldier's stomach, and he grunted as if punched. His Luger continued out of the holster and was pointed at Leo when Ernst fired the second round into his throat, which exploded in blood and bone and he collapsed. A whistle blew down the street; the crash of boots and clatter of rifles being readied.

Leo stared dumbfounded at the dead man. Ernst snatched the Luger and

500

dragged Leo deeper into the alley, where they crouched in the dark, hearing soldiers run to attend their fallen comrade. A light beam shone down the alley but Ernst covered their faces and there was no pursuit. After some minutes he took Leo's hand and led him slowly through the pitch-black until they emerged in the rubble-strewn courtyard on Rue d'Epice, near the willow tree across the street from his apartment.

Rue d'Epice was quiet, but the commotion from surrounding blocks closed in like a thunderstorm. Ernst pulled Leo up the three flights. He had not counted on this distraction. He had a picture in his mind of how this would go. He would warn Puck in time and they would flee. Maybe he would be back in Switzerland in just a few days. But, he thought, nothing ever happens the way one imagines. Something unexpected, something from nowhere materializes – Leo – and that ultimately determines the course of events. His key trembled so that he had to steady it with two hands. The lock gave and behind the open door Puck leveled a pistol. The room was full of smoke.

"Ernst!" Puck pulled him in and embraced him. "Thank God you're all right. Do you hear what's going on? Get in here and help me burn everything."

Ernst dragged Leo inside, then shut and bolted the door. Puck looked from Leo to Ernst.

"I found him – outside. His name is Leo."

Puck stared at the blood on Ernst's overcoat and right hand. "A German," Ernst said. "Just now. We're all right."

Leo's jaw still quivered and his breath shuddered as he stared at the blood-stained Luger Ernst put on the table.

"I came to warn you, but..."

Puck returned to the smoldering stove. "Burn everything!"

The shattering of glass from the street door three stories below. Boots thundered up the stairs, crescendoing, shaking the floors.

Puck exhaled sharply and his shoulders slumped. "It's done."

Ernst knelt by Leo and gripped his shoulders. He found his eyes and said, "Look at me, Leo! Listen carefully. In the street, I will create a distraction by trying to flee. When I do, you run in exactly the opposite direction, into an alley." He scribbled an address and a coded message onto a piece of paper and held it up for the boy to read. "Give this to Robert at Sept Petit Pècheurs. Do you understand?"

Leo nodded, his mouth ajar, his green eyes wide.

The door to their flat crashed open and three soldiers burst through, their weapons leveled, helmets shading their eyes. Only their mouths differentiated them. An officer strutted in and directed one of the soldiers to douse the cook stove. A great cloud of steam condensed. He emptied the ashes into a canvas bag. Another soldier collected the pistols.

"Quite an arsenal for innocents to possess, don't you think?" He walked up to Puck. "I believe they call you Puck, Herr Isaacs?" The officer removed his peaked cap, straightened his light brown hair, and walked around the room, circling his prisoners. "And you are Toussaint. Or should I say Tessier?" He picked up the dead German's Luger. "Whose blood is this?" He pointed the pistol at the boy's forehead. "Henri said nothing of a child." He knelt down to Leo's eye level and pulled back the hammer. "Which one of these men killed the soldier?"

Leo licked his lips; his saucer-wide eyes darted back and forth. A great tear coursed down one grimy cheek inscribing an immaculate vein.

The barrel touched his smooth forehead. Leo quivered and shook, eyes closed tightly.

"I shot him." Puck stepped forward.

"No, it was me," Ernst pulled back on Puck's elbow. "You old fool!" he hissed.

A soldier brought the record player down from the shelf and set it on the table. Ernst's heart missed a beat. The officer opened the phonograph and studied its mechanics. He turned to a huge shadow waiting outside. "Klaus. Open this."

Klaus was so tall that he had to bend his head to pass through the doorjamb. A heavy ax hung from his hand. In one motion, he swung the ax, as if a toy, onto the record player, which shattered and split in two. The officer picked through the wreckage and held up the remains of a wireless headset, bent but clearly recognizable. One vacuum tube was till intact.

"Espionage is a capital offense. A pity to drag the boy into your misery." He turned to the soldiers. "Take them outside!" Then back to Ernst and Puck. "The Gestapo wish to interrogate you both."

The street churned with rushing troops, harsh German orders, crying women and children, metal on wood, leather on cobblestone. A green-coated German soldier dragged a man into the middle of the street followed by a woman holding a baby, a crying toddler clutching at her night-dress. The Vichy paramilitary Milice in black uniforms with silver buttons on each lapel loaded families into the lorries. A clamor of French weeping, swearing, and bewilderment, flew from the maw of the lorry like blackbirds disturbed; four children whimpered under a street lamp flanked by the menacing rifles of two German soldiers.

Ernst, Puck and Leo were brought to a Milice officer who adjusted his black beret, beside him a stout German officer in khaki. Behind them in the shadows, a tall man in a black pea coat lit a cigarette. In the match's flash Ernst recognized Henri. Henri whispered to the Milice officer and nodded his head.

The Milice reported to the German officer. "He says that one is Ernest Toussaint, a spy for the British. He doesn't know the other one."

"And the boy?" the German officer asked in primitive French.

Henri shrugged his shoulders.

"Old enough to be deported." He reverted to German and snapped his head in the direction of the lorry.

Leo's breath came shallow and fast. Ernst squeezed his hand to give him courage, to signal his attention. He stared hard at Henri. "How could you?" Ernst called to him.

Henri crushed his cigarette and walked closer, so he could speak more privately. "Turning you in feeds my children for two, maybe three weeks." He spat on the ground and walked away.

"These two go to headquarters!" the German officer in charge ordered. Cloaked Milice Agents Française led them towards a Black Maria separate from the lorries.

Ernst looked around desperately. He knew where all the narrow alleys were, alleys so slender only a small boy could pass through. He knew the inevitable end, his only choice now to decide how it would unfold. There was no escaping, only choosing how to die. No time for goodbye, for heartache, and maybe that was for the best.

He didn't want his last feeling on earth to be anguish and he clung to one image – his father in the National Gallery. Only this time Alfred Techow looked down at young Ernst and smiled. He smiled at his boy as if he truly loved him.

They were almost at the lone willow growing in the rubble filled lot. There was an alley directly opposite.

His father pointed to a painting – Monet's Water Lillies.

Ernst stumbled and fell, feigning injury. The Milice guard bent to help him, an instinctive kindness, and in that moment Ernst lunged and drove his head into the guard's stomach. The man's breath hissed out. Without even regaining his feet, Ernst snagged the legs of the soldier holding Leo and upended him. All three fell in a heap. Puck restrained his own guard, tripping him by his boots.

"Run, Leo! Run!" Ernst punched the Milice in the face and stumbled across the cobblestones. He scrambled to his feet and ran toward the willow. He heard the first discharge of a rifle and cries from behind.

"Halt! Achtung! Arreté!"

He lunged for the willow. A night breeze blew the willow's branches like a woman's hair. He didn't hear the next rifle shot, but a steel spike drilled into his back. Then another, higher up below his shoulder. The trip-hammer of his heart, racing and hot, pounded in his ear, the cobblestones suddenly cool against his cheek. He did not recall falling; the pain burned deep, insistent but detached, like a phantasm. He tried to distinguish the clatter of boots from the sound of his own pulse and realized it was preposterous; his ears felt full of cotton. He tasted salty blood.

The willow shone silver, then yellow in unexpected light, branches waving gently. Each cobblestone glowed with street light, like moonbeams on a windy lake, a jewel-studded river of light leading to the willow tree. Behind the willow Ernst saw Wannseestrasse, Gemeiner Goldregen, golden flowers cascading over the south fence. He heard the tiny Zaunkönig, the Fence King, rhapsodizing from the bushes.

The pulse in his ear slowed and he heard Margo Lion singing:

> Peter, Peter, may I have this dance
> Peter, Peter, give me one more chance
> Peter, Peter, tell me what to do
> Peter, Peter, I'm still in love with you

Each cobblestone's reflected light softened, diffused, became a lily pad in a black pond. "See, Ernst," his father's arm around his shoulder. "The painting of the light."

A shrinking tunnel. The street darkened.

★   ★   ★   ★   ★   ★   ★   ★   ★   ★

THE END

EPILOGUE

(* Historical persons)

Lisa Schmidt remained with Margaret in Geneva for the duration of the war, where they continued to receive displaced and orphaned children. After the war their Relocation Home became the *Wandervogel* House, a center for children and troubled youth. Every summer she and Margaret visited Marseille, where they left a bouquet of flowers by Eglise St. Laurent, the Romanesque church on the Quai. Lisa died in 1989 at the age of 87.

Puck (Julius Isaacs) was true to his determination never to be imprisoned again. In the Black Maria he swallowed two cyanide capsules. When the officer opened the back door to the paddy wagon at Gestapo Headquarters, he was dead.

Gertrude Techow worked at the Charité Hospital until she was killed on January 28, 1944 during one of the heaviest bombing raids on Berlin.

Leo Techow died somewhere near Stalingrad. His unit disappeared in a snowstorm. His body was never found.

* **Hans Gerd Techow** joined the Nazi party and the SA. After the war he worked as a lawyer, journalist and publisher. He died in 1992.

Katherine Techow moved with her son, Alexander to Uncle Erwin's estate in Jacobsdorf where they survived the war. When peace returned, she became a social worker and founded a social work society to assist displaced persons.

Alexander Techow came to America to study at Columbia University where he obtained a PhD in philosophy. He lives in Vermont and is a Professor Emeritus at Middlebury College.

Erwin Behrens continued to operate his estate in Jacobsdorf until 1945 when he was called to duty as a Home Guard to protect the shattering Reich. He became a prisoner of the Russians after the fall of Berlin and died in a POW camp from Typhoid Fever. In his last will and testament, written after the death of his sister, he left his entire estate to his nephews, Ernst and Alexander. Hans Gerd received nothing.

Fritz Sommers rose to the rank of SS *Obersturmführer* and was arrested after the war as one of Eichmann's collaborators. He faced the Nürmberg War Crimes Tribunal, which sentenced him to 20 years in prison. Fritz, unrepentant to the end, refused to acknowledge the jurisdiction of the tribunal and offered the Nazi salute as he was led away after his trial. After his release, he continued to work for a marginalized Neo-Nazi party, soliciting, handing out leaflets and booklets. He began to suffer from dementia in 1960, and by 1965 he required constant care in a nursing home, where he was often violent. He died two years later at the age of 67.

Adolph 'Adi' Sommers was called up to fight in 1942 when only 16. Fritz secured his son a privileged and safe position with the Home Guard. After D-Day, Adi's unit was sent to the Belgium frontier where he was killed by a sniper's bullet in July 1944.

Wilhelm Rathenau joined the Free French and fought with distinction against Rommel's Afrika Corps in the North African campaign. He received the Pour le Merité for his heroism. After the war he married and continued his studies first at the Sorbonne, then obtained his PhD in contemporary German history from Harvard University. Though retired from teaching, he continues to write at Boston College and lives in Cambridge with his wife. They have three children.

* **Varian Fry** offered aid to over 4,000 people trapped in Vichy France. Of these, he was able to rescue between 1,200 and 1,800. Among others, Fry saved the artists Marc Chagall, Marcel Duchamp, Max Ernst and Wilfredo Lam, the sculptor Jacques Lipchitz, novelists Lion Feuchtwanger and Franz Werfel and his wife, Alma Mahler Gropius Werfel, and political and social scientist Hannah Arendt. The Emergency Rescue Committee he headed enlisted smugglers, black marketers and forgers to assist

Jewish and anti-fascist intellectuals and artists to escape, rescue downed British pilots, report on internment camps, and establish illegal escape routes across the mountains, all with a staff of inexperienced relief workers, wealthy socialites, students and the refugees themselves. After the war, Fry retired to near obscurity and died in 1967 virtually unrecognized. In 1995 he was honored as a gentile who was "righteous among the nations," joining Oskar Schindler, Irena Sendler, and Raoul Wallenberg at Yad Vashem, Israel's national Holocaust Memorial.

* **Mary Jayne Gold** lived out her life in France and died at the age of 88. She confided to a friend, the filmmaker Pierre Sauvage, that she "felt that only one year in her life really mattered and it was the year she spent in Marseille." The heiress from Chicago gave huge sums of money to Varian Fry's Emergency Rescue Committee to purchase visas and passports on the black market. She never married.

* **Danny Bénédite** continued fighting the Nazis as a Resistance fighter until he was captured by the German army in 1944 and sentenced to death. Danny managed to escape after the Allied landing along the coast of Provence. After the war he became a journalist and newspaper executive. For his wartime heroism he was made a Chevalier de la Légion d'Honneur in 1951.

* **Theodora (Theo) Prins** went underground with her husband Danny Bénédite and their newborn daughter Caroline. After Danny was arrested, she became director of their Maquis (guerrilla) camp. Their first child, Peterkin, escaped Marseille in 1941 with his grandmother, Eva. He became a geophysicist. She and Danny divorced after the war and Theo worked for UNESCO. She retired to Provence.

* **William Freier (Spira)** was deported to Poland, where he was imprisoned in a sub-camp of Auschwitz, then transferred to other concentrations camps including Buchenwald and Theresienstadt. He survived the war and after liberation he reunited with Mina and their 4-year-old son, Francois. He took back his legal name, Spira. Tragically, after their reunion, Mina suffered a breakdown, which left her incapacitated and she died in an asylum in 1953. Spira remained in Paris as a cartoonist and photographer until his death in 2000.

POSTSCRIPT

Before the Court of Heaven was inspired by an article published in *Harpers* magazine in April 1943. The article, "My Favorite Assassin" by George Herald, purported to be an historical account of Ernst Werner Techow's turn from evil and his redemption. Assuming that it was true, Rabbi Fritz Rothschild based his 1992 Yom Kippur sermon at Middlebury College on the story. Subsequently, noted German scholar Martin Sabrow demonstrated that, though based on actual events – Techow's trial, Frau Rathenau's letter, Techow's increasing disillusion with the Nazi party – much of Herald's account was a fiction.

What is known of Ernst Werner Techow's life is that after his release from prison in 1930 he worked on the editorial staff of Goebbels' newspaper *Der Angriff*, became disillusioned with Hitler, and was involved in the anti-Hitler Stennes Putsch in March 1931, after which he was expelled from the Nazi party. Ernst von Salomon described an incident during the Stennes uprising in which Techow slapped Goebbels in the face. Techow declared, "We didn't kill Rathenau for swine like you!" After the Stennes Putsch was quelled, Techow left *Der Angriff* and opened a photography shop.

Following the German occupation of territory in Austria and the Sudetenland, Techow worked for the Deutsche Umsiedlungs-Treuhand-Gesellschaft (German Resettlement Trust Company) charged with administering and safeguarding the property rights of ethnic Germans in newly occupied territories. Its charge included handing over confiscated Jewish assets and properties. In May 1941 he joined the German navy as a war correspondent. His ship was sunk in October 1942. He was injured but survived. Towards the end of the war he joined the *Volkssturm*, the German Home Guard, a last-ditch effort against the Allies. He was captured near Dresden by Russian troops and became a POW. On May 9, 1945 he was involved in an altercation with a Russian guard who struck him on the head with a shovel. He died from the injury.

There is no evidence that Ernst joined the French Foreign Legion or participated in the rescue of Jews from Marseille. However, Varian Fry, an American journalist and his co-conspirators did rescue between 2,000 and 4,000 Jews from Marseille, including Hannah Arendt, Marc Chagall, Max Ernst, Lion Feuchtwanger, Wilfredo Lam, Arthur Koestler, Wanda Landowska, Claude Levi-Strauss, Jacques Lipchitz, Kurt and Helen Wolf, and Franz Werfel.

Puck, Lisa, and Fritz are fictional characters.

Fiction illuminates the truth. Thus I was moved by Rabbi Rothschild's sermon to craft *Before the Court of Heaven*. I believe such stories touch something vital and unique in us: the human capacity for decency. They speak to our better angels. They are an immunization against the recurrence of horrors such as Nazism, and inspire us to do our part toward the repair of the world – toward *Tikkun Olam*.

A bibliography is available upon request.

CPSIA information can be obtained at www.ICGtesting.com
Printed in the USA
LVOW11s1536070916

503614LV00003B/599/P